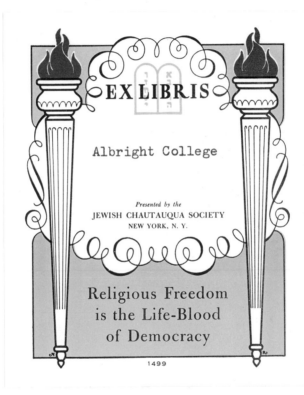

# FAITH and REASON

## Essays in Judaism

# FAITH and REASON
## Essays in Judaism

*edited by*

ROBERT GORDIS and RUTH B. WAXMAN

KTAV PUBLISHING HOUSE, INC.

NEW YORK

1973

SBN 87068-188-5

LIBRARY OF CONGRESS CATALOG CARD NUMBER: 72-429
MANUFACTURED IN THE UNITED STATES OF AMERICA

# TABLE OF CONTENTS

# INTRODUCTION

## I

It may seem anomalous, in an introduction to a collection of Jewish theological essays, to suggest that the term "Jewish theology" is itself alien to the Jewish tradition! One linguistic observation may help buttress this contention. Thomas Aquinas called his great presentation of Catholic religious thought *Summa Theologica*. Yet, throughout the Middle Ages, when theology was the queen of the sciences, the term *theology*, "the study of God," never entered the Hebrew language. On the other hand, the term *philosophy*, "the love of wisdom," which is likewise Greek in origin, was borrowed by the medieval Jewish thinkers because it met a felt need. While faith in God has always been the cornerstone of the Jewish religion, it has shared honors with two other pillars, as in the classic statement derived from the Zohar, "God, Torah and Israel are one." (*Idra*). In fact, a case may be made for the proposition that of these three equally significant elements, Torah is more equal than the others! On the one hand, there is the striking utterance which the Rabbis attribute to God, "Would that men forgot Me but kept My Torah" (P. *Hagigah* 1:7). On the other, the tenth century philosopher, Saadia, declared, "We are a people only by virtue of the Torah" (*Emunot Vedeot*, Chapter 3). By juxtaposing both pronouncements, one may conclude that both God and Israel are dependent on Torah, which is the most fundamental of all.

*Torah,* which properly means "teaching, guidance," is, like every important term, untranslatable. The Greek rendering, *nomos,* would not have proved so inadequate if the full spectrum of meaning which it enjoys in classical Greek literature had been kept in mind. Unfortunately, *nomos,* a term beloved of Paul in his polemic against normative Judaism, was restricted to "law," "law" was equated with "legalism" and "legalism" was, by definition "soulless." No wonder it has proved a stumbling-block to Christians and even to Jews who seek to understand the content of Torah. As the use of *Torah* for the Pentateuch makes clear, it includes narrative as well as enactment, tradition as well as prescription. It presupposes a doctrine; it commands the deed. It is a repository of faith; it rarely, if ever, enunciates dogma.

With the Five Books of Moses as its starting point, Torah was broadened to encompass the Prophetic books in the Bible, which include both the historical works and the utterances of the great seers. It embraces the varied works of Biblical Wisdom which, incidentally, includes the Book of Psalms. The stream of Torah has continued to grow wider and deeper. The Midrash, though differing in form and substance from the Qumran *pesharim* that have come to light in the last few decades, is, like these sectarian expositions of Biblical books, a massive commentary on the Bible. The Talmud and all succeeding Rabbinic literature, which took the form of treatises, responsa and codes, became part of Torah. The lucubrations of the mystics, no less than the analyses of the philosophers, constitute a commentary on Torah. Maimonides deepened the concept of Torah without violating its spirit by subsuming under it the teachings of science as revelatory of the ways of God, and insisting, "Accept the truth whatever its source" (Maimonides, *Introduction to Commentary on Abot*).

Whenever the Jew has grappled with the duty and the destiny of man, whether in literature or philosophy, in science or mysticism, he has been enlarging the boundaries of Torah, which is "longer than the earth in measure and broader than the sea." These words, which Zophar uses in the Book of *Job* to describe the greatness of the Divine Wisdom, the Rabbis applied to the dimensions of Torah, with which they identified it. The length and breadth of Torah, its height and depth, ruled out any narrow, monolithic conception of its content. The Hebraic tradition is the distillation of the millennial experience of an entire people. As the great Jewish exegete, Arnold B. Ehrlich, declared, the Hebrew Bible, unlike the New Testament, is not a collection of religious texts, but "a national literature on a religious foundation."

This national-cultural characteristic of Torah strengthened the tendency in Judaism to avoid the formulation of abstract principles either in belief or conduct and to favor, instead, concrete rules of action, whether in ritual or in ethics. Thus, the *Dialogues* of Plato explore with incomparable brilliance the meaning and implications of justice. The Hebrew Prophets do not speculate on this question. Micah declares, "He has told you, O man, what is good and what the Lord your God requires of you, only to do justice and to love mercy and to walk humbly with your God" (Micah 6:8). The Hebrew Scriptures do not urge the virtue of loving one's enemy— though, to be sure, the statement that they command hating one's enemy is a calumny. Instead, the Torah commands, "If you see the ox of your foe crouching beneath his burden, you shall surely help him" (Exodus 23:4, 5). Even the realistic Wisdom teacher in Proverbs says, "If your enemy is hungry, feed him. If he is thirsty, give him water to drink, for you are heaping coals upon his head and God will reward you" (Proverbs 25:21 f.). Similarly, the thousands of pages of the Talmud contain very few theoretical discussions of religious doctrines or even of ethical norms. Everywhere the concern is with the concrete fact, the existential situation, the decisive act.

Perhaps the closest one comes in the Talmud to a formulation of dogma as a condition of salvation is the passage in the Mishnah (*Sanhedrin* 10:1), "He who denies the Divine revelation of the Torah (literally, that the Torah is from Heaven) or the resurrection of the dead, has no share in the world to come." It is noteworthy that the statement is couched in the negative, evidence that it is a polemic response to challenges that arose in the Hellenistic-Roman period. The first doctrine, the promulgation of the Divine origin of the Torah, was the reaction of traditional Judaism to the claim advanced with ever greater insistence by the rising Christian Church that the authority of the Old Covenant had been abrogated by the New. The affirmation of the resurrection of the dead was the rejoinder of normative or Pharisaic Judaism to the Sadducees, who denied the belief, both because of their literal reading of Scripture, and their innate skeptical tendencies, which are characteristic of upper-class circles. These heretical ideas did not disappear with the destruction of the Temple, as has become increasingly clear. Whatever the reasons, Rabbinic literature, like its Biblical fountainhead, is rarely concerned with abstractions.

While this trait gives a realistic quality to Jewish literature, Biblical and post-Biblical, it does not facilitate the task of the philosopher and the theologian. It is not easy to extrapolate fundamental attitudes from specific cases. One can never be sure that he has penetrated to the rationale behind any specific ruling in Talmudic law. Similarly, when one reaches back to underlying ethical and philosophic principles, there is the ever-present danger of apologetics, giving an interpretation which is more *eisegesis,* reading one's views *into* the text, than *exegesis,* reading the author's views out of it.

Moreover, the Bible itself is characterized by a vast variety of outlook, content and temper. The law-giver, the historian, the prophet, the poet and the sage have each made their contribution to the Book of Books and endowed it with an extraordinary breadth of outlook and a deep humanity that distinguish it from all other sacred books. As for the second great fountainhead of Judaism, the Talmud, it is a massive monument to controversy. Its three thousand pages reproduce the arguments and discussions of over two thousand authorities living in two countries during a period of nearly a millennium. The variety becomes even more extensive in the Codes and Responsa, both medieval and modern.

In view of the extraordinary divergence of attitude reflected in the multitudinous sources of Torah, it is no wonder that some scholars have been led to deny altogether the existence of a mainstream in the tradition, arguing that each current is equally normative. On the other hand, in the face of this bewildering variety, others have fashioned the image of one "authentic" Judaism that always coincides with their own pattern. Many have sought to take refuge in the snug harbor of a final authority, be it a code, a council or a charismatic figure. The truth, as is so often the case, does not lie with either extreme. Jewish tradition is best compared to a mighty river containing a principal stream and many minor currents, all of which affect the flow of the water and, in turn, are affected by the contours of the shore and the structure of the river-bed.

To determine what is primary and what is secondary, what is fundamental and what is of lesser significance in the tradition, requires comprehensive knowledge of the sources and deep sympathy and insight into that tradition. Even when these qualities are present, there remains the danger of faulty interpretation. Fortunately, the limitations of one scholar tend to be corrected by another, so long as the lines of communication remain intact. As the *Pereq Qinyan Torah* declares, *pilpul hatalmidim,* "the discussion of students" constitutes one of the forty-eight qualities needed for the acquisition of Torah (Mishnah, *Abot*, chap. 6).

These are the basic characteristics of the Jewish tradition, particularly in its greatest and most creative periods, the eras of the Bible and the Talmud, and they have moulded the character of Judaism ever since. Nevertheless, modern Jews are spiritual citizens of Western civilization, as well as children of the Jewish tradition. Hence, they have inevitably been influenced by Western modes of thought, including such fundamentals as the categories of logical structure and relevance which are our heritage from the Greeks. This "Westernization" of Judaism produced Jewish philosophy, of which the first-century Philo of Alexandria was the lonely and premature forerunner, the twelfth-century Maimonides, the climax, and the seventeenth-century Spinoza, the less than grateful heir.

Medieval Jewish thought represents an intellectual and spiritual undertaking of impressive proportions. It sought, if we may borrow the Rabbinic phrase, to bring "the beauty of Japhet into the tents of Shem" (*B. Megillah* 9b) or, to put it more precisely, to pour the wine of Hebrew faith into Hellenic bottles. To a very high degree, the enterprise succeeded. That in the process some degree of distortion took place was inevitable, but a substantial measure of enrichment of the Jewish tradition resulted from the encounter.

Many of the problems of medieval Jewish philosophy are remote from modern men, as are the solutions arrived at. On the other hand, there are many aspects of medieval Jewish thought and special insights that are still relevant today. Beyond any concrete achievements of these thinkers,—Saadia, ibn Gabirol, Halevi, Maimonides, Crescas, and their co-workers—they established for all time the legitimacy and the necessity for interpreting the Jewish tradition in terms of the needs, attitudes and ideals of every generation.

The problems and pitfalls confronting Jewish theology today are omnipresent, but equally real are the challenges it faces and the needs it seeks to meet. The nineteenth century witnessed an all too brief efflorescence of Jewish religious thought in Europe, primarily, but not exclusively, in Germany. The twentieth century has been marked by a far more extensive burgeoning of Jewish philosophy and theology in the United States, Western Europe and Israel, that is impressive in its content, depth and variety. This intellectual and spiritual renascence bears witness to the relevance for the modern Jew of the Jewish tradition in its Biblical, Rabbinic and medieval embodiments, as he seeks to discover the nature of his identity both as a man and as a Jew.

It was to assist in this perennial quest that JUDAISM was founded more than two decades ago. It is to serve this goal that this volume is being published.

## II

At the time of the launching of JUDAISM, the greater part of Jewish energies and talents were absorbed in the practical, indeed desperate, problem of Jewish survival in the most literal sense. The Nazi program for the extermination of the Jewish people had all but achieved its objective, and six million dead were mute testimony to the large measure of success that had met the Nazi campaign. The smell of the crematoria was still strong and hundreds of thousands of survivors of the concentration camps bore the scars of their harrowing experience on their bodies and in their souls. The impact of this massive tragedy was too great for its consequences to be assessed at the time. The effort had scarcely begun to come to grips with the implications of the catastrophe, both for Jewish faith and for the meaning of human existence in general.

Nor was this all. Two other great events dominated the Jewish landscape. The State of Israel was in its infancy and required nurture, care and perpetual vigilance. The American-Jewish community was still in the process of integrating itself into the social, economic, cultural and political life of the country.

It is, therefore, perhaps no wonder that while lip-service was paid on every hand to the religious and ethical heritage of Judaism, there was no all-inclusive forum for the elucidation of Jewish religion, philosophy and ethics, and for the application of the insights of the Jewish tradition to the contemporary scene. In 1950, Professor Horace M. Kallen, Dr. Milton R. Konvitz, Rabbi Morris Goldfarb and I conceived of a plan for such a quarterly. I then presented the idea to the American Jewish Congress, which agreed to sponsor the journal. At its inception in 1952, and for several years thereafter, I served as Chairman of the Board of Editors, which has continued to include many of the most creative thinkers and scholars in America, Europe and Israel. A succession of dedicated and gifted editors—Will Herberg, Felix A. Levy, Theodore Friedman and Steven S. Schwarzschild—established JUDAISM as a uniquely significant journal, attracting contributors, both famous and unknown, from every school of thought within Judaism and without. At the end of 1969, I assumed the active post of Editor.

The unique position of the journal in Jewish life derives from another factor as well. It has been a forum for cross-fertilization and mutual influence transcending all schools of thought. It has served as a non-partisan, non-denominational arena in which religionists and secularists, believers and non-believers, adherents of Orthodoxy, Conservatism, Reform and Reconstructionism, Zionists and non-Zionists, radical, liberal and conservative Jews and non-Jews have all been able to speak with one another. In an age of hardening party lines—noticeable in Jewish, as well as in general, life—JUDAISM has been a major highway of communication.

In the two decades since JUDAISM was founded, the maturation of American Jewry has proceeded apace, at least for a minority of American Jews. This saving remnant is, fortunately, growing, and includes many of the most creative elements of our youth. It has become clear that Jewish survival for its own sake cannot serve as a sufficient ideal for Jewish loyalty. Nor can it supply adequate motivation for the sacrifices involved in self-identification with a minority group. The world-view of the Jewish religion, the content of the Jewish ethical tradition and the bearing of both upon the nature of Jewish belonging and the needs of the human condition—it is these factors that constitute the referents upon which the loyalty of the individual Jew, and, by that token, the survival of the Jewish people must be based.

I believe that among the resources available to all interested in embarking upon this enterprise of Jewish discovery, the twenty volumes of JUDAISM occupy an honored place. The twelve hundred papers that have appeared in its columns, which are now easily accessible by virtue of the *Cumulative Index to JUDAISM* published early in 1972, are, by and large, distinguished by their high quality and their catholicity and breadth of attitude.

It has, therefore, seemed worthwhile to select from this embarassment of riches an anthology of material dealing with Jewish religious thought. Equally significant volumes dealing with other themes, such as the authority and validity of Jewish law, the application of Halakhah to various areas of contemporary concern, and various departments of Jewish scholarship can be culled from the pages of the journal. The present volume, however, is concerned with Jewish theology.

This anthology represents the joint effort of the Editor of JUDAISM and its Managing Editor, Dr. Ruth B. Waxman, who are responsible for the selection and the organization of the material, as well as for seeing the volume through the press. In this task, we have had the assistance of our most capable secretary, Mrs. Trudy Kramberg.

The papers included within these covers have been structured so as to provide a systematic presentation of Jewish religious thought from its inception to the present. By its very nature, an anthology cannot present a complete treatment of so vast and variegated a theme. Had not Solomon Schechter virtually pre-empted the title in his classic work, the present volume might well have been called, "Aspects of Jewish Theology."

It should not be necessary to point out that the authors may have modified their views since the original publication of their contributions. We hope that readers will be stimulated by these papers to explore more fully the themes treated by the various writers, many of whose later and most extensive writings are indicated in the Index of Contributors at the end of the volume.

Since the volume is printed by offset, there are unavoidable variations in the orthography, the mode of transliteration, and even the physical appearance of the pages. For the same reason, the biographical data originally attached to each paper should be supplemented by the information given in the Index of Contributors.

## III

The structure of this anthology will, we hope, commend itself to the reader as both logical and chronological, being based upon the conviction that while history is not a sufficient condition, it is a necessary one for genuine understanding.

The first section, "The Framework of Jewish Theology," constitutes a brief introduction to the work as a whole, dealing with the fundamentals of Jewish theology. David S. Shapiro, in his paper, *The Existence of God,* deals with this basic concern of medieval Jewish philosophy. Even Kant's famous demolition of the "proofs of the existence of God" has not been able to exorcise this approach from the thought of believers and non-believers alike. Alexander Altmann presents an overall discussion of *The Divine Attributes,* with which classical religious philosophy was as much preoccupied as with the existence of God.

The second section, "Jewish Religious Thought Through the Ages," includes three papers dealing with "The Biblical Foundations." Abraham J. Heschel presents what he regards as the basic category of prophetic theology in his paper, *The Divine Pathos.* The Book of Job continues to fascinate and stimulate scholars and thinkers, as well as lovers of literature and general readers. This is clear from treatments of Job as disparate as those of the philosophers, Maimonides, Gersonides, and Immanuel Kant, psychologists like Carl Jung, and writers like Archibald Macleish. In this volume, two papers, *The Temptation of Job—Tradition versus Experience in Religion,* by Robert Gordis, and *Job's Problem,* by Morris Stockhammer, offer varying interpretations of the essence of Job's existential tragedy. By that token, they represent different approaches to the significance of what Thomas Carlyle called "the grandest book ever written with pen."

In the sub-section entitled, "The Rabbinic World View," varied aspects of normative Judaism are illumined.

In the periods following the Talmud, the Aggadah, the religio-ethical material embedded in Rabbinic literature, was downgraded both for practical and theoretic reasons. During the medieval religious dispensations which the Church forced upon Jewish communities in Western Europe, isolated Aggadic passages would be cited, always out of context and often mistranslated. The practice was designed to show that Judaism was contemptuous of other faiths, particularly Christianity, and indifferent to the rights of non-Jews. In response, the de-

fenders of Judaism, like Naḥmanides, declared that the Aggadah represented individual views not binding upon the Jewish
people, and that only the Halakhah established norms authoritative for all Jews. In the modern period, the Aggadah,
with its fanciful and hyperbolic language, its legends and folklore, was looked at askance by the Maskilim and other up-
holders of rationalism, who saw in it a farrago of poetry and
superstition, homely wisdom and popular magic. It is primarily in our age that a deeper understanding of the uses of
language for connotation as well as denotation, for suggestive-
ness as well as for specific delimitation of ideas, has come into
being. As a result, the Aggadah has sustained a rehabilitation
in the esteem of modern Jews. Witness Bialik and Ravnitski's
classic work, *Sefer Ha'aggadah* among many others less well
known. Today, the Aggadah is recognized as a rich treasure-
house of wisdom and insight into those aspects of the world
that go beyond normal experience and which beggar description. Samuel E. Karff presents an appreciation of this basic
aspect of the Jewish heritage in his paper, *Aggadah—The
Language of Jewish "God-talk."*

Avraham Holtz discusses fundamental religio-ethical concepts in his paper, *Kiddush and Hillul Hashem.* In his paper,
*God's Omnipotence in Rabbinic Judaism*, Richard L. Rubenstein addresses himself to a traditional attribute of God which
has proved a major difficulty for contemporary theologians, as
the "death of God" theology demonstrates.

Another concern of twentieth century thinkers has been the
validity of the concept of the Judeo-Christian tradition, which
has been affirmed and denied with passion and vigor on both
sides. Elsewhere, I have argued that instead of adopting either
approach, it would be far more significant and fruitful to
explore the nature of the relationship between Judaism and
Christianity, noting the areas of confluence on the one hand
and divergence on the other. (See *Judaism in a Christian
World,* McGraw-Hill, 1966, Chapter 7, "The Judeo-Christian
Tradition—Illusion or Reality.") In the present volume, four
stimulating papers shed light on this question. The late Paul
Tillich affirms the truth of the concept in his paper, *Is There*

*a Judeo-Christian Tradition?* The late Joseph Klausner, whose studies on Jesus, Paul, and Christian origins are pioneering and classic works in this area by a Jewish scholar, calls attention to the differences in *Christian and Jewish Ethics*.

The rise of existentialism has led to a resurgence of interest in the Danish religious thinker, Soren Kierkegaard. Marvin Fox highlights the differences between the Danish philosopher and traditional Judaism in his paper, *Kierkegaard and Rabbinic Judaism*. Contrary-wise, Jacob L. Halevi maintains that there is warrant in Jewish traditional sources for Kierkegaard's famous doctrine of "the teleological suspension of the ethical" and presents his evidence in his paper, *Kierkegaard and the Midrash*.

The year 1967 marked the four hundredth anniversary of the publication of Joseph Karo's *Shulhan Arukh,* by all odds the most influential law book in the history of Judaism, and today regarded in Orthodox circles as the ultimate authority. Isadore Twersky discusses the historical background of this great work, the motivations of its author, its scope and its abiding influence in, *The Shulhan 'Aruk: Enduring Code of Jewish Law*.

The third sub-section, "Modern Interpretations of the Tradition," underscores the continued creativity of Jewish religious thought after the Emancipation. Noah H. Rosenbloom surveys the ideas of David Samuel Luzzato in his paper, *Judaism and Natural Religion*. Simon Kaplan presents a conspectus of *Hermann Cohen's Philosophy of Judaism*. Maurice Friedman highlights the elements of novelty in *Martin Buber's New View of Evil,* while Zvi E. Kurzweil presents important aspects of the thought of Martin Buber, Franz Rosenzweig and Samson Raphael Hirsch in his paper, *Three Views on Revelation and Law*. His presentation helps to remind the reader of an important truth. Without derogating from the importance of such general theological themes as the existence and the attributes of God, the problem of evil, or the sanctions of ethics, Judaism has always placed at the center of its concern the specific Jewish concept of law, its source and authority, its scope and methodology, and, by no means least, its validity and relevance.

The third and largest section of this book is concerned with "Contemporary Jewish Theology." Under the first rubric, "God," several Jewish theologians set forth the outlines of their personal credos. Monford Harris argues, in *Interim Theology,* that Jewish theology today must be concerned primarily with Jewish existence and allegiance, rather than with abstract theological principles. On the other hand, Jakob J. Petuchowski stresses the need for an all-inclusive theology in his paper, *The Question of Jewish Theology.* What Harris denies and Petuchowski argues for, an all-embracing doctrine of God and man, is presented by Emil L. Fackenheim in his paper, *An Outline of Modern Jewish Theology,* which he has since expanded in several full length works. The late Solomon Simon, who was a leader in Yiddish cultural activity, in his article, *Illusion or Wish,* offers moving testimony of the yearning for faith in circles seemingly far removed from traditional religious forms and institutions.

The political and civic emancipation of the Jews of Western and Central Europe and the concommitant Enlightenment which ushered in "The Modern Period in Jewish Life and Thought" saw the abandonment, in wide circles, of traditional Jewish doctrines and attitudes. In our age, which has been described as "post-modern," the viability and the significance of these traditional doctrines have been warmly reaffirmed. The present volume contains two papers that seek to rehabilitate discarded values of the past: *The Personal Messiah— Toward the Restoration of a Discarded Doctrine* by Steven S. Schwarzschild, and *Jewish Mysticism in the Modern Age* by Nochumm J. Schealtiel.

The second sub-section, "Torah," focuses attention on the nature of revelation. Jacob M. Chinitz, in *The Elusive Revelation,* offers a critique of Buber who understands revelation as an experience of God but not as a body of content to be derived from Him and embodied in the Torah. The same issue is approached from a different vantage-point by Arthur A. Cohen in his paper, *Revelation and Law.* The need for a doctrine of revelation in Reform Judaism is underscored by Joseph H. Gumbiner in his paper, *Revelation and Liberal Jewish Faith.*

Torah, all-encompassing as it is, places ethics at the center of God's concern and man's duty. Jack J. Cohen presents an analysis of the Sixth Commandment, "Thou shalt not kill," from a Reconstructionist point-of-view in his paper, *Toward a Theology of Ethics*. Samuel H. Dresner highlights several traditional virtues which were particularly characteristic of Hasidism in his paper, *Prayer, Humility and Compassion*, which later appeared in expanded form as a book.

In the next sub-section, the third element in the triad of God, Torah and Israel is treated from the perspective of the Jewish religion. The late Samuel S. Cohon calls attention to the creative tension between *The Universal and the Particular in Judaism*, which is one of its unique characteristics. His paper should help to enlighten many observers, both within Judaism and without, who, lacking the breadth of sympathy and insight characteristic of the greatest exemplars of Judaism in the past, find it impossible to comprehend the relationship. As a result, they are driven either to denigrate Jewish particularism or to deny Jewish universalism. Whether their motives be laudatory or pejorative, both schools fail to embrace the totality of the Jewish world-view and, therefore, they inevitably distort its character and content.

Z. M. Schachter presents *A Contemporary Attempt at the Perennal Questions* from what may, perhaps, be described as a neo-Hasidic vantage point. A critique of Jewish nationalism from a theological position is presented by Will Herberg, in his paper, *Jewish Existence and Survival: A Theological View*. On the other hand, Emanuel Rackman offers a reinterpretation in modern terms of the organic relationship of Jewish peoplehood and religion in his essay, *Israel and God, Reflections on Their Encounter*.

The fourth and final sub-section of the volume, "God, Israel and the Holocaust" is dedicated to the greatest catastrophe in Jewish experience. More than a quarter of a century has elapsed since the most vicious and successful attempt at the extermination of the Jewish people was carried out by the Nazi butchers, with the active collaboration of their allies and the silent acquiescense of their foes. The phrase "the death of the six million" comes all too trippingly to the tongue, but it represents the most agonizing tragedy experienced in thirty centuries by a people inured to sorrow and familiar with pain. The implications of the Holocaust for faith, whether in God or in man, are only now beginning to be explored.

The monstrous inhumanity of man to man, of which the Nazi Holocaust is only the most striking aspect, has led many sensitive men of faith to espouse a "death of God" theology. In his paper, *Death of a God,* Eliezer Berkovits argues that this conclusion may be congenial to Christian theology but is both irrelevant and unnecessary for Jewish religious thought. Seymour Cain presents a summary and critical analysis of the views of three contemporary Jewish theologians, Ignaz Maybaum, Richard L. Rubenstein and Emil L. Fackenheim, in his paper, *The Question and the Answers After Auschwitz.* These views represent only a sampling of the vast amount of attention that the Nazi Holocaust has been receiving at the hands of Jewish theologians and philosophers. There are signs, too, that some Christian thinkers are being led to re-examine the relationship of Christian theology and the Christian Church to the Holocaust, on the one hand, and to the existence of the State of Israel on the other.

However stimulating and, indeed, indispensable such intellectual activity is, the fact remains that the vast majority of Nazi survivors are neither philosophers nor theologians. Many of them are men and women of simple faith, who did not pretend to understand the role of God during the bloody decades of the 1930's and 40's. They were content to struggle to keep body and soul alive, preserving themselves physically for a better day and cleaving spiritually to the conviction that what is veiled and dark for man is part of God's plan. In the depth of their anguish they echoed the words of the patient Job, "Shall we accept good from God and not accept evil?" Their faith, which survived the buffetings of cruel circumstance, is the subject of Charles W. Steckel's paper, *God and the Holocaust.*

This entire volume, dedicated to keeping Jewish faith alive in the hearts of men, is offered as a loving and humble tribute to these martyrs and heroes, whom we are proud to call our brothers.

ROBERT GORDIS

# I. The Framework of Jewish Theology

# THE EXISTENCE OF GOD

## DAVID S. SHAPIRO

### I

The existence of God has been the subject of philosophic speculation for thousands of years. It has been maintained variously that there must be a first cause, that the law and order that obtain in the physical world point to a Creator, that our idea of perfection implies the existence of the Perfect One. These demonstrations, known respectively as the cosmological, the teleological, and ontological proofs of God's existence, have been subjected to penetrating criticisms, particularly by Hume and Kant. It has been maintained that cause and effect belong to the phenomenal world. We have no right to make the leap to a world beyond our experience. The idea of perfection does not necessarily imply existence. The argument from law and order ("the argument from design") was treated by Kant with a great deal of respect, but he regarded it not as a proof for the existence of a Creator, but rather of an artist and designer employing already-given materials to produce his work. Kant, however, insisted that just as it is impossible to demonstrate in rigorous mathematical manner the existence of a Creator, so it is impossible to negate His existence. Where this intellectual vacuum

DAVID S. SHAPIRO is the author of several works in Hebrew on Jewish ethics and philosophy. He is a rabbi in Milwaukee, Wisconsin.

exists, faith can come in and take its place.

Regardless of the cogency of philosophic argumentation for the existence of God, we still have before us the problem as to the possibility of demonstrating the existence of a God who stands in relationship with humanity and human beings. Even if a Creator exists, how can we know that he is the God of justice and love? The following reflections are intended to meet this crucial question, religion's central axiom.

There obtains in human life a discontent that can never be satisfied. There is a restlessness which constantly drives us onward. We are also aware of a yearning in our hearts for something beyond the mundane. How did this restlessness and striving come into existence? The unhappiness which spurs a Moses and a Buddha to accomplish great things for mankind cannot be the product of natural selection. It serves no biological purpose. The creative pains which great spirits experience in intense measure, and which all human beings go through to some extent, even where there is no survival-value in that suffering, are evidence that man's spirit transcends itself, and touches a realm where the ego and its own are not the ultimate values.

There is a striving in human beings for justice, for goodness, for beauty, and for truth, which goes beyond concern for themselves. The symphonies of Beethoven, the formulas of Einstein, the art of Da Vinci, of what survival-value are they? And yet they are the most significant achievements of the race. There is a readiness, in many instances, to give up one's life for the realization of these values. What is the origin of this concern with the non-self? Would nature produce, maintain, and perpetuate characteristics which are self-defeating to organisms in their struggle for survival? Nature has produced beings who lack the properties that make for survival, but would it produce and perpetuate beings with propensities for self-destruction? Would nature give birth to organisms which cannot live merely *biologically*, but must find some *raison d'etre* for their existence? Going back farther, could nature which is devoid of intelligence, personality, vision, and spirituality produce and preserve these very qualities in the organisms it generates? These facts point to the existence, if not of a Creator *ex nihilo*, then certainly of a Power who alone makes possible the emergence of qualities which lift organisms above themselves to transcendent heights. He who brings forth these values, must of necessity bear some relationship to these values. The source of intelligence and personality and the striving for righteousness cannot be totally unconcerned with, and completely abstracted from, these aspects of existence.

The problem of evil is generally regarded as a powerful argument against Theism. If there is a God, and if God is good, how can He tolerate evil? Why do the righteous suffer and the wicked prosper? Why does death have the last word? Without attempting to minimize this problem, this writer submits that the basic problem is not suffering itself, but our concern with its seeming immorality. We are troubled not so much by our own suffering as by suffering as such. Evil in the universe becomes a problem once we become aware of its immoral nature. We have here adopted standards of right and wrong by which we appraise the happenings in the universe. Without relating the problem to objective standards we have no question to raise. All we can do is utter a cry of anguish when we are in pain. In raising the problem of evil, we tacitly admit that there are standards that are ultimate. We thus reach a paradox where we can only question God's existence by silently affirming it. And again the question arises: Whence does our basic faith in impersonal standards arise, standards whose only purpose seems to be to thwart us and torment us in the face of the tremendous struggle that arises in our soul? Their origin can be only in a Transcendent Spirit who has established within us the great moral ideals to which we find so much in the world that is contradictory. We can thus conclude that whereas we may derive the Architect of the physical world from the contemplation of nature, we can derive His relationship to morality and spiritual values from a contemplation of the noble strivings that stir the human breast.

That life has meaning and value is an intuition that makes our life tolerable in spite of all adversities and hardships. Every normal human being, in spite of reverses, somehow feels most of the time, that life is worthwhile, that it has a place in the cosmic scheme. Not only is life at times enjoyable, but we feel that it has a higher meaning, that it has a significance in the complete fabric of existence. This certainty which colors our entire existence, and which also gives rise to much of our misery when we face phenomena which seem to be out of joint with this basic intuition, is based on an awareness that there is a God who makes our lives meaningful and everlastingly significant. This feeling likewise must derive from a Transcendent Being who has implanted within us this assurance. For purposes of mere survival it need not have originated. The euphoria experienced by animals is sufficient for the well-being of organisms.

Men have directly experienced God as the great friend of humanity, as well as the righteous judge and loving father: men in all climes, at all times, men of all races, colors, and religions. The mystics of India, the saints of Christendom, Islam, and Judaism have known Him in varying degrees. This experience which can be duplicated by all who lead a righteous, saintly, and God-seeking life, has as much validity as our intellectual and aesthetic experiences. The common denominator of all religious experience is the presence of a Divine Providence who enters into a close relationship with all who seek Him in truth. That there have been negative aspects to this experience need not deter us from accepting its validity any more than we need to refrain from using either reason or science because of the mental aberrations of crackpots or the employment of science to destroy Hiroshima.

Human history represents the titanic struggle between great ideals and those who stand in the way of their realization. The bearers of ideals and those who battle for them are few and they struggle against great odds. They may falter and fall. Numberless obstacles may be in their path. Their enemies are mighty. Power is on their side. And yet, in the upward struggle of man, the mighty armies are crushed, and empires based on sheer force crumble to the dust. And yet ideals remain forever, even though their bearers may perish in the struggle. Who carries these ideals through thick and thin to gradual and ultimate realization? Who has saved the Word and the Truth from being crushed? Is it not the hand of God that has done this? "Grass withereth and the flower fadeth, but the word of our God remaineth forever".

## II

What is the Jewish attitude towards the problem of God's existence? It is not surprising that in Jewish writings, both ancient and medieval, we read little about actual denial of God's existence, although much is said of denying His Providence. All of Jewish history and Jewish letters revolves around God, and the relationship of God to Man and the inextricable bond which links the two are the *leitmotifs* of all our life and lore. What are the grounds for this unquestioning certainty of His existence and His concern for man that is so basic in the Jewish outlook?

The religious experience is the fundamental datum of Biblical religion. The Bible takes it for granted that man can communicate with God. It maintains that the communication between man and God is a matter of record. Factually, the entire Bible is the record of God's actual and attempted communication with man from the dawn of history to the early days of the Second Commonwealth. Moreover, the Sacred

Writings assume that this dialogic relationship between the Creator and man is a perfectly normal relationship, as that between man and his fellow. The exchange of speech between God and man ceases not because God refuses to speak to the children of men, but because man turns his back to God and refuses to hear His word. This communication does not assume a mythological form in the Bible. God does not appear bodily to human beings. He makes known His word and reveals His nature through the media of speech, dream, and vision.

It may seem paradoxical, yet it is true that the problem of God's existence could arise in all its acuity only against the background of spiritual Monotheism. In the polytheistic atmosphere that pervaded the entire civilized world, the question, is there a God, could not arise. All existence is divine. The whole world is full of gods, as Thales put it (Aristotle, *De Anima,* 411A). Only when the world revealed to our senses is not recognized as divine, does the question of God's existence come to the fore. There is a world. Is there also a God? Either we deny God's existence, or we affirm the divine nature of all existence, or we posit the existence of God who is the Creator.

Scripture seldom engages in formal philosophic reasoning. But there is no doubt that the Biblical writers were not only God-intoxicated men, but also profound thinkers and observers of nature. Their belief in God was the product of more than their personal experience of God.

The basic postulate of the Biblical writers regarding the sensual world is that, by and of itself, it is dead. Matter is not a God nor is it full of gods. Alone, it is completely inanimate. This view very likely was the result of observation of the processes of generation and decay. Everything that possesses the spirit (*ruach*) of life is born and dies. The spirit is not an inseparable aspect of the essence of living things. "Thou withdrawest their spirit (*ruach*), they perish, and return to their dust; Thou sendest forth Thy spirit (*ruach*), they are created; and Thou renewest the face of the earth" (Psalm 104.29-30). Plants, animals, and man are all mortal. They are kindred to inanimate matter. Only the spirit of life distinguishes them from matter. The spirit of life is not an essential part of nature as it appears and evanesces. Neither matter nor the spirit of life is divine. What then is the source of this spirit in animate and vegetative creation? What is the source of motion in the inanimate world? The answer is: God whose Spirit (*ruach*) infuses all creation and gives life and movement to all beings.

The first chapter of Genesis contains more than a record of the order of creation. It presents an implicit demonstration of the existence of God, the Creator and Fashioner, based on this new conception of the nature of matter. The creation-story contains no mythological elements, in spite of the arbitrary attempt of some scholars to identify the *tehom* (abyss) of Genesis 1.2, with the Akkadian deity Tiamat. We are told in this verse: "Now the earth was *tohu vavohu* and darkness was on the face of the deep". The word-combination *tohu-bohu* is found in two other places in the Bible (Isaiah 34.11; Jeremiah 4.23). From the use of this phrase in these other instances, it is evident that *tohu-bohu* means waste, desolate, lifeless. Matter itself, the writer emphasizes, is completely devoid of life. Even light itself, which makes life possible, is in itself also lifeless. It is the creation of God. Since all matter, as such, is inanimate it must, like light, be the product of God's creative word. All matter and all life originate in the spirit of God which hovered over the face of the waters. The Bible does not speak of God as hovering over the face of the waters but of His spirit (*ruach*), through which life and motion are imparted to all beings.

The argument from design which we meet in philosophic literature also appears in the Bible. In Isaiah 40.26: "Lift up your eyes on high, and see who hath created these? He that bringeth out their host by number, He calleth them all by name; By the greatness of His might, and for that He is strong in power, not one faileth". The argument here seems to be that since the heavenly host make their regular appearance without fail, they must have been created by God. Were they divine beings or independent powers they could not be under the absolute and complete rule of God. There would be havoc and disorder in the heavens above. The regularity of the processions of the heavenly bodies, as well as the regularity of all natural phenomena, is spoken of as "the ordinances (*chukkim*) of heaven and earth" (Jeremiah 33:25; 39:35-36; cf. 5:22, 24; Psalm 148:6; Job 38:33) or as "God's covenant with the day and the night" (Jeremiah 33:20). The existence of these ordinances is evidence to the Biblical writers that there is one harmony that informs the entire universe. This makes the accepted hypothesis of a multiplicity of divine powers either impossible, if they are supposedly in conflict among themselves, or totally superfluous, if we are to assume that there was cooperative endeavour among them. Since there is only one divine Power everything must have originated in His creative will. By themselves, heaven and earth and all their hosts are not divine but natural phenomena. Their existence is contingent and temporary. "Of old Thou didst lay the foundation of the earth, and the heavens are the work of Thy hands; they shall perish, but Thou shalt endure; yea, all of them shall wax old like a garment; as a vesture shalt Thou change them, and they shall pass away" (Psalm 102:26-27; cf. Isaiah 51:6).

The wisdom that is apparent in the universe aroused not only the wonder of the Biblical writers. It served them as proof of the existence of a Creator and a beneficent Providence. The infinite variety of creatures in the world is evidence of a divine wisdom. "How manifold are Thy works, O Lord! In wisdom hast Thou made them all; the earth is full of Thy creatures" (Psalm 104:24). The human artist is "filled with the spirit of God to work in all manner of workmanship, to devise skilful works, to work in gold, silver, brass, and in cutting of stones, and in carving of wood" (Exodus 31:3-5). All this varied ability, the gift of God, constitutes man's wisdom, understanding, and knowledge (Ibid. 3), and is but a meager reflection of the divine wisdom which operates with all sorts of materials to fashion its manifold works.

However, this divine wisdom manifests itself not only in the diversity of the physical properties of the various creatures. The provisions that every creature finds ready-made for its sustenance, the wonderful adaptation of all creatures to their environment, the perpetuation of species, are all to the Biblical

7

writers evidence, not of a chance relationship, but of the conscious activity of a superhuman Providence that watches over, and cares for, all creatures with wisdom (Psalm 104:10 ff; 145:15; Job 38:39; 39; 40:11-41). Even more are the wonders of the human body, its development from the embryo into a full-grown human being, regarded as evidence for a wise and beneficent Creator (Ps. 139).

It is the regularity of natural phenomena, the wisdom manifested in the variety of creatures, the adaptation of life to the world, in addition to the wondrous beauty of the heavens and earth that lead the Psalmist to break forth in song: "O Lord, our Lord, how glorious is Thy name in all the earth! whose majesty is rehearsed above the heavens" (Psalms 8:2). "The heavens declare the glory of God, and the firmament showeth His handiwork" (Ibid. 19:2). Cf. Isaiah 5:12; Psalm 92:6.

An explicit argument for divine Providence is found in Psalm 94:7 ff. "Yet they say, the Lord shall not see, neither shall the God of Jacob regard it. Understand ye brutish among the people; and ye fools, when will ye be wise? He that planteth the ear, shall He not hear? He that formed the eye, shall He not see? He that chastiseth the nations shall not He correct? He that teacheth man knowledge? The Lord knoweth the thoughts of man . . . " It is true that we need not assume that God eats because He created stomachs, but we cannot preclude from Him consciousness and knowledge. When the source of life brings forth mind, purpose, quality, and value, we can hardly assume that the source is blind, unaware of purpose, and unresponsive to value.

The existence of God and His Providence is derived by the Biblical writers from the evidence of His presence in human history. The redemption of Israel from Egypt is explained as the result of divine intervention. Israel, crushed and hopeless, could not have been liberated from its powerful enslaver unless God had lifted His mighty arm to redeem His people. This tremendous historical episode is explicitly brought forward as evidence of God's existence in Deuteronomy 4.34: "Or hath God assayed to go and take Him a nation from the midst of another nation by trials, by signs, and by wonders, and by war, and by a mighty hand, and by an outstretched arm, and by great terrors, according to all that the Lord your God did for you in Egypt before your eyes? Unto thee it was shown, that thou mightest know that the Lord He is God, there is none else beside Him". The entire course of Jewish history as well as the history of the nations is determined by the Law of Righteousness promulgated by God, and in the light of this Law all of history is interpreted. (See Deuteronomy 32:9-43, Psalm 92:5 ff., and diverse passages throughout the prophetic writings and the Hagiographa.)

# The Divine Attributes

## An Historical Survey of the Jewish Discussion

### ALEXANDER ALTMANN

THE DISCUSSION, IN JEWISH PHILOSOPHY, OF the attributes or predicates (Hebr. *to'arim;* Arab. *sifāt*) of God concerns the question how God whose essence is presumed to be unknowable can yet be spoken of in meaningful terms. This problem had not arisen in classical Greek philosophy. The Stoic distinction between mythical and philosophical theology (which goes back to Xenophanes) led only to the postulate to speak of the gods or of God in a way "befitting the divine nature" (*theoprepés*), and to the allegorical interpretation of the Homeric tales (cf. W. Jaeger, *The Theology of the Early Greek Philosophers,* 1947, 50; *Early Christianity and Greek Paideia,* 1961, 128). Greek philosophers did not clearly assert the unknowability of the essence of God (H. A. Wolfson, "The Knowability and Describability of God in Plato and Aristotle," *Harvard Studies in Classical Philology,* 56-57, 1947, 233-249). This notion was first introduced by Philo.

## I

PHILO DERIVED THE DOCTRINE OF THE unknowability of God from the Bible (cf. C. Siegfried, *Philo von Alexandria als Ausleger des Alten Testaments,* 1875, 203-204; Wolfson, *Philo: Foundations of Religious Philosophy in Judaism, Christianity, and Islam,* 1947; Third Printing, 1962, II, 86-90; 119-126). In several passages he interpreted Moses' prayer, "Reveal Thyself to me" (according to the Septuagint version of *Ex.* 33:18), as one for the knowledge of God's essence, and God's answer as pointing out that only His existence could be known, while His essence was unknowable to any created being (Wolfson, *Philo,* II, 86-87). The reason given by Philo is the incomparability of God stated in *Num.* 23:19 (according to the Septuagint: "God is not like a man"; Wolfson, *Philo,* II, 97). From God's unlikeness to any other being follows His simplicity (i.e. indivisibility) and His being "without quality" (i.e. without "accidents" such as inhere in corporeal objects, and without "form" such as inheres in matter). God belongs to no class. He is without genus or species, and consequently no concept can be formed of Him. Hence He is incomprehensible both to the senses and the mind (Wolfson, *Philo,* II, 97-110). The Scriptural passages describing God in anthropomorphic and anthropopathic terms must therefore be understood as serving a merely pedagogical purpose "for the sake of instruction and admonition" (*Immut.* II, 53-54).

ALEXANDER ALTMANN, *Philip W. Lown Professor of Jewish Philosophy at Brandeis University, has published extensively in the fields of medieval and modern thought. The present essay represents an enlarged version of an article on the subject prepared by the author for the forthcoming* Encyclopaedia Judaica.

In what sense can any attributes be ascribed to God if His essence is unknowable? According to Aristotle (*Topica*, I, 4, 101b, 25), predicables in relation to a subject in a proposition may be one of the following four: property or definition or genus or accident. On the grounds already established neither definition nor genus nor accident is applicable to God. Property, however, Philo asserts, may be attributed to God, for a property, though belonging to the subject in virtue of its own essence, is not of the essence itself. The attributes which Scripture predicates of God are therefore so many properties, and they can be reduced to one single property, *viz.* that of action. For action is in fact a property only of God, while all other beings are created and "suffer action" (*Cher.* 24, 77). "God never pauses in His activity"; He is "the source of action" in the universe (*Leg. All.* I, 3, 5; Wolfson, *Philo* II, 130-135). In other words, all the predicates of God in Scripture describe Him only by what is known of Him by the proofs of His existence, and they refer only to the casual relation of God to the world. Informally, however, Philo adds another theory of divine predicates, *viz.* negations. The unlikeness of God to any other being invites the use of negative descriptions of God such as unborn, invisible, ineffable, etc. (Wolfson, *Philo*, II, 126-127; "Albinus and Plotinus on Divine attributes," *Harvard Theological Review*, 45, 1952, 117). This theory is, however, not developed by him.

Building most probably on the foundations laid by Philo, as Wolfson has shown, Albinus and Plotinus elaborate this doctrine of divine attributes by offering a threefold classification which is reduceable to a twofold one: divine attributes are essentially either negations or references to God's casual relation to the world. "Therefore, let us take away everything from Him and let us affirm nothing of Him . . . And so also, let us not attribute to Him any of the things posterior to Him or inferior to Him, but let us bear in mind that, being above all of them, He is their cause" (*Enn.* V, 5, 13). Moreover, according to Albinus and Plotinus, God may be described by predicates which are positive or non-active in form, provided they are understood as being negative or active in meaning. Thus, God may be described as "complete in Himself" in the sense of being "without want" or as "one" in the sense of "indivisible." The term used by both Albinus and Plotinus to express the negative description of God is "abstraction" (*aphairesis*) which corresponds to the Aristotelian term "negation" (*apophasis*) and has its equivalents in the medieval Arabic, Hebrew and Latin terms used to denote the negative way of speaking about God (*salb, shelilah, negatio;* and *nafy, harḥaqah* or *biṭṭul or silluq, remotio*).

## II

ALBINUS' AND PLOTINUS' CLASSIFICATION OF DIVINE ATTRIBUTES was adopted by John of Damascus (*ca.* 676-*ca.* 749), who was the connecting link between the Church Fathers and early Islam, and other patristic writers (see Wolfson, "Philosophical Implications of the Problem of Divine Attributes in the Kalam," *JAOS*, 79, 1959, 74, 76 quoting *De fide ortho-doxa*, 1, 2, 9, 12). The discussion of the semantic value of divine attributes was thereby introduced into Islamic theology. The problem became, how-ever, more complicated as a result of two factors, *viz.* the influence of the Christian doctrine of the trinity and the consideration of the ontological status of the divine properties. As for the first, it appears that Islamic theologians, while rejecting the trinitarian concept as incompatible with the teaching of the Koran (*Sura* 4: 169; 5: 77), took the attributes of "life," "knowledge," and "power," by which some Christian theologians had characterized the Son and the Holy Spirit, as real beings or "things" existing in God from eternity and inseparable from Him (see Wolfson, "The Muslim Attributes and the Christian Trinity," *Harvard Theological Review*, 49, 1956, 1-18). This list of attributes was later increased to in-clude "will" as well as "hearing," "seeing," and "speaking." The second factor is linked to the first. The rejection of attributes in the sense of real beings by the Mu'tazilites, who well perceived the Christian implications of this doctrine, led to a differentiation between divine properties as real things and their interpretation as mere "modes" (*ahwal*), i.e. as interme-diate between "real" and "non-real" (purely conceptual). The attack upon the "realists" (termed "attributists," *sifatiyya*) was opened by Wāṣil ibn 'Aṭa' (d. 748), who, however, did not touch upon the semantic aspect. His contemporary, Jahm ibn Ṣafwān (d. 746) was the first to discuss the problem of attributes from the semantic viewpoint by stating the imper-missiveness of describing God by terms by which His creatures are des-cribed, since this would be tantamount to "likening" (tashbih) the Creator to the created. Only terms asserting God's casual relation to the world were acceptable (see Wolfson, "Philososphical Implications," 75). The nega-tive interpretation of divine attributes was first stated in Islamic theology by al-Najjār and Dirār (750-840) who denied the existence of real attri-butes in God and interpreted all affirmative predictions of God as being negative in meaning. The discussion was carried a stage further by al-Nazzām (d. 845) and Abū al-Hudhayl (d. 849) who differed as to whether the properties attributed to God are negative or causal in meaning. Their dispute concerns, as Wolfson suggests, the interpretation of the Aristotelian phrase "in virtue of itself" (*kat' hautén*) used in the passage (*Met.* XII, 7, 1072b, 26-30): "Life belongs to God, for the actuality of thought is life, and God is that actuality; and God's actu-ality in virtue of itself is life most good and eternal." An Arabic doxo-graphy of Greek philosophers has paraphrased this statement to read that "God is living in virtue of His essence (*bi-dhatihi*) and is eternal in virtue of His essence." Abū al-Hudhayl interpreted this to mean that knowledge and life signify in the case of God His very essence, and, inasmuch as His essence is unknowable, must be understood negatively: "God is knowing in virtue of a knowledge which is Himself (or His essence) ." Al-Nazzām, on the other hand, regarded Aristotle's statement to mean that the properties attributed to God have a causal or active meaning: "God is continuously knowing, living . . . in virture of Himself (bi-nafsihi) but not in virtue of knowledge, life . . ." (see Wolfson, "Philosophical Implications," 77-78) . From al-Shahrastānī's report (Milal, 34) it would appear that the controversy concerned not the difference between a negative and a causal view of Divine properties but the difference between the acceptance or non-acceptance of the doctrine of modes: Abū al-Hudhayl affirmed and al-Nazzām rejected the notion of Divine properties as "modes," i.e. ontologicaly intermediate between the real and the merely conceptual. Both are represented by al-Shahrastānī as precursors of the famous controversy about modes (cf. Milal, 55-57, 67) .

The Jewish theologians who followed the pattern of Kalam made use both of its arguments in rejecting the notion of trinity (as well as Manichean dualism) and of its formulae in dealing with the Divine attributes. The Karaite Dāwūd ibn Marwān al-Muqammiṣ, the earliest representative of Jewish Kalam, argued against the trinitarian concept as interpreted by Abu Rā'iṭa, Jacobite bishop of Takrīt (first half 9th cent.) and Nonnos (Nānā) , who, on the testimony of al-Qirqisānī, was al-Muqammiṣ' teacher (cf. G. Vajda, "Le problème de l'unité de Dieu d'après Dawud ibn Marwan al-Muqammiṣ" in: Jewish Medieval and Renaissance Studies, ed. A. Altmann, 1966) . Having established the unity of God as a "simplicity" unlike everything else, he posed the question of the Divine attributes. God's essence cannot be defined, but we may speak of Him as living, wise, hearing and seeing, provided these attributes are understood in a ṣense totally different from their normal connotation. Moreover, His life and wisdom are not distinct from His essence—an assertion of this effect would be tantamount to the Christian view—but identical with it. Al-Muqammiṣ employs al-Nazzām's formula: "He is living not by virtue of life but by virtue of Himself." He does not approve Abū al-Hudhayl's formulation since it seems to him only verbally different from the Christian one. He makes the further point that the different attributes ascribed to God do not imply distinct aspects in God. They merely represent so many negations of deficiencies in Him. By saying, "He is living" we remove the notion of death from Him, etc. Al-Muqammiṣ thus arrives at the negative interpretation of the attributes. He also reflects in some way the concept of "analogy" which Albinus had introduced in describing the causal relation between God and the world. Following Plato, Albinus had applied to it the analogy between God and the sun. Al-Muqammiṣ uses the same analogy in order to point out that the sun radiates light by its very essence and not by virtue of light acquired from outside itself, and that, a fortiori, God must be held

12

to be living and wise by His essence (see *'Ishrūn Maqālāt,* IX, quoted in a Hebrew version in Judah Barzilai's *Perush Sefer Yeṣirah,* ed. D. Kaufmann, Berlin, 1885, 77-82; edited in the original Arabic by I. O. Ginzburg, in *Zapiski Kollegii Vostokovedov,* V, 1930, 481-571). Similarly Samuel b. Ḥofni, Gaon of Sura, and Nissim b. Jacob of Kairuan reflect the Kalam treatment of the Divine attributes. The former adopts the formula that God is living, wise and powerful by His essence and not by life, wisdom and power (see W. Bacher, "Le commentaire de Samuel ibn Ḥofni sur le Pentateuque," *REJ, XVI,* 118). The latter opens his *Sefer ha-mafteaḥ* (ed. J. Goldenthal, Vienna, 1847, 1a) with a eulogy of God describing Him as "wise Himself, His wisdom being not something other than Him; knowing Himself, His knowledge not being acquired by Him from another; living eternally, not by virtue of life given to Him." The most elaborate Jewish Kalam discussion of attributes is, however, found in Saʿadya Gaon's *Book of Doctrines and Beliefs.*

Saadya finds in Scripture the following attributes assigned to God: He is one, living, powerful, wise, and unlike any other being. His unity and incomparability follow logically from the notion of "Creator" (I, 1), and the remaining three, *viz.,* life, power and knowledge are also implied in the same concept. For it is inconceivable that one not living should create, or that one not possessing power should create, or that any perfect handiwork should proceed from one not knowing how to act. These three aspects of God, although grasped at one blow, must needs be expressed by three different words, but they denote one single idea, i.e. that of Creator. Thence these three attributes do not imply a diversity in God. Just as the attribute of "Creator" does not add anything to the essence of God but merely expresses His causal relation to the world, so do the attributes of Life, Power and Wisdom, which explain the term Creator, add nothing to His essence but merely denote the existence of a world created by Him (I, 4). It would seem to follow that the three attributes are in the ultimate analysis active, not essential attributes, but this is not Saʿadya's ultimate meaning. He makes the point that whereas the life of a human being is distinct from his essence because it is followed by death, and likewise his knowledge is distinct from his essence because he is affected also by ignorance, the position is different in the case of God who is eternally, and therefore, intrinsically, alive and knowing (II, 5). Saʿadya thus upholds positive essential attributes (life, knowledge, power), although he reduces their semantic value to that of God's causality as Creator. He distinctly states that there is a difference between the essential and the active attributes of God, as explained in his *Commentary* on *Exodus* (II, 12). What he meant by active attributes as distinct from essential ones may be gathered from his statement that such Scriptural attributes as merciful, gracious, jealous and avenging "go back, so far as their ultimate mean-

13

ing is concerned, to God's works" (*ibid.*), i.e. "to His creatures, since
. . . He is free from all affect" (V, 7; see D. Kaufmann, *Geschichte der
Attributenlehre* . . ., 1877, 68-69, note 127). These attributes are active in
the sense that they express a certain affection of the creatures by the causality of God (I, 12).

By interpreting the three essential attributes as ultimately expressing God's causal relation to the world Sa'adya managed to steer clear
of the Mu'tazilite formulae discussed above. On the other hand, Sa'adya's
discussion of the three attributes bears a close resemblence to the treatment of the same theme in al-Ash'arī's (d. 935) *Kitāb al-Luma'* (Richard
J. McCarthy S.J., *The Theology of Al-Ash'arī*, Beyrouth, 1935, 12-19).
Sa'adya's originality and profundity are revealed in his elaborate exegetical treatment of the anthropomorphic references to God in Scripture (II, 9-12; see the analysis by S. Rawidowicz in *Saadya Studies*, ed.
E. I. J. Rosenthal, 1943, 139-165). The anthropomorphic terms are classified and interpreted in a non-literal, figurative sense under ten heads signifying the ten Aristotelian categories (substance, quantity, quality,, relation,
place, time, possession, posture, activity, passivity), none of which are
applicable to God. Of great interest is also Sa'adya's refutation of the
Christian doctrine of trinity (II, 5-7). The sects mentioned by him have
been identified as the Jacobites, Nestorians, Malkites, and a group which
sought to accomodate Christian doctrine to Islam (H. A. Wolfson,
"Saadia on the Trinity and Incarnation," in: *Studies and Essays in Honor
of Abraham A. Neuman*, 1962, 547-568).

### III

IN JEWISH NEOPLATONIC WRITINGS the Kalam formulae are largely eclipsed
by a new emphasis on the unity of God, based chiefly on Neoplatonic
and Pythagorean sources, the latter developing the concept of unity
found in Nicomachus of Gerasa's *Introductio Arithmetica*. At the same
time, the notion of the will of God obtrudes itself upon the discussion.
In the Long Arabic recension of the pseudepigraphical *Theology of
Aristotle* (shown by S. Pines to exhibit Isma'ilian traces) the will (*irāda*)
or command (*amr*) of God is hypostatized and identical with the word
(*kalima*) which is said also to contain the power (*qudra*) and the knowledge ('*ilm*) of God (Pines, *Revue des Études Islamiques*, 1954, 7-20). The
prominence of the concept of the will of God in the Jewish Neoplatonists may be partly due to the influence of this source. The extant writings
of Isaac Israeli, the earliest Jewish Neoplatonist, contain but few references to the attributes (cf. A. Altmann and S. M. Stern, *Isaac Israeli*, 1958,
151-158). Solomon ibn Gabirol's views are more pronounced. They appear both in his Fons Vitae and in his poem *Keter Malkhut*. God is "the
truly one" (*F. V.* III, 4; V, 30). In His unity there is no plurality, and to
Him there applies only the question "whether" He is; the questions
"what," "how," "why," or "where" can expect no answer in His case.

We hear echoes of the Kalam formulae in the *Keter Malkhut*: "Thou art alive but not by virtue of a living soul"; "Thou art wise . . . without having acquired knowledge from elsewhere." Negative terms are used particularly with reference to the "mystery" (*sod*) of the Divine unity concerning which we do not know "what it is" but which we may describe as unaffected by plurality and change, by attribute (*to'ar*) and designation (*kinnuy*). "There is no distinction between Thy Divinity and Thy Oneness, Thy eternity and Thy existence, for all is one mystery, and though the terms of each differ, they all go back to one place" (i.e. they are identical in meaning). This clear-cut negative interpretation of the Divine attributes is, however, complicated by Ibn Gabirol's doctrine that matter and form, the two constitutive principles of all created beings, derive from the essence and the will of God respectively. Matter (which is originally "spiritual" matter) proceeds from the very essence of God, and form is impressed upon, and diffused in, matter by virtue of the will. While in Plotinus the will is identical with the essence of One and implies no voluntaristic or dynamic principle, Ibn Gabirol's will tends to assume the character of a hypostatized dynamic power akin to Philo's Logos and intermediate between God and the world. In certain respects it shares in the Divine absoluteness; it cannot be described (V, 38); it is not diverse in itself (V, 37); it is the power of unity (V, 39); and it is the agent cause (IV, 20). Like the Long Recension of the *Theology*, Ibn Gabirol identifies it with the word of God (V, 36) and His wisdom (V, 42). There is, however, no precedent in the *Theology* for the dynamic character of the Will (see the discussion of this notion in Kaufmann, *Attributenlehre*, 95-115; Julius Guttmann, *Philosophies of Judaism*, 1964, 100-103; A. Altmann, Tarbiṣ, *XXVII*, 1958, 504-507).

Baḥya ibn Paquda's elaborate treatment of the attributes in the "Chapter on the Unity" in the *Ḥobot ha-lebabot* starts from the thesis that from the existence and order of the universe the existence of one single Creator can be inferred. God is one—but what is the meaning of the unity ascribed to Him? Baḥya distinguishes between two fundamentally different senses of the term "one," *viz.* the "truly one" and the "figuratively one" (I, 8; cf. Aristotle, *Met.*, V, vi, 1015b 16-17, where a distinction is made between the "accidental" and "absolute" senses of the term "one"). The truly one is "substantial" and "enduring" while the figuratively one is accidental. The latter divides (1) into the oneness attaching to pluralities under the aspects of generic, specific, or composite unity; and (2) into the oneness attaching to individual things which are in themselves composite in nature. The truly one divides into (1) the "ideational one" which is the concept of numerical unity or the "root of number" and exists in the mind only; and (2) into the truly one which exists in actuality and is identical with God. It does not multiply nor change, and it cannot be described by the attributes of bodies; it is unaffected by generation and corruption; it has no end, and it is motionless; it resembles no other thing, nor does anything resemble it; it does not associate with anything but is absolutely one and the root of all multiplicity. This table of distinctions, though ultimately indebted to Aristotle, has its immediate predecessor in a Pythagorean doxography (see al-Shahrastānī, *Milal*, 266-7) which differentiates between the essential unity which belongs to God and the accidental unity which is the "root of number." Baḥya, as we have noted, counts the root of number among essential unity but follows his source in subsuming the other senses of the term "one" under accidental unity. On the other hand, Baḥya, like his source, applies the term "the truly One" "in its true sense" to God alone who is incomparable and unique (I, 9). Having established the Neoplatonic sense of the unity of God, Baḥya proceeds to discuss the meaning of the attributes. They may be classified again under two heads, *viz.* essential and active. The essential attributes are three in number: existence, unity and eternity. They do not imply a plurality within God's essence but are negative attributes in disguise. They must be interpreted to mean that God is not non-existent; that there is no plurality in Him; and that He is not a created being. Moreover, each of the three logically implies the rest. The three attributes are therefore really one in concept, although many in linguistic terms. Baḥya is applying here to the essential attributes listed by him the argument used by Sa'adya with reference to the attributes of life, power and wisdom (which Baḥya, too, mentions in an earlier context (I, 7), together with existence, unity and eternity, as being implied in the concept of creation). The active attributes are twofold: they describe God's actions either in anthropomorphic terms or in terms of corporeal motions and acts. The Targumists have already shown us the way of interpreting these attributes in a manner befitting God's honor, and Sa'adya Gaon has discussed this subject sufficiently in his works (*Emunot we-de'ot; Com. on Torah; Com. Sefer Yeṣira*). Scripture uses these attributes in order to establish the belief in God in the souls of men (I, 10), i.e. for pedagogical reasons. Since the essence of God is unknowable, we have to exert ourselves to know Him from the "traces" of His actions. God is near to us from the aspect of His actions and far from us from the aspect of His essence. Baḥya quotes a number of Neoplatonic dicta conveying the notion of *docta ignorantia*: "He who knows most of God is the most ignorant . . ." (see D. Kaufmann, "Die Theologie des Bachja ibn Pakuda," *Gesammelte Schriften*, II, 1910, 273-4; for similar sayings as quoted by Jewish authors see Kaufmann, *Attributenlehre*, 444, n. 127, and Vajda, *Isaac Albalag*, 1960, 127, n. 5).

Like Baḥya, Josef ibn Ṣaddiq, in his *Sefer ha-'olam ha-qatan* (ed. S. Horovitz, 1903), treats the subject of the attributes after having established the true nature of the Divine unity. He adds, however, by way

16

of introduction, an incisive critique of the Kalam doctrine (known to him from the writings of the Mu'tazilite Karaite Abū Ya'qūb Yūsuf al-Bāṣir) concerning the "created will" and the attributes of God (pp. 43-47). Moreover, he advances some hints as to his own view of the Will, following pseudo-Empedocles. Unlike Baḥya, he does not clearly differentiate between the One as "root of number" and the actual Divine Unity, but this distinction would seem to be taken for granted by him, as it was in the *Epistles* of the Ikhwān (see the passages quoted by Kaufmann, *Attributenlehre*, 286-8). The One is described as the root of number and yet itself outside, prior to, and unaffected by number. It is the first and the last, the cause of all plurality and actually existent in all numbers. Calling God "one" implies no quantity; for quantity is an accident residing in a substance, and every substance is created. God's is "the true unity" which is identical with His essence. It signifies the uniqueness of God as the Creator (pp. 49-51). In his discussion of the attributes (pp. 57-59) Ibn Ṣaddiq points out that they are not separate from God's essence and that the Divine essence is not separate from the attributes. They constitute the solitary nature of God and have to be interpreted not in the sense of negating imperfections but in the sense of affirming the absolute perfection of God. True, it is better to remove positive attributes from God by negating them than to affirm them, but this is so only because the Divine perfections cannot be adequately expressed in positive terms and can be only approximations, according to human intellectual capacity, to the true Unity comprising them. The most fitting term for it is, therefore, that of "truth," i.e. "the true Being," as stated by the philosophers and Scripture (*Jer.* 10:10; see Kaufmann, *Attributenlehre*, 333-4). The Kalam formulae "living but not by virtue of life," "powerful but not by virtue of power," etc. are not only open to refutation on logical grounds but fail to take care of the eminently positive character of the Divine Unity. Similarly, the Kalam notion of the "created Will' is shown to imply absurdities. God's Will is not created but identical with the Divine essence (pp. 53-4).

The neo-Pythagorean notion of the One as "the root of number," itself being no number, plays a notable part also in Abraham ibn Ezra (*Yesod Mora,*' ch. 12; *Sefer ha-Shem*, ch. 3; *Sefer ha-Eḥad*, ch. i), but it is interpreted in a pantheistic sense: "God is the One; He is the former of All (*yoṣer ha-kol*), and He is All" (*Com. Gen.* 1:26); "For He is All, and All is from Him" (*Com. Ex.* 23:21; more passages in David Rosin's "*Die Religionsphilosophie Abraham Ibn Ezra's,*" MGWJ, 42, 1898, 60-61; see also Julius Guttmann, *Philosophies of Judaism,* 119). This concept of God being "All" does not however, imply an absolute immanentism. God is incorporeal (He has no "likeness or image"), and His simplicity excludes the duality of matter and form which is inherent in all created beings, including the angles.

17

## IV

IN JEWISH ARISTOTELIANISM the discussion of the Divine attributes reached a new level, reflecting the influence of Avicenna and, subsequently, of Averroes. The notion of God as the "necessary Being" which was introduced by Avicenna, contested by al-Ghazālī, and modified by Averroes, replaced in some measure the Neoplatonic concept of the One. Moreover, the problem of the semantic value of terms like "one" and "being" came to the fore. The traditional interpretation of these terms as either causal (relational) or negative in meaning was recognized by al-Fārābī and Avicenna but was held to require further elucidation. For even though these terms were predicated of God in a peculiar sense, they seemed to bear a generic sense as well in which they were predicated of God and other beings. They therefore appeared to be common terms with a certain difference of meaning and to amount to definitions, contrary to the assumption that God has no genus and no difference and hence no definition. Al-Fārābī answered this question by stating that common terms of this kind are predicated of God "firstly" or "in a prior manner" and of other beings "secondly" or "in a posterior manner," i.e. that the perfections implied by the predicate concerned derive from God as their cause or exemplar. According to Avicenna, the term "one" is predicated of God and other beings "in an ambiguous sense" (see H. A. Wolfson, "Avicenna, Algazali, and Averroes on Divine Attributes," in: *Homenaje a Milla's-Vallicrosa*, 1956, II, 352-358; Ibn Sina, *Livre des Directives et Remarques*, tr. A.-M. Goichon, Beyrouth-Paris, 1951, 366-369). The assertion of the "ambiguous" character of the terms in question implies the doctrine of the "analogy" of being (cf. Goichon, *loc. cit.*, note 2), a view which was not at first adopted by the Jewish Aristotelians (Abraham ibn Da'ud; Maimonides) who substituted for it the notion of the purely homonymous character of these terms. Only under the influence of Averroes did it eventually command the assent of Jewish Aristotelians (notably Gersonides).

Abraham ibn Da'ud (*Sefer ha-'emuna ha-rama*, ed. S. Weil, 48-57; German tr. 60-72) follows Avicenna in establishing the existence of God as the "necessary Being" in the sense that God's essence necessarily implies His existence, while in the cases of all other beings their existence is only "possible" and extrinsic to their essence. He compares this concept with the neo-Pythagorean concept of the One which is presupposed in all number, thus echoing the older, Neoplatonic treatment of the theme. In a manner reminiscent of Baḥya's he then reviews the various senses of the term "one" and distinguishes the "true unity" of God from all other senses of the term. Only the "necessary Being" (God) is truly one because it contains no compositeness. The angels, though free from matter (as he asserts against the view of Ibn Gabirol), are still composed of possibility of existence *per se* and necessity of existence as imparted by God. True unity is therefore established in the case of

God by virtue of His intrinsic necessary existence. Ibn Da'ud then turns to a discussion of the various attributes of which he enumerates seven: unity, truth, life, knowledge, will, power, and being. They do not constitute a plurality in God but describe the unknowable unitary essence of God from the narrow angle of our human way of thinking, much as a defective eye will see as double what is really one. Nor do the attributes imply definitions of God. They have to be interpreted as either negations or asserting God's causality. The latter, being relational attributes, do not affect His essence. The former merely signify the uniqueness and incomparability of God. Reflecting Avicenna's denial of the generic character of the term "being" as applied to God, Ibn Da'ud says that speaking of God as an incomparable Being is not to be understood in the sense that God possesses the genus "being" and the differentia "incomparable" and is thus defined. For the meaning of the term "being" in the case of God is absolutely different from the meaning of this term as applied to all other beings. Unlike Avicenna, he thus asserts the homonymity of this term. The negative meaning of the seven attributes is explained as follows: God's unity means His uniqueness and incomparability. His truth (see Aristotle, *Met.* IX, 10, 1051b 1, where being in the strictest sense is said to be truth; S. van den Bergh, *Averroes' Tahafut al-Tahafut*, II, London, 1954, 103) signifies eternal existence in the sense of His never-not-being. Life means not-non-living (or, relationally interpreted: Giver of all life). Knowledge in the sense of omniscience means absolute freedom from matter (for it is matter which impedes in the case of man the functioning of the intellect). Will is asserted of God in order to deny unconscious activity (such as happens in the operations of nature) on His part. Power means the tremendous force which moves either directly or indirectly the all-encompassing sphere. Ibn Da'ud, in this instance, uses no negation, but he seems to suggest that God's power can be spoken of only as non-identical with, and superior to, the power of the sphere. Finally, the being of God is necessary and true being because it alone has an underived and independent existence. If we realize that God's existence is undeniable and that His essence is unknowable (except, perhaps, in the afterlife) we possess the whole truth concerning God open to man. Ibn Da'ud quotes a number of Scriptural passages (*Ex.* 3: 14; *Jer.* 10: 10; etc.) which seem to him to indicate that the prophets knew by the grace of God what the philosophers had to establish by way of laborious inquiry.

## V

THE MOST INCISIVE AND, IN MANY WAYS, original treatment of the attributes is found in Maimonides' *Guide to the Perplexed* (I, 56-60). Its net result is that every attribute predicated of God is an attribute of action, or, if the attribute is intended for the apprehension of His essence and not of His action, it signifies the negation of the privation of the attribute in question (I, 58). Maimonides' overriding concern is to show that there cannot be affirmative essential attributes, i.e. affirmative predications relating to the unknowable essence of God. He makes the radical statement that "he who affirms that God has positive attributes . . . has abolished his belief in the existence of the Deity without being aware of it" (I, 60), since by superadding notions to the essence of God he denies His true reality. He deplores the liberal use of attributes by the poets (*paytanim*) and preachers as constituting a denial of faith (I, 59), for faith uninformed by correct notions is meaningless (I, 50). The anthropomorphic and anthropopathic descriptions of God in Scripture have to be understood as attributes of action or as assertions of God's absolute perfection (I, 53).

Novel elements in Maimonides' discussion of the theme are his fivefold classification of atttributes; his rejection of relational attributes; and his interpretation of negative attributes. His classification of attributes, for which there is no precedent, combines Porphry's five predicables with the nine accidental categories of Aristotle, and adds as a final class the attributes of action (see H. A. Wolfson, "The Aristotelian Predicables and Maimonides' Division of Attributes," in: *Essays and Studies in Memory of Linda R. Miller*, 1938, 151-173). Maimonides lists and discusses the following attributes: (1) A thing may have its definition and thereby its essence predicated of it. In the case of God who cannot be defined this kind of attribute is impossible. (2) A part of a definition may be predicated. This, again, is inapplicable to God; for if He had a part of an essence, His essence would be composite, which is absurd. (3) a quality subsisting in an essence may be predicated. There are four genera of qualities: (a) habits or dispositions; (b) natural power; (c) passive qualities or affections; (d) quantity. None of these is applicable to God. (4) A relation to something other than itself may be predicated of a thing, *viz.* a relation to a time or to a place or to another individual. Notions of this kind do not touch the essence of a thing nor do they indicate something subsisting in the essence, as qualities do. Yet they are inadmissible in the case of God who is not related to time or place and not even to any of the substances created by Him, for there can be no relation between two objects belonging to different genera (e.g. knowledge and sweetness), and *a fortiori* there can be no relation between God whose existence is necessary and His creatures whose existence is accidental. (5) The action performed by a certain agent may be predicated of him. This kind of attribute makes no affirmation of his essence or quality and is therefore admissible in the case of God (I, 52). Maimonides makes the point that not only the many attributes of God used in Scripture but also the four intellectually conceived attributes of life, power, knowledge and will are attributes of action and not essential attributes (I, 53). The "thirteen attributes of mercy" revealed by God to Moses (*Ex.* 34:6-7) are attributes of action. They do not denote affects (e.g. compassion) on the part of God but merely express the actions proceeding from Him in terms drawn from analogous human experiences (e.g. a father's compassion, a ruler's act of punishment). Moses' prayer to be shown the essence ("glory") of God was answered: "Thou canst not see My face" (*Ex.* 33:20) (I, 54). The reason for the unknowability of God lies in His absolute uniqueness and unlikeness to anything known to us (I, 55). Those who claim that the four attributes of life, power, knowledge and will denote His essence lose sight of the fact that these attributes when predicated of God are purely equivocal in meaning and have nothing in common with these attributions when applied to us (I, 56). Maimonides extends this verdict also to the meaning of the terms "existence" and "oneness." They normally denote accidents distinct from the essence of things, whereas in the case of God they are identical with His essence and hence bear a totally different meaning. God exists, but not through an existence other than His essence, and He is one not through oneness, even as He lives, but not through life, and is powerful and knows, but not through power and knowledge. Maimonides obviously follows Avicenna's interpretation of Aristotle's discussion of the terms "being" and "oneness" as accidental to essence (I, 57; as for the exact meaning of the term "accidental" in this context see Alexander Altmann, "Essence and Existence in Maimonides," *Bulletin of the John Rylands Library*, 35, 1953, 294-315).

Bearing in mind the equivocal nature of the terms mentioned, their use can only be described as "looseness of expression" (I, 57) and as "indulging in facile language" (I, 58). The only correct way of speaking of God's essence is that of negation. The affirmative predication of certain terms is shown to be an emphasis of the negation of opposite terms. Maimonides lists eight terms (existence, life, incorporeality, first-ness, power, knowledge, will, unity), all of which are interpreted as negative in meaning and as expressing the dissimilarity between God and all other beings. They have this logical function by negating "privations" in God; e.g. "God exists" means "God is not absent"; "He is powerful" means "He is not weak." The Aristotelian term "privation" denotes a special type of "opposites," i.e. the opposite of "habit" (e.g. blindness is a privation as the opposite of sight). The negation of a privation, therefore, logically amounts to an implied affirmation of the corresponding habit. In what sense, then, is there any advantage to be gained by interpreting affirmative predications of God as negations of privations? Obviously in order to obviate this difficulty Maimonides makes use of the Aristotelian distinction between "private negations" and "negations," the former applying when something normally belonging to a subject (e.g. sight in man) is negated (e.g. in the sentence "The man is blind") ; the latter being in place when something normally not found in a subject is denied (e.g. in the sentence "The wall is not seeing"). Maimonides clearly wishes the negations implied in affirmative predications of God to be understood as of the latter type. He uses the example of "a wall that is not seeing" (which is taken from Alexander of Aphrodisias' *Commentary* on Aristotle's *Metaphysics;* see Wolfson, *Harvard Theological Review,* 45, 1952) in order to make this point. It follows that the negation of certain terms in regard to God does not imply that its opposite is indirectly predicated of God. The negation only means that the term in question (e.g. "weak") is inapplicable to God. It also means that the affirmative term (e.g. "powerful") is equally inapplicable, and that it can be used only in an equivocal sense. Maimonides also uses another method of expressing negative attributes, i.e. by the affirmation of privation, i.e. by affirming of God terms with a negative prefix. As Wolfson has shown, Maimonides' use of the sentence "a wall that is not seeing" (*lā bāṣir*) should really be translated "a wall that is unseeing." In this form the sentence is equivalent to the former. It is, however, logically impermissible to cast it in the form "a wall that is non-seeing" (Aristotle's "indefinite term") since this would be equivalent to saying "a wall that is blind" which is logically faulty. In his early study in *JQR*, N. S. 7 (1916), pp. 20-22, Wolfson had suggested that by negative attributes Maimonides meant affirmative propositions with indefinite predicates (called "infinite judgments" by Kant) —an interpretation that had already been suggested by Hermann Cohen—but this interprtation has been shown by him to be incorrect (see for the entire above account Wolfson's essay "Maimonides on negative attributes," in *Louis Ginzberg Jubilee Volume.* 1945, 411-446).

Maimonides' doctrine of attributes reflects, fundamentally, Avicenna's position as presented by al-Ghazālī in his *Tahāfut al-falāsifa* (i.e. denial of essential attributes based on the concept of God's "necessary existence," which in turn is based on the Avicennian ontological distinction between essence and existence in the cases of all beings except God) but goes beyond Avicenna in rejecting relational attributes. It ignores al-Ghazālī's critique of the notion of necessary existence as implying absolute simplicity to the exclusion of affirmative attributes, and stresses, like Avicenna, the negative meaning of all predications of God's essence, including the one of God's "knowledge." He is most emphatic on the point that the term "knowledge" is equivocally used in regard to God and all other intelligent beings (II, 20). Unlike Avicenna, he does, not however, designate the term "intellect" when used of God as a negation of matter (as did Ibn Da'ud) but speaks of God as an intellect *in actu* in which there is a complete and permanent identity of knowing, knower and known (I, 68). The inconsistency of this usage with his negative interpretation of all other attributes was noted and severely criticized by the anonymous author of the "Treatise on the Unity of the Creator" (ed. A. Altmann, *Tarbiz,* 27, 1958, 301-309). Maimonides follows here the Aristotelian tradition (see *ibid.,* 301) which Averroes was to assert with particular emphasis against Avicenna. While agreeing with Avicenna's interpretation of the attributes as either relational or negative in meaning, Averroes differed from him by describing intellect as "the most special appelation for His (*sc.* God's) essence" ("*Tahāfut al-Tahāfut,* 310; van den Bergh, 185-186).

<h1 style="text-align:center">VI</h1>

IN POST-MAIMONIDEAN JEWISH PHILOSOPHY, the influence of Averroes became increasingly pronounced. Averroes' attack on Avicenna's ontological distinction between essence and existence (*Tahāfut al-Tahāfut,* 302-305; v.d. Bergh, 179-181; *et passim*) achieved particular prominence and led to the adoption of the theory that the Divine attributes (e.g. existence, oneness, knowledge) did not imply homonymous terms but were to be understood to denote properties related to the properties of all other beings as their infinitely superior and perfect sources of exemplars (*secundum prius et posterius*). Averroes had shown that Avicenna had confounded the logical meaning of the term "being" (signifying, as the copula in a proposition, the conformity between the concept of a thing and its corresponding reality outside the mind) and its ontological meaning (denoting essence). The latter meaning of the term referred to both substances and the other nine Aristotelian categories in an analogical sense (*secundum prius et posterius*). Being or existence was, therefore, not a general notion but an analogical one, applying to substances and the other categories in different ways, yet not as distinct from the essence. Avicenna's designation of existence as an accident to essence was in his view destructive of the fundamental character of Aristotelian philosophy (see the detailed analysis in Léon Gauthier, *Ibn Rochd,* 1948, 152–159). Essence and existence were, therefore, identical in all beings, not only in God, and the same applied to the notion of "oneness."

Isaac Albalag, one of the most rigorous medieval Jewish philosophers, followed Averroes' critique of Avicenna but tried to solve certain inconsistencies in the Averroean position by showing that the term "essence" was an equivocal term denoting the "individual essence" which exists outside the mind, and the universal essence which is a concept of the mind. Correspondingly, there are two species of existence (see G. Vajda, *Isaac Albalag,* 34-40). Following Averroes, he also adopts the doctrine of the identity in God of knowing, knower and known but amplifies this theory by establishing a hierarchy of minds culminating in the Divine intellect. The totality of forms appears at each level in different degrees of simplicity, and the essence of God is but the absolutely simple form of the entire universe. Hence God is called "the Form of the world" (ibid., 81-88). He describes the Christian notion of trinity as a vulgarized expression of the philosophical notion of the unity of knowing, knower and known in God (ibid., 89). Although Albalag admitted the legitimacy of the term "knowledge" when speaking of God secundum prius et posterius, thus repudiating the notion of absolute homonymity, he nevertheless affirmed the impossibility of our knowing the mode of God's knowledge. Similitude was in name only and not in the sense of analogy. The essence of God is existence pure and simple, and hence unknowable. All we can achieve is knowing by way of demonstration that knowing Him is impossible; to establish the fact of His existence; and to deny any similarity between Him and all other beings (ibid., 125-129). Albalag thus arrived at a negative theology not essentially different from Maimonides'.

The full implications of Averroes' critique of Avicenna appear in the more radical doctrine of Gersonides (Milḥamot Adonai, III, 3). The attributes are not to be interpreted as equivocal in meaning, since such an assumption would render invalid the difference between attributes to be affirmed and attributes to be negated. If existence is to be understood as equivocal, why not corporeality likewise? Hence attributes are to be understood secundum prius et posterius. They do not thereby imply a kind of relation and similarity between God and other beings, nor do they involve plurality. The latter point is explained by differentiating between the subject of discourse and the existential subject. God is the subject of discourse of the attributes predicated of Him, and as such may be said to have many attributes without injury to His unity. "For not every proposition in which something is affirmed of something implies plurality of that thing. There is implication of plurality only when one part of the proposition is the subject with respect to existence of the other part. But if it is not its subject with respect to existence, though it is its subject in the proposition, it does not follow that the subject is composite. For instance, if we state about a definite redness that it is a red color, it does not follow that the redness is composed of color and red, for color is not the existent subject of red, but its subject of discourse only." In other words, when predicating attributes of God we really state a relation of identity (cf. H. A. Wolfson's interpretation of this passage in JQR, N. S., 7, 38-39). Gersonides quotes Scriptural passages affirming God's oneness (Dcut. 6:4) and existence (Ex. 4:13), and he concludes from them that the attributes of intellect, life, goodness, power and will must likewise be predicated of God in a positive sense.

## VII

THE LAST SIGNIFICANT DEVELOPMENT OF THE DOCTRINE of Divine attributes in medieval Jewish philosophy is found in Ḥasday Crescas (*Or Adonai*, I, 3, 1-6). He distinguishes between the essence of God which is unknowable and essential predicates which are knowable. The latter are neither identical with God's essence nor merely accidental to it, but inseparable from it in the sense that the one cannot be thought of without the other, just as the essence and the radiative quality of a luminous object cannot be thought of separately. This mental distinction between essence and essential attribute is not in conflict with the notion of God's absolute simplicity. We may, therefore, predicate power and knowledge of God in an affirmative sense, it being understood that these attributes apply to God and other beings *secundum prius et posterius*. Nor is God's unlikeness to any other being thereby denied, seeing that the incomparability of God's necessary and infinite being and the absolute perfection of those attributes in God negate any notion of likeness. Crescas quotes the famous phrase of the *Sefer Yeṣirah* (I, 7), "as the flame is united with the coal" in order to illustrate the inseparability of God's essence and the attributes (I, 3, 3). There are, however, some attributes which are, in the final analysis, negative in meaning, *viz.* existence, unity and eternity. They denote negations of non-being, plurality and createdness respectively (*ibid.*). Yet they, too, are not equivocal terms. They apply to God and all other beings—admitting the possibility of the world's eternity—*secundum prius et posterius*. Crescas shows that existence and oneness are neither accidental to essence, as Avicenna held them to be, nor identical with the essence, as Averroes maintained, but "essential" to essence in the sense that without them essence would not be essence. They signify the non-subjectivity and non-plurality of essence, and they apply in this general connotation to God and all other beings *secundum prius et posterius* (I, 3, 1). Crescas thus firmly rejects the denial of affirmative attributes which held sway in the traditional views on the subject, and suggests that such denial may be interpreted as really referring only to God's essence, where it is, of course, legitimate, but not to His essential attributes (I, 3, 3 end).

Unlike the Aristotelians who identify God's essence with His intellect, Crescas sees the unifying principle which connects the attributes with the essence of God in His goodness. By the same token, he regards the bliss of God ("in whose abode is joy," according to the rabbinic formula) not as the joy of thinking (Aristotle, *Met.* XII, vii, 1072b 25) but as the joy of benefiting His creatures (I, 3, 5). Crescas evolves his theory of attributes largely in confrontation with Maimonides' of which he gives an excellent summary (I, 3, 3). He first raises a number of queries, showing inconsistencies and other flaws; he then makes the point that Maimonides failed to demonstrate his thesis, and, finally, he asserts

25

that Maimonides doctrine of negative attributes cannot be upheld and that the implied affirmations must refer to essential attributes and not to the essence of God itself (see H. A. Wolfson, *JQR*, N. S. 7, 182-185). Crescas re-interprets Moses' prayer to be shown God's glory as referring to the essential attributes (not to the Divine essence, as Philo and all subsequent philosophers, including Maimonides, had understood it), and God's answer (*Ex.* 33:19-23) as signifying that, while the attributes of action would be fully revealed, those termed "essential attributes" could not be perfectly grasped but visualized, as it were, "from the rear" (*secundum posterius?*). The tetragrammaton and the twelve-lettered name of God likewise indicated essential attributes.

Crescas' assertion of affirmative essential attributes non-identical with, yet unified in, the Divine essence was criticized by some scholars (according to Isaac ben Shemtob, who translated Crescas' *Refutation of the Christian Principles* from Spanish into Hebrew) as being open to the very charges which Crescas himself had leveled against the trinitarian concept. Abraham Shalom (*Neve shalom*, XII, i, 3) and Isaac Abrabanel (*Comm.* on Maimonides' *Guide*, I, 51) attacked Crescas' doctrine of essence and essential attributes as logically meaningless. The influence of Crescas is, however, traceable in his pupil's, Joseph Albo's *Sefer ha-'iqqarim* which sought to synthesize the various theories on the attributes in its elaborate discussion of the theme (II, 6-30). Necessary existence, Albo suggests, implies unity, incorporeality, timelessness, and freedom from defect. The notion of unity precludes attributes such as wisdom and power which are either esential or accidental to the essence. Incorporeality rules out bodily emotions, timelessness, relation and similarity, and freedom from defect negates every kind of deficiency. The attributes of wisdom, life, power, will are to be interpreted negatively as freedom from defects. The infinite perfection of God is implied in His timelessness. God's incorporeality establishes his having no genus, species, or accident (II, 6-7). The attributes are accordingly interpreted as terms explaining the meaning of necessary existence or as negations or as actions (II, 8) or as relations (*ibid.*). In a manner reminiscent of Crescas, Albo eventually admits affirmative attributes, i.e. those denoting perfections, as inseparable from the Divine essence and unified in Him (II, 21). He includes the attributes of action in the class of attributes of perfection (II, 22) but maintains that attributes like one, eternal, true must be interpreted in a negative way (II, 23). As for existence, Albo seems to reject both Avicenna's view which regards it as accidental to essence, and Crescas' which describes its as "essential" (II, 1, according to Wolfson's interpretation, *JQR*, N. S. 7, 215-216). In the case of God existence denotes nothing else but God's *essence* (*ibid*). Albo is obviously not consistent in this admission of essential attributes. He takes no notice of Crescas' re-interpretation of Moses' prayer but follows Maimonides (*ibid.*).

## VIII

IN MODERN JEWISH PHILOSOPHY, THE DIVINE ATTRIBUTES are no longer discussed with the stringency imposed by the medieval tradition inherited from Philo and the Neoplatonists and modified by the Aristotelians. Nevertheless, the concepts evolved by the medieval thinkers are not entirely lost. Both Moses Mendelssohn and Hermann Cohen, whose views shall be briefly reviewed, reflect in different ways, according to their respective positions, essential elements of the earlier discussion.

Mendelssohn upholds the affirmative meaning of the negative attributes (*Gesammelte Schriften* II, 1843, 114). He deals with the attributes particularly in his small treatise *Sache Gottes oder die gerettete Vorsehung* (1784), which is devoted to proving Divine providence and rectifying, from a Jewish standpoint, the theodicy offered by Leibnitz' *Causa Dei* (see Leo Strauss' incisive analysis in his essay on the subject written as an introduction to Vol. IIIb of the Jubilee edition of Mendelssohn's Works and published in *Einsichten,* Gerhard Krüger zum 60. Geburtstag, 1963, 361-375). Mendenssohn asserts in the name of "the true religion of reason" the conjunction in God of His "greatness" and His "goodness." He quotes R. Yoḥanan's dictum (*Megilla* 31a) concerning God's "greatness" and "humility" (rendering the second term by "condescending goodness") as characteristic of the Biblical notion of God (#2; in his *Morgenstunden,* ch. XV he quotes *Ps.* 113: 5-6). The greatness of God contains two parts, *viz.* His power or omnipotence and His wisdom or omniscience (#3 *seq.*). His power denotes His independence as the supreme Being which is "necessary Being" (here the Avicennian concept is re-affirmed in the Leibnitzian interpretation; see *Morgenstunden,* ch. XII) and absolutely free in its actions (#6). The wisdom of God comprises the necessary and the accidental or possible which becomes real by virtue of the Divine Will which chooses the best (#18, 26, 39). The discussion of the Divine attributes (Mendelssohn does not use this term) is directed toward the problem of theodicy, and its details need not be elaborated in our context. The essential point is that in Mendelssohn's view the infinite wisdom of God is allied to His infinite goodness (#46). The term "wise goodness" ("Betrachtungen über Bonnet's Palingenesie," *Gesammelte Schriften,* III, 166) expresses Mendelssohn's key-notion concerning God: "The laws of wisdom and of goodness cannot contradict each other" ("Jerusalem," *Ges. Schr.,* III, 270). The goodness of God connected with wisdom constitutes His "justice" which apportions to every rational being as much happiness as is compatible with the general good (#50). In its highest degree justice is "holiness" in which equity and mercy are included (*ibid.*). Mendelssohn rejects the Christian doctrine of "eternal damnation" of the impious, which Leibnitz had defended, as irreconcilable with the justice of God (#60). The concept of the goodness of God implies that God's punishment of the sinner, is meant for the sake of the sinner's improvement. Hence no punishment can be eternal (see the analysis in L. Strauss' essay, 368 *seq.*). Mendelssohn lays great stress on the agreement between Judaism ("our religion") and Reason in this matter (#60; *Ges. Schr.*, III, 131; V, 565) which formed an important topic of discussion in the Age of Enlightenment (cf. G. E. Lessing's "Leibnitz von den ewigen Strafen.")

Hermann Cohen presents his concept of the attributes of God in much closer dependence on the medieval Islamic and Jewish philosophers, particularly on Maimonides. He repudiates, however, the notions of essence and existence as they appear in medieval ontologism (Anselm's argument for the existence of God), and sharply differentiates between the "idea" of God and the assertion of His "reality." God cannot be "real" since reality is related to apperception by the senses. He is an "idea" in the specific sense which this term has in Cohen's Neo-Kantian idealism. He sees the entire history of Jewish monotheism as moving toward this idea. Its denial, in many ways, of anthropomorphism is in his view a case in point. The concept of the unity of God in Judaism must not be confounded with that of a mere oneness. From Xenophanes onward (who "looking upon the entire Heaven said that the One was God") the notions of being, oneness, and God appear related to one another. This pantheistic viewpoint is, however, not religion in the Jewish sense. Nor does the term "oneness" suffice. For it is merely negative in meaning. Cohen adopts the term "uniqueness" (*Einzigkeit*), which he identifies with the term *eḥad* in the Shema‘ and the "rabbinic" term *yiḥud* (*Religion der Vernunft aus den Quellen des Judentums*, 1919, 46-48; *Jüdische Schriften*, ed. Bruno Strauss, 1924, I, 87-92). It denotes God as the only Being in the true sense of the word, and it signifies also His incomparability (*Isa.* 40:25), eternity and causality (*Religion der Vernuft*, 51-54; 70). Cohen recognizes the doctrine of negative attributes as a significant philosophical achievement for the safeguarding of the monotheistic concept (*loc. cit.*, 70-71). He interprets Maimonides' theory of negative attributes in the sense of Kant's term "infinite judgment," thereby giving such propositions as e.g. "God is not weak" the logical form "God is not non-active" which implies the absolute negation of negativity and the affirmation of positivity in the most eminent sense (*Jüdische Schriften*, 252, 257; *Religion der Vernunft*, 72-73). Moreover, he links this alleged use of the infinite judgment in Maimonides with his own concept of *Ursprung* (*principium;* Greek: *arché*) which he had introduced in his *Logic of Pure Reason* as the thinking which alone can produce what

28

may be considered as being, and which does not depend on the data of sense experience. In analogy to this concept of logic, the attribute of activity discovered by the afore-mentioned infinite judgment in relation to God denotes the idea of God as the *Ursprung* or principle of all activity (*Religion der Vernunft*, 73-74). As the unique Being God is the ground of all being. The finite has its origin in the Infinite, in the negation of its privation. The concept of God as Creator follows from the concept of God's uniqueness (*loc. cit.*, 73-77).

Cohen interprets Maimonides' attributes of action as expressing the "correlation" between God and men. (On the concept of correlation in Cohen, see A. Altmann, *In Zwei Welten*, ed. H. Tramer, 1962, 377–399.) They denote exemplars for man's actions rather than qualities in God (*Religion der Vernunft*, 109 *seq.*; 252, 313). They can be reduced to two: love and justice. They, and not the "essence" of God, were revealed to Moses (*loc. cit.*, 92-94; 110). These moral attributes are identical with holiness (understood as a moral quality) and goodness (*loc. cit.*, III). In Cohen's ethical monotheism the attributes of God become "concepts of virtue for man" (*loc. cit.*, 476, 480).

# II. Jewish Religious Thought Through the Ages

## A. The Biblical Foundations

# THE DIVINE PATHOS

*The Basic Category of Prophetic Theology*

ABRAHAM J. HESCHEL

How can we define the prophetic consciousness in relation to God? The prophetic consciousness was, of course, a consciousness about the world, but the prophets did not see the world as a superficial succession of causes and effects in the world; they saw it rather as a meaningful relation among events. History revealed the work of God and therefore needed interpretation. To the prophet God is never an object; He is always a person, a subject. The prophet does not think of God as of something absolute in the sense of unrelated; he thinks of Him primarily as of One who takes a direct part in the events of the world.

The prophets never ask: *"What* is God?" They are interested only in His activity and influence in human affairs. Even their views of what we would call basic principles took the form of concrete aims and tasks. It is from this point of view that we must try to answer the questions: What is typically prophetic theology like? What attitude to God defines the meaning of prophecy? Which

aspect of the monotheism they affirmed had the most decisive influence upon their thought and feeling?

To the prophet, as we have noted, God does not reveal himself in an abstract absoluteness, but in a specific and unique way — in a personal and *intimate* relation to the world. God does not simply command and expect obedience; he is also moved and affected by what happens in the world and he *reacts* accordingly. Events and human actions arouse in Him joy or sorrow, pleasure or wrath. He is not conceived as judging facts so to speak "objectively," in detached impassivity. He reacts in an intimate and subjective manner, and thus determines the value of events. Quite obviously in the biblical view man's deeds can move Him, affect Him, grieve Him, or, on the other hand, gladden and please Him. This notion that God can be intimately affected, that he possesses not merely intelligence and will, but also feeling and *pathos*, basically defines the prophetic consciousness of God.

*Pathos* is not, however, to be understood as mere feeling. Pathos is an act formed with intention, depending on free will, the result of decision and determination. The divine *pathos* is the theme of the prophetic mission. The aim of the prophet is to reorient the people by communicating to them the divine

ABRAHAM J. HESCHEL is Associate Professor of Jewish Ethics and Mysticism at the Jewish Theological Seminary and is the author of a number of studies in Jewish theology. The present paper is an excerpt of Part 3, Chapter 1 of his Die Prophetie, Cracow 1936 and is the work of Mr. William Wolf.

*pathos* which, by impelling the people to "return", is itself transformed. Even "in the moment of anger" (Jer. 18:7), what God intends is not that His anger should be executed but that it should be appeased and annulled by the people's repentance.

The divine *pathos* is not merely intentional; it is also transitive. The gods of mythology are self-centered, egoistic. Their passions — erotic· love, jealousy, envy — are determined by considerations of self. *Pathos,* on the other hand, is not a self-centered and self-contained state; it is always, in prophetic thinking, directed outward; it always expresses a relation to man. It is therefore not one of God's attributes as such. It has not a reflective, but rather a transitive character. Hence, whereas in the mythological genealogy of the gods man plays no part, the "history" of God cannot be separated from the history of the People Israel: the history of the divine *pathos* is embedded in human affairs.

In primitive religion, God's anger is something arbitrary, and unrelated to any conditions. The prophetic thought that human actions bring about divine *pathos,* emphasizes the unique position that man occupies in his relation to God. The divine *pathos* rooted though it is in God's free will, emerges in the context of conditions which are quite clearly human conditions.

The prophets know two different kinds of divine *pathos:* from the point of view of man, the *pathos* of redemption and that of affliction; from the point of view of God, the *pathos* of sympathy and that of rejection. But the fact that rejection seems to occur more frequently in the biblical account should not be taken to prove that wrath is inherently one of God's chief attributes. On the contrary, prophecy aims at the annulment of the *pathos* of affliction and rejection. The prophets experience God's wrath as suffering which He receives at the hand of man. It is the incredible disloyalty of His people which arouses in Him the *pathos* which afflicts. God's word comes as an appeal and a warning to His people not to arouse His anger.

The basic features emerging from the above analysis indicate that the divine *pathos* is not conceived as an essential attribute of God. The *pathos* is not felt as something objective, as a finality with which man is confronted, but as an expression of God's will; it is a functional rather than a substantial reality. The prophets never identify God's *pathos* with His essence, because it is for them not something absolute, but a form of relation. Indeed, prophecy would be impossible were the divine *pathos* in its particular structure a necessary attribute of God. If the structure of the *pathos* were immutable and remained unchanged even after the people had "turned", prophecy would lose its function, which is precisely so to influence men as to bring about a change in the divine pathos of rejection and affliction.

God's *pathos* is obviously not to be understood as a powerful wave of emotion which overwhelms and sweeps everything away since for the prophets justice is a basic feature of God's ways. *Pathos* and *ethos* do not simply exist side by side, opposing one another; they pass into each another. Because God is the absolute source of value, His *pathos* is always ethical. The divine *pathos* is a form of expression of God's absolute value.

*Pathos* is not something created arbitrarily. Its inner law is the moral law, for *ethos* is immanent in *pathos.* God is concerned about the world and shares in its fate. How could His *ethos* express itself more deeply and more immediately than by this intimate and emotional participation? But to identify God with the moral idea would be contrary to the very meaning of prophetic theology. God is not the appointed guardian of the moral order. He is not an intermediary between a transcendental idea of the good and man. The prophet does not think of Him as a being whose function it is to supervise the moral order and to bring about the realization of an autonomous morality. Morality is the norm, not the structure of the relation between God and man. As love cannot be identified with the values found in it, so the relation between God and man cannot be associated simply with the value of the moral idea. The *pathos*-structure of divine *ethos* implied and follows from the unlimited sovereignty of God. If the moral law were something absolute and final, it would represent a destiny to which God Himself would be subject. Far from being sovereign, God would then fall into dependence on rigid, objective norms.

The subjection of the moral idea to the divine *pathos* is the indispensable assumption of prophetic religion. Mercy, repentence, forgiveness, would be impossible if moral principle were held to be superior to God. God's call to man, which figures so frequently in the writings of the prophets, presupposes subjective ethics. God's repenting a decision which was based on moral grounds clearly shows the supremacy of *pathos*. Let us take the idea of retaliation as an example. Whereas in Hindu religion retaliation is automatic, punishment following crime; in prophetic religion, it is seen not as a blind movement of mechanical power, but as directed by the *pathos* of conscience and will. This is why it was only in Biblical religion that the powerful and paradoxical idea could be developed.

A comparison with other theological systems can help to reveal the unique-ness of the prophetic idea of God. The Stoics considered *pathos* to be unreasonable and unnatural emotion, whereas apathy — the subduing and the overcoming of the emotions — was taken to be supreme moral task. Spinoza held feeling to be "confused ideas." Laotse's *Tao* (the "divine way") is the eternal silence, the everlasting calm and the unchangeable law of the cosmic order. In accordance with *Tao*, man is to rid himself of desire and sympathy, greed and passion, and humbly and quietly become like *Tao*. Zeal and unrest are to be avoided. To live according to *Tao* means to live passively. The God of the prophets, however, is not the Law, but the Lawgiver. The order emanating from Him is not a rigid, unchangeable structure, but a historic-dynamical reality. Aristotle's god ever rests in itself. Things long for it and thus are set into motion; it is in this sense the "prime mover," but is itself immovable. Aristotle's God knows no feeling or suffering; it is simply pure thought thinking itself. The prophet's God is concerned with the world, and His thoughts are about it. He is the God of the fathers, the God of the covenant. The divine *pathos* expresses itself in the relation between God and His people. God is the "Holy One of Israel."

Many civilizations too, know an inescapable, unyielding power standing above the gods. Fate is supreme; it cannot be evaded. The divine *pathos*, on the other hand, strives at overcoming destiny. Its dynamic character, which makes every decision provisional, conquers fate. In Greek theology, the highest power does not need man. Events are a monologue. But Jewish religion starts with the covenant: God *and* man. An apathetical, immobile conception of God could not possibly fit into prophetic religion.

The divine *pathos*, though it is rooted in His freedom, is not simply will. God as pure will is found in Islam. In the Koran, Allah is represented as a will removed from all considerations, working without any relation to actuality. Since everything is rigorously determined, the dialogue is again reduced to a monologue. Central is not the relation between Allah and man, but simply Allah himself. The prophets explicitly fought against the idea, widespread even in Palestine, that God was the Creator of the world but did not interfere with the course of nature and history. This essentially deistic notion has no place for the divine *pathos* because it has no place for any genuine connection between God and the world.

The decisive importance of the idea of divine *pathos* emerges clearly when we consider the possible forms in which God's relation to the world may present itself. A purely ethical monotheism in which God, the guardian of the moral order, keeps the world subject to the law, would restrict the scope of God's knowledge and concern to what is of ethical significance. God's relation to man would, in general, run along the lines of a universal principle. The divine *pathos* alone is able to break through this rigidity and create new dimensions for the unique, the specific, and the particular.

The idea of divine *pathos* throws light on many types of relation between God and man unknown in apathetic religion. The covenant between God and Israel is an example. The category of divine *pathos* leads to the basic affirmation that God is interested in human history, that every deed and event in the world concerns Him and arouses His reaction. What is characteristic of the prophets is not foreknowledge of the future but insight into the present *pathos* of God.

The idea of divine *pathos* has also its anthropological significance. Man has his relation to God. A religion without man is as impossible as a religion without God. That God takes man seriously is shown by his concern for human existence. It finds its deepest expression in the fact that God can actually suffer. At the heart of the prophetic affirmation is the certainty that God is concerned about the world to the point of suffering.

In sum, the divine *pathos* is the unity of the eternal and the temporal, of the rational and the irrational, of the metaphysical and the historical. It is the real basis of the relation between God and man, of the correlation of Creator and creation, of the dialogue between the Holy One of Israel and His people.

The meaning of the divine *pathos* was often misunderstood by Jewish as well as by Christian and Islamic religious philosophy, which tended to overlook its specific form and content and to interpret it as simply an aspect of anthropomorphism, or to be more precise, of anthropopathism.

Marcion, the gnostic leader, bitterly assailed anthropopathism. In the polemics of Jews and Christians against heathenism, the emotions of the pagan gods formed a favorite target of attack. In more modern times, too, exception was frequently taken to God's wrath, which was held to be incompatible with His justice and love. But, of course, God's wrath is not something in itself but is part of the entire structure of the divine *pathos*. God's anger is conditioned by God's will and aroused by man's sins; it can be dissipated by the "return" of the people. Divine wrath is not opposed to love, but rather its counterpart. It is the very evidence of God's love. Only because God loves His people is He capable of being kindled with anger against them. God's love, justice, and wrath are part of the same structure of divine *pathos*.

Embarrassment over the "emotional"

and irrational features of the biblical account of God induced the so-called historical school of Bible criticism to assume an evolutionary development. In ancient times, it was alleged, Israel knew only the awe-inspiring God; in later times, however, they came to think of God as a kind and loving God. This view is neither true to fact nor in line with the fundamental biblical outlook. It likewise ignores the crucial polarity — love and anger, justice and mercy — which characterizes the divine *pathos*.

Whether philosophical or historical, the objections to anthropopathism have generally prevailed. Why? What has been the strength of this opposition to the idea of divine *pathos*? It seems to us to be due to a combination of various tendencies which have their origin in Greek classical philosophy. The Eleatics taught that whatever exists is unchangeable. This ontological view was very soon put to use to determine the nature of God. Xenophanes, Anaxagoras, Plato, and Aristotle followed in much the same line. The principle that mutability cannot be attributed to God is thus an ontological dogma, and as such it has become the common property of religious philosophers.

It is easy to see how on the basis of the ontological view of the Eleatics there emerged a static conception of God. According to Greek thinking, impassivity and immobility are characteristic of the divine. Now since in Greek psychology, affects or feelings are described as emotions (movements) of the soul, it is obvious that they cannot be brought into harmony with the idea of God. The ontological basis of this system of thought may, of course, be challenged by another ontological system which sees in changeability the very sign of real being. Such a system will lead to a dynamic rather than static idea of God.

Since Plato, we have become familiar with the distinction between a rational immortal component of the human soul and one that is irrational and mortal. The rational component is believed to be indivisible, whereas the irrational one is usually subdivided into a noble and a less noble part, the former comprising the passions, the latter the evil desires. In medieval philosophy, the three elements are reduced to two, but in either case the life of the emotions is separated from the realm of the rational. The dualism of values thus engendered has deeply penetrated Western thinking. To the degree that theology has subscribed to this dualism of values, it has attributed to God the power of thinking, but excluded the emotions. But this dualism is utterly foreign to Biblical thinking. The emotions are part of the entire spiritual structure, and Scripture never demeans them.

The wisdom of the Greek exalted reason above the passions. Zeno even demanded the complete extinction of the feelings on moral grounds. All the other schools of Greek ethics acknowledged the inferior character of the irrational emotions as against the rational part of the soul. This opinion was projected into theology. The ideal of the sage was made to find its realization in God. Plato constantly stressed the notion that the gods are without emotions, desires, or needs.

The Greek word *pathos* implies suffering. In the Greek view, *pathos* is necessarily passive; in the state of *pathos*, one is affected and directed by another from the outside. From very early times, it was felt that God could not be affected in such a way. God, the Supreme Cause, could not possibly suffer from or be affected by something which is effected by Himself. Passivity was held to be incompatible with the dignity of the Divine. It was on these grounds that anthropopathism was rejected. But this whole line of thinking makes little sense in biblical terms. In the Bible, God desires to be loved.

Authentic Jewish thought evaluates the emotions in a manner diametrically opposed to the Greek view. The emotions have often been regarded as inspirations from God, as the reflection of a higher power. Neither in the legal nor in the moral parts of the Bible is there a suggestion that the desires and the passions are to be negated. Asceticism was not the ideal of biblical man. Since the feelings were considered valuable, there was no reason to eliminate them from the conception of God. An apathetic and ascetic God would have struck biblical man with a sense not of dignity and grandeur but rather of poverty and emptiness. Only through arbitrary allegorizing was later religious philosophy able to find an apathetic God in the Bible.

Recognizing the motives lying behind the Greek rejection of anthropopathism helps us get an insight into the meaning of the teaching itself. We can see how very questionable are the presuppositions in terms of which anthropopathism was for centuries repudiated by religious philosophy. Present-day philosophy has abandoned many of these axioms taken over from ancient Greek philosophy and it will also have to revise its attitude towards anthropopathism.

The mystic strives to experience God as something final, immediate. In mythical thinking, too, God Himself is the object of the imagination. For the aborigines, indeed, God dwells in the visible symbol. Once religious thinking proclaimed God to be invisible and different from man, there would seem to be no escaping agnosticism. The prophets overcame this dilemma by separating essence and expression. They were not out to experience God Himself, but rather His expressions in the image of vision, in the word of inspiration, in the acts of history. Prophetic revelation, indeed, does not reveal anything about God's essence. What the prophet knows about God is God's *pathos*, but this is not experienced as a part of the divine essence. Not God Himself is the object of understanding, but only His relation to Israel and to the world. Hence revelation means not that God makes Himself known, but that He makes His will known. In the separation of essence and relation the prophetic knowledge of God becomes possible.

The prophets are familiar with various forms of the divine *pathos:* love and anger, mercy and indignation, kindness and wrath. But what is, so to speak, the intrinsic property of the divine *pathos?*

In every one of its forms, the divine *pathos* points to a connection between God and man — a connection which originates with God. God "looks at" the world and its events. He experiences and judges them; this means that He is concerned with man and is somehow related to His people. The basic feature of the divine *pathos* is God's transcendental attention to man.

Yet even here we must not think that we reach God's essence. God's transcendental attention merely defines the limits of the prophet's understanding of God. The prophet never speculates about God's real being. In the divine *pathos,* which is a manifestation of God's transcendental attention, he finds the answer to the events of life. For in it is implied God's interest in the world and His concern for it.

The world is looked upon by God. God knows us. God can be experienced by us only if and when we are aware of His attention to us, of His being concerned with us. The prophet is impressed by God's concern with the world. This is the ultimate reality for prophetic spirituality.

God's transcendental attention engenders in man the sense of being the object of the divine subject. In all that the prophets knew about God, they never found in Him a desire which did not bear upon man. God is not the object of religious discovery, but the sovereign subject of revelation. He is the supreme subject.

# THE TEMPTATION OF JOB—
# TRADITION VERSUS EXPERIENCE
# IN RELIGION

## ROBERT GORDIS

**E**ver since Matthew Arnold called attention to Hellas and Israel as the two sources of Western civilization, it has been a widespread practice to draw contrasts, eloquent or epigrammatic, between these two creative cultures. Greece was the home of philosophy and reason; Palestine, of religion and morality. Hellas invented science, Israel discovered conscience. The Greek ethos was predominently intellectual and skeptical, its highest symbol being the philosopher; the Hebrew ethos basically emotional and moral, rooted in faith, its noblest exemplar being the prophet.

Now the fundamental unity of the human spirit should have made us wary in advance of drawing such sharp distinctions between two peoples. As modern scholarship has explored all the facets of life in both centers, it has documented the similarities of the Greeks and the Hebrews, as well as their differences. Notable progress has been registered in the study of Greek reli-

Robert Gordis is Associate Professor of Bible at the Jewish Theological Seminary and Adjunct Professor of Religion at Columbia University. His most recent publication is a volume entitled *Judaism for the Modern Age*. The present paper was read at the Institute of Religious and Social Studies of the Jewish Theological Seminary.

gion, expressed both in public rites, which spoke for the group, and in the mystery cults, which appealed to the individual. These investigations have served to reveal the emotional, non-rational aspects of the Greek spirit. Conversely, contemporary research into Biblical Wisdom literature has indicated a strong intellectual cast in Jewish religious thought. Divergences undoubtedly exist between the Greek and the Hebrew spirit, but they are largely differences in emphasis, significant, to be sure, but not mutually exclusive.

Consider, for example, what may perhaps be described as the supreme embodiment of the creative genius of the two peoples, the *Dialogues of Plato* and the *Book of Job*. Here the distinctions between the two cultures are most striking. The *Dialogues* are, of course, the expression of an incisive intelligence, seeking to establish the proper norms of human conduct through the exercise of reason. In Books I and II of *The Republic,* the effort is made to analyze the concept of justice, discarding false notions and arriving at a true understanding. It is the same theme that preoccupies the author of Job, but what a world of difference in temperament and method, in the mode of expression and in the conclusions reached! Nowhere in Job is there an analysis undertaken of the nature of right and wrong. What the Greek philosopher sought to discover through the mind, the Hebrew poet knew through the heart. It is not merely Job's antagonists in the Debate who are certain that right is right and wrong is wrong. He, himself, never differs with them on the nature of righteousness. To raise such questions is possible only for sinners who wish to confuse their fellows so that they may despoil them.

Woe unto them that call evil good,
And good evil;
That change darkness into light,
And light into darkness;
That change bitter into sweet,
And sweet into bitter! (Isa. 5:20)

For honorable men, however, the truth was clear: "It hath been told thee, O man, what is good and what the Lord thy God doth require of thee, to do justice, to love mercy, and to walk humbly with thy God" (Micah 6:8). Man knows the good because God has revealed it to him—and justice and mercy are recognizable by their presence or absence in human affairs.

The far-reaching difference between Plato and Job, in content and temper, is reflected in the striking variation of form. The Greek *Dialogues* are prose, the Hebrew *Dialogues*, exalted poetry. If we seek a parallel to Job in the Hellenic world, we must turn to Aeschylus, perhaps the most "Hebraic" of the Greeks.

Having noted the vast distinctions between Plato and Job, we should not ignore the affinities, recognizing that what is primary in the one is likely to be secondary in the other. It would be a grave error to underestimate the emotional drive underlying the ostensibly cool analysis of the Socratic dialogues. It was the poet in Plato that led him to banish poets from his Republic, for he knew the strength of the irrational, creative aspects of human nature, which brook no discipline and confound the neatest blueprints of the future. The entire structure of Platonic ideas is a creation of the poetic faculty, a myth which seeks to interpret the nature of reality. To ignore the emotional underpinning of the Platonic dialogues is fatal to their understanding.

## II

Equally disastrous is the failure to recognize the strong intellectual content of the book of *Job*. It is not merely that the author of *Job* is, in Pfeiffer's words, the most learned ancient before Plato; indeed, he possesses a range of knowledge and perhaps of experience that recalls that of Shakespeare. The Temptation of Job, the heart of the tragedy and the triumph is, to be sure, expressed in passionately emotional terms, but it is intellectual as much as it is moral. Beyond the specific issue of the problem of suffering, with which it is concerned, the book posits a problem as enduring as man himself, who remembers the past, but lives in the present, and it points the way to an answer. *This perennial issue is the conflict between the accepted tradition of the group and the personal experience of the individual.* Though Job has suffered the full gamut of human misery, the accepted religious doctrine of his day has a ready answer: suffering is the result and, consequently, the sign of sin. Heretofore, Job has never had cause to doubt the proposition, for it was a logical consequence of his faith in a world ruled by a just God. In fact, Job's prosperity and well-being was the best evidence of the truth of the conventional doctrine! Now he has been exposed to a rapid succession of calamities that have destroyed his wealth, decimated his family and wracked his body with loathsome disease.

For his Friends, the severity of Job's affliction serves only to demonstrate the gravity of his offences. A few months ago, Job himself, would not have doubted the conclusion. Had it been reported to him during the period of his well-being that some individual had been visited by such devastating blows, the God-fearing Job would have reacted exactly as do his Friends.

Hence, the discussion does not begin as a debate at the outset. When the Friends come to comfort Job in his affliction, they naturally take it for granted that his faith is unshaken. For even his tragic lament on the day of his birth (ch. 3) is couched in general terms; it is not yet directed against God. Eliphaz is certain that all that is required is to remind Job of the basic religious truth that has been momentarily darkened for him by his suffering:

If one venture a word unto thee,
   wilt thou be weary?
But now it is come unto thee, and
   thou canst not bear it,
It toucheth thee, and thou art
   affrighted.
Remember, I pray thee, who ever
   perished, being innocent?
            (Job 4:2, 5, 7)

Soon enough, Eliphaz and his colleagues discover that it is a vastly changed Job that confronts them. Job has undergone a shattering personal experience, but he knows, with the knowledge that defies all logic, that he is innocent. He must now choose between tradition and experience, between the body of convictions and beliefs accumulated by the generations, on the one hand, and the testimony of his own

senses and reactions on the other. For the individual to set himself up against the generality of mankind is both a tragic and a heroic enterprise. Its pathos in Job's case is heightened by the feeling, which he himself had always shared, that the body of religious truth which he now opposes is the very bedrock of morality. His adversaries can, therefore, accuse him in all sincerity of undermining the foundations of society. In Bildad's words:

Thou that tearest thyself in thine
   anger,
Shall the earth be forsaken for thee?
Or shall the rock be removed out
   of its place?
            (Job 18:4)

The personal suffering involved is intense for all concerned, for Job, who now recognizes his loneliness in a world where once he was at home, and for his Friends, who stand helplessly by as the chasm opens between them.

### III

Job's tragedy, however, goes deeper, for he is compelled to challenge no superficial body of ideas, but the very heart and essence of Biblical thought. The axis on which all of Hebrew religion turns is the tension between the two poles, one that of faith in God, the just Ruler of the universe, the other, the widespread phenomenon of human suffering. The profoundest spirits in Israel had labored to resolve the tragic paradox of evil in God's world. In the process, an imposing body of thought had grown up in which the lawgiver, the prophet, the historian and the sage had each played a part, either in emphasizing one pole or the other, or in seeking to reconcile the contradiction through a theodicy justifying the ways of God to man.

At the very beginning of Israel's meeting with God, the process had begun. For the Decalogue proclaimed on Sinai rests on faith in the justice of God as an effective force in the universe. In that immortal Code, God has introduced Himself, as Judah Halevi had noted in another connection, not as the Creator of heaven and earth, but as the author of liberty, who had brought Israel out of the house of bondage. The implication of the First Commandment, probably not immediately apparent to all of Moses' contemporaries, was that God held universal sway and was no merely national deity limited to his own territorial domain, like the gods of the Canaanites, the Ammonites or the Moabites. The God of Israel, who had delivered the weak from slavery in a foreign land and had executed judgment upon their oppressors, was by that token both all-powerful and all-just.

From this basic conviction, the Pentateuchal doctrine of retribution followed naturally; righteousness would be rewarded and wickedness would receive its condign punishment. The doctrine was expressed in the famous Deuteronomic passage incorporated into the Shema (Deut. 11:13-17). The principle was elaborated with graphic power in the Comminations, which set forth the reward of righteousness and the penalty of sin for the nation (Lev. chap. 26 and Deut. chap. 28).

The doctrine of retribution could be held with total conviction, because it arose early in Hebrew history, when group-consciousness was all powerful and the individual was conceived of as little more than a cell in the larger organism. A man's personal destiny had no existence apart from the clan and the nation to which he belonged.

The Biblical historians, the authors of Joshua, Judges, Samuel and Kings, made the doctrine of national retribution the cornerstone of their philosophy of history, explaining the ebb and flow of Hebrew prosperity and disaster in terms of the people's fluctuating obedience or resistance to the word of God. The prophet, Hosea, emphasized that the law of consequence was rooted in the universe, by expressing it in a metaphor drawn from nature:

For they sow the wind, and they
  shall reap the whirlwind . . .
Sow to yourselves in righteousness,
  reap in mercy,
Break up the fallow ground,
For it is time to seek the Lord,
Till he come and teach you right-
  eousness.
Ye have plowed wickedness, you
  have reaped iniquity,
Ye have eaten the fruit of lies.
        (Hosea 8:7; 10:12,13)

Hosea's older contemporary, Amos, had applied the same principle of justice as the law of history to contemporary world affairs and found in it the key to the destiny of all the neighboring nations and not only of Israel (Amos, chap. 1, 2).

Even in its collective form, the doctrine of retribution created immense difficulties. In their effort to resolve these problems, the Prophets deepened the content of Hebrew religion. If God is all-righteous, it follows that a sinful people, even if it be Israel, deserves to perish. The Prophets of Israel loved God, but they loved their people too, and could not make their peace with this logical but devastating conclusion. Thus, Amos, confronted by the iniquitous Kingdom of Israel, which refused even to hear his message, let alone reorder its national existence, foretold the annihilation of the northern state. But the total disappearance of his people was an intolerable prospect for the Hebrew prophet, both because of his natural attachment to his kinsmen and his conviction that God's word needed a spokesman in an idolatrous world. After his expulsion from the Northern Kingdom, Amos transferred his hopes for the future to the smaller and weaker kingdom of Judah (Amos 9:8 ff.).

A generation later, his spiritual descendant, Isaiah of Jerusalem, faced the same heart-rending challenge of a righteous God judging His sinful people. Incomparably the greatest intellect among the Prophets, Isaiah refined still further Amos' faith that part of the Hebrew people would survive, by enunciating his doctrine of the Saving Remnant. Not all of Judah, but some of Judah, would be saved. History was a process of the survival of the spiritually fittest, directed by God, who would reveal those capable of regeneration and salvation.

Another challenge confronted Isaiah's faith in the God of hosts who is exalted in righteousness. The Assyrian conqueror, infinitely more arrogant and cruel than Israel had ever been, was treading all other nations, including Israel, under foot. How could that spectacle of evil triumphant be reconciled with a just and almighty God? This contradiction Isaiah resolved by another profound insight, the concept of "the rod of God's anger". Assyria, pitiful in its conceit, was merely an instrument in God's hand for rooting out the evil and ushering in the good. When its function would be accomplished, it would pay the penalty for its crime against God and Man (Isa. 10:5-7; 12, 13,15).

The same challenge, in a far more agonizing form, confronted Isaiah's anonymous name-sake, Deutero-Isaiah, a century and a half later. The people of Judah were now in ignominious exile under the heel of the Babylonian empire. How to explain the misery and degradation of Israel? It could not be justified in terms of Israel's sin, for at its worst, Israel was better than its pagan conqueror. Unless these tormenting doubts were met, the people would be plunged into a despair that would be the prelude to dissolution. A message of hope and courage was needed, not only for Israel's sake, but for God's cause, for this people, weak and imperfect, remained "God's witnesses" (Isa. 43:10). A rabbinic comment spells out the implications of the Deutero-Isaianic metaphor: "Ye are My witnesses, saith the Lord. If ye are my witnesses, I am the Lord, but if ye are not my witnesses, I am not the Lord."[1] The great prophet of the Exile accordingly evolved the doctrine of the Suffering Servant of the Lord.[2] Israel is not merely God's witness, but man's teacher, whose suffering at the hands of the nations is evidence of their moral immaturity. These tribulations are destined to end when they recognize Israel's true greatness:

---

[1] Cited in the name of the Tannaitic sage, Simeon bar Yohai in *Sifre, Deut.* sec. 346; Cf. also *Pesikta*, ed. Buber, p. 102b and *Yalkut Shimeoni, Isaiah*, sec. 455.

[2] Cf. the careful study of the theme in C. R. North, *The Suffering Servant in Deutero-Isaiah* (Oxford 1948) and the briefer survey of the various theories in H. H. Rowley, *The Servant of the Lord and other Essays*, (London 1952). The view adopted in the text, that the Servant is Israel in its ideal sense, is still the most acceptable position, particularly when the fruitful concept of "fluid personality" is taken into account. See H. W. Robinson, "*The Cross of the Servant—A Study in Deutero-Isaiah*" (London, 1928) and see our remarks in "Hosea's Marriage and Message" in *Hebrew Union College Annual*, vol. 25 (1954) pp. 15ff.

Behold, My servant shall prosper,
He shall be exalted and lifted up,
    and shall be very high.
Surely our diseases he did bear, and
    our pains he carried;
Whereas    we    did    esteem    him
    stricken,
Smitten of God, and afflicted.
But he was wounded because of our
    transgressions,
He was crushed because of our ini-
    quities;
The chastisement of our welfare
    was upon him,
And with his stripes we were
    healed.
Therefore will I divide him a por-
    tion among the great,
And he shall divide the spoil with
    the mighty;
Because he bared his soul unto
    death,
And was numbered with the trans-
    gressors;
Yet he bore the sin of many,
And made intercession for the
    transgressors.
                    (Isa. 52:13; 53;4, 5, 12)

Thus, for the first time the Prophet affirmed the possibility of national suffering that was not the consequence of sin, but, on the contrary, an integral element in the process of the moral education of the race. This insight of Deutero-Isaiah was not lost on the author of *Job*.

The tension between God's justice and the triumph of wickedness was also met in another way by the Prophets, who deepened an older folk-belief in the Day of the Lord. The people had long believed that the day would come when the Lord of Israel would give His people victory over its foes and establish its hegemony over all. This chauvinistic doctrine has its parallels in ancient and in modern times among all peoples. The Hebrew prophets did not attack or denounce the doctrine—they moralized it. They agreed that the day would come when the Lord of Israel would

arise and bring victory to His cause, but that did not mean the inevitable triumph of Israel, as it stood, only of a vastly better, righteous Israel. For several of the prophets, notably Isaiah and Micah, the instrument for God's purpose in the world would be the Messiah, the anointed scion of the house of David. The Messiah would restore the scales of justice to their true balance, by ushering in freedom and plenty for Israel, and peace and brotherhood for the world. The Messianic age represents the triumph of the righteousness of God in an imperfect world. Justice would prevail—what was needed was patience in the present and faith in the future.

In sum, the contradiction, the tension between the doctrine of retribution and the spectacle of injustice in the world created most of the deepest insights of Biblical religion.

IV

To wait patiently for the triumph of God's retribution was relatively easy, so long as the nation was the unit under consideration, for God has eternity at His command, and nations are long-lived. This is particularly true of Israel. In Ben Sira's words:

The life of man is but a few days,
But the life of Jeshurun, days with-
    out number.
                    (37:25)

Yet, from the beginning, the individual played a part in the religious consciousness. His hope and desires, his fears and frustrations, could not be submerged wholly in the destiny of the nation. The people might prosper and a man might be miserable; the status of society might be critical, yet the individual could find life tolerable. The Law of God demanded obedience from the individual; was it unfair to expect that righteousness or sinfulness would receive their reward or punishment in the life of the individual as well? Imperceptibly, the problem emerged in the days of the First Temple. Isaiah had taken the simplest course by reaffirming the traditional doctrine and applying it to the individual:

> Say ye of the righteous, that it shall
> be well with him;
> For they shall eat the fruit of their
> doings.
> Woe unto the wicked! It shall be
> ill with him;
> For the work of his hands shall be
> done to him.          (3:10f.)

As inexorable doom began descending on the nation and the small Judean state saw its life-blood ebbing away, the mere reiteration of conventional ideas was not enough. Now there was no comfort or compensation in collective retribution. Moreover, since the individual was now the unit and the scale of judgment, the counsel of long-range patience was pathetically irrelevant, for man flowers but a brief instant. The prophets, Jeremiah and Ezekiel, whose tragic destiny it was to foretell and to witness the destruction of the Temple and the Babylonian exile, agonized over the prosperity of the wicked and the suffering of the righteous:

> Right wouldest Thou be, O Lord,
> Were I to contend with Thee,
> Yet will I reason with Thee:
> Wherefore doth the way of the
> wicked prosper?
> Wherefore are all the traitors
> secure?
>                              (Jer. 12:1)

Both prophets protested energetically against the popular doctrine enshrined in a folk-saying: "The fathers have eaten sour grapes and the children's teeth are set on edge" (Jer. 31:28; Ez. 18:2). Ezekiel, in particular, emphasized the doctrine of individual responsibility

and individual retribution. He was content to bolster ethical living without formulating a complete theodicy. Other men of faith, psalmists and poets, urged obedience to God's will, buttressed by the faith that righteousness would soon triumph in the life of the individual:

> For His anger is but for a moment,
> His favour is for a life-time;
> Weeping may tarry for the night,
> But joy cometh in the morning.
>                              (Ps. 30:6).

> The Lord is good unto them that
> wait for Him,
> To the soul that seeketh Him.
> It is good that a man should
> quietly wait
> For the salvation of the Lord.
>                         (Lam. 3:25, 26)

Thus, Biblical religion, resting on the cornerstone of faith in a just and powerful God, met all challenges and held fast to its faith that justice prevails in God's world. On this faith every generation in Israel had been nurtured, drawing from it the motive for obedience to God's law, the strength to bear affliction, and the patience to await the hour of vindication.

Job, too, had always accepted this body of religious teaching as the truth. Then came the crisis, catastrophe following catastrophe, leaving the temple of his existence a mass of rubble. We who have read the tale of the wager between God and Satan in the Prologue, know that Job's misery and degradation is part of a cosmic experiment to discover whether man is capable of serving the ideal for its own sake, without the hope of reward. Job has no such inkling —for him, *the accepted religious convictions of a lifetime are now contradicted by his personal experience,* by his unshakable knowledge that he is no sinner, certainly not sinful enough to deserve such a succession of blows upon his defenseless head.

Of Job's inner travail the Friends are unaware. Eliphaz, the oldest and the wisest of the three, proceeds to remind Job of the truths by which he has lived. It is noteworthy that the author, whose sympathies are clearly on Job's side,[3] nevertheless gives the fullest and fairest presentation of the conventional theology. Divine justice does prevail in the world, the apparent contradictions in the world of reality notwithstanding. In the first instance, the process of retribution takes time and so Job must have patience. The righteous are never destroyed, while the wicked, or at least, their children, are ultimately punished. Eliphaz then describes a vision from on high which disclosed to him the truth all men are imperfect, so that not even the righteous may justly complain if he suffers. God is not responsible for sin, for it is a human creation (5:6, 7). Moreover, suffering is a discipline—and hence a mark of God's love. (5:17). Ultimately, the righteous are saved and find peace and contentment.

In his later speeches, Eliphaz will emphasize the familiar doctrine of God's visiting the sins of the fathers upon the children, and will extend it. For by the side of this "vertical responsibility" linking all the generations through time, there is "horizontal responsibility" in space, uniting all men in a given generation. Thus, the entire people is visited by a plague because of King David's

sin. (II Sam. 24:11ff.). On the other hand, it is this interdependence of mankind which makes it possible for the saint, by his presence, to redeem his sinful contemporaries, as when Abraham sought to save Sodom for the sake of a righteous minority. Accordingly, Eliphaz promises Job that if he repents and makes his peace with God, he will be able to intercede with Him for sinners and save them:

> Thou wilt then issue a decree, and
> it will be fulfilled for thee,
> And upon thy ways, light will
> shine.
> When men are brought low, thou
> wilt say, "Rise up!"
> And the humble will be saved.
> Even the guilty will escape punishment
> Escaping through the cleanness of
> thy hands.[4]
>
> (Job 22:28-30).

Job has scarcely heard, let alone been persuaded by, Eliphaz's arguments or by the considerably more heated and less illuminating speeches of the other Friends. He has no theory to propose as a substitute, merely his consciousness that he is suffering without cause. He does not claim to be perfect, but insists he is not a willful sinner. Against the conventional ideas he sets the testimony of his own experience, which he will not deny, whatever the consequences. As the round of debate continues, Job's fury mounts, as does the helpless wrath of his Friends. For his attacks upon their disloyalty, his pathetic description of his physical pain and mental anguish, his indignant rejection of their deeply held faith, serve all the more to convince them that he is a sinner. For do not arrogance and the assumption of innocence by man, with the im-

---

[3] This is clear from the greater length and eloquence of the Job speeches and from the Divine judgment on the Friends in Job 42:8. This verse is part of the "jointures" (12:11-13; 42:7-10), the links written by the poet to connect the prose-tale, which he utilizes as Prologue and Epilogue, with the poetic Dialogue. On the critical problems involved, see our study, "All Men's Book—A New Introduction to Job" in *Menorah Journal*, Winter 1947, pp. 329-58.

[4] Cf. the writer's "Corporate Responsibility in Job" in *Journal of Near Eastern Studies*, vol. 4, 1945, and the references cited there.

plied right and capacity to pass judgment on God, constitute the height of impiety?

Bildad paints a picture of the destruction of the wicked and the ultimate restoration of the righteous, and he hymns the power of God. Job dismisses this as irrelevant, for he does not deny God's power; it is His justice that he calls into question. Zophar, the youngest and least discreet of the Friends, summons Job to repent of his secret sins.

With bitter irony, Job turns again upon his friends who, in their security and ease, can afford to indulge in artificial arguments far removed from the painful realities of life. In a passage long misunderstood, he parodies their speeches on the greatness of God and concludes that their defense of God, dishonest and biased as it is, will not likely win His favor.[5]

As the First Cycle ends, Job has been fortified in his conviction that he is right. What he experiences existentially cannot be refuted theoretically; it must be taken into account in any conception of reality.

Job is aware of the contention that morality depends upon faith in Divine justice. Denying the latter, how can he maintain the former? Job is driven to a desperate expedient, which is to prove one of the great liberating ideas in religion; he cuts the nexus between virtue and reward. Honest men will tremble at his undeserved suffering, but will not on that account be deterred from righteousness:

> Upright men are astonished at this,
> And the innocent stirreth up himself against the godless.

---

[5] For this passage cf. "Quotations as a Literary Usage in Biblical, and Oriental Literature" in *Hebrew Union College Annual*, vol. 22, 1949, pp. 214 ff.

> Yet the righteous holdeth on his way,
> And he that hath clean hands waxeth stronger and stronger.
> (Job 17: 8, 9)

The Mishnah (*Sotah* 5:5) quite correctly contends that Job served God from love and not from fear. God's ways still remain to be justified, but in the interim, man's ways must be just.

In the succeeding Cycles, Eliphaz adds a supplement to the traditional position. He emphasizes that there is more to the punishment of the wicked than his ultimate destruction, whether in his own person or in that of his offspring. During the very period of his ostensible prosperity he lives in trepidation, never knowing when the blow will fall. Otherwise, the same ideas are reiterated, but with greater vehemence. The conventional theodicy, maintained by the Friends, has exhausted itself.

## V

The full meaning of Job's existential tragedy now begins to disclose itself. Increasingly, Job has become convinced, not merely that the Friends have maligned him, but that they have traduced God. In the First Cycle, Job has ventured a hope that some impartial arbiter might decide between him and God:

> For He is not a man, as I am, that I should answer him,
> That we should come together in judgment.
> Would that there were an arbiter between us,
> That might lay his hand upon us both,
> Were he to take His rod away from me,
> And not let His terror make me afraid,
> I should speak and not fear,
> For I am not so with myself.
> (9:32-35)

As the Friends proceed to attack Job's integrity with less and less restraint, the contact between Job and them all but disappears. Their conception of God is meaningless for him. He proceeds to discover a new faith, forged in the crucible of his undeserved suffering, as unshakable as his experience of his own innocence—behind the cruel reality of suffering, a just order must exist in the world. He can find no sympathy or understanding among his erstwhile Friends; then there must be, there would be, a witness on his behalf later:

O earth, cover not my blood,
And let my cry have no resting-place.
Even now, behold, my Witness is in heaven,
And He that testifies for me is on high.
Are my intercessors to be my Friends?
Unto God does my eye pour out tears!
For He would prove a man right even when he contends with God
As between one man and his fellow!
(16:18-21)

As the debate reaches a crescendo of fury, Job attains a crescendo of faith. The longing he first expressed for an arbiter (mokhiah) has become a conviction of a witness ('edh) ready to speak on his behalf. Now he reaches the peak of faith. In a moment of mystic ecstasy, he sees his vindication through a Redeemer, who will act to avenge his suffering. The term he uses, go'el, means a kinsman, a blood-avenger, who, in earlier Hebrew law, was duty-bound to see that justice was done to his aggrieved brother.

The inherent difficulties of communicating a mystic vision are aggravated by textual problems in the famous passage, which, we believe, should be rendered as follows:

Oh that my words were now written!
Oh that they were inscribed in a book!
That with an iron pen and lead
They were graven in the rock for ever!
But as for me, I know that my Redeemer liveth!
Though He be the last to arise upon earth.
For from within my skin, this has been marked,
And from my flesh do I see God,
Whom I see for myself,
My own eyes behold, not another's!

But the momentary vision of God arising to redeem him fades; Job cannot hold the ecstasy—

My veins are consumed with longing within me.    (19:23-27)

Similarly, the modern saint, Rabbi Abraham Isaac Kuk, has sought to describe the ecstasy of the experience of "the nearness of God" which extends beyond "the walls of deed, logic, ethics and laws." But exaltation is followed by depression, as the mystic sinks back "into the gray and tasteless world of conflict, contradiction and doubt."[6]

Job, however, in spite of his experience, is no mystic, who can find peace in the beatific vision. Even after the ecstasy has faded, he demands vindication. Only if God appears to him and answers, will he know that his suffering is not meaningless, that it counts for something in the universe. In his last speech, which sets forth his code of conduct, he closes with a plea:

Would that I had someone to hear me,
Lo, this is my desire, that God answer me
And that I had the indictment my foe has written,

---

[6] Cf. the brief but illuminating summary of Rabbi Kuk's religious philosophy in J. B. Agus, "Guideposts of Modern Judaism", New York 1954, pp. 53f.

I would surely carry it on my
shoulder
And bind it as a crown for myself!
I would announce to Him the
number of my steps,
Like a prince would I confront
Him!
                    (Job 31:35-37)

Who is this arbiter, this witness, this
redeemer to whom Job looks for salvation and comfort? Job's refuge is the
God of righteousness, who lives and
rules the world behind the sway of the
God of power. The dichotomy never
becomes a dualism; for the Hebrew
author, as for his hero, these two aspects
merge as one. In the end, the two aspects of the Divine are reunited when
the God of reality not only ignores the
defenses of the Friends in his speeches,
but castigates them, "for ye have not
spoken the truth about Me as has my
servant Job" (42:7, 8) so that Job must
intercede for them. God's power and
God's righteousness, the attribute of justice and the attribute of mercy are one
in Him; it is only to man's limited and
imperfect gaze that they seem distinct,
if not contradictory.

Centuries later, the medieval Hebrew
poet, Solomon Ibn Gabirol, in his
*Royal Crown*, echoed the heart-beat of
Job in his affliction, but like him, retained his faith in the One Living God
of the universe:

Therefore though Thou shouldst
slay me, yet will I trust in Thee.
For if Thou shouldst pursue my
iniquity,
I will flee from Thee to Thyself,
And I will shelter myself from Thy
wrath in Thy shadow,
And to the skirts of Thy mercies I
will lay hold,
Until Thou hast had mercy on me,
And I will not let Thee go till
Thou has blessed me.[7]

---

[7] Cf. I. Davidson ed. *Selected Religious Poems
of Solomon Ibn Gabirol*, Phila. 1944, pp. 118.

The later poet, Immanuel of Rome,
rephrased the same thought:

I shall flee for help, from Thee to
Thee,
And cover myself with thy wings
in the day of trouble
And from thy wrath flee to thy
shadow.[8]

Job's final speech is no longer addressed
to his Friends. Like his opening lament
(ch. 3), his closing Confession of Innocence (ch. 31) is a soliloquy.

## VI

There now appears a brash young
character named Elihu, of whom, we
are to assume, the dignified elders have
previously taken no notice. He has over-
heard the debate and feels impelled to
inject himself into the discussion. For
a variety of reasons, many scholars regard the Elihu speeches (chap. 32-37)
as a later interpolation, an easy method
which solves little. What has been generally overlooked is the basic fact that
in the architecture of the book, they
perform a vital function. Increasingly,
the study of ancient literatures, like that
of the Homeric epics, has been focussing
attention upon the unity and meaning
of the whole rather than upon the dis-
parity of the parts. That the indiscrimi-
nate, and even accidental lumping together of scattered literary fragments by
an obtuse redactor, who often did not
understand the material he was working
with, will produce a masterpiece—that
naive faith of nineteenth century literary critics is no longer widely shared
today.[9]

---

[8] Cf. his *Mahbarot*, chap. 19.

[9] Cf. the trenchant observations of H. D. F.
Kitto, *The Greeks* (Harmondsworth 1951) p.
63. "The attribution (of the *Iliad* and the
*Odyssey* to Homer) was accepted quite whole-
heartedly until modern times, when closer investigation showed all sorts of discrepancies of

The differences between the Elihu chapters and the rest of the Book, which are fewer than is generally alleged, may perhaps be explained by the assumption that they were added by our author at a later period in his career. The creation of a masterpiece like *Job* might well have been a lifetime undertaking and Goethe's *Faust* is a case in point. The *Urfaust* goes back to the poet's *Sturm und Drang* period, when he was in his twenties. The First Part of *Faust* did not appear until more than thirty years later, in 1808; and the Second Part was completed shortly before his death, more than two decades later, in 1832. In the long process, Goethe's conception of his theme underwent a profound transformation. Something like that may well have been the case with the author of Job.

It is noteworthy that Elihu is at least as antagonistic to the Friends as he is to Job. Actually he denies the truth of both positions. The Friends have maintained that God is just and that, therefore, suffering is both the penalty and the proof of sin. Job has countered by insisting that his suffering is not the result of sin and, therefore, he charges God with injustice. Elihu denies the conclusions of both sides by injecting a virtually new idea, adumbrated in another form in Deutero-Isaiah and referred to in one verse by Eliphaz.[10] Elihu declares that God is just, and yet suffering may rightly come to the innocent, as a discipline and a warning. Job has contended that God avoids contact with man. On the contrary, Elihu insists, God does communicate with man through dreams and visions, and when these fail, through illness and suffering.

This recognition of the uses of pain is the kind of mature insight that would come to a man through years of experience. For life teaches, at every hand, how insufferable are those who have never suffered and that frustration and sorrow are men's passport to fellowship and sympathy with their brothers.

The author of *Job* would thus wish to express this observation. Yet suffering as a discipline is certainly not the whole truth regarding the problem of evil. How could the idea be given its proper weight? Obviously the doctrine could not be placed in the mouth of Job, who denies that there is any justice in suffering. Nor could it be presented by the Friends, for the author wishes to negate their standpoint, as we have seen. Finally, were this idea included in the subsequent God-speeches, it would weaken the force of the principal answer. By creating the

---

fact, style and language, both between the two epics and between the various parts of each. The immediate result of this was the minute and confident division of the two poems, but especially the *Iliad* into seperate layers of different periods, appropriately called 'strata' by critics, who imperfectly distinguished between artistic and geological composition. The study of the epic poetry of other races, and of the methods used by poets working in this traditional medium, has done a great deal to restore confidence in the substantial unity of each poem; that is to say, that what we have in each case is not a short poem by one original 'Homer' to which later poets have added more or less indiscriminately. but a poem, conceived as a unity by a relatively later 'Homer' who worked over and incorporated much traditional material—though the present *Iliad* certainly contains some passages which were not part of Homer's original design."

---

[10] Eliphaz had briefly referred to the idea of suffering as a discipline in one verse (5:16), but had not referred to it again or explored its implications. Deutero-Isaiah's doctrine of the Servant of the Lord describes the Servant's suffering as inflicted by other men, not as emanating directly from God. The affinities are, however, noteworthy.

character of Elihu, who opposes the attitude of the Friends as well as that of Job, the author is able to express this secondary idea, giving it due place in his world-view.

## VII

Elihu's words end as a storm is seen rising in the east. The Lord himself appears in the whirlwind and speaks to Job. The argumentation of the Friends that Job must be a sinner is treated with the silence it deserves. Nowhere does God refer to Job's alleged misdoings. Instead, the entire problem is raised to another dimension. Can Job comprehend, let alone govern, the universe that he weighs and finds wanting? Earth and sea, cloud and darkness and dawn, snow and hail, rain and thunder, snow and ice, and the stars above—all these wonders are beyond Job. Nor do these exhaust God's power. With a vividness born of deep love and careful observation, the poet pictures the beasts, remote from man, yet precious to their Maker. The lion and the mountain goat, the wild ass and the buffalo, the ostrich, the horse, and the hawk, all testify to the glory of God. For all their variety, these creatures have one element in common—they are not under the sway of man, or even intended for his use. Even the ponderous hippopotamus and the fearsome crocodile, far from conventionally beautiful, reveal the creative power of God and His joy in the world. Moreover, God declares, were Job able to destroy evil in the world, even He would be prepared to relinquish His throne to him—a moving acknowledgment by God that the world-order is not perfect!

Job is not overwhelmed, as is often alleged, by God's physical power. For that had failed to cow Job into silence during the earlier debate with the Friends. It is the essential truth of God's position that impels Job to submit. His surrender, however, is still a victory, for his wish has been granted:

I had heard of thee by the hearing
  of the ear,
But now mine eye has seen thee.
Wherefore I abhor my words, and
  repent,
Seeing I am dust and ashes.
        Job 42:5, 6)

Job's triumph lies in the fact that God speaks to him and does not ignore him. The confrontation of God is Job's vindication.

But that is not all. In rebelling against tradition because of his experience, Job has enriched tradition. For religious truth, like all truth, can grow only through the evidence derived from the experience of life. To use the language of the hour, Job's protest is existential, but it contributes to a deeper essential religion. It compels a reconsideration of the conventional theology, which the author incidentally does not reject out of hand; he merely regards it as inadequate. The author's positive ideas, one major, the other minor, are stated in the two closing sections of the book.

The minor thought is expressed by Elihu, who stresses that suffering frequently serves as a source of moral discipline and is thus a spur to high ethical attainment.

The principal idea is reserved for the God-speeches, where the implications, in accordance with widespread Semitic usage, are at least as important as their explicit content.

The vivid and joyous description of nature in these chapters testifies that nature is more than a mystery; it is a cosmos, a thing of beauty. The force of the analogy is not lost upon Job. Just as there is order and harmony in the natural world, so there is order and meaning in the moral sphere. Man cannot fathom the meaning of the natural order, yet he is aware of its beauty and harmony. Similarly, if he cannot expect to comprehend the moral order, he must believe that there is rationality and justice within it. As Kant pointed out, if it is arrogant to defend God, it is even more arrogant to assail Him. After all legitimate explanations of suffering are taken into account, a mystery still remains. Any view of the universe that fully explains it is, on that very account, untrue. The analogy of the natural order gives the believer in God the grounds for facing the mystery with a courage born of faith in the essential rightness of things. What cannot be comprehended through reason must be embraced in love. For the author of *Job*, as for Judaism always, God is one and indivisible. As nature is instinct with morality. so the moral order is rooted in the natural world.

One other significant contribution to religion emerges from the Book of Job. For the poet, the harmony of the universe is important not only as an idea but as an experience, not only logically but esthetically. When man steeps himself in the beauty of the world, his troubles grow petty, not because they are unreal, but because they dissolve within the larger plan, like the tiny dabs of oil in a masterpiece of painting. The beauty of the world becomes an anodyne to man's suffering.

The author of *Job* is not merely a great artist and poet. He is too deep a religious thinker to believe that any neatly articulated system of man can comprehend the beauty and the tragedy of existence. Yet he is too great an intellect to abdicate the use of reason and reflection in pondering on the mystery of evil and comprehending as much of it as we can. He would endorse the unemotional words of the third century sage, Jannai: "It is not in our power to understand the suffering of the righteous or the well-being of the wicked" (*Aboth* 4:15). There is a residuum of the Unknown in the world, but we have good grounds for holding fast to the faith that harmony and beauty pervade God's world. The mystery is also a miracle.

When Job found that the tradition of the past was contradicted by his personal experience, he resisted the temptation to submit to the platitudes of the past. Because of his unswerving allegiance to the truth, he refused to echo accepted truths, however respectable and ancient their source. His steadfastness and agony found their reward—for out of his suffering emerged a deeper vision of the Eternal and His ways.

# JOB'S PROBLEM

## MORRIS STOCKHAMMER

THROUGHOUT his trial, Job[1] remains unaware of the dialogue between God and Satan (chapters one and two). Hence, he cannot know the purpose of his sufferings. The reader, however, is immediately apprised of the dialogue in the Heavenly Court and of God's decision. Job shall be put to a test. What is problematical to the hero, is clear to the reader. Thus the scene in the Heavenly Court clarifies for us the meaning of the tragedy: the hero's faith and trust in God are to be tested.

That Job is to remain in the dark concerning the purpose of his sufferings is indeed strange, but not unusual. Many tragic heroes are ignorant of the background of their inner experiences. Apparently, the editor of the Book of Job was not aware of the obvious implication to be drawn from the drama he presents. The motif he offers spells a humanization of God, a humanization that upon reflection would have revolted his philosophical sensibilities. Human understanding, being limited, may have to

test a friend occasionally. But God, being omniscient, knows who is loyal to Him and who is not and does not have to have recourse to testing His subjects. And why should God wish to convince Satan of Job's righteousness? Is it reasonable to torment a righteous man, just to please Satan? Thus the prologue of our book has its palpable weakness.

Humanizing God, then, is unsatisfactory, for it leads to a contradiction — namely, to a human God. One cannot conceive of God as being both human and superhuman. To affirm the one, the other must be rejected. To think that God must be either just or unjust, is to be guilty of the same error — that of humanizing God. An infinite Being — and God's infinity is a supposition generally acknowledged — can not be provided with a finite attribute. All finite attributes must be sacrificed, if Divine infinity is to be maintained. This means that God is neither just or unjust, since He is beyond these two concepts. Once we have gained this insight, we do not have to declare God to be unjust, only because we cannot find him to be just. Only man must be either just or unjust. God is neither just nor unjust, but infinite. Under the unavoidable supposition of God's infinity it becomes illogical to look for God's justice or His injustice, even though our feelings may revolt at this thought. (Similarly, the mathematician cannot operate with finite quantities in the realm of the infinite. Therefore, the attempt to understand God's infinity

---

[1] For a religio-historical criticism it would be essential to describe the literary development of the Book of Job from its original form to the present one. Such research, however, does not bear on the philosophical viewpoint which is only concerned with the content of the book and not with the literary problems involved.

The writer of this essay holds a Doctorate in Political Philosophy from the University of Vienna and has published widely in European journals in the fields of philosophy of law, psychology and esthetics. The present article was translated from the German by William Wolf.

must not end in the resignation of the agnostic, as long as it is not concerned with a detailed characterization).

Job is deeply cognizant of the Infinite ground of all things: " "He (God) is not a man as I am" (9:32); "Hast thou eyes of flesh, or seest thou as man seeth? Are thy days as the days of man? Are thy years as man's days?" (10:4, 5) "What? Shall we receive good at the hand of God, and shall we not receive evil?" (2:10); "He destroyeth the innocent and the wicked". (9:22). Therefore Job is not quite logical, if he imagines, as he does, God to be just or unjust: "He (the wicked man) may prepare it (the raiment), but the just shall put it on, and the innocent shall divide the silver (heaped up by the wicked man)". (27:17). "Thou art become cruel to me". (30:21). Even the Divine voice "out of the whirlwind" makes this concrete and finite assumption: "Wilt thou even make void My judgment?" (40:8). Job's friends, too, use this hypothesis which limits God's qualities: "Who ever perished, being innocent?" (4:7); "Doth God pervert judgment? Or doth the Almighty pervert justice?" (8:3); "But the eyes of the wicked shall fail, and they shall have no way to flee, and their hope shall be as the giving up of the ghost." (11:20); "Far be it from God that He should do wickedness, and from the Almighty, that He should commit iniquity." (34:10). But Job's last word of wisdom "Wherefore I abhor myself, and repent" (42:6) — frees itself from the error of limiting God. God's omnipotence, which does not allow of any limitation — and the axiom of Divine justice would be a limitation too — is also stressed by Job's friends: "Canst thou by searching find out God? Canst thou find out the Almighty unto perfection? It is as high as heaven; what canst thou do? Deeper than hell; what canst thou know? The measure thereof is longer than the earth and broader than the sea." (11:7–9). But the search for an invisible, infinite God is not hopeless. Only the idea of a concrete God and the simultaneous belief in His infinity (omnipotence) and His justice or injustice do not go together. One may argue that a strong faith can overcome the paralyzing effects of an inscrutable God. But God's infinity is imaginable by us. It is a weakness of faith which furnishes an infinite Being with finite attributes; this is what is inconceivable.

The sharp difference of opinion between Job and his friends over the former's righteousness relates to a secondary question, and should not distract the reader's attention from the main problem: God's justice. And it is here that Job and his friends do agree. Both parties, without sensing the contradiction, believe in God's infinity and in His justice, i.e. His finity. For a Being which "does not give an account" cannot be termed just or unjust. He who cannot be thought "unto perfection", cannot be characterized by any single attribute. Jastrow[2] says: "The position reached by independent inquiry is superlatively painful, because the choice lies between an ethical view of Divine rule and a non-ethical Power, representing a force of nature to whom no appeal for either justice or mercy is possible...The value of the Book of Job lies precisely in this sharp formulation of the situation — either a God Who is cruel, or a blind force." But all positive (either — or) or negative (neither — nor) alternatives are false, because all we have is an infinite series: this and this and —. Our thesis that God is neither just nor unjust must be expanded this way: God is just *and* unjust, a seeing *and* a blind Power, and so ad infinitum. God is everything, a just Ruler and blind Nature, He is omnipotent. Thus the painfulness of our posi-

---

[2]*The Book of Job*, 1920, p. 153s.

tion is lessened to a certain degree. For even if we cannot appeal to a God who is a blind natural Force, we can still turn to Him as a gracious Ruler of the world. We do not deny that the idea of the infinite encounters some difficulties, but the naive and uncritical way of furnishing God with one attribute (He is just, He is unjust, etc.) cannot be maintained, unless one is to give up His infinity.

Spinoza[3] is described as expressing this thought in this way: "He attempted a synthesis of the whole of reality...The system of course would be more than one attribute. For each attribute is only infinite in its kind; the system of all the attributes is absolutely infinite, it exhausts the whole of reality...God consists of attributes. God as the complete system of attributes is absolutely infinite or complete, each attribute is only infinite of its kind...Spinoza realized the difference between the mental and the material, but rejected the conception of their antagonism. So he did not hesitate to attribute to God both extension and thought. And man, a finite mode of God, is thus both physical and mental, and functions in both ways concurrently, even if each series of events is self-contained...He described extension and thought as attributes, reserving the term "substance" for the system which they constitute between them. This change of description was not intended to deny that extension and thought are substances in the sense of being self-existent. It was only intended to express their coherence in one system." The difficulty becomes clear: the system of nature and the system of the mind (= value) are self-contained and yet they are to be presented as parts of a super-imposed system. But there is hardly any sense in conceiving God other than infinite. And is not the infinite opposed to any systemization?

How short-sighted, therefore, is Job's demand: "Oh that I knew where I might find Him, that I might come even to His seat" (23:3). But God is everywhere and yet unsearchable, being without a "seat" in the infinite: "But the thunder of His power who can understand?" (26:14). So we see that Job is well aware of infinity, and still he goes on searching for a limited God.

In considering God's infinity, man senses his own unworthiness: "How then can man be just with God?" "What is man that he should be clean?" (15:14). "Shall mortal man be more just than God? Shall a man be more pure than his maker?" (4:17). But man cannot be denied the possibility of being just. That the righteous man gets his share of misfortune is something else again, which does not however impair his capacity for being righteous. Man is not more or less just than God; basically, he may only be said to be just or unjust, or rather: more or less just than somebody else. The comparison between just and unjust beings is meaningful only among human beings.

The key to justice is compensation: reward for righteousness and punishment for unrighteousness. Thus the logic of Job's friends is indisputable. But one must not thereupon conclude, as do Job's friends, that misfortune must be the effect of sinfulness. It is not the principle of compensation which is at fault, but the anthropomorphism which tries to apply that principle to Divinity and makes Job's sufferings the consequences of moral impurity. The thesis that God rewards and thus is finite cannot be maintained in the presence of the "voice out of the whirlwind." Even the belief in a future reward for the good in the hereafter limits God's infinity, and would

---

[3]Encyclopedia Britannica, s.v. Spinoza.

therefore not answer Job's query, but only postpone a reply to it.

Jastrow[4] states: "What hope is there that the tiny human intellect can by mere discussion penetrate into a mind of such infinite magnitude?... The symposium, with its abandonment of the problem as one incapable of solution through the processes of reasoning, and the nature poems with their insistence upon human faith in a Divine will (of which nature furnishes the evidence) as the only solution of the problem — both have their message for us of the present day." But problems of a theoretical or theological nature can only be solved by way of reason. To ascribe the human intellect as "tiny" is to do it less than justice; certainly it is less tiny than our five senses. What other path of faith is there but that of reason? The nature poems in the Book of Job describe only the awe inspiring works of nature and not her blind cruelties. A comprehensive description of nature would have a crushing as well as an elevating effect on our mind, without, however, bringing us closer to the Unknown. God's infinity can only be conceived by the mind. "I have heard of Thee by the hearing of the ear; but now mine eye seeth Thee." (42:5). Divine infinity, however, is more than indefinite hearsay, because it is perceived less through our senses — seeing or hearing — than through our intelligence. Job puts it this way: "I know that Thou canst do everything". (42:2): note that he does not say: "I see, or I hear that Thou canst do everything." The "spirit of God that hovereth over the waters" is only accessible through an act of reasoning.

To quote Jastrow[5] again: "In the third speech of Elihu we are introduced to a new thought. Since man's deeds — good or bad — affect him alone, and God is neither benefited by the virtues of the good nor injured by the sins of the wicked, man and not God should be held responsible for the ills that befall one. It is proper to appeal to God of help, but not with the thought that the misfortune has come from God."

Although God cannot be held responsible — "For He giveth no account of any of His matters" (33:13) — it does not follow that suffering does not stem from Him. God sends everything — good fortune and bad fortune — and still He is not responsible. The paradox is more apparent than real. Are parents responsible for their children's sins, are they condemned together with their ill-begotten descendants? (A good father may have an evil son, and vice versa). To cause or to create something does not necessarily mean to be responsible for it. One can only say that certain causes create certain effects, not that they are responsible for the latter. The idea of responsibility does not occur in nature, it is independent of any causality. Man is responsible, not as part and parcel of nature as created by God, but because he ought to fulfill the laws ordained by God. The Divine commandments are the source of man's responsibility, it is they that make him responsible, not God as his Creator.[6] Thus man alone is respon-

---

[6]"A curious explanation is given why the whole human race originated from one man: 'Because of the righteous and the wicked, that the righteous should not say "We are the descendants of a righteous ancestor", and the wicked shall not say "We are the descendants of a wicked ancestor." (Sanhedrin 38a). The moral is that neither can plead hereditary influence as the deciding factor in their character." (A. Cohen, Everyman's Talmud, 1949, p. 94). This is not a "curious" reason; on the contrary, it is the essential reason. The contrast here is between man's natural character which is dependent on the physical factors included in heredity and man's moral character. The principle of causality reigns in nature; in the realm of ethics alone — man's moral character — must one recognize the principle of responsibility.

---

[4]op. cit., pp. 168, 191.
[5]ib., p. 164.

sible for his deed: "Man's deeds affect him alone". (Jastrow), and this because of the commandments given him, and not because God does not derive any benefit or disadvantage from man's conduct. The latter statement is correct, but it has nothing to do with man's responsibility, which derives solely from God's commandments. Hence, just as God cannot be termed righteous, so too can He not be termed responsible. He is neither responsible nor non-responsible, but simply infinite. The essence of God's substance comprises all attributes, but it cannot be expressed by any of them.

This view would indicate that the biblical prohibition against pictorial presentation of God was a mark of intellectual progress, because it takes into account the fact that the infinity of the God-idea cannot be represented in any way. This has not escaped the attention of Thomas Mann who writes, in his story "The Tables of the Law": To the children of Midian this numen, named YHWH, was merely one god amongst others...Moses, on the contrary, was deeply impressed by just this feature of YHWH's invisibility. He felt that no visible god could vie in sanctity with one not visible, and he was amazed that the children of Midian set so little store by a quality which seemed to him so full of incalculable implications. The infinite *is* immeasurable, and yet the mathematicians calculate with it."

Even the designation of an infinite God as being a "first cause" (prima causa), may be a blasphemy, because it contains a limitation. In the realm of the immeasurable, even the fact of creation may lose its meaning, as Kant once perceived:[7] "The physical-nature world has no beginning and cannot have been created; only ideas can be created. There

_____
[7]Kritik der praktischen Vernunft, I 3.

is a supreme law, but no supreme cause." Thus Kant concludes with bold objectivity: "Where there is no beginning, there cannot be a creation."
Goethe's Faust speculates in similar vein:

'Tis written: In the beginning was the Word.
Here am I balked; who now can help afford?
The Word? Impossible so high to rate it,
And otherwise must I translate it,
If by the Spirit I am truly taught.
Then thus: "In the beginning was the Thought."
This first line let me weigh completely,
Lest my impatient pen proceed too fleetly.
Is it the Thought, which works, creates, indeed?
"In the beginning was the Power", I read.
Yet, as I write, a warning is suggested,
That I the sense may not have fairly tested.
The Spirit aids me: Now I see the light:
"In the beginning was the Act", I write.

That the Thought and, with it, the Word, were in the beginning, is also evident from the story of the creation, as reported in the Book of Genesis: "In the beginning God created the heaven and the earth. Now the earth was unformed and void, and darkness was upon the face of the deep; and the spirit of God hovered over the face of the waters. And God said: "Let there be light".... and God saw the light that it was good, and God divided the light from the darkness." Thus, the work of creation begins with light, i.e. the light of thought and moral revelation. In the cosmology of Genesis, the phrase "it was good" — the leitmotif of the moral world order, as created by the Word and the Spirit of God, occurs no less than six times. It is really the light of cognition, of thought, without which everything would be "unformed and void." And since moral ideas are beyond space and time, one can well understand Philo's opinion, that the world has only a moral, but not a "time-ly" origin. "To Philo of Alexandria, Creation was altogether outside time."[8] Good and bad are those very light phenomena, which are created by the moral aspect. "In the Bible account of creation everything centers around man and is viewed from his angle." The specific angle of man is the concept of good and evil. "And God divided the light from the darkness."

Edgar Allan Poe, too, belongs to the theologians among the poets. He writes: "If we cannot comprehend God in his visible works, how then in his inconceivable thoughts, that call the works into being? If we cannot understand Him in his objective creatures, how then in his substantive moods and phases of creation?" (The Imp of the Perverse) Thus man wrestles with the angel from beyond, and he swings to and fro in restless search. Since man does not feel at home in the infinite, he attributes to the Divine Being finite qualities (creative power, prima causa, transcendence, extension, thought, justice, responsibility, etc.) qualities which he again denies Him, once he admits the hopelessness of his attempts at limiting Him. "From eternity to eternity" sounds empty and void, but it is the only greeting which is sure to reach us. "Things too wonderful" (Job 42:3) should not be handled with inadequate methods. Andre Gide expresses this thought thus: "Do not hope to find God here or there — but everywhere. Every creature points to God, none of them revealing Him. Every creature beheld by us removes us from God." He who is used to God's infinity is not surprised by the thought that God cannot be presented as human; justice, nature, spirit, etc., cannot be His. For all these attributes are "definitions", which stand between ourselves and God's illimitability.

[8] J. H. Hertz, Pentateuch, 1950, p. 193.

The age-old self-contradiction which presents God at once as both finite (the burning bush), and infinite (the bush is never consumed), and which does not come to a clear-cut decision, is also typical for Rilke's idea of God. In his poetical cycle, Das Stundenbuch, he crowns God with the most tender, yet concrete metaphors, and still he leaves Him indefinite. The poet's god, of whom we have only an obscure knowledge (*"eine dunkle Kunde"*), dwells in the infinite rather than in the finite.[9] The more one meditates on Divine infinity, the more readily does one grow accustomed to refraining from adorning Him with finite attributes. But once one has the courage

[9] All those familiar with the poetical work of the German writer Rainer Maria Rilke (1876–1920) will agree that the ordinary difficulties involved in translating any poem are enormously magnified in his case. I most humbly submit this timid attempt to render the stanzas referred to by the author. (translator)

Thou art the Master, Thou alone.
Who ever saw Thee learn?
Coming from far, to us unknown,
'Round Whom, with humble or with pompous tone,
Men's songs and stories turn.

Thou carest not for the questioning mind;
But Thou art kind
To those who carry the burden.

All those who walk behind Thee, try Thee;
And those who find Thee; tie Thee
To image and appearance;
But I wish to know Thee
As does nature;
And as I mature,
So make I grow — Thee.

I do not vainly wish to prove Thee,
Knowing that Time cannot move Thee.

Of all the things Thou art the very essence,
But what it is, Thou lettest not pass Thy lips;
To different viewers Thou showest a different presence:
To the ships as a shore, and to the shore as ships.

The image we make of Thee is like a wall
(A thousand walls surround Thee!)
So do our pious hands hide Thee from us all,
Although our hearts have found Thee.

to face this alternative, it loses some of its self-contradictory character. Thus Job's problem, as to whether God is just or unjust is solved. He should not be subjected to any attributive limitation, because, being almighty, He may do anything.

We admit that the idea of God's infinity leads to some difficulties. In *The Magic Mountain,* Thomas Mann writes: "Is not this affirmation of the eternal and the infinite the logical-mathematical destruction of every and any limit in time or space, and the reduction of them, more or less, to zero? Is it possible, in eternity, to conceive of a sequence of events, or in the infinite, of a succession of space-occupying bodies? Conceptions of distance, movement, change, even of the existence of finite bodies in the universe — how do these fare? Are they consistent with the necessary hypothesis of eternity and infinity we have been driven to adopt? Again we ask, and again an echo answers." Ludwig Mieses, the contemporary national economist, too, saw the contradiction: "Scholastic philosophers and likewise theists and deists of the Age of Reason conceived an absolute and perfect Being, unchangeable, omnipotent, and yet planning and acting, aiming at ends and employing means. .For an almighty being the categories of ends and means do not exist...It is beyond the facilities of the human mind to think the concept of almightiness consistently to its ultimate logical consequences. The paradoxes are insoluble."[10] But faith must overcome these doubts, too.

---

[10]*Human Action,* 1949, p. 70. Yale University Press.

# B. The Rabbinic World View

# Aggadah—The Language
# of Jewish "God-talk"

SAMUEL E. KARFF

## I.

NO REASONABLY SENSITIVE MORTAL NEEDS TO BE reminded that we live in a "secular age." That term covers a multitude of truths, but the sign of secularity which most directly concerns us here was crisply stated by Langdon Gilkey: ". . . religious or mythical language is difficult if not unintelligible to our age. By mythical or religious language I mean not just an older mythical cosmology, but all those types of discourse . . . which contain transempirical language, referring to what is transcendent to, and yet active in nature and history."[1]

Such is the language of the Hebrew Bible. Building on biblical foundations, the early rabbis spun elaborate tales of God's relation to Israel. They called this "God-talk," *aggadah*. In the world of aggadah God's conversations with the Patriarchs and Prophets were freely reconstructed, His continuing activity in the world celebrated, and His abiding covenant with Israel reaffirmed.

Much of aggadah was homiletical. The rabbis, drawing on the God-talk of the Bible, spoke to the people of God's past encounters with Israel, of His unfailing power in the present and of His trustworthy promise of future redemption. Rabbinic God-talk articulated this theological consensus of the pre-modern Jew:

> I am a son of Abraham, Isaac and Jacob. God called my people (Israel) into being when He redeemed us from bondage and entered into a covenant with us at Sinai. The terms of that covenant (Torah) are the touchstone by which I may measure my faithfulness to God. By observing the Torah I beome what God intended me to become and fulfill my part of Israel's vocation in the world. The God who appeared unto my fathers is present in my experience. The God who commanded my fathers commands me. The God who redeemed them will redeem me.

This theological consensus finds no better formulation than the testimony of the Zohar. "God, Torah and Israel are inextricably bound up one with the other."[2] A Jewish community which acknowledged the significance and interdependence of these three terms could appreciate and unselfconsciously employ the language of aggadah. To describe the crisis in self-understanding of the modern Jew we need only note that

1. Gilkey, L. "The Contribution of Culture to the Reign of God," *The Future as the Presence of Shared Hope*. ed. M. Muckenhirn, New York: Sheed & Ward, p. 43.
2. Zohar to Leviticus (*Aḥare Mot*) 73b.

RABBI KARFF *is spiritual leader of Sinai Temple in Chicago, Ill.*

both the terms themselves and their interdependence are now problematical. This religious predicament is not uniquely Jewish. Sam Keen describes the "crisis in self-understanding" of Western man by contrasting the perspective of traditional and modern cultures:

> . . . traditional man may best be understood as *homo-admirans*—wondering man. He accepted his life and his environment as a meaningful gift which filled him with admiration and gratitude and responded actively by creating a community in harmony with patterns, meaning and value which he believed were homogenized into the cosmos. By contrast, modern man increasingly experiences himself in anxiety as the sole value-creating force in what is still called a uni-verse but what for many has become a chaotic multi-verse, devoid of intrinsic meaning.[3]

Richard Rubenstein has argued that with the modern Jew's loss of the "gift of meaning" the traditional language of faith has lost its function and power. "I can appreciate the aggadah" he writes, "only . . . in terms of what it did for those who lived within the framework of its myths and symbols . . . ."[4] Rubenstein believes that the world view of the aggadah is no longer real or credible for the modern Jew.

Though Rubenstein may overstate the case, the problem he dramatizes is real enough. Classic rabbinic God-talk assumed *two primary forms*. The aggadah was in part *traditional homiletics*—the sermons or sermon fragments by which the ancient sages spoke of God's abiding relation to the people Israel. The modern preacher finds considerably more resistance (or at least a diminished congregation) when he speaks of God's active presence in history and in the life of the people Israel.

The aggadah was also *liturgical*. It provided the symbolic language by which Israel spoke to and about the God of their fathers. Today worship even more than preaching is in desuetude.

Our awkwardness with aggadah is the hallmark of our "secularity." Can classical aggadah mediate the religious quest of a Jew in our time? That broad question prompts the present essay. We shall focus on several functions of the aggadah in the "pre-modern" world and consider whether such needs are evident in contemporary life and under what conditions the aggadah might be reappropriated to meet them.

## II.

At Yabneh, following the siege and destruction of Jerusalem by the Romans, the foundations of rabbinic Judaism were consolidated. The sages decided which books were to be included in the biblical canon. This fateful judgment determined both the basis for defining faithfulness to the covenant (halakhah) and the norm for all talk of God's relation to Israel (aggadah).

Thus the biblical text informed both the judicial dicta and the

---

3. Keen, S. *Apology For Wonder*. New York: Harper & Row, 1969, p. 61.
4. Rubenstein, R. *The Religious Imagination*. Indianapolis: Bobbs-Merrill, 1968, p. 172.

"religious imagination" of the ancient rabbis. Halakhah and aggadah embraced a single assumption: Though the age of prophecy has ended we have been given a sufficient and valid transcript of divine revelation.

For all the Torah's completeness, creative rabbinic exegesis was required to establish continuity between biblical injunctions and present needs. Such exegesis was authorized by the ingenious concept of two revelations at Sinai—the written and the oral Torah. The attempt to ground rabbinic law in biblical texts was called Midrash Halakhah.

Similarly, biblical God-talk could not directly mediate the religious experience of post-biblical Israel. How could the sages justify such discourse when prophecy had ended? The answer was found in Midrash Aggadah which embodied the faith, doubt and hope of a new generation.

The most creative period of classical aggadah occurred in the centuries following the destruction of the Second Temple. Unlike the more neatly structured halakhah, aggadah tolerated and even encouraged contradictory visions. One rabbi could describe the theophany at Sinai as Israel's voluntary response to a divine summons, another portrayed Israel's reluctant submission to an overpowering and coercive God: "If you accept, all is well; if not, there shall be your burial."[5]

Such tolerance for contradiction seems to confirm the secondary place of aggadah in the hierarchy of rabbinic value. A Jew fulfilled the covenant by performing God's commandments, not by the effusions of his or the rabbis' religious imagination. A son of the covenant would be judged by his deeds rather than his words.

Some rabbinic texts suggest that aggadah was indeed a conceit of the rabbis, a momentary escape from the rigors of halakhah, while the folk sought in aggadah a balm of soothing rhetoric for troubled times. The basis for such judgments is the interpretation of Chap. 2, verse 5 from the Song of Songs: "Stay ye me with dainties. Refresh me with apples; for I am love-sick."

> One of the sages taught: when a man is well he will eat anything he finds. When he is sick he seeks to eat all kinds of dainties. Rabbi Isaac said that in former times the main outlines of the Torah were known to all, and the people sought to hear a lesson of the Mishnah or of the Talmud. But now that the main outlines of the Torah are not known people seek to hear a lesson of scripture and of aggadah. Rabbi Levi said, in former times when people had means people were eager to learn something of the Mishnah, the Halakhah or the Talmud. Now when they are impoverished and sick from bondage they no longer seek to hear anything but words of blessing and consolation (i.e., aggadah).[6]

Yet, there is also rabbinic evidence that aggadah *was* highly valued. "Do you wish to know who spoke and the world came into being?" asks the Sifre rhetorically. The answer: "Then study aggadah for thereby you

5. B. Shabbat 88a, cf. *Abodah Zarah* 2b; also Sifre 142b, ed. M. Friedmann, Vienna 1864.
6. Midrash on Song of Songs II:14, Levin-Epstein, Warsaw 1924.

may come to know the Holy One, blessed be He, and to follow His ways."[7] We may better judge the importance of aggadah in ancient Israel by pinpointing three of its historic functions in the life of the people. We shall consider aggadah as the language by which the pre-modern Jew (1) perceived contemporary Jewish fate and human history under the sign of the covenant, (2) affirmed the inextricable bond between his personal identity and his covenant consciousness, and (3) resolved his crises of faith.

## III.

The Torah spoke of a commanding Presence who had singled out the people Israel for particular covenant and who acted in its history. History became revelation when the liberation of slaves from Egyptian bondage was received as an act of divine power and love, the destruction of the First Temple an act of divine retribution and the restoration under Cyrus, a sign that "my kindness shall not depart from thee, neither shall my covenant of peace be removed, saith the Lord that has compassion on thee." (Isaiah 54:10) *Through aggadah the rabbis were able to speak of God's continuing power and love for Israel in an age when prophecy had ended.*

The end of the Second Commonwealth, the destruction of the Temple, and the exile of the people by the Romans were all traumatic events in the life of Israel. Through aggadah, Edom became a code name for Rome and Israel's present degradation a sign of divine chastening. Rabbi Johanan ben Zakkai (1st century) could say to his people in quasi-prophetic terms: "You were unwilling to repair the roads and streets leading up to the Temple; now you have to keep in repair the posts and stations on the road to the royal cities, and thus it says: 'because you did not serve the Lord your God, therefore you shall serve your enemy . . . (Deut. 28:47f) .' "[8]

Again the aggadah asks: Why was the first sanctuary destroyed? Because of three things which prevailed therein: idolatry, immorality, bloodshed . . . but why was the second sanctuary destroyed, seeing that in its time they were occupying themselves with Torah, precepts and the practice of *tzedakah?* Because hatred without just cause prevailed therein. This teaches you that groundless hatred is considered of even greater gravity than the above three sins . . ."[9] Through aggadah post-biblical Jewish fate was understood under the sign of the covenant. God continues to call Israel to account for its faithlessness. The decisive word in history belongs to the Sovereign of the World.

Roman dominion was one of two major events which required a

---

7. Sifre 85a.
8. Mekilta, Baḥodesh, Vol. II ed. Lauterbach, p. 194.
9. B. Yoma 9b.

theological response. The second was Christianity's emergence as an aggressive rival and usurper. Rabbinic Judaism combated the Christian challenge by mustering the arsenal of aggadah. Indeed, the polemic between the early church and the synagogue may be viewed as a conflict of aggadic midrashim.

New Testament God-talk—its claim that Jesus embodied the complete divine revelation to man—was supported by texts from the Hebrew Bible. Matthew 2:6 quotes Micah 5:1: "For from you . . . (Bethlehem) shall come a ruler who will govern my people Israel." Jesus' suffering, described in Matthew 8:17 is understood as the fulfillment of a Hebrew prophecy: "Surely our diseases he did bear and our pains he carried" (Isaiah 53:4).

The sages denied the validity of Christian claims by also invoking biblical texts. God has no son, says R. Abbahu (3rd century). Commenting on Exodus 20:2, he writes: "Compare therewith a king of flesh and blood. He reigns and has a father or a brother or a son—The Holy One—blessed be His name—said, 'Not so am I' . . ."[10] Resh Lakish (3rd century) interprets Numbers 24:23 as Balaam's rebuke of one "who declared himself to be God."[11]

The Christian aggadists buttressed their claims to being the New Israel by invoking the razing of Jerusalem and the destruction of the Temple as divine judgment upon Israel for failing to believe in Jesus. Such is the argument of Chapter 16 of the Epistle of Barnabas (2nd century) which Eugene Mihaly reconstructs in this paraphrase:

> How do you explain . . . the destruction of the Temple, the fall of Jerusalem, the miserable lot of your people? Is this not the decisive proof that God has rejected you Jews and has delivered you for destruction at the hands of your enemies? . . . Now there is only one true temple, not the temple built by hand which was in fact a 'nest of idolatry and a haunt of demons . . .' but the spiritual temple in us—that is where God really dwells.[12]

The rabbis ignited the fuel for this Christian polemic when, entirely in the spirit of the Biblical prophets, they interpreted the destruction of the Temple as a sign of God's judgment. To counter the Christian claim it was now necessary to affirm that, even in the aftermath of divine wrath, God will not forsake His people. Mihaly suggests that the aggadists searched for "a clear biblical text which speaks not of an event in the past but one that looks to the future—a prophecy that sees Israel's degradation as part of a grand divine scheme of history which culminates in the final redemption."[13] The rabbis found such a verse,

10. Exodus Rabba 29:4, ed. Levin-Epstein, Warsaw 1924.
11. B. Sanhedrin 106b.
12. Mihaly, E. "A Rabbinic Defense of the Election of Israel," Hebrew Union College Annual, Vol. XXXV, p. 129.
13. *Ibid.*, p. 130.

Mihaly contends, in Jeremiah 10:16—"Not like these is the portion of Jacob for he is the former of all things and Israel is the tribe of his inheritance. The Lord of Hosts is his name." This verse is frequently used in the consolatory sermons of that era. It may be taken as a code symbol for the assertion that the Christian claim is invalid. God's chastening is but the prelude to redemption. Israel remains God's chosen one.

The sages also transmuted Israel's lowly estate from a sign of divine wrath into a badge of divine service. The aggadists frequently cite Psalms 44:22 to make the point: "Because of Thee we are slaughtered all day long, we are counted as sheep for the slaughter."[14]

A rabbinic commentary on Deuteronomy 6:5 expounds: "Even if he takes your soul as it says 'for thy sake we are slain every day.' "[15] The Talmud speaks of 400 Jewish youth and maidens taken captive and transported to a house of ill repute. Learning of their fate the maidens and then the youths choose death. They jumped into the sea proclaiming, "For thy sake are we killed all day long."[16]

Rabbi Akiba (2nd century), himself a martyr, recounts that Israel's fate leads the nations to ask: "What is your beloved more than another beloved . . . that you die for Him and that you are slain for Him, as it says . . . 'for thy sake are we slain all day . . .' " Akiba answers that Israel resists the blandishment of the nations, standing prepared to die for God's sake in a world which does not acknowledge his sovereignty.[17]

It is evident that Psalms 44:22 provides a code symbol by which Israel's present suffering becomes not a sign of divine rejection but the price of bearing the yoke of the covenant in an unredeemed world. In countering the Christian claim, aggadah served as the language through which God's abiding relation to Israel was reaffirmed. *In aggadah, contemporary Jewish fate was understood in terms consistent with the biblical view of the covenant.*

In contemporary Jewish life two primary events have cried out for theological understanding: the Holocaust and the rebirth of Israel. Aggadah was the language by which the post-biblical Jew affirmed the continued presence of God in history. Is the God who redeemed slaves from Egypt, brought them to the Promised Land and exiled them from their home, the selfsame God who let 6,000,000 die in the ovens of Hitler and 30 years later revealed His power in the rebirth of Zion? Can the contemporary Jew fashion an aggadah which embraces both the past and present experience of his people? An authentic Jewish God-talk may seek no less, either by reappropriating the traditional aggadah or by reshaping it.

---

14. Tanhuma B. 48b, cf. Midrash on Song of Songs I:15.
15. Sifre 73a-b.
16. B. Gittin 57b.
17. Midrash on Song of Songs II:16.

Throuogh rabbinic aggadah Roman dominion was perceived by post-biblical Jews as an act of divine chastening. No Jewish theologian of any stature has sought to understand Auschwitz in these terms. The "professional" theological response has assumed these general forms: (1) the God of the covenant is a revaling and a hiding God. Auschwitz is a sign of God in eclipse. (2) Hitler reminded us that the Jew, a charter witness to the vision of God's Kingdom, remains especially vulnerable in a world where that vision has not been fulfilled. The Jew still suffers for God since the Messiah has not yet come. (3) Rather than sound the death knell for the God of history (*à la* Rubenstein), Jewish theologians and preachers have felt compelled to acknowledge the essential or self-imposed limits of God's power in a world where men are created for responsibility and freedom. *All such efforts at theological understanding reveal some vestigial yearning to interpret contemporary Jewish fate under the sign of the covenant.*

Classical aggadah invested the restoration of Jewish sovereignty in Palestine with eschatological significance. While no Jewish theologian has contended that Israel's rebirth represents the advent of the Messiah, most have felt impelled to relate this event to the classical understanding of Jewish destiny and hope. To many it is a sign of desperately needed grace bestowed upon a people on the verge of despair.

Even today's secular Jew lives with some awareness of a particular Jewish destiny, a special vulnerability attached to being a son of the covenant in an unjust world. The premonition of anti-Semitism, whether in reaction to America's "betrayal" in Vietnam or as the bitter fruit of growing racial ferment, finds Jews speaking as if their Jewish burden is an old and familiar story. Even if they do not invoke the name of God they continue to understand Jewish experience as the price of the covenant.

Similarly the most secularized Israeli sees the present struggle of his nation in a hostile world as part of the peculiar fate of a historic people. Moshe Dayan, drawing on the biblical saga, told a group of Israeli cadets recently, "Tranquility and home have always been an ardent desire for our people and not a reality. If from time to time we achieved them it was only as temporary stops along the way, pauses to replenish our spirit and draw strength and courage to go on with the struggle."[18]

The modern secular Jew also acknowledges man's accountability for the quality of his life. He admits that man must create an ordered world or face nuclear destruction. In this sense he appears to understand "current events" under the sign of the covenant but in demythologized form. Nevertheless, such social thought contains at least intimations of

18. Jerusalem Post, August 11, 1969.

transcendence. Beyond strict empiricism it appeals to a "moral structure of the universe."

We have suggested that aggadah expressed symbolically the unbroken continuity of Jewish covenant existence. Even in this secular age this perception of continuity persists. Aggadah may be reappropriated only by those who detect a relation between the meaning of Jewish fate disclosed in ancient rabbinic tales and the destiny of the Jewish people in the contemporary world; those Jews perceive signs in the daily newspapers that the God of the covenant is very much alive.

## IV.

To this day the liturgy of the ancient synagogue and home remains the language in which the Jew speaks to and about God. Harvey Cox has described the religious man as "one who grasps his own life within a larger historical and cosmic setting. He sees himself as part of a greater whole, a larger story in which he plays a part."[19]

Liturgical aggadah—the God-talk of Jewish worship—nurtured and confirmed the Jew's consciousness of himself as a member of the people Israel. In turn his self-understanding as a creature of God was shaped by his concept of Israel's covenant with God. In liturgy he affirmed that his personal deity was in truth the God who appeared unto his fathers. Through liturgical aggadah he did "grasp his own life within a larger historical and cosmic setting."

The *Haggadah* (same root as aggadah), celebrating Israel's redemption from Egyptian bondage, provided the language of faith by which the Jew could acknowledge God's mighty acts as events having special claim upon him. Clearly the Jew is summoned to celebrate this event as a significant milestone in his *personal* life. It was "incumbent upon an individual in every generation to regard himself as if he went forth out of Egypt."[20]

This was no less true in the daily and Sabbath liturgy. The God-talk of the worship service lent presentness to decisive moments in Israel's past. As Heinemann suggests, "Every man of Israel was empowered to say 'we' in speaking of his fathers, and the exodus from Egypt and the standing at Mt. Sinai became as close to us as to those who actually were privileged to be there in truth."[21]

The worshipper daily recited the words attributed to ancient Israel upon their redemption from Egypt. The Morning Service quotes Exodus 14:30–15:18:

> From Egypt Thou didst redeem us, O Lord our God, from the house of bondage Thou didst deliver us . . . Wherefore . . . Moses and the children

19. Cox, H. *Feast of Fools.* Harvard Univ. Press, 1969, p. 14.
20. B. Pesaḥim 116b.
21. Heinemann, I. *Darkhe Ha-Aggadah*, Massada, Israel, 1954, p. 43.

of Israel sang a song unto Thee with great joy, saying together "Who is like unto Thee, O Lord, among the mighty" "Who is like unto Thee, glorious in holiness, revered in praises, doing wonders.. ? With a new song the redeemed people offered praises unto Thy name. At the seashore, they gave thanks together and proclaimed Thy sovereignty as they said: The Lord shall reign forever and forever.[22]

With minor variations, the same responses are recited in the Evening Service. Thus did the liturgical aggadah enable the individual to enlarge the scope and significance of his selfhood by sharing in the sacred history of his people. It also permitted his *personal* trust in God to be conditioned by what God had done for *Israel*. His experiences with God were identified with Israel's life under the covenant. Present hopes were grounded in the remembrance of things past.

Similarly, petitions on behalf of self are indistinguishable from prayers on behalf of Israel. The fate of the individual is inextricably bound up with the fate of his people. Here are two examples. The eighth benediction of the *Amidah* prayer reads: "Heal us, O Lord, and we shall be healed. Save us and we shall be saved. For Thou art our praise. Grant a perfect healing to all our wounds for Thou, almighty God, art a faithful and merciful physician. Blessed art Thou, O Lord, who healest the sick of Thy people Israel."[23] A voluntary prayer may then be inserted naming the individual for whose recovery one is praying. Clearly the individual's prayer on an occasion of illness which personally affects him is tied up with his acknowledgment of God as the healer of the people Israel. *The liturgy both preserves and confirms the indissoluble bond between a Jew's personhood and his Jewishness.*

In the liturgy for weddings, the significance of the personal love bond between two persons is again linked to membership in the household of Israel. Prayers for personal bliss are tied up with petitions for the redemption of Israel and the restoration of Jerusalem.

> Praised be Thou, O Lord, our God, King of the Universe, who hast created joy and gladness, bridegroom and bride, rejoicing song, pleasure and delight, love and brotherhood, peace and fellowship. Soon may there be heard in the cities of Judah and in the streets of Jerusalem the voice of joy and gladness, the voice of the bridegroom and the voice of the bride, the jubilant voice of the bridegrooms from their nuptial canopies and of youth from their feasts of song. Praised be Thou, O Lord, who gladdenest the bridegroom and the bride.[24]

Halakhah defined the Jew's obligation as a Jewish person. Such definition was compelling because of the role of aggadah in cementing the bond between a Jew's self-understanding and his membership in the community of Israel.

Revelation may have ended with prophecy but personal religious ex-

---

22. Daily Prayerbook, ed. J. Hertz, New York: Bloch, 1948, pp. 128–9.
23. *Ibid.*, p. 141.
24. Ketubot 8a.

71

perience did not depart from the house of Israel. Jewish worship, mediated by aggadah, linked the personal religious experience of the Jew to the encounter between God and the people. The Bible speaks at times of the visual experience of God: "So have I beheld Thee in the sanctuary to see Thy strength and glory (Ps. 63:3)." In rabbinic literature sensory experiences of God were associated with the Temple service. "Everybody felt," writes Kadushin, "that the sacrificial services took place in so to speak the proximity of God, a proximity that, when all conditions were fulfilled, would be visibly manifest."[25]

Although some rabbis nurtured expectations of an auditory or visual religious experience even in the aftermath of the Temple destruction, most felt that such an event belonged to the past and to the future. Kadushin describes the religious experience encouraged by halakhah and aggadah as "normal mysticism." He defines normal mysticism as "the experience of God without visions or locutions or other sense phenomena."[27]

Despite its social models (God-Israel) for personal religious experience, the aggadah did not unduly cramp the individual's spiritual style. Its splendid variety testified to individual differences among rabbis and to diverse experiences within an individual rabbinic soul. One aggadah may celebrate God's nearness, another his hiddenness. This fluidity permitted the God-talk of rabbinic Judaism effectively to express the personal experience of the traditional Jew.

Nevertheless, the structure of rabbinic thought also imposed normative limits upon personal religious experience. The Jew was not invited to understand his relation to God in terms other than those defined by the covenant between God and Israel. Meaningful God-talk was possible for our ancestors because it embodied a common covenant consciousness.

What has happened to that consensus in the modern world? Moses Mendelssohn, a man whom many called the first modern Jew, once wrote a letter to Herder in which he claimed that "Moses, the human being (*mensch*) is writing to Herder, the human being, and not the Jew to the Christian preacher."[28] Mendelssohn implied that his Jewishness and personhood were separable. That statement charts the "identity crisis" of the post-emancipation Jew.

Mendelssohn's descendants, those who remained Jewish, are able to ask a question which would have been unintelligible to their rabbinic

25. Kadushin, M. *Worship and Ethics*. Northwestern Univ. Press, 1964, p. 164.
26. *Ibid.*, p. 167.
27. Kadushin, M. *The Rabbinic Mind*. New York: Jewish Theological Seminary, 1952, pp. 257–8.
28. Kayserling, *Moses Mendelssohn*, quoted in J. Katz, *Exclusiveness and Tolerance*, Oxford, 1961, p. 170.

forebears: "Which am I first, a man or a Jew?" The question may take several forms. For some the traditional identity of personal fate with the fate of the Jewish people has itself become negotiable. "What obligations can a fellowship which is only an accident of birth impose upon me?" Others disclaim the integral bond between their personal faith and the faith of Israel. Enticed by the new self-understanding of secular man, some deny meaning to the religious quest itself. Others may hunger for God but find their personal needs better served by Eastern mysticism than by the obligations of covenant theology. They feel no compulsion to be guided in their spiritual quest by the faith of their fathers. They are willing to consider Judaism as one option among many—without conceding its priority in advance.

In at least some respects the 20th century has helped mend the breach which Mendelssohn articulated. Hitler proved that even a German person of Mosaic persuasion, and even a baptized Jew, could find his personhood threatened by his Jewishness—that the defense of one could not be divorced from the defense of the other. Through his fervent identification with his Israeli brethren the post-Holocaust diaspora Jew registers that he has gotten the message. The resurgence of "Black Peoplehood" has further dramatized the failure of that classical liberal model which envisaged a neutral society in which a rarefied American consciousness, purged of all other particularisms, would be made manifest. On some level the Jew carries his Jewishness (and the Black his negritude) wherever he goes—and his personal self-consciousness is defined by it. Significantly even those "under 30" collegiates, who most stridently disavow the primary claim of Jewish faith or fate, seek encompassing loyalties and communities which will define and enhance their personhood.

Nonetheless, it remains true that Samson Raphel Hirsch's concept of a *"Yisroel-mensch"* is mocked by that recurring question: Which am I first, a man or a Jew? The integrity of Jewish person-hood has been broken as much, and by the same forces, as the traditional interdependence of God, Torah and Israel. The aggadah may only be reappropriated by a Jew who is disturbed by the breach and is at least struggling to mend it.

*In the world of aggadah the individual Jew stood before God as a member of the people Israel. His self-understanding and his ethnic identity were intrinsically bound together.* Aggadah may function in the life of a Jew who acknowledges at least some vestigial bond between his yearning for religious meaning and his membership in the fellowship of Israel. Aggadah may only be reappropriated by a Jew who believes his "Jewishness" must in some primary way mediate his personal quest for an authentic existence.

73

## V.

The rabbis of the aggadah lived in an era which challenged their trust in the promise of life. Not only did they witness such personal tragedies as illness, premature death, drought, etc.—but they also suffered the pain of Jewish homelessness in the face of a militant and triumphant church. *Aggadah was the language in which these crises of faith were acknowledged, expressed and overcome.*

Such crises are amply foreshadowed in biblical tales depicting Israel's dialogues with God. Sheldon Blank has called these confrontations "the promethean element" in biblical literature. Certain individuals are featured and "properly the name of Moses leads all the rest; for he more often than others, and more successfully, takes issue with God,"[29] Earlier Blank characterizes the biblical promethean figures ". . . not among the rebels . . . but among the faithful. They hold fast to God even while they question His decrees. Though they defy they do not deny him."[30]

On biblical foundations the rabbis reconstruct their own elaborate confrontations between Israel and the God of the covenant. The tense is past but the struggle is contemporary.

Aggadah finds God and Abraham encountering each other amid the ruins of the Temple in Jerusalem. When God asks Abraham to explain his presence Abraham declares his intention to represent his children as plaintiffs before God. Abraham is told that Israel sinned and was therefore exiled. Undaunted, the Patriarch presents a whole range of possible mitigating circumstances: perhaps only a few sinned; besides, what about God's commitment to remember the covenant symbolized by circumcision? And if God has waited for them they might have repented! After the Lord responds to each challenge, Abraham bows his head in acknowledgement of divine justice as he inquires yearningly of the possibilities of ultimate restoration. He is then assured that as the olive's fulfillment lies in its final end, so Israel's promise lay in a destiny yet to unfold.[31] Even the modern reader needs little prod to discern in this aggadah a rabbinic need for reassurance that God is worthy of trust and that there is hope for the future.

At times, by boldly extracting a confession from God the Midrash will vindicate His people Israel: "The School of Rab said: Four things God regrets that He created and one of them is exile.[32] When God seeks to comfort the fallen city of Jerusalem she will say,

> Master of the Universe, before you gave the Torah to Israel Thou didst go round offering it to all the 70 nations, not one of which would accept it. It was finally Israel who accepted it and since it was they who accepted

---

29. Blank, S. *Prophetic Faith in Isaiah.* New York: Harper, 1958, p. 198.
30. *Ibid.,* p. 197.
31. B. Menakhot 53b.
32. B. Sukkah 52b.

it how couldst Thou have done to them what Thou hast done? At once
the Holy One, blessed be He, will accept the reproof from Jerusalem and
will say: "I was unfortunately arbitrary with you," as is said, "I acted in
lordly fashion towards you" (Jer. 3:14). Jerusalem will reply: Master of
the Universe, is it right that what Thou art saying be kept only between
us? Who will let the nations of the earth know about me that I have done
Thy Will? . . . (God replies): I shall speak to the nations of the earth about
thee and make known thy works of righteousness.[33]

Prompted by the destruction of Jerusalem, the rabbis elsewhere
attribute to God even more daring confessions of failure. In a burst of self-
deprecation the Lord exclaims, "Woe unto the king who in his youth succeeded and in old age failed."[34] The rhetoric of aggadah registers the rabbinic struggle for faith and on occasion mends the breach by compromising divine perfection.

Again the need for such confirmation of faith is reflected when
Israel is portrayed patiently waiting for God's redemption. The aggadah
seeks to justify Israel's steadfast loyalty in the absence of redemption.
The tense is past but the struggle is present. According to the aggadah
the nations of the world woo the covenant people to forsake its be-
nighted fate: "How long shall you continue to die on account of your
God? . . . Consider all the retribution He hath inflicted upon you, how
many despoilers He hath brought upon you . . . return unto us . . ."
Israel replies:

> And (the children of) Israel enter their houses of worship and study and
> they open the Torah and read therein "I will turn toward you and make
> you fruitful and multiply you. I will establish my covenant with you." (Lev.
> 26:9). And by these words the people were comforted and on the morrow
> when the end shall come the Holy One, blessed be He, will say to Israel:
> My sons I am amazed how you were able to tarry for me all these years, to
> which Israel shall reply, Were it not for the promises of your Torah the
> nations of the world long since would have caused us to defect from you.[35]

Israel's suffering is received not as punishment for faithlessness but
as the price of being God's covenant people in an unredeemed world.
It is not Israel's loyalty, but that of God which is in need of vindication.
In fact, God is amazed at his people's steadfastness.

Often the rabbis portray a God who shares in the suffering of His
people. His self-fulfillment is contingent upon His people's redemption.
The image of an infinite God caring for and affected by the plight of
His people is paradoxical. Recognizing this, the rabbis frequently employed the qualifying term *kavyakhol*—"as it were"—to suggest both the
inadequacy and indispensability of symbolic language if we are to speak
of God from man's perspective.

Aggadah accentuates divine involvement in the traumas of man.

---

33. Pesikta Rabbati, Piska 30:4. ed. and trans. W. Braude, Vol. II, p. 597, Yale University Press, 1968.
34. Midrash on Lamentations, Introduction #24. Levin-Epstein, Warsaw, 1924.
35. Pesikta Rabbati 106b. ed. M. Friedmann, Vilna 1880.

"When Israel is enslaved God, as it were, is enslaved with them."[36] God says to Moses: "I have been with you in the midst of this enslavement and shall abide with you when you are enslaved by the nations."[37] Of Israel's redemption from Egypt God says: "You *and* I went forth from Egypt."[38] God weeps over the destruction of the Temple and Israel's exile from its land. He requires consolation no less than His children. He follows His children into exile as a sign of His abiding love.[39]

Aggadah indicates that our forebears were not strangers to crises of faith. The rhetoric of aggadah offered a language in which anger and doubt could be openly expressed and trust in life's meaning reaffirmed.

The rabbis did not resolve the issue between God and Israel simply by blaming themselves for all their woes. Such is the contention of Richard L. Rubenstein in *The Religious Imagination*. By an act of reductionism Rubenstein treats aggadah as the projection of the rabbinic unconscious. In a chapter entitled "God's Omnipotence in Rabbinic Judaism" Rubenstein suggests that "the ceding of ultimate power and authority to God's inscrutable will left the religious Jew with two alternatives: He could blame himself for his misfortunes or he could proclaim the death of the omnipotent Lord of history, reluctantly regarding the cosmos as hopelessly absurd, as do such modern existentialists as Sartre and Camus."[40] Given that choice, says Rubenstein, the rabbis affirmed God. "Self-reproach was therefore the principal reaction to the destruction of Jerusalem by Vespasian and Hadrian. There were other possible reactions, there was always the temptation to accuse God," but such accusation could only be done obliquely by placing personal doubts in the mouths of "heavies" like Korah because "the protest against God could not be expressed openly in rabbinic times."[41]

Rubinstein's formulation of rabbinic alternatives does scant justice to the aggadah. While self-accusation is a strong motif, there is no reluctance to argue with God and it is not only "heavies" who do so. Abraham, Moses, and the people Israel are numbered among the challengers. Moreover, Rubenstein totally ignores the aggadah's justification of the Jew at divine expense, or the God who shares in the affliction of His people, or the concept of suffering as the price of bearing witness to God in a world not yet redeemed.

Unless he has settled into a comfortable agnosticism or a glib atheism, every Jew grapples in some form with the "problem of evil." In moments of most fervent doubt one may detect this tacit plea: Give me reason

---

36. Mekhilta, Piska, Vol. I. ed. Lauterbach, p. 113.
37. B. Berakot 9b.
38. Exodus Rabba 15:13; Leviticus Rabba 9:3, Levin-Epstein, Warsaw, 1924.
39. Pesikta Rabbati 139a. ed. M. Friedmann, Vienna, 1880.
40. Rubenstein, R. *op. cit.,* p. 135.
41. *Ibid.,* p. 130.

to confirm my primordial faith in life's meaning. Schubert Ogden is correct when he insists that "religions are by their very nature *representative,* they never originate our faith in life's meaning but rather provide us with particular symbolic forms through which that faith may be more or less adequately reaffirmed at the level of self-conscious belief."[42] Aggadah may speak for and to the Jew who experiences the threat of doubt and yearns to confirm the "gift of meaning." Several attempts have been made by professional Jewish theologians to hew a contemporary theodicy from the quarry of aggadah.

Henry Slonimsky turned to aggadah as a bold anticipation of contemporary process thought. The world is unfinished; man and God must jointly fulfill the promise of creation. The relation between them is one of "give and take or reciprocal enrichment resulting in the slow change in growth not merely of man but God."[43] Slonimsky makes much of those passages which affirm God's need for man, noting for example the Sifre's comment on Psalms 123:1, "Unto Thee I lift up mine eyes, O Thou that sittest in the heavens": אשׂא עיני אל ההרים.

> If it were not for me (if I did not lift up my eyes) Thou, O God, wouldst not be sitting in the heavens.[44]

The ancient Jew's struggle for faith in a world pocked by unmerited suffering grounds Slonimsky's own affirmation. "God in the full meaning of the term seems to stand at the end not at the beginning, 'on that day He shall be One and His name shall be One.' He must be made One and man is the agent in whose hands it is left to make or to mar that supreme integration."[45]

If this be the major thrust of the aggadah and the cornerstone of its theodicy, what purpose is served by the mythic framework? Slonimsky commends aggadah for creating "an atmosphere or medium of freedom and unconstraint, by providing themes and images to guide and influence the listener and all the workings of his mind and still (retaining) the fluidity of a story as of the myths to which Plato resorts when his themes outdistance his concepts."[46] Slonimsky elaborates: "Whatever in philosophy is capable of translation or transformation into poetry is alone vital and valuable; and secondly . . . whatever has originally been conceived as myth is alone real and effective for it is something capable of being believed and therefore loved."[47]

Like Slonimsky, Emil Fackenheim finds that aggadah is a unique and viable rhetoric of faith. It's language uniquely captures the dialectic of

---

42. Ogden, S. *The Reality of God.* New York: Harper, 1966, p. 34.
43. Slonimsky, H. *Essays,* Chicago: Quadrangle Press, 1967, p. 63.
44. Sifre 144a.
45. Slonimsky, *op. cit.,* p. 15.
46. *Ibid.,* p. 13.
47. *Ibid.,* p. 62.

a relation between an infinite God and finite man. "Midrash," writes Fackenheim,

> is dialectical because it must hold fast to contradictory affirmations which thought can hold together only in the form of symbols and metaphor. Divine power transcends all things human—yet divine love becomes involved with things human, and man, made a partner of God, can 'as it were' augment or diminish divine power. . . . Man must wait for redemption as though all depended on God—and work for it as though all depended on man. The Messiah will come when all men are just—or all wicked. These affirmations must be held together unless thought is to lose either divine infinity or finite humanity or the relation beween them. Yet they cannot be held together except in stories, parables and metaphor . . . there is what may be called a midrashic framework which systematically resists philosophical or religious dissipation of its central affirmations. Midrashic thought resists the fatalism which dissipates human freedom . . . and a paganism which limits divine power literally for the sake of human freedom. . . . There are times in history when evil can be explained as deserved punishment, others . . . when divine power is 'as it were' suspended and God Himself suffers in exile.[48]

Slonimsky and Fackenheim use aggadah to express and overcome the "problem of evil." Each, however, interprets the midrashic framework differently. Slonimsky discovers evidence of a limited God in the process of becoming. Fackenheim discovers a dialectical tension between infinite divine power and finite human power which resists philosophical resolution but may be reconciled in the life of faith.

We have suggested that aggadah was the language in which the Jew's classic argument with God was both expressed and resolved. Sam Keen contends that the function of religion is to "nourish and restore the sense of basic trust by affirming in symbolic language that the ultimate context of life is succoring and trustworthy." Keen illustrates his position with the following image:

> . . . the most comprehensive, immediate symbol for the human condition might well be: ? (+ — 0)? Each individual's life is a parenthesis which includes mixed experiences of pleasure, pain and neutrality. Outside the parenthesis—before birth, after death, and beyond the limits of the present temporal imagination—there is the ? (mystery). . . . Theology making use of the rich emotive language of love, trust, memory and grace, affirms that the source out of which life comes and into which it disappears . . . is trustworthy. Religion places a plus at the heart of the mystery.[49]

That function was performed exquisitely by the aggadah. The modern Jew, no less than his forebear, must struggle with the issue of life's transcendent meaning. Can aggadah still mediate this quest? It may do so only for those who affirm in spite of everything that there is "a plus at the heart of the mystery."

---

48. Fackenheim, E. *Quest for Past and Future.* Bloomington: Indiana U. Press, 1968, pp. 16–17.
49. Keen, S. *op. cit.,* pp. 204–5.

# KIDDUSH AND HILLUL HASHEM[1]

## AVRAHAM HOLTZ

### I

The dual concepts of Ḥillul (defamation) and Kiddush (sanctification) are among the basic concepts of Judaism. They have been a major and constant influence in the shaping of the Jewish mind and attitude, and are fundamental to an understanding of the relationships between the Jews and the Gentiles not only in times of crisis, but in peaceful and less eventful periods of Jewish history.[2]

The attitude of ultimate seriousness manifested towards these concepts was not unique to any one age but was a result of a long and fascinating development. Retaining certain fixed relationships, these concepts nonetheless were redefined and reconstituted. As all Jewish concepts, they have their roots in the Bible, were developed in a very characteristic way during the Rabbinic period and were preserved for popular edification in the Siddur, the compendium of Jewish belief and practice.

Kiddush and Ḥillul Hashem are complimentary concepts since they are always used together and the elucidation of the one will shed light on the other. These concepts in their original verb-form and detailed application appear in several books of the Bible.[3] The clearest statements of these concepts are to be found, in my opinion, in the Book of Ezekiel. Though the possibility exists that Ezekiel screened these concepts through his most imaginative and complex mind and is, therefore, not to be considered as faithful evidence for the biblical view, I think that the evidence will support the conclusion that Ezekiel did *not* alter the original view. Ezekiel in his unique style merely rendered a more elaborate, and in this instance, a more lucid, presentation, one which can

---

The growth and actual transformation of the twin concepts of Sanctification and Desecration of the Name of God (*Kiddush* and *Ḥillul Hashem*) is here traced. The shift in emphasis the author underscores forms a significant aspect of the growth of Jewish religious thought. The author serves as Instructor in Modern Hebrew Literature at the Jewish Theological Seminary.

3 We use as examples only those references in which the word *shem* (name) immediately follows the verb. v. Lev. 18:21, 19:12, 20:3 Ez 20:39, 36:20, 39:7 Amos 2:7 Ez 36:23, in the *niphal* Lev. 10:3, 22:32 Ez 20:41, 28:22, 28:25, 39:27.

serve as a key to the other books of the Bible. I will quote the verses *in toto* to eliminate the need for referring to the texts and for greater clarity.[4]

Ezekiel 20:9 But I wrought for my name's sake, that it *should not be profaned in the sight of the nations,* among whom they were, in whose sight I made myself known...
20:41 With your sweet savour will I accept you, when I bring you out from the peoples, and gather you out of the countries wherein you have been scattered; *and I will sanctify myself in (by) you in the sight of the nations.*[5]
36:20 And when they came unto the nations whither they came, they profaned My Holy Name, in that men said of them: These are the people of the Lord, and are gone forth from His land. (21) But I had pity for My holy name, which ye have profaned among the nations, whither ye came. (23) And I will sanctify My great name, which ye have profaned in their midst; and the nations shall know that I am the Lord, saith the Lord God, when I shall sanctify myself in you before their eyes... (35) And they shall say: "This land that was desolate is become like the garden of Eden... (36) Then the nations that are left round about you shall know that I the Lord have builded the ruined places.
39:4 Thou (Gog) shall fall upon the mountains of Israel. Thou, and all thy bands, and the peoples that are with thee... (5) Thou shall fall upon the open field . . . (7) And My holy name will I make known in the midst of my people Israel; neither will I suffer my holy name to be profaned any more; and the nations shall know that I am the Lord . . ."

The above-quoted verses saliently expose the several indispensable and organically-related elements which constitute the framework for the concretization of these concepts. The constituent elements are: the people Israel, the nations, an action (or better, a reaction, a response, by the nations) and the Lord who is the subject and fulfiller of His plans.

The words "in the sight (presence) of the nations" are the central-terms in the pattern of the concepts of Kiddush Hashem, for without the awareness of the nations apparently no Kiddush Hashem can take place, the Lord can not be sanctified without the awareness of the nations.

The Lord unfolds his plans and exhibits them through Israel, by means of the people Israel. The people Israel is passive, the Lord restores His people to the land of Israel, perhaps, against their will. They are not active participants in this drama, but rather play a supporting role; they are the stage on which the drama is unfolded and as such need not react, neither positively nor negatively. The nations, on the other hand, are involved in the sanctification of the Lord's name for only with their response can it be effected. The Israelites do not and can not sanctify the Lord's name. The sanctification is reserved for the Lord Himself; He alone is concerned about the fate of His name and He alone must rectify any deeds which, though caused by the iniquity of His people, have led to the defamation of His name. The nations, by their positive response to the manifestations of

---

[4] *The Holy Scriptures*, J.P.S.A. 1917 (1953 printing) is the basic text for all biblical translations in this article. Wherever my translation differs from this one I will note the reason for the change in a footnote.
[5] The *niphal* form in the Bible is usually used as a Middle voice form. It is not to be rendered in the English by the passive forms. cf. Isa. 5:16 (appears sanctified) Gen. 7:11 (opened) v. *Gesenius' Hebrew Grammar* (second English edition by A. E. Cowley) 51 c-e.

the Lord's deeds with Israel do finally effect the sanctification.[6] The nations must become aware that the wonders wrought on Israel are from the Lord of Israel and their reaction is a prerequisite to Kiddush Hashem. This fusion of elements: the Lord as sanctified of His name, the people of Israel as the stage for the drama, the reactions of the nations—is the biblical view of Kiddush Hashem.

Since the Lord has bound His name with the fate of the people Israel, the actions of His people can directly defame His name. In the biblical view, though the Israelites cannot sanctify the Lord's name, they are held responsible for defaming it.

A negative response on the part of the nations to a deed performed by the Lord or by the Israelites, the bearers of the Lord's name on earth, causes Hillul Hashem. If by the actions or condition of Israel the nations reflect: "Where is their God?"[7] then His name has been defamed. In the view of the nations, the Lord himself is manifest through the actions of his people and through the conditions in which they find themselves. The nations, for example, upon seeing the Israelites cast into exile, ejected from their land naturally exclaim: "These are the Lord's people, they have been driven from His land." The nations in their narrow-mindedness misinterpret this act of the Lord as a clear indication of His weakness and loss of strength; this is surely a defamation of His name.

But Israel stands helpless since it can do nothing to retrieve the Lord's name and reclaim it to its proper place for this rests with the Lord alone. Israel can prevent the defamation of His name by restricting itself to good deeds thereby preventing any reprisals from the Lord which ultimately lead to Hillul Hashem but the Lord must himself restore His glory.

As Assyria was the rod of the Lord's wrath to chastise Israel so Israel is the rod in the Lord's hand for the purpose of Kiddush Hashem. Lest Israel, like Assyria, reason that it deserves the glory bestowed upon it, it must be reminded that it is only a tool in the Creator's hands.[8] The prophet reminds Israel that were not the Lord's name imperilled they on their own merit would never be redeemed. The covenant by which the Lord has bound himself to Israel is irrevocable, at least in the eyes of the nations.

At each time of crisis the Israelites as they stood in prayer would call to the Lord in supplication and when all channels of petition were sealed, they would turn to the Lord and use His tune, but in a new key. As one pleading before a king, the author of Psalm 115 stands before the Lord: "Not for our sake, not for our sake, But unto thy name give glory ... in order that[9] the nations should not say: "Where is their God?" (and thereby your name is defamed. You who are in charge of your sanctification must rescue us—for though we know that) "our God is in heaven, whatsoever pleased Him He hath done" (of this *we*

---

[6] The verb form *kadesh* in the *piel*, from which the noun form *kiddush hashem* derives, is used, in the Bible, exclusively for the Lord's demonstration of his power which he displays in the presence of the nations.

[7] v. Ps 79:10 cf. II Ki 18:34 (Isa 36:19) Joel 2:17 Ps 42:4, 115:2.

[8] Ez 36:22, 32.

[9] The word *lammah* often means "in order that not," "lest." Cf. Song of Songs 1:7 (The Aramaic word *dilma*, perhaps.) Ex 32:12, Numbers 14:3, II Sam 2:22, Dan 1:10 and others cf. Deut. 9:28.

are convinced despite the wretchedness of our lot and we know too) that "Their idols are silver and gold, the work of men's hands." (The nations in whose midst your name is being profaned are as convinced that their gods must be superior to you, for to them our miserable state of existence indicates a failure of strength of our god. You must therefore demonstrate your powers in their presence and set the world and your name aright.) The petitioner has used the words of the Lord against Him, as it were. The Lord has often said to Israel "Not for your sake Israel but for the sake of my name." The author following a long tradition here turns to the Lord and begs: "Not for our sake but for Yours." The author of this psalm followed an ancient tradition when he introduced this divine concern lest the name be defamed. Abraham implied it,[10] Moses stated it explicitly,[11] and many other prophets were able thereby to arouse the Lord to pity on His people.[12]

## II

With the conclusions arrived at in the preceding section, we can hope to elucidate the relevant texts in Leviticus parts of which were a major influence on the prophet Ezekiel.

Leviticus
(a) 18:21 Thou shalt not give any of thy seed to set them apart to Molekh, neither shalt thou profane the name of thy God, I am the Lord.
(b) 19:11 And ye shall not steal; neither shall ye deal falsely, nor lie one to another. (12) And ye shall not swear by My name falsely, so that thou profane the name of thy God. I am the Lord. 13) Thou shalt not oppress thy neighbor.
(c) 20:2 Whosoever . . . that giveth of his seed unto Molekh . . . (3) I also will set My face against that man . . . because he hath given of his seed unto Molekh, thereby[13] defiling my sanctuary and profaning My name.
(d) 21:5 They (the priests) shall not make baldness upon their head neither shall they shave off the corners of their beard, nor make any cuttings' in their flesh. (6) They shall be holy until their God, and not profane the name of their Lord.
(e) 22:2 Speak unto Aaron and to his sons, that they separate themselves from the holy things of the children of Israel, which they hallow unto Me, and that they profane not My holy name.
(f) 22:31 And ye shall keep My commandments, and do them; I am the Lord. (32) And ye shall not profane My holy name, but I will hallow myself among the children of Israel . . .

In the verses whose meaning is clear (a-d, and f,) all the elements of these dual concepts appear. The priests, who are the possessors of the Torah,[14] must be extra cautious in their behaviour. The people of Israel must ever be conscious lest their actions with their neighbours result in the defamation of the Lord's name, that is lest the neighbor come to feel the superiority of his deity.[15]

An Israelite who delivered his son as a sacrifice to Molekh inadvertently declared the supremacy of the foreign deity and thereby boldly denied the Lord's power to help. Every sacrifice of

---

[10] Gen 18:25.

[11] Ex 32:11–14, Numbers 14–11 ff., Deut 9:25–29.

[12] Joshua 7:9, Jer 14:7.

[13] *l'maan* often means "with the result that" and not "in order that" cf. Deut. 16:3, Amos 2:7 (clearly the lads did not go to the harlots to anger the Lord!).

[14] v. Jer. 2:8, Haggai 2:10ff.

[15] Tanḥuma, Jerusalem, 1953 p. 98a Rashi on Exodus 21:1.

this type which was offered for a blessing or a future reward was by its very nature a public offering and Molekh's worshippers, recognizing the Israelite who too was sacrificing a son to Molekh, night haughtily ask "Their God must be powerless to help, for if not why would he come to ours for help?" The father's action leads to a meaningless burning of the son and to the defamation of God's name.

Using our premises, we shall hazard a guess as to the ideational foundations of the laws prohibiting the Kohen's shaving, leaving a bald spot, etc. Apparently these visible acts were connected somehow with the ritual of foreign deities. The Kohen were he to follow in their patterns of ritual would thereby enhance the foreign deity and strengthen the faith of the foreign worshippers and thus diminish the Lord's esteem in the eyes of all concerned.

There are two separate clauses in "e" and "f" and two distinct reasons for the prohibitions: one is purely an intra-Israelite reason, the other concerns the Israelite as he relates to a non-Israelite. The people of Israel in their relationships with other Israelites must be faithful to their Lord and His precepts, but they are also instructed in their behaviour with foreign peoples. They are cautioned about the possible effect of their actions on strangers. "Foreign-relations" are most significant for they may result in Hillul Hashem.

In verse 19:12 the Israelite is cautioned not to lie, be deceitful, or cheat. If he commits any of these in his relationships with another Israelite, he obviously transgresses the commandment of his Lord, but here the prohibition concludes with the phrase: "he defames My name." Applying our principle that

defamation is applicable only in Israelite-non-Israelite relations, we may support the hypothesis that the prohibitions here are intended to caution the Israelite in his dealings with his neighbor. (cf. v. 13) If an Israelite transgresses with his non-Hebrew neighbor he not only disobeys the law between man and his fellow man but directly causes Hillul Hashem.[16]

Verse "e" is difficult and only when we discover the answer to the question why the children of Aaron must be separate will we be able to fully test the applicability of our premise to this verse.

Ezekiel expounded the principles inherent in these verses. He followed the pattern set forth in 19:12 which is directed to all Israelites and he elaborated their actions which result in Hillul Hashem.

Further, in the Book of Leviticus it states "I will appear holy in the midst (through) the children of Israel, I the Lord make them holy..." (22:33)[17] Ezekiel, analyzing this process of Kiddush Hashem through the children of Israel, undertook to answer the questions How? When? and Where? Additional responses to the ones discussed in the previous section are rendered in his chapters on the battles of Gog and Magog.[18]

The chapters on the battles of Gog and Magog are in essence illustrations of the method by which the Lord will sanctify His own name in the presence of the nations through the children of Israel. In full accord with Isaiah's description of the defeat of Assyria[19] on

---

16 cf. Tosefta, *Baba Kama* 10:8 (*Sefer Ḥasidim* paragraph 600). The Tosefta reads: "Stealing from a non-Jew is more serious than stealing from a Jew for Hillul Hashem is involved."

17 The translation is mine.

18 Ezekiel ccs. 38–39.

19 Isa. 10:12ff, cf. Daniel 11. See H. L. Gins-

the land of Israel, Ezekiel paints a more vivid picture. The nations will be brought to Eretz Yisrael, will be utterly defeated there in order that the Lord's name may be sanctified by them—in their very presence, indeed, on their very persons. The nations will be forced to recognize the fact that their defeat was the result of the Lord's intervention and will thus come to know His mighty hand.

Ezekiel has thus introduced two possible methods of the Lord's preparing for His Kiddush Hashem. Either the nations will realize the Lord's power by their own visual and mental observations of His deeds in Israel or they will be forced to this conclusion by God's own act. The Lord's name will be sanctified either voluntarily or under duress.

### III

An Israelite who, in the biblical view, could actively cause the defamation of the Lord's name could not sanctify His name. He was able, however, to glorify[20] His name. Isaiah says: "The Lord of hosts, Him shall ye extol" and further in 29:23 "When he (Jacob) seeth his children, the work of My hands, in the midst of him, that they extol My name; Yea they shall glorify the Holy One of Jacob, and shall stand in awe of the God of Israel." The children of Israel, upon experiencing the ingathering of the exiles will praise God's name, that is they will magnify and acclaim it. The nations are not involved in this process and there is no mention of them. This is an internal, national and popular reaction. The one action on the part of the Lord, His returning to the exiles, has resulted in the sanctification and in

the glorification of His name; they are distinct reactions. The *Hakdashah* (glorification) is one in which the Israelites are active, they praise, they stand in awe, they extol. In the Kiddush Hashem they are passive, the Lord and the nations are active. The momentous historic event of the return of the exiles and rebirth of Israel will have world wide ramifications. The Israelites, finally will recognize the hand of the Lord in their history and will sing praises to Him (*Hakdashath Hashem*). At the very same time and for the same reasons the nations of the world will also realize the power of the Lord as He reveals His might and fashions a new Israel and sanctifies His name.

### IV

There are three major Talmudic sources for our two concepts.[19a] There are many Midrashic commentaries that elucidate the Rabbinic view of these concepts. Nor do I feel it necessary to repeat the very brilliant discussions of Dr. Kadushin who has already drawn the basic conclusions from these sources.[21] Kiddush Hashem is possible, according to these sources, when the act is carried out even in the presence of ten Israelites —a *minyan*.[22] The difference between the biblical and rabbinic view becomes

---

19a *Sanhedrin* 74a, b; Yerushalmi *Abodah Zarah* 27b; M. *Sheb'iit* 4:2.

20 The *hiph'il hakdish* is incorrectly translated in the J.P.S. translation as though it were the *pi'el*. Clearly in these verses the verb "*takdishu*" is parallel to the verb *ta'a'riz u* which means to revere, to extol. Therefore once again the translation is my own.

21 Kadushin, *The Theology of Seder Eliahu,* N.Y. 1932 pp. 64 ff especially p. 65 note 164 and p. 149 note 162. *Organic Thinking*, p. 63. Evelyn Garfiel, *Service of the Heart*, N.Y. 1958 pp. 78ff.

22 *Sanhedrin* 74 b see Katz p. 97 note 38.

---

berg, *Studies in Daniel*, J.T.S.A. 1948 p. 78 note 21b.

apparent. First, the Jew has it in *his* power to be *mekadesh hashem*, not only need he not perform his act of Kiddush Hashem in the presence of non-Jews, a synagogal ritual can now be referred to as Kiddush Hashem.[23]

Prof. Kadushin has emphasized the daily aspects of Kiddush Hashem. "The name is sanctified when Torah is prized by men; the name is profaned when Torah is cheapened among men ... When they (the learned) deal honestly in their transactions in the market place . . . with their fellow men people say, 'Happy is so-and-so who studied Torah . . . let us study Torah and teach our sons Torah' "[24] Here we may note that the verbal, conscious, reaction of the non-Jew in the market place is still essential.

In light of the first three sections of this study we can observe the variations and deviations in the rabbinic interpretations of this concept. All the Rabbinic sources assume that not only can a Jew defame the Lord's name in the presence of non-Jews, but *he can* sanctify the Lord's name in the presence of Jews and non-Jews alike. The very fact that a Jew is henceforth capable of sanctifying God's name (which function, it will be recalled was divine prerogative) is indicative of a bold and fruitful transformation. It is only after this interpretation that the Jew was granted the divine and sacred privilege of sanctifying the Lord's name by his daily behaviour and ultimately by his death. Moses and Aaron,[24] the spokesmen for God, had been especially privileged since they could sanc-

tify the Lord's name, but they did not fulfill their God-given gift so that until the rabbinic period no mortal had actually sanctified God's name. In the rabbinic period this right no longer remains sealed in the heavenly spheres, but is placed in the hands of the Jews. The Lord, as it were, had relinquished and abrogated his right to sanctify His name to the Jewish people. The Jews could defame and sanctify the Lord's name.

Though the Rabbis stated that Kiddush Hashem could take place in the presence of ten Jews they nevertheless continued to emphasize these concepts as basic to Jewish and non-Jewish relations. The Jew could be *mekadesh Hashem* in his intra and inter-communal relations. In the Middle Ages these concepts were stressed to caution the Jews in their relations with the Gentile world. Even if a certain action might be legally permissible it was often prohibited lest it cause *Hillul Hashem*. The Jew was to feel a greater sense of responsibility for he was the bearer of the Lord's name. They were crusaders of the true faith of the Lord to the outside world.

It is essential to add, that even in the moment of supreme sacrifice the martyrs of the Middle Ages inadvertently reflected the original intent of the biblical and rabbinical views. These martyrs, as Katz indicates, hoped that the *nations* would awaken to the recognition of their beastly behaviour and would come to realize the ways of the true Lord.[25] The Jewish martyr replaces the Lord as he forces the world to recognize Him by his devotion and willingness to die for his faith. No longer is the Lord the divine actor in this drama; the Jews are now the active participants and wield a decisive influence in the change of at-

---

[23] See above note 21 and *The Rabbinic Mind* p. 44.

[24] In Deut. 32:51 Moses and Aaron are chastised for not having sanctified the Lord in the midst of the children of Israel. But in this exception the *piel* form followed directly by the noun refers to the Lord.

[25] Katz, p. 64ff. and p. 97ff.

titude which must precede the future days. The Jews sanctify the Lord's name, actively and vitally. They need no longer await the Lord, they initiate the actions by their daily acts and by their death.

Sanctification by death is a complete reversal of the biblical concept of the sanctification of the Name by miraculous but joyous, events in history. There still dimly flickers the hope that the Lord must sanctify His name by the restitution of the Jewish people, but the sanctification is redemptive only in that it redeems the martyr from the chaos of the present. This redemption may bring, it is hoped, the final acceptance and recognition of the kingship of the Lord in this world.

The concepts of Kiddush and Ḥillul Hashem have played a decisive role in Jewish thought and action and have persisted most forcefully in their rabbinic reinterpertations. This was inevitable since in their biblical form they were passive concepts for the Jew could not by any act in his lifetime concretize the concept of Kiddush Hashem. It was only through the rabbinic re-orientation and the Jews' re-application of these concepts in their daily action that the concepts became concrete, real and thereby served as dynamic forces in Jewish life. How, when, and why this re-valuation of concepts actually took place cannot be precisely established, but once they were transformed they were sanctified and revered.

# GOD'S OMNIPOTENCE IN RABBINIC JUDAISM

### RICHARD L. RUBENSTEIN

Theology as a contemporary discipline is concerned with problems which were not explicitly dealt with in normative Rabbinic Judaism. Nowhere did the Rabbis deal systematically with such questions as the existence of God, the meaning of God's omnipotence, or the problem of religious authority. Their attitudes towards theological issues were implicit in what they said and did. This was not, as some critics have suggested, because they were naive and childlike in their religious meanings. It is difficult to imagine that the personalities who exhibited such enormous sophistication in the growth and development of Jewish legal institutions could have been utterly without reflective capacity when they turned to validating their religious affirmations. It is more likely that they lacked the first prerequisite of good theological statement in the modern sense—they were incapable of setting themselves at a distance from their deepest

Taking as his point of departure, the singular elaboration the Pentateuchal story of Korah's rebellion received at the hands of the Rabbis, the author proceeds to examine the motivations, patent and unconscious, that inform these Rabbinic legends. These motivations represent—such is the author's thesis—rabbinic feeling and thinking on the theologumen of God's omnipotence. Aside from the alternatives faced by the Sages and their wrestling with the problem, the author tentatively explores another psychological possibility, one clearly reflective of a contemporary mood.

beliefs and saying "no" to them as a precondition to a theological "yes." Theology as a systematic discipline only exists after the theologian has experienced doubt's intensity and has sought to counter its deeply felt challenge. The involvements of the Rabbis in their religious affirmations were too immediate and too urgent to permit themselves the luxury of a reduplicated glance at their own commitments. Theology is a problem for the modern Jew because Judaism is a problem for him. Theology could not be a problem for the Rabbis in the same sense because they were incapable of calling Judaism as radically into question as do modern Jews.

It would, however, be a mistake to assume that the Rabbis either lacked a theology or had one which was so childlike as to be unworthy of examination by contemporary thinkers. Insofar as theology attempts to express man's word about the living God and the life-entailments of that word, the Rabbis most certainly had a theology. Furthermore, for all of the Rabbinic disagreements on details, the Rabbinic system is surprisingly unanimous on basic religious issues. Theology for the Rabbis, though all-pervasive, was entirely implicit. One of the tasks of contemporary Jewish thinking is to make their affirmations explicit.

One of the most serious religious questions confronting the believer is that of determining the meaning of God's omnipotence and the ultimate source of authority in the religious system he accepts. If his religious system demands obedience to prescribed norms, it is of importance that he be clear as to the reasons why such obedience is sought. In Rabbinic Judaism obedience to prescribed norms was a central issue. It was also the point of greatest stress on the loyalties of Jews committed to the system. One of the persistent signs of the decay of normative Judaism has been the increasing unwillingness of many Jews to accept these norms. Although this is an evident problem in our day, it is hardly likely that Jewish life was ever entirely devoid of its pressure.

The Rabbinic legends on Korah's rebellion are especially significant in eliciting the real feelings of the Rabbis towards these issues. Scripture offers ample evidence af the extreme reluctance of the children of Israel to accept the religious disciplines offered to them by Moses. There were continual resistances and backslidings in the first generation as well as in subsequent generations. As recorded in Scripture, Korah's rebellion was one of the most important crises faced by Moses during the wilderness sojourn. Korah rejected the sacerdotal and political authority of the religious leaders of Israel, Moses and Aaron. In so doing, he offered a paradigm of all future challenges to religious authority in both Judaism and Christianity. His rejection was grounded on the contention that the entire congregation was holy and that no special sacerdotal privilege adhered to Moses and Aaron which set them above the people. (Num. 16.1-3) Throughout the history of religion, the assertion of the holiness of the people

and the denial of the special sacerdotal claims of the priesthood has frequently been the central platform of religious rebellions.

As the Rabbis read and studied the Korah story, its special relevance to their situation did not escape them. Though they claimed no priestly prerogatives, they were leaders of a community in which religious authority was indispensible. Religious knowledge garnered at the price of years of toil, heartbreak, and diligence were the prerequisites of Rabbinic authority. There were always members of the community prepared to deny the value or relevance of this scholarly emblem of authority as Korah had earlier denied the priestly emblem. Leadership is, in any event, a precarious pre-eminence in the human community. Behind the Korah story, there is to be found an instance of the instability of leadership and authority in any human society. The large number of discussions and anecdotes concerning Korah in the Aggadah testify to the extent to which this story impressed itself upon the Rabbis and became a matter of concern for them.

The Rabbis did not attempt to minimize Korah's challenge. They could have represented it as the effort of a small group of trouble makers to disturb the harmony of a unified community. Instead, they maintained that the threat to Moses' authority was complete and that the entire community sided with Korah against Moses and Aaron.[1] There is the possibility that this reflected an intuition on the part of the Rabbis of the extent to which the Jewish community as a whole was ambivalent about the disciples they accepted.

---

1 *B'midbar* R. 18.10-11; Tanhuma Korah 6-7; *Tanhuma*, Edition Buber, IV. pp. 90-91.

One of the most interesting aspects of the Korah story is that as one reads the Aggadic accounts, one is never quite sure who the real villain is. In many of the sources, Korah is depicted as attacking Moses and his laws as cruel, without equity, and irrational. It is, of course, pointed out that an element of personal envy moves Korah to his attack, yet Korah's arguments are extremely telling. Furthermore, although Korah's denunciations have no explicit warrant in Scripture and are obviously the product of the Rabbinic assimilation of the legend to the needs of a later time, Korah's arguments are never directly answered by Moses. Moses seeks to appease Korah, but he never answers him. When Moses fails to win Korah over, he is depicted as turning to God and declaring that if God does not efface the rebel, then he, too, (Moses) will become an unbeliever and a heretic! The victory won by Moses is clearly a victory of superior numinous power. All of the rational arguments mustered by Korah become irrelevant when the earth opens up and swallows him. There is no hint of an answer by Moses which gives communicable assurance that the Law is in fact humane and equitable. Though the Rabbis were able to invent Korah's attack on the Law, they were either incapable of, or thought it unnecessary to invent an answer. In the end, the Rabbis depict Korah as won over, but only when the earth opens up and Korah and his band are swallowed alive amidst ascending flames. The issue is settled by superior numinous force and by it alone. This is heightened in some legends which depict Korah as stirred around in Gehenna like flesh in a pot crying out "Moses is true and the Torah is true and we are liars." The flames

of hell prove adequate in the absence of the arguments of Moses.

The moral of the legends is plain. One accepts the Law irrespective of human comprehension of its rationality or its equity. The Rabbis never doubted either its rationality or its ultimate equity. They were convinced that the Author of existence and the Author of the Torah were one and the same. Nevertheless, the capacity to defend this conviction is irrelevant in the last analysis. Righteousness manifests itself in obedience to the will of God. Moses proves that his doctrine comes from God by superior numinous power rather than by argument. This is a vindication of God's Lordship over both the moral and physical universe. Korah offers extremely telling arguments but fails. He can offer no such evidence of numinous power. This incident resembles that of Elijah and the priests of Baal. There, too, the issue is decided by a similar test. The ultimate validation of this type of theonomous system is graphically portrayed in the Legends.

Korah's attack on the Law as it is found in the *Aggadah* is divided into two parts. He attacks the system as irrational and cruel. In one tradition, which is to be found with variants in a number of sources, Korah is depicted as asking Moses whether an entirely purple garment required the addition of a fringe of purple in fulfillment of the law in Numbers 15.38 Moses replied that it was required. Korah sardonically commented:

"A garment which is entirely purple does not suffice to fulfill the commandment, yet four threads suffice!" Korah is pictured as then asking if a house full of sacred books sufficed to fulfill the commandment that a Mezuzzah with its two sections from the Torah be placed upon the doorpost. Moses replied that a Mezuzzah was nevertheless necessary. Korah comments ironically that a house full of books does not suffice to fulfill the commandment, yet the two small sections attached to the door do suffice! This tradition is further elaborated[2] where Korah asks Moses whether a man was unclean if his skin showed a small bright (leprous) spot. Moses replied that he was. Korah then asked whether he was unclean if the bright spot spread over his entire skin. In accordance with the law, Moses replied that he was clean. The point of Korah's challenges was to demonstrate the arbitrary character of the Law. Elsewhere, Korah is depicted as thereupon turning on Moses and exclaiming:

"These words were not commanded upon them (the Israelites) but you devised them in your own heart!"[3]

Again, Korah exclaims:

"There is no Torah from Heaven, and Moses is not a prophet, and Aaron is not a High Priest!"[4]

Apparently the Rabbis derived their conviction that the Laws of Fringes was involved in the rebellion from the hermeneutical rule of *simuchim* "juxtaposition" which implies that there is an associative connection between two Scriptural passages which are "near" each other. This is the opinion of L. Ginzberg.[5] The Law of Fringes is enunciated in Numbers 15.38-41 (end of the chapter) and Korah's rebellion is narrated immediately thereafter in Numbers 16. Beyond this hermeneutic principle, there is no warrant in Scripture for assuming that the irrationality of the Law of Fringes was an issue with Korah. The associative connection is purely the result of Rabbinic invention. There is, at least, the possibility that this tells more of Rabbinic intuition of ambivalence towards the Law than it does of the causes of Korah's revolt.

In addition to the irrationality of the Law, the Rabbis depict Korah as rebelling against the inequities and cruelties of both the Law and Jewish religious leadership. In Midrash *Tehillim*, Korah is depicted as assembling the congregation of Israel against Moses and Aaron and reciting the following anecdote:

"In my neghborhood there was a widow, and with her were two fatherless daughters. The widow had only one field, and when she was about to plow, Moses said to her: *'Thou Shalt Not Plow Thy Field With an Ox and an Ass Together'* (Deut. 22.10) When she was about to sow, Moses said to her: *.Thou Shalt Not Sow Thy Field with Two Kinds of Seed'* (Lev. 19.19) When she was about to reap the harvest and to stack the sheaves, Moses said to her: *'Thou Shalt Not Harvest the Gleanings, the .Overlooked Sheaves, and the Corners of the Field.'* (Lev. 19.9; Cf. Deut. 24.19) When she was about to bring the harvest into the granary, Moses said to her: 'Give me the heave-offering, the tithe, and the second-tithe." She submitted to God's decree and gave them to him. What did the poor woman do then? She sold the field and bought two sheep, so that she might clothe herself in wool shorn from them, and so that she might profit out of the lambs. As soon as the sheep brought forth their young, Aaron came and said to the widow: 'Give me the firstling males, for this

2 J. Sanhedrin.

3 Tanhuma, Korah 2; Tanhuma, Edition Buber, IV, pp. 85-86.

4 J. Sanhedrin 10, 27d-28a.

5 Cf. *Legends*, Volume VI, p. 100, n. 566.

is what the Holy One, blessed be He, said to me: '*All the Firstling Males That Are Born of Thy Herd and Out of Thy Flock Thou Shalt Sancify Unto The Lord Thy God*' (Deut. 15.79)

Korah continues in the same vein offering a narration of the poor woman's progressive impoverishment due directly to the enforcement of the Law of Moses. The story ends with Aaron taking the whole sheep which was all that remained to the woman. She and her daughters are left weeping and stripped of what little possessions they had.[6]

Korah's story contains two objections to the Law: It is cruel and it exacts an unnecessary price from those who can afford it least; it benefits the priestly class and the rulers at the expense of the people. None of this detailed rejection of the Law on rational and humanitarian grounds is to be found in Scripture. It is placed in the mouth of Korah, but this detailed analysis of the Law's failings which presupposes considerable religious knowledge is invented by the Rabbis.

A comparsion of the *Aggadot* on Korah with Kierkegaard's discussion in *Fear and Trembling* is instructive. The resemblances are only superficial, Kierkegaard is also interested in the nature of the divine authority and the meaning of God's omnipotence. He shows that in the *Akedah* there is a conflict between Abraham's ethical values and his religious obligation. As a thoroughly skilled dialectician, Kierkegaard deliberately chose a problem in which the conflict between human judgment and

God's demand at its most mysterious is extreme. He concluded that in such a conflict there is a teleological suspension of the ethical; obedience to God's will cancels out all other claims. In the Korah story, some of this conflict seems to be present though not in the sharpened dialectic form in which Kierkegaard presented it. The challenge does not come from God to man to demonstrate his obedience. It comes from Korah in the midst of an act of disobedience. His ethical arguments do not deal with extreme instances in which the conflict is absolute; ethical argument is used to discredit the entailments of obedience. To follow God, Abraham must violate the ethical category. For Korah, the ethical is not in open conflict with the religious but with Moses' interpretation of what is religious. Were the Rabbis pressed, there is every indication that they would have contended that man's *understanding* of the ethical is irrelevant before God's will; the truly ethical, though imperfectly understood by man, is never in conflict with God's demand. This is, of course, a conjecture since the Rabbis do not address themselves directly to the problem as Kierkegaard saw it. The distinction is based upon the fact that there were real differences in the existential contexts out of which each religious affirmation arose. Kierkegaard was a solitary and was alienated from any decisive human community; the Rabbis were responsible for the preservation of a fragile and beset community whose existence, they believed, was a central concern in the divine scheme. The religious solitary can ignore the ethical; the Rabbis could not; communities cannot exist where the ethical dimension is threatened.

---

[6] Midrash *Tehillim*, Ed. Buber, 1, p. 14; English translation from *The Midrash on Psalms*, edited and translated by William Braude, Yale University Press, New Haven, 1958.

By placing the allegations of immorality and hypocrisy in the mouth of Korah, the Rabbis may have attempted to suggest their own reactions to similar if not identical accusations by the Christian movement and its founder. There is also the possibility that Gnostic elements are involved, especially among ascetic Gnostics who regarded the God of the Old Testament as the corrupt ruler of the world of flesh. Nevertheless, the accusations must have had some cogency else they would not have been repeated. This does not mean that they were true. There is no evidence of any violations, but there may have been a psychological basis for the legend. Leaders and authority figures are frequently psychic-surrogates for the father who has had as one of his prerogatives the possession of the desired woman—the mother. The imputation of immorality to Moses in such a way that each of the rebels suspects his own wife of adultery would fit into such a pattern. The rebel is psychologically a son-figure. The likelihood that this type of psychological dynamic can explain the legend is heightened by the absence of any evidence that the legend had a manifest reality-basis.

There is even a legend concerning an attempt by the rebels to murder Moses. In this tradition the rebels seek to do away with Moses by stoning. There is again no hint of this in Scripture.[7] This does not by any means prove the hypothesis advanced by Freud in *Moses and Monotheism*, but it does show that the Rabbis intuited the murderous intentions of the rebels against the leader. In reality, there is no way of verifying Freud's etiological myth; its significance may

very well lie in what it tells us about the ambivalent feelings of submission and murderous rebellion present as a component in the instability of any human community.

The final end of the band is preceded in the Rabbinic traditions by Moses' demand that God manifest his power lest these men die the common death of all mankind. This follows Scripture. In the Bible, Moses demands that God manifest His power as proof of His authority; In the *Aggadah*, Moses says that if these men live, he, too, will become an unbeliever and a heretic *(kofer)*.[8] Thus the final test is the same for both sides! What is at stake cannot be settled by discussion. In *B'midbar Rabbah*, Moses' demand that God manifest his power is associated with similar demands by Elijah and Micah. In each case the matter is not settled by argument but by superior numinous power.

The final end came with the opening up of the earth and the swallowing up of the rebels by the earth. (Numbers 16.32 f.) There is considerable elaboration of this theme in the Rabbinic sources. When the end came Korah is depicted as going down while crying aloud:

"Moses is King and Aaron is High Priest and the Torah is given from Heaven."[9]

There can be no doubt as to the final validation of religious authority in these legends. The Rabbis may not have left to us systematic discussions of their opinions on the subject of the problem of religious authority. However, their meanings become en-

---

7 *B'midbar* R. 18.4.

8 *B'midbar* R. 18.12; *Tanhuma*, Ed. Buber, IV, 96.

9 *Tanhuma*, Ed. Buber, IV, p. 97; Cf. Targum Yerushalmi on Numbers 16.22-24.

tirely clear when the *Aggadah* is systematically examined.

If the Rabbis believed, as they apparently did, that the final validation of their religious system lay in God's omnipotence, they, nevertheless, could not escape another terrible dilemma which stemmed directly from their conception of the ultimate nature of religious authority. The point of the legends we have examined is that the sign was given to Moses rather than Korah. This, and this alone, rather than any argument settled the matter. Ultimately, Korah's disaster is proof of the fallacious character of his intentions.

This type of proof, unfortunately, can be double-edged. It was hardly calculated to offer the Rabbis or their followers much comfort. Justin Martyr in his *Dialogue With Trypho* used exactly the same type of logic to prove that the Jews were the rejected by God and that Christianity had the superior numinous power. Furthermore, he had very good evidence when one measures the truth of one's religious doctrine by such standards. For Justin, Jewish disaster was a convincing proof of Christianity's truth. The whole Jewish world had been twice overturned under Vespasian and Hadrian. The revolt under Trajan had hardly resulted in Jewish good fortune. Nor was Justin unique. Countless Christian polemicists have used the same argument. Just as the Rabbis could and did assert that Moses was the true prophet and Korah false because of Korah's fate, so, too, Christians could point to the disasters which befell Israel and Jerusalem as proof of the truth of Christianity. Some Christians may even have wondered why the Jews did not exclaim that the Christ was true as Korah had done as he sank into the earth. In terms of the

logic employed, it was at least a thinkable question.

There were other alternatives to the facts of Jewish disaster. This type of thinking could reflect and sharpen Jewish anxiety and self-blame. If God had treated them as he had Korah, it was likely that they had been guilty as had Korah. If God was in any event right and if all power lay with Him, then the disasters of the Jewish people could only have come from Him. The disasters of 67-70 C.E. and 132-135 C.E. could only have befallen the people because God was punishing them for their sins. They did not, of course, agree with the Christians that God was punishing them for rejecting the Christ. They did agree that God was punishing them, but for other sins. Rabbinic sources are replete with the extent to which the Jewish people blamed themselves for their disasters. In the phrase *"mipnei hata-enu . . ."* "because of our sins we were exiled from our land", the liturgy reflects this self-blame. The conclusion was inescapable to anybody who took the logic of these Legends seriously. In some measure the Jewish people were like Korah and other rebels. Had they acted differently, a merciful God would never have afflicted them so devastatingly. Overwhelming disaster had convinced Korah of the error of his ways. Perhaps overwhelming disaster might also convince the Jewish people of their errors. A terrible sense of guilt and self-blame is implicit in these legends as elsewhere in Jewish sources.

If there was self-blame, there was also accusation against Moses and God. In the Legends, Dathan and Abiram are pictured as declaring to Moses that he has not fulfilled his promises. Korah is seen as examining the Law and finding in it much that is arbitrary and inhumane. The Jewish people had been given signs—the wrong signs. They were unlike the signs demanded by Moses—disaster to the enemy and the rebel. As a matter of fact, had Moses received the signs the Jewish people had, he would, according to the spirit of the legend, have become an unbeliever. Though the protest and the accusation is muted and inferential, it is nevertheless present. Yet, the protest could not abide. That, of course, was the unhappy reason of the Korah legends. By settling the problem of religious authority in favor of God's total power, Jewish anxiety and the feeling of guilt among the Jews were enormously strengthened. In effect, the legends reinforced the feeling that before God man is always in the wrong. The Jewish people had been treated like Korah. The moral was clear and as such it was preached and continues to be preached to the congregation of Israel—mend your ways —"Return O Israel unto the Lord thy God." The insistence on repentance became very great. A theme which had its origin in the literature of the prophets was sharpened in Rabbinic Judaism. But the call for repentance and the proclamation of God's total power presupposes deep and abiding feelings of guilt. These feelings predominate in the literature and are part and parcel of the Korah story.

There was a third alternative which was not consciously taken at this time. One could, for lack of a supporting sign, become an unbeliever as Moses had threatened. The threat is invented by the Rabbis and is indicative of a mood which one could only entertain in fantasy. The Jewish community was hardly in a position to support the luxury of atheism or extreme heresy.

It was, after the Hadrianic war, a defeated and beleaguered minority under extraordinary pressure to maintain internal unity. To splinter the group even further would have been disastrous. Doubts were the sort of luxury which a minority community could not embody in action. Furthermore, the need to find some meaning and, consequently some hope was very great.

In their book, *The Psychology of Rumor,* Gordon Allport and Bernard Postman speak of the way in which human beings pursue an *effort after meaning* so that their world is somehow manageable. They suggest on the basis of their experiments, that rumors which express blame tend to justify, relieve, and explain the subject's tension. In terms of the logic of Biblica and Rabbinic Judaism, God could very well be blamed for Jewish disaster since as the All-powerful He is responsible for it. Yet, there is too much anxiety involved in blaming God. As bitter as is self-accusation, it is both safer and less anxiety-producing. Self-blame relieves a primary emotional need—the need to counter-aggress against an enemy when the only safe place to counter-aggress is against oneself. Above all self-accusation *explains* and *offers hope.* In such a psychic world there may be anxiety, but it is not a world devoid of hope. Hannah Arendt has pointed out that one of the most difficult aspects of the Nazi death-camp was that it was deliberately made so irrational that all hope disappeared. This was part of the planned program of human degradation. Even treason and betrayal were unavailable to the inmate who was denied every possible opportunity of learning what the system was and how he could adjust to it. Even the blackest of tyrannies have a certain rationality about them if they make it clear that submission means safety and rebellion means death. The Nazi death-camps allowed no such intrusion of even the rationality of submission and surrender.

In the case of Rabbinic Judaism, the ceding of all power and authority to God's inscrutable will left the Jew with two alternatives—he could either blame himself for his disasters or he could by rejecting God's omnipotence accept the universe as hopelessly irrational and gratuitous. Had he accepted the latter alternative, he would have had to assert that there is no necessary connection between man's virtue and his *external fate.* Allport, Postman, and a host of other psychological researchers have offered their testimony as to the extraordinary psychological difficulties involved in accepting fate as arbitrary and gratuitous. Such a point of view seems to go completely against the structure of the human psyche. Furthermore, there is implicit in such a view a denial of hope, an attitude which was both needed and precious to a beset and overwhelmed community.

In the end, the path of doubt and denial was not a realistic one. Self-blame and guilt, with the resolve to repent and make one's peace with an omnipotent Deity was the only viable alternative and certainly the only psychologically tenable one. Yet Korah's rebellion was to remain an ever-present issue for the Jewish people. When the terms of their existence were such that self-determination and self-realization were again tenable alternatives, there was bound to be a change in sentiment. Many were quick to abandon the religion or at least the disciplines of Moses while retaining their Jewish identities. Frequently, their abandonment of Jewish practice was based upon reasons which were not unlike those which the Rabbis placed in the mouths of Korah and Dathan and Dathan and Abiram. Perhaps, too, some have acquired such inner resources of strength that the alternative of an irrational and only partly understood universe devoid of an omnipotent God no longer frightens them. Their need to make the effort after meaning in the cosmos may very well diminish as they come to find greater inner meaning. With this diminution, there may, also come a diminution in Israel's pathetic and gratuitous need to blame itself for all of its misfortunes. Before God man may not be entirely in the wrong.

# IS THERE A JUDEO – CHRISTIAN TRADITION?

## PAUL TILLICH

### I

JEWS AS WELL as Christians always have asked whether the hyphen in the word Jewish-Christian is justified. Both have asked whether Christianity was right in making the Jewish Bible a part — and by far the largest part — of its own Bible. Since Marcion, the gnostic, tried to cut out of the biblical text not only the Old Testament but also everything in the New Testament reminding him of the Old, the Church has not ceased asking the question of the hyphen. Harnack, the greatest representative of modern liberal theology, dedicated his most recent study, entitled *Marcion,* to this problem, and Jewish writers have sometimes suggested that Christianity committed a kind of theft when it appropriated the Old Testament to itself.

There is, of course, a way of understanding — I would say, misunderstanding — the meaning of our question, namely, by referring it to the traditions which have developed in both groups independently after the establishment of Christianity as a religion of its own. These traditions, rites, symbols, organiza-

tions, doctrinal statements, psychological attitudes diverge considerably from each other. But this fact is too obvious to be discussed. It is more a truism than a problem.

What our question really means can be expressed in the following explanatory questions: Is there a unique series of events which is considered revelatory by both Jews and Christians? Is this common basis still visible in both groups, in spite of the fact that a special event has produced differing interpretations concerning the event itself and implicitly of all events leading to it? Are the common elements in both so strong that in comparison with other religions Judaism and Christianity belong to each other? Is it meaningful to say that Christianity is a Jewish or that Judaism is a Christian heresy? I answer in the affirmative to all these questions! And if theological and historical studies had left any doubt in my mind, the encounter with Jews who live through the presence of their God and who are able to give expression to it, would have convinced me. For a Christian the reality and seriousness of the Jewish consciousness of *the* God who alone *is* God is a great experience, and an experience which he may not so often have when he encounters Christians. He becomes aware of the God of Abraham, Isaac, and Jacob whom Pascal, at the moment of his conversion, contrasted with the non-serious gods of the philosophers.

•••••••••••••••••••••••••••••••••••••••••••••••••••••••

PAUL TILLICH, professor of theology at Union Theological Seminary in New York, is author of many works, including *The Interpretation of History, The Protestant Era, The Shaking of the Foundations,* and *Systematic Theology.* He came to this country from Germany in 1933. He has been designated to deliver the Gifford Lectures in 1953–54.

## II

The first point in which Christianity has continued the Jewish tradition is the idea of God in terms of exclusive monotheism. Exclusive monotheism is different from the monarchic monotheism of a highly developed polytheism; it is different from the acosmic monotheism of all mystical systems; and it is different from the ontological monotheism of the philosophers. In opposition to the mystical and ontological forms, exclusive monotheism maintains the concreteness of God; in opposition to the monarchic form, it emphasizes the absoluteness, universality, and exclusiveness of God. The exclusive God is a jealous God who demands unconditional devotion and who does not share His honor with other gods. At the same time, He preserves His historical definiteness. He is the God who revealed Himself through Moses, for Jews and Christians; the God who revealed Himself in Jesus, for the Christians. Christianity never gave up the exclusive monotheism of the Old Testament. It was for this that the great fight against the Roman Empire as well as against gnostic syncretism was waged. And when, in connection with the christological struggles, the Christ was interpreted as a second, inferior god beside God, Athanasius and, following him, the official church — though not heretic groups and popular primitivism — resisted every sign of ditheism or tritheism which might endanger the exclusiveness of the God of the prophets. A theology for which the trinitarian doctrine is something else than a symbolic description of the living God, who is *one* God, cannot claim to be Christian. The problem, on the other hand, which Christianity has expressed in christological terms is not strange to Judaism. The more the God of the Old Testament became the universal and radically transcendent God, the more He lost His ancient anthropomorphic dynamics, the greater grew the desire for mediating forces and beings — as, for instance, Wisdom and the Messiah. Modern theism, both Jewish and Christian, is not aware of this problem and has created a God who is little more than an hypostatized moral ideal without the power and majesty of the God of both classical Judaism and classical Christianity.

The second point in which Christianity has continued the Jewish tradition is the assertion that the exclusive God has the right to be exclusive because He is the God of justice and righteousness. He is the God who, because of His universal justice, may reject even His elected nation and who cannot be reconciled by cult and sacrifices if righteousness is not done. Justice, *zedakah,* is not legality; it is the whole of righteous being and acting *of* God and *towards* God — towards God as well as towards men. Christian theology never has obscured the unconditional character of the demand of righteousness in the relation between God and man. Certainly, in sacramental practice, supported sometimes by questionable theological formulas and popular superstitions, magical abuses have developed. But for classical theology, especially in its Protestant restatement, faith and sacraments without implicit and consequent righteousness are demonic distortions. Here again a genuine theological problem common to Jews and Christians lies in the background, namely, the question how the divine gifts and promises are related to human activity and perfection. And here again the other alternative must be taken into consideration, a legalistic and utopian interpretation of righteousness, as we find it in modern forms of Protestantism and Judaism equally. The result is self-righteousness and social illusion in the first stage, neurosis and social disillusionment in the second; and this has occurred perhaps more frequently among Jews and Protestants than among other groups.

The third point in which Christianity has continued the Jewish tradition is the interpretation of man's historical existence. God is manifest through the historical event. In the history of mankind, He fights and conquers the antidivine forces. History has an end in the double sense of goal and finish. In a unique, irreversible process, history drives towards this end, which combines ultimate judgment and ultimate fulfilment, the two great themes of Jewish-Christian eschatology. Nobody, I think, can doubt the justification of the hyphen at this point.

Since history has an end, it also has a beginning — the dual, supra-historical event of creation and fall. Perhaps the one word creation would have been a sufficient answer to the question of a Jewish-Christian tradition. For while there is a Persian eschatology and interpretation of history which probably has deeply influenced Jews and Christians, there is no Persian doctrine of the creation of everything by the *one* God and therefore no certainty that everything that is, is good insofar as it has being. And the same can be said about the doctrine of the fall. Platonism and other forms of mystical philosophy have a doctrine of the fall. But the fall is understood as an ontological process and implies a devaluation of the material world, which makes historical revelation and historical salvation impossible.

Since history has an end and a beginning, it also has a center, the event in which the meaning of the whole process becomes manifest and is embodied in an historical representative, an elected nation, or an elected group within it, or elected people from all nations or the elected one, the Messiah, the Christ.

Thereby, history becomes a history of salvation, whether salvation is seen predominantly in a future time, as taught by Jewish prophetism and Protestant social gospel, or as predominantly beyond time, as taught by the Jewish apocalyptics and conservative-ecclesiastical Christianity. The tension between the inner-historical and the trans-historical element in the history of salvation in Christian theology is a Jewish heritage, and it is an inescapable problem for both groups, even if it appears as if the emphasis of Judaism were more on the inner-historical and the emphasis of Christianity more on the trans-historical element.

### III

Now, however, we have reached the point where the divergence of ideas and traditions sets in. Christianity asserts that Jesus of Nazareth is the expected Christ; Judaism rejects this claim and expects the Messiah in an indefinite future at the end of history. Judaism, on the other hand, claims that the Torah, the teaching of God, as given through Moses, is valid through all history, a claim which is rejected by Christianity in the doctrine that the Christ is the end of the law.

But the contradiction is not as simple as this. The Jews have an argument which was taken seriously by the early Christians and should be taken more seriously by the Christians of today. It is the argument that Jesus cannot be the Christ because he did not achieve what the Messiah is supposed to do: he did not bring the new aeon. The early Christians took this argument so seriously that they answered with the doctrine of the second coming of the Christ. The end delays, the world is not changed, the Christians are living between the times: the Christ *has* come; but he must come *again*. This is, so to speak, the tribute paid by the Christians to the Jews, which means, in the first period, largely to themselves as Jews. There is a counter-tribute, paid by the Jews to the Christians long before Christianity appeared: the law is in Jewish conviction a gift before it is a command. The Torah, the divine instruction, is eternal, pre-existent and post-existent. It is the expression of the true relation between God and man, and the world is created for it. It is given to the Jewish people in a covenant which is the cause of highest blessing and deepest suffering together. And it contains a problem as difficult for the Jews as the unchanged world for the Christians, the problem, namely, of how the divine covenant can be kept by God if it is not kept by Israel. And neither Israel as a people, nor the remnants of the divine judgments, nor any special groups, are able to follow, even for a single day, the divine instructions. Through such questions, the Christian answer was prepared, the answer indicated by the prophets that God is the God of forgiveness and that His gift precedes all human doing and running.

But in spite of this mutual tribute in the center of their divergence, the divergence *does* exist and has many religious, theological, and historical consequences.

The Christian faith that the new aeon has already arrived, though visible only for the Spiritual eye, changes the Jewish tradition in some basic points: it replaces the conditioned universalism of the Jews by an unconditional universalism; in the new aeon, the Spirit, given to everybody, replaces the authoritarian law (as Jeremiah and Joel have prophesied). Therefore, the privilege of those who have first received the law is abolished, and the nationally and historically conditioned elements of it have lost their validity. To enter the new aeon, only communion is needed with the Spiritual power which has brought it, Jesus the Christ and his assembly, the Church. But the law is not abolished. Those elements in it which are independent of the Jewish national vocation are restated and actualized in the new aeon. This is the first point of a basic transformation of the Jewish tradition. And the second is the nature of the new aeon. If Jesus can be the Christ *in spite,* or more exactly *through,* his defeat, it is not the change of the world which makes the new aeon new, but the change of the heart of those who, though defeated externally, are victorious internally; they can influence the external world — for instance, the social realm — only indirectly and never completely and never without defeats. But inspite of this invisibility of the kingdom of heaven, they believe that it has already appeared and that they are living in it. It is impossible for Jewish faith to accept this. For in Jewish faith, *expectation* is the basic attitude, just because the kingdom of God has not yet appeared visibly. Those differences can not be denied and must not be underestimated.

## IV

But if some one shaped and nourished by the Hindu or the Buddhist or the Confucian or the Greek tradition were to hear what I have said, would he not be astonished at the identity of structure at all points, and at the identity of content in most? Would he not, if he compared all this with his own tradition, answer the question: Is there a Jewish-Christian tradition?, with an unhesitating and unambiguous, Yes? I think he would!

# CHRISTIAN AND JEWISH ETHICS

## JOSEPH KLAUSNER

WHAT ARE Christian ethics? In what way do they differ from the ethics of Judaism?

Christian ethics are so closely derived from the Old Testament and the Talmud that, as Geiger and Graetz have both rightly concluded, there is not a single ethical sentence in the whole New Testament which cannot be parallelled either in the Old Testament, in the literature of the Apocrypha and Pseudepigrapha, or in the Talmudic and Midrashic literature of the era of Jesus and Paul.[1] Nevertheless, there is something distinctive and specific in the moral law of Christianity which is not found in the moral law of Judaism.

But this "something" is bound up with the Christian conception of God, a conception essentially different from that of Judaism.

There is no doubt that Jesus of Nazareth did not regard himself as God. It is sufficient to mention the saying attributed to him: "Why callest thou me good? None is good save one,[2] even God"; or

---

[1] v. J. Klausner, *Jesus of Nazareth*, 5th ed., 1945, pp. 418–419.
[2] Mk. 10:18; Lk. 18:19.

••••••••••••••••••••••••••••••••••••••••••••••

JOSEPH KLAUSNER, professor emeritus of modern Hebrew literature at the Hebrew University in Jerusalem, is the author of *History of the Second Temple, The Messianic Idea in Israel, Jesus of Nazareth, From Jesus to Paul,* and other works. A companion piece by him on "Monotheism and Ethics in Judaism" appeared in the October issue of this Journal.

the tradition that, when Jesus was nailed to the cross, he cried in Aramaic: "My God, my God, why hast thou forsaken me?"[3] This is enough to prove that, like every Jew in the time of the Second Temple, Jesus set an unbridgeable gulf between God and even the greatest and holiest of men — the Messiah. Jesus did not regard himself as either God or the Son of God. He regarded himself as the Messiah. Not without reason is he known to history as "Jesus the Messiah", and not without reason were the adherents of his doctrine called, immediately after the crucifixion, "Messianists". The division of the Godhead into three, or more correctly two, parts, the Christian conception of God the Father and God the son — (the Holy Ghost is a later development to explain how a son was born to God) — appeared in the course of time as a development of Jesus' Messianic claim. In alluding to this claim, Jesus borrows from The Book of Daniel[4] the title "Son of Man", an appellation already regarded as messianic in one of the early pseudepigraphical works.[5] Moreover, Jesus frequently calls God "Father", "my Father", "my Father who is in Heaven." Although these are thoroughly Hebraic expressions, the extreme emphasis which Jesus gave them could be misleading. Thus, Jesus is reported as saying: "But of that day and hour (of the end of the world) knoweth no one, not even the angels of

---

[3] Mk. 15:34; Matt. 27:46.
[4] Dan. 7:13.
[5] Book of Enoch (c. 70 B.C.E.) 46:1–6.

heaven, neither the Son, but the Father only."[6] Here, on the one hand, "the Son" is distinguished from God; but, on the other hand, "the Son" is placed between "the angels of Heaven" and "the Father". Jesus, then, as Messiah, occupies a special place in the universe. This is based on the Psalm which opens with: "And the rulers take counsel together, against the Lord and against his anointed"[7] and further says: "The Lord said unto me, Thou art my son: this day have I begotten thee".[8] The Messiah, then, is the Son of God; not indeed in the later Christian sense, according to which "the Son" is divine, though at the some time remaining human: still, as Messiah he stands between God and the angels, he will come with "the clouds of heaven", will draw near to "the ancient of days" and sit at his right hand — "at the right hand of power".[9] Without intending it and without willing it, Jesus nevertheless brought it about that, in the course of time, he was raised to the level of divinity. What was still inchoate and implicit in the words of Jesus was gradually made definite and explicit by Paul.

Paul too, like Jesus, is still far from a threefold, or even a twofold, division of the Godhead. For him too there is only "one God and Father of all, who is over all, and through all, and in all" [10] For him too "God is one",[11] and "the same God who worketh all things in all"[12]: and so forth. Even at the end of days, when death shall be swallowed up forever and there shall be brought to pass what is written in the verse, "Thou hast put all things under his feet",[13] — i.e. un-

der the feet of God — even "then shall the Son also himself be subjected to him that did subject all things unto him, that God may be all in all".[14] Nonetheless, the pure monotheism of Judaism was clouded and blurred by Paul: primarily through the belief in spirits and the fear of spirits, which are together responsible for the important part played by Satan in Paul's creed. Satan is here almost the anti-God, just as he was later the anti-Messiah (anti-Christ). This alone is sufficient to create an affinity between Paul and the dualistic religion of Persia.

But there was a second reason. Paul could not portray Jesus as a Messiah of flesh and blood, as the Jews had always portrayed their Messiah, despite the high esteem in which they held him. If the Messiah is terrestrial, a creature of flesh and blood, it follows that he is King Messiah"; and if he is "King Messiah," then he must re-establish the Kingdom of the House of David. The propagation amongst the Gentiles of the belief in such a Messiah — terrestrial and political — would not have been tolerated by the Romans; and this propagation was Paul's life-work.

There was also a third reason. Paul was not a disciple of the earthly Jesus: indeed, he had at first persecuted him and his disciples. Hence Paul had a sense of inferiority in relation to James, the brother of Jesus; to Peter, and to the other disciples who had enjoyed the intimacy of Jesus throughout his Messiahship on earth. Paul knew Jesus, or recognized Jesus, only after Jesus had appeared to him in a vision on his journey to Damascus, when Jesus shone on him as a "light out of heaven".[15] Paul was therefore compelled to dwell more and more on the spiritual Jesus, and to re-

[6]Matt. 24:36.
[7]Ps. 2:2.
[8]ibid 2:7.
[9]Mk. 14:62; Matt. 26:64; Lk. 22:69.
[10]Ephesians 4:6.
[11]Galatians 3:20.
[12]I. Cor. 12:6.
[13]Ps. 8:6.

[14]I. Cor. 15.24:28.
[15]Acts. 9:3; 22:9; 26:19.

move him ever further from the Jewish conception of the Messiah, which is terrestrial and political. Thus Jesus became for him "the image of the invisible."[16] "the mystery of God",[17] "the man of heaven",[18] who is the complete antithesis of "the first man of earth".[19] To Paul, then, Jesus is, like the "logos" of Philo, "a man without bodily form". Eventually, the result of this process was that, instead of the words of the prophet: "Unto me (God) every knee shall bow, every tongue shall swear",[20] words which Jews repeat three times a day in the "Alenu" prayer, Paul says: "That in the name of Jesus every knee should bow, of things in heaven and things on earth and things under the earth".[21] Instead of "the day of the Lord", we find in Paul "the day of the Messiah" or "the day of Lord Jesus", on which the judgment of all the earth's inhabitants, and even of the whole creation, shall be entrusted to Jesus alone, as Messiah.[22] It is he — Jesus, the Messiah, and not God — who shall overthrow Satan, put an end to sin and abolish death.[23] It is true that all this will be done "in the name of God" and "to the glory of God the Father"; but anyone who performs cosmic acts of this nature is already himself God — "God the Son," to whom "God the Father" has entrusted complete control over the creation, and in whose hands he has placed the whole destiny of man, so that he himself, "The Father," has, in truth, nothing more to do in his universe.

Such a Messiah has outsoared the bounds of humanity. Of the Jewish Messiah it can be said: "Thou hast made him but little lower than God",[24] but this "little" is a great deal: it prevents the unitarian faith of Israel being turned from a pure monotheism into a blurred monotheism. Judaism emphasized the fundamental difference between God and man. Christianity denied the fundamental quality of this difference; and thus it removed the barrier between God and man, and arrived at the belief in a second god born of the Holy Ghost — the third god — through the Virgin Mary, who is the "mother of God". Such conceptions are essentially foreign to Judaism and are largely influenced by Hellenistic idolatry in its later, syncretistic phase.

This conception of the Deity, altogether irrational and illogical, and derived from a mystic conception of Messiahship, is closely connected with the Christian ethic, which in its uncompromising extremism is also irrational and unnatural.

Jesus as Messiah is exalted above the angels. He is, as we have already noted, a man without bodily form. How then could it happen that he was cruelly flogged and suffered crucifixion, the vilest of deaths? There can be only one answer: that he took this strange death upon himself of his own free will and for a higher purpose.

Christianity took over from Judaism the idea of "original sin", which in Judaism is called "the sin of the first man".[25] Now Jesus is the antithesis of "the first man": he is the "last man". Therefore he took upon himself suffering on the cross and cruel death, in order by his blood to redeem mankind from "the sin of the first man." Judaism holds that man is delivered from sin by the Law, by repentance and by good deeds. According

---

[16]Colossians 1:15; II. Cor. 4:4.
[17]Colossians 2:2.
[18]I. Cor. 15:47.
[19]Romans 5:12–19; I. Cor. 15:21–22, 45–49.
[20]Is. 45:23.
[21]Philip. 2:10–11.
[22]I. Cor. 1:8; 5:5; Rom. 2:16, et al.
[23]I. Cor. 15:22–28.

[24]Ps. 8:5.
[25]Sifre, Deut. Par. 223, ed. Friedmann, p. 138a; IV Ezra 7:116–118; Syrian Baruch 17:2–3; ibid. 23:4.

to Christianity, mankind was purified of all iniquity after the crucifixion of Jesus.

But men continued to sin, even after Jesus had redeemed them from their sins by his blood. Hence Paul's view that, since it is impossible for man not to sin when sin is part and parcel of "the nature of man's flesh", he can only be saved by faith — faith in Jesus. "Flesh" and sin are identical for Paul: and man, "flesh and blood", being by nature sinful, can be saved only by the grace of Jesus — "unmerited grace". This led, quite logically, to the belittlement of the ceremonial laws. So far was this attitude carried that one of the most important Church Fathers, Jerome, complains of the sages of Israel that they waste their time practising medicine.[26] And, if memory serves, it is Augustine who asks: "What need have Christians of science? Have they not been give the word of God?" In contrast to this, the Talmud praises the Sages for their scientific interests. For example: R. Simeon bar Halafta studied the life of the ant, and even carried out experiments for this purpose;[27] R. Simeon bar Johai studied the ways of the hoopoe;[28] and Rab Asi studied the life of the raven.[29]

Jesus and Paul set repentance and ethical deeds above the ceremonial laws. In this they followed in the footsteps of the prophets. But the prophets, from Ezekiel and Second Isaiah onwards, also emphasize the importance of the ceremonial laws: Sabbath observance, circumcision and even sacrifice.[30] Jesus and Paul failed to realize that ethico-religious ideas which are not embodied in actions will never be taken up by the masses of the people, but will remain the exclusive possession of individuals; and even these individual thinkers will not always be able to remain true to their convictions in difficult times. Obviously, Jesus did not reckon with the fact that no people can, in daily life, retain its distinctiveness solely by means of abstract ethical views, and that, if Israel were to abandon the ceremonial laws peculiar to itself, it would be absorbed into the Gentiles and would disappear. Paul did not actually make the absorption of the Jews his aim, but he certainly would not have regretted it, since to his mind, in Christianity "there is neither Jew nor Greek".[31]

In Paul's moral doctrine there is not much which is original, apart from his view of love as a fundamental ethical quality. Most of the ethical teachings of Jesus, too, are common to him and to the Prophets, and also to the Jewish Sages who were his contemporaries. Is there then anything which distinguishes his moral preachment from the moral law of Israel?

In my opinion, there is a basic distinction. After all, in most of Jesus' ethical sayings, especially "the Sermon on the Mount", it is clearly emphasized that his morality differs from that of all who have preceded him: "It hath been said unto you thus but I say unto you thus and thus", i.e. I say something which differs from the established tradition of the Jewish people.

The following is a summary of the points in which the moral teaching of Jesus, as found in The Gospels, in the Acts, and to some extent in the Apocryphal Gospels, professes to differ from the established tradition of Jewish ethics.[32]

---

[26] v. Hieronymus; Prol. ad Oseam, ed. Migne, XXV. 820.

[27] Hullin 57b.

[28] Vayyikra Rabba, 22.

[29] ibid. 19, beg.

[30] Hagg. 2:11-13; Mal. 1:7-8.

[31] v. J. Klausner: *From Jesus to Paul, II* (1940), pp. 233-246.

[32] Index of passages in J. Klausner, *Jesus of Nazareth*, 5th ed., (1945) pp. 415-418.

He who divorces his wife is an adulterer, and the divorced wife who has married another man is an adulteress: for
what God hath joined together, let no
man put asunder. But, in general, it
is better that a man should not marry
at all.

It is forbidden to swear an oath, even a
true oath.

It is forbidden to fight against evil.

If anyone strike thy right cheek offer
him the left, and if anyone take thy cloak
from thee, give him thy tunic too.

Love your enemies and pray for those
that persecute thee, for if ye love those
that love thee, what is your reward? See,
even the tax-gatherers do thus. But as for
ye, be ye perfect, even as your Father in
Heaven is perfect.

A man must not take thought for the
morrow. Sufficient unto the day is the
evil thereof. Consider the lilies of the
field: they toil not neither do they spin,
yet King Solomon in all his glory was
not arrayed as one of these.

It is forbidden to summon any man to
judgment: "Judge not, that ye be not
judged".

Whatever ye would have men do unto
you, that do ye also unto them.

The blessed, whose reward is great in
heaven, are the poor, the hungry and
thirsty, the simple and innocent ("the
poor in spirit"), the humble, the mourn-
ers, the compassionate, the peace-lovers,
the persecuted, the reproached and reviled.

"Man is Lord of the Sabbath", and "it
is permitted to do good on the Sabbath",
even if this involves work.

Vows do not bind a man through the
"utterance of the lips", nor does the non-
fulfilment of the commandment of wash-
ing the hands defile him: What defiles
are evil thoughts and evil deeds: murder,
theft and robbery, adultery, false-witness
and blasphemy; for it is not what goes

into the mouth, but what comes out of
it that defiles.

The greatest commandment is: "Thou
shalt love the Lord thy God with all thy
heart and with all thy soul", and equally
great is: "Thou shalt love thy neighbor
as thyself"; and "on these depend the
Law and the prophets".

He who would obtain everlasting life,
let him sell all his possessions and distribute his wealth to the poor. For "it is
easier for a camel to pass through the eye
of a needle, than for a rich man to enter
the Kingdom of Heaven."

The sin of the Scribes and Pharisees
is twofold: first, that they make the in-
essential essential, and the essential in-
essential; and secondly, that the words
of a verse in the Law are more important
to them than its inner meaning.

Let him who feels himself free of sin
cast the first stone at the harlot.

These are moral sayings in which it
would appear that Jesus himself saw
something new. It is unnecessary to remark that, in the other moral sayings of
Jesus, which have not been quoted here,
there is nothing that is not found in the
Prophets or in the Tannaitic Midrashim.
But even in the case of the great majority of the moral sayings which I have
selected, where Jesus emphasizes his opposition to earlier teaching, it is not difficult to find parallels in Jewish literature of the periods of the First and Second Temple. As I have observed elsewhere: "Sometimes the resemblance between the sayings of Jesus and the sayings
of our ancients is so close that the former
seem to us a deliberate anthology of what
is found in Talmud and Midrash".[33]
And yet the ethics of Jesus are not precisely the ethics of Judaism.

For Judaism has never held that a man

---

[33] J. Klausner, *Jesus of Nazareth*, 4th ed., p.
438; 5th ed., p. 423.

should not marry at all, or that he who divorces his wife is an adulterer and the divorced wife who marries again an adulteress. Judaism has never held that one should not swear at all: or that one should not go to law at all. Judaism has never held that, if anyone strikes your right cheek, you should offer him the left as well; nor has it ever held that man must distribute all his possessions to the poor, in order to gain the Kingdom of Heaven for himself: on the contrary, it requires that "he who is spendthrift (for charitable purposes) should not squander more than a fifth (of his possessions)".[34] Judaism has never required of man that he should be as perfect as God; nor has it ever taught that only the poor and "the poor in spirit", the hungry and thirsty, the reproached and reviled, and they alone, have a great reward in heaven.

These extreme ethical views had practical consequences. Society cannot exist without family life, without true oaths, without law and justice, and without private property; and it is not in man's nature to meet a blow in the face with a request for a second, nor is he capable of loving his enemies or of praying for his persecutors. Hence, he who wishes to save his soul and to live according to the ethics of Jesus has no choice but to withdraw to the wilderness or shut himself up in a monastery. Such a man, who is concerned only with his own soul, has nothing to do with the improvement of society, nation and state, or with any kind of community, much less with humanity as a whole. It is his own soul that he is concerned with — and society, nation and state may do as they please.

This was not the way of our Prophets. Amos goes from Judah to the Kingdom of Samaria to prophesy against the house of Jeroboam, son of Joash. The First Isaiah encourages Hezekiah in his war with Sennacherib; Jeremiah fights a long and bitter battle with those who would revolt against Nebuchadrezzar; Ezekiel in his prophecies marks out the way of national regeneration in the Babylonian Exile and draws up the blue-print of a new state for the exiles who are to return to their land; the Second Isaiah gives the title "mine Anointed" to the alien Cyrus, and preaches the Return to Zion; and Haggai and Zechariah urge the renewal of the building of the Second Temple. Again, almost all the prophets without exception prophesy not only about Israel, but about all the Asian and African peoples known to them. Jonah, son of Amittai, who is unwilling to bring back Ninevah to repentance and save it from the threatening disaster, is taught a striking lesson by God through the medium of a storm at sea and a gourd. It is true that Jeremiah says: "Oh that I had in the wilderness a lodging place of wayfaring men; that I might leave my people, and go from them!"[35] But in fact he remains amongst his people, and up to his last day actively shares in the bitter destiny of his nation and state. There were Essenes in Israel who withdrew from the life of the State (though even then not permanently: they too fought against the Romans in the great war which preceded the Second Destruction); but they have passed away like a shadow, and even their name would have been forgotten in Israel, if it had not been preserved in Greek by Josephus and Philo. What was the origin of this difference between Jewish and Christian ethics?

In my view, the difference originates in Christian monotheism, which is essentially different from the monotheistic faith of Israel. As we have seen, the trinitarian

---

[34] Ketuboth 67b.

[35] Jer. 9:1.

belief arose from the Messianic faith of Jesus and his disciples. As Messiah, Jesus proclaimed: "The time is fulfilled, and the Kingdom of God is at hand: repent ye, and believe in the gospel".[36] Now, if the Kingdom of God, which is the same as the Kingdom of the Messiah, "is at hand" because "the time is fulfilled", it follows that the Messiah cannot attach any importance to the life of the actual present: his gaze is fixed on the life of "future days", the life of "the days of the Messiah". Hence the superhuman moral conduct which Jesus demands of man. Not that his moral law is really a "transitional morality" (*Interims-Ethik* of the German theologians), which is appropriate only to the short period preceding the coming of the Messiah; it is a morality without which the coming of the Messiah cannot be hastened; and therefore it cannot be a normal, human, realistic morality suited to the life of the present. Nor is this all.

The Jewish Messiah is, above all, the redeemer of his people and of his country, and also the redeemer of mankind. He redeems it from war ("nation shall not lift up sword against nation"); he redeems it from tyranny ("and he shall smite the earth (tyrant) with the rod of his mouth and with the breath of his lips shall he slay the wicked"); and he makes peace in the world ("and the wolf shall dwell with the lamb"). But nowhere is it stated that the Jewish Messiah will redeem mankind by his blood, and that by his death (the death of the Jewish Messiah is a natural death[37]) will atonement be made for all sins. It may be conjectured that Jesus too dreamt of redeeming his people from Roman bondage. But he did not associate this redemption with rebellion against Rome, at least not *only* with political and military rebel-

lion: fundamentally, he associated the redemption with repentance and good deeds. Paul glossed over this national and political aspect, since it was, as we have already remarked, dangerous to give it prominence in the time of Roman rule. The whole activity of the Messiah was turned by Paul into something purely spiritual, something which the Romans did not understand and in which they were not particularly interested. To them it was simply a "superstition", which there was no obvious reason to persecute. Thus the Christian Messiah became entirely spiritual and entirely mystical. His spiritual and mystical nature was gradually raised into something supernatural, something beyond actuality — beyond the needs of society and state.

The God of Israel is the God of goodness, but he is also the God of truth and righteousness, even as His prophets are prophets of truth and righteousness. The prophets always speak of the good in store for the righteous in this world, but, at the same time, as God of righteousness, "the Lord is a God of vengeance" who does not let sin pass unpunished. Furthermore, since the God of Israel "summons the generations from the beginning; He is the first and with the last there is He",[38] He is the God of history through whom the sins of one generation certainly bring subsequent punishment upon the second and the third generation: "visiting the iniquity of the fathers upon the children, upon the third and upon the fourth generation of them that hate me".[39]

Christianity is the faith of mercy, the religion of love. But even Jesus himself could not remain true to his own teaching. He threatened his opponents, the Pharisees, that upon them would "come all the righteous blood shed on the

[36] Mk. 1:15.
[37] IV Ezra 7:29.

[38] Is. 44:6.
[39] Ex. 20:5.

earth";[40] and he threatened Capernaum, Chorazin and Bethsaida,[41] and every city which should not receive his disciples, that "it shall be better for Sodom and Gomorrah on the Day of Judgment than for it".[42] The Gospels contain violent curses from Jesus' lips which[43] are every whit as harsh and savage as those found in some of the Psalms. However, since "none is good save one, namely God", and since this actual workaday world with its evil and wickedness, is no more than a transition to the impending Messianic age, Jesus' moral teaching ceased to provide a firm basis for the life of human society. True Christianity, the Christianity of the Sermon on the Mount, cannot be practised in an organized Society or State, where there must be resistance to evil, there must be law and justice, there must be family life, there must be security of life and property. Christianity does not embrace all life's needs. It seeks to live as the "lilies of the field", without care for the morrow. This means despising the ceaseless advance of human civilization with the good and evil which it inevitably brings in its train. Moreover, despite "the Day of Judgment" for sinners, the God of Christianity is no longer the God of history, because He is not the God of righteousness, but the God of love and "unmerited grace": "He maketh His sun to rise on the evil and the good"[44] — without distinction. This attitude stands in sharp contrast to that underlying the Biblical story of the Flood as it stands in opposition to the main trend of Rabbinic ethics.

Judaism too sees in God the God of love and mercy, and it was Judaism which coined the expression, "our Father who art in heaven." But it also frequently employs the compound expression, "our Father, our King": the God of Israel is the "merciful Father", but at the same time He is the "just King" (cf. Shemoneh Esreh prayer).

Judaism created the great ideal which is summed up in the hope that a day will come when "the golden age will be established by the kingdom of the Almighty" — the ideal of "the Kingdom of Heaven". Judaism knows of only one, unique God, the God of goodness; and just as it is impossible that the one God should be conquered, so it is impossible that good should be conquered by evil — that the divine goodness should not be realized in the universe of the God of goodness. But Judaism took into account the reality of evil as well, and therefore recognized and understood that absolute good can be only a great and lofty aspiration, capable of realization only "at the end of days". Man is made better by aspiring to goodness and by embodying it, bit by bit, in life. This is man's moral obligation, which he can hope to fulfil when the miraculous end comes. But it is a long way to "the end"; and the "moral obligation", which for Judaism is the essence of spiritual life, must take account of the fact that man is not an angel: that man is "flesh and blood", that the inclination to good and the inclination to evil are inextricably intertwined in him and struggle with each other all his life. Therefore, Judaism recognized that "the Law was not given to the ministering angels,[45] and that "an ordinance can be imposed on the community only when the majority of the community are able to observe it".[46] Hence Judaism has never demanded of man that which is beyond human nature: complete monastic withdrawal from society, asceticism

---

[40] Matt. 23:35.
[41] ibid. 11:20–24.
[42] Mk. 6:11.
[43] cf. e.g. Matt. 13:3, 23:33–36, 24:51, 25 et al.
[44] Matt. 5:45.

[45] Berakhoth 25b.
[46] Baba Qama 79b.

and self-imposed isolation are not in the spirit of Judaism, while to Christianity and Buddhism these are regarded as the acme of piety. Herein lies the superiority of Judaism: it takes account of man's evil inclination no less than of his good inclination. Certainly the evil inclination must be held in check: its activity must be restricted as much as possible. But it cannot be crushed completely. A Haggadic story relates that the evil inclination was once caught and imprisoned — and a new-laid egg could not be found for a sick man.[47] Indeed, Judaism went so far as to maintain that, in the Biblical description of the Creation, it is said of the evil inclination too "and behold it was very good"; since, "but for the evil inclination, man would not have built a house, nor taken a wife, nor begotten children, nor engaged in trade."[48] The Judaism which taught: "A man should always be of the persecuted and not of the persecutors"[49] and which praised "those who are insulted but do not insult, who hear themselves reviled but make no reply";[50] the Judaism which included in the Prophets the Book of Jonah, containing a lofty moral demand for the deliverance of Ninevah, the destroyer of the Kingdom of Samaria, because there were in it tens of thousands of infants and "much cattle", this same Judaism could say: "Great is vengeance, for it is placed between two divine names, as it is said, "A God of vengeance is the Lord".[51] There is no teaching so opposed to warfare and bloodshed in all their forms as Judaism throughout the ages. Its greatest prophet envisaged everlasting peace, a time when the nations "shall beat their swords into plowshares, and their spears into pruning hooks",

when "nation shall not lift up sword against nation, neither shall they learn war any more".[52] The Jewish Messiah is depicted by the same prophet as "smiting the earth (tyrant)" *not by the* sword but "with the rod of his mouth, and with the breath of his lips shall he slay the wicked", and in his days "the wolf shall dwell with the lamb".[53] Nevertheless, this same Judaism speaks of "a war waged in a righteous cause" and "a war waged in duty bound", (as opposed to "a war waged of free choice"), in both of which "all go forth (to war), even the bridegroom out of his chamber and the bride out of her bridal canopy".[54] And the King Messiah — both the Messiah ben Joseph who is killed and the Messiah ben David who is victorious — will fight the war of Gog and Magog and the other wars which must be fought against the enemies of Israel. This is so opposed to the conception of a Messiah who becomes the Son of God, or himself divine, and to a one-sided and irrational moral law, that there is ground for thinking that, if the Jews mounted the pyre rather than embrace Christianity, this was not only because they refused to believe in a biform or tri-form Godhead, but also because, perhaps subconsciously, they rejected an ethico-religious *Weltanschauung* which was completely unacceptable to the Jewish mind.

For there is here not only a religious conflict: there is a distinctive attitude to the whole of human history. In judging world events, Judaism never adopted an attitude of sterile doctrinairism. It saw reality just as it is. True, it measured reality by the yardstick of the eternal ideal; but it did not demand of present reality what pertains to the future ideal. It never cherished a Tolstoyean

---

[47]Sanhedrin 64a.
[48]Bershith Rabba, 89.
[49]Baba Qama, 93a.
[50]Shabbat 88b.
[51]Berakhoth 33a.

[52]Is. 2:2–4.
[53]ibid. 11:4–9.
[54]Mishnah, Sotah viii:7.

ideal of "non-resistance to evil" in all circumstances. Certainly, Judaism was pacifist in principle: could it have been otherwise with a nation that continually pondered the prophecies of Isaiah and Jeremiah, and the teaching of the elder Hillel and Rabban Johanan ben Zakkai? But, at the same time, Judaism did not forget that in its Holy Law there are verses such as: "thou shalt put away the evil from the midst of thee",[55] "thou shalt blot out the remembrance of Amalek",[56] "thou shalt save alive nothing that breatheth",[57] "Who is this that cometh from Edom with crimsoned garments?"[58] "when the wicked perish there is shouting",[59] and many similar passages. There are historical circumstances which, in exceptional times, in particularly desperate situations and when there is no alternative, make it necessary to repay the evildoers in the coin of their wickedness, since no other course is possible. Such a situation arose in our own lifetime only a few years ago, when Hitler, together with the feudal lords of Japan, attempted to bring the whole world under the yoke of their tyranny. Let us suppose that the relations of the democratic countries with Hitler and the Japanese had been guided by the principle of "thou shalt not resist evil" and "offer thy left cheek": what aspect would humanity now bear?

There are contradictions in Judaism. Sometimes it seems to us that Judaism has diverged from the path of pure morality. In fact, the contradictions and inconsistencies in Judaism result from contradictions and divergences in life itself. Judaism, as a creed of life, a creed which embraces all the needs of nation and state, cannot ignore changes and developments in the political and national situation. Therefore, in a certain situation, a profoundly ethical book like the Psalms calls for "vengeance on the nations and chastisement of the peoples",[60] and one of the poems in this holy book begins with: "Blessed be the Lord my rock, who teacheth my hands to war, and my fingers to fight".[61] Second (or, according to some, Third) Isaiah, the sublimity of whose universalist morality is unsurpassed, boasts that God has "trodden the winepress" in Edom, and, in the name of God, says of Israel's foes, the Edomites: "I trod them in mine anger and trampled them in my fury", simply because "the day of vengeance was in my heart".[62] Judaism does not shrink from combining into a single chapter the exalted prophecy of Isaiah and Micah about beating swords into ploughshares, and the prophecy of Micah which contradicts it: "Arise and thresh, O daughter of Zion, for I will make thine horn iron, and I will make thy hoofs brass: and thou shalt beat in pieces many peoples."[63] Moreover, Judaism can put into the mouth of another prophet the complete antithesis of the great prophecy of peace which it attributes to Isaiah and Micah: the prophet Joel, son of Pethuel, demands: "Beat your ploughshares into swords, and your pruning-hooks into spears: let the weak say, I am strong!"[64] Everything depends on the time and the situation.

Generally speaking, the differences between various books of the Old Testament can be traced to differences in the spirit of their times. The Book of Jonah, with its sublime love of one's enemy, is a holy book. But the scroll of Esther too, which recounts the hanging of Haman

---

[55] Deut. 17:7.
[56] Deut. 25:19.
[57] Deut. 20:16.
[58] Is. 63:1.
[59] Pr. 11:10.

[60] Ps. 149:8.
[61] ibid., 114:1.
[62] Is. 63:1-5.
[63] Cf. Mic. 4:1-3 and 4:13.
[64] Joel 3:10.

the Agagite, the enemy of the Jews, together with his ten sons (who may, or may not, have sinned), and which states explicitly that "the Jews smote all their enemies with the stroke of the sword, and with slaughter and destruction" to the number of 74,000 men, while in Shushan the capital they slew 800,[65] this scroll of Esther too is a holy book which is read on Purim in every Jewish community. This is the scroll of which the Talmud says: "Esther was uttered in the holy spirit",[66] and this is the scroll on which a whole Talmudic tractate was based — the tractate Megillah. Judaism is kaleidoscopic in its ethical attitudes, just as life is kaleidoscopic in its phenomena.

It is true that Gentile scholars regard this as moral imperfection; and they adduce it as proof that Judaism is merely "a forerunner of Christianity". For my part, I find in it a distinctive *Weltanschauung:* here we have before us a comprehension of the two aspects of the human soul, of which the one, absolute good, will completely and finally vanquish the other only "at the end of days": This is the secret of Judaism's immortality. It has grasped the eternal contradiction in the human soul: the contradiction between the good inclination and the evil inclination. Christianity either did not grasp this contradiction, or grasped it but failed to seriously reckon with it. It imposed upon man an obligation which he cannot fulfil: to be perfect even as God is perfect.[67] The demand of Judaism is: "Ye shall be holy: for I the Lord your God am holy"[68] — holy *to* God,[69] but not holy *as* God. And what were the results? If there is a people

which fulfils the moral commandments ordained by Jesus, insofar as human beings can fulfil them, it is none other than the Jewish people. Whereas the Gentile nations, which formally adhere to the religion of love and the creed of mercy, have always gone from one extreme to the other — from "loving one's enemy" and "offering the left cheek" to the deeds of Torquemada, St. Bartholomew's night, the mediaeval holocaust of unbelievers in Europe, the extermination of whole peoples in America, Africa and Australia, and to the massacre of six million Jews in the Second World War. What did the great thinker Blaise Pascal say? "Whoever would be an angel, becomes a brute". Indeed, is it mere chance that the very people which produced Immanuel Kant with his "ethical absolutism" produced also the Asmodeus of our generation, who by systematic sadism destroyed a third of an ancient nation?

Judaism has never produced such atrocities, because it has never imposed too tight a curb on human nature. Consequently, in Jewish life, human nature has never gotten entirely out of hand, except when the horrors perpetrated by Gentiles against the Jews have strained their endurance to breaking-point. Judaism's attitude to the evil inclination is not one of weak indulgence, nor yet of pretence that it does not exist. Hence Judaism does not demand of man what he cannot perform.

Judaism knows that love, real love, of one's enemy runs counter to human nature. Therefore it contents itself with the ethical commandments: "Thou shalt not hate they brother in thy heart", and "thou shalt not take vengeance, nor bear any grudge".[70] If Judaism does ordain love of one's enemy, it tries to find a natural, human basis for this command-

---

[65] Esther 9:5–15.
[66] Megillah 7a.
[67] Matt. 5:48.
[68] Lev. 19:2.
[69] Cf. Deut. 14:2: "for thou art an holy people unto the Lord thy God."

[70] Lev. 19:17–18.

ment. It says: "If thine enemy be hungry, give him bread to eat; and if he be thirsty, give him water to drink." Certainly this is a commandment to show love to one's enemy; but immediately after this commandment come two natural — I had almost said human, all-too-human — reasons: "For thou shalt heap coals of fire upon his head, and the Lord shall reward thee".[71] That is to say, in return for the good deed which you do your enemy by mastering your hatred of him, you will have the pleasure of seeing his chagrin, and you will also be rewarded by God. The same is true of a second passage which warns us against rejoicing over the sufferings of our enemies, a passage which was frequently on the lips of Samuel, the Small, a Tanna of the first century: "Rejoice not when thine enemy falleth, and let not thine heart be glad when he is overthrown"; and immediately the human, the all-too-human reason follows: "Lest the Lord see it, and it displease Him, and He turn away His wrath from him".[72] Rashi sensed that the reason given for not rejoicing at the fall of one's enemy was not particularly ethical, and he added this explanation: "lest His anger turn away from him and come upon you".[73] And it is worth remarking that in the Middle Ages, one of the blackest periods of Jewish history, the righteous, pious and humble Rashi composed the rhymed diatribe beginning "Thou wilt bring shame upon them"[74] — a composition full of vitriolic curses upon the enemies of Israel, the like of which can hardly be found in our literature. The time and the situation were responsible.

It is also worth remarking that when Rashbam, Rashi's grandson, in his commentary on the Torah, came to the "great principle of the Law", "thou shalt love thy neighbor as thyself",[75] he thought fit to interpret: "Thy neighbour — if he is good, but not if he is wicked, as it is written: To fear the Lord is to hate evil". And who in our time was capable of loving the enemy of Israel and the foe of mankind, Hitler?

Love of one's enemy found clear expression in the verse: "If thou see the ass of him that hateth thee lying under his burden and wouldst forbear to help him, thou shalt surely help with him".[76] Yet in Deuteronomy — the most ethical of the Five Books of Moses — we read, in place of this verse, one which is similar yet different: "Thou shalt not see thy brother's ass or his ox fallen down by the way, and hide thyself from them: thou shalt surely help him to lift them up again."[77] "Thy brother's ass", in place of "the ass of him that hateth thee".

It is true to say that Judaism, in its original form, before it was subjected to outside influences, did not develop an absolutist ethics. For this reason, Essenism did not take a firm hold in Judaism; and for this reason, (quite apart from the irrational conception of the Deity), Judaism did not accept Christianity. Judaism did not build monasteries for itself, nor did it for long adopt the ascetic morality of the Middle Ages, though it was inevitably infected with it during the long, bitter exile in a strange and hostile world, in which there was no respite from massacres and persecutions. Judaism always remembers that man is only flesh and blood, and that human society and the state are founded in part, it is true, upon lofty human emotions of mercy, kindliness and righteousness, but not less on human weaknesses and upon inclinations and passions which cannot

[71] Pr. 25:21–22.
[72] ibid. 24:17–18 cf. Mishnah, Aboth iv. 19.
[73] v. Rashi's Commentary on Aboth, ibid.
[74] A. H. Freiman in Tarbiz, XII (1941), 70–74.

[75] Lev. 19:18.
[76] Ex. 23:5.
[77] Deut. 22:4.

be dismissed simply by turning a blind eye to them, and which, if thrust out by the door, creep in again by the window. Judaism curbs the passions and fights incessantly against brutal savagery and bestial grossness, training man to a truly humane morality in his relations with individuals and with society. But it never for a moment forgets that "the Law was not given to the ministering angels".[78]

In the two World Wars mankind lost its God. A vacuum formed in the spiritual life alike of individuals, communities and states. For with the loss of God, human morality too has been lost. Where there is no God, everything is permissible. Everything becomes "relative" and subjective and there is no check, no curb, no fence. Why then should what is thought wrong to-day be wrong? Because it is so written in the Law? Or because such is the convention of society? If there is no God, there is no Law either.

Seventy years ago, Dr. Felix Adler tried to fill the vacuum caused by the ever-growing decline of faith by founding "ethical brotherhoods" which treated morality as independent of religion. Ahad Ha'am, in his article "National Ethics",[79] tried to follow in the path of this movement founded by Felix Adler — the movement of "Ethical Culture", which made a clear distinction between faith and morality and sought "to strengthen the moral sense of its own members and of others outside it *without the slightest reference of any kind to religion*".[80] The movement did not exert a wide influence. The "moral sense" alone, unaccompanied by God, cannot resist the evil inclination, especially where the lives of the masses are concerned. The destruction of faith must inevitably lead to the liquidation of the "moral sense". There is an intrinsic connection between the unity of God and the moral commandments in man's heart. In no nation, and in no period of history, has polytheism produced prophets of truth and righteousness; and such prophets have never prophesied except in the name of the one, unique God, the God of goodness.

Hence all those whom I would call "spiritual Christianizers", such as Sholem Asch, and of course the "Jewish Christians", were and are wrong in their attempts to break down the barrier between Judaism and Christianity, and to represent Judaism's whole rejection of the teaching of Jesus and Paul as a mistake, or as the act of wicked men motivated by self-interest. These "compromisers" between Judaism and Christianity do not ask themselves: Is it possible that a whole people would endure for almost two thousand years the burden of unheard of sufferings — pogroms, massacres, thousands of cramping laws, and hundreds of restrictions at every step — merely through an ancient error, or because wicked men refused to recognize the religion which grew out of their own people?

No, there must of necessity be a deeper reason for this obstinate rejection, which has continued for nearly two thousand years! This deeper reason is the subconscious feeling, and perhaps also the conscious realization, that Christianity, both in its conception of God and in its moral law, which are interdependent, is not a *creed of life* like Judaism, but an abstract and irrational creed, which runs counter to the course of human life, and which men do not attempt to put into practice because it is incapable of being put into practice — except perhaps at the millennium, when human nature shall have been changed by processes which

---

[78]Berakhoth 25b.

[79]One-volume edition of Ahad Ha'am's complete works (1947) pp. 159–164.

[80]ibid. p. 164 (Ahad Ha'am's italics).

we should try to help forward, but the full completion of which we cannot foresee.

Everyone who reads the Old Testament and the Haggadic literature of the Talmud and Midrash, and even the works of Maimonides—the most authoritative voice of later Judaism—cannot but admit that the definition of Judaism given by Micah of Moresheth—"He hath told thee, O man, what is good; and what doth the Lord require of thee, but to do justly, and to love mercy, and to walk humbly with thy God?"[81]—sums up the whole Law in three brief ethical commandments. Moreover, he will recognize that this teaching sets "doing justly" in the first place, even above "loving mercy". Without the love of mercy the human individual cannot exist, but without justice there is no moral order in the world. Is there really anyone who, on the principle of loving one's enemy, would accept the view that those who systematically and deliberately destroyed millions of human beings ought not to receive their due punishment? Possibly, Tolstoy the Russian and Gandhi the Indian would have accepted this; but then, the former was a Christian who regarded Judaism and its ceremonial laws as idolatry, and the latter was a Buddhist who did not recognize the religion of Judaism at all.

Mankind has lost its morality, because it has lost its God. Perhaps it has lost both, because of the irrational element in both of them......

Judaism has a conception of God which, for all its mysticism, remains rational, and therefore the ethics of Judaism have not taken an extreme, superhuman form. It will be a disaster for Judaism if it removes the barrier which divides it from Christianity or from Buddhism. For then it will be lost in an ocean of belief and morality foreign to its spirit. The difference in beliefs and in religious and ethical views between Judaism and Christianity must not be eliminated or glossed over. If we professing Jews eliminate or gloss over this difference, we shall become conscious of that spiritual emptiness which the rest of humanity feels to-day.

For whoever has eyes to see will not deny that, with the loss of God, an empty void has formed in mankind's universe. This empty void has given rise to that "horror vacui", that "fear of emptiness" so wonderfully described by Zalman Schneur in his poem "On the Banks of the Seine":

Man is afraid. The space of the whole universe is emptied
When God dies.
Blue is the void in summer and winter grey,
But empty and always frightening when there is no God.

This "fear of emptiness" will eventually drive man to seek his God again. Where shall He be found?

There was a similar situation in the ancient world, not long before the destruction of the Second Temple. Then too "the space of all the universe was emptied, when God died" — when, in the void of the world of idolatry, there was heard the shattering cry of despair: "Great Pan is dead!" Then the idolatrous world turned in its spiritual affliction, not to Greece, which at that time had subdued almost all the known world by its philosophy, its poetry and its faith — by Hellenism — but to tiny Judea, the conquered and despised. And why? Because there it found a God without bodily form and a human morality at once lofty and realistic.

In our time too, when mankind begins to search for its God, it will not find Him

---

[81] Mi. 4:6.

in Christianity with its trinity, its hypostatization of man, and its "Mother of God" — an irrational conception of the Divine nature involving an abstract and absolutist moral law beyond the natural capacity of "flesh and blood". Neither will lost and perplexed humanity find Him in the backward Islam of the desert, nor yet in Buddhism with its ideal of "Nirvana". It will find God only in Judaism, with its pure monotheism, its God "who has no body, is not subject to the accidents of matter and cannot be compared to any object" — that is to say, who is a transcendent power, abstract in the highest degree, an entity raised above the whole of creation as a cosmic sublimity infinitely beyond man's comprehension. Man, for all his wisdom and ingenuity, cannot be considered as the final reality in the whole cosmic existence known to

him. Humanity, which has lost its way, will find this "transcendent God" linked to a moral law which has the lofty and exalted aim of improving human nature and ennobling human relations; but which is not beyond humanity and outside reality: a moral law of love, mercy and compassion, but also of truth and righteousness, of justice and equity; a law of whose commandments it is said "that he may live by them — and not die by them".[82]

Only this human Judaism is fitted to save humanity — and first of all itself — in these days of spiritual confusion. For Judaism is eternal in its rational faith and its human morality, and "in the end of days", when the sway of the irrational creeds is ended, "all the nations shall come streaming to it".

---

[82] Yoma 80b.

# KIERKEGAARD AND RABBINIC JUDAISM

MARVIN FOX

THE RELIGIOUS thought of Kierkegaard is clearly among the dominant religious philosophies of our time. Its influence has been strongly felt in Christian circles and has also penetrated through various routes into contemporary Jewish thought. Numbers of Jewish thinkers, some eminent names among them, have discovered religion anew through the influence of Kierkegaardian existentialism. They have rejected the rabbinic tradition, or in some cases have been ignorant of it, and are determined to cast Judaism into a Kierkegaardian mold. Whatever the merits of Kierkegaard's work, and they are many, I think it can be shown effectively that his doctrines are, on the whole, antithetical to traditional Jewish beliefs. Any man has the right to follow Kierkegaard if this is the direction in which his thought and experience lead him. But no man has the right to ascribe to Judaism ideas and attitudes which violate the very spirit of the Jewish tradition. Yet, such violations have occurred with increasing frequency in recent years. Kierkegaard and the crisis theologies, more than the Bible and the Talmud, are supplying both the impulse and the direction of much contemporary Jewish thought. Under these influences such attitudes as despair, dread, pessimism, anxiety are being championed as the necessary consequences of religious maturity. As a result, the usual Jewish optimism is rejected as naive, and the concept of salvation in history through good works is abandoned in favor of a doctrine of divine grace whose workings no man can grasp. While I would admit quite readily that this side of the religious life has a legitimate place in Judaism or in any mature religion, I would deny categorically that these doctrines are the whole of Judaism or even that, so far as they go, they are normative Judaism.

In what follows, I shall attempt to show how far the rabbinic tradition, which is after all, apart from the Bible, the most fundamental source of Jewish doctrine, differs from Kierkegaard's views. If we examine the interpretation of the *akedah*, the story of the offering of Isaac, as it occurs in the Talmud and the various Midrashim and contrast it with Kierkegaard's treatment of the same event in *Fear and Trembling* we shall discover a very different religious world from that in which Kierkegaard moved. It is not the primary purpose of this essay to argue for the Rabbis and against Kierkegaard. It is its purpose to show how the Rabbis' understanding of the *akedah* differs from Kierkegaard's, and to insist that a properly *Jewish* theology must follow the rabbinic teachings and reject the views of Kierkegaard. Jewish thinkers should learn readily from every source of instruction. But they must take heed lest they be overwhelmed by doctrines which are at best directive, but can never be normative for Judaism.

MARVIN FOX is a member of the Department of Philosophy of Ohio State University.

## II

The few recent efforts to analyze the *akedah* through the understanding and insights of Jewish sources have been commendable but partial.[1] They tend to be polemical and their polemic centers on the problem of the relationship between the ethical and the religious. Kierkegaard understands the *akedah* as involving a teleological suspension of the ethical. Though our ordinary moral norms would make the murder of one's own child one of the most repellent of all crimes, in the *akedah* Abraham's readiness to perform such an act is transformed into a perfect expression of love of God and of faith in God. To Kierkegaard this means that the "knight of faith" when he confronts God directly may have to abandon even his deepest moral commitments, and an act which, in other circumstances, is ugly and wicked becomes sublime when it is an act of perfect faith. The religious, as thus conceived, is beyond the ethical, is absolutely distinct from the ethical, and even requires a suspension of the ethical. A man of true faith must be ready to violate the universal moral law when God requires it of him.

The main burden of argument in the first of the articles to which reference was made above, is merely that Judaism makes no such break between the ethical and the religious. As its author, Rabbi Gumbiner, understands the matter, the ethical and the religious are identical. There can be no conflict between the moral law and the life of faith. God does not permit, and certainly He does not require, the violation of ethical obligations. For Rabbi Gumbiner the prime significance of the *akedah* lies in the fact that

it "is a prophetic tract designed to show that God does not demand and will not accept the sacrifice of a child.... The story had been told to demonstrate the fact that God did *not* demand the sacrifice, that men should understand that ethical conduct was the mode of worship demanded by God."[2] He concludes that Kierkegaard's doctrine of the teleological suspension of the ethical is a "Christian doctrine historically unfounded, dialectically unnecessary, and, from the Jewish standpoint ethically and religiously impossible."[3] Dr. Baumgardt, in his article, does not deny the essential correctness of Gumbiner's strictures. But he adds a caution, namely that we must not forget that Kierkegaard also emphasizes an important point when he stresses the "truly paradoxical nature of the divine command in the Abraham and Isaac story... the 'absurdity' of the moral conflict involved, and the torment, the fear and trembling endured."[4]

## III

One of Kierkegaard's most deeply held convictions is that religious faith is not rational in character. With some of the early Church Fathers he believes that a genuine religious commitment is one which says, *"Credo quia absurdum est."* Man's reason is not adequate to an understanding of God, nor is reason sufficient to bring man into proper relationship with God. On the contrary, if man had to rely on his intelligence alone, then faith would be impossible, according to Kierkegaard. Faith transcends intelligence and even violates intelligence. "A man can become a tragic hero by his own powers — but not a knight of faith.... To him who follows the narrow way of faith no one can give counsel, him no

---

[1]Cf., Joseph H. Gumbiner, "Existentialism and Father Abraham", *Commentary*, February, 1948, and David Baumgardt, "Man's Morals and God's Will", *Ibid.*, March, 1950.

[2]Gumbiner, *op. cit.*, pp. 144 and 148.
[3]*Ibid.*, p. 148.
[4]Baumgardt, *op. cit.*, p. 247.

one can understand. Faith is a miracle...."[5]

It is from this point of view that Kierkegaard understands Abraham's part in the *akedah*. Abraham's faith was a belief by virtue of the absurd. Human reason, presumably, could never understand or justify God's ways with Abraham. The biblical version of the episode is terse and cryptic and, therefore, is open to interpretation. God demands the sacrifice of Isaac, while He acknowledges that he is "thy son, thine only son, whom thou dost love." God demands the sacrifice of a child whom He brought into the world through His own personal intervention, a child who, He had previously promised, would carry on Abraham's work and his teaching. But for this most incomprehensible demand God gives no reasons and Abraham requires no reasons. Instead "Abraham arose early in the morning", hastening to fulfil the divine command. This is all that we are told in the Bible, and with this text before him Kierkegaard does a brilliant job of exhibiting the absurdity of God's demand and the perfect quality of Abraham's faith. No human intelligence can understand God's demand for the sacrifice of Isaac. Intelligence would see here only a violation of God's own promises and purposes, and, even worse, a violation both of the most elementary rules of moral decency and of natural sentiment. But Abraham's faith, his love of God, was so complete that he hastened to comply with the commandment, asking no questions and raising no objections. Such faith is truly a miracle; it is a true instance of belief by virtue of the absurd. Kierkegaard gives his readers the feeling that Abraham believed, not in spite of the absurdity, but precisely because of the absurdity. As a distinguished Kierke-

gaard scholar has expressed it, "The various determinants of faith are by Kierkegaard concentrated in the single category of the *absurd*, since the movement of faith seems paradoxical to the ordinary consciousness from which faith emerges."[6]

Such a view is appropriate within the framework of the Christian tradition, since many of the articles of Christian faith are mysteries. The very foundations of Christian doctrine utterly transcend man's intelligence, and in some instances actively violate human intelligence. Thus, the belief in a triune God or the belief in a God-man are paradoxes whose very nature is to be incomprehensible to man's reason. But this need not be embarassing to orthodox Christianity since it is a system of belief which acknowledges readily the inadequacy of man's reason. Faith is necessary at the very point at which understanding has reached its limits. *"Credo quia absurdum est"*, is neither a failure of nerve nor an abdication of reason. It does not make every absurdity worthy of belief, for while it sees the divine as absurd, it never sees the absurd as divine. It is merely a humble acknowledgement that there are severe limits to human understanding, and that the mysterious aspects of the universe are those with which man's inner being needs most to come to terms.

While Judaism admits the limitations of man's intellect and the presence of certain cosmic mysteries it does not lay its primary stress on this side of things. Instead one finds in the rabbinic sources a rather steady inclination to make sense out of the apparently senseless. As one surveys the rabbinic literature dealing with the *akedah* it becomes clear that the tendency of the rabbis was to reject the view that Abraham's ready compliance with God's commandment was an act of

---

[5]S. Kierkegaard, *Fear and Trembling*, (Princeton, 1945), p. 100.

[6]*Ibid.*, p. xxiii, quoted in Editor's Preface.

*blind* faith. Certainly no one would deny that Abraham acted out of faith and love. But his faith, according to the rabbinic view was not blind. The absurdity is apparent so long as we rely only on the scriptural text. Jewish tradition, however, was unwilling to admit that the scriptural story was the whole story, precisely because as it stands the story is absurd. If God, who is the foundation of all morality, requires Abraham to perform a wicked and immoral act, if God, whose word is eternal requires the performance of an act whose result will be the violation of His own promises concerning the future of Abraham's children, and if Abraham goes forth quietly and unquestioningly to do as he is bidden — could anything be more senseless?

It is the very absurdity of the story as it stands that forced the rabbis to expand it and to give it a different meaning. Kierkegaard, in presenting Abraham as a prototype of the "knight of faith", tends either to forget or to misread other episodes in Abraham's career. The same Abraham on other occasions openly doubts God's promises and questions His justice. Though God has repeatedly assured him that he will have a legitimate son who will be his heir, Abraham laughs at the idea. In fact, so profound is his skepticism that his only response to the divine promise is the request that at least Ishmael be permitted to live. That Sarah should bear him a son is something that Abraham refuses to believe will ever happen. This Abraham is so skeptical that he questions God's justice when he learns of the impending destruction of Sodom and Gomorrah. [6a] Yet, in Kierke-

gaard's interpretation, this same man is ready to offer up his own son without a single murmur of protest at God's behest, though the command is absurd, or better yet, because the command is absurd.

This is a view which is wholly unacceptable to the teachings of the rabbis. Instead as they fill out the story of the *akedah* they give us a doctrine that is insistent on turning an apparent absurdity into a perfectly understandable and reasonable event. Just as Abraham was not required to accept the apparently absurd in other instances so was he not required to do so here. In the cases of the promised birth of Isaac and of the threatened destruction of Sodom and Gomorrah Abraham openly expresses his doubts and his objections. And God does not grow angry with him, because there is very good reason to doubt. Judaism does not require a man to believe what intelligence clearly cannot accept. Maimonides laid down the principle that even "a miracle cannot prove that which is impossible; it is useful only as a confirmation of that which is possible."[7]

In this framework, the rabbis taught that in actuality God's demand for the sacrifice of Isaac was not a moral absurdity at all. On the contrary, God, Abraham, the angels, and even Isaac, all knew and understood that there were very

---

[6a]Kierkegaard holds that "When the righteous punishment was decreed upon Sodom and Gomora...Abraham came forward with his prayers." But it is quite clear from the Biblical text that things were quite different. Abraham does not acknowledge the righteousness of the punishment, but questions it. He does not pray

for Sodom and Gomora; but demands that justice be done. Moreover, he is clear and unequivocal in his suggestion that God is not doing justice. But when Kierkegaard reads even such an open text he sees it through the transforming powers of his own conception of Abraham.

Kierkegaard stresses the fact that Abraham pleaded the cause of Sodom and Gomora, but that when God demanded the sacrifice of Isaac "he did not pray for himself." What Kierkegaard overlooks completely is that Abraham might have prayed for Isaac; he might have seen this as Isaac's cause, as well as his own. Kierkegaard does not see at all that the son has to be spared, not only the father.

[7]Maimonides, *Guide for the Perplexed*, Part III, Ch. XXIV.

good reasons for God's demand, and these reasons were far more earnest than a mere protest against child-sacrifice. The midrashim pivot around a central theme. The scriptural text relates that when Isaac grew and was weaned Abraham made a great celebration. It was then that God tested him. The rabbis describe what happened in this way:

Satan said to the Almighty: 'Sovereign of the Universe! To this old man Thou didst graciously vouchsafe the fruit of the womb at the age of a hundred, yet of all the banquet which he prepared, he did not have one turtle-dove or pigeon to sacrifice before Thee! Hath he done aught but in honor of his son!' Replied He, 'Yet were I to say to him, "Sacrifice thy son before Me", he would do so without hesitation. Straightway, "God did tempt Abraham..."[8]

In another version Abraham is represented as realizing himself that in his joy over his son he had neglected to give thanks to God. Thus he says, "I have rejoiced and caused all to rejoice, but I did not set aside even a ram or a bullock for God."[9] Still another interpretation has the ministering angels present the same complaint before God.

In any case it is clear that the rabbinic teachings did not conceive of God's demand as arbitrary or incomprehensible. Nor is Abraham's act of faith based on a moral absurdity. On the contrary, there is a perfectly understandable reason why God asks and Abraham is ready to offer up such a sacrifice. Nor does the comprehensibility of the act lessen its significance as an act of faith. Even when a man knows why the sacrifice is required of him he still must be distinguished by his love of God and his faith in God to be able to do as God commands. In Kierkegaard's version Abraham did not argue or protest because he was faced with a demand which made argument or questioning inappropriate, and even impossible. The Jewish version remembers that this is still the Abraham who argued and protested, questioning God's justice, even in behalf of the wicked Sodomites. How then could he do less in behalf of his own son? The answer is that what struck him dumb was not the utter paradox and absurdity of God's demand, but rather the recognition of the truth of the charges brought against him. Words would have been meaningless at this point. As a man of faith, understanding what was required of him, he could only go forth at once to justify himself.

The rabbis took pains even to give the episode a special meaning for Isaac. In the rabbinic view Isaac was not an innocent child being led to the slaughter. According to the usual count Isaac was thirty seven years old, and for him, too, this was a meaningful and comprehensible event. He is represented as he compares his own merits with those of Ishmael. Ishmael argues that he is superior in God's sight because he was already thirteen years old when he was circumcised yet he made no effort to run away from the painful operation, while Isaac was only eight days old at his circumcision and thus had made no real sacrifice for God. To this Isaac replies that unlike Ishmael who served God with only one limb he would be prepared to offer up his very life if God should require it of him. As with Abraham we have here great faith and great love, but not an act whose foundations are absurdity. Like Abraham, Isaac too understands why he is being bound to the altar.[10]

Moreover the *akedah* is an event which is meaningful for all mankind, in the interpretation of the rabbis. Its purpose

[8] *B. Talmud, Sanhedrin*, 89b, Soncino translation.

[9] *Bereshith Rabbah*, XLV.

[10] Cf. *B. Talmud Sanhedrin*, 89b; also *Tanchuma*, Vayera, 42.

was to demonstrate to all men that God does not act arbitrarily. Lest any man might think that God chose Abraham arbitrarily or that He gave him a pre-eminent position for no special reason, he was commanded to sacrifice his son so that all the world would know how great was Abraham's love of God. The *Midrash Tanchuma* expresses this idea in a magnificent passage. It pictures Abraham standing before God and arguing in the following manner:

Master of the Universe! A man ordinarily tests his friend because he does not know what is in another's heart. But You, who examine the hearts and reins of men, should you have found it necessary to test me in this way? Surely it must have been evident to you that if you commanded me to offer up my son I would hasten to do so with a perfect heart. The Holy One, Blessed be He, answered him: I did it only to let the peoples of the world know that I did not choose you arbitrarily.[11]

What more striking instance could there be of the Jewish conception of the reasonableness and comprehensibility of the *akedah!* One could not imagine Kierkegaard's Abraham addressing God in this way, nor Kierkegaard's God replying in this way.

## IV

·The heart of the issue lies in the fact that for Kierkegaard the paradox of faith "is rooted in an antithesis...between God and man, between God's understanding of what human life ought to be, and man's."[12] Judaism is rather inclined to emphasize the close tie between God and man, and the common elements of understanding that bind God and man together. Man's highest life is one in which his understanding of his ideal ends

coincides with God's understanding. One of the ultimate purposes of the revelation at Sinai is to give man a clear picture of what human life ought to be in God's sight. The very center of this conception of religion is the belief that God is not far removed from man, but is instead closely bound to him. Kierkegaard's God transcends the world absolutely. He is completely separated from man, perhaps even opposed to man, and, therefore, there is, according to his doctrine, almost inevitably an antithesis between God's view of things and man's view of things. The Jewish God is "nigh unto all them that call upon Him, to all that call upon Him in truth." Jewish teaching frequently goes so far as to suggest that God is, in some degree, dependent on man, and even that he is bound by the laws of men.

These ideas are developed in a striking way in some of the rabbinic commentary on the *akedah*. In much of the commentary one finds the feeling that the *akedah* is not only Abraham's trial, but also God's trial. God must prove himself to humanity, just as Abraham must prove himself. It would be a mistake to think of this view as blasphemy, since what underlies it is a very deep and sensitive piety joined together with a profound love of humanity. So long as men are imperfect God is necessarily on trial. It may be that an Abraham can achieve perfect faith even when God hides his purposes from him, though, as we have shown, the rabbis did not think so. The Torah teaches, in the story of the water issuing forth from the rock, that Moses lost faith momentarily. If Abraham, who is the father of faith, sometimes questions God, if Moses, who alone spoke with God directly, could lose faith, then what can be expected of ordinary men? God is always on trial. In times of trouble men are forced to doubt, and God must prove Himself if humanity is to be redeemed.

---

[11] *Tanchuma*, Vayera, 46.
[12] From a review by David Swenson, quoted in the Editor's Preface to *Fear and Trembling*, p. xxiv.

How else will men come to a knowledge of God? Judaism, in its classic form, does not teach that God arbitrarily bestows His grace on some men, while in His detachment from humanity he leaves others to remain ignorant of His glory. He is rather the ever loving Father who seeks to redeem and elevate every one of His children. He is ready to stand trial in man's court of justice. Through His prophets He pleads His own cause. "Thus saith the Lord! What unrighteousness have your fathers found in Me, that they are gone far away from Me?" And as God pleads, his witness is man. More than signs and wonders, more than every miracle, the testimony of the man of true faith justifies God and brings him close to men.

We see this feeling expressed in a well known comment on the *akedah* in which the rabbis picture God as coming to Abraham with the following words:

I have tried you with many trials and you have passed them all successfully. Now, I beg of you, for my sake, withstand also this trial, so that men will not say that all the earlier ones were without true worth.[18]

God acknowledges his dependence on Abraham, for if men are to find their way to Him then they must be led by Abraham. If Abraham fails, then God, too, has failed. As Schechter has expressed it, "it is this witnessing...to revelation by which God is God: without it He could not be God."[14] Indeed, we find Abraham saying, according to the Midrash, "Before I made Him known to His creatures He was only the God of the heavens; but once I made Him known to his creatures he is also the God of the earth."[15]

The angels, too, are aware of God's need for man. Interpreting the verse in which the angel calls to Abraham to stop him from killing Isaac, the tradition tells the story in this way. As Abraham lifted the knife, the angels began to cry bitterly before God, reminding Him of His promise that Isaac would carry on Abraham's line. But if Abraham slaughters Isaac, they demanded, "to whom will you say at Sinai: I am the Lord your God; and who will sing before you at the sea; This is my God and I will glorify Him"?[16] Just as man needs God, for without Him he becomes a beast, so does God need man, else he remains unknown to the world. For His own sake, say the angels, God must not permit his faithful to be destroyed.

Of course, this is only one side of the picture. Judaism also recognizes God's majesty, and knows that there are times when man can do little more than prostrate himself before God. There are many familiar instances in the traditional liturgy where man humbly and tearfully acknowledges his own unworthiness. Judaism never ceases to impress man with his own creatureliness, and with the consequent fact that he is limited and imperfect. So far Judaism has no quarrel with Kierkegaard. The quarrel arises when Kierkegaard makes this the whole of man's relationship to God, while Judaism teaches that prostrating oneself is only one way of approaching God.

The difference can be even more sharply delineated if we reflect on the fact that the rabbis did not only teach that God sometimes needs man, but even that he is sometimes bound and judged by the laws of men. The classic instance in which Rabbi Levi Yitzchok of Berditchev called God to judgement before a court of men is by no means an isolated occurrence. It is just one in a series of episodes of this general character. The

---

[13]*B. Talmud, Sanhedrin*, 89b.
[14]Solomon Schechter, *Some Aspects of Rabbinic Theology*, (New York, 1910), p. 24.
[15]*Bereshith Rabbah*, XLIX.

[16]Cited in *Torah Shelemah*, Vol. 3, Tome 4, p. 897, item 131.

epitomization of this idea is contained in the midrashic explanation of the meaning of "Moriah". Depending on the relationship of "Moriah" to the root which means "teaching", the rabbis explain that the name refers to "the place at which the righteous issue forth their teaching before the Holy One, Blessed be He, and He carries out their instruction."[17] Or in an even stronger version they speak of Moriah as "the land from which the righteous give forth their teaching, issuing decrees to God which He fulfils." This same conception of God as bound by the laws of men is evident in a number of other rabbinic comments on the *akedah*. The Jewish God is not opposed to man. His own fulfillment depends on man, even as man's fulfillment depends on God. It would be blasphemous to suggest that God and man are on the same level. But it is equally wrong to forget that man is the culmination of God's creative work, that he is made in the divine image, that he is "but little lower than the angels". Such a man must recognize his limits and, in deep humility, pay homage to his Creator. But such a man is also duty-bound to recognize his highest possibilities, to know where he stands in the cosmic scheme, and to insist on his rights, even before God, as well as to do his duty with unquestioning obedience.

## V

The essential opposition between Kierkegaard and the Jewish tradition is also apparent in another aspect of the interpretation of the *akedah*. For Kierkegaard Abraham is "the knight of faith who in the solitude of the universe never hears any human voice but walks alone with his dreadful responsibility."[18] In the moment of trial when a man faces God he stands completely alone, according to Kierkegaard. He is neither understood by others, nor does he seek to guide others. His detachment from the world is complete, and Kierkegaard applauds this as a very high achievement. "The true knight of faith," says he, "is a witness, never a teacher, and therein lies his deep humanity, which is worth a good deal more than this silly participation in others' weal and woe which is honored by the name of sympathy, whereas in fact it is nothing but vanity".[19]

This is a doctrine which violates one of the most deeply rooted convictions of Judaism. When a Jew stands before God, even in the moment of trial, he is not completely alone. He is a member of *k'lal Yisrael*, of the community of Israel. He bears with him responsibility for his people, and his own merit is increased through *z'chuth avoth*, the merits of the fathers. When he stands before God, even on Yom Kippur, he does not pray only for himself, but for the group. The very confession of sins is expressed in a plural form — "for the sin which *we* have sinned before Thee". Kierkegaard is filled with contempt for "silly participation in others' weal and woe". Judaism has always considered such participation one of man's highest duties.

It is for this reason that Kierkegaard imagines Abraham as standing before God in complete solitude, totally detached from the rest of mankind. But the Jewish tradition was certain that at the very moment of his trial Abraham did not stand alone, but that, at the very least, he must have asked God's mercy for the future of Israel. One of the most typical expressions of this view is found in a comment on the words, "By myself have I sworn, saith the Lord". One rabbinic tradition describes the scene this way:

[17] Cited in *ibid.*, p. 775, item 37, and footnote.
[18] *Fear and Trembling*, p. 122.

[19] *Ibid.*, pp. 122-123.

The Holy One, Blessed be He, opened the firmament and the darkness [as witnesses] and said: By myself have I sworn. Abraham said to Him: You have sworn Your oath, but I too have sworn an oath that I shall not leave this altar until I have said all that needs to be said. God told him to speak. Said Abraham: Did You not once promise me that my children would be numerous as the sands on the shore of the sea and as the stars in the heavens? Yet when You commanded me to offer up Isaac I did not answer by reminding You of Your promise [but I went directly to do Your will]. Therefore, I ask that in the future when Isaac's children will sin and will suffer that You shall remember in their behalf the binding of Isaac.[20]

One of the measures of Abraham's greatness is that he did not stand alone before God. It is to his eternal credit that in the midst of the severest trial which any man can suffer he remembered to ask God's mercy for his future generations. Because the rabbinic tradition could not imagine a great spirit doing otherwise it was only natural for it to picture Abraham in this way. Abraham's act would be far less impressive if he did not, in the midst of his own suffering, participate in "others' weal and woe".

To Kierkegaard this appears to be a kind of vanity. To the Jewish tradition such participation in the lives of others is one of man's highest duties. A truly pious man never approaches God in the solitude which isolates him from his fellow men. Even when the high priest stands all alone in the holy of holies he prays not only for himself, but for his household and for all Israel. Abraham could do no less.

One can hardly resist at this point a brief mention of an earlier episode in Abraham's career. We are told that "the Lord appeared unto him by the terebinths of Mamre, as he sat in the tent door in the heat of the day; and he lifted up his eyes and looked, and, lo, three men stood over against him." The Torah goes on to tell how Abraham ran toward the men and pleaded with them to accept his hospitality. From this the rabbis drew a lesson concerning the importance of hospitality. Abraham, though he was ill, and though it was hot, ran to the strangers in order to offer them what comforts he could. But most important of all, the rabbis conclude, is that Abraham left the divine presence in order to extend a hand of welcome to strangers who were hungry and weary. For this reason the rabbis rule that hospitality to a needy traveller is an even greater act than receiving the Presence of God. For Abraham left God in order to receive the wanderers. To Kierkegaard this would be utterly incomprehensible. In his view, when a man stands before God he is completely detached from men. In the Jewish view, a man's worthiness to stand before God is directly related to his love and concern for his fellow men.

### VI

This leads us to one final comment which in its own way illuminates the fundamental difference between Kierkegaard's Abraham and the Jewish Abraham. The only emotion that Kierkegaard attributes to Abraham during the *akedah* episodes is "fear and trembling". He stresses the dread which Abraham suffers when he has to make the terrible choice between his love for his son and his desire to fulfil God's commandment. Kierkegaard describes with artistic mastery the father's anguish during those three long days of the journey to Moriah, as well as the horror which must have been Abraham's as he lifted the knife to slaughter his beloved son. How else could it be?

But the rabbinic tradition is able to

---

[20]Cited in *Torah Shelemah, op. cit.,* p. 909, item 184 note.

imagine the events in another way. It would be foolish to think that Abraham was so lacking in ordinary human sentiment that he could prepare to slaughter his son without feeling any pain. But even in the midst of his tears, the rabbis tell us, he also felt joy.

"And Abraham stretched forth his hand and took the knife to slay his son." He stretched forth his hand to take the knife, and tears fell from his eyes into the eyes of Isaac, because he felt the mercy of a father. *But in spite of this he went joyfully to do the will of his Creator.*[21]

This same idea is expressed in a number of other places. Abraham hastens to do God's will, and even when it requires of him the greatest sacrifice which any man can make he is still able to do it with joy, because he knows that he is fulfilling a divine commandment. He feels the joy because he is not performing an act which is absurd, but one which is meaningful. He feels the joy because he does not stand before God alone, but as a representative of the children of Israel. He rejoices because he knows that his personal suffering may be the source of Israel's future redemption. Above all else the Jewish Abraham can rejoice even in such trying circumstances because he knows that he is doing God's will. The Psalmist teaches, "Happy is the man that feareth the Lord, that delighteth greatly in his commandments."

---

[21]*Bereshith Rabbah*, XLVI.

It is clear that what distinguishes Jewish doctrine from Kierkegaard's doctrine is the Jewish conception of the religious life as involving a kind of dialectical movement. Kierkegaard is aware of only one dimension of religious reality, namely the dimension in which man is so overpowered by the sense of his own unworthiness that he can do nothing but prostrate himself before God. Judaism sees this as only one aspect of the religious life, and conceives of man as moving between a humble acknowledgement of God's majesty and a forthright assertion before God Himself of human claims and human rights. Kierkegaard sees only the somber and solitary side of the religious life. Judaism sees instead a movement between the somber and the joyous, between solitude and sociality.

I am very much aware that in this essay I have, at best, pointed to many fundamental questions while dealing with them at the surface. To pursue all of these questions to their proper depth would require far more space than is available to any article. My main purpose has been only to illuminate some of the most fundamental differences between Kierkegaard's *akedah* and the Jewish *akedah,* and to show how far the differences between the Kierkegaardian Abraham and the Jewish Abraham are symptomatic of the differences between Kierkegaardian religion and Jewish religion.

# KIERKEGAARD AND THE MIDRASH

JACOB L. HALEVI

The article, "Kierkegaard and Rabbinic Judaism,"[1] by Marvin Fox is the latest effort by a Jewish critic to discredit Kierkegaard's interpretation of *Fear and Trembling*, one of his most noted books. To bolster and lend authority to his argument, Mr. Fox draws liberally upon the Midrash. But a study of the Midrashim he adduces serves only to reveal the futility of his attempt to squeeze from them his own type of rationalistic interpretation of the *akedah*, the sacrifice of Isaac. His essay only emphasizes the fact that, like other predecessors of his, he attempts to answer Kierkegaard without a clear understanding of Kierkegaard's ideas, or of the Midrash.

In his essay he charges that under the influence of "Kierkegaard and the crisis theologies . . . such attitudes as despair, dread, pessimism, anxiety are championed as the necessary consequences of religious maturity." I do not essay to speak for the "crisis theologies", whatever they affirm. I speak only in behalf of Kierkegaard's thought. To say that

he held the view that despair is the sign of religious maturity is fantastic and the very opposite of the truth. In fact, Kierkegaard speaks specifically of the "immaturity of despair",[2] a viewpoint which is implicit in all his works from his big book *Either/Or* to the last issue of the *Instant* which he wrote on his death bed.

In the preface to his book *The Sickness Unto Death*, the inadequacy of despair for the life of faith is explicitly stated thus: "I would call attention once for all to the fact that in this whole book, as the title indeed says, despair is conceived as the sickness, not as the cure."[3] Further on in the same work he declares, "despair is precisely to have lost the eternal and oneself."[4] Transposed into Rabbinic terms, the view expressed in this work is that despair is present in varying degree in all forms of *chayei sha'ah* and is transcended only in *chayei olam*.

Kierkegaard was primarily an ethicist and not a speculative philosopher. In the Midrash it is revealed that Rabbi Eliezer and Simeon ben Zoma imply that if there were but a single man in the whole world who heeded the eternal

JACOB L. HALEVI is rabbi of Congregation Beth El, San Pedro, California. He is a graduate of the Hebrew Union College, Cincinnati, Ohio. The present essay marks his first appearance in the pages of JUDAISM.

[1] *Judaism*, April 1953, 160-69.

[2] *Stages on Life's Way*, tr. by Walter Lowrie (Princeton 1945), Appendix, p. 462.
[3] *The Sickness Unto Death*, tr. by Walter Lowrie (Princeton 1951), p. 5.
[4] *Ibid.*, 99.

demands of the ethical, it was for his sake that the world was created.[5] Kierkegaard hews to this line of thought in declaring, "Whoever does not apprehend the eternal validity of the ethical, even if it concerned him alone in all the world, does not really apprehend the ethical."[6]

With the human reason Kierkegaard went every inch of the way, but he did not retreat from his position that the imagination and feeling are every whit as important as the intellect. Therefore, though as an author he often used his considerable aesthetic talent to express his ideas strikingly and with poetry and passion, in his personal life and thought he was an ethicist who aspired to the highest level of the religious as expressed in repentance and the ideal of an eternal becoming. His powerful imagination and feeling made him sensitive to the allurements of the aesthetic, but his equally powerful intellect and ethical nature revealed its limitations and the despair and perdition it led to when enthroned as the highest.[7]

Many who reject Kierkegaard do so not only because they misunderstand his ideas but, sometimes even more, because they misconstrue his terms.

In his article, Mr. Fox suggests that Kierkegaard's concept of faith, as represented in his interpretation of Abraham, is *"blind"*. In addition, he takes his concept of the absurd to be synonymous with the senseless. His attempt to discredit Kierkegaard by implying that, as a Christian, he must naturally have been strongly influenced by the stress placed upon mystery in the doc-

trines of Christianity misses the mark. Kierkegaard's interest in Christianity was almost wholly ethical and religious, not doctrinal or mystical. "Christianity," he declared, "is really not a collection of teachings but is—the development of character."[8]

If, as a Christian, he wrestled valiantly in his *Philosophical Fragments* with the paradox of the God-Man, it was fundamentally for the same reason that a pious, philosophical Jew must wrestle with the problem presented by the entrance of eternity into time in any specific revelation of God to man. The problem of revelation as such is equally valid in both Judaism and Christianity, or in any similar faith. It is only the special form which it takes in Christianity that makes it offensive to the Jew. Kierkegaard came as close to Judaism as it is possible for a Christian to come by stipulating that the God-Man would, in any event, have been incognito to ordinary human perception; and any view to the contrary only makes this concept a purely pagan one and, "from the Jewish point of view, idolatry."[9]

What did Kierkegaard understand by faith, and the absurd? Existentially, "faith is the anticipation of the eternal," and brings God into the world as an active spirit in human life. As he stated it, "When an existing individual has not got faith God *is* not, neither does God *exist*."[10] The Rabbis expressed the same idea in a midrash to Isaiah 43.10, Ye are My witnesses, saith the Lord: "When ye are My witnesses, I am God;

---

[5] *Yalkut Shimoni*, Sec. 979, end.
[6] *Concluding Postscript*, tr. by David F. Swenson and Walter Lowrie (Princeton 1944), p. 128.
[7] See *ibid.*, 349.

[8] *The Journals of Soren Kierkegaard*, selected, by Alexander Dru (Oxford University Press 1938), No. 1294.
[9] *Postscript*, 188.
[10] *Journals*, No. 605.

and when ye are not My witnesses, I am not, as it were, God."[11]

Faith, therefore, is not "an easy thing", but "the greatest and the hardest".[12] It is not an endowment so much of the intellect and imagination as of character and feeling. It is a "passion" and consequently cannot be conferred by science, philosophy or reflection,[13] for in such case it would be available principally to the most cultured, whereas it is precisely culture which is often found to be one of the greatest obstacles to faith.

Faith may be possessed by the simplest soul as by the greatest philosopher. For the paradox of faith, according to Kierkegaard, consists in that decisive attitude of the soul which empowers a man to pursue his ideal ends sustained by a belief in a righteous God despite the contradictions, often glaring and tragic, which confound his existence.[14] Hence faith is allied to the category of the absurd,[15] a term used by Kierkegaard to denote not the ridiculous and senseless but the logical contradictions which beset a man when he seeks, in humility and truth, to face the problem of his existence in the world of men in the full consciousness of his God-relationship.

When God commanded Abraham to offer up his beloved son Isaac, this came as a direct contradiction of His promise to Abraham that "in Isaac shall seed be called to thee" (Gen. 21.12). In this contradiction between God's command and His earlier promise Marvin Fox sees the circumstance which renders the episode of the *akedah* unreasonable and even senseless, aside from the even more terrible contradiction that it is God who commands Abraham to offer up his son. Hence he jumps to the conclusion that the Rabbis in the Midrash conceived it as their task to interpret the story in such wise as to enable it to be grasped by the understanding and thus turn, as he says, "an apparent absurdity into a perfectly reasonable event."

In all the Midrashim I have perused, I have not met with one where it is even remotely intimated that the *akedah* was unreasonable or did not make sense. In fact, the opposite is true. Commenting on the verse in Genesis 22.6, "He took in his hand the fire and the knife", the Rabbis declared: "All eating (*akhiloth*) which Israel enjoy in this world, they enjoy only in the merit of that *Ma'akheleth* (knife)."[16] Again, the ass upon which Abraham rode to Mount Moriah, one Midrash says, is the same as that upon which Moses rode on his return to Egypt from Midian, and the same as that upon which the son of

---

11 *Yalkut Shimoni*, Sec. 455, beginning.

12 *Fear and Trembling*, tr. by Walter Lowrie (Princeton 1945), p. 75.

13 Among the most misunderstood of Kierkegaard's terms is that of the "leap of faith". As used by him, this signifies an act of decision which cannot be the product of reflection, and where it appears to be so it is an illusion. See *Journals*, No. 871; *Fear and Trembling*, p. 59, note at bottom, and p. 100. See also *Postscript*, 15 and 90-97.

14 See *Postscript*, 182ff · also *Sickness Unto Death*, 60.

15 According to Kierkegaard, the ultimate expression for the absurd is the figure of the God-Man who represents the paradoxical character of existence at its highest, therefore demands a faith brought to white-hot incandescence in which love of God and trust in Him are expressed with the utmost degree of intensity. As predicated of faith, this is biblical-rabbinic. Its union with the figure of the God-Man is the Christian element. See *Postscript*, 187-91; also *Journals*, No. 871.

16 *Ber. Rabba*, 56.3 (Soncino translation, Vol. I, 493).

David (the Messiah) is destined to come in the future.[17]

In the Midrash, Abraham is revealed considering whether to disclose to Sarah the reason for his journey to Mount Moriah. He decided in the negative on the ground that such revelation could only result in confusion of mind and disaster to her.[18] Abraham's motive in sacrificing Isaac was so private, so inaccessible to any other understanding than his own that it could not be made intelligible to others. This insight of the Midrash, which Kierkegaard in *Fear and Trembling* arrived at independently, is the only standpoint from which the *akedah* makes sense.

The paradox of Abraham's trial consists in the circumstance that it was the result of an individual God-relationship which put him in an "absolute relation to the absolute"[19] and not a God-relationship which could be mediated through the universal, i.e. the group. Under such circumstances Abraham's act cannot be understood or justified from the universal standpoint at all, and Abraham therefore could not attempt to speak and explain the motive for his action. For the essence of language consists in the factor that communication, to be effective, must be reduced to terms of the universal, which is precisely what Abraham could not do with respect to his individual God-relationship and the demand it made upon him.

*Fear and Trembling* represents the work of a man who found in the *akedah* episode, just as it appears in Genesis 22, the answer to the most pressing and agonizing problem of his own life. Kierkegaard staked his whole existence on the proposition that no man could go higher than Abraham as he is revealed in the sacrifice of Isaac, and he set himself the ideal of emulating Abraham's faith though he felt himself far inadequate to the task. Mr. Fox chides Kierkegaard for not presenting Abraham in an attitude of protest against God's command to sacrifice Isaac as he protested to God the destruction of Sodom and Gomorrah. But Kierkegaard in *Fear and Trembling* takes pains to point out that had Abraham wavered, had he prayed to be saved from the ordeal, had he raised his voice in protest against God's command, he could not have become the father of faith and "the guiding star which saves the anguished".[20] And in this viewpoint the Midrash supports Kierkegaard against all censure.

In both the Midrash and *Fear and Trembling* Abraham is revealed going forth joyfully[21] to fulfill the command of God. Despite his agony, he did not relinquish his faith in God's promise that in Isaac he would have an heir who would carry on his name and ideal. This belief could not save him from the anguish he experienced, yet had he been bereft of this faith he could not have become the epitome of faith for the generations.

There is indeed a universal kind of faith, inborn in man, which Kierkegaard names "the first immediacy"[22] and classifies in the sphere of the aesthetical. But the faith which he denominates as such is "not an immediate instinct of

---

[17] See *Rashi* to Exodus 4.20, where the source is given.

[18] *Yalkut Shimoni*, Sec. 101, middle. Cf. Ginzberg, *Legends of the Jews*, Vol. I, 286.

[19] *Fear and Trembling*, 82, 92f., 143.

[20] *Fear and Trembling*, 26.

[21] *Ibid.*, 27. Marvin Fox (*Judaism*, op. cit., 168.) wrongfully accuses Kierkegaard's Abraham of expressing distress but not joy in fulfilling God's command.

[22] *Ibid.*, 125.

the heart", nor "the first immediacy but a subsequent immediacy". This faith of a higher immediacy no man acquires by mere birth. It is not to be possessed without anxiety and dread, yet it does not preclude profound and vibrant joy. Such was the faith which God accounted to Abraham as righteousness, which enabled him to resign Isaac infinitely yet persist in the passionate expectation that God would respond justly and mercifully to his utter trust in Him.

Truly, the righteous man has only his faith as security, for "without risk there is no faith". He who would be absolutely secured in his faith by his reason, or by any other power or property, cannot have faith such as Abraham's. Though Abraham used reason to the limit of his strength, he was not content ultimately with trying to understand God with his mind, a task essentially aesthetical, but leaped to the acceptance of God in the inwardness of his heart as a motivation to self-transformation in the direction of the ethical and religious life.

Kierkegaard's definition of truth coincides with his conception of faith, making the realization of truth for the individual dependent on the existential quality of his faith.[23] This is in harmony with the Rabbinic view of the Torah, the truth for mortals presented by Heaven to earth, which finds its reality fulfilled in a learning that is predicated on a doing.[24] Little wonder that Kierkegaard admonished men not to belittle faith but to regard it as the "greatest and the hardest".

That the *akedah* marks the highest test of Abraham's religious integrity is emphasized in the Midrash and forms

the crux as well of *Fear and Trembling*. In the course of his attempt to clarify the nature of Abraham's trial, Kierkegaard develops the distinction between two types of transgression of the ethical. In the first type, the tragic, one level of the ethical is transgressed for the sake of preserving a higher level of the ethical; but the ethical as such is not transcended. King Agamemnon's sacrifice of his daughter Iphigenia[25] and King Mesha's sacrifice of his son[26] are two examples of such. Had the sacrifice of Isaac been of such a type, had it been done for the sake of preserving a tribe or state from destruction, it would have presented no difficulty to the understanding. The difficulty arises from the factor that the reason for the act does not stem from the sphere of the ethical but from that of the religious. This is a case in which the ethical is itself the temptation, in which Abraham can fulfill the will of God which he has accepted as his duty only by utterly transcending the ethical at the point where it collides with the religious. As it is expressed in *Fear and Trembling*, "What ordinarily tempts a man is that which would keep him from doing his duty, but in this case the temptation is itself the ethical . . . which would keep him from doing God's will."[27]

This is the condition for the concept of the "teleological suspension of the ethical" which Kierkegaard developed in *Fear and Trembling*. Before proceeding to explain the nature of this concept, it is necessary for the sake of clarity to have some notion of what he

---

23 *Postscript*, 181-82.
24 *Pirke Aboth*, I.17.

25 *Fear and Trembling*, 84f., and 201, note 43.
26 II Kings, 3.27.
27 *Fear and Trembling*, 89. Cf. *Postscript*, 231.

meant by the ethical as distinguished from the religious.

By the ethical Kierkegaard meant the "universal". The religious he described as the "universal which stands above the universal".[28] When one's understanding of his religious duty is derived from the ethical, i.e. the universal, the group, there is no essential conflict between the religious and the ethical because both issue from the universal. A conflict between them arises only when the individual relates himself to God in such a direct manner as to suspend the validity of the ethical, the universal, for him. In such a collision there can be no understanding of the individual by the universal, and all attempts at reconciliation are vain for the individual has stepped outside the universal within which alone an explanation can make sense.

The command to sacrifice Isaac represents just such a collision in which the reason for the act cannot be made intelligible to the universal. It is not that Abraham has no reason, but his reason is comprehensible to God and the angels and cannot be made clear in terms of the existing society, Abraham's family.

Perhaps this thought can be illuminated by a comparison with the earlier Abraham who heeded God's command to forsake his father's house for the land which God would show him. According to one Midrash, this earlier command was similar in character to the later command to sacrifice Isaac, a relationship the Midrash establishes by showing, in the first place, that in both the first and last tests God's command to Abraham began with lekh lekha (get

thee) ; and, furthermore, by showing that the numerical value of the Hebrew letters comprising these two words is an hundred, the age at which Abraham begot Isaac.[29]

The Midrash reveals the earlier Abraham as an iconoclast who, by virtue of a new God-relationship, came into conflict with his father's ethic, and that of the society he was born into, so decisively as to preclude any possibility of reconciliation.[30] Eventually, when Abraham heard the command of God to forsake his father's house, a conflict between the ethical and the religious stirred within him. He recognized at once the irony and ambiguity of his position. In God's command there was implicit the command to leave his father in his old age. Thus, in the name of the religious he was bidden to suspend a basic ethical principle, Kibbud Ab, the honor and respect which a son owes to his parents. According to the Rabbis, Abraham remonstrated with God over the command to forsake his father, which would only serve to discredit the Divine Name before the people. But God, according to the Midrash, silenced and reassured Abraham in the following words: "I exempt thee from the duty of honouring thy parents, though I exempt no one else from this duty."[31]

In the Midrash above, we have a pure example of what Kierkegaard in Fear and Trembling meant by the "teleological suspension of the ethical", a term

---

28 Fear and Trembling, 79, 89-90, 102.

29 Yalkut Shimoni, Sec. 62, end; (also Genesis 12.1 and 22.2),

30 See Legends of the · Jews, Vol. I, 195-202, 210-14.

31 Ber. Rabba, 39.7 (Soncino translation, Vol. I, 315-16). Cf. Legends of the Jews I, 217f.

representing a concept[32] for which he has been sharply reproached and condemned in the name of Judaism by his Jewish critics[33] who have judged him without understanding him or the Midrash.

In leaving his father despite his reverence for the principle of *Kibbud Ab*, Abraham did not intend to *abolish* the ethical principle that the son must respect and honor his parents. However, when such an ethical rule conflicts with the demand which the religious makes upon the individual, then *in such instance* the ethical must be suspended in favor of the higher religious *telos*, even at the risk of having the act falsely interpreted as a sign of hate or disrespect. In truth, had Abraham hated his father there could have been no teleological suspension, for then he would have left him because he hated him and not *despite* the fact that he honored him. Where there is no love for the ethical there cannot be a teleological suspension of the ethical, for the latter results from choosing the religious over the ethical in a conflict between the two within the same individual,[33a] and not out of a reaction caused by hate or vengefulness.

Similarly in the *akedah* episode, the ethical rule that the father must love his son is not abrogated. Abraham loves Isaac as much as or more than himself. Therefore the universal would forbid him from slaying his son except for a reason which is clear to it. But since

---

[32] Even Dr. Walter Lowrie, Kierkegaard's eminent translator, biographer and interpreter does not seem to have a *clear* notion of this concept. The illustration from "merciful killing" which he gives in his big book *Kierkegaard* (New York 1938), pp. 329-30, is not, in this writer's opinion, a true example of a teleological suspension of the ethical.

In this connection it might be noted that Kierkegaard mentions another form of this same concept "in relation to the communication of truth" which also has its counterpart in Rabbinic thought. See *The Point of View*, tr. by Walter Lowrie (New York 1939), p. 91, also *Stages on Life's Way*, p. 218, and *Rashi* to Exodus 3.14. The manner in which Kierkegaard applied this form of teleological suspension in the relation of Jesus to the Apostles may be noted in his work *Training in Christianity*, tr by Walter Lowrie (Princeton 1944), p. 184.

[33] Besides Marvin Fox in *Judaism*, op. cit.,— Rabbi Joseph Gumbiner, "Existentialism and Father Abraham," in *Commentary*, February 1948; and the late Rabbi Milton Steinberg, "Kierkegaard and Judaism," in the *Menorah Journal*, Spring 1949. Martin Buber's essays on Kierkegaard are dealt with at the end of the present article.

[33a] To forestall possible criticism that Kierkegaard's concept of the teleological suspension of the ethical opens the way to justification of persecution by one religious group of another, such as the persecution by the Inquisition of the Jews, the following points may be offered:

(1) As presented by Kierkegaard, this concept can apply only to the individual in relation to his group, large or small, with which he comes into conflict. The individual, as the result of his unique stand, may thus be made to suffer, on the part of his group, isolation, ostracism, persecution, and even the attempt upon his life—all of which indeed, as depicted in the Midrash, Abraham suffered at the hands of his father and the tyrant Nimrod. But this concept cannot apply to a dominant individual or group.

(2) Kierkegaard's religious views caused him to stand unalterably opposed to a union of the State with religion, and to the use of material force in any form, including that of the State, to enforce the religious. Therefore he fought the Established Church in his native land Denmark. It was his contention that when Christianity early in its history became united with the State, it ceased to be the authentic Christianity of Jesus, the Apostles, and the "witnesses to the truth", but became instead, for this and other reasons, the opposite of the original while holding on to the name. Hence Kierkegaard regarded it as his life's work to expose the "deceit", as he called it, and to begin the task, in a religious manner, of reintroducing Christianity into Christendom.

God's command to Abraham to sacrifice Isaac cannot be made clear to the universal, Abraham must appear to it as a murderer. This precisely is the point that is stressed both in the Midrash and in *Fear and Trembling.* In the Midrash the point is brought out in Satan's warning to Abraham that viewed from the standpoint of the universal, the *din*[34] or law, he cannot be judged in any other light than as guilty, a consequence Abraham accepted. The Midrash stresses the conflict in Abraham's soul between the religious and the ethical, precisely as Kierkegaard delineated it in *Fear and Trembling.*

Kierkegaard saw in Abraham's life only one instance of a teleological suspension of the ethical. But, as indicated above, the Rabbis noted two such instances. Rabbi Levi bar Chayyatha[35] declared that as between the first and last temptations imposed upon Abraham by his God-relationship, namely the command to leave his father and the command to sacrifice his son, it was the last which endeared him most to God. The Midrash leaves no opening for any insipid rationalization. Abraham's last (tenth) trial, it is affirmed, "was as weighty as all the rest together, and had he not submitted to it, all would have been lost."[36]

As depicted in the Midrash, between Abraham and Isaac there existed a perfect accord: Isaac was as strongly moved to be sacrificed [37] as Abraham was to sacrifice him. Kierkegaard's position, however, which *Fear and Trembling* poetized, was different. Like Abraham, he too heeded the divine voice within

him which bade him sacrifice his Isaac, the girl he loved. But unlike Isaac, Regina rebelled desperately against being sacrificed, that is to say, she refused to grant him his freedom at his request in an amicable severance of their engagement. The paradox he could not explain directly, that it was for her sake as much as his own, from love of her and not from disaffection, that he was inspired to dissolve the engagement, he felt under compulsion to explain through the indirect medium which only poetry permitted. This was one of his chief motives in writing *Fear and Trembling* as a "dialectical lyric" and revealing himself to the extent that this could be done in a Midrash on Abraham's sacrifice of Isaac. But this also explains in part the title of the book, the deeper implications of which Marvin Fox, and others, have misconstrued.

To Kierkegaard, Abraham was the prototype of the single individual who is faced by the necessity of reaching a determination in which no other man can help him and which will be decisive for his whole existence. The voice of God he hears within him, which bids him sacrifice his beloved Isaac, is this God's voice or only an hallucination and self-delusion? This is what makes his decision so filled with dread and fear and trembling. "If the individual had misunderstood the deity—what can save him? . . . If then the solitary man who ascends Mount Moriah . . . if this man is disordered in his mind, if he had made a mistake!"[38]

This problem raised by Kierkegaard is precisely the problem presented in the Midrash through the figure of Samael who admonishes Abraham to consider whether his intended act is not

[34] *Yalkut Shimoni,* Sec. 98, end.

[35] *Ber. Rabbah,* 55.7 (Soncino translation I, p. 487).

[36] *Ibid.,* 56.11 (Soncino tr., I p. 501).

[37] *Ibid.,* 55.4 (Soncino tr., I p. 485).

[38] *Fear and Trembling,* 90f.

the act of a man of disordered mind. Is this veritably God's command? Consider, Samael warns, "Tomorrow He will say to thee, 'Thou art a murderer, and art guilty!'"[39] To which Abraham replied simply, "Still am I content!" the only reply the man of faith can make who decides in the purity of his heart and consciousness. And when Samael approached Isaac with the same appeal, he too replied simply, "I accept my fate."

It is a tribute to Kierkegaard's love of truth that he did not fear ridicule and misunderstanding as much as he feared self-deception, a trait which saved him from fanaticism and enabled him to see himself with as much irony and humor as he viewed others. He justified his breach with Regina as a teleological suspension of the ethical duty to marry. By this sacrifice he believed, with as much certainty as human calculation and foresight could assure, that he accomplished two things in one stroke: he saved her as well as himself from future unhappiness and ruination, and simultaneously returned as a penitent with undiminished spirit to the full measure of his God-relationship.

Like any Midrash worth its salt, Kierkegaard's interpretation of Abraham in *Fear and Trembling* mirrors his own existential and intellectual collisions. This point is no less true of the Rabbis in the Midrash who poured into the figures of Abraham and Isaac their own idealizations of the ethico-religious life.

As the Rabbis saw Abraham, the two highest points in his life were his submission to the command to leave his father's house and the command which set him on the journey to Mount Moriah. In his youth he had not hesitated to suspend even his livelihood when it

clashed with the higher *telos* of his God-relationship. This was the Abraham who later prayed that his ideal might be secured by a son to whom it might be transmitted. But with Isaac's birth, the Midrash implies, he shrank from relating his beloved son to the hard demands of the lofty ideal which had been the substance of his own life.

Before Isaac was born, Satan complained before God, Abraham "served Thee and erected altars to Thee wherever he came, and he brought offerings upon them, and he proclaimed Thy name continually to all the children of the earth. And now his son Isaac is born to him, he has forsaken Thee." The gist of Satan's charge was that Abraham having got in Isaac the son he prayed for, "he therefore forsook Thee." This, Satan declared, was the common trait of mankind who serve and remember God when "they require aught" from Him; but, "when Thou givest them what they require from Thee, then they forsake Thee, and they remember Thee no more."[40]

In these Midrashim, Satan is not portrayed as the mighty antagonist who struggles with God for the souls of men and delights in their downfall. On the contrary, he is depicted as God's protagonist, man's guilty conscience and the accuser before the bar of his highest God-relationship. Having got the son he desired in Isaac, Satan implied, Abraham was content thereafter to sink back into the life of the natural man whose highest goal is not concern for the poor but the achievement of honor and self-esteem among his fellows with an undisturbed, pagan-like contentment and happiness.

---

[39] *Ber. Rabbah*, 56.4 (Soncino tr., I, p. 494).

[40] See *Legends of the Jews*, Vol. I, 272-73.

Thus, instead of strengthening Abraham in his ideal, Isaac innocently became the occasion of Abraham's relapse from his God-relationship. The trial to which God put him at the instigation of Satan was therefore a test to prove him. The journey to Mount Moriah is the act of a repentant soul seeking to make atonement before his God. In the light of repentance one course lay open to Abraham: he must dedicate Isaac to God, sacrifice and resign him without reservation. To the question, how the sacrifice was to be effected, the crashing climax came with a suddenness that left him dazed. The sacrifice was not to be made in a bloody slaughter upon the altar (the ram which suddenly appeared could fulfill that category),[41] but by devoting his son to the promise for which he had been given in the first place, an ideal which would demand its full toll in spiritual as well as physical distress and suffering.

What is confusing to the ordinary mind about the *akedah* is that Isaac was not sacrificed at once upon the altar like the son of Mesha, the Moabite king, whom the Midrash condemns for literally slaughtering his son, in the manner of a tragic hero, as an act of repentance for the sake of the state. Had Abraham sacrificed Isaac in this manner, the Midrash declares, his sacrifice would have been as unacceptable to God as Mesha's. Abraham's sacrifice was acceptable because it was made in humility before God, not for the sake of victory and power in themselves, but to the cause of doing justice and loving mercy.[42]

In the view of tragic heroism, it is in the surrender of the beloved to death that the heroism manifests itself. To the universal hero, life in the midst of and dedicated to his people is the highest good, and death which cuts off is the terrible. But to the knight of faith it is not by death but by his life that he becomes a hero and the beloved of God. To the hero of faith who loves the universal, yet may be pitted against it by his devotion to the ethico-religious as the highest, it is existence which is fraught with risk and suffering, existence which is the terrible, in which he dies the death, and death itself when it comes is often only a release. Thus Jeremiah wept for the day he was born, not for the day he would die: "Woe is me, my mother, that thou hast born me, a man of strife and a man of contention to the whole earth!"[43]

The ram caught by its horns in the thickets, in its struggles to reach the altar which Abraham erected for the sacrifice of Isaac, was identified by the Rabbis in the Midrash with the descendants of Isaac caught in the successive oppressions of the nations and empires, yet determined, despite this, to exist by the divine Law and to make this existence the highest and truest form of worship and sacrifice to God.

It is from this aspect of dedication to the ethico-religious life that Abraham's sacrifice of Isaac must be seen to understand its true significance and its differentiation from the sacrifice of Mesha's son. The sacrifice for the sake of victory is immediately recognizable and applauded by the universal mass of men. But the sacrifice for the sake of the idea is rarely so obvious and therein lies its lonely suffering, on account of which the mass of mankind shun it with horror.

---

41 *Ber. Rabbah*, 56.9 (Soncino tr., I, p. 499).
42 *Ibid.*, 55.5; see especially Soncino tr., I, p. 485 and note 3.

43 Jeremiah 15.10; see also 20.14.

In the existence of the natural man, the allurement of some type of worldly reward is the motivation. But in a God-relationship such as Abraham espoused and transmitted to Isaac, suffering is the highest that may be anticipated, which will come to an end only when God blows upon the horn that will sound the signal for the final redemption. Thus the *akedah* denotes the sacrifice of the natural man's disposition to Torah, and its transmutation in the direction of *yirah*, the religious, with self-commitment to the ethical life which the religious presumes. In this effort at transformation of the self, enjoyment and gladness are not outlawed but are sublimated into the *simchah shel mitzvah*, the joy in which existence is sanctified to God, and not mere natural enjoyment which the natural man makes the only measure of worthwhile existence and which finds its fruition, as in the child and youth, in the functioning of the human endowments and capacities for their own sake.

Similarly, to Kierkegaard Christianity implied a confession which, to be authentic, must be activated in a persistent struggle away from the instinctive, unreflective natural man, i.e. immediacy. The goal envisaged is a change in character in conformity with the religious as it passes through the ethical, resulting in a suffering which can never cease because the end of the process can never be reached. When Christianity is tied in with privileges so that it becomes a positive handicap and disadvantage not to be a Christian in the formal sense, that is a sure sign that that which is paraded and espoused is not Christianity.

What Kierkegaard fought against was the watering down of the ethico-religious requirements to the point where religion is reduced to a matter of doctrine, a conventional triviality, or mere childish sentimentality. True Christianity, he held, was an ideal to be striven after, a becoming, not a sapped and devitalized entity of little ethical consequence from a practical standpoint. Therefore, from the very beginning, he ironically disclaimed *being* a Christian, but claimed only that his life was dedicated to *becoming* one. Far from dissociating himself from Christendom, his attack upon it, towards the end of his life, was inspired by a feeling of concern for its future and the future of authentic religion.

Stripped of its dialectic, Kierkegaard's life-view was extraordinarily simple, so much so indeed as to brand as a simpleton in the eyes of the world the man who would live by it. "The highest of all," he contended, "is not to understand the highest but to act upon it."[44] Understanding the highest was not so difficult and often enough earned the world's honor and esteem. But to act upon it was to end by earning the world's contumely, and it was for this that he braced himself, though not without dread.

"Humbug" is the word he uses to denote the modern pseudo-religious, shallow faith which frowns on dread and bans fear of God from its teaching of love of God. He contended that in authentic religious faith dread (*Angest*) is a prime factor. But though he made much of the term, he was thoroughly aware that the concept itself is rooted

[44] Journals, op. cit., No. 1248. Compare with statements in *Training in Christianity*, op. cit., p. 201: "Christianly understood, the truth consists not in knowing the truth but in being the truth." "No man knows more of the truth than what he is of the truth."

in the Jewish faith. "It is commonly said," he wrote, "that Judaism represents the standpoint of the law. This, however, may be expressed also by saying that Judaism lies in dread" and proves by this fact that it "is further advanced than Hellenism".[45]

The presence of dread, according to Kierkegaard, is a sign that the individual possesses spirit, and its absence is the mark of spiritlessness. What superficial religiousness tries to hide from is that there is a dread of the good as well as of the evil. Immanuel Kant adumbrated this thought which Kierkegaard developed in his book *The Concept of Dread*. "Love to the law," declared Kant, "must be the constant though unattainable goal . . . what we highly esteem, but yet (on account of the consciousness of our weakness) dread."[46]

In Kierkegaard's analysis, dread is given a dual character, being at one and the same time "sympathetic" and "antipathetic". That the Jews should have joyfully accepted the Torah after the tribes and nations of the world rejected it, as the Midrash relates, represents the sympathetic aspect of the concept of dread. The antipathetic aspect is exemplified by the Midrash in which the Israelites are shown accepting the Torah only under duress, after having been warned that their refusal would only result in their being crushed under the mountain.

The gladness and fear alike which characterize Judaism and Jewish worship is admirably expressed in the admonition of the Psalmist: "Serve the

Lord with fear, and rejoice with trembling" (Psalms 2.11). Similarly, the Midrashim quoted above emphasize that the Law, the covenant with God to obey His commands and hearken to His Torah, is at once the source of Israel's glory and the occasion of its guilt. The Law will not lessen its demands because of the fear that men will be unable to fulfill its requirements and so come to grief in guilt. In his dread of guilt, Paul the apostle renounced the Law in the name of faith. But unlike Paul, Kierkegaard, as I understand him, would not abrogate the Law, for after guilt there is always repentance from which to make a new beginning in the Law's fulfilment. According to him, not to annihilate dread, but to prevail over it, is the task given to faith by "continually developing itself out of the death throe of dread", precisely as in the *Yamim Nora'im* (The Days of Dread) in Judaism where faith and trust prevail over dread.

If despair, as Kierkegaard affirmed, is the mark of immaturity and the "lack of the eternal", then dread is the sign, particularly in Judaism, that the individual has attained to maturity and has become aware of the absolute claim which the ethical and religious make upon his existence.

Kierkegaard's interpretation in *Fear and Trembling* differs from the account of the *akedah* as interpreted in the Midrash in one important respect, namely in the figure of Isaac. Hewing to the biblical account, as usually understood, Kierkegaard presents Isaac as a beloved but wholly subordinate character who has no bond of understanding with his father. Isaac is put into the category of the universal along with Sarah and Eleazar. He has no independent God-

---

45 *The Concept of Dread*, tr. by Walter Lowrie (Princeton 1946), p. 92. For what follows see also pp. 84ff., 104, and the section on the "Dread of the Good, beginning p. 105.

46 See Kant: Selections, ed. by T. M. Greene (Charles Scribner's Sons 1929), p. 330.

relationship of his own. He no more than Sarah can be told in a way that can make sense to him why he is to be sacrificed. At the last moment, when the true purpose of the journey to Mount Moriah is revealed to him and he falls at his father's feet in a piteous plea for his life, Abraham must turn upon him in the guise of a madman, so as not to appear to his son as a murderer, and strangle him with his hand before slaying him with the knife.[47]

As revealed in the Midrash, however, Isaac possesses a God-relationship which is his not at second hand but by virtue of a free act of his own will. It was only after he prayed to become a sacrifice to God that God imposed the trial upon Abraham. The Midrash derives the unity of spirit which bound father and son from the fact that the place whither God commanded Abraham to go was rendered visible to both of them by the sign of a pillar of fire "and a heavy cloud in which the glory of God was seen".[48] This sign was not rendered visible to Ishmael and Eleazar who accompanied them, by which a spiritual distinction was indicated.

In *Fear and Trembling* and in the Midrash alike Abraham is depicted as a figure who towers aloft as a "knight of faith", to use the term employed in Kierkegaard's work to distinguish Abraham from the "tragic hero". But what the Midrash also shows is Isaac's equally strong and self-sustaining spirit which enabled him to respond to the demands which the God-relationship of his father made indirectly upon him. For Abraham's trial was simultaneously a test of Isaac. Each acted independently, each

was a "knight of faith" in his own right. Indeed, there is a Jewish tradition which lauds Isaac as a hero of faith above Abraham.

With his acute grasp of biblical Hebrew, the noted commentator Arnold B. Ehrlich indicates that in the verse from Genesis 22.8, "They went both of them together," the word "together" implies here, as it does in Amos 3.3, concerted action springing from an independent resolution on the part of each of the participants.[48a] Thus Ehrlich, through pure textual exegesis, substantiates the view that the interpretation of Isaac in the Midrash as a hero of faith in his own right is not in opposition to the Bible, artificially imposed upon it by Rabbinic tradition, but is implicit within the biblical text itself. Although the commonly-accepted view of Isaac as a passive figure comported best with Kierkegaard's own existential situation adumbrated in *Fear and Trembling*, nevertheless, with his typically whimsical and sharp-witted insight, he acknowledged, through his pseudonym Johannes *de silentio*, that if only "he had known Hebrew",[48b] this might have helped him more truly to understand Abraham and the sacrifice of Isaac.

As depicted in the Midrash, Isaac's independent faith and self-dedication, which made it possible for the father to confide in the son and for the son to receive the confidence, must have been crucial in effecting the restoration of the son to the father. But in the case of Kierkegaard and Regina (his Isaac), what caused him ultimately to repel her

---

[47] See *Fear and Trembling*, 11f.
[48] *Legends of the Jews*, I, 278; also *Ber. Rabbah* 56.2 (Soncino tr. I, 491).

[48a] Ehrlich *Randglossen zur Hebraischen Bibel* (Leipsig 1908), Vol. I, 95, and Vol. V, 234. This writer has Dr. Robert Gordis to thank for pointing out the existence of this comment by Ehrlich.
[48b] *Fear and Trembling*, 10.

(for her sake even more than his own) despite his undying love for her was that his spirit, which enfolded his love and his faith alike, was not matched in her by an independent spirit to which he could reveal and confide himself in his "idea", a point he deemed essential to validate the ethical character of the marriage. Therefore he resigned her in a finite sense and only in eternity did he hope to be joined with her.

Kierkegaard believed that *Fear and Trembling* alone, aside from his other works, was destined to make his name famous and to be translated into many languages. In this work, with no knowledge of the Midrash and only by the prodigious powers of his dialectical mind and imagination, he re-created single-handedly the essential features of the Rabbinic interpretation of Abraham. His comments on this book in his *Journals* and in his *Concluding Postscript* give no hint that he had any notion that his superb interpretation of Abraham had already been accomplished centuries before him by the Rabbis.

In common with Christians of his age (and, with the exception of a bare handful, of ours as well), he had only a distorted notion of the true character and spiritual creativeness of Rabbinic Judaism in the time of Jesus. (In the *Postscript* he characterized it as "superannuated"). Like nearly all Christians, he appropriated as Christian what he liked in the Hebrew Scriptures, added this to what he liked in the Greek Testament; then with the usual Christian ignorance of Rabbinic Judaism, he performed the exercise of exhibiting the superiority of Christianity (as he interpreted it) over Judaism. However, what distinguishes him from other Christian theologians and philosophers

(including Immanuel Kant) [49] is the absence in his works of all signs of vindictiveness against Jews and Judaism. He would undoubtedly have been amazed to learn that the category of the ethico-religious, which he championed in his works and desired to reintroduce into Christianity as its predominant feature above the doctrinal and historical, constitutes the core of Rabbinic Judaism as it stands revealed in the Midrash.

As in Judaism, Kierkegaard subordinated aesthetics, philosophy and the sciences to the ethico-religious as the highest. He was not thankless for what culture had to offer and not unaware of its benefits, but he perceived that to give it the status of the highest was to give up authentic religion and open the gateway to paganism, despair and pessimism. In the sphere of faith, he contended, the simple man and the cultured stood equally on the common level of their simple humanity, except that faith was perhaps easier for the simple man to embrace than for the philosopher and the scientist. Yet faith was the highest pinnacle for human beings because it signalized the ethico-religious and provided the latter with its dynamic power and movement.

Kierkegaard possessed a midrashic type of thinking and expression which, to my mind, makes his works valuable to one who would penetrate to the heart of Judaism in its Haggadic form. Conversely, a knowledge of the Midrash helps to illuminate Kierkegaard's works and type of thinking. Of his several Jewish critics, only Martin Buber has something to say about him which shows any appreciation and understanding of

---

[49] See Kant *Religion Within the Limits of Reason Alone*, tr. by T. M. Greene and H. H. Hudson (Chicago 1934), 117ff.

his ideas. But even he cannot be relied upon as a guide and interpreter of Kierkegaard without the greatest caution. To give one example. In his essay, "On the Suspension of the Ethical,"[50] Buber charges that in *Fear and Trembling* it is "self-evident" for Kierkegaard, because of his Christian tradition, that the voice Abraham heard commanding him to sacrifice his son was veritably the voice of God, without considering the problem that it might only be a satanic voice. In fact, however, this is a question which not only Kierkegaard, but the Midrash as well, considered, as was shown above in this article (p. 39).

To give another example. In his essay, "The Question to the Single One,"[51] Buber gravely misrepresents Kierkegaard by implying that he regarded himself (consciously or not) as a religious genius. The fact is that, though Kierkegaard frankly knew himself to be a genius, it was one of his most dearly held articles of faith that there was no such thing as a *religious* genius, and he continued in this conviction despite all apparent evidence to the contrary. The ethico-religious life-view to which he held (which while embracing the temporal did not stop there but swept on to the eternal), a life-view basic to Judaism as well, Kierkegaard believed could be the possession of every one who willed it with enough passion and tenacity, "whether he be Abraham or a slave in Abraham's house, whether he be a professor of philosophy or a servant-girl."[52] The difference between the simple man and the genius in the sphere of the existential, the ethical, was not to be found, he held, in the possibility of ethical action but only in the profundity of the reflection. "*Poetic* pathos is differential pathos," he asserted. But "*existential* pathos is poor man's pathos, pathos for every man. Every human being can act within himself, and one sometimes finds in a servant-girl the pathos which one seeks for in vain in the existence of a poet."[53] (My italics.)

It is certain in my own mind that when he wrote "The Question to the Single One," Buber did not have an adequate conception of what Kierkegaard meant to convey by such terms as the "individual", the "crowd", the "religious", the "monastery". He shows the questionable tendency of making massive generalizations on individual striking utterances without sufficiently taking into account the vast existential and intellectual hinterland out of which the utterances emerge and which they poetically represent. Thus he commits a serious injustice to Kierkegaard's name by wilfully concluding that Kierkegaard's not marrying Regina can be taken as a symbol of his rejection of woman and the world.[54] He seems totally unaware in his essay that his refutations of Kierkegaard's thought as he apprehended it are often only a reitera-

---

[50] In Martin Buber *Eclipse of God* (New York 1952), 152f.

[51] In Martin Buber *Between Man And Man*, tr. by Ronald Gregor Smith (London 1947), p. 57.

[52] *Fear and Trembling*, 51.

[53] *Postscript*, 353. See also *Point of View*, pp. 119, 126, 129; *Training In Christianity*, 235.

[54] See Buber *Between Man and Man*, op. cit., 59f. Kierkegaard indeed censures the type of marriage in which the woman's influence is exerted in weakening the ethico-religious fiber of the man. See *Training in Christianity*, op. cit., p. 119. Like the prophets of the Bible he also rejected the "world", that is, the natural man's world, but aimed to replace it with the religious man's world.

tion in his own words of what Kierkegaard himself said. Nevertheless, Buber's essay shows an appreciation of Kierkegaard's thinking and a perception of his importance which his other Jewish critics, among them Marvin Fox, lack entirely.

Kierkegaard was aware that he gave a new ethical meaning to the concept of faith which before him did not exist in Christianity (but is present in the Hebrew Scriptures). He implanted the religious so deeply at the core of his own existence that the orthodox might well be beguiled into the error of claiming him as one of themselves. While he was sympathetic to the external practices of the religious life, what he emphasized pre-eminently was the spirit that awoke the individual to ethical awareness. He held that the only reality of which a person could be sure was his own ethical reality, and this is the meaning of his dictum, which constitutes the heart of the *Concluding Postscript,* that "truth is subjectivity".

Did Kierkegaard look upon himself in some sort of way as a prophet or apostle? Decidedly not, for he recognized that genius by itself belongs to a wholly different category. Did he consider himself at least as a wise or holy man? Again, no. Kierkegaard saw himself simply as a "fellow student",[55] in Rabbinic terms, a *talmid chakham.* He looked upon his books as the development of his own education. This explains in part why he sought no disciples for he considered himself throughout most of his life as only a learner and not a teacher. It was only near the end of his life that he felt his own education to be sufficiently complete to come forth boldly and enunciate his message to the populace in the simple language of the common man.

If the applications which Kierkegaard, as a Christian, makes in his works to the God-Man and other Christian *sancta* are discounted, it must be admitted that a study of his books and writings reveals a remarkable coincidence between his and the Rabbinic type of thinking found in Midrash Haggadah which can only be described as extraordinary. Futhermore, a comparison between his ideas and life-goal and Ahad Ha-am's famous essay, "Priest and Prophet,"[56] will testify that it was the prophetic, in contrast to the priestly, spirit which he invoked,—which indeed he interpreted as being identical with true Christianity,[57]—and which he attempted unconditionally and uncompromisingly to follow in his own life and thought. His category of the "single individual" which enables one "to be an independent force in the world",[58] which he held to be the highest religious category and by which he strove to model his own existence while calling upon all without exception to do the same, is practically identical with Ahad Ha-am's exposition of the prophetic character and role in life.

The nature of his own life task Kierkegaard summed up in a judgment which he uttered upon himself: "He himself was 'that individual', if no one else was, and he became that more and more."

---

[55] *The Point of View,* op. cit., 75.

[56] In Ahad Ha'am *Selected Essays,* tr. by Leon Simon (Philadelphia, 1912). In Hebrew, *Al Parashath D'rachim,* Vol. I.

[57] "Christianity is the absolute". See Kierkegaard *For Self-Examination and Judge for Yourselves!* tr. by Walter Lowrie (Princeton 1944) p. 125; also 123, 128, 167, etc. This corresponds to Ahad Ha'am's view that the prophetic is equivalent to the absolute.

[58] See *Training in Christianity,* op. cit., p. 57, translator's note at bottom.

# The Shulhan 'Aruk:
# Enduring Code of Jewish Law

ISADORE TWERSKY

*Shulḥan 'Aruk,* A TERM TAKEN OVER FROM early rabbinic exegesis in the Midrash[1] and applied to one of the most influential, truly epochal literary creations of Jewish history, has a double or even triple meaning, and its use therefore necessitates precise definition or description. *Shulḥan 'Aruk* is the title given by R. Joseph Karo (1488-1575) to a brief, four-part code of Jewish law which was published in 1565-66, just over four hundred years ago. *Shulḥan 'Aruk* also designates a composite, collaborative work, combining this original text of R. Joseph Karo, a Spanish emigré from Toledo (1492) who lived and studied in Turkey and finally settled in Palestine in a period of turbulence and instability and apocalyptic stirrings, with the detailed glosses —both strictures and supplements—of R. Moses Isserles (c. 1525-1572), a well-to-do Polish scholar, proud of his Germanic background, who studied in Lublin and became de facto chief rabbi of Cracow in a period of relative stability and tranquillity. This unpremeditated literary symbiosis then generated a spate of commentaries and supercommentaries, brief or expansive, defensive or dissenting, from the *Sefer Me'irat 'Enayim* of R. Joshua Falk and the *Sefer Siftei Kohen* of R. Shabbetai ha-Kohen to the *Mishnah Berurah* of R. Israel Meir ha- Kohen; and the term *Shulḥan 'Aruk* continued to be applied to this multi-dimensional, multi-generational, ever-expanding folio volume—a fact which attests the resiliency and buoyancy of the Halachic tradition in Judaism. A person must, therefore, define his frame of reference when he purports to glorify or vilify, to acclaim or condemn—or, if he is able to avoid value judgments,

---

1. *Mekilta* on *Exodus* 21:1, ed. J. Z. Lauterbach (Philadelphia, 1935), v. III, p. 1: " 'And these are the ordinances which thou shalt set before them.' Arrange them in proper order before them like a set table (*shulḥan 'aruk*)." See Rashi on this verse, who adds, "like a table set before a person with everything ready for eating." Attention should be paid to the identical use of this phrase in the thirteenth century by R. Menahem ha-Me'iri to describe his Talmudic opus; see introduction to *Bet ha-Beḥirah* on *Berakot* (Jerusalem, 1960), p. 31. Also, R. Solomon ibn Adret uses this metaphor in verbal form in the introduction to his *Torat ha-BaByit.*

Leo Baeck, *This People Israel* (Philadelphia, 1965), p. 301, suggests another association: "When Joseph Karo chose his title, he almost certainly had in mind that psalm which begins, 'He Who is my shepherd; I shall not want' and continues, 'Thou preparest a table before me in the presence of mine enemies' (*Ps.* 23)."

---

ISADORE TWERSKY *is Nathan Littauer Professor of Hebrew Literature and Chairman of the Department of Near Eastern Languages and Literatures at Harvard University.*

to describe historically.[2] The genuinely modest purpose of the following remarks is, first, to chronicle the emergence of the *Shulḥan ʿAruk*, especially in its first and second meanings, and then to describe a few of its salient literary and substantive characteristics. "The rest is commentary," which we should go and study.

## I

IN THE YEAR 1522,[3] R. JOSEPH KARO, a young, struggling, volatile and ascetic scholar, having settled temporarily and discontentedly in Adrianople, Turkey, launched a massive literary project that would preoccupy him, sometimes at a frenetic pace, for over thirty years—twenty years in the composition and about twelve years in editorial revision and refinement.[4] The stimulus was provided by the worrisome decline in scholarship—" and the wisdom of their wise men shall perish"—[5] coming in the wake of the rigors and vicissitudes of exile, the endless turbulence of history, and the increasing human imperfection.[6] The need was great for a comprehensive as well as authoritative guide, which would stem the

2. Contemporaries would sometimes criticize the *Shulḥan ʿAruk*, even stridently, but it was left for modern, post-Enlighenment writers to vilify it. See, for example, the references in L. Greenwald, *R. Joseph Karo u-Zemano* (New York, 1954), pp. 174–176; B. Cohen, *Law and Tradition in Judaism* (New York, 1959), pp. 66–68; R. J. Z. Werblowsky, *Joseph Karo* (Oxford, 1962), p. 7; *Jewish Encyclopedia*, III, p. 588.

Actually, there is no need even for devotees of the *Shulḥan ʿAruk* to indulge in meta-historical panegyrics, for supernatural phenomena carry no weight in Halachic matters. The *Shulḥan ʿAruk* is not a revealed canon, nor is it a hypostasis of the Law. In the long, creative history of the Oral Law, it is one major link connecting R. Hai Gaon, Maimonides, Naḥmanides and R. Solomon ibn Adret with R. Elijah Gaon of Vilna, R. Akiba Eiger, and R. Yosef Rosen. It is a significant work which, for a variety of reasons, became a repository and stimulus, a treasure and inspiration for Halachah, both practice and study.

3. What follows is based essentially on the authors' own, often autobiographical narratives: R. Joseph Karo's introductions to the *Bet Yosef* and R. Moses Isserles' introduction to the *Darke Mosheh*, which can conveniently be found in the Jerusalem, 1958 reprint of the *Turim*. I have interpolated historical or other explanatory comments, but have not seen fit to burden the reader with cumbersome references. I wanted simply to recount their tale.

4. He came to Palestine and settled in Safed in the year 1536. See Professor Z. Dimitovsky in *Sefunot*, VII, p. 62, n. 137.

5. The verse is *Isaiah* 29:14 and is quoted in similar context by Maimonides, introduction to the *Mishneh Torah*. The correlation of political adversity and intellectual decline becomes a constant theme and appears almost as a stereotype justification for Halachic abridgements or codifications. Difficult times necessitate the composition of books which would facilitate the study and perpetuate the practice of Halachah. Note, for example, the introduction to the *Turim*. See my *Rabad of Posquières* (Cambridge, 1962), pp. 133–134, n. 9.

6. This reflects the widespread attitude of humility, even self-effacement, expressed in the Talmudic dictum: "If those before us were sons of angels, we are sons of men, and if those before us were sons of men, we are like asses" (*Shabbat*, 122b; *Yoma*, 9b). It is typical of the deep-rooted veneration traditionally displayed by later scholars to early masters. However, it did not, as we shall see, restrict independence of mind or stifle creative innovation. Fidelity and freedom were felicitously combined.

undesirable and almost uncontrollable proliferation of texts and provide a measure of religious uniformity in this period of great turmoil and dislocation. This would be accomplished, however, not by producing another compact, sinewy manual—a small volume such as the *Agur*, which R. Karo treats perjoratively[7]—but by reviewing the practical Halachah in its totality. The oracular type of code, containing curt, staccato directives and pronouncements, was neither adequate nor reliable. It did not provide for intellectual stimulus and expansion of the mind, nor did it offer correct guidance in religious practice.

R. Joseph Karo's ambitious undertaking in the field of rabbinic literature, entitled the *Bet Yosef (House of Joseph)*,[8] was thus motivated by the need to review "all the practical laws of Judaism, explaining their roots and origins in the Talmud" and all the conflicting interpretations concerning them. No extant work answered to this need. In order to avoid duplication or reduce it to a bare minimum, he decided to build his own work around an existing code that was popular and authoritative. He selected the *Turim* of R. Jacob b. Asher (c. 1280-1340) rather than the more famous and widespread *Mishneh Torah* of R. Moses b. Maimon, because the latter was too concise and monolithic, presenting, on the whole, unilateral, undocumented decisions, while the former was expansive and more interpretive, citing alternate views and divergent explanations. At this stage, then, the text of the *Turim* was only a pretext for his own work.[9] His method was to explain every single law in the text, note its original source, and indicate whether the formulation found in the *Turim* was the result of consensus or was subject to dispute. He would, furthermore, explain the alternate interpretations and formulations which the *Turim* referred to but rejected. In addition, he would introduce and elucidate those views which the *Turim* had totally omitted from consideration. As a purely theoretical increment, he promised to examine and explain those views of predecessors—especially Maimonides—which were problematic or remained obscure despite the availability

---

7. Why this small work, written by R. Jacob Landau at the end of the fifteenth century, is singled out for special criticism is not clear. The reason may be that it was simply one of the most recent representatives of this genre. Or was R. Joseph Karo provoked by the author's declaration that he produced this compendium in order to satisfy the minimal needs of Halachic study in the most economical way so as to provide ample time for philosophic study?

8. He thus incorporated his first name into the title—again, pretty much standard literary procedure. There is, however, an added homiletical explanation: just as the house of Joseph in Egypt supplied bodily nourishment, so this book will supply spiritual nourishment.

9. Actually, the *Mishneh Torah*, with its theoretical approach, which included all laws and concepts, even those temporarily devoid of practical value, would not have been consonant with R. Joseph Karo's practical orientation, while the *Turim*, with its limited scope, did coincide with the latter goal. Another reason for selecting the *Turim* could have been the fact that the *Turim* was the most popular textbook at the time.

of such commentaries as the *Maggid Mishneh*.[10] He would, incidentally, correct the text of the *Turim*, which suffered many scribal corruptions. That he intended his encyclopedic review of Halachah to be used as a study-guide is indicated by his promise always to give exact bibliographical references in order to enable his readers to consult original texts or check quotations in their original contexts. However, having completed this panoramic presentation and almost detached, academic analysis of a law, he would regularly indicate the normative conclusion, for the "goal is that we should have one Torah and one law." The function of this massive work is thus twofold: to flesh out the bare-bones codifications which are too brief and uninformative, but preserve their sinewiness and pragmatic advantage by unequivocally stating the *pesak*, the binding regulation, in each case.[11] Certitude and finality are among the top-priority items that will be guaranteed.[12]

In connection with this, the author lays bare his juridical methodology, a methodology that was to be vigorously contested, as we shall see. The judicial process was complex. A Talmudist could arrive at the normative conclusion by critically reviewing and appraising all arguments and demonstrations marshalled by his predecessors and then selecting the most cogent, persuasive view. His guide would be examination of underlying texts, relying, in the final analysis, upon his autonomous judgment and not on appeal to authority.[13] This independent, assertive

---

10. This foreshadows his later work, the *Kesef Mishneh*, in which he reveals himself as an astute, sympathetic and resourceful student of the *Mishneh Torah*.

11. Later commentators—e.g., the authors of the *Sefer Me'irat 'Enayim* and the *Bayit Hadash*—felt that R. Joseph Karo's ultimate codificatory aim vitiated his commentatorial one and that the former prevailed at the expense of the latter. Their own works, which were intended exclusively as faithful text commentaries, were thus urgent desiderata. Contemporaries such as R. Solomon Luria (*Yam shel Shelomoh*, *Hullin*, introduction) note the extraordinarily wide bibliographic coverage and unusual erudition of the *Bet Yosef*.

12. His striving for a powerful, central authority is unmistakable (and, incidentally, something he shared with his Sephardic teachers and colleagues—e.g., the great R. Jacob Berab). This aspiration is quite prominent also in the *Maggid Mesharim*, a revealing and intriguing diary of instructions and messages received from his angelic mentor. Analysis of this work is the main concern of Professor Werblowsky's study. Professor Dimitrovsky's article in *Sefunot*, VII provides much background information; it is important and suggestive.

13. The following passage from Benjamin Cardozo, *The Nature of the Judicial Process* (New Haven, 1921), p. 10, comes to mind:

> What is it that I do when I decide a case?-To what sources of information do I appeal for guidance? In what proportions do I permit them to contribute to the result? . . . If a precedent is applicable, when do I refuse to follow it? If no precedent is applicable, how do I reach the rule that will make a precedent for the future? If I am seeking logical consistency, the symmetry of the legal structure, how far shall I seek it? At what point shall the quest be halted by some discrepant custom, by some consideration of the social welfare, by my own or the common standards of justice and morals?

The most forceful contemporary exponent of this approach was R. Solomon

approach is unqualifiedly repudiated by R. Joseph Karo for two reasons: 1) it would be presumptuous to scrutinize the judgment of such giants as R. Moses b. Naḥman, R. Solomon b. Adret, R. Nissim, and the Tosafists and then pass judgment on them—we are not qualified or competent; 2) even if the task were not beyond our powers and capacities, the process would be too long and arduous. Forcefully underscoring his subservience and *apparently* forfeiting his judicial prerogatives, he chose to arrive at the normative conclusion in each case by following the consensus or at least the majority rule of the greatest medieval codifiers—R. Isaac Alfasi (d. 1103), Maimonides (d. 1204), and R. Asher ben Yeḥiel (d. 1328).[14] Contemporary legislation, innovation, and native usage are given no role whatsoever—almost as if the law were all logic and no experience. In other words, in the realm of commentary R. Joseph Karo was bold and resourceful, while in the realm of adjudication he was laconic, almost self-effacing.

At about the same time, in entirely different circumstances and with a totally different motivation, R. Moses Isserles, born into comfort and affluence,[15] son of a prominent communal leader who was also a gentleman scholar and (for a while) son-in-law of the greatest Talmudic teacher in Poland (R. Shalom Shakna), also began to compile an exhaustive commentary on the *Turim*. He reveals the immediate stimulus which led to his project: having been persuaded by friends to assume rabbinic duties in Cracow—his youth, immaturity, and unripe scholarship notwithstanding—he found himself deciding many Halachic problems and issuing numerous judicial opinions. It was his practice to turn directly to the Talmud and consult its authoritative expositors, among whom he mentions R. Isaac Alfasi, R. Moses b. Naḥman, and R. Asher b. Yeḥiel. He found, however, that he was repeatedly subjected to criticism for having ignored the rulings of the most recent scholars (e.g., R. Jacob Weil, R. Israel Isserlein, R. Israel Bruna) who were really the progenitors of contemporary Polish Jewry and gave it its creative and directive vital force. They introduced, *inter alia*, many preventive

Luria, as exemplified in his *Yam shel Shelomoh*. He was preceded in this by R. Isaiah of Trani. See, generally, my *Rabad of Posquières*, pp. 216–219.

14. This distinguished triumvirate was already recognized as authoritative before the time of R. Joseph Karo, as he himself implies. Explicit confirmation is found in the *Responsa* of R. David b. Zimra (Radbaz), v. IV, n. 626. R. Moses Isserles (introduction to *Shulḥan 'Aruk*) and R. Joshua Falk (introduction to *Sefer Me'irat 'Enayim*) suggest that the Sephardic view would automatically prevail inasmuch as Alfasi and Maimonides would always coalesce to determine the majority view. The truth is that R. Asher b. Yeḥiel was not fully representative of the Tosafistic school of France and Germany and was at a very early date accepted in Spain, to the exclusion of other Tosafists. This was noted in the introduction to the commentary *Ma'adane Yom Tob* and also in an anonymous responsum in R. Joseph Karo's *Abkat Rokel*, n. 18, which refers to R. Asher as a "Spanish rabbi." See the literary tudy by José Faur in the *Proceedings of the American Academy for Jewish Research*, XXIII (1965).

15. See his *Responsa*, nn. 45, 95, 109, and others.

ordinances and stringent practices which tended to nullify earlier decisions, and as a result no picture of Halachah could be true to life which did not reflect these resources, motifs and developments. This put R. Moses Isserles in a bad light, and he and his colleagues were, therefore, subjected to much severe criticism, the validity of which he fully appreciated and accepted, as we shall see.

Impromptu, *ad hoc* review—and judicious, instantaneous application —of all this material, this panoply of interpretations and traditions, would be cumbersome, if not impossible. It therefore occurred to R. Moses Isserles that the way out was to prepare a digest and anthology of all opinions and record them alongside of a standard code. The best book was the *Turim,* for its arrangement was very attractive and useful, and it was easily intelligible to all. He set out, with great determination and commensurate perseverance, to implement this literary plan (he vividly describes his frenetic, indefatigable activity, without ease and without quiet). At a rather advanced stage of his work, he was electrified by the news that "the light of Israel, head of the exile" R. Joseph Karo had composed a comparable commentary on the *Turim,* the *Bet Yosef,* the excellence of which was immediately evident. R. Moses Isserles' anxiety was indescribable; just as he neared the hour of consummation, it appeared that his efforts and privations would turn out to be a wearying exercise in futility. He acknowledges—with what seems to be a blend of modesty and realism—that he could not hold a candle to R. Joseph Karo. However, shock did not lead to paralysis. His peace of mind and momentum were restored when, reassessing the situation, he realized that the field had not been completely preempted and that he was still in a position to make a substantive contribution.

There were three areas in which he could realign his material and operate creatively and meaningfully:

1) He would compress the material, almost encyclopedic in its present proportions, and present a more precise formulation of the law. Length, as Maimonides notes, is one of the deterrents of study.[16] Nevertheless, R. Moses Isserles is somewhat apologetic at this point, because he was fully aware of the pitfalls of excessive brevity; indeed, it had been the codificatory syndrome—the rigidities and inadequacies of delphic manuals—that initially impelled him to disavow the methodology of existing codes. As a compromise, he determined to cite—not to reproduce or summarize—all sources, so that the inquisitive or dissatisfied but learned reader will be able to pursue matters further, while the less sophisticated and less talented reader will still benefit and not be able to argue that the material is too lengthy and complicated.

---

16. The reference is probably to the *Guide for the Perplexed,* I, 34 (tr. S. Pines [Chicago, 1963], p. 73): "For man has in his nature a desire to seek the ends; and he often finds preliminaries tedious and refuses to engage in them."

2) The *Bet Yosef* was too "classical," somewhat remote, for Germanic-Polish Jewry: it failed to represent equally the more recent codifiers and commentators. His work, the *Darke Mosheh*, would do justice to them by incorporating their positions. It would reflect the historical consciousness of R. Moses Isserles and his colleagues who looked upon themselves as heirs and continuators of the Ashkenazi tradition. On one hand, therefore, the *Darke Mosheh* would be an abridgement of the *Bet Yosef*, and, on the other, it would expand its scope. Clearly, R. Moses Isserles had taken the words of his earlier critics to heart.

3) Perhaps the most radical divergence between the two works appeared in the methodology of *pesak*, formulating the normative conclusion and obligatory pattern of behavior. Unlike R. Joseph Karo, who cautiously claimed to follow the *communis opinio*, or majority rule, of early codifiers, and unlike those who would freely exercise independent judgment in arriving at practical conclusions, R. Moses Isserles adopted a third stance: to follow most recent authorities—*halakah ke-batra'e*.[17] This method would preserve established precedent and respect local custom. It is reflected stylistically in R. Moses Isserles' habit of underwriting the most valid view by adding "and this is customary" and then identifying the source or by noting candidly "and so it appears to me."[18] He is thus more independent and resourceful than R. Joseph Karo, though less so than R. Solomon Luria.[19] In short, as R. Moses Isserles puts it in a rhetorical flourish, "And Moses took the bones of Joseph"[20] —he adapted and transformed the essence of the *Bet Yosef* and abandoned the rest.

This ends the first chapter of our story in which R. Joseph Karo made it to the press before R. Moses Isserles and forced the latter to revise his initial prospectus in light of a changed literary reality. What is,

---

17. In formulating this principle, R. Moses Isserles relies—with good effect—upon the authority of R. Isaac Alfasi. See *Darke Mosheh*, introduction, and *Yoreh De'ah*, 35:13. An anonymous contemporary, writing against R. Joseph Karo, advances the same position; *Abkat Rokel*, n. 18. Note R. Joseph Karo's important discussion in *Kesef Mishneh, Hilkot Mamrim*, II:1.

18. It is noteworthy that R. Hayyim b. Bezalel, a former classmate and colleague of R. Moses Isserles, took him to task for not going far enough in his vindication of local custom. The *Wikkuah Mayyim Hayyim* is built on this premise. This work is significant also in that it opts for still another possibility of juridical methodology. The author's contention is that a code should simply review all the different opinions and arrange them systematically but leave the final determination to the specific rabbinic authority that is responsible for a given decision. He protests forcefully against "levelling" books which tend to obliterate the distinctions between scholar and layman and implicitly undermine the authority of the scholar. A code should be an auxiliary manual for the judge and scholar, not an explicit, monolithic work.

19. See n. 13. R. Solomon Luria also displays an anti-Spanish, especially anti-Maimonidean, animus or polemicism, which is not found in R. Moses Isserles.

20. *Exodus* 13:19, with a play on the word "bones" (*'azmot*), which may be interpreted as essence (*'azmut*).

of course, striking is the remarkable parallelism and similarity of attitudes between these two Talmudists, both seeking to push back the frontiers of Halachic literature, both convinced of the need to review individual laws in their totality and not rely upon delphic manuals, and both selecting the same code *(Turim)* as their springboard.

## II

TEN YEARS LATER, IN THE COURSE OF WHICH the *Bet Yosef* spread far and wide and his authority was increasingly respected, R. Joseph Karo came full cycle in his own attitude towards the oracular-type code. Having previously and persuasively argued against the utility and wisdom of the apodictic compendium, he now conceded its need and efficacy. He himself abridged the voluminous *Bet Yosef*—"gathered the lilies, the sapphires"—and called his new work the *Shulḥan 'Aruk*, "because in it the reader will find all kinds of delicacies" fastidiously arranged and systematized and clarified. He was persuaded that the *Shulḥan 'Aruk* would serve the needs of a diffuse and heterogeneous audience. Scholars will use it as a handy reference book, so that every matter of law will be perfectly clear and the answer to questions concerning Halachic practice will be immediate and decisive. Young, untutored students will also benefit by committing the *Shulḥan 'Aruk* to memory, for even rote knowledge is not to be underestimated.[21]

When the *Shulḥan 'Aruk* appeared, it elicited praise and provoked criticism; the former could be exuberant, and the latter, abrasive. Some contemporaries needed only to resuscitate R. Joseph Karo's initial stance and refurbish his arguments against such works as the *Agur*. R. Moses Isserles' reaction moved along the same lines which had determined his reaction to the *Bet Yosef*.[22] He could not—like R. Solomon Luria or R. Yom Tob Lipman Heller—take unqualified exception to the codificatory aim and form,[23] for he had already, in his revised *Darke Mosheh*, aligned himself in principle with this tendency and had eloquently defended it. He could, however, press his substantive and methodological attack on Karo: the latter had neglected Ashkenazic tradition and had failed to abide by the most recent rulings, thereby ignoring custom which was such an important ingredient of the normative law.[24] Moreover, just as R. Joseph Karo drew upon his *Bet Yosef*, so R. Moses Isserles

21. See *Berakot*, 38b. It is interesting that Maimonides also intended his *Mishneh Torah* to be used by "great and small," learned and simple.
22. See *Rabad of Posquières*, p. 113, and pp. 96–97.
23. A helpful review of these attitudes can be found in H. Tchernovitz, *Toledot ha-Poskim*, v. III. The rationale of this position is eloquently stated by the Maharal of Prague in *Netibot 'Olam*, *Netib ha-Torah*, ch. 15. I say "unqualified exception" because the fact is that R. Moses Isserles' contribution to the *Shulḥan 'Aruk* is significantly more expansive than that of R. Joseph Karo.
24. See, e.g., *Oraḥ Ḥayyim*, 619; *Yoreh De'ah*, 381, 386.

drew upon his *Darke Mosheh*;[25] both, coming full cycle, moved from lively judicial symposium to soulless legislative soliloquy. If R. Joseph Karo produced a "set table," R. Moses Isserles spread a "tablecloth" over it.[26] It is certain that the "table" would never have been universally accepted if it had not been covered and adorned with the "tablecloth." R. Moses Isserles' glosses, both strictures and annotations, were the ultimate validation of the *Shulḥan 'Aruk*. The full dialectic has here played itself out, radical opposition to codes giving way to radical codification, almost with a vengeance; for the *Shulḥan 'Aruk* is the leanest of all codes in Jewish history—from the *Bet Yosef* to the *Shulḥan 'Aruk*, from the baroque to the bare.

It is not this dialectical movement *per se* which is novel or note-worthy, for this characterizes much of the history of post-Talmudic rabbinic literature. Attempts to compress the Halachah by formal codification alternate with counter-attempts to preserve the fulness and richness of both the method and substance of the Halachah by engaging in interpretation, analogy, logical inference, and only then formulating the resultant normative conclusion. Any student who follows the course of rabbinic literature from the Geonic works of the eighth century through the *Mishneh Torah* and *Turim* and on down to the *Shulḥan 'Aruk* cannot ignore this see-saw tendency. The tension is ever present and usually catalytic. No sooner is the need for codification met than a wave of non-codificatory work rises. A code could provide guidance and certitude for a while but not finality.[27] *'Arvak 'arva zarik*—"your bondsman requires a bondsman." A code, even in the eyes of its admirers, required vigilant explanation and judicious application. The heartbeat had constantly to be checked and the pulse had to be counted. It became part of a life organism that was never complete or static. What is striking, therefore, in the case of the *Shulḥan 'Aruk* is that the dialectical movement plays itself out in the attitudes and achievements of the same person—"surfing" on the "sea of the Talmud," rising and falling on the crests of analysis and thoughts of argumentation, and then trying to "gather the water into one area," to construct a dike that would produce a slow, smooth flow of its waters. The *Shulḥan 'Aruk* thus offers an instructive example of the dialectical movement in rabbinic literature as a whole.

This whole story is important, I believe, because it expands the historical background against which the *Shulḥan 'Aruk* is to be seen and cautions against excessive preoccupation with purely sociological

---

25. See his *Responsa*, nn. 35, 131.

26. The imagery is provided by R. Moses Isserles himself. The "table" was bare and uninviting without his "tablecloth."

27. See B. Cardozo, *The Nature of the Judicial Process*, p. 18: "Justinian's prohibition of any commentary on the product of his codifiers is remembered only for its futility."

data, with contemporary stimuli and contingencies. It makes the *Shulḥan 'Aruk* understandable in terms of the general history of Halachic literature and its major trends. It provides an obvious vertical perspective—i.e. literary categories seen as part of an ongoing Halachic enterprise—to be used alongside of an, at best, implicit horizontal perspective—i.e. historical pressures and eschatological hopes—for an explanation of the emergence of the *Shulḥan 'Aruk*.[28] This is strengthened by the striking parallelism between the literary careers of R. Moses Isserles and R. Joseph Karo; their historical situations, environmental influences, social contexts (in a phrase of contemporary jargon, their *sitz-im-leben*) are so different, but their aspirations and attainments are so similar.

### III

WHEN WE COME TO GAUGE AND APPRAISE the impact of the *Shulḥan 'Aruk*, it is idle to speculate whether R. Joseph Karo intended the *Shulḥan 'Aruk* to circulate and be used independently, as a literary unit sufficient to itself, or to be used only as a companion volume together with the *Bet Yosef*. His intention has been disputed and variously construed. Some condemned those who studied the *Shulḥan 'Aruk in vacuo*, thereby acquiring superficial acquaintance with Halachah, claiming that this contravened the author's intention. Others treated the *Shulḥan 'Aruk* in a manner reminiscent of R. Joseph Karo's original attitude as found in the preface to the *Bet Yosef*. In this case, however, the original intention of the author is eclipsed by the historical fact, abetted or perhaps made possible by R. Moses Isserles' glosses,[29] that the *Shulḥan 'Aruk* and

---

28. This important vertical perspective is usually left out of the picture. See e.g., R. Werblowsky, *Joseph Karo*, pp. 7, 95, 167. There can be little doubt that R. Joseph Karo was preoccupied with eschatological hopes and that he saw the catastrophic nature of his period as having messianic significance. This is attested, *inter alia*, in the introduction to *Sefer Ḥaredim*.

It would indeed be strange if the mood of that generation—physically uprooted, emotionally shattered, but spiritually exuberant—did not leave an imprint on the *Shulḥan 'Aruk*. Note in this connection the author's novel emphasis upon the desirability of unflagging awareness of the state of exile, dispersion and destruction. After reproducing (*Oraḥ Ḥayyim* 1:2) the statement of the *Turim* concerning nocturnal prayer dealing with the destruction and the dispersion, R. Joseph Karo adds in a separate entry that "it is proper for every God-fearing person to grieve and worry about the destruction of the Holy Temple." This is a cardinal principle, part of one's consciousness—over and beyond any concrete expression.

29. The fact is that R. Moses Isserles' strictures are very radical, but low-keyed and disarmingly calm. They are free of the stridency and impetuosity which punctuate the glosses of R. Abraham b. David on the *Mishneh Torah*, but are nevertheless uncompromising in their criticism. While they contain explanations, amplifications and supplements, most were designed simply to supersede R. Joseph Karo's conclusions. It is only the harmonious literary form that avoided an overt struggle for Halachic hegemony such as occurred in other periods—for example, in the 13th century when Spanish students of the great Naḥmanides attempted to impose their customs and interpretations on Provence. There was no diluion of diversity in this case, either, but there was at least a formal fusion of Ashkenazi and Sephardi Halachah in one work. Sephardim continued to rely on R. Joseph Karo, pointing to the verse, "Go unto

not the *Bet Yosef* became R. Joseph Karo's main claim to fame, and its existence was completely separate from and independent of the *Bet Yosef*. Commentators such as R. Abraham Gumbiner in the *Magen Abraham* effectively and irreparably cut the umbilical cord which may have linked the *Shulḥan 'Aruk* with the *Bet Yosef*. What some literary critics have said about poetry may then be applied here: "The design of intention of the author is neither available nor desirable as a standard for judging the success of a work of literary art."[30] In our case, consequently, we should simply see what are some of the characteristics of the *Shulḥan 'Aruk* and some of the repercussions of its great historical success.

Perhaps the single most important feature of the *Shulḥan 'Aruk* is its unswerving concentration on prescribed patterns of behavior to the exclusion of any significant amount of theoretical data. The *Shulḥan 'Aruk* is a manual for practical guidance, not academic study. This practical orientation is discernible in many areas and on different levels.

First of all, by initially adopting the classification of the *Turim*, R. Joseph Karo capitulated unconditionally to the practical orientation. The import of this becomes more vivid when we contrast the two major codes on this point. The *Mishneh Torah* is all-inclusive in scope, obliterating all distinctions between practice and theory, and devoting sustained attention to those laws and concepts momentarily devoid of practical value or temporarily in abeyance because of historical and geographical contingencies. Laws of prayer and of the Temple ceremonial are given equal treatment. Laws concerning the *sotah*, the unfaithful wife (abrogated by R. Johanan b. Zakkai in the first century), are codified in the same detail as the ever practical marriage laws. The present time during which part of the law was in abeyance was, in Maimonides' opinion, an historical anomaly, a fleeting moment in the pattern of eternity. The real historical dimensions were those in which the Torah and its precepts were fully realized, that is, the time after the restoration of the Davidic dynasty, when "all the ancient laws will be reinstituted . . . sacrifices will again be offered, the Sabbatical and Jubilee years will again be observed in accordance with the commandments set forth in the Law."[31] The Oral Law was, therefore, to be codified and studied exhaustively. The *Turim*, on the other hand, addresses itself only to those laws that are relevant, to those concrete problems and issues whose validity and applicability are not confined either temporally or geographically. For while both Maimonides and R. Jacob b. Asher were of

---

Joseph; what he saith to you, do" (*Genesis* 41:55); Ashkenazim continued to rely on R. Moses Isserles, adapting the verse, "For the children of Israel go out with upraised hands" (*beyad ramah*—and "Ramah" was the acrostic for R. Moses Isserles).

30. W. K. Wimsatt and M. C. Beardsley, "The Intentional Fallacy," *Sewanee Review*, LIV (1946), 468.

31. *Hilkot Melakim*, XI:1. See Rabbi J. B. Soloveitchik, "Ish ha-Halakah," *Talpiyot*, 1944, pp. 668 ff.

one mind in abandoning the sequence of the Talmudic treatises and seeking an independent classification of Halachah, they differed in their goals: Maimonides sought to create a topical-conceptual arrangement that would provide a new interpretive mold for study and would also be educationally sound, while R. Jacob b. Asher was guided only by functionality and as a result was less rigorous conceptually. It involved a lesser degree of logical analysis and abstraction, and did not hesitate to group disparate items together. A code, according to this conception should facilitate the understanding of the operative laws and guide people in translating concepts into rules of conduct.

The *Shulḥan ʿAruk* adds a further rigorism to the practicality of the *Turim*. The *Turim*'s practicality expresses itself in the rigid selection of material, in the circumscribed scope, but not in the method of presentation, which is rich, varied, and suggestive, containing as it does much textual interpretation and brief discussion of divergent views, while the functionality of the *Shulḥan ʿAruk* is so radical that it brooks no expansiveness whatsoever. The judicial *process* is of no concern to the codifier; exegesis, interpretation, derivation, awareness of controversy —all these matters are totally dispensable, even undesirable, for the codifier.[32] In this respect, the *Shulḥan ʿAruk* has greater affinities with

32. This is, of course, a codificatory utopia, never achieved. First, all the author's protestations notwithstanding, the *Shulḥan ʿAruk* is not a mechanical, scissors-and-paste compilation. For all his veneration and authority and his *a priori* declaration of subservience to the three great medieval codifiers, the author writes selectively and discriminatingly. Already his contemporary, R. Ḥayyim b. Bezalel, observed (in the *Wikkuaḥ Mayyim Ḥayyim*) that Karo did not really follow the standards he outlined theoretically. Similarly, R. Moses Isserles in the introduction to the *Darke Mosheh* called attention to inconsistencies and discrepancies between the statement of intention and actual performance. There are many examples which show how subtly but steadily the author of the *Shulḥan ʿAruk* modified positions and expressed his own judgment. This is often indicated by the deletion of a phrase or addition of a word in what is otherwise a verbatim reproduction of a source. Note *Yoreh Deʿah* 246:4, which is almost an exact quotation of Maimonides, *Hilkot Talmud Torah*, I:11, 12. The author has, however, expunged the sentence which makes philosophy (*pardes*) an integral, even paramount component of the Oral Tradition, for this statement obviously caused him more than a twinge of discomfiture. R. Moses Isserles reinserts this reference less conspicuously and more restrainedly toward the end of his gloss. The author's censure of the writings of Immanuel of Rome (*Oraḥ Ḥayyim*, 307:16) is an example of a novel, emphatic addition.

Second, all the author's statements about certitude, finality, and unilateral formulations notwithstanding, there are many paragraphs which cite multiple views. Sometimes reference is even made to the authorship of these divergent views. See, e.g., *Oraḥ Ḥayyim*, 18:1; 32:9; 422:2 and many others. This area of indecision is one of the major concerns of the 19th-century work, *ʿAruk ha-Shulḥan* by Rabbi Y. M. Epstein, and such earlier works as *Halacha Aḥaronah we-Kuntros ha-Reʾayot*.

Third, there is a sparse amount of interpretive and exegetical material. See, e.g., *Oraḥ Ḥayyim*, 6:1, which contains the explanation of a liturgical text. Note also 11:15, 14:1, 14:3, 15:4, 17:1 and many others where reasons are briefly adduced or the Halachic process is traced. What is more, even the self-sufficiency of the work is weakened when, for example, the author says (*Oraḥ Ḥayyim*, 597), "this is explained well in the *Tur* in this section."

the *Mishneh Torah,* which also purports to eliminate conflicting interpretations and rambling discussions and to present *ex cathedra* legislative, unilateral views, without sources and without explanations. The fact is that the *Shulḥan 'Aruk* is much closer to this codificatory ideal than the *Mishneh Torah,* which, after all, is as much commentary as it is code. One has only to compare, at random, parallel sections of the *Turim* and *Shulḥan 'Aruk* to realize fully and directly, almost palpably, the extent to which the *Shulḥan 'Aruk* pruned the *Turim,* relentlessly excising midrashic embellishments, ethical perceptions, and theoretical amplifications. It promised to give the "fixed, final law, without speech and without words." It left little to discretion or imagination.

There is yet another area in which this austere functionality comes to the surface—in the virtually complete elimination of ideology, theology, and teleology. The *Shulḥan 'Aruk,* unlike the *Mishneh Torah* or the *Sefer ha-Rokeaḥ,* has no philosophical or Kabbalistic prolegomenon or peroration. The *Shulḥan 'Aruk,* unlike the *Mishneh Torah* or the *Turim,* does not abound in extra-Halachic comments, guiding tenets and ideological directives.[33] While, as I have tried to prove elsewhere, the *Mishneh Torah* does reveal the full intellectualistic posture of Maimonides,[34] the *Shulḥan 'Aruk* does not even afford an oblique glimpse of the Kabbalistic posture of R. Joseph Karo, who appears here in the guise of the civil lawyer for whom "nothing was more pointless, nothing more inept than a law with a preamble."[35] He was concerned exclusively with what Max Weber called the "methodology of sanctification" which produces a "continuous personality pattern," not with its charismatic goals or stimuli, the ethical underpinning or theological vision which suffuse

---

33. One striking illustration is provided by the prologue of the *Turim* to the *Ḥoshen Mishpat,* where the instrumental role of positive law is expounded. The point of departure is the apparent contradiction between two statements in the first chapter of *Pirke Abot.* One reads: "Upon three things the world stands, upon Torah, upon divine service, and upon acts of lovingkindness." The other reads: "By three things is the world sustained, by justice, truth, and peace." These are means; the others are ends. The author of the *Shulḥan 'Aruk* omits all preambles and plunges directly into the legal-institutional details. Compare the two also at *Oraḥ Ḥayyim,* 61, 125, 242 (introduction to the laws of Sabbath) and others. At *Yoreh De'ah,* 335 (visitation of the sick), the *Turim* starts unhurriedly with a midrashic motif used by Naḥmanides at the beginning of his code *Torat ha-Adam,* while the *Shulḥan 'Aruk* plunges *medias in res.* It has no time—or need—for adornment.

34. In my article "Some Non-Halakic Aspects of the Mishneh Torah," which is scheduled to appear soon in *Medieval and Renaissance Studies,* ed. A. Altman (Cambridge, 1967).

35. J. W. Jones, *The Law and Legal Theory of the Greeks,* p. 8. R. Moses Isserles fleshed out a good number of the lean formulations in the *Shulḥan 'Aruk,* introducing many Kabbalistic motifs and explanations. See, for example, *Oraḥ Ḥayyim,* 426 (on New Moon), 583 (on Hoshanah Rabbah), 664 (on *kapparot*), and others. See also 290, in comparison with the *Turim.* He is thus much less reserved and less reticent than his Sephardic counterpart.

the Halachah with significance, guarantee its radical, ineradicable spirituality and thereby nurture the religious consciousness. The *Shulḥan 'Aruk* gives the concrete idea, but omits what Dilthey called *Erlebniss,* the experiential component. In the *Shulḥan 'Aruk* the Halachah manifests itself as the *regula iuris,* a rule of life characterized by stability, regularity, and fixedness, making known to people "the way they are to go and the practices they are to follow" (*Exodus* 18:20). These specific, visible practices are not coordinated with invisible meaning or unspecified experience. One can say, in general, that there are two major means by which apparently trans-Halachic material has been organically linked with the Halachah proper: 1) construction of an ideational framework which indicates the ultimate concerns and gives coherence, direction and vitality to the concrete actions; 2) elaboration of either a rationale of the law or a mystique of the law which suggests explanations and motives for the detailed commandments. The *Shulḥan 'Aruk,* for reasons of its own, about which we may only conjecture, attempts neither.

## IV

THIS RESTRICTIVE, ALMOST STYPTIC TRAIT of the *Shulḥan 'Aruk* was noticed—and criticized—by contemporaries, foremost among whom was R. Mordecai Jaffe (1530-1612), disciple of R. Moses Isserles and R. Solomon Luria and successor of R. Judah Loewe, the famous Maharal, of Prague. It is worth re-telling the story of the composition of his major, multi-volume work, known as the *Lebush,* inasmuch as it zeroes in on the radical functionality of the *Shulḥan 'Aruk* and also briefly reviews the tense dialectic surrounding codification which we discussed above.

R. Mordecai Jaffe, a very articulate, sophisticated writer who was well acquainted with the contemporary scene, describes the enthusiastic reception accorded to the *Bet Yosef* because people imagined it would serve as a concise, spirited compendium, obviating the need for constant, wearisome recourse to dozens of rabbinic volumes in order to determine the proper Halachic course. He shared this feeling and heightened anticipation, but enthusiasm gave way to disillusionment as he realized that the *Bet Yosef* was anything but concise. Inasmuch as a comprehensive and compact compendium remained an urgent desideratum, he began a condensation of the *Bet Yosef* that would serve this purpose. External factors—an edict of expulsion by the Austrian emperor, which compelled him to flee Bohemia and settle in Italy—interrupted his work. In Italy, where so much Hebrew printing was being done, he heard that R. Joseph Karo himself had made arrangements to print an abridgement. Again he desisted, for he could not presume to improve upon the original author who would unquestionably produce the most balanced, incisive abridgement of his own work. R. Jaffe adds parenthetically—but with remarkable candor—that there was a pragmatic consideration as well: even if he persisted and completed his work, he could not hope to compete publicly with such a prestigious master as R. Joseph Karo—and to do it just for personal consumption, to satisfy his own needs, would be extravagant.

However, upon preliminary examination of the *Shulḥan 'Aruk*—in Venice—he noted two serious deficiencies. First, it was too short and astringent, having no reasons or explanations—"like a sealed book, a dream which had no interpretation or meaning." He describes it as "a table well prepared with all kinds of refreshments, but the dishes are tasteless, lacking the salt of reasoning which makes the broth boil and warms the individual"—i.e., lacking a minimum of explanatory and exhortatory material to embellish and spiritualize the bald Halachic directives. Second, it was almost exclusively Maimonidean, or Sephardic, and Ashkenazic communities could not, therefore, be guided by it—an argument that had been tellingly and uncompromisingly put forward by both his teachers (Isserles and Luria). Again he started work on a new composition which would fill the gap, and again he abandoned his plans in deference to R. Moses Isserles who was reported to have undertaken this task. When the full *Shulḥan 'Aruk* appeared—the text of R. Joseph Karo and the glosses of R. Moses Isserles—he quickly realized that only the second deficiency had been remedied, that Ashkenazic Halachah had found a worthy and zealous spokesman, but the first deficiency remained—and this was glaring. Some measure of explanation was as indispensable for law as salt was for food. So, for the third time, he turned to producing a code which would a) strive for a golden mean between inordinate length (the *Bet Yosef*) and excessive brevity (the *Shulḥan 'Aruk*); and b) would explain, motivate, and spiritualize the law, often with the help of new Kabbalistic doctrines.

In effect, R. Mordecai Jaffe—whose code was a potential but short-lived rival to the *Shulḥan 'Aruk*—addressed himself to the problem which great Halachists, ethicists, philosophers and mystics have constantly confronted: how to maintain a rigid, punctilious observance of the law and concomitantly avoid externalization and routinization. On one hand, we hear the echoes of Maimonides, R. Eleazar ha-Rokeaḥ of Worms, and R. Menaḥem b. Zeraḥ (author of the *Zedah la-Derek*), who attempt to combine laws with their reasons and rationale, as well as R. Baḥya ibn Pakuda, R. Jonah Gerondi, and R. Isaac Abuhab, to mention just a few of his predecessors. On the other hand, this tone continues to reverberate in the *Shulḥan 'Aruk* of R. Shneur Zalman of Ladi, as well as in the writings of R. Isaiah Hurwitz and R. Moses Ḥayyim Luzzato, to mention just a few of his successors. The common denominator here is the concern that the Halachic enterprise always be rooted in and related to spirituality, to knowledge of God obtained through study and experience. All difficulties notwithstanding, it was generally felt that even when dealing with the corpus of practical, clearly definable law, an attempt should be made to express the—perhaps incommunicable —values and aspirations of religious experience and spiritual existence.

## V

HOWEVER, WHEN ALL IS SAID, it would be incorrect and insensitive to assert unqualifiedly that the *Shulḥan 'Aruk*, that embodiment of Halachah which Jewish history has proclaimed supreme, is a spiritless, formalistic, even timid work. Its opening sentence, especially as elaborated by R. Moses Isserles, acts as the nerve center of the entire Halachic system and the fountain of its strength.

> A man should make himself strong and brave as a lion[36] to rise in the morning for the service of his Creator, so that he should "awake the dawn" (*Psalms* 57:9)[37] . . .

> "I have set the Lord always before me" (*Psalms* 16:8). This is a cardinal principle in the Torah and in the perfect (noble) ways of the righteous who walk before God. For[38] man does not sit, move, and occupy himself when he is alone in his house, as he sits, moves, and occupies himself when he is in the presence of a great king; nor does he speak and rejoice while he is with his family and relatives as he speaks in the king's council. How much more so when man takes to heart that the Great King, the Holy One, blessed be He, whose "glory fills the whole earth" (*Isaiah* 6:3), is always standing by him and observing all his doings, as it is said in Scripture: "Can a man hide himself in secret places that I shall not see him?" (*Jeremiah* 23:24). Cognizant of this, he will immediately achieve reverence and humility, fear and shame before the Lord, blessed be He, at all times.

Law is dry and its details are burdensome only if its observance lacks vital commitment, but if all actions of a person are infused with the radical awareness that he is acting in the presence of God, then every detail becomes meaningful and relevant. Such an awareness rules out routine, mechanical actions; everything must be conscious and purposive in a God-oriented universe, where every step of man is directed towards God. Halachah, like nature, abhors a vacuum; it recognizes no twilight zone of neutrality or futility.[39] It is all-inclusive. Consequently, every

---

36. See *Pirke Abot*, V: 23.
37. This verse, meaning that man "awakens the dawn and not that the dawn awakens man," is elaborated in the Palestinian Talmud, *Berakot*, ch. 1 and is cited by the *Turim*.
38. What follows is part quotation, part paraphrase from the *Guide for the Perplexed*, III, 52. Maimonides refers in this context to the Talmudic saying in *Kiddushin*, 31a fobidding a person to "walk about proudly, with erect stature," because of the verse, "the whole earth is full of His glory." He concludes: "This purpose to which I have drawn your attention is the purpose of all the actions prescribed by the Law."
39. See Maimonides' definition of futile action in *Guide for the Perplexed* III, 25:

action—even tying one's shoes[40]—can be and is invested with symbolic meaning. Nothing is accidental, behavioral, purely biological. Even unavoidable routine is made less perfunctory. The opening paragraph of the *Shulḥan ʿAruk* is thus a clear and resounding declaration concerning the workings and the searchings of the spirit. Its tone should reverberate throughout all the subsequent laws and regulations. It provides—as does also paragraph 231, which urges man to see to it that *all* his deeds be "for the sake of heaven"—an implicit rationale for the entire Halachah, but it is a rationale that must be kept alive by the individual. It cannot be passively taken for granted; it must be passionately pursued.

What I am saying, in other words, is that to a certain extent the *Shulḥan ʿAruk* and Halachah are coterminous and that the "problem" of the *Shulḥan ʿAruk* is precisely the "problem" of Halachah as a whole. Halachah itself is a tense, vibrant, dialectical system which regularly insists upon normativeness in action and inwardness in feeling and thought.[41] It undertook to give concrete and continuous expression to theological ideals, ethical norms, ecstatic moods, and historical concepts but never superseded or eliminated these ideals and concepts. Halachah itself is, therefore, a coincidence of opposites: prophecy and law, charisma and institution, mood and medium, image and reality, the thought of eternity and the life of temporality. Halachah itself, therefore, in its own behalf, demands the coordination of inner meaning and external observance—and it is most difficult to comply with such a demand and sustain such a delicate, highly sensitized synthesis.[42]

There can be no doubt that R. Joseph Karo, the arch mystic passionately yearning for ever greater spiritual heights, could not have intended to create a new concept of orthopraxis, of punctilious observance of the law divorced, as it were, from all spiritual tension. While this may indeed have been one of the unintended repercussions of the *Shulḥan ʿAruk*—while it may unknowingly have contributed to the notion, maintained by a strange assortment of people, that Judaism is all deed and no creed, all letter and no spirit—its author would certainly discountenance such an interpretation and dissociate himself from it. If the

---

"A futile action is that action by which no end is aimed at at all, as when some people play with their hands while thinking and like the actions of the negligent and the inattentive."

40. *Oraḥ Ḥayyim*, 2:4.

41. See the brief discussion of this in my article in *Tradition*, V (1963), pp. 144–45. For a clear, almost unnoticed example of this correlation, see *Yoreh Deʿah*, 335:4 where it is stated that the external action of visiting a sick person without the concomitant feeling of compassion and inward action of prayer for his recovery does not constitute the fulfillment of a *mizvah*.

42. See in this connection G. Van der Leeuw, *Religion in Essence and Manifestation* (Harper, 1963), II, p. 459 ff; Joachim Wach, *Sociology of Religion* (Chicago, 1944), p. 17 ff.

*Shulḥan 'Aruk* only charts a specific way of life but does not impart a specific version or vision of meta-Halachah, it is because the latter is to be supplied and experienced independently.[43] The valiant attempt of so many scholars to compress the incompressible, imponderable values of religious experience into cold words and neat formulae, alongside of generally lucid Halachic prescriptions, did not elicit the support of R. Joseph Karo. Halachah could be integrated with and invigorated by disparate, mutually exclusive systems, operating with different motives and aspirations, as long as these agreed on the means and directives. I would suggest that R. Mordecai Jaffe's parenthetical apology for his expansive-interpretive approach to Halachah—that every person spices his food differently, that every wise person will find a different reason or taste in the law, and this reason should not be codified or legislated —may well be what prompted R. Joseph Karo, generally reticent about spiritual matters, to limit his attention to the concrete particularization of Halachah. This could be presented with a good measure of certitude and finality, but its spiritual coordinates required special and separate, if complementary, treatment.[44]

* * *

As a personal postcript, or "concluding unscientific postcript," I would like to suggest that, if the Psalmist's awareness of "I have set God before me continually" *(Psalm* 16:8) —the motto of the *Shulḥan 'Aruk—is* one of the standards of saintliness,[45] then all *"Shulḥan 'Aruk* Jews,"* all who abide by its regulations while penetrating to its essence and its real motive powers, should be men who strive for saintliness. But strive they must, zealously, imaginatively, and with unrelenting commitment.[46]

---

43. The introduction to the *Shulḥan 'Aruk* should perhaps be re-examined at this point. After stating that this compendium will serve the needs of the veteran scholar and the uninitiated student, the author refers to the pleasures which the *maskilim,* the wise men, will derive from his work. *Maskilim* is a common epithet for Kabbalists, for mystics proficient in esoteric lore. "The wise will shine like the brightness of heaven when they shall have rest from their travail and the labor of their hands." Does this suggest that the *Shulḥan 'Aruk* will provide a compass with the help of which the *maskilim* will be able to chart their own course in the lofty spiritual realms?

It should also be noted that R. Joseph Karo is for the most part uncommunicative about his inner world, his spiritual *Anschauung,* and even about such contemporary issues in which he was deeply involved, as the attempted re-institution of ordination in Safed. I would add that even in the *Kesef Mishnah* he remains remarkably reticent (see, e.g., *Hilkot Talmud Torah,* I:11, 12), and only occasionally is a subdued comment forthcoming (e.g., *Yesode ha-Torah,* I:10; *Teshubah* III:7; X:6).

The introduction to the *Bet Yosef* has a single laconic reference to the *Zohar.* R. Moses Isserles is more expressive in this respect; see n. 33.

44. See the balanced remarks of Werblowsky, pp. 290–92; also pp. 146–47.

45. S. Schechter, *Studies in Judaism* (New York, 1958), p. 147.

46. See R. Moses Ḥayyim Luzzatto, *Mesillat Yesharim* (Philadelphia, 1948), pp. 3–4.

# C. Modern Interpretations of the Tradition

# JUDAISM AND NATURAL RELIGION

NOAH H. ROSENBLOOM

## I

Many of the intellectual tensions, philosophical perplexities and ethical tensions that plague modern man hark back to the Cartesian-Newtonian outlook, which revolutionized man's concept of nature and its relationship to faith. This new concept toppled the neatly established dualistic view of the Middle Ages of a "realm of nature" and a "realm of grace".

The advocates of nature, who heretofore were satisfied to serve as the handmaiden of faith, rebelled now against this subordination. They refused to concede to the inferior position assigned to nature in the belief that it was acted upon from without. Nature suddenly became elevated to the sphere of the Divine. God was not revealed through a one-time-act of revelation but His presence constantly manifests itself in the dynamism of the multifarious phenomena of nature. The latter was, therefore, not only the realm of man but the realm of God as well. The new philosophy was not reversed medieval *weltaschauung* claiming the supremacy of naturalism over supernaturalism but actually left no room for the latter.

The discovery of law in nature accessible to human reason endowed man with a sense of security. It changed his universe from a bewildering capricious phantasmagoria of phenomena, whose permutations were unintelligible to him, into a unified rational cosmos of law and order. The optimism engendered by the rationality and mathematical regularity in nature intoxicated its advocates to associate *natural* with *rational*. Since nature represents the most perfect order of God, therefore, it seems logical to conclude that what is *natural* ought to be considered also *reasonable*.

This alliance between nature and reason made the battle between them and faith fierce and acrimonious. Their respective followers drifted further and further apart. A harmonious reconciliation was becoming utterly impossible. Both groups had extremists who refused to compromise. The militant rationalists exclaimed: *Ecrassez l'infame*. The stubborn traditionalists derisively boasted, *Crede quia absurdum* or *Credible quia*

---

The paradox of a universalistic faith in a nationalistic framework, to use Yechezkel Kaufman's descriptive phrase for Judaism, has drawn the repeated attention of Jewish thinkers. Samuel David Luzzatto, the nineteenth century polyhistor, is shown, in Dr. Rosenbloom's present study, to have attempted a full scale resolution of the antinomy. The attempt involved the positing of two distinct phases in Judaism's development—the Abrahamic phase, natural and hence potentially universal, and the Mosaic, particularistic and hence nationalistic. How such conceptual framework might strengthen the present traditionalist position forms the conclusion of the author's exposition on a neglected aspect of Luzzatto's thinking.

*non intellectum est.* Not, however, all traditionalists and rationalists were swept down the maelstrom of extremism and radicalism. Some tried to steer a more moderate course. They endeavored to find a more conciliatory approach to these ever-widening currents of thought. Firmly believing that laws of reason could be found in all fields of endeavor, they were certain that it could be found in religion too. All that was necessary was to divest the historical religions of their accidental elements, superstitious accretions and sacerdotal practices and a rational religion would emerge. This idea was already expressed by the humanists and particularly by Nicholas of Cusa: *Una est religio in rituum varietate.*

The criterion for what constitutes a rational religion was not too difficult to find. Since during this period nature was rational and reasonable, consequently, whatever religious ideas and values could be discovered in nature ought be considered natural religion, hence the religion of reason. In their eagerness to unearth what was "natural" and "reasonable" in religion, it became fashionable to explore and study the religions and cultures of the Oriental peoples who have escaped the ravages of artificial and unnatural Western civilization. The common denominator of these religions would constitute the fundamental and universal principles of natural religion. The interest in oriental cultures and religions so different from their occidental counterparts brought about an infatuation with the most primitive and uncivilized ones. The more primitive a society, the more ancient a culture, the more primeval a religion, the more natural it was considered to be. The religion of the *bon savage* was thus the closest to universal reason, eternal truth and natural religion.

This veneration of the primitive and uncivilized cultures gave raise to the assumption of a Golden Age in remote antiquity which was universal, rational, and natural in every respect. Only with the advent of civilization and the manipulation of scheming priests, was this pure and unadulterated natural religion corrupted. The pristine kernel of natural religion was overladen with an encrustation of dogmas, doctrines, theologies and rituals.

## II

The danger to the existing historical and traditional religions was apparent. Small wonder that many Christian thinkers and theologians made a frantic effort at a higher synthesis. They attempted to identify Christianity with the principles of the religion of reason and, subsequently, with those of natural religion. Thus, they expected to save Christianity from the powerful and devastating attacks by the proponents of nature and reason. At the height of the popularity of Cartesianism, Fenelon, Bossuet and Malebranche tried to reconstruct religious traditions upon the new philosophic ideas. Similar attempts were made by Isaac Newton, John Locke and Samuel Clarke. Other attempts to synthesize Christianity with natural religion were made by John Toland, who endeavored to prove that Christianity was not mysterious. Matthew Tindal, in his book *Christianity as Old as Creation* or *The Gospel a Republication of the Religion of Nature* emphasized the identity between the old faith and natural religion. Accordingly, there was no essential difference between them. There was no distinction between natural morality and religion. The former taught man to act in accordance with reason and the latter taught him to act also according to reason as the manifest will of God. Joseph Butler saw in revelation a mere "republication of natural religion". John Tilloston argued that "Natural religion is the foundation of all revealed religion and revelation is assigned simply to establish its duties". Accordingly, there is no fundamental difference between natural and supernatural religion. The latter does not contain anything not already inherent in the former. Leibniz considered Christianity meritorious since it had transformed the religion of the philosophers into the religion of the people.

### III

The only man who seriously attempted to synthesize Judaism with natural religion and thus vindicate its traditional aspects was Samuel David Luzzatto. His attempt at harmonization was propounded by him in his well known but often misunderstood, and even more frequently misinterpreted, concept of *Abrahamism*. The latter is ordinarily considered to represent Luzzatto's particular concept of Judaism as opposed to Atticism. Judaism and Atticism were two diametrically opposed cultures. Atticism emphasized reason; Judaism stressed emotion. The former extolled mind over heart, preferred outer form to inner spirit, worshipped holiness of beauty over beauty of holiness. Judaism, on the other hand, exalted heart over mind, revered holiness, and elevated it over beauty and stressed compassion, love, righteousness and simplicity.

Since these latter ideals and values were pursued by the progenitor of the Jewish people, Abraham, Luzzatto, ac-

cordingly, denoted his moral concept of Judaism by the term Abrahamism. According to this interpretation, the general term Judaism is too broad and all-inclusive. It embraces a multitude of concepts and a variety of views frequently conflicting and antithetical. They range from extreme rationalism professed by Maimonides and Ibn-Ezra, to extreme mysticism, professed by the followers of the Lurianic school. In order to emphasize the moral, compassionate and altruistic aspect of Judaism, Luzzatto termed his specific concept—Abrahamism.

In a letter writen in 1839 in Italian to Isaac Samuel Regio, Luzzatto tells of a new idea that overwhelmed him completely. Luzzatto, however, hesitated to expound his new theory in public which he considered novel, spontaneous and, perhaps, radical. In that letter, Luzzatto sets forth the theory of *Abrahamism* and *Mosaism*. Both constitute two distinct, separate but successive periods in the development of Judaism. The former began with Abraham and lasted until the Revelation on Sinai. The latter began immediately upon the termination of the former and continued uninterruptedly until the present time.[1] This theory appears in many of Luzzatto's writings and in his letters as well as in his book *Yesodei Hatorah*. He repeats it with emphasis as an accepted concept. A careful analysis will show that Luzzatto was actually proposing a higher synthesis between Judaism and natural religion, not unlike many of the Christian theologians in the eighteenth century, who made similar attempts with regard to Christianity. Judaism or Mosaism was merely a republication of natural religion or *Abrahamism*. Luzzatto

---

[1] S. D. Luzzato—*Epistalorio*, pp. 295-301.

was familiar with the writings of the exponents of reconciliation between the traditional religion and the religion of nature,[2] and he apparently made an effort to apply the same methods to Judaism.

The period of Abrahamism corresponds to the original state of mankind, when man lived in accordance with the dictates of nature. No laws and no regulations fettered man, no Torah was imposed by God amidst thunder and lightning. There was no need for precepts or commandments. Man felt what was naturally good and chose it, or what was wicked and avoided it. It was an era when man was completely free and happy and in that freedom he sought God rather than God seeking him, since the gulf between man and God was hardly distinguishable. During that period, Abraham found God by himself, without any supernatural assistance or "grace". It was Abraham, who discovered God, and clung to Him and not *vice versa*. Having recognized God, Abraham forsook idolatry and followed Him without any compulsion but of his own free will in a natural manner just as a child follows his father. In that early period, the belief in God was not based upon reason, speculation nor philosophical argumentation, but was simple and natural, flowing out of the yearning of the heart. This kind of faith was characteristic of the Patriarchs and the early Hebrews until the time of Moses.

Reconstructing from the Biblical narratives the Patriarchs' views, thoughts and outlook, during the period of Abra-

hamism, we find "that they believed in one God creator of heaven and earth, judge of the world, protector of those who fear Him, rewarding them and punishing the evildoers according to the work of their hands. Hence, we see also that they believed in miracles, angels and prophecy. They were concerned with the place where they would be interred (hence we may conclude that they believed in immortality and resurrection). We see that they prayed to God in time of trouble, as well as for others (Abraham for Abimelech), they made vows and when they were rescued—they praised Him and brought sacrifices. The way of God that Abraham taught his children—his household—was to do justice and righteousness.[3]

This was Judaism in its first phase of history. It was Abraham, who first recognized God and, as a result, God elected him and his descendants and set them apart from all other people of the world. In this Abrahamistic period, Judaism was natural and spontaneous. Its precepts were carried out, not in response to a superimposed heteronomous authority or by the threat of coercion, but in an autonomous fashion, in accordance with the dictates of the heart. In the course of time, with the increase of man upon earth, the children of Abraham, Isaac and Jacob, too, multiplied and grew from a small family into a people of six hundred thousand strong. They were liberated from the Egyptian bondage and went to establish a land of their own, to constitute an independent nation. In their new land the descendents of Abraham would be surrounded by many people, who were steeped in various pagan cults. It was,

2 Noah H. Rosenblomm, "The Conservative Rationalist School and its Influence on Luzzatto" (Hebrew) *Sura*, Vol. 2, Jerusalem, 1956, pp. 181-205.

3 S. D. Luzzatto, *Yesode Hatorah*, Part 1, pp. 9-11.

therefore, necessary to strengthen and fortify the natural ethics, morality and religion, which were self-evident and natural in the Abrahamistic period by giving to the nation that now replaced the old family a Divine code in revealed form in the times of Moses.

Thus, the period of Abrahamism terminated and the period of Mosaism began. During this new era, the Jews came in contact with the corrupt civilization of their neighbors. Natural religion could not be depended upon any longer. There was a need now for a revealed morality, based upon authority and enforced by coercion. The new revealed code, however, did not contain anything which was unknown during the period of natural religion in the time of Abrahamism. The changes, however, that took place during the crucial period between the Exodus and the conquest of Canaan, made it imperative that revealed, authoritative Mosaism should supersede natural Abrahamism. Essentially, as far as the content was concerned, Mosaism only gave legal and authoritative validity to the simple self-evident tenets recognized and practiced out of free will by Abraham.

This distinction of two different phases in the historical development of Judaism, Abrahamism and Mosaism, the first which represented natural Judaism, when man sought God, and the second revealed Judaism when God sought man, is not dissimilar to the distinction drawn by many Christian theologians during the eighteenth century. Luzzatto, like those Christian theologians, attempted to reconcile historic religion with natural religion, and thus validate the former on the grounds that it is a mere duplication of the latter. Unlike his Christian predecessors, Luzzatto

failed to draw the inherent inferences from his basic premise. His theory, however, was replete with far-reaching philosophical and theological implications.

## IV

Luzzatto's theory obliterated the medieval distinction between the "realm of grace" and the "realm of reason". Actually, nature preceded grace chronologically, but essentially, from the point of view of content, there was no difference between them. Mosaism, which was synonymous with grace, did not differ from Abrahamism, which connoted nature. We have already pointed out that Luzzatto endeavored to prove that Judaism was not a heteronomous religion, which superimposes upon its adherents duties which are not in accordance with nature. The heteronomous view was considered objectionable by the Deist rationalists, the exponents of the Enlightenment period, as well as by the theorists of the Jewish Reform movement. The latter eliminated a great portion of the Law due to its heteronomic character. The laws and observances that they left, were only those which had an autonomous basis.

The heteronomous view brought about a dilemma that either Judaism was not natural, since it had to be imposed upon man against his will and contrary to his nature, or that nature was not perfect due to the fact that an outside force, unnatural or supernatural, was required to complete it. Both horns of the dilemma were unacceptable to Luzzatto, since they would have introduced a dichotomy between Judaism and nature. By distinguishing two distinct historical eras in the development of Judaism, this dilemma was avoided. During the first period of Abrahamism,

JUDAISM AND NATURAL RELIGION

Judaism was not revealed and was not heteronomous. It was adhered to, nevertheless, due to the fact that Judaism then was natural. Abraham and his children discovered Judaism and fulfilled its laws and precepts on an autonomous basis. They abided by the laws of Judaism, as by the laws of nature. Their faith in the existence of God was just as unshakable as their knowledge of the existence of the world. The distinction between good and evil was as clear to them as the distinction between light and darkness. Judaism did not emanate from a Book, nor from a supernatural authority, but from the heart. Only when man became unnatural, when an invisible wall arose and separated man from nature, did Judaism begin to appear unnatural. Its laws, which in the Abrahamic period were autonomous, became subsequently heteronomous. When man became estranged from nature, alienated from his own true self, and corrupted by civilization, it was necessary to transform natural Judaism from its Abrahamic state into an authoritative Mosaism. Essentially, Judaism is nature and its laws autonomous.

The exponents of natural religion argued that all traditional and historic religions will eventually disappear or be superseded by other religions. "Everything that has a beginning will sometime have an end, and *vice versa*, that which has never had a beginning can never perish", said Diderot. Accordingly, natural religion alone is the only true and eternal religion, which will never be replaced in the course of historical development.[4] By making Judaism, in its Abrahamic stage, synonymous

with natural religion, Luzzatto thus established that Judaism was not a religion which began at a certain moment in history, but was always in existence. Consequently, Judaism was, and will be eternal.

Luzzatto's theory answered an old but serious question about the "chosen people" idea. Why did God elect Israel and not any other nation to receive the Torah? This problem seemed to disappear in the light of Luzzatto's explanation. Accordingly, God did not favor Israel, nor did He choose Abraham out of all the people of the world. It was Abraham, who sought and found God, followed in His ways, executed His principles and taught his own children justice, righteousness and the laws of God. It was, therefore, only reasonable that God should give the Torah, in its revealed manifestation, to Abraham's descendents, who knew it already as a family tradition, and had fulfilled it for many centuries, in accordance with their natural inclination. God did not elect Israel for any particular esoteric reasons, but merely gave Divine authority (the Torah) to a way of life which had been in existence for a long time, based heretofore upon natural and traditional foundations.

Luzzatto's theory that Revelation was preceded by a period of Abrahamism explained still another old, vexing problem, namely, the reason that the Torah, which is the source of religion and knowledge of God, does not deal with any metaphysical or eschatological problems or theological doctrines. Accepting the premise that the Torah was already known and practiced in its Abrahamistic form, there was every reason to assume that those basic principles were already axiomatically accepted, and

---

4 Ernst Cassirer, *The Philosophy of the Enlightenment*, Boston, Beacon Press, 1955, pp. 170-171.

there was no need to reiterate them. Otherwise, all the other practices could not have been taken for granted. The revealed Torah did not have to contain those axioms which were never questioned or doubted. The only need was to write down the laws and commandments which, due to the changes of conditions and circumstances, were in danger of being forgotten.

### V

The narrative portion of the Bible has always aroused a number of questions. Why did the Torah, which is eternal and Divine, dwell so extensively and minutely upon the personal biographies and histories of the Patriarchs? Why did the Torah describe all these seemingly insignificant episodes in such elaborate detail? In the light of Luzzatto's theory, this enigma was solved. The Torah includes both periods of Judaism, the Abrahamistic and the Mosaic. The Mosaic religion appears in the form of legislation and exhortation, whereas the Abrahamistic religion is described in simple narrative. Reading the stories and the biographies of the Patriarchs and their descendents, reading the details of their domestic life, their customs, their conversations and relationships, we learn about their outlook on Judaism in that early and naturalistic era. We also see the striking similarity between both phases of Judaism, which were identical in all respects and represented only two different aspects of the same way of life.

The criticism, leveled by early Christianity against the excessive legalism and formalism of the Pharasees, became one of the cardinal motifs of subsequent Christian theology and even influenced

the subsequent philosophic appraisal of Judaism. Spinoza considered his ancestral religion a legal system which was neither religious nor moral, but aimed primarily at the political and social welfare of the Jewish nation.[5] Kant, too, saw in Judaism a religion devoid of moral imperatives and religious feeling. The Jewish religion simply insisted upon legal and moral conformity. Even the commandments of the Decalogue ought not to be viewed as moral precepts, but rather as legal enactments.[6] Due to the lack of moral insight in Judaism, Kant seriously recommended that the Jews incorporate into their religion the ethical principles of the Gospels.[7] That Judaism was legalistic was not even disputed by Mendelssohn, who considered Judaism rationally superior to Christianity. Mendelssohn maintained that Judaism was Revealed Law and, therefore, it implied immutability.

Luzzatto seemed to have removed this stigma of excessive legalism and formalism hurled at Judaism by theologians and philosophers. While Mosaism has many legal aspects, they are not devoid of religious feeling or a sense of morality. Behind the legal and formalistic facade of Mosaism, there is the foundation of Abrahamism, which shows that in the period of natural religion, before these acts and precepts were legally formulated, they were executed on a voluntary basis as emanating from the heart, nature and moral consciousness.

The concept of Revelation was repugnant to many rationalists due to its particularistic aspect. Since Revelation implied personal salvation, it was decried

---

[5] Julius Guttman, *Dat Umada*, Jerusalem 1956, pp. 195-196.

[6] *Ibid*, pp. 222.

[7] *Ibid*, pp.223.

as immoral since God had revealed Himself to only a small segment of humanity, leaving the rest of mankind in darkness. The problem of salvation also affected the generations who lived prior to the historic act of revelation. It was thought unreasonable and unethical that all those generations, as well as most of humanity, should be deprived of salvation from which they were excluded by time or space, or lack of knowledge.

Again, Luzzatto's theory of Abrahamism seemed to solve this vexing problem. While Judaism was revealed to the Jews only, due to historic and cultural circumstances, Abrahamism was open to everyone. Any person, whenever and wherever he lived, could have attained salvation by following Judaism in its natural form. Though Judaism, in its Mosaic aspect, appeared to be particularistic it was, nevertheless, universal in its Abrahamic one. Any person, at any time, could follow Judaism in its natural state and have the same advantage as those to whom these very same principles were revealed authoritatively and supernaturally.

Luzzatto does not draw the distinction between *traditional* precepts, which are not inherently, right or wrong, but are the commands of God and rational ones which are approved or disapproved by our reason. This distinction, prevalent in most of the works of Jewish medieval philosophers,[8] could not be accepted by Luzzato, since it would have implied that there are heteronomous laws which are not natural and of which man, without supernatural aid could not be aware of. Therefore, we noticed that Luzzato included the offering of sacrifices in the Abrahamic era, not as

---

8 Isaac Husik, *A History of Medieval Jewish Philosophy*, Philadelphia, 1941, pp. 38-39.

a heteronomous law unacceptable to reason, but rather as an expression of gratitude emanating from man's feeling of thankfulness to God. The differentiation between the two groups of commandments is rather due to our being removed from nature and natural religion. Consequently, many things which could formerly be categorized as "rational" became relegated to the position "traditional" or actually non-rational.

## VI

The synthesis of Luzzato, between Judaism and natural religion, would have had undoubtedly a tremendous impact upon the intellectual circles in his day when nature and natural ideas and concepts were valued highly. It is, therefore, to be regretted that S. D. Luzzatto, who propounded this profound theory of Abrahamism and Mosaism, left it in its embryonic state, arrested in its initial stages. Neither he nor his followers ever elaborated upon it, nor did they investigate its possibilities and inherent applications. However, in spite of its embryonic nature, the implications necessary for the reconciliation and harmonization of Judaism and natural religion are inherent in his theory, and evident to everyone able to draw out its implicit ideas. Though Luzzatto's theory was primarily designed to meet the challenges of his time and harmonize Judaism with the philosophic ideas of his age, many of its inherent implications still seem of interest to the contemporary traditionalist, who endeavors to hold on precariously to both pillars—revelation and reason.

For the avowed secularist, who negates revelation completely, or to the modern religious relativist, who considers it a mere figure of speech, Luzzatto's views have only a literary and historical significance. For the contemporary traditionalist, who though operating in a religious universe of discourse not dissimilar to that of his ancestors, is still sensitive to the outer intellectual climate of his times, Luzzatto's view possesses more than historical interest. Accepting the historicity of the fact of revelation on Sinai, the contemporary traditionalist, like Luzzatto, is in search of a rationale for its particularistic manifestation. Though he firmly believes in its universality, its timelessness, and its redemptive purpose for all mankind, he is, nevertheless, acutely cognizant that its temporal and local aspect is unacceptable. Luzzatto's view that historical conditions necessitated the revelation of God on Sinai, in order to prevent the disintegration of natural Abrahamism, and to fortify the Israelites against the corroding influencs of heathenism, may mitigate the difficulty of the problem.

The contemporary traditionalist, like his predecessors, accepts the idea of the election of Israel. He is aware, however, that its ethnocentric aspect meets with misunderstanding and objection. Living in a democratic society and imbued with the ideal of human equality, he finds it difficult to reconcile the latter with the concept of "chosenness". Luzzatto's explanation that Israel was not selected by God, due to its racial or ethnic singularity, but due to the fact that it was already in possession as a family tradition of the verities of subsequent revelation, makes it plausible even in modern times. Furthermore, the idea that cognition of God, morality, religious truth and salvation of mankind, are not contingent upon historic revelation and can be achieved by anyone through its natural manifestation, vindicates the universal and democratic aspect of Judaism and minimizes the objections to its historic revelation.

Subscribing to the Divinity and veracity of the Scriptures the contemporary traditionalist is aware of the criticism leveled against its quantitative elaborations and its seemingly irrelevant biographies and historical narratives. He, too, is mystified by the lack of metaphysics, theology, philosophy and eschatology in the Bible, an interest he shares with all perplexed moderns. Luzzatto's explanation that these fundamental ideas were known and accepted in early Israelite society so that there was no need of elaboration, while not satisfactory in full, may serve as an apologetic pawn. Luzzatto's distinction that the Bible contains two parts, a naturalistic-Abrahamic portion, which is reflected in its biographic and narrative sections, and the corresponding theophanic-Mosaic part, which is stated in legal terms, may validate the excessive narrative elaborations.

The contemporary traditionalist, who is under the impact of the various anti-intellectual philosophies of modern times, may not be as anxious as S. D. Luzzatto or Samson Raphael Hirsch to rationalize the entire regimen of commandments, precepts, rites and rituals. Nevertheless, he would feel more comfortable if he could point to the non-mystical and autonomous aspect of the *Mitzvoth*, as well as to their moral values behind the outer formalistic and legalistic encrustation. Rejecting relativism in religion, affirming the historicity of revelation, the validity of the Bible, the eternity of Judaism, and the immutable character of the *Mitzvoth*, the contemporary traditionalist will find many ideas in common with Luzzatto's interpretation of Judaism.

But this is not to expect that Luzzatto's views can serve as a cure-all to the numerous theological and philosophical problems that beset the contemporary traditionalist. Though the latter's religious universe of discourse has not appreciably changed, the outer intellectual climate to which he is sensitive, and to which he has to relate his theological views, is in a state of fluidity. Nevertheless, amidst the changes and the fluctuations of the general contemporary intellectual climate, Luzzatto's attempt at a higher synthesis between traditional Judaism and the philosophy of his time may prove both philosophically provoking and theologically fructifying.

# HERMANN COHEN'S PHILOSOPHY OF JUDAISM

SIMON KAPLAN

# HERMANN COHEN'S PHILOSOPHY OF JUDAISM

SIMON KAPLAN

TWO EVENTS put an end to the spiritual isolation in which European Jewry had lived up to the midde of the eighteenth century. One, the personality and philosophy of Moses Mendelssohn, erupted from within; the other, coming from without, was the French Revolution, which began three years after Mendelssohn's death.

After Mendelssohn and the French Revolution, the German Jews followed, by and large, the general trend of the Enlightenment in Europe. The essence of religion was not merely to affirm divine revelation but to examine and comprehend it by the light of reason; revelation became dependent upon its harmony with "natural reason", especially "ethical reason." Among Jews, this attitude found its expression chiefly in religious reform, and in the quickening and renewal of the scientific study of Judaism (*Wissenschaft des Judentums*). The traditional foundations of Judaism were examined from the point of view of rational religion and brought closer to the secular spirit of the time. The consequences of this activity

were the abandonment by many Jews of traditional Jewish law, a widespread movement to eliminate whatever civil laws restricted Jewish rights, and the creation of secular Jewish nationalism.

Hermann Cohen's mature work was done in the final period of the Reform movement in Germany at the end of the nineteenth and the beginning of the twentieth century. Reform Judaism and its antithesis, Neo-Orthodoxy, were by then well established. Just as the ideas of the Enlightenment had inspired Mendelssohn to reinterpret traditional Judaism, so it was through the ethics and theology of Kant that Cohen, one of the leading German philosophers of his time, approached Reform Judaism, whose ideas he systematized. The vigor of his thinking, together with his reverence for the sources of Judaism, made Cohen the greatest exponent of Jewish thought since the beginning of the Enlightenment — of which he is the culminating point in Jewish thought.

## I

Two interrelated ideas dominate Cohen's thinking: the *ethical idea of the one God* and the resulting idea of an *ethical mankind*. Jewish monotheism is for Cohen the original source of these ideas, and the moral improvement of mankind is to him the specific task of the Jews.

Cohen rejected both Orthodoxy and Zionism. His rejection of the traditional

SIMON KAPLAN is professor at St. John's College in Annapolis, Md. He is author of *Das Problem der Geschichte in H. Cohens System der Philosophie* (1930). — This article is the second in the department "Teachers and Thinkers". The first was Nahum N. Glatzer's "Franz Rosenzweig: the Story of a Conversion", which appeared in the last issue of this Journal. Other studies in this department will be published in forthcoming issues.

law followed from his reinterpretation of revelation as a revelation of ethical reason. The underlying reason for his rejection of Zionism was his affirmation of Galut (diaspora-exile). For Cohen, Galut is the heart and core of Israel's world-mission and symbolizes its election to love the One God and suffer the "martyrdom of monotheism." Thus Cohen combined in his thinking the ethics of the Enlightenment and the traditional doctrine of the love of God and suffering for His sake.

In 1880, when Cohen was thirty-six, he published an article entitled *Ein Bekenntnis zur Judenfrage (My Position on the Jewish Question)*. Years later, Cohen himself designated 1880 as the year of his "return". For although he had received a good Jewish upbringing and education—in childhood and youth from his father, and later in the Rabbinical Seminary at Breslau — he had hitherto devoted himself almost entirely to philosophy. Two of his basic works on Kant had already appeared before the publication of this article, one of which, *Kant's Theory of Experience*, did more than any other work of its time to bring about the rediscovery of Kant. The ideas developed in it later became the foundation of Cohen's own system of neo-Kantian idealism.

After publication of his *Bekenntnis*, Hermann Cohen never lost his interest in Jewish problems. The older he grew, the more fervently did he apply himself to religious studies, and this in turn affected his own system of philosophy. The idea of the One God, as well as the teachings of the prophets, were infused into his ethical system, though in such a form as to make religion a mere complement to ethics, in which it is entirely absorbed. "Ethics simply cannot recognize the independence of religion...it can recognize religion only as a natural

process which in its cultural maturity coincides with ethics," wrote Cohen in 1907 in his *Ethik des reinen Willens (Ethics of Pure Will)*. Yet the problem of individuality, which found no solution within his system of ethics, led Cohen eventually to revise this view.

In his *Begriff der Religion im System der Philosophie (Concept of Religion in the System of Philosophy)*, which appeared in 1915, three years before his death, Cohen assigned to religion a "special" task within the framework of ethics. This special task of religion, as distinguished from ethics, is to supply a foundation for individuality. Ethics knows only the general law of duty. In the presence of the individual with his imperfections and frailties, it stands silent and helpless. Man, in the consciousness of his frailty, realizes that he himself cannot be the source of forgiveness for his own transgression. In his helplessness, he finds and recognizes God as the sole source of forgiveness. To cognize God, however, means, in monotheistic religion, to re-cognize, to acknowledge God; it means to love Him. And thus the ethical knowledge of man's guilt is transformed into the religious love of God. But the love of God, according to the biblical commandment, involves the whole man: he must love God with all his heart, with all his soul, with all his strength. Religious love embraces every aspect of the human consciousness. "The love of God", says Cohen, "must unite all things and all problems of the world."

Along with the love of God, religion reveals God's love of man, for God is the forgiver. In religion thus arises the reciprocal relation — the "correlation", as Cohen puts it — of God to man and man to God. This correlation is the special content that distinguishes religion from ethics; it corresponds to the biblical concept of the "covenant" with God. In

Cohen's view, however, the religious concept of love has no independence, but only a "privileged position," within the field of ethics. Hence Cohen interprets the love of God as the love of the ethical ideal, whose "prototype" is God.

## II

It was with this concept of religion that Cohen approached the traditional sources of Judaism. The result was his mature work, *Die Religion der Vernunft aus den Quellen des Judentums (Religion of Reason as Drawn from the Sources of Judaism)*, which appeared posthumously. According to the subtitle originally intended by the author, it is a "Jewish philosophy of religion and a Jewish ethics."

The "uniqueness" of God is the concept from which Cohen develops the doctrine of monotheism. He distinguishes between "uniqueness" and "oneness." The latter expresses merely a negation of the manyness of the polytheistic gods. The statement, God is "one", as in the *Shema,* is not merely a negation of God's manyness, but carries also the positive meaning of God's exclusive uniqueness. Uniqueness, as expressed in the rabbinical term *yihud,* signifies the exclusive otherness and incommensurability of God's being in relation to other modes of being. Positively expressed, God's uniqueness means that His divine being transcends all human or natural existence. Therefore pantheism, which teaches the identity of God and nature, is incompatible with monotheism. This essential "otherness" or "yonderness" of God excludes the possibility of an intermediary: whether between God and nature, as in the logos of Philo, or between God and man, as in the person of the Christian savior. Similarly, the uniqueness of God excludes the "incorporation" of God in the Trinity, for the Trinity compromises the exclusive uniqueness of God.

Divine being, which is the only true being, and in relation to which all other being is "only appearance" or mere "existence," does not imply that God stands outside all relation to the world and to man. A relation to the world and to man, a relation compatible with His uniqueness, is inherent in God's being: the unique God is Creator and Revealer.

For Cohen, however, creation does not have the literal-"mythological" sense of the biblical narrative. Nor does it have the meaning ascribed to it by the theory of emanation, according to which the genesis of the world is contained in God's being. If that were true, says Cohen, "God and nature would be the same thing," and then God could not be the Creator. Cohen also discards the traditional concept of creation as a single event in time, a "work in the beginning". This he replaces with the later concept of "renewal of the world". In accordance with his logic, he interprets the latter as a continuous preservation and renewal of the world, thus deviating from the traditional teaching of the unique act of "creation out of nothing."

The biblical narrative of the creation distinguishes the creation of nature and of animals, who were created "after their kind", from the creation of man, who was created in God's "image". Man created in God's image is conceived not only as a particular species of animal, but as a creature endowed with knowledge, above all the knowledge of good and evil. By virtue of the creation of man's reason, which for Cohen is eminently ethical reason, man transcends the world of animals and enters into the realm proper and peculiar to himself, the realm of correlation to God. This correlation to God, which constitutes the content of religion, is the "characteristic difference that distinguishes man from animals." Thus the creation of man's reason determines his being, a being separated from all living creatures for the sake of his relation to God. Cohen finds this separation formulated in the words of the *neilah* prayer: "Thou hast distinguished man from the very beginning and hast acknowledged him worthy to stand before Thee."

Even though man's reason is derived from God, man is free to choose between "life and Good and death and Evil" (Deut. 30:15). Cohen invokes the talmudic saying: "Everything is in the hand of God, except the fear of God," which in this context means that man should "stand" before God only in freedom.

As the traditional term of "standing" before God indicates, the relation of man to God is not a contemplative one. Since God is "unique," God cannot, as medieval thought believed, become an object of knowledge, not even "analogically." God's relation to man in revelation is no "unveiling" *(revelatio)* of God's being. The traditional term for revelation is "the giving of the Torah". In the "laws and ordinances", as in the Torah in general, God reveals not His being but His will, and He does not reveal His will in respect to His being, but in respect to man. Even in speaking to Moses "face to face," God says nothing more of His being than " I am that I am." He reveals to Moses not His being but only His "back", that is to say, the "wake" or effects of God's actions, which the Jewish tradition interprets as God's works in distinction to His being. The "works" are not God's qualities but rather His "actions" with regard to man: they should be understood as "normative" for the actions of man. Basing himself on Maimonides, Cohen interprets the "thirteen qualities" that God reveals to Moses (Exod. 34:6,7) not as qualities of God,

but as "attributes of God's action," *i.e.*, as norms for the road of man's ascent to ethical perfection.

Cohen sums up the "thirteen qualities" in two concepts: love and justice. These are not revealed in order that man should know God through them, but in order that man should worship God through love and justice in his own actions. To "know" God means to "recognize" Him as the Father of mankind, to love Him. But the love of God as the Father of mankind implies for man God's forgiveness. In his worship of God, man's love of his fellow-men corresponds to God's love of man: for only because God is the common "Father" do "other men" become "fellow-men," or brothers.

Cohen finds the mutual relation of God and man expressed in the biblical passage: "Ye shall be holy, for I the Lord your God am holy" (Lev. 19:2). Thus holiness becomes common to God and man, with the distinction that God *is* holy, while man should *become* holy. To Cohen, this means that God as the ethical prototype prescribes man's ethical ideal. Hence God's holiness means for man the "infinite task" of man's ethical perfection. The chasm between God and man remains unbridgeable, and there is no end to man's striving to achieve the ethical ideal of holiness.

### III

It now becomes clear that for Cohen the revelation of the Torah does not have the traditional sense of definite "laws and ordinances." In the Torah, the eternal law, the eternal "source" of ethical reason, is revealed as a "foundation" for historically changing "laws and ordinances." For Cohen, this justifies the reform of certain laws in the light of historical development, though the reform must harmonize with the eternal "source" of ethical reason. Nor is revelation to be understood as an isolated historical event occurring on Mount Sinai. Cohen interprets the Rabbinical tradition, according to which the whole Torah, including the Oral Tradition, was given "to Moses on Mount Sinai," as implying that the revelation is a "living and renewable continuity." The words from Deuteronomy, "The Lord made not this covenant with our fathers, but with us, even us, who are all of us here alive this day" (5:3), are taken to mean that the living continuity of revelation extends to the Jew of every present and future, and is not limited to the single historical event on Mount Sinai.

Revelation did not begin on Mount Sinai, for through Noah God concluded a covenant with the whole human race. The "seven commandments of the sons of Noah", which God revealed to Noah, constitute an "ethical foundation" for the entire human race. Upon this "ethical foundation" will arise "the pious men of the nations of the world," who like the Israelites have a share in the "world-to-come". For Cohen this equality, this participation of all the pious — Jews and non-Jews alike — in eternal life, is the ethical consequence of the idea of the One God, which alone can shape the idea of one mankind.

In the development of monotheism, the idea of one mankind culminated in prophetic messianism. The prophets, as Cohen interprets them, transfer the revelation from the various ordinances given on Mount Sinai to the "heart of man," which is equated with the ethical. God reveals "what is good" (Micah 8:6), that is, the ethical, and in their vision of the messianic age, the prophets establish the ethical ideal of one mankind. Cohen interprets the messianic age, not as the end of time, but as the dawn of a new era, the ethical age, in which the nations of the earth will find reconciliation and

peace. The messianic peace is not merely negative: it means not merely that war, this specifically human struggle, will cease; it also carries the positive significance of inner peace for the human soul and a united mankind. It is in this sense, Cohen believes, that the Messiah is proclaimed the "prince of peace."

With the messianic ideal, the prophets introduce a new concept of history unknown to the Greeks. For the Greeks, history was the "knowledge of the past"; for the prophets, history is "the province of the seer," the vision of the ideal future. The Greeks oriented their concept of history "in space"; for them, the world was divided into their own society, and the barbarian world outside its borders; there was no concept of one mankind. The vision of the prophets orients history not in space, but in time, and this time is the future. In this future, despite all present and past experience, the ethical ideal of a united mankind will be realized. Thus, history is not "eternal recurrence", as Plato conceived it, but a development toward the ideal future of mankind.

God's covenant with Noah guarantees the realization of this future. His covenant with the earth guarantees the preservation of nature for the realization of the ethical ideal. His "providence for the human race" creates in the messianic age "new heavens and a new earth" (Isaiah 65:17), i.e. a "new historical reality." Only then will true history, the history of a united mankind, dawn and the "victory of the good" be realized. It is in this sense that Cohen affirms: "Monotheism is the true consolation of history."

### IV

The unique God is not only mankind's "God of history." He is in equal measure the consolation of the individual person, of erring, frail man, in his "specifically human" quality of sinfulness. In consonance with the Jewish tradition, Cohen rejects the doctrine of Original Sin; man does not sin because Adam transmitted to his descendents a vitiated nature. Man does not sin in consequence of Adam's sin, but because of his own transgression. But man's guilt is not man's tragic end: it shall not be his ruin, for God has no "pleasure at all that the wicked should die...." God's pleasure is rather "that he should return from his ways and live" (Ezek. 18:23).

The traditional way of "return" from sin is *teshubah.* This word means both conversion and turning back and is usually translated as "repentance," which does not exactly render the concept. While repentance primarily expresses the recogniton of guilt and an attitude of regret, *teshubah* implies the act of "turning away" from one manner of life and "returning" to another. Sin is a "turning away" from God, and *teshubah* enables man to "return" to God, to become free from sin and achieve forgiveness.

The pre-exilic concept of *teshubah* led to the ritual of sacrifice. The blood of the sacrificial animal replaces the blood, *i.e.,* the life, of the sinner. In the blood of the animal, the sinner sacrifices himself. He lays his life in God's hand and only God can give back to him his life cleansed of sin. Because of this cleansing through *teshubah,* the prophet Ezekiel attached especial importance to sacrifice. Cohen, however, although invoking Ezekiel, believes that the instrument of *Teshubah* required by Ezekiel — sacrifice — was merely historically determined. The mediation of priest and sacrifice distorted the "immediate" relation of the sinful man to God. Cohen cites the psalm, "The sacrifices of God are a broken spirit, a broken and a contrite heart" (Ps. 51:17), which he takes to mean that man himself, without the mediation of sacrifice or

priest, must stand "immediately" before God.

In *teshubah,* man recognizes himself, and himself alone, as the author of his sinful deed. Sin, as the knowledge that one has "turned away" from God's will, thus becomes a "turning into" oneself, an avowal of the sin, and this is self-condemnation. Out of the depths of despair in himself as sinner, man recognizes his own isolation from God and men. He recognizes his guilt and the suffering that he has brought on himself and which no other man can forgive or take away. From this isolation in suffering, man recognizes that only God can forgive his sin. Thus the knowledge of sin leads man to the knowledge of God, or rather, to the avowal of his sin before God. Between the "turning away" from God and the "turning back" to God, there occurs a transformation in which the human self, cleansed of sin, is born. In *teshubah* God gives to man "a new heart...and a new spirit" (Ezek. 36:26). Man, "conceived in sin" (Ps. 51:5), attains his true self, his purified "humanity," only when he is "reborn" in *teshubah,* which is when the truly human individual is born.

Does man — erring and sinful man — ever reach the moment in which he is freed from sin and forgiven by God? Man ever knows only the commandment to cast off his sin; he knows only the labor of self-purification, the endless task of achieving holiness, the goal of which is the holiness of God. But the sure knowledge of achievement and forgiveness is denied him. Man's hope is his firm "trust" *(emunah)* in God, the merciful and forgiving.

This "reliance" or "trust" or "fidelity", as the word *emunah* should be translated, must be distinguished from "faith". Faith aims at the knowledge of, or participation in, the very *essence* of God, as, for example, faith in the passion and resurrection of Christ. Faith in the sacrament whereby bread and wine are transformed into the body and blood of Christ, even when this is conceived symbolically, implies an act which imitates or participates in the essence of God. Jewish "trust", however, never applies to the essence of God's being but to His will and actions *with regard to man* exclusively.

The expression of God's will towards man is the law, which is therefore the object of "fidelity" and the connecting link between man and God. But the law never prescribes an action intended to imitate or to participate in the essence of God, for its aim is not to know but to obey God. The law does, it is true, provide for symbols, such as circumcision, phylacteries, fringes, etc., but their only meaning is to bring one to "remember all the commandments of the Lord, and do them" (Num. 15:39).

"Trust" in God is thus at the same time "fidelity" to the "lawful," *i.e.*, the ethical act. And the meaning of "trust" is precisely that from his "trust" in God's forgiveness, the erring and sinful man gathers the strength for the ethical act of self-purification. Or in the words of the Midrash which Cohen cites, "only after the action" that man performs "does the holy spirit rest upon him."

While in Christian teaching forgiveness of sin rests essentially on faith and the grace of God, in the Jewish meaning of trust, according to Cohen, the act of self-purification incumbent upon man is strictly separate from the grace of God. No one can relieve man of his task of self-purification from sin; man himself must perform it. And only God can forgive sin; "no son of God shall purify you, but your Father alone." Cohen finds this relation of man to God and God to man expressed in the words of Rabbi Akiba: "Happy are you, Israel: who purifies you

and before whom do you purify yourself? It is your Father in heaven."

Cohen sees penance *(teshubah)* as the climax and epitome of all purification; and the words of the Mishnah, "Do penance a day before your death," are to be taken as an injunction to do penance every day of our lives. Penance should not, however, be performed in the mystical isolation of the individual; it should take place in public, in the community of the "participants in guilt and fellow-worshipers." On the Day of Atonement the sin of the entire community of Israel is forgiven.

In the rhythm of the Jewish year, the Day of Atonement is the climax towards which man strives. After man has taken on himself all the pain and suffering of self-purification, God makes him pure and guiltless on the Day of Atonement. This is the moment for which man has been waiting in all his self-purification. This is the moment when eternity penetrates time, when man's penance is transformed into reconciliation with God, and when man is reborn in innocence. But it is "only for a moment" that man is freed from his guilt and suffering and the "road to life" is again opened to him. Afterwards he may "strive and err" again, for as Ecclesiastes says, "there is not a just man on earth that doeth good, and sinneth not" (Eccl. 7:20). But the words of Ezekiel still remain in force: sin shall not be man's ruin, but shall lead to repentance. Repentance elevates man to the heights of reconciliation with God, so that, according to the Talmud: "In the place where the repentant man stands, the perfectly righteous may not stand."

V

Just as the individual stands before God in repentance and hopes for forgiveness, so the whole people of Israel, apart from other peoples, stands before God and hopes for forgiveness and redemption. In Balaam's words, Israel is a people that "shall dwell alone and shall not be reckoned among the nations" (Num. 23:9). The real history of Israel, Cohen believes, confirms this statement of the heathen prophet, for Israel lacks the common characteristics of a nation: soil, language, state. The soil of Israel is hallowed soil, the language the holy language, and the state the future kingdom of God. Israel's history begins with the call to Abraham: "Get thee out of thy country and from thy kindred and from thy father's house" (Gen. 12:1). Israel's history begins with the exile. Even the gathering of Israel into a state was only a transitory phenomenon; in reality it was a "gathering for exile." It is a "miracle" that the Jewish people has been preserved in dispersion, for the "peoples of the world" disappear with the loss of state.

Among the Jews, the state was replaced by the community, the sword by the law, for in the words of Saadya, quoted by Cohen: "Our people is a people only by virtue of its Torah." The community became the community of those who studied the Torah and were faithful to the law; it became "people and religion" at once. This community has "isolated" itself from the "peoples of the world" through the idea of the unique God and His law. Cohen regards the entire law as an instrument of this separation. In obedience to the commandments, this separation becomes a living relation to God.

God's commandment — the *mitzvah* — has the double meaning of commandment and duty. The commandment comes from God, but duty comes from man. It is the function of the *mitzvah* to integrate the entire life of the Jew and all his acts through the eternal law. Thus

the difference between profane and sacred falls away, for every act stands in the service of the "ideal of holiness." All earthly activity is embraced and illumined by the divine law: "God gives the Torah as He gives everything, life and bread, and death too." With the *mitzvah*, the Jew takes upon himself the "yoke of the kingdom of God," and all his acts serve the "sanctification of God's Name."

Their election for the "sanctification of the Name" is the "greatest happiness" of the community of Israel, just as the commandment "to lay down their life for the holiness of the divine Name" has become the "greatest martyrdom" in history. All other peoples, to be sure, have also suffered in history, but their suffering was contingent on shifts in political power. With the disappearance of their political power, the peoples disappeared too. The history of Israel has taken a different course: only with the loss of its state, with the emergence of the "world-mission" of realizing the messianic ideal, did the true historical existence of the people of Israel begin. The "uniqueness" of the history of Israel rests precisely on the fact that its historical mission in the world began only with the loss of all earthly power and treasure, with "political defenselessness." Political defenselessness, suffering, and martyrdom become the true "historical characteristics" of the history of Israel: "It passes through history like a Job."

Non-Jewish peoples, with a "self-righteousness dangerous for their own morality," interpret this suffering as God's punishment for the sins of Israel. It is true that the sufferings of Israel have this significance as punishment; or rather, Israel is "chosen" by God for punishment: "You only have I known of all the families of the earth: therefore I will punish you for all your iniquities" (Amos

3:2). But this election for punishment does not exhaust the meaning of the suffering of Israel. Israel's suffering has another, quite independent meaning.

Job is the prophet who reveals this meaning through his own suffering. Job's suffering is not brought about by his sins, as his friends in blind "self-righteousness" assume; no, Job suffers innocently. Thus Job reveals the truth that there is a suffering that is not punishment, not the consequence of sin. He does not suffer for his sins, but "for others," for his friends, for the world, which does not understand the meaning of this suffering. Job reveals the truth that the sufferings of men belong to the "divine plan of salvation." Suffering is no "defect" in human history; it is "integrated with the divine organization of the world" as the source of purification for redemption. The true "saving forces" of history are not the state, not power and earthly happiness, but the purifying suffering that binds man to the true goal of history, redemption. Israel knows and freely professes this revelation of suffering, and if Israel has throughout its history been "a people of suffering," suffering has also become "its vital force," from which it has gathered purification for redemption.

Traditional Jewish exegesis, to which Cohen adheres, sees the people of Israel in the suffering "servant of God" (Isaiah 52, 53), in the Messiah. "But thou, Israel, art my servant...whom I have chosen... and said unto thee: Thou art my servant" (Isaiah 41:8, 9). Israel is the messianic people; it suffers "for the peoples who do not accept the unique God." This suffering should indeed be the punishment visited upon the other peoples, who are unwilling to accept the unique God. But because Israel has been chosen to recognize the unique God, it sees the guilt and the sins of other peoples and takes their suffering voluntarily upon itself. "By his knowledge shall my righteous servant justify many, for he shall bear their iniquities" (Isaiah 53:11). Thus Israel has been chosen to be the "servant" of many peoples, to "suffer in their place." "He was wounded for our transgressions, he was bruised for our iniquities: the chastisement of our peace was upon him" (Isaiah 53:5). The peoples of the world do not "consider" the sacrificial sufferings of Israel. They do not realize that Israel's suffering is the "suffering of love" for the sake of their redemption, that Israel suffers "the martyrdom of monotheism."

God loves Israel because He loves those who suffer. Israel is therefore God's vessel on earth, His "treasure", through which God's will on earth will be fulfilled. "God loves in Israel nothing but the human race," says Cohen, for Israel takes upon itself a yoke of suffering for the redemption of all mankind, which will also be the redemption of Israel. In its suffering, Israel longs for the messianic age, when "the Lord will be one and His name one" (Zech. 14:9) for the entire human race.

## VI

Cohen's religious philosophy breathes traditional Jewish religion. Cohen did ask the radical question whether the revelation on Mount Sinai could be brought into harmony with philosophy — with the love of self-sufficient reason — that originated in pagan Greece. His answer invoked the philosophy of Jewish medieval rationalism, in which, he believed, "reason is made into the root of the content of revelation"; and he approached the traditional sources with the basic assumption that "the origin of revelation is reason." By reason, Cohen meant "consciousness" as expressed in science and philosophy, the ethical reason of idealism. Cohen, the philosopher, looked for ethical reason in the sources of Judaism in order to construct a religion that would be a religion of reason. As a philosopher, he was primarily interested in the contribution of Jewish monotheism to ethical reason and progress in history.

But as a Jew, Cohen cried out in deep piety: "Psychologically, monotheism is a mystery.... The survival of the Jews is a miracle." This dialogue between Cohen, the philosopher, and Cohen, the Jew, beginning in his middle years, continued into his old age, and in the course of it his piety towards the one God and his historical vessel — the Jewish people — steadily increased.

Let us try to indicate Cohen's position as the leading exponent in Jewish thinking of the Enlightenment. Cohen raised religious reform to the rank of a system of rational ethics. But Cohen also, based his religion on the love of God and on suffering, which have no source in ethics. He himself attributed a "special nature" to these religious concepts, as distinct from rational ethics. Thus he set limits to ethics, and by leading it back to the traditional source of religion, he completed the Enlightenment and the reformation in Jewish religious thought.

Cohen's influence on Jewish thought cannot yet be fully estimated. His great accomplishment might perhaps be designated as a kind of mission within the ranks of German liberal Jewry. Cohen's living piety, the force of his thinking, contributed greatly to bring liberal Jewry back to the depths of tradition. His great admirer and successor, Franz Rosenzweig, made still further advances in the Jewish philosophy of religion. But his outlook was no longer along the lines of the Enlightenment but rather along the metaphysical tendencies of his own time.

# MARTIN BUBER'S NEW VIEW OF EVIL

MAURICE S. FRIEDMAN

IN THE Preface to *Images of Good and Evil*, Buber writes that he has been preoccupied with the problem of evil since his youth. It was not until the year following the first World War, however, that he approached it independently, and it is only in this, one of the very latest of his books, that he has achieved full maturity and clarity on the subject.[1] *Images of Good and Evil* is without question one of the clearest, most profound, and most concrete treatments of good and evil to appear in modern times. It is particularly significant for its wholly unsentimental realism and for its treatment of evil on the concrete base of philosophical anthropology rather than in the customary terms of metaphysics and theology.

The Yehudi in Buber's Hasidic chronicle-novel *For the Sake of Heaven* reproaches the Seer of Lublin for dwelling on Gog, the mythical incarnation of an external, metaphysical evil:

He can exist in the outer world only because he exists within us. He pointed to his own breast. The darkness out of which he was hewn needed to be taken from nowhere else than from our sloth-

ful and malicious hearts. Our betrayal of God has made Gog to grow so great.[2]

It is to this speech of the Yehudi's that Buber points in the preface to *Images of Good and Evil* as the answer to the question of the point of attack for the struggle against evil. This point of attack must not be understood simply as man against that which is not man but as that which the individual knows from his own inner experience as against that which he encounters outside of himself.

I certainly gain no experience of evil when I meet my fellowman. For in that case I can grasp it only from without, estrangedly or with hatred and contempt, in which case it really does not enter my vision; or else, I overcome it with my love and in that case I have no vision of it either. I experience it when I meet myself.[3]

Man knows evil when he recognizes the condition in which he finds himself as the "evil" and knows the condition he has thereby lost and cannot, for the time being, regain as the good. It is through this inner encounter alone that evil becomes accessible and demonstrable in the world; for "it exists in the world apart from man only in the form of quite general opposites," embracing good and ill and good and bad as well as good and evil. The specific opposition good-evil is peculiar to man because it can only be perceived introspectively:

A man only knows factually what 'evil' is insofar as he knows about himself, ev-

---

[1] Martin Buber, *Good and Evil, Two Interpretations*, Scribner's, 1953, p. 63ff.

The author of the present study is a member of the faculties of Philosophy and Literature at Sarah Lawrence College. This study will form a chapter in a projected volume by Dr. Friedman, entitled "*The Narrow Ridge: A Study of Martin Buber*", scheduled for publication early in 1954.

[2] *For the Sake of Heaven*, 1946, p. 54.
[3] *Ibid.*, p. 57.

erything else to which he gives this name is merely mirrored illusion;... self-perception and self-relationship are the peculiarly human, the irruption of a strange element into nature, the inner lot of man.[4]

When the demon is encountered at the inner threshold, there is no longer any room for taking attitudes toward it: "the struggle must now be fought out." The Yehudi recognizes the real difficulty of this inner struggle when he says: " 'Within me, where no element of strangeness has divisive force and no love has redeeming force, there do I directly experience that something which would force me to betray God and which seeks to use for that purpose the powers of my own soul.' "[5] Despite the power of evil, man can overcome temptation and turn back to God. For if evil, in Buber's conception, is rebellion against God with the power He has given man to do evil, good is the turning toward God with this same power. If evil is a lack of direction, good is a finding of direction, of *the* direction toward God. If evil is the predominance of the "I-It" relation, to use the terminology of *I and Thou*, good is the meeting with the "Thou," the permeation of "I-It" by "I-Thou." Thus in each case good and evil are bound together as they could not be if evil were an independent substance with an existence of its own.

Good and evil, then, cannot be a pair of opposites like right and left or above and beneath. "Good" is the movement in the direction of home, "evil" is the aimless whirl of human potentialities without which nothing can be achieved and by which, if they take no direction but remain trapped in themselves, everything goes awry.[6]

Good and evil are usually thought of as "two structurally similar qualities situated at opposite poles." But this is because they are treated as ethical abstractions rather than as existent states of human reality. When one looks at them "in the factual context of the life of the human person," one discovers their "fundamental dissimilarity in nature, structure, and dynamics."[7]

Evil, for Buber, is both absence of direction and absence of genuine relation, for relation and direction as he uses them are different aspects of the same reality. The man who cannot say "Thou" with his whole being to God or man may have "the sublime illusion of detached thought that he is a self-contained self; as man he is lost." Similarly, the man who does not keep to the One direction as far as he is able may have "the life of the spirit, in all freedom and fruitfulness, all standing and status — existence there is none for him without it."[8]

The clearest illustration of the ultimate identity, for Buber, of evil as absence of direction and evil as absence of relation is his treatment of "conscience." Conscience, to him, is the voice which calls one to fulfill the personal intention of being for which he was created. It is "the individual's awareness of what he 'really' is, of what in his unique and nonrepeatable created existence he is intended to be." Hence it implies both dialogue and direction—the dialogue of the person with an "other" than he now is which gives him an intimation of the direction he is meant to take. This presentiment of purpose is "inherent in all men though in the most varied strengths and degrees of consciousness and for the most part stifled by them." When it is

---

[4] *Good and Evil*, pp. 75f., 87f.

[5] *For the Sake of Heaven*, p. 57.

[6] Martin Buber, *Between Man and Man*, Kegan Paul, 1947, "The Question to the Single One," p. 78f.

[7] *Good and Evil*, pp. 64, 121.

[8] *Between Man and Man*, "What Is Man?," p. 168; *Good and Evil*, p. 143.

not stifled, it compares that which one is with that which one is called to become and thereby distinguishes and decides between right and wrong. Through this comparison, also, one comes to feel guilt.

Each one who knows himself...as called to a work which he has not done, each one who has not fulfilled a task which he knows to be his own, each who did not remain faithful to his vocation which he had become certain of — each such person knows what it means to say that "his conscience smites him."[9]

Guilt is the product of not taking the direction toward God. The guilty man is he who shuns the dialogue with God, and this means also he who does not enter into the dialogue with man and the world. "Original guilt consists in remaining with oneself." If the being before whom this hour places one is not met with the truth of one's whole life, then one is guilty.

Heidegger is right to say that...we are able to discover a primal guilt. But we are not able to do this by isolating a part of life, the part where the existence is related to itself and to its own being, but by becoming aware of the whole life without reduction, the life in which the individual, in fact, is essentially related to something other than himself.[10]

The fact that one discovers guilt in relation with something other than oneself does not contradict the fact that one discovers evil first of all in the meeting with oneself. This meeting takes place only if one remains aware of the voice of conscience. The man who fails to face the evil within him or affirms it as good is precisely the man who remains with himself and suppresses his awareness of

direction, his awareness of the address of God which comes to him from that which is "other" than he.

The specific structure of evil in the human person cannot be explained as a result of the 'moral censorship' of society. "There can be no question at all here of the psychology of 'inhibitions' and 'repressions', which operate no less against some social convention or other than when it is a matter of that which is felt to be evil in the full meaning of the word." One's inner encounter with evil does not presuppose that "self-analysis" of modern psychology which seeks to penetrate "behind" the experience, "to 'reduce' it to the real elements assumed to have been 'repressed'." What is needed here, rather, is the technique of the philosophical anthropologist who first participates in the experience and then gains the distance indispensable for objective knowledge, "Our business is to call to mind an occurrence as reliably, concretely and completely remembered as possible, which is entirely unreduced and undissected." The state of evil is experienced within ourselves in such a way that "its differentiation from every other state of the soul is unmistakable." This experience leads us to inquire as to the existence of evil as an ontological reality.[11]

If this inquiry is to be successful, says Buber, it must make use of the truth found in the myths of the origin of evil. The experience which has taken place in countless factual encounters with evil has been directly embodied in these myths without passing through any conceptual form. Rightly interpreted, therefore, "they tell us of the human constitution and movement of evil" and of its relation to good. We can only interpret them rightly, however, if we accord to

---

[9]Martin Buber, *Eclipse of God*, Harpers, 1952, pp. 115f., 125f.

[10]Buber, *At the Turning*, Farrar, Straus & Young 1952, p. 56; *Between Man and Man*, "What Is Man?," p. 165f.

[11]*Good and Evil*, pp. 117f., 121ff.

their account that manner of belief which comes from our personal experience of evil. "Only out of the conjunction of these two, primordial mythic intuition and directly experienced reality, does the light of the legitimate concept arise for this sphere too, probably the most obscure of all." The concept which arises from this conjunction serves as an indispensable bridge between myth and reality which enables man to see the two together. Without it man "listens to the myth of Lucifer and hushes it up in his own life."[12]

The myths that Buber interprets in *Images of Good and Evil* are the Biblical and the Zoroastrian, for, in his opinion, "these correspond with two fundamentally different kinds and stages of evil." He portrays the first of these stages, decisionlessness, through an interpretation of the myths of Adam and Eve, Cain, and the flood. When Adam and Eve take the fruit, they do not make a decision between good and evil but rather image possibilities of action and then act almost without knowing it, sunk in "a strange, dreamlike kind of contemplation." Cain, similarly, does not decide to kill Abel — he does not even know what death and killing are. Rather he intensifies and confirms his indecision. "In the vortex of indecision,...at the point of greatest provocation and least resistance," he strikes out. Man grasps at every possibility "in order to overcome the tension of omnipossibility" and thus makes incarnate a reality which is "no longer divine but his, his capriciously constructed, indestinate reality." It is this, in the story of the flood, which causes God to repent of having made man. The wickedness of man's actions does not derive from a corruption of the soul but from the intervention of the evil "imagery." This imagery is a "play with pos-

sibility," a "self-temptation, from which ever and again violence springs." The place of the real, perceived fruit is taken by a possible, devised, fabricated one which *can be* and finally *is* made into the real one. Imagination, or "imagery," is not entirely evil, however. It is man's greatest danger and greatest opportunity, a power which can be left undirected or directed to the good. It is in this understanding of imagery that the Talmudic doctrine of the two "urges" originated. *Yetser*, the Biblical word for "imagery," is identical, in fact, with the Talmudic word for the evil and good urges. The evil "urge" is especially close to the "imagery of man's heart" which the Bible speaks of as "evil from his youth," for it is identical with "passion, that is, the power peculiar to man, without which he can neither beget nor bring forth, but which, left to itself, remains without direction and leads astray."[13]

Man becomes aware of possibility, writes Buber, "in a period of evolution which generally coincides with puberty without being tied to it." This possibility takes the form of possible actions which threaten to submerge him in their swirling chaos. To escape from this dizzy whirl the soul either sets out upon the difficult path of bringing itself toward unity or it clutches at any object past which the vortex happens to carry it and casts its passion upon it. In this latter case, "it exchanges an undirected possibility for an undirected reality, in which it does what it wills not to do, what is preposterous to it, the alien, the 'evil.'" It breaks violently out of the state of undirected surging passion "wherever a breach can be forced" and enters into a pathless maze of pseudo-decision, a "flight into delusion and ultimately into mania." Evil, then, is lack of direction and that which is done in and out of it:

---

[12]*Ibid.*, pp. 115–118, 66.

[13]*Ibid.*, pp. 67–97.

"the grasping, seizing, devouring, compelling, seducing, exploiting, humiliating, torturing and destroying of what offers itself." It is not an action, for "action is only the type of evil happening which makes evil manifest." The evil itself lies in the intention: "The project of the sin and the reflecting upon it and not its execution is the real guilt."[14]

Evil is not the result of a decision, for true decision is not partial but is made with the whole soul. "Evil cannot be done with the whole soul; good can only be done with the whole soul." There can be no wholeness "where downtrodden appetites lurk in the corners" or where the soul's highest forces watch the action, "pressed back and powerless, but shining in the protest of the spirit."[15] The absence of personal wholeness is a complement, therefore, to the absence of direction and the absence of relation. If one does not become what one is meant to be, if one does not set out in the direction of God, if one does not bring one's scattered passions under the transforming and unifying guidance of direction, then no wholeness of the person is possible. Conversely, without attaining personal wholeness one can neither keep to direction nor enter into full relation.

Buber portrays the second stage of evil, the actual decision to evil, through an interpretation of the Zoroastrian myths found in the Avesta and in post-Avestic literature. Here we meet good and evil as primal moving spirits set in real opposition to one another, and here, for the first time, evil assumes a substantial and independent nature. In the hymns of Zoroaster, God's primal act is a decision within himself which prepares and makes possible the self-choice of good and evil by which each is first

rendered effectual and factual. Created man, similarly, finds himself ever again confronted by the necessity of distinguishing deception from truth and deciding between them. The primal spirits stand between God and man and like them choose between good and evil. But in the case of Ahriman, the evil spirit, this choice takes place in pure paradox since in choosing he acknowledges himself precisely as the evil.

This paradox is developed further in the saga of the primeval king Yima, who assumes dominion over the world at the bidding of the highest God, Ahura Mazdah. After a flood similar to the Biblical one, Yima lets loose the demons whom he has hitherto held in check and allows the lie to enter through lauding and blessing himself. Yima's lie is "the primal lie...of humanity as a whole which ascribes the conquest of the power of nature to its own superpower". It is the existential lie against being in which man sees himself as a self-creator. Man chooses in decisive hours between being-true and being-false, between strengthening, covering, and confirming being at the point of his own existence or weakening, desecrating, and dispossessing it. He who chooses the lie in preference to the truth intervenes directly in the decisions of the world-conflict. "But this takes effect in the very first instance at just his point of being": by giving himself over to non-being which poses as being, he falls victim to it. Thus Yima falls into the power of the demons whose companion he has become and is destroyed by them.

Corresponding to the myth of Yima's rebellion and of his self-deification and fall are the Old Testament stories of the tower of Babel and of the foolhardy angels, such as Lucifer (Isaiah 14), who imagined themselves godlike and were cast down. Similarly, good and evil appear

<hr>

[14]*Ibid.*, pp. 125–132, 139f.; Buber, *Two Types of Faith*, Macmillan, 1952, p. 64f.
[15]*Good and Evil*, p. 129f.

again and again in the Old Testament, as in the Avesta, as alternative paths before which man stands and which he must choose between as between life and death (Deut. 30:19).

This second stage of evil as decision follows from the first stage of evil as indecision. The repeated experiences of indecision merge in self-knowledge into "a course of indecision," a fixation in it. "As long as the will to simple self-preservation dominates that to being-able-to-affirm oneself," this self-knowledge is repressed. But when the will to affirm oneself asserts itself, man calls himself in question. Buber explains the crisis of the self which results from this questioning through a development of his philosophical anthropology. For this anthropology, man is the creature of possibility who needs confirmation by others and by himself in order that he may be and become the particular man that he is. "Again and again the Yes must be spoken to him ...to liberate him from the dread of abandonment, which is a foretaste of death." If one's own self-confirmation reaches a high enough pitch, one can do without confirmation from others, but one cannot, even with the encouragement of one's fellows, do without self-confirmation. When a person's self-knowledge demands inner rejection, he either falls into a pathologically fragile and intricate relationship to himself, readjusts self-knowledge through that extreme effort of unification called "conversion," or displaces his knowledge of himself by an absolute self-affirmation. In this last case, the image of what he is intended to be is totally extinguished, and in its place he wills or chooses himself just as he is, just as he has resolved to intend himself. This self-affirmation in no sense means real personal wholeness but just its opposite — a crystallized inner division. "They are recognisable,

those who dominate their own self-knowledge, by the spastic pressure of the lips, the spastic tension of the muscles of the hand and the spastic tread of the foot."

The man who thus affirms himself resembles Yima who proclaims himself his own creator. It is in this light too that we can understand the paradoxical myth of the two spirits, one of whom chose evil precisely as evil. The "wicked" spirit, in whom evil is already present in a nascent state, has to choose between the affirmation of himself and the affirmation of the order which establishes good and evil. "If he affirms the order he must himself become 'good', and that means he must deny and overcome his present state of being. If he affirms himself he must deny and reverse the order." The "good" is now just that which he is, for he can no longer say no to anything that is his. This absolute self-affirmation is the lie against being, for through it truth is no longer what he experiences as truth but what he ordains to be true.[16]

In "Imitatio Dei," Buber says that Adam's fall consisted in his wanting to reach the likeness to God intended for him in his creation by other means than that of the imitation of the unknown God. This substitution of self-deification for the "imitation of God" lies at the heart not only of the fall of Adam but also that of Yima. In Adam's case, however, it is a matter of "becoming-like-God" through knowing good and evil, whereas in Yima's it is a matter of "being-like-God" through proclaiming oneself as the creator both of one's existence and of the values by which that existence is judged. The first stage of evil does not yet contain a "radical evil" since the misdeeds which are committed in it are slid into rather than chosen as such. But in the second stage evil becomes radical

---

[16]*Ibid.*, pp. 99–113, 118f., 133–138.

because there man wills what he finds in himself. He affirms what he has time and again recognized in the depths of self-awareness as that which should be negated and thereby gives evil "the substantial character which it did not previously possess." "If we may compare the occurrence of the first stage to an eccentric whirling movement, the process of the freezing of flowing water may serve as a simile to illustrate the second."[17]

In his interpretation of Psalm 1 in *Right and Wrong*, Buber makes an essential distinction between the "wicked" man and the "sinner" corresponding to the two stages of evil which we have discussed. The sinner misses God's way again and again while the wicked opposes it. "Sinner" describes a condition which from time to time overcomes a man without adhering to him whereas "wicked" describes a kind of man, a persistent disposition. "The sinner *does* evil, the wicked man *is* evil. That is why it is said only of the wicked, and not of the sinners, that their way vanishes..." Although the sinner is not confirmed by the human community, he may be able to stand before God, and even entry into the human community is not closed to him if he carries out that turning into God's way which he desires in the depths of his heart. The "wicked," in contrast, does not "stand" in the judgment before God. His way is his own judgment: since he has negated his existence, he ends in nothing. Does this mean that the way of God is closed to the wicked man? "It is not closed from God's side,...but it is closed from the side of the wicked themselves. For in distinction to the sinners they do not wish to be able to turn." Here there arises for us the question of how an evil will can exist when God exists. To this question, says Buber, no

human word knows the answer: "The abyss which is opened by this question advances still more uncannily than the abyss of Job's question onto the darkness of the divine mystery."[18]

There is undoubtedly a close relation between Buber's growing tendency to ascribe reality to evil and the events of the past decades — in particular, the Nazi's persecution of the Jews, World War II, and the war in Palestine ("for me the most grievous of the three [wars]"). In the Preface to his chronicle-novel Buber says that the necessary impetus to writing it came to him only with the outbreak of the second World War and in the form of a vision in a half-dream of a demon with the features of a Judaized Goebbels. Correspondingly, the central theme of this novel, as we have seen, is that the power of evil is great in the world because it is great in our hearts.[19]

Does Buber's new emphasis on a "radical" and "substantive" evil mean that we can no longer place him in that middle position between non-dualism and dualism which regards evil as real but redeemable, thus refusing to ascribe to it an absolute and independent reality? Does his use of the Iranian myths, the most important historical fountainhead of dualism, not only serve to illustrate an anthropological reality but also imply a dualistic metaphysics?

*Images of Good and Evil* itself supplies the answer to our question. Buber makes it clear there that it is not man's nature which is evil but only his use of that nature. There are, to be sure, wicked men whose end is non-existence — this accords with the simple facts — but there are no men whom God cuts

---

[17]Buber, *Israel and the World*, 1947, p. 73; *Good and Evil*, pp. 120, 140.

[18]*Good and Evil*, "Right and Wrong," Chap. V. "The Ways."

[19]*Two Types of Faith*, p. 15; Buber, *Gog und Magog*, Lambert Schneider, 1949, p. 405; *Good and Evil*, p. 65.

off as simply evil and therefore by nature hostile to His purpose. If some men bring evil to a "radical" stage where it possesses a substantial quality, this does not mean that evil is here independent and absolute, nor even ultimately unredeemable, but only that it has crystallized into a settled opposition by the individual to becoming that which he is meant to become. "Good... retains the character of direction at both stages," writes Buber, indicating clearly that there *is* a good for the second stage even as for the first. This good is the realization by man of the right unique purposes for him in creation. The Biblical attitude toward creation to which Buber refers here precludes, in his opinion, the existence of any evil power which God allows independent existence for longer than the purpose of temptation.[20]

Further evidence that Buber has not left the "narrow ridge" in his attitude toward evil is his discussion of "God's will to harden" in *Two Types of Faith* (1951). On the three occasions when the Old Testament speaks of God as "hardening the heart" of a person or people, it is because of his or their persistent turning away. The hardening comes in an extreme situation as a consequence of perversion "and..., dreadfully enough,...makes the going astray into a state of having gone-astray from which there is no returning." "Sin is not an undertaking which man can break off when the situation becomes critical," Buber explains, "but a process started by him, the control of which is withdrawn from him at a fixed moment."[21]

The "special strength to persevere in sin" which God grants the sinner when He "hardens" his heart is a counterpart, we may surmise, of that absolute self-affirmation with which the "wicked" closes himself off from God. God will not abridge the freedom which He has given man in creation, and therefore He allows this process of closing off to take place. His "hardening" is His response to man's decision against Him. It is at once the judgment with which He confirms the wicked in his non-existence and the "severe grace" with which He points out to him the one road back to real existence.

Even in the dark hour after he has become guilty against his brother, man is not abandoned to the forces of chaos. God Himself seeks him out, and even when He comes to call him to account, His coming is salvation.

Despite the importance in Buber's recent thought of such terms as contradiction, tragedy, eclipse of God, and "radical evil", Buber remains essentially different from even the least extreme of the dualists. His affirmation of the oneness of God and the ultimate oneness of God and the world has deepened in its paradoxical quality as he has taken more and more realistic cognizance of the evil of the world, but it has not wavered or weakened. The great significance, indeed, of that second stage of evil which is the newest development in Buber's thought is its concrete base in human existence which makes understandable such extreme phenomena as Hitler and the Nazis without resorting to the dogma of original sin or agreeing with the assertion of Jean-Paul Sartre that the events of recent years make it necessary to recognize evil as absolute and unredeemable.

---

[20]*Good and Evil*, pp. 91, 132, 140ff.
[21]*Two Types of Faith*, pp. 83–88.

185

# THREE VIEWS ON REVELATION AND LAW

## ZVI E. KURZWEIL

In his polemic essay against the Swiss psychologist C. G. Jung, Buber expounds his theory of revelation in the following words: "It must be mentioned here, for the sake of full clarity, that my own belief in revelation, which is not mixed up with any 'orthodoxy', does not mean that I believe that finished statements about God were handed down from Heaven to earth. Rather it means that the human substance is melted by the spiritual fire which visits it, and there now breaks forth from it a word, a statement, which is human in its meaning and form, human conception and human speech, and yet witnesses to Him, who stimulated it and to His will. We are revealed to ourselves—and cannot express it otherwise than as something revealed."[1]

In this statement, Buber clearly rejects the traditional interpretation of revelation as the transmission to man of Divine statements about God and the right conduct of man. The metaphor of "the

human substances being melted by the spiritual fire which visits it" constitutes an attempt to express in human language those physiological and psychological changes occurring in man when "visited" by God, which are fully described in books such as James' *The Varieties of Religious Experience*. Finally, we note that according to Buber the result of that Divine "visitation" is a word or a statement which is human in its meaning and form and, therefore, cannot claim any infallible authority over any other ways of apprehending truth. The mere fact of the human transmission of the word of God is of very great importance. Elsewhere, Buber underscores this point when he says that "ever there clings to the word commanded a trace of the present character of human speech"[2]. In other words: revelation itself is a Divine phenomenon witnessing to the presence of God who "visits" man, but the content of revelation, the message or "word" evinced by it, bears an essentially human character.

In this passage, Buber characterizes revelation as an individual phenomenon in the sense of what is generally termed in theological literature, religious experience. Elsewhere in his writings the term revelation seems to denote the revela-

[1] *Eclipse of God*, p. 135.

The starting point, as well as the point of perennial return of Jewish theology, past and present, is the doctrine of *Torah M'Sinai*. Here, Dr. Kurzweil submits to exposition and analysis three modern interpretations of that doctrine, those of Buber, Rosenzweig and Rosenheim, respectively. In broad terms, these afford the basis, consciously or unconsciously, of the current tri-partite denominations of contemporary Jewish religion.

[2] '*Immer haftet am gebietenden Wort die Gegenwartsspur des Sprechens.*' viz. Simon: Buber and Jewish Faith' in IYYUN, January 1958.

tion on Mount Sinai, for he bases the faith of Judaism on "the threefold cord of Creation, Revelation and Redemption"[3] and, in that context, Revelation seems to mean the Divine Revelation on Mount Sinai, whose aim it was "to lay a message upon the whole man". He says: "There is . . . one important subject within the sphere of Judaism about which I do not feel myself called upon to speak, and that is 'the Law'. My point of view with regard to this subject diverges widely from that which has been handed down to us; it is not without its basis of law, but neither is it entirely based on law. For this reason I should neither attempt to present tradition, nor substitute my own personal standpoint for the information you have desired of me. Besides, the problem of the law does not seem to me to belong at all to the subject with which I have to deal. It would be a different thing were it my duty to present to you the teaching of Judaism. For Judaism comes from Sinai; it is the teaching of Moses. But the soul of Judaism was before Sinai; it is the soul which drew near on Sinai, and there received what it did receive; it is older than Moses; it is of the Patriarchs, a soul of Abraham, or more truly as it concerns the product of a primordial age, it is a soul of Jacob. The law joined itself to it, and it cannot henceforth ever again be understood outside of it, but it, itself, is not of the law"[4].

This passage from *Mamre* is extremely interesting. Like the one quoted previously, it contains a frank rejection of traditional Judaism ("My point of view diverges widely from that which has been handed down to us"). On the other hand, it reflects belief in the Revelation of Sinai. ("The teaching of Judaism comes from Sinai"). What distinguishes Buber's standpoint from that of traditional Judaism is his attitude to the Law.

Whereas traditional Judaism admits of no differentiation between the Judaism of the Patriarchs and that of Sinai, in fact according to the Talmud, the Patriarchs anticipated and actually kept all the Commandments of the Torah, Buber discerns an essential difference between these two expressions of Judaism. The teaching of Judaism comes from Sinai. It is essentially Law. However, the "soul" of Judaism is the Abrahamistic Judaism, or the Judaism of the Patriarchs to which later the Law joined itself. This Abrahamistic Judaism is, as Buber points out later, mainly characterized by faith. It is said of Abraham: "And he believed in the Lord and its omission was counted to him as righteousness". Buber accepts Franz Baader's characterization of faith "as pledge, that is, as a tying of oneself, a betrothing of oneself, an entering into a covenant". This faith, then, is the "soul" of Judaism. The Patriarchs seek God and they find him and place themselves into a direct relationship to Him. Thus the "dialogic" situation between God and man is created, crowned by faith in the sense of trust, fealty and betrothal, and this relationship is formally acknowledged by the covenant and outwardly symbolized by a number of laws which epitomize the covenant. Sinaitic Judaism, however, is marked by a predominance of Law over faith. This Law is, "a hard protecting shell", it endows the soul with the attribute of permanency, it gives the chosen people enhanced power of endurance.

There are, however, other passages in Buber's writings which witness to a

---

[3] *Mamre*, p. 14.
[4] Opus Cit. 18, 19.

fuller appreciation of the Law on the part of the writer and indicate an interpretation of the Law clearly transcending that of the "protective" function. . . . the giving of the Law at Sinai', says Buber, "is properly understood as the body of rules which the Divine Ruler conferred upon His people in the hour of His ascension to the throne". All the prescriptions of this body of rules, both the ritual and the ethical, are intended to lead beyond themselves into the sphere of the "holy". The people's goal was set not by their being bidden to become a "good" people, but a "holy" one. Thus, every moral demand is set forth as one that shall raise man, the human people, to the sphere where the ethical merges into the religious, or rather where the difference between the ethical and the religious is suspended in the breathing space of the Divine. This is expressed with unsurpassable clarity in the reason given for the goal that is set. Israel shall become "holy", "for I am holy". The imitation of God by man, the "following in His way", can be fulfilled naturally only in those divine attributes turned towards the human ethos, in justice and love, and all the attributes are transparent into the Holiness above the attributes, to be reproduced in the radically different human dimension"[5]. In this passage, Buber finds the Law eminently meaningful inasmuch as it is intended to make the Jewish people a "holy" nation. It is to be noted that in this passage, Buber attaches to the ritual law the same importance as to the ethical, because both reach out beyond themselves and merge in the sphere of the "holy".

Following the teaching of the Hebrew prophets, Buber stresses the importance of faith as the basis of Law. The fulfillment of Law is meaningful and legitimate only if carried out "with a full intention of faith". This point is brought out clearly in Buber's polemic with Pauline theology. "The Pauline and Paulinistic theology depreciated works for the sake of faith. It left undeveloped that which bound the two together, the demand for intention of faith, intention of work out of faith, the demand which underlays the proclamation of that which is pleasing to God, from the first Biblical prophets to the Sermon on the Mount'[6].

The question arising here is that of defining the nature of faith that makes the fulfillment of the Divine commandments meaningful and legitimate. Is it, according to Buber, merely faith in God, or does Buber imply faith in the Divine origin of the entire body of Law? Professor Ernst Simon, an eminent disciple of Buber, argues (on the strength of a number of relevant passages from Buber's writings) that "according to Buber, a Jew has to be a Fundamentalist in order to feel justified to fulfill the Commandments and he must fulfill them all, he has to wear "the protective shell of the Law" complete as it is, i.e., he has to fulfill all the laws without exception, if his observance is to be regarded as legitimate from a religious point of view".

The reader will, not doubt, be surprised at such a conclusion, particularly in view of the fact that Buber, himself, is by no means a Fundamentalist and does not believe in "verbal inspiration". Upon a close study of the passages quoted by Simon, in support of his rather surprising interpretation of Buber, the present writer cannot help

---

[5] Eclipse of God, p. 104, 105.

[6] Opus cit., p. 106–7.

doubting whether they really prove the point he argues[7].

For the sake of fairness it must be admitted that Simon, himself, expresses doubts as to whether the view put forward by him still represents Buber's attitude to-day. However this may be, it is one thing to believe that the Law is meaningful and quite another that it is binding, i.e., that it has to be obeyed irrespective of one's faith. And here we have to come back again to Buber's controversy with Jung mentioned at the beginning of this article. The point at issue between Buber and Jung is this: Is God merely an archtype of the human unconscious, that is to say a purely psychic phenomenon, or does He also exist outside the psyche of man? Buber takes the second, Jung the first view. Buber criticizes Jung for his overstepping the proper limits of psychology by making statements about the existence or non-existence of an extra-psychic being. The only attitude that properly belongs to the science of psychology in this connection is a reasoned restraint. Jung does not exercise such a restraint when he explains that God cannot exist independent of man. For, once again, if this is a statement about an archetype called God, then the emphatic assurance that it is a psychic factor is certainly unnecessary. (What else could it be?) But if it is a statement about some extra-psychical Being which corresponds to this factor, namely the statement that no such Being exists, then we have here instead of the indicated restraint, an illicit overstepping of boundaries[8].

Buber's criticism of Jung seems cogent enough, at least at first sight. Buber, himself, is not a scientist but a theologian and, therefore, he may be justified in seeing in revelation a phenomenon that witnesses "to Him who stimulated it and to His will". What he asserts is the unshakeable "Existentialist" faith of the person who has a revelation in the extra-psychic existence of the Being who "visits" him. On the other hand, Buber regards the content of revelation i.e., the word, statement or message "breaking forth" from man as the result of the Divine visitation as impaired by the fact that it is human in its meaning and form, a human conception and human speech. Here we note a serious inconsistency in Buber's thought. If he relies on the Existentialist certainty of man's faith in the existence of an extra-psychic Being, why does he exclude from this certainty the word or message breaking forth from man? Buber answers that this message is delivered in human speech. To this we may reply that revelation, too, is a psychic and, therefore, human phenomenon. If the human factor in revelation impairs its content, it invalidates the whole phenomenon and Jung's attitude appears more consistent.

## II

Franz Rosenzweig's theory of revelation finds its full expression in the sec-

---

[7] Simon quotes the following passage from 'Reden' (Der heilige Weg), p. 183: 'We respect the law, that protective armour of our people which was forged by forces deserving respect; we respect everyone who goes forth with us . . . to the battlefield out of full trust that the Lord himself has clad His people in this coat of armour as it is. . . ."

[8] The second passage is from Haruach Vehametziuth, p. 1920: 'I shall not touch a man who faithfully believes in the full content of the written and oral Torah.' From the fact that Buber expresses respect for the fully observant Jew it does not follow (non sequitur) that Fundamentalism is the only precondition for keeping the Law.

ond volume of his *Star of Redemption* where revelation is conceived of as the meeting point between God and man, on one hand, and as the continuation of creation, which may also be regarded as revelation, on the other hand. In the beginning God reveals Himself in the powerful deeds of His creative acts, but immediately withdraws behind the natural laws of His creation. Now prompted by His love to man, He reveals Himself once more, this time in a revelation proper, i.e., in a revelation which is 'nothing else but revelation'. In Rosenzweig's own words: "Here begins that completion of the Divine revelation which had only started in the acts of creation. . . . In order to reaffirm His actual existence which was in danger of being lost (by man) in consequence of His being hidden, His first revelation in the infiniteness of creative deeds was not sufficient; there was the danger of His remaining the mere "origin" of creation and thus a hidden God which he had ceased to be by virtue of creation. Something else than mere creative power must come out of the dark of His hiddenness; something in which the immensity of creative deeds becomes visibly displayed, lest God withdraw again behind His deeds into the unknown"[9].

This passage from *The Star of Redemption* seems to disprove Professor Bergman's interpretation of Rosenzweig's philosophy of revelation. According to Bergman[10], Rosenzweig's conception of revelation is identical with personal revelation or "mystical experience", such as Pascal refers to in his wonderful prayer known as "the Memorial". The

very juxtaposition of creation and revelation in the above quoted passage, the fact that Rosenzweig sees in revelation the continuation of creation suggests that he had in mind a more spectacular phenomenon such as the Revelation of God on Mount Sinai and not revelation as a phenomenon of the individual psyche. Moreover, it is as we have said, God's love for man that prompts Him to reappear from behind "the infiniteness of His creative deeds" and reveal Himself to man once more. It does not seem plausible, within the context of Rosenzweig's thought, to interpret "revelation proper" as the revelation of God to those individuals, who, like Pascal, are sure of having been "visited" by Him. God's love for man is universal. It seems more likely that Rosenzweig had in mind the Sinaitic Revelation whose content was transmitted by the Jewish people to the whole of mankind.

Rosenzweig's attitude to the Law, as the content of revelation, is extremely intricate and difficult to define. He affirms the election of Israel and, therefore, fully accepts the implications of the blessing 'who hast chosen us from all peoples and hast given us Thy Torah'. His spiritual development led him to the acceptance of the Law as a whole, that is to say he asserted and understood its *raison d'être*, (on grounds similar to those adduced by Buber), but on the other hand, he did not find it possible to accept a number of specific *mitzvot* which remained 'alien' 'to him'[11] In his later years he came, in actual religious observance, very near to traditional Judaism. 'An outsider looking on at the observance of the Sabbath in

---

9 *Der Erloesung*, pp. 93–4.

10 '*Revelation, Prayer and Redemption in the Teaching of Franz Rosenzweig*,' p. 43–4, Beth Hillel Publication: *On Franz Rosenzweig*, The Magnes Press).

11 '*Grade zum Ganzen hat uns unser Weg wieder geführt, aber das Einzelne suchen wir.*' Franz Rosenzweig: Briefe, p. 521.

Franz Rosenzweig's home, with prayer, benediction, song and scrupulous abstinence from all proscribed manner of work, would expect to find a strictly Orthodox Jew'[12], but this fact must not blind us to the profound difference between his attitude to the Law and that of Orthodoxy. Like Buber, Rosenzweig did not believe in revelation in the sense of "verbal inspiration". In a letter to Jacob Rosenheim he says: "Where we differ from Orthodoxy is in our reluctance to draw from our belief in the holiness or uniqueness of the Torah and in its character of revelation, any conclusions as to its literary genesis and the philological value of the text as it has come down to us. If all of Wellhausen's theories were correct and the Samaritans really had the better text, our faith would not be shaken in the least. This is the profound difference between you (Orthodoxy) and us—a difference which, it seems to me, may be bridged by mutual esteem, but not by understanding"; and he continues in the same letter: "For us, too, the Torah is the work of one spirit; we do not know who its author was; we cannot believe that it was Moses. Whosoever it was and whatever sources he may have used, he was our teacher and his theology is our teaching"[13]

From these presuppositions there follow important consequences for Rosenzweig's attitude to religious observance. According to Rosenzweig, Judaism contains, strictly speaking, no laws but merely precepts (Gebote), i.e., mitzvot, which should be freely adopted, chosen and 'blessed'. The ultimate decision as to the acceptance or non-acceptance of

Mitzvoth rests with the individual and the only criterion is "the choice of ability" (die Auswahl des Kennens), that is, the inner readiness of the individual to choose the precept and "bless" it. As time went on, Rosenzweig's own readiness to freely embrace the mitzvot of the Torah grew steadily. Once when asked whether he was "laying tefilin" he answered "not yet" which, of course, implied "but soon I will". In fact, he wrote down in his diary the date when he started "laying tefilin". He loved the Talmud and was emotionally disposed to embrace the Law in toto. He intended to write a book about the mitzvot of Judaism, but did not live long enough to be able to carry out this plan. His attitude to Judaism was very much that of a ba'al teshuva, and this is the reason why representatives of Orthodoxy saw in him the reincarnation of Rabbi Meir, whereas Buber appeared to them—quite injustly —as Elisha be Abuya.[14] In actual fact, the difference between his attitude to the Law and that of Buber is practical and temperamental rather than theological.

It cannot be denied that Rosenzweig's attitude to the Law must lead to an arbitrary adoption or rejection of precepts on the part of the individual Jew. This may lead to chaos in matters of Jewish religious observance. Rosenzweig, himself, faces this issue. In another letter to Jacob Rosenheim he says: 'On one point, however, I may set your mind at ease. The danger of individualism exists only for the individual Jew, but not for the whole people. For the choice of Mitzvot according to one's ability is made from the spiritual stock of the whole people, and only inability is in-

---

12 Nahum N. Glatzer: Franz Rosenzweig, p. IX–X.
13 Briefe, p. 582.

14 Jacob Rosenheim in a series of articles in the Israelit, viz. 'Briefe,' footnote to page 521.

dividual'.[15] In other words, what unites us all is the objective existence of the corpus of tradition, which is not impaired by the individual's choice.

Professor Bergmann offers another answer which seems to supplement that of Rosenzweig. He frankly admits the danger of "religious anarchy" inherent in Rosenzweig's teaching and says that there is no rational solution to this problem. We can only trust in God that He will not allow us to disintegrate as a community. He who has promised us that "My words which I have put in try mouth shall not depart out of thy mouth, nor out of the mouth of thy seed, nor out of the mouth of thy seed's seed from henceforth and for ever" will not allow us to become disunited.[16]

### III

The traditional philosophy of revelation was very lucidly presented by Samson Raphael Hirsch. Like Yehuda Halevi, he based Judaism on the Sinaitic Revelation and accepted the Torah as revealed Law and as 'real as Heaven and earth', a Divine creation analogous to the very creation of nature itself. The twofold revelation of God, in nature and the Torah, is a conception underlying Jewish medieval philosophy, but Hirsch developed it further and gave it a rather incisive formulation. And this is what he says on the analogy between Torah and nature in the 18th of his *Nineteen Letters about Judaism*:

'Two revelations are open before us, nature—and Torah. In nature all phenomena stand before us as indisputable facts, and we can only endeavour

*a posteriori* to ascertain the law of each and the connection of all... The right method is to verify our assumptions by the known facts, and the highest attainable degree of certainty is to say, "The facts agree with our assumption"—that is, all observed phenomena can be explained according to our theory. A single contradictory phenomenon will make our theory untenable. We must, therefore, acquire all possible knowledge concerning the object of our investigation, and know it, if possible, in its totality. If, however, all efforts should fail in disclosing the inner Law and connection of phenomena revealed to us as facts of nature, the facts remain, nevertheless, undeniable, and cannot be reasoned away. The same principles must be applied to the investigation of the Torah. In the Torah, as in nature, God is the ultimate cause; in the Torah, as in nature, no fact may be denied, even though the reason and the connection may not be comprehended; as in nature, so in the Torah, the traces of Divine wisdom must ever be sought for. Its ordinances must be accepted in their entirety as undeniable phenomena, and must be studied in accordance to their connection with each other, and the subject to which they relate. But as in nature, the phenomena are recognized as facts, though their cause and relation to each other may not be understood, and are independent of our investigation, but rather the contrary is the case; in the same way the ordinances of the Torah must be Law for us, even if we do not comprehend the reason and the purpose of a single one'.

Hirsch's accentuation of obedience to the Law—even if we do not comprehend the reason and purpose of a single one of God's Commandments—reminds us of the Rabbinic saying: "Would that they forgot Me and kept my Commandments!"

Professor Nathan Rottenstreich makes the following interesting comment on Hirsch's attitude to the Law:

---

[15] Ibid. p. 522.
[16] Hugo Bergmann in 'On Franz Rosenzweig,' p. 52-3.

'Hirsch thought it possible to save the (Judaic) legal order which is innately static and not easily altered, from the corrosive action of the historical process. The legal sphere is one where permanent features are more prominent than transient ones, the enduring has sway over the mutable. The preference of the factor of the Law to that of doctrine and faith, reflects a certain conception of the essence of Judaism. Opposition to the subjectivisation of religion is formulated as the preference of the objective panoply of Jewish Law, and preference for Jewish Law reflects a tendency to withdraw the true essence of Judaism from the historical process, posing it incontravertibly as Divinely revealed and an eternal statute'.[17]

It must be admitted that Hirsch's analogy between Torah and nature is part of our spiritual heritage. It is implicit in Psalm 19 where immediately after 'The heavens declare the glory of God, and the firmament showeth His handiwork' follows: 'The teaching of the Lord is perfect . . . the precepts of the Lord are right'. The same conception is embodied in our Prayer Book, where immediately after the blessing 'Who formest light and createst darkness. . . . How manifold are Thy works, O Lord, In wisdom hast thou made them all', there follows the *Ahavah* prayer with 'Enlighten our eyes in Thy Torah and let our hearts cleave to Thy Commandments. . . .'

The weak point in Hirsch's conception of revelation and Law is the dogmatism inherent in it; it may rightly be asked whether he has not "overstretched" the points of comparison between To-

rah and nature. Already his contemporary and former friend, Abraham Geiger, took issue with Hirsch on this point.[18]

In his critical survey of Samson Raphael Hirsch's *Nineteen Letters*, Geiger rejects vehemently the analogy of Torah and nature. Hirsch surely cannot seriously believe, writes Geiger, that his apodictic statement that Torah is as immutable as Heaven and earth, expresses an alternative theory to the historical proof. In this way, all religions could attribute absolute authority to the books on which they base their ideas, such as the Koran and the New Testament. How can one compare Torah to nature when the latter is a lofty and incomprehensible creation which cannot be examined exhaustively, whose beginning and end are difficult to grasp and which stands above the powers of man? On the other hand, Torah is a book intended solely for us and is subjected to the historical process; its age can be estimated accurately. Geiger concludes this paragraph of criticism with the words: "For goodness' sake, what an error have we here: May God save Israel from such a spirit!"

The three philosophies of revelation presented in this paper are somewhat related to, though not quite identical with the doctrinal foundations of the three main streams in present-day Judaism: Liberal, Conservative and Orthodox. The critical presentation of all three should bring home to the reader the urgent need of further thought on this important subject. And by the way, it is interesting to note that all the three theories were developed by the religious genius of German Jewry.

17 *Jewish Thought in Modern Times, Vol.* I, p. 115.

18 Abraham Geiger, *Leben und Lebenswerk*, Ludwig Geiger, Berlin 1910, p. 293.

# III. Contemporary Jewish Theology

## A. God

# INTERIM THEOLOGY

## MONFORD HARRIS

A Jewish theology is in a sense a con-tradiction in terms for a genuine Jewish theology is its own gravedigger. What I mean by this is not the truth that theology must ultimately keep silent before the Living God, Who is beyond any final formulations of theology, but that Jewish theology, if it is true to its Jewish sources must ultimately cancel itself out.

For the fundamental fact of Jewish theology, the central point of reflection for the Jewish thinker, *qua* Jewish think-er, is Jewish existence. The existence in this world of Jewish existence and how each Jew is to link his private existence to Jewish existence sets into motion a *Jewish* theological enterprise.

There are certain themes of theological thinking in Western civilization which are so fundamental that whether or not they occur in traditional form they may be called classical. One of these is the problem of the nature of Man. This has always been and in the nature of the case always will be fundamental for Christian thought. There is also no doubt of the fact that throughout classical Jewish literature there is *implicit* a notion of Man's nature. But none of the great classical Jewish texts or medieval Jewish books are explicitly and systematically interested in describing or analyzing *Man's* nature.[1] The crude and untrue quip that the church "invented" the idea of Man as sinner so that it could convince people that they needed salvation and thereby the church became a powerful institution does contain a certain truth, namely: unredeemed man must first be made aware of his miserable state before he can be redeemed. This is, of course, part of the genuine outlook of Christianity. Christianity's theological endeavor must always analyze for Man his nature so as to show him his actual misery. It is only then that Man can attain his grandeur.

Jewish thought, however, has never devoted itself in any explicit way to the nature of Man.[2] Classical Judaism does have in itself the notion of the double *yetzer* but Jewish thought has not developed in any sustained and systematic way an outlook on the fundamental nature of Man. It has kept its thoughts on the subject muted. Man, alone and single, has not been a primary subject for discussion. It is unthinkable for even a modern Jewish thinker, as *Jewish*

---

[1] Cf. M. Kadushin, *Organic Thinking*, N.Y., 1938, p. 267. Rabbi Max Ticktin kindly recalled this reference for me.

[2] David Hoffmann showed that *ADAM* the basic Hebrew word for man eventually gets to mean a Hebrew man. Cf. his famous commentary on Leviticus (Leviticus 1:2, p. 80 of the Hebrew translation, Jerusalem, 1953). Rabbi Maurice Pekarsky pointed out to me in private conversation that the very title of the legal compendium "Chaye Adam" is one of the many instances in Jewish thought where Man means a Jewish man.

thinker, to write a book entitled (like R. Niebhur's major work) *The Nature and Destiny of Man*.

Neither has there been any systematic attempt in classical Jewish sources to deal with the problem of revelation. In Christianity revelation has been perhaps the fundamental problem if we consider the question of incarnation under this rubric. Why and how did God become man? Much serious theologizing was done on such questions as homoousianism (that the son is of the *same* substance as the Father) and homoiousianism (of *like* substance). These terms may sound esoteric and irrelevant to us but the problems they represent are in a way serious problems for Christian theology even today. The relationship of revelation and reason, or, the divine foolishness of Calvary to the human wisdom of Athens, has also been a cardinal problem of Christian theologizing.

Nothing like the first problem of God becoming man can even present itself in Judaism. But there is an issue in Judaism that one might have expected to see treated in as sustained a fashion as Christianity treated incarnation. This issue is, obviously, the revelation at Sinai. In Exodus 19:20 we are told that "the Lord came down at Mount Sinai." This is a serious statement and the Biblical writer, whether we call him Moshe, or Redactor, or *Rabenu* (to use Franz Rosenzweig's synthesis of Biblical criticism and Torah) was not writing loosely. Yet in all of Jewish tradition there has been no systematic analysis of how God came down on Mount Sinai. One might have thought this statement which was taken seriously would have received some analysis.

And the problem of revelation/reason is also neglected. It is true that thinkers such as Saadia and Maimonides deal with this problem and many others, too numerous to mention, devote themselves to finding a solution. This is one of the major issues for Jewish thinkers during the middle ages. Yet this does not contradict our observation that Jewish thought never really came to grips with the problem of revelation/reason. For the first five centuries of the common era—five centuries of sustained Christian thought on this problem—the Jewish mind which also did not slumber ignored this question. The Babylonian Talmud (and the other material in its wake) is a highly reasoned work. Yet none of these rabbinic minds ever worked on this problem. If in the aggadic literature there are hints that they thought about the relationship of revelation to reason they certainly did not consider it important enough to devote even a chapter in all of their immense literary corpus to this question. It might be said that they never raised the problem of revelation versus reason because they solved it at the very beginning, since the hermeneutic rules that they employed they considered to be granted them through revelation. But the fact remains that it was their human reasoning powers that had to apply the "revealed logic."[3] Nevertheless, no one worked on this problem in any systematic way (comparable to an halachic discussion) in all the literature of the Talmudic period. Even the philosophers (or the theologians, depending on one's estimate of the respective functions and use of terms) such as Saadia and Maimonides who discuss revelation and reason do so only in solving the conflicts with reason in what we call the narrative portions of the Bible. But Saadia

---

3 Cf. Baba Metziah 59b.

and Maimonides never raise the issue in the crucial area of Pharisaic thought: the Halacha.

It can rightly be said that the first five centuries of the common era form the classical period of both Jewish and Christian "expounding" of their "Bibles." The classical Christian endeavor during this period was theological; the classical Jewish was (pharisaic) halachic. And this difference is not accidental. Controlling this difference is something crucial.[4]

No major halachic exegete or pharisee was a convert to Judaism. Some were descendants of converts, but even these were very few. The Pharisees did not come to Jewishness from the outside; they were born Jews. But the overwhelming majority of the Christian thinkers of the first five centuries were not born into "Christian nations," but were converts to Christianity. This rather obvious difference has many important ramifications but it points to something at the root of our question.

The Christian thinker of these first five centuries was by virtue of his experience *necessarily a theologian* for his becoming Christian necessitated squaring some way or other (depending on the individual) his former assumptions as a pagan thinker with his "new birth" as a Christian. This is the situation which gives birth to theology: *The pagan mind still has its problem that the baptized heart knows not of.* And so the pagan mind must formulate answers to bring both heart and mind into consonance (though in some respects it is doubtful that this is ever solved).

Jewish thought, however, was devoted to the halacha. The Jew had in the

world only the four ells of halacha and the major emphasis of systematic thought in classical Judaism was the halacha. Outside of these four cubits many things were going on but for Jewish thought the most important subject was existence within this comparatively small area. The task of the halachic thinker was not to unite a new heart with an old mentality (such as the Christian thinker had to do) but to keep mining the four ells long ago staked out, or, to put it another way, as new situations arise how are we to live our Jewishness.

Now halacha has of course some crucial religious pre-suppositions. But the main Jewish systematic activity was not the theological analysis of the pre-suppositions but working the halacha itself. It is true that there is the aggadah. No one can justifiably maintain that the aggadah is simply musings of minds tired from halachic labors or stories to entertain children. But even if one were to question Nachmanides reservation about the aggadah (which was stated under the duress of the Barcelona debate) and even if one were to assert that the aggadah was of great importance it is certainly true that aggadah was not systematic theology and was not the decisive area of the rabbinic mind.

In the light of this analysis it would seem that theological writing in the classical sense of the term is foreign to Judaism.

It is not the misery of man, nor the paradox of reason/revelation that is the dynamic for Jewish thought. It is Jewish existence that sets into motion a Jewish "theology."

At the watershed of the twentieth century Jewish existence finds itself in a different situation than it did at the beginning of the period of emancipa-

---

4 I treat here an issue, on an historical level, which is ultimately "metahistorical."

tion. Self hatred is not as common a phenomenon as it was at one time. Simone Weil's self hatred seems archaic, a case of nineteenth century atavism but not symptomatic of a general *malaise*. Whether because of the existence of a Jewish state or because of the reaction to Hitler, or because of the specific sociological pattern of American life, or these factors in combination, young Jews are *not* forsaking their Jewishness.[5] It is here that a Jewish theology or Jewishology—if we can be forgiven a crude neologism —can play a genuine Jewish role. With the fact of Jewishness neither forgotten nor forsaken, a Jewish theology—to reverse the Midrash's description of the angel presiding at birth—can give the fillip of recall, the shock of recognition of what Jewishness really is. This shock treatment for Jews is the function of a twentieth century Jewish theology. What is the situation today in which a Jewish theology must speak, for an authentic Jewish theology always speaks in terms of specific historic situations?

The most important and universally rampant question in the Jewish community today, whether its segments are in America or in the State of Israel, is not the question of God's Oneness and Uniqueness but the question of Jewry's oneness and uniqueness. Religious Jews, non-religious Jews, anti-religious Jews, all share this concern. Even the American Council for Judaism by the very passion of its protests reveals its entanglement.

In the Middle Ages the various Jewries did not know the problem of relationship to one another. Only in the last ten years have we known this.

Jews have always been interested in

one another. Ben Baboi in the ninth century wrote a compendium describing the differences in customs between Palestinian and Babylonian Jewries. Spanish Jewry was, for various reasons, interested in the Khazar Jews. Benjamin of Tudela and Petahya of Regensburg wrote travel diaries recording information about different Jewish communities. But none of these writers, and many more examples could be given, were concerned about the communities growing apart. Yet these writers and travelers were astute and sensitive enough to see deep differences. For them there was no problem.

Only today is this problem felt and only in reference to the State of Israel. We have not been concerned about Indian Jewry, for example; nor has Indian Jewry been concerned about us.

We are concerned today specifically about Diaspora and Israeli Jewry because the State of Israel presents the possibility of a basic "normalization" of a segment of Jewry. No other Jewry in the last two thousand years has found itself in this situation. Both inside and outside the State, Jews are concerned lest this normalization bring a segment of Jewry to live a life like unto the nations. Israeli Jewry also knows this concern. Both feel the common concern yet there are tensions between these two communities because each approaches this common concern from its own specific situation. American Jewry, to take the most blatant (in more ways than one) example of Diaspora Jewry, nurtures its guilt, envious of Israeli Jewry's "fulfillment." Mixed with genuine concern lest Israelis become like unto the nations is American Jewry's desire to be at one with the nations, to make America its promised land. In turn the people of

---

[5] Cf. W. Herberg, *Protestant, Catholic, Jew,* N.Y., 1955, chp. VIII.

the State of Israel in spite of the vaunted normalization are concerned about the problem of becoming like unto the nations.

Because of these tensions, our uniqueness and our desire for normalization, we talk about "bridges of understanding," "what can we offer one another," etc. This was unknown in the Middle Ages. Even the tensions between Polish and Lithuanian Jewry, for example, were peripheral in the sense that they were due to ordinary human pride and distrust of differences. Polish and Lithuanian Jewry were never concerned about cultural bridges and drifting apart. They were committed to the notion that they were one people. The famous kaddish of Reb Levi Isaac of Berditschev implicitly affirms this. Shneur Zalman of Ladi, founder of Habad, and caught in many battles, was convinced that in every Jew there was implanted a love for all Israel, a love inherited from the patriarchs.

But today we have a new problem, a segment of catholic Israel traveling a new road. This is a new situation.

A Jewish theology for our time must speak in a new way for the situation is new but it speaks about the old themes. A Jewish theology must start with the question: what does it mean to be a Jew.

We must be clear in our minds that this is not at all similar to the Christian theological problem: how does one *become* a Christian. Jewish theology is not Christian theology minus Jesus so as to be addressable to Jews. Jewish theology is fundamentally different because it talks of a fundamentally different kind of fact: a different kind of existence. Christian theology is concerned with conversion, rebirth, becoming. Jewish theology is involved with recall, return-

ing, being. To Christianity no one can come except he be as a "little child," i.e., reborn. To Judaism only the convert, fairly rare, is described as newborn. The central problem of Christianity is how to be something *new*, how to be reborn, how to become a Christian. This accounts for the agony and travail at the heart of authentic Christianity. The stigmata, to take an admittedly extreme example, reveal much about Christianity. This groaning is the pain and travail of rebirth.

We have intentionally referred to the stigmata for it brings us to Francis of Assisi. No stigmatics are known before the thirteenth century; Francis was the first of a long line. In spite of the self abnegation and mystical exercises practiced by Jews in the Middle Ages it is worth noting that the travail and agony objectivized in the stigmata are never found among Jewish mystics. It has been said that Judah the Pious, the thirteenth century focal point for the Hassidai Ashkenaz, was a kind of Jewish Francis of Assisi. There are, it is true, some superficial parallels between the two men. But a closer look shows a profound difference and it is this which is a basic difference between Judaism and Christianity.

The initial story about each life is the significant clue for the dynamic of the total life; and each life itself illuminates each tradition.

It is recorded[6] that Francis of Assisi was a wayward, young man, living a life of intemperance and extravagance. An illness caused him to reflect. He decided to dedicate himself to God. The father interested in Francis' carrying on the

---

6 *The Life of St. Francis* by St. Bonaventura, London and New York, 1941 (Everyman's Edition), p. 313.

family name and business interfered with the decision. Francis was forced to break with his father, going so far as to cast off the clothes provided by his father saying: "Hitherto I have called you my father on earth; henceforth I desire to say only, 'Our Father Who Art in Heaven.'" So Francis broke with his father, his past.

Judah the Pious[7] also was a wayward young man. His father was not wealthy so Judah did not have the possibility of living extravagantly. But he is pictured as spending his time in play. A young student of his father's comments on this. The father offers to give Judah instruction in Torah, etc. Judah accepts and when the session begins an effulgence fills the synagogue.

Common to both biographies is the early waywardness of each hero. But that is all. Francis breaks with his father so as to *become* a genuine Christian. Judah *returns* to his father in which act he returns to what he always was. Here there is no struggle, no renunciation, no break with the father. Here there is reconciliation. Seven centuries separate Judah the Pious from the twentieth century Jew and profound differences exist between the two communities yet the dynamic is the same. A Jewish theology is one of recall. The immediate task of a Jewish theology is not the exploration of dogma or a formulation of dogmatics. The immediate problem, intensified by the specific situation, is a renewed understanding of the covenantal people. The primary goal of an authentic Jewish twentieth century theology is the revitalization of the awareness of our uniqueness.

It is only after this has been done or at least attempted that we can come to

grips with the Torah. This is not to say that Torah is anthropocentric but it does take seriously the Biblical assumption of two major personalities, God and the people of Israel. Both make the Torah what it is. And so it is only after first understanding the data immediately before our eyes—our life as a corporate personality—that we can hope to understand what is implied by revelation.

This brings us to the problem that we cannot evade: the question of halacha. There have been serious attempts in our day to formulate a Jewish Biblical theology; but in spite of the claim that these were genuine Biblical theologies they have turned out to be pretentious. For these Biblical theologies have avoided the immense corpus of Biblical laws. A Christian Biblical theology can do this. For the "old" testament is seen by Christianity through the eyes of the "new." But through what eyes does a Jew view Torah? He has two legitimate possibilities: the normative rabbinic tradition, or the collective experience of the people down the ages. It may be that these two possibilities ultimately converge and it may be argued that they remain separate. In any case, each position necessitates an acceptance of an halachic centered existence. The only other alternatives for viewing the halacha is the Christian claim, which it is presumed the modern Jewish Biblical theologians reject, or general nineteenth and twentieth century humanistic assumptions which the modern Jewish Biblical theologians glory in rejecting as an idolatry.

An honest Biblically centered theology for Jews must be halachic. And this opens up a vast territory for exploration. All the fumbling attempts in the community today indicate this deep

---

[7] Moses Gaster, *Maaseh Book*, Philadelphia, 1934, vol. II, p. 336.

awareness on our part, if only unconscious, that halacha is an integral part of an authentic Jewish theology.

There have been many attempts to formulate a "philosophy" of halacha.[8] This had not been a major concern of Jewish thought but at most a minor footnote to halachic efforts. But in our times this has to be at least a prolegomenon to living the halacha. For after we re-explore and thereby rediscover what our Jewishness is we must live it. There is this endemic pragmatism about our tradition, from the days of the people's response at Sinai where "action" spoke prior to "understanding," which demands application of all theoretical insight to living.

Alongside the corroding of applied halacha from our lives in the twentieth century there has been some quiet but significant formulations which indicate the possibility of an approach for our time.

Bialik in a very suggestive essay *Halacha and Aggadah* tried to show that these two are interrelated. Professor Chaim Tchernowitz in his major study *Toledot HaHalacha* which does not attempt to be more than just a history did explore in passing, an idea which a Jewish theology could use with great advantage. Tchernowitz observed, very circumspectly, it must be noted, that the

specific laws of the Biblical halacha in most cases have their parallels in specific events of the patriarchal narratives. And Tchernowitz summed up with an important generalization:[9] that which was direction (halichot) originally for the Patriarchs became directive (halachot) for the sons.

This is a bold formulation which, so far as I know, has no parallel though Tchernowitz argued that this is implicit in the rabbinic notion that the patriarchs observed the entire law. But this idea that the practices of the fathers became the way of the sons can help a twentieth century Jewish theology move from covenantal recall to covenantal living.

Jewish theology, then, is an interim theology. It is not a continuous challenge to mankind, to the old Adam. But it addresses itself to the children of Abraham, to the Jew. And it speaks only when Jews have forgotten the meaning of their existence or why and how to live this existence. This theological enterprise must view itself with a rather sceptical eye; it must see itself as a product of sickness rather than as the queen of Jewish knowledge. For Jewish knowledge must pass beyond a Jewish theology and become knowledge in the original sense of the Hebrew term. When this happens the covenantal people are happily rid of theology; for so often in our time has theology been a barrier between us and life.

---

8 I. Heinemann in his *Taamei Ha Mitzvot,* Jerusalem, 1949, has brought together all the relevant material.

9 Vol. I part 1, N.Y., 1934, pp. 201ff.

# THE QUESTION OF JEWISH THEOLOGY

## JAKOB J. PETUCHOWSKI

In one of the books of his trilogy about the *Lost Son*, Soma Morgenstern describes the following scene at a *"Knessijoh Gedauloh"* of the *Agudah* which took place in Vienna: — An orthodox scholar with a thorough Western training (probably a reference to Nathan Birnbaum) was scheduled for a lecture on the Jewish belief in God. After the speaker had begun his lecture, individual members of the audience began to leave one by one, until the hall was practically empty. Where, then, did all these pious souls go while this profound lecture on theology was in progress? They were assembling in one of the corridors to *davven minchah!*

I have often thought of this story when, in conversations with strictly ob-

*The revival, in our day, of Jewish Theology raises, if only by implication, at least two fundamental questions. Does Judaism need a theology? Is a Jewish theology possible today? To both questions, Dr. Petuchowski, Professor of Jewish Theology at Hebrew Union College—Jewish Institute of Religion, responds in the affirmative. While granting that a systematic Jewish theology may be the concern of only a scanty few, he insists that without such concern and convictions Jewish group existence in America will be compelled to rest on nothing more enduring than the ever-shifting currents of purely sociological forces.*

servant orthodox Jews, my admission of interest in theology was greeted by raised eyebrows. There is good historical precedent for this, too. We only have to recall Abarbanel's opposition to the Maimonidean Creed. The formulation of dogmas in Judaism, according to Abarbanel, was a mistake, an erroneous copying of what the non-Jewish philosophers were doing. For the Jew, every word of the Torah has to be considered as constituting a dogma. At the same time, it is well for us to be mindful of what Schechter had to say about this: "It is idle talk to cite this school in aid of the modern theory that Judaism has no dogmas. As we have seen, it was rather an *embarras de richesse* that prevented Abarbanel from accepting the Thirteen Articles of Maimonides. To him and to the Cabbalists the Torah consists of at least 613 Articles."[1]

Inasmuch as dogmas are, by definition, theological, and inasmuch as one of the branches of theology deals with Dogmatics, we may here for our purposes take this reference to dogma as a *pars pro toto* for theology in general. We need not, at this point, discuss the perennial problem whether Judaism has dogmas or not. This problem can be argued till doomsday. Rather would we follow the rabbinic advice *puk chaze ma amma dabbar*, in the sense of the homely truth that "the proof of the pudding is in the eating."

---

[1] *Studies in Judaism*, First Series, p. 174.

Think for a moment of a rabbi who many a time thunders forth from his pulpit the broadmindedness of Judaism, —a broadmindedness which manifests itself in the absence of any dogmas. Imagine him one Sunday morning, after his customary lecture, adjourning to his study. There he is to meet Miss McCarthy who, in view of her engagement to Mr. Cohen, has expressed her desire to seek refuge under the wings of the Shekhinah. The rabbi, just having delivered himself of another utterance on the absence of dogmas, now turns to page 31 of the CCAR's *Rabbi's Manual*, and has Miss McCarthy solemnly pledge that she believes that God is One, Almighty, Allwise and Most Holy; that man is created in the image of God; that he is a free-will agent; that Israel is God's priest-people, the world's teacher in religion and righteousness as expressed in our Bible and interpreted in the spirit of Jewish tradition; etc., etc. No doubt, a week later our rabbi will again hold forth on the "dogma-lessness" of Judaism.

This illustration, which may not be at all *too* hypothetical, establishes the existence of Jewish dogmas on a pragmatic level, — whatever else may be said on the subject in theory. Perhaps Bernard Felsenthal hit the nail on the head when he said: "Therefore it is quite possible to speak of a *history* of dogma in Judaism, but hardly of immovably fixed absolute dogmatics."[2]

It is the evolution of Jewish religious ideas which makes it impossible for us to regard them as being on the same level with the permanent unchanging dogma of the Church, — this, and the other important fact to which we shall return later on, that, in contrast to the Christian scheme of things, belief in dogmas alone is no key to the Jewish *'olam habba*. Again, Felsenthal is right in saying: "And thus it turns out in the end that every one of us has his individual dogmas, every one holds fast to certain thoughts as his fundamental religious thoughts. Everybody has his own dogmatics."[3]

But even if in Judaism we have dogmas only in a pragmatic and ephemeral sense, "dogmas" there are. And to that extent we have, or should have, a theology, — the sort of thing which Kaufmann Kohler defines as "the presentation of one specific system of faith after some logical method."[4]

Is it then impossible to have a religion *without* a theology? This is not a new question. An important discussion took place on the floor of the CCAR in 1903, when Max L. Margolis presented his learned paper on *"The Theological Aspects of Reformed Judaism"*. Margolis made the statement that "no religion can be without a theology". This statement was attacked by Marcus Friedlander who, on the basis of Frazer's *Golden Bough* and Spencer's *Principles of Sociology*, argued that it could hardly be said that "the bewildering jungle of all manner of wild practices in early savage religion had a theology."[5]

This, of course, is neither here nor there. We happen to deal with a highly developed kind of religion, called Judaism, and not with early savage religion. But, I submit, it *is* possible (or, at any rate, it used to be possible) for a Jew

---

[2] *"Gibt es Dogmen im Judenthum?"*, in *Juedische Fragen*, Chicago 1896, p. 13.

[3] op cit., p. 10.

[4] *Jewish Theology*, p. 1.

[5] *Discussion of The Theological Aspects of Reformed Judaism*, Oakland, Calif., 1905, pp. 10 ff.

to live a pious and religious life on the basis of only an unconscious and inarticulate theology.

I do not want to set myself up as a judge in deciding who, in the story we alluded to before was more pleasing to the *ribbono shel 'olam*: the Westernized Jew who had given much thought to the theological problems of Jewish Monotheism, or the Eastern Jew whose religion was so "built-in" into the very mechanism of his watch that, when *minchah*-time arrived, it was the most natural thing on earth for him to *shtell sich aveg davvenen*. But I do know this: that the piety of the "automatic" *minchah-davvener* was the kind of piety which the late Dr. Leo Baeck described as *Milieu-Froemmigkeit*. Its practitioners, once removed from their environment, were liable to throw their *tefillin*-bags overboard the moment their ship came within sight of the Statue of Liberty. And I also know that the theological pre-occupations and teachings of a Samson Raphael Hirsch or a Nathan Birnbaum enabled a not inconsiderable section of German Jewry to combine their strict observance of orthodox Judaism with a full participation in Western culture and in civic life. (*Torah 'im Derekh Eretz!*)

Note, however, that in *both* instances there is no question as to the actual obligation to recite the daily *minchah* service! Both types, the "instinctive" as well as the "verbalized", agree on the binding character of traditional Jewish Law.

But what happens when the *mitzvoth ma'asiyoth* are given up, when practical Jewish observance can no longer be taken for granted? Samuel Holdheim, a foremost theoretician of radical Reform, furnishes us with a suggestive an-

swer. He asserts[6] that "until now" Jewry has felt no need to set up fixed norms of Jewish faith. This, in a somewhat Paulinian way of speaking, he attributes to the "externalism" of pharisaic-rabbinic Judaism.

Says Holdheim, characterizing the rabbinic position which he rejects: "Only through the transgression of the divine laws can the truth be denied, even as it is only through the observance of them that this truth can be made known and confessed. In order to be a Jew, that is to say in order to confess the faith of Judaism, it is, therefore, not sufficient to bear the truths of Judaism in one's mind and heart, without a factual confession (*factisches Bekenntniss*) by means of the practice of the Law. The mere spiritual confession without a symbolical activation (*symbolische Bethaetigung*) of it is considered to be just as worthless as it is considered impossible to deny the truths which are attested through the deed."[7] Furthermore, there is the fact that you are *born* a Jew, so that, however sinful you may turn out to be, you can never get away from it.

As against these traditional notions, Holdheim maintains for himself and his *Reform-Genossenschaft*: (i) that the essence of Judaism is exclusively defined by the morally free confession of the truths of Judaism and the inward conviction of the mind and the heart, "without the necessity to activate this inward faith by means of external ceremonies"; and (ii) that it is not the accident of birth which determines one's belonging to Judaism, but, again, exclusively one's

---

[6] *Die Religions principien des reformirten Judenthums*, Berlin 1847, p. 10.

[7] op. cit., p. 11.

inner convictions combined with the practice of morality.[8]

In consequence of this, "since, according to the conviction of the *Genossenschaft,* the external deed ... is of no consequence (*gleichgueltig*), the spiritual thought, on the other hand, and the inner conviction of supreme importance", Holdheim now feels compelled to determine and to proclaim the "basic truths of Judaism" (*Grundwahrheiten des Judenthums*) according to his latter-day convictions.

We may, for our part, hail or bewail what Holdheim and his successors have done to the spirit and the structure of traditional Judaism. The fact remains that the break-down of the system of *mitzvoth ma'asiyoth,* which Holdheim regarded as a desideratum, stares us in the face as an actual *fact!* Like Holdheim, therefore, we are compelled—whether we like it or not—to determine and proclaim the *Grundwahrheiten des Judenthums* according to our latter-day convictions. In short, we cannot do without a theology, — whatever may have been the legitimacy or otherwise of theology in Judaism before.

Yet, as soon as we say this we find ourselves in a dilemma. There is, after all, something to Franz Rosenzweig's criticism of 19th century Jewish Liberalism, when he finds fault with the Liberals for determining their principles before acting according to them. "The fundamental principles remained fathers without children, even as those who fought for them were but officers without soldiers."[9] Like Rosenzweig, there may be those among us who would prefer to say: "We begin with the deeds. May we

or some others on some future occasion find the underlying principles for them." (A nice modern variant on the old theme of *mittokh shelo lishmah ba lishmah!*)

But those of us who have been concerned over the years with the problem of a modern Halakhah—and by this I do *not* mean the facile manufacture and acceptance of "ceremonial pageantry"— know very well that such a Halakhah can be "sold" to our people only on a "theological" basis. The recent *"Guide"* prepared by Doppelt and Polish, for example, is predicated on a prior acceptance of at least a God who, at certain points of Jewish History, has "met" His people.

We may mention in passing that the current pre-occupation with Halakhah in Conservative Judaism (with, of course, such notable exceptions as Jacob Agus) may be criticized precisely on this score: that the whole complex of Halakhah is being dealt with in complete isolation from its *theological* basis. Naturally, *mutatis mutandis,* the Reform movement is guilty of the same thing. There is no relation in the *Columbus Platform* between the "customs, symbols, and ceremonies possessing inspirational value", which are recommended, and the idea of a God Who commands.[10]

As I said before, we find ourselves in a dilemma. There may be no pat solution. It was my intention primarily to clarify the problem. Who knows but that in our case, too, the old rabbinic preference for *midrash* over *ma'aseh* (since *midrash* is bound to lead to *ma'aseh*) holds good, — only that *ma'aseh*

---

8 op. cit., p. 13f.

9 Franz Rosenzweig, *Briefe,* ed. Edith Rosenzweig, Berlin, Schocken, 1935, p. 425.

10 Cf. the present writer's article, *"Problems of Reform Halakhah",* in the Fall 1955 issue of *JUDAISM.*

for us will have to include the theological principles as much as the deeds. Yet even the *midrash* itself will have to be a "theological" *midrash*, an earnest inquiry into the very sources of our being, with at least the possibility of a personal commitment to the implications of our findings.

And if, with Franz Rosenzweig, we like to insist that "Das juedische 'Lernen' ist *keine* Theologie"[11], let it be clearly understood that there is a *"Theologie"* and a*"Theologie"*. Rosenzweig was right in maintaining that Jewish "learning" is not identical with *Christian* theology. But is it not just possible that there is such a thing as a *Jewish* Theology?! The desirability of one, at any rate, it has been our purpose thus far to demonstrate. But the mere fact that we can speak about "The *Question* of Jewish Theology" certainly indicates the possibility that this question might be answered in the negative. "Jewish Theology?" "There is no such thing!"

There are, as a matter of fact, many conscious and committed Jews who shy away from theology; — not, of course, in the sense in which the participants at the *"Knessijoh Gedauloh"* did, but as a result of a superior sophistication. Theology sounds so narrow and medieval when contrasted with such more respectable and acceptable terms as "religious philosophy" and "religious thought". There is no denying that the three·fields we have just mentioned have a number of overlapping areas. But this still does not mean that they are all identical, or that we could substitute one term for another.

Theology which, as we have seen, is charged with "the presentation of one specific system of faith after some logi-

11 *Briefe*, p. 412.

cal method" has to rely to a certain extent on the materials furnished by religious philosophy. And whatever ideas are expressed in theology are, of course, "religious thought". Nevertheless not all religious thought goes into the making of theology. The doctrines of Elisha ben Abuyah, for example, are, in a manner of speaking, "Jewish Religious Thought", and so, I suppose, are the writings of St. Paul. But are they "Jewish Theology"?!

With this we have come to a decisive point. What do we mean by "Jewish"? Here we have to go back to a point made by Holdheim to which we have briefly referred before. In contrast to the Talmudic view that you cannot check in or out of Judaism (*af 'al pi shechata yisrael hu*), Holdheim wants to do away with the "accidental" nature of Judaism, and, by disregarding the mere fact of birth, he makes membership in Judaism *exclusively* dependent upon one's religious convictions and practice of morality. This, of course, is the way it works in the Christian Church, and, for all we know, this is the way it may one day work for Judaism, too. But this is *hilkhetha demeshicha!* In the meantime there is still such a thing as a Jewish people, — however we may care to define it. And membership in this people, if no longer by the authority of the Talmud, then at least by the established findings of the science of sociology, is "automatic", and becomes effective with and through the "accident" of birth.

As far back as 1895, in a lecture before the *Verein Chicagoer Rabbiner*, Bernard Felsenthal drew attention to such things as Jewish newspapers, which were by no means restricted to "religious" news, but dealt with all problems facing Jews *qua* "Stammesjuden" ("Jews by descent"); to the Jewish clubs of which it could hardly be said that they were organizations for the promotion of religious aims; to the Jewish dances, and the Jewish picnics.[12]

In other words, it is not at all our theology which determines our "Jewishness" or the "Jewishness" of our projects and activities. We would still be Jews even if we believed nothing. Just as certain as it is that affirmation of certain theological tenets makes a person a Christian, so certain it is that no such affirmation is required to make a person born of Jewish parents a Jew. Now, these are the facts. And the additional fact that, in the past, the Jews interpreted their existence primarily, if not exclusively, in *religious* terms is a fact which even the secularist-nationalist could accept as being of historical interest, — without, however, bearing any present-day implications for him.

In short, just as a non-nationalist cannot deny the existence of the Jewish people (the members of the American Council for Judaism do not deny it either the moment they join a "Jewish" country club), so the mere *existence* of "Jewish Religious Thought" cannot be denied by the nationalist, the secularist, and the humanist. But the fact that, from the point of view of both the assimilationist and the "survivalist", no such thing as a Jewish theology is necessary or desirable does not at all have as its consequence that such a thing is not *possible*.

Certainly, there can be a *historical* theology. Felsenthal, who, as we have seen, was opposed to the formulation of binding Jewish *dogmatics*, nevertheless admitted the existence of a *history* of Jewish dogmas. It is only when we get to *Systematic* Theology that the problem really arises. Systematic Theology, according to Kaufmann Kohler, "presents the ... doctrines in comprehensive form as a fixed system, as they have finally been elaborated and accepted upon the basis of the sacred scriptures and their authoritative interpretation."[13] It is the "fixed" and "authoritative nature of the thing which frightens the opponents of Jewish theology away.

If, as we have seen, Holdheim notwithstanding, one's "Jewishness" is "automatic", it can be argued that no authority can tell *me* what is required in order to make me "Jewish"! Why should I even *try* to bring my own religious convictions into relation with Bible, Talmud and Maimonides?! Inasmuch as I am a Jew to begin with, my own "religious thought" is as authentically "Jewish" as that of, say Yehudah Halevi. Why bother with a systematic theology?!

We might as well admit it: There is no hope of formulating a systematic theology which will be both meaningful and acceptable to *kelal yisrael*. But perhaps, for practical purposes, we have to modify the concept of *kelal yisrael*. In his book, *Judaism for the Modern Age*, Robert Gordis has tried to do the same thing, — albeit in a different context. The old 19th century Conservative view of *"vox populi vox dei"*, that *kelal yisrael* determines what is, and what is not, Halakhah, would lead to dire consequences in this age of general non-observance. Consequently, Gordis restricts the halakhic franchise, as it were, to those Jews who still regard themselves as living halakhically. *They* are the *kelal yisrael* who determine the conservation, changes and adaptations of the traditional Halakhah.

---

12 *Juedische Fragen*, p. 36.

13 op. cit., p. 1.

That this procedure is fraught with certain logical—let alone practical—difficulties is obvious. But how otherwise can a meaningful concept of *kelal yisrael* be put to *practical* use in this 20th century? And it seems that those of us who reckon with the possibility or the desirability of a modern Jewish theology are pretty much in the same position. We have nothing to say to those who do not want a Jewish theology. We have neither the desire nor the power to read them out of the fold if they do not subscribe to our formulations. But, by the same token, we cannot allow our own religious needs to suffer on account of their lack of interest.

For ourselves, we are not satisfied with a mere study of *historical* theology, a mere contemplation of "religious thought" in either past or present. Something within us has been touched by our study of past Jewish religious thought. We have no desire to create religiously *ex nihilo*. We think that it is possible to see ourselves theologically as the present-day (though by no means as the last) link in a chain that reaches back to Sinai and before. With all the credit we may wish to claim for our own insights, we happen to think that the insights of our predecessors were not so poor either. With the late Chief Rabbi Kook we would like to say: *hayashan yithchaddesh, hechadash yithkaddesh* ("Let the old be renewed, and the new sanctified") — where the "new" would gain some of its sanctity by being viewed from the perspective of what has been Judaism in the past. And what all this adds up to is an affirmative answer to the question of Jewish theology.

True, the formulation of such a theology may come to be regarded as the idiosyncrasy of a few cranks representing nobody. The bulk of Jewry will continue to "muddle through" theologically or otherwise as heretofore. The existence of the State of Israel, with its supposed "survivalist" implications and its actual danger of a "vicarious Judaism", may make some feel the need for a theology less than ever. But there will come a time—if not in our generation, then in the next—when the novelty of the Jewish State will have worn off, when the inevitable assimilation to the pastimes of the environment will have taken place of whatever Jewish "folkways" had previously been practised (I mean "folkways", — not *mitzvoth*), and when the only possible form of Jewish existence in the Diaspora will be the *religious* existence. When that time comes, there better be a theology, there better be some material for the Jewish father to fulfill the commandment of "Thou shalt tell it to thy son", when the son, as invariably he must, will ask: "What is the meaning of this service to you?".

We need a Jewish theology which will make it clear that Judaism does not simply mean "everything, and nothing in particular"; a theology which can point out in the words of the title (though not necessarily in all of the contents) of Abba Hillel Silver's latest book, *"Where Judaism Differed"*. And this Theology will have to give these answers not only to our children, but also, last not least, to the *ben hanekhar hanilvah el adonai* ("the stranger who has joined himself to the Lord", — Isa. 56:6), whom we attract in the performance of our mission to mankind.

# AN OUTLINE OF A MODERN
# JEWISH THEOLOGY

### EMIL L. FACKENHEIM

WHATEVER their differences, all present schools of Jewish theology would seem to have a common failing. This is the lack of system. To illustrate this contention, we need only cast a brief glance at the two main schools, the so-called humanists and the so-called existentialists.

The members of the former school tend to draw heavily on the support of the sciences, and it is perfectly logical that they should. For inasmuch as they deny such articles of faith as supernatural revelation, it follows that Jewish religion (as all religion) is based on natural insights closely related to other natural insights, whether they be philosophical, moral, aesthetic or scientific. But one looks in vain in their writings for a systematic account of the relation between Jewish religion (and religion as such), on the one hand, and all the other forms of human insight, on the other. For example, it is fashionable to relate Judaism to the insights of modern psychology. But the attempts to establish such a relation, frequent though they are, content themselves with random illustrations; they never seem to get down to first principles. The thoughtful read-

The author of this essay is Assistant Professor of Philosophy at the University of Toronto. Professor Fackenheim was last represented in the pages of *Judaism* by a review that appeared in our October 1953 issue.

er is therefore forever left wondering whether Jewish religious insight is meant to give the standard of what is valuable in modern psychology, or whether psychology is to be the standard of what is valid in Jewish tradition; whether the whole enterprise is a mere apologetic which assures us that Jews knew long ago what psychology discovered only recently, or whether Judaism still gives us something which nothing else can give; and if the latter, what this something is. The Jewish humanist makes similar attempts to relate Jewish religious insight to pragmatism, sociology, and even modern physics. And in each case the reader is left in a similar state of bewilderment. All this does not prove that the humanist version of Judaism is untenable; but it does prove that the case at present made for it is poor indeed. And what makes it poor is the lack of system.

The existentialists, too, must be criticized in this respect, though (at least in the opinion of this perhaps not unbiased writer) not quite so severely. They tend to emphasize the difference between religious truth (and consequently Judaism), on the one hand, and all ordinary forms of knowledge and experience, on the other. Again this is perfectly logical. For it is perhaps the principal tenet of this school that faith constitutes a unique form of commitment; and it asserts

211

realities removed from natural insight, such as revelation. But again, the fact that this commitment is in some sense outside our ordinary system of knowledge does not mean that one cannot give a systematic account of it. And the fact that religious truth must here be set apart from other forms of truth does not absolve us of the theological duty to relate what in some sense is separated. For the moment we are told of the existential commitment we can raise a number of legitimate questions. Is the commitment possible? What is its meaning, in relation to the rest of human knowledge and experience? Why one commitment rather than another? These are questions which can be answered only in systematic form. And while it may be true that the actual act of commitment transcends all system, there can (and for the theologian must) be system both before and after: before, to explain why and where to leap; after, to clarify the consequences of the leap. The existentialists have been the object of many unjust accusations, such as obscurantism, "failure of nerve" and the like. What has lent such accusations a semblance of justice has been the fact that the existentialists, too, have failed wholly to live up to the demands of system.

System in theology is needed for two reasons, one theoretical and one practical. Whatever theology may be, it is thinking. And thinking is systematic. The function of theology is to save religious faith from obscurantism and arbitrariness. And it can fulfill this function only by giving a consistent account of faith, consistent both in itself and in relation to everything else asserted as true. Thus, theology without system is a contradiction in terms. This is the theoretical reason for the need for system in theology.

From this follows the practical reason. Theologians, no matter how different their stand, can argue with each other. Untheological believers often cannot. This is because theologians, merely by virtue of being theologians, are all agreed on at least one criterion of truth: consistency. And in this lies the principal practical value of theology. But where theologians fail to give adequate attention to system they can no longer argue with one another. They can only either sermonize or vituperate. And there has been in Jewish theological discussion far too much rhetoric and vituperation, and too little argument. To this writer it seems that the existentialists have been the primary victims; but it is possible that his own leanings have biased his judgment in this matter. At any rate, what concerns us here is the cause of the undue prevalence of vituperation and rhetoric in contemporary Jewish theology, a phenomenon undoubtedly traceable to the insufficient heed paid to system in all quarters.

There are, of course, some excellent reasons for this situation. If English-speaking Jewry has failed to produce impressive works in systematic theology, this is not entirely due to theological incompetence. The Jewish spiritual situation in the modern world is such a to make it doubtful whether even the most gifted theologian could produce a systematic theology adequate in all details. But this is no excuse for ignoring the idea of system. For we might be able to produce at least fragments of a system, and we certainly could, by keeping the ideas of system and consistency perpetually in mind, reach a level of theological debate at which rhetoric and invective are left behind, and the followers of opposing schools can genuinely argue with one another.

The article which follows these introductory remarks may seem singularly ill-fitted as an illustration of the virtues which we have exalted. For, as a mere outline of a theology, it cannot substantiate by argument any of the doctrines it puts forward. But the idea of system which we have urged means two things: argument of details, and the fitting of all details into a Whole. The outline which follows makes no claim to adequate substantiation of detail; but it seeks to offer a conception, however sketchy, of a Whole.

## I

Theology is the attempt to give a coherent account of religious faith; Jewish Theology is the attempt to give a coherent account of Jewish faith. Theology thus differs from religion, which is the life of faith itself; it also differs from philosophy and science, which are either not concerned with religious faith at all, or else cannot accept it as an irreducible source of truth.

As every other religion, Judaism requires a theology. To be sure, in many ages Judaism did not produce a theology; but in such ages the immediacy of faith was strong enough to make its intellectual clarification practically superfluous. No such immediacy is to be found today. Hence the disparagement of theology in some quarters merely indicates confusion, or else indifference to the substance of Jewish faith.

Modern theology often fails to distinguish itself sharply from philosophy, or some such science as psychology. This failure is a specifically modern phenomenon. Since the Enlightenment, modern man has questioned or denied the actuality, or even possibility, of supernatural revelation, once regarded as the autonomous source of religious truth, and the basis of theology. Because of that denial, a defence of religious truth, if attempted at all, had to be sought elsewhere—in philosophical argument or, more recently, in scientific evidence. But it is more than likely that this sort of defence is futile, and that the attempted fusion of theology with either philosophy or science is a confusion. As regards the specific tasks of Jewish theology, it is a priori evident, not only that this *is* a confusion, but that it is a confusion fatal to the tasks of Jewish theology. For the categories of philosophy and science are, one and all, universal; but from such *universal categories* no conclusions can be derived which might be a theological justification of the *particular* existence of the Jewish people. Hence the ceaseless, but futile, endeavours in modern Jewish thought to explain and justify Jewish existence in universal categories, such as a nation, denomination and the like. If we should have to conclude that the only course left open to the modern Jew is to base his thinking in Jewish matters exclusively on the grounds of science or philosophy, then this would be tantamount to concluding that, in the modern world, a Jewish theology is impossible.

The substance of Jewish faith is the direct relation, not only of man in general, but also of Israel in particular, to God. Jewish theology must seek to defend this faith. And it can defend it only if it can defend this relation as immediate, unmediated by general categories. In other words, if it can defend a supernatural God, and a relation to such a God. To justify the substance of Jewish faith, theology must turn its back not only on secularism, but also on all attempts to found Judaism on anything less than an irreducible faith in the Supernatural.

But modern Jewish theology may not simply assume that a defence of Jewish faith is possible. It must not close its eyes to modern criticism which has seriously put this in question. The method of modern Jewish theology must differ from that of classical theology. This latter "worked its way down", i.e., assumed from the start what to modern man is the thing most in question: the actuality of a divine revelation given to man and Israel. Modern theology must "work its way up", i.e., show, by an analysis of the human condition, that man's existence, properly understood, forces him to raise the question of the Supernatural, and the existential problem of the "leap into faith". That human existence is indeed of this sort is implicit, and sometimes explicitly stated, in the whole of Jewish tradition. But whether the traditional view is correct is a question to be considered independently, by unbiased analysis. Only if such an analysis does in fact find this thesis correct can we go a single step further. For if human existence is not such as to raise necessarily the questions to which faith is the answer, then faith is a relic of an unenlightened age which modern man can do without. *From this it follows that the analysis of the human condition constitutes the necessary prolegomenon for all modern Jewish and, indeed, all modern theology.* On the adequacy of this prolegomenon depend the foundations of its sequel, theology proper. For theology is the explication of the faith into which a leap has been made, and the analysis of the human condition alone can justify the leap into faith itself.

Theology proper, in the case of Jewish theology, will fall into two major parts: (1) the explication of the faith by which the Jew lives insofar as he is a man. If this faith is the true answer to the question raised by human existence, it must be true for all men; (2) the faith by which the Jew lives insofar as he is a Jew; this faith, involving the nature and destiny of Israel before God, is confined to Israel alone.

We have said that faith, to be acceptable to modern man, must reveal itself as the sole positive response to questions inherent in the human condition; and we have further asserted that this view is implicit in the Jewish tradition. If this is true, then the task of Jewish theology proper will largely consist of trying to understand Jewish tradition in this light: as reflecting a faith which is the response to perennial human problems. If we may assume that Jewish tradition reflects (along with much that is incidental and inauthentic) also the essential and authentic, then modern Jewish theology will in no way seek to alter the essence of Jewish faith; though it may very well alter traditional Jewish theology. For the task of modern Jewish theology is to understand Jewish faith in terms compatible with modern thought.

## II

Philosophical analysis reveals that man is, as it were, half-angel, half-brute. Unlike all other beings, he is not all of one piece. If he interprets himself as an overgrown animal—different from other animals only in complexity—he finds that his natural needs and urges fit into this interpretation, but his moral and spiritual nature do not. Yet if he interprets himself as an unfinished angel he fares no better: nature in him forever refuses to be transcended. Every effort to make himself all of one piece is doomed to ultimate failure, and history is littered with philosophies (as well as so-called sciences) reflecting this failure. Man is in perennial contradiction with himself—a "broken vessel". To mitigate this contradiction may be a task set to human prudence and moral wisdom; but to resolve it is possible, if at all, only for a God.

History reflects the human condition. If man were but a complex animal he would have no history. He would realize no meaning beyond what is already inherent in his essence. His history would be but quantitative variation, in other words, not history at all. If, on the other hand, man were an unfinished angel, all that is evil and unmeaning in history would be mere temporary accident. History would be necessary progress, and man would be wholly competent to bring about its moral perfection. In truth, history is a domain of meaning, but of a meaning forever partially thwarted. Moral progress is exposed to tragic frustration. Man can mitigate the tragic and evil in history but cannot eliminate it: history, like man, is in need of redemption.

The domain of human freedom is defined by moral law. The moral "ought" marks the perennial human ability and task to transcend an "is". The tension between "is" and "ought" not only constitutes freedom in its profoundest sense: it defines man's very humanity. But any "is" is finite whereas the "ought" is infinite. This means that there are no a priori limits to human freedom and responsibility: man must always strive further upward. But it also means that the tension between "is" and "ought" is never resolved: by his own moral judgment, man is always a sinner. Moral knowledge, and perhaps even moral life, need no God. But man's moral situation raises not only moral but also religious questions. The question is not only: what ought I to do? but also: what is the meaning of my sinfulness, which remains no matter what I do? If the religious question is left open, then the demands of the moral law leave life an unsolved riddle; and if God is denied that riddle becomes a tragedy.

The moral tension of human existence is only one of many, though perhaps the most significant. But perhaps others, raised by problems such as death and solitude, are no less significant after all. All these ultimate tensions derive from the fundamental tension of existence, above described. They all, jointly or separately, pose the fundamental religious question: is the contradictoriness of existence as final as it is seen by our finite reason? Reason can still state this question, but it can no longer answer it. To answer this question, affirmatively or negatively, we require a leap, an act of decision and commitment. A commitment to a negative answer is a commitment to tragic existence, to a way of life lived in the conviction that existence is in its core paradoxical. The affirmative answer is the decision of faith. *Faith may be defined as the positive answer, given by way of personal commitment, to existential questions of ultimate significance, which reason can still raise, but no longer answer.* Faith asserts that the human contradiction is not final but ultimately redeemed; that what naturally cannot come to pass yet does come to pass; that not one, but both sides of the human contradiction are redeemed, and nothing is lost. Faith asserts the existence of a God who is Creator of all, and Redeemer of all.

Faith is thus neither knowledge nor superstition; not knowledge because its evidence is subjective, and outside rational proof; not superstition, because its object transcends refutation as well as proof, and because it is not arbitrary. Faith is a leap into the dark but, again, not an arbitrary leap—one of many possible leaps, each of which is equally meaningful. It is the sole possible positive answer to the fundamental question posed by existence itself.

Because it is faith, faith in God is an absolute risk. Because it is faith in God —Creator of all and Redeemer of all— it is a risk involving existence in its entirety.

### III

Theology is the organized statement of religious faith. Faith consists in the commitment to a positive answer to problems of human existence which reason can state but not answer. Thus every doctrine of faith must reflect a contradiction in human existence which it resolves; and it is part of the business of theology to exhibit this reflection. Jewish theology, too, has this business. What marks it as specifically Jewish is that the faith which is its subject is the faith by which the Jew lives, not only as a man, but also as a Jew.

The God whose existence faith asserts is a mystery. Asserting His existence, faith dares not make any assertion about His nature as it may be in itself. God's nature, if intelligible, is not the subject of faith. Faith is concerned with God only insofar as He is related to human existence: as the God who has made, and will reconcile, a paradox. The language of faith therefore does not include words such as "Substance", "Force", "Cause", etc., but only terms such as "Creator" and "Redeemer". The God of faith must redeem man, but not by making him less than human, or by transforming him into an angel. To assert either would be to assert that hu-

man existence as such is meaningless, a contradiction to no purpose. But faith must assert (if it asserts anything) that what is contradictory to finite understanding is yet ultimately not contradictory. The God of faith must redeem man by preserving the contradictory elements which constitute his humanity, but by transforming them in such a way (unintelligible to finite understanding) as to take the sting out of the contradiction. God thus relates Himself to man in ways which appear contradictory to finite understanding. He is at once a God of Justice who makes absolute demands on human freedom, and a God of Mercy who heals absolutely the contradictions which arise from the use of that freedom. Before Him as Judge all men are radically sinful; yet before Him as Father all sins are radically forgiven. For the same reason, man's moral freedom, and the importance of its responsible use, is at once everything and nothing. It is everything because God makes demands upon men, as if He Himself were impotent, and man the sole agent of history; it is nothing because, after all, God is omnipotent, and history is safe in His hands despite the evil done by men.

God is therefore Person. For whenever a person is in *mutual* relation with another, that other is person as well.

Yet when we speak of the justice, mercy, and personality of God we speak symbolically only. God's nature is a mystery, and only insofar as He is related to man may faith speak of God; yet even in relation to man God remains a mystery. For God is infinite and man is finite; and a mutual relation between a God who is infinite and men who are finite passes finite understanding. Nevertheless, faith must assert the reality of this relation. Man is forever tempted to deny such a mutual relation, either by making God a mere ideal which does not act, or by making man a mere plaything of an omnipotent God. But neither doctrine is a genuine doctrine of faith; for both fail to resolve the human contradiction. The latter denies the very fact (i.e., moral freedom) which gives rise to the human paradox; the former fails to resolve that paradox. Faith, then, in asserting a mutual relation between man and God, cannot speak literally. But to be unable to speak literally cannot mean to remain silent: for, to faith, that relation itself is a reality, demanding participation on the part of man. Man addresses God, obeys His law, prays for and trusts in His mercy. He must treat God as if He were literally Person, Judge and Father. Man must speak, but speak symbolically, or (if we wish) anthropomorphically: for he speaks from his finite situation. But anthropomorphic language, not being absolute truth, is not therefore falsehood: it is the truth about the God-man-relation as it appears from the standpoint of man; and that relation is itself a reality. How it appears from the standpoint of God man cannot fathom, nor is it his business to fathom it.

No religious doctrine is more baffling than that of revelation; yet none is more essential.

Two alternative interpretations present themselves of which neither appears intelligible. Either revelation reveals what man may discover by means lying within his nature: but then revelation is superfluous. Or else revelation reveals what lies beyond human means of discovery: but then it would seem to lie beyond human comprehension also, and the recipient of a revelation cannot understand it. This dilemma cannot be avoided by fashionable equivocations.

To associate revelation with poetic inspiration is to make it the product of man; but revelation is either the direct gift of God or not revelation at all.

Yet no doctrine is more essential than revelation, unless it be faith in God itself. Creation establishes time and history, whereas redemption consummates and redeems them. Revelation is an incursion of God *into* time and history; eternity here breaks into time without dissolving time's particularity. Creation and redemption establish the significance of time and history in *general*. Revelation establishes the significance of the *here and now* as unique; it is the religious category of existentiality as such.

If revelation is impossible then there is significance only to the human situation in general, even though God is accepted. And the law as well as the promise known to man remains in strict universality. But this makes individual men and historic moments universally interchangeable. God may then be related to man in general: He is only indirectly and accidentally related to myself, my people, my historic situation.

Existence, however, is of inexorable particularity. The moral law to which I am obligated may be universal, but the situation in which I must realize it is unique. A historic situation reflects what history as such is, but it is nevertheless something all its own. Israel is a manifestation of mankind, but what makes her Israel is unrepeatable and uninterchangeable. If there is no revelation, the particular in existence is a meaningless weight upon time and history, from creation until redemption. History in that case has meaning only at its beginning and at its end: nothing essential goes on within it.

But faith must assert that revelation is possible. For only if revelation is possible does the here and now have relevance before God. And if the here and now has no such relevance the human contradiction remains at least partly unresolved. Only if there is, or at least can be, revelation does the God of mankind become my God; only then does the universal God of the philosophers become the God of Abraham, Isaac and Jacob.

This explains the dialectical character of revelation, above described. An incursion of the eternal into the temporal which destroyed either the temporality of the temporal or its own eternity would provide no essential difficulty for the human understanding; but an incursion which preserves both its own eternity and the particularity of the temporal is a paradox. But faith *must* hold fast to this paradox if the particular is to have meaning before God; it *may* hold fast to it because there is no reason why what is paradoxical to finite understanding should be impossible to God. Revelation, like all doctrines of faith, reflects in its own dialectical character the nature of the human problem to which, as a doctrine of faith, it corresponds.

This character is reflected also in the content of revelation. It lights up the particular as such, in its obligation and promise: it must therefore reveal. Yet in passing into time it becomes transformed: hence it must remain concealed as well. That God speaks, or has spoken, is a simple fact to the man of faith; but what He has said is expressed in human language; it is inexorably shot through with interpretation and hence remains, even while revealed, a mystery.

The modernists of all times distort revelation by transforming it into natural inspiration; the orthodox distort it no less by equating the human interpretation of, and reaction to the Encounter with the Encounter itself.

A history without God is an unmitigated tragedy, i.e., a domain of frustrated meaning. A history which is, as a whole, in the hands of God, but in which no revelation is possible, is as a whole beyond tragedy; but the particular as such remains a weight without meaning. A history in which revelation is possible is one in which every event, no matter how insignificant, may in its stark particularity acquire unique meaning. It is a history characterized by the all-important possibility of Fulfillment *within* history; not merely the ultimate Fulfillment of redemption, which can fulfill only by abolishing history.[1]

The assertion of faith that revelation as such is possible and, indeed, necessary, is still a universal assertion. It is concerned with the *category* of the particular, not any special particular. A leap is therefore required before it is possible to assert the *actuality* of a specific revelation.

Not unnaturally religions divide at this point. While atheist, agnostic and religious believer can agree on the human condition and its need for redemption; while all who have made the leap of faith can agree on the general implications of that leap, and on the general thesis that the contradictions of existence are not final: it is not possible to arrive at the actuality of a particular revelation by means of universal considerations of this sort. Theological reflection, even after the leap into faith, takes us no further than to the estab-

---

[1] For a fuller treatment of the concept of revelation, cf. my article "Can There Be Judaism Without Revelation?" *Commentary* Vol. X[II], New York, 1951, pp. 564-572.

lishment of the possibility of revelation as such. The assertion of the actuality of a particular revelation entails a second absolute leap, and a second absolute risk.

There is a second, and perhaps even profounder reason why religions should divide at this point. Only at the point when an actual revelation is asserted do we enter the realm of concrete, unique, unrepeatable existence. Here individuals, peoples, historic situations begin to know of, and live in, their unique condition. And, by the same token, here they begin to be ignorant of the uniqueness of other individuals, peoples and historic situations. Thus, for example, the Jew who asserts a revelation addressed to himself as Jew, speaks of something of which others are necessarily ignorant; at the same time, he is himself ignorant of what may establish the religious significance of the concrete existence of others. The extent to which the adherent of one faith may understand, and pass judgment on, the faith of another is clearly limited. Here, then, religions divide in their claims; but here, also, different claims cease to be mutually exclusive.

Judaism rests on the assertion of the actuality of a series of revelations which have constituted Israel as a historic community destined to serve a specific purpose. Where it speaks of mankind and the God of mankind, Judaism is nothing beyond what a universally human religion might be; only at the point where, leaping into the particular, it is concerned with Israel and the God of Israel, does Judaism separate off from universal truths of faith.

Jewish existence is established by, and responsible to, divine revelation. Hence it shares the dialectical character of all revelation. That Jewish existence has a meaning is vouchsafed by the faith which accepts the reality of revelation; of a revelation which has established Jewish existence. But the nature of that meaning is involved in the dialectic of the paradox. All revelation both reveals and conceals: thus the meaning of Israel's existence, too, is both revealed and concealed. It must remain concealed: for the divine plan for Israel remains unfathomable. Yet it must also be revealed: for Israel is to play a responsible part in that plan. Since the Jew is to live a consciously Jewish life before God he must have at least a partial grasp of its meaning; but in its fullness that meaning is not disclosed: for his Jewishness is only partly the Jew's own doing. The Jew both makes, and is made by his destiny.

The God-man-relation demands of man a free response, the response through moral law. The God-Israel-relation demands of the Jew, in addition to the moral response, a response expressing his Jewishness in all its particularity. This response is Halakhah. Moral law, mediated through the leap of faith, becomes the divine law to man. Halakhah is Jewish custom and ceremony mediated through the leap into Jewish faith; and it thereby becomes the divine law to Israel. In themselves, all customs, ceremonies and folklore (including those Jewish, and those contained in the book called Torah) are mere human self-expression, the self-expression of men alone among themselves. But through the leap of faith any one of them (and pre-eminently those of the Torah) have the potency of becoming human reflections of a real God-Israel encounter. And thus each of them has the potency of becoming Halakhah, commanded and fulfilled: if fulfilled, not as self-expression but as response on the part of Israel to a divine challenge to Israel; as the gift of the Jewish self to God. Thus no particular set of ceremonies is, as such, divine law: this is an error flowing from the orthodox misunderstanding of the nature of revelation. But, on the other hand, all customs which flow from the concreteness of Jewish life have the potency of becoming divine law, and are a challenge to fulfillment. The denial of the religious significance of any law which is not moral is an error flowing from the modernistic misunderstanding of the nature of the concrete before God.

We have said that, as all revelation, the revelation of God to Israel both reveals and conceals; and that, correspondingly, the Jew both makes, and is made by his destiny. Thus, whether the Jew practices Halakhah is, on the one hand, not constitutive of his Jewishness; on the other, it is not indifferent to his Jewishness. If the former were the case, the Jew would wholly make his Jewish destiny; if the latter, he would be wholly made by it.

Thus the meaning of Israel's destiny is in part revealed: it is to respond, ever again, to a divine challenge; to become. of her own free choice, a people of God; to give perpetual realization to this decision in thought and practice. Situations change, and with them the content of the response they require: but the fact of challenge, and the need for response, remain the same.

Yet the meaning of Israel's destiny is also concealed. Man cannot understand the final reasons for the tensions of his existence; the Jew cannot understand the final reasons why he was chosen to exemplify these tensions. Hence the Jew is also unable to decide whether or not Israel will continue to exist. He is, to be sure, free to decide whether to be a devout or stiff-necked Jew, whether to heed or to ignore the divine challenge. But if it is really true that God has a plan for Israel, Israel is as little free to alter that plan as she is able to understand its final meaning.

# ILLUSION OR WISH?

SOLOMON SIMON.

Mediaeval Hebrew literature found no place for the human species within the traditional threefold division of all nature into animal, vegetable and mineral. Instead, it created a fourth category—the "articulate," *M'daber*. For man alone is endowed with the power of language; it is his greatest gift. This gift made man the elect among creatures, the ruler of the earth. But it is an imperfect gift, limited by the fact that it is exercised by a living creature, dependent on his senses. To be sure, the oldest inscriptions, out of antiquity, show us that language was not even then limited to symbols for concrete objects; already we find expressions for the finest nuances of abstracts, concepts and emotional variations. Nevertheless, language today still falls short of being a perfect instrument for complete communication between humans. Different people may use the same word; but for each of them it often has different connotations, and dissimilar emotional overtones.

---

The anthropomorphisms of the Bible may, in a sense, be regarded as the beginning point and impetus to Jewish philosophy. Here, Dr. Simon, the author of several works in Yiddish (among them *Toch Yiddishkeit*, 1954) on the ideological aspects of Judaism, outlines a modern approach to the concept of revelation in the context of the traditional philosophical resolution of the problem of Biblical anthropomorphisms. The essay was translated from the Yiddish by S. Gershon Levi.

Despite these limitations, language is still an efficient enough instrument for human conversation; because no matter how various human beings are, they still share a modicum of common intelligence. The most ignorant person possesses a degree of intelligence which reaches, at least, the lowest level of the greatest intellectual. Only with those devoid of the minimum of human understanding is it completely impossible to speak. Language is useless as a means of communication with the hundred per cent idiot, or with the infant below a given age.

As for the animals, man can communicate with them only in a limited fashion; and with the greatest difficulty. Human language is not suited for their level of intelligence. To be sure, it is possible that birds and beasts can converse with one another as easily as man with his fellow. There may be some truth in the Midrashic statement that "each species of animal has its own language". Perhaps even plants have a language of their own. There are many legends in the folklore of various peoples—and they are common in Jewish folklore—about people who understood the language of animals and birds, and even of plants. But the gap between human and animal intelligence is too great for any measure of real communication.

Still greater is the distance between man and the transcendental power that governs the universe. Man is, after all, a sensory creature, but his mind tells him that no trace of corporeality may enter into his conception of God. Says Rabbi Moses Cordovero (1522–70):

"Should your reason tell you that God exists, do not imagine that He exists in the way you think He exists; for if that were so, then His existence would be limited by being contained in your understanding. It would partake of corporeality. You may only conclude that He must exist—and then draw back in haste. For if you begin to conceive anything more of Him, the result will be that you will think of Him as an individual; and the human imagination is limited, tied to the physical. You must, therefore, put a check-rein on your thoughts, that you may avoid describing Him. Affirm His existence, but do not let your thoughts try to grasp Him. Advance— and draw back. Go forward to assert His existence; then flee, lest you circumscribe Him with your definition, for our human imagination treads hard on the heels of our reason. Therefore does the *Sefer Yezirah* say: 'If your heart pulls you forward—turn back.' "[1]

The question then arises, how can there be any communication at all with God, seeing that we dare not attempt to describe Him, or define Him? How is it possible that He reveal Himself to us? Certainly it is within His power, but how can we possibly receive such a revelation? It is as though a tree were to try to absorb the speech of a human being. How can we, who perceive with our senses, apprehend that which is beyond the world, beyond ourselves, and beyond our senses?

For thousands of years man has wrestled with this problem. In the Bible, two God-concepts are found, side by side—one abstract, the other anthropomorphic. The prophets conceived of God as a power over and above the world of matter, outside of nature. He is spirit untrammeled, not tied to natural law, not subject to fate. The God of the prophets is supra-mythological and supra-natural. This is the basic difference between the Jewish and the pagan world-views. To the pagans, the gods were part of nature, subject to its laws, bound by fate. They shared man's weaknesses, experienced the same desires, and like him underwent the same sorrows.

But the God of the prophets is also described, both in the Torah and in prophetic literature, in corporeal terms. To be sure, the Bible does contain varying God-concepts, stemming from different periods. But, in every part of the Bible one finds a representation of the Divinity which includes such elements as these: He dwells in the Heavens, where there is a mansion, a throne, a chariot. His appearance is as that of a man. He commands heavenly hosts. There are clear-cuts accounts of God appearing to the patriarchs in human form, or revealing Himself to the whole people on Mt. Sinai through phenomena sensed in specific form.

The sages of the Talmud and the philosophers of the Middle Ages, who believed in a historically unique theophany, resolved the Biblical paradox by declaring that the Torah had to speak to humans in human terms, and that the prophets, too, used allegorical terms so as to make Divinity understandable. "The Torah speaks the language of man", says the Talmud (*Berakhot* 31b). Language is a human instrument and is, therefore, the only means for com-

---

1 *Torat Ha-Kabbalah* of R. Moses Cordovero, edited by S. A. Horodetsky, s.v. "Unity".

municating with human beings. Another Talmudic saying goes even further: "The Torah speaks the language of exaggeration; so do the prophets, and even the sages," (*Hullin* 90b). (Rashi explains: "This means, the ordinary language of ordinary people, who are not exact in their speech, and say things which are not so. This is not because they deliberately lie, but rather because, in their ignorance, they are inaccurate.") The *Gemara* gives examples of such exaggerations. "It is said that the altar in the Temple contained an ash-bin, with a capacity of 300 Kur. Says Rabha: 'it is an exaggeration' ". Other examples are: "Great cities, with fortifications reaching the Heavens" (Deut. 1:28); "The earth was split open by their shouts", (I Kings 1:40). "These" says the *Gemara*, "are *dibhre habhai*—exaggerations", (*Hullin*, ibid).

Both Bahya ibn Pakuda and Maimonides take this statement of the *Gemara* as their point of departure for their own rationalistic interpretations of the anthropomorphisms in the Bible. Says Bahya: "Our human limitations force us to speak of God in physical terms, to ascribe creaturely attributes to Him, in order to make His existence comprehensible to people. So it is that the prophets use corporeal terms, comprehensible to the common man. Had they described God as befits Him, using abstract words and concepts, we should have understood neither the words nor the concepts. How then could we have worshipped what we could not understand? It was, therefore, necessary to use terms and ideas within the range of our mental grasp... Only later, as we grow wiser, do we discern that all this is a figure of speech; that the matter is really so refined and elevated.

that it is beyond our understanding. The really refined intelligence will make the effort to peel away the verbal wrappings from the idea itself, rising in thought from stage to stage, until he approaches as near to the true concept as his abilities will take him. The foolish and the ignorant, on the other hand, will take the metaphors literally... The Biblical anthroporphisms will bring no harm to the intellectual, for he will perceive the true meaning of the figurative language; while the ignorant will, at least, be helped to realize that he has a Creator, whom he must serve. Otherwise, most of the human race would remain without any religion, for the truly thinking people are in the minority. The matter may be compared to a man, who was the guest of a wealthy friend. The host supplied great quantities of fodder for his vast flocks and herds, but he served his guest comparatively little provender, albeit sufficient for his needs. Even so, Scripture abounds in picturesque descriptions of the Deity, using terms of speech familiar to the common man; whereas only here and there does it furnish brief hints that God is really a spiritual essence. Of the former instances, the Rabbis say 'The Torah speaks the language of men'; of the latter, the Book of Proverbs writes: "They that seek the Lord will understand all," (Prov 28).

Maimonides also deals, after his own rational fashion, with the anthromorphisms of the Bible:

"It is explicitly stated in the Torah and the Prophets, that God is not corporeal, for it is written: 'The Lord your God is in the Heavens above and on the earth below', (Joshua 2:11). A physical being could not be in two places at the same time. 'To whom will you com-

223

pare Me?', (Isaiah 40:25). If He had a body, it would be possible to compare Him to other bodies. This being so, why then does the Torah state, in speaking of the vision of God granted to the Elders of Israel: "Under His feet was a floor of sapphire, and like the Heavens themselves for brightness'; and so with similar references to God's hand, His ears and so forth? The answer is that all these passages are designed for the understanding of those people who can only grasp what is concrete, so Scripture speaks as human beings speak. All these terms are descriptives, metaphors, attributes—a picturesque manner of speech. For, look you, it is written (Deut: 32:41) 'I have sharpened the flash of my sword'. Does God then wield a literal sword? Obviously, this is a *Mashal*—an allegory. This is proven by the fact that one prophet sees Him dressed in white wool, (Daniel 7:9); while another beholds Him clothed in red, (Isaiah 53:1); and there are many other variations All of this means that God has no physical appearance at all, but that prophetic visions take many forms. The truth is, that human intetlligence is incapable of comprehending Him. This is the meaning of Job 11:7; 'Canst thou search out the depths of God?' "

Rabbi Moses Cordovero, whom we have quoted above, explains the anthropomorphic passages in the Bible in the same way as do Bahya and Maimonides, but he adds his own characteristic nuance. For him, these expressions are not just metaphors, but actually stand for concepts. Says he: "A hand is not a hand because of its flesh and bone, but because of its function. Thus, the Talmud asks, 'Does a female minor have a hand or not?' Obviously, the question is not whether her hand has been amputated, but rather, does she have the legal power to consent to marriage or to receive a divorce. The term is not anatomical, it refers to function."

All these explanations are valid for believers, who hold not only to the belief that the entire Bible is compact of eternal values, but also that its framework and form are eternal and unchanging. For them, to tamper with any detail is to bring the whole structure down; so that it becomes necessary to resolve all Biblical inconsistencies by a method which calls into question no single phrase of Scripture.

It is odd that so many enlightened moderns apply the same yardstick to the Bible. They, too, claim that every expression in the Torah, the Prophets and the Hagiographa must agree with the last word of modern science. But since this is not so they say, therefore, the Bible is nothing but a literary compilation of the folklore of a primitive people. It is childish of Genesis to describe creation as having taken place in six days, whereas we know it took a good deal longer. Hence, there is no point in delving into Biblical cosmogony, which teaches that the universe arose, with meaning and purpose, from the harmonious unfolding of the will of a transcendental power, rather than from the blind collision of physical elements. Those who reason this way point out that the so-called perfect Bible is ignorant of modern anatomy and physiology, for Scripture speaks of the heart as the organ of thought, and describes the kidneys as the seat of conscience. In the face of such error, they conclude, the whole ethical approach of the Bible is also mistaken.

On the other hand, there have been, and still are, those who read the findings of modern science into the Biblical text, in their zeal to defend its infallibillity. Familiar is the argument that reconciles Genesis with the evolutionary theory, by claiming that "a day" in the story of creation stands not for twenty-four hours, but rather for a millennium, or an aeon. Similarly, it is claimed, do not the Biblical laws of purity reveal a profound knowledge of modern hygiene? It must be said that these attempts at reconciling the Bible with contemporary knowledge are a good deal more primitive than the efforts of the medieval Jewish philosophers. Bahya and Maimonides had a method, based on the philosophical principles of their times. Many of their propositions are still valid for our day. But the latter-apologetes work with an amalgam of mere homiletics and rank anachronism.

Modern Biblical scholars hold, quite rightly, that contradictions in the Bible are not to be resolved by one key formula. Indeed, they cannot always be explained, nor is it important to do so. For the Bible contains lasting values, transmitted in a framework contemporary not to us, but to its time of origin. Not only does "the Torah speak the language of men"; the phrase can be revised to read: "The Torah speaks to each generation in the terms of that generation".

The prophets enunciated the concept that God's will rules the cosmos. They freed Him from any subservience to either nature or to fate. But they thought of Him also as a God, who reveals Himself to men; not as a deity so abstract that he has nothing to do with the world, so static that the affairs of men do not concern Him. He is a God who commands, who remembers, who bestows kindness, saves, metes out retribution for sin, and rewards righteousness. The prophets thought of Him as a God of will and deed. It is not only man, who seeks to rise to Godliness; God, himself, comes down to man, and teaches him how to walk in His ways.

The prophets conceived of God as transcendental, beyond nature and outside of nature, a deity all-inclusive. He rules over all; everything in the universe is responsive to His will. But, at the same time, they thought of Him in anthropomorphic terms. He reveals Himself in specific forms to his elect. (This summary is drawn from Yehezkel Kaufman). Certainly, there is a paradox here, but we are not bound to resolve the inconsistency. We can simply say: these were the concepts of those times. The prophets did think their way through to a transcendental God; but the concept of an abstract deity, completely incorporeal—this is a later development.

So the old problem remains. Agreed that the interpretations of Bahya, Maimonides, Cordovero and other Jewish philosophers are later views, read into the Biblical text; still, how can mortal man, bound by his five senses, be in communication with an abstract God, of whom we may posit only His existence, and then forbid ourselves any attempts to grasp His essence. We must deal with the paradox through our own modes of thought, without the authority of scriptural proof-texts. We have to arrive at the God idea within the framework of a cultural-historical universe of discourse.

First of all, we posit the existence of

a power beyond ourselves, a creative power that rules the cosmos, and created the world with a goal and a purpose. Science cannot disprove the existence of such a power; nor can we perceive it with our senses. But ever since man achieved consciousness, and found his way around in the forces of his environment, he has had an awareness of such a supra-natural power, which we call God. To this power, which is beyond the reach of his sense-perception, he has applied his own, human, attributes. Awareness of the existence of such a power is an eternal truth; the form in which it is conceived, the attributes applied to the idea—these have always been conditioned by the outlook of the times, and hence have been mutable.

There is, of course, the opinion that the God-idea is an illusion, as Sigmund Freud would have it. Mankind has fashioned for itself the image of an eternal father-figure, because mankind is still immature. Man feels himself helpless against the forces of nature. Overpowered by emotions, fearful of disease and of death, he has fashioned for himself a super-father, who protects him in life and provides for him after death. When man really grows up, he will not need a protecting father-figure. He will then be able to rely on his own powers, and will no longer need to comfort himself with the illusion of a father who keeps an eye on him from the cradle to the beyond.

But it is very difficult to accept so simple a division between spirit and matter. Within man, as in the world around him, the spiritual is as recognizable, as real, as the material. It does not even appeal to our sense of rational probability to accept the hypothesis that mere blind chance accounts for the harmony of the cosmos, the wonderful regularity of natural law, man's struggle with the forces of nature, and even his battle with the forces within him.

Indeed, it doesn't matter whether we believe that the spiritual in man is implanted by a transcendental force, at birth or after birth, or whether we subscribe to the surmise that man's spirituality is the resultant of the combination of the physical elements that produced man. Such a surmise is as miraculous, supernatural, and non-rational as the belief in the separate existence of the soul. Either way, one is positing a manifestation of the divine.

This being so, it becomes reasonable to believe that the existence of a transcendental power, or being, indescribable, because description depends on our sense-perception—that this existence is an eternal truth; a truth that man felt within him, and surmised because of the spirit which is within him. That very spirit is also a part, or an aspect, of the transcendental.

Therefore, man is moved by a constant yearning for the divine, a striving to make himself over into the likeness of God. The God-idea is not an illusion, but rather a wish. Man has always desired that perfect ethical being of whom he is aware by reason of his own existence; he represents Him, to himself, in terms of his conceptual stature, in terms of his cultural climate, at any given time. It is not the idea of God's existence, but rather the quality of the prevalent God-idea, which mirrors the culture of any period in history.

This thought is not as new as Professor Erwin Goodenough seems to think, (see his *Towards a Mature Faith*). The

Midrash contains a clear implication that *mitsvot* are not only commands of God, but man's desire to be like God. The clearest statement is in the *Sifra*: "It is written (Joel 3:5) 'And it shall come to pass that whosoever shall call on the name of the Lord, shall be delivered'. Now, how can a man call God's name? But it means, that even as God is named 'Merciful and Compassionate', be thou also merciful and compassionate, doing good to everyone without expectation of reward".

The same idea is expressed by many Jewish philosophers. Understandably, they all drew their ideas from Jewish sources. This can help us understand how man can communicate with God, finding his way to God through a constant process of revelation.

Man was not created perfect, whole. He has developed from lower to higher stages, both physically and spiritually. But all human capabilities were always potentially present in him. This, too, is no new heretical idea. "R. Tanhuma said, in the name of R. Benaya, and R. Berechia quoted R. Eliezar to the same effect, as follows: 'God created man a *golem*' ", (*Bereshit Rabbah* 24:2). As Bialik explains, man was not fully formed, but was created as raw material. His powers and potentialities remained to be developed, as the Midrash puts it: "With each generation and its wise men, its leaders, its creative spirits, its righteous." Hence, does Scripture say, in describing creation: 'This is the book of the generations of man' ".

We may explain the matter thus: In his beginnings, man had little awareness and understanding wherewith to recognize God. God became greater as man's understanding grew. The more man learned about the world of nature around him, about the universe above him, the more he probed into his own difficulties, and became acquainted with the mechanisms of his own body, the greater the ability he acquired to get nearer to an understanding of the transcendental. As man develops, he approaches closer to his goal, which is to understand that power which is beyond his senses.

Let us consider an analogy. Man fashions an instrument—a table, for example. In every table there inheres something of human intelligence and skill. But the table, a lifeless object, can in no wise be aware of its purpose, of its role in man's environment. But let us imagine that the craftsman has somehow succeeded in infusing into the table some glimmer of his own appreciation of the purpose for which the table was made. The table, inert object though it be, begins little by little, to become aware of its creator, and of the latter's intentions regarding it. How many years would it take that inanimate thing to understand its true role around the house; how much longer to apprehend the part it plays in human civilization? The table would have to become acquainted with thousands of objects, with hundreds of environments. Now let us apply the analogy to man, himself. We have acquired, somehow, the ability to conceive that the universe has a purpose. But we are limited by five senses, *vis-a-vis*, our Creator, to whom our relationship is as that of the table to its maker. Occasionally, we get a glimpse of the blinding light; sometimes we catch sight of a reflection of the eternal, and garner for ourselves a little nugget of truth—and our little knowledge confuses us even more.

227

Our search for God is very like experimentation in the exact sciences. We run into more failures than successes. But we have achieved something; we have discovered a goodly portion of nature's secrets. In seeking God, we must also be prepared for the same kind of struggles. We must gird ourselves with patience, rejoice at what we do achieve, but avoid either satisfaction with our successes, or disappointment with our failures. As in the laboratory, here, too, we must regard every achievement not as a dogma, but rather as a stage in our ongoing search for the truth. Doubts, insoluble mysteries, failures, false concepts and suppositions, need not lead us to disbelief or negation. They ought rather to drive us onward in our search, in the hope that a day will come, perhaps in some distant future, when we will know so much that we will be able to apprehend God with rational and positive clarity, even as the God-seekers of yore apprehended Him with their imagination and their intuition.

This is our contemporary version of revelation. An approach like this will strengthen our faith. For the more we discover the secrets of nature, the more we achieve in science, the firmer will become our faith.

# THE PERSONAL MESSIAH—TOWARDS THE RESTORATION OF A DISCARDED DOCTRINE

STEVEN S. SCHWARZSCHILD

Into the first blessing of the Eighteen-Prayer, liberal Judaism has introduced one change which is linguistically minor but doctrinally major. The traditional formulation—He "brings a Redeemer"—now reads, He "brings redemption." This changed liturgical formula persists in pratically all authorized liberal prayer-books to this day (including the "Conservative" version of Reconstructionism), although the theological reasons which induced the change were among the very earliest issues raised against Orthodoxy at the beginning of the 19th century.

Much, if not most, of the liberal Jewish platform has been modified in these 150 years, and the trend of such modifications has almost unexceptionally been in the direction of a gradual and limited return to the original, traditional position of Judaism. The doctrine of the peoplehood of Israel and the concommitant significance of the earthly Jerusalem for Jewish hopes have long been restored to non-Orthodox religious thinking; the meaningfulness of ritual and ceremonial has been emphatically re-asserted; even the validity of the continuous authoritativeness of Jewish law, if not actually re-established, is certainly increasingly becoming a matter of major concern to Reform Jews. It is, therefore, a little surprising that almost the only basic claim of pristine Jewish liberalism which has not been subjected to this process of re-evaluation in the course of time, should be the doctrine of the Messiah.[1]

The resason for this comparative neglect may well be that the doctrine of the Messiah superficially appears to be merely a matter of theory. The question whether the Messianic fulfillment is to be brought about by the instrumentality of a single, individual person or through the collective progress of mankind seems of little moment when put side-by-side with such pressing, concrete problems as Zionism, the homogeneity of the Jewish community, the observance of Jewish practice and obedience to Jewish law. If this assumption were correct, it would be perfectly proper to relegate so theoretical a ques-

The author of this paper has contributed within recent years to the discussion of Jewish theology in various journals. The present essay marks his first appearance in *Judaism*. He is a rabbi in Fargo, North Dakota.

[1] The only theologian who seems to have concerned himself with the problem, and he with his customary perspicacity and ardor, is the much neglected Max Wiener, *Der Messiasgedanke in der Tradition und seine Umbiegung im modernen Liberalismus*, in *Festgabe für Claude G. Montefiore*, pp. 151-156.

tion to the background. And yet, it is very easy to demonstrate that the messianic doctrine is not academic at all but, on the contrary, exceedingly "practical"; perhaps it can even be proved that it, too, requires re-investigation within the framework of contemporary, non-Orthodox Jewish thinking and life.

There were basically three reasons why liberal Judaism in the first half of the 19th century was moved to transform the doctrine of the personal Messiah into the doctrine of the messianic age—or, to use the phraseology of the Eighteen-Prayer, the doctrine of the Redeemer into the doctrine of redemption. These three reasons can be described respectively as anti-nationalistic, anti-miraculous and optimistic.

In the minds of the early reformers, lay as well as rabbinical, the foremost consideration in favor of the depersonalization of the Messiah certainly seems to have been the fact that they regarded the personal Messiah as inextricably interwoven with the hope of the eventual restoration of the people of Israel from the lands of the Diaspora to Palestine, the re-establishment of the Temple and the sacrificial cult. For the present, it implied the foreign character of Jews in the countries of their domicile. These premises, or implications, of the belief in the personal Messiah they rejected most strenuously. They had begun to receive civil rights in Germany and throughout Western Europe, where Reform had its origin; together with non-Jewish liberals, they continued to agitate for expansion and completion of their citizenship rights; and they confidently looked forward to an early consummation of these aspirations. To declare, at this juncture of history, that they were still awaiting a person who

would lead them from their present homes and re-constitute them a separate nation in a distant land struck them as aiding and abetting their antagonists who insisted on refusing them their civil rights on the grounds that they neither were nor wished to be members of their host-nations. Thus, in his report of the pertinent discussions at the Rabbinical Conferences of 1844-1846, Philipson relates that Dr. Mendel Hess identified the personal with the "political" Messiah.[2] Even earlier, the Frankfort Society of the Friends of Reform, in the single substantive statement of its beliefs, had announced: "A Messiah who is to lead back the Israelites to the land of Palestine is neither expected nor desired by us. (The non-expectation is understandable and, in this context, logical; the undesirability evokes the ironical picture of the Messiah appearing in Frankfort and being received at the city gates by a delegation of respectable Jewish citizens with the urgent request kindly to remove himself since his presence was likely to obstruct current attempts at the complete emancipation of German Jews.) We know no fatherland except that to which we belong by birth or citizenship." And, in another hemisphere as well, many years later, K. Kohler still says: "A complete change in the religious aspiration of the Jew was brought about by the transformation of his political status and hopes in the nineteenth century. The new era witnessed his admission in many lands to full citizenship on an equality with his fellow-citizens of other faiths ... He therefore necessarily identified himself completely with the nation whose language and literature had nurtured his

---

[2] *The Reform Movement in Judaism*, pp. 5, 122, 173-180.

mind, and whose political and social destinies he shared with true patriotic fervor. He stood apart from the rest only by virtue of his religion ... Consequently the hope voiced in the Synagogal liturgy for a return to Palestine, the formation of a Jewish State under a king of the house of David, and the restoration of the sacrificial cult, no longer expressed the views of the Jew in Western civilization. The prayer for the rebuilding of Jerusalem and the restoration of the Temple with its priestly cult could no longer voice his religious hope. Thus the leaders of Reform Judaism in the middle of the nineteenth century declared themselves unanimously opposed to retaining the belief in a personal messiah ... They accentuated all the more strongly Israel's hope for a Messianic age, a time of universal knowledge of God and love of man, so intimately interwoven with the religious mission of the Jewish people ..."[3]

It may be taken for granted that this particular reason for the abolition of the doctrine of the personal Messiah in liberal Judaism need no longer be taken seriously in the middle of the 20th century. In the further pursuit of the argument quoted above, Kohler explains that Eastern-European Jewry, still subject to disenfranchisement and persecution, continues to adhere to the Orthodox longing for a Jewish political restoration—that for this reason Zionism was born there as an answer to anti-Semitism—and that both of these situations are inapplicable to Western Europe in the first place, and must, in the second place, be made superfluous everywhere else by social progress. The irreconcilability of Zionism with liberal Judaism has long been given the lie in

theory as well as in practice and need no longer be argued. But one additional observation must still be made in this connection before we proceed to the next point. It is surely an ironical paradox that Reform Judaism eliminated the personal Messiah because it was held that belief in him was inevitably accompanied by Jewish nationalism, while extreme right-wing orthodoxy of the *Aggudat Yisrael* brand rejected Jewish nationalism because it awaited the advent of this very Messiah! The *Aggudah* argued exactly the other way around: the personal Messiah will redeem the Jewish people; therefore, we must not attempt to anticipate by human action what he will do on divine instruction. Reform remained aloof from Zionism because it did not believe in the personal Messiah, the *Aggudah* remained aloof because it did.

This ironical paradox conclusively illustrates the essential *non-sequitur* of Reform reasoning on this point: whether one believes in the personal Messiah or not has nothing whatever to do with Jewish nationalism. Theoretically, there is no reason why the personal Messiah must mean Jewish nationalism and the messianic age must mean "universalism." It is just as possible, logically, to believe that the Messianic person will bring universal redemption rather than the ingathering of the Jewish people, and that the messianic stage in human history will bring with it the national restoration of Israel rather than its complete absorption among the converted nations of the world.[4] Practically speaking, the

---

[3] *Jewish Theology*, pp. 388f.

[4] The identification of the personal Messiah with nationalism was based on the traditional identity of the Messiah as a descendant of David the King. Thus, the Jewish monarchy was believed to be involved and with it all the features of a re-constituted state.

outstanding Reform Jews who, during the last half century, were also Zionist leaders do not seem to have been inhibited in their Jewish nationalism by their rejection of the belief in the personal Messiah.

In short, not only has the anti-nationalistic argument against the doctrine of the personal Messiah been refuted in theory and in fact, but it can be shown never to have been a cogent argument in the first place.

A logically more tenable argument against the personal Messiah was the belief that to await him implied in fact expectation of a miracle. Traditionally, in Bible, Talmud, and post-Talmudic Jewish literature, the functions which the Messiah would fulfill were regarded as being indeed miraculous: nature itself would be transformed to accord with moral requirements, human life would be rid of all natural or moral deficiencies, Israel and Judaism would be established in their proper place of spiritual primacy.[5] But such a doctrine ran counter, of course, to the positivistic, scientific outlook of 19th century liberals. As Kohler put it straight-forwardly: "Our entire mode of thinking demands the complete recognition of the empire of law throughout the universe, manifesting the all-pervasive will of God. The whole cosmic order is one miracle. No room is left for single or exceptional miracles. Only a primitive age could think of God as altering the order of nature which He had fixed, so as to let iron float on water like wood to please one person..."[6]

On closer analysis, however, even on its own premises, also this objection to the doctrine of the personal Messiah on "scientific," anti-miraculous grounds cannot long be maintained. In the first place, it is very difficult to understand why the achievement of the messianic aims by many ordinary men—which is, after all, what the concept of the messianic age boils down to—is any less miraculous than their achievement by one extraordinary person. Even if it be granted that the state of the world in messianic times must be considered a miracle from our perspective, a notion which, as we shall see immediately, is not necessary to the doctrine as such, it presumably will be miraculous regardless of the agency through which it is brought about. In one sense, therefore, the transformation of the doctrine does not accomplish this declared aim of rationalization. In the second place, however, it is not at all certain that miraculousness is necessarily one of the ingredients of the messianic state. Long before the 19th century reformers came along, the mediaeval Jewish scholastic rationalists, at their head, Maimonides himself, on occasion objected to a supernatural interpretation of this tenet: "Let it not occur to anyone that in the days of the Messiah a single thing will be changed in the natural course of the world or that there will be any kind of innovation in nature. Rather, the world will continue to exist as it always has... The Messiah will come exclusively in order to bring peace to the world... How all these things will come about none can know until they have actually come about."[7] And yet they certainly anticipated the arrival of the person of the Messiah "though he may tarry, at any time." Therefore, as in the case of the anti-nationalistic objec-

---

[5] Cf. J. Klausner, *The Messianic Concept in Israel*, Jerusalem, 5710, p. 138f.
[6] *op. cit.*, p. 165.

[7] *Mishneh Torah*, Laws of the Kings, 12.1.

tion to the doctrine of the personal Messiah, here, too, a complete *non-sequitur* in the liberal argumentation must be noted: in fact, people, and often "better people than we," have believed in him without subscribing to his miraculous advent. In theory, messianism is bound up with miraculousness either in both of its variants, the personal and the collective, or in neither. Thus, miraculousness cannot decide the issue between them.

We have stated that miraculousness is inherent in the messianic doctrine even when it is re-formulated in liberalistic, collective terms. Apart from the common-sensical argument already adduced to that effect, no better evidence can perhaps be added than that of Hermann Cohen, the man who was rightly described by Klatzkin as "a spiritual giant who guarded the inheritance of an impoverished generation,"[8]—the liberal generation. In him, liberal theology, including the depersonalization of the Messiah, reached its grand consummation—and if it failed here it must be regarded as having failed *in toto*.

History was for Cohen the infinite human process of striving for the ideal, and messianism is the term designating the completion of this infinite process. But how can infinity be completed? If, to use an analogy of which Cohen was fond, the ideal state of the future lies on an axis which the curve of human history approaches ever more closely but cannot actually touch, like an asymptote, then perfection is not an ideal whose reality is guaranteed at some point however far removed but a mathematical impossibility—and there is no guarantee of success at all; to the contrary, there is only a guarantee of relative fail-

ure.[9] The conception of the Messiah as an age leaves man swimming desperately in the ocean of history without a shore where he might eventually reach safety. Guttman had pointed out that Cohen's depersonalization of the concept of God had deprived it of the ability to perform the real, historical and ontological function which Cohen himself had ascribed to it.[10] The same must be said of his view of messianism.[11] In fact, the rational picture presents itself in this manner: that there may be such a thing as history at all, progress must be possible; for progress to be possible there must be a logical guarantee of the eventual attainability of the goal of progress; by Cohen's own admission the goal of progress, perfection, is unattainable through human endeavor. If, therefore, the goal is to be reached at all, it can be reached only by a divine intercession at the end-point of history. And once the theological, even the philosophical necessity of divine, i.e. miraculous intercession is established, it becomes absurd and arrogant to declare the concept of the miraculous, personal Messiah out-of-bounds. To say that the messianic state must be miraculously brought about, if at all, but not through the miraculous agency of a person, is clearly a purely arbitrary assertion.

Another, usually unexpressed, reason may have contributed to the hostility

---

8 *Hermann Cohen,* Berlin, 1921, p. 11.

9 Cf. *Rosenzweig,* Glatzer, p. 358: "According to the words of a philosopher whom I regard as an authority even greater than Hermann Cohen, what is not to come save in eternity will not come in all eternity."

10 *Die Philosophie des Judentums,* p. 351.

11 Cf. Cohen, *Religion der Vernunft,* pp. 276-313. I have discussed this point somewhat more lengthily in "The Democratic Socialism of Hermann Cohen," *Hebrew Union College Annual,* vol. XXVII, "Conclusion."

which the reformers of the last century felt toward the concept of the individual Messiah. Maimonides had stipulated the belief in the bodily Messiah as a fundamental doctrine of Judaism and declared the denyer thereof to be a heretic.[12] Taenzer has convincingly demonstrated that Albo relegated this doctrine to a very much lower level of Jewish obligatoriness. On this level, belief or disbelief in the personal Messiah by the individual Jew would be without effect on his full religious status.[13] In effect, Albo proclaimed not only that a Jew need not necessarily believe in the Messiah but actually, by implication, recommended against such belief. The historical conditions under which he lived explain his attitude. By his time, the doctrine had become a serious obstacle to Jewish theological self-assertion, for it was used to good effect by Christians in formal as well as informal religious disputations. "Also the others (!) make out of it (the messianic doctrine) a basic principle with which to refute the Torah of Moses."[14] Once the principle of an individual Messiah was accepted, and with the narratives of the New Testament difficult to refute in an age bereft of historical or literary criticism, the crucial issue between Jews and Christians seemed to become one of picking the right person to fit the messianic pre-requisites—an unproductive quarrel at best. By eliminating the messianic doctrine, Albo hoped to prevent further unconstructive controversies and even to strengthen the Jewish position which could then actually turn the argument around: the Messiah having been declared to be irrelevant to true religion, a religion which made him the central test of faith demonstrated its own unauthenticity.

From the Jewish point of view, the phenomenon of Christological Christianity is, of course, only one of many pseudo-messianisms. By the 19th century there had been many such movements in Jewish history; some of them extremely unsettling. If enlightened, rationalistic, liberal Christians of that era were embarrassed by the traditional claims of Christianity regarding the historical Jesus, as indeed they were, how much more eager must liberal Jews have been to rid themselves of all the theological pre-conditions which might again lead, as they had done so often in the past, to the recurrence of enthusiastic messianic claims. One recalls Graetz's immoderate observations on the subject.[15] How easier to answer the claims of traditional Christianity, than to dissociate oneself from Jewish pseudo-messianisms and the entire Jewish messianic doctrine, and thus prove the rationality of Judaism. In short, this was Joseph Albo in 19th century disguise.

Perhaps it is no longer necessary to show both the uselessness and the invalidity of this procedure. It is truly a case of throwing out the true gods together with the false ones. If a doctrine is to be rejected because it can be or even has been abused, the very belief in God must be dispensed with, since men have also often represented themselves as God and created havoc by the falsehoods announced in his name. Fur-

---

12 Cf. Thirteen Principles, last no.; *Mishneh Torah*, Laws of Repentance, 3:6.
13 *Die Religionsphilosophie Josef Albo's*, pp. 34-37.
14 *Ikarim*, I, 4.

15 Cf. *History*, vol. 10, pp. 190f., 312f., 387f. The Zohar, the source of much late Jewish messianism he never refers to other than as "the book of lies."

thermore, Buber quotes the pointed Chassidic story which compares the pseudo-messianic movements to wet compresses that keep the patient awake until the doctor comes: "When God saw that the soul of Israel had fallen sick, he covered it with the painful shawl of the *Galuth*. So that it could bear the pains, however, He bestowed upon it the sleep of numbness. Again, so that it would not be destroyed, He awakens it each hour with a false messianic hope and then lulls it to sleep again until the night will have passed and the real Messiah will appear. For the sake of this work, the eyes of the wise are occasionally blinded."[16] Franz Rosenzweig made the same point in a less anecdotal, more theological and poetic fashion: "The expectation of the coming of the Messiah, by which and because of which Judaism lives, would be a meaningless theologumenon, a mere 'idea' in the philosophical sense, empty babble, if the appearance again and again of a 'false Messiah' did not render it reality and unreality, illusion and disillusion. The false Messiah is as old as the hope for the true Messiah. He is the changing form of this changeless hope. He separates every Jewish generation into those whose faith is strong enough to give themselves up to an illusion, and those whose hope is so strong that they do not allow themselves to be deluded. The former are the better, the latter the stronger. The former bleed as victims on the altar of the eternity of the people, the latter are the priests who perform the service at this altar. And this goes on until the day when all will be reversed, when the belief of the believers will become truth, and the hope of the hoping a lie. Then—and no one knows whether this "then" will not be this very day—the task of the hoping will come to an end and, when the morning of that day breaks, everyone who still belongs among those who hope and not among those who believe will run the risk of being rejected. This danger hovers over the apparently less endangered life of the hopeful."[17] Herein also lies the answer to those who will always worry: if the belief in the personal Messiah as such is granted, why not Jesus? It is true that if I wish to be married I may chose the wrong wife, but does that prove that I should not look for a wife at all and entirely reject the possibility of marriage?

Underlying all these motivations for the depersonalization of the Messiah-concept lay an optimism about the future of the Jewish people and of mankind as a whole. This optimism resulted in the belief that, as already indicated, the redeemer had become not only impossible and undesirable, but also unnecessary. After all, the Messiah was logically and historically a product of need. In the former sense, the anticipation of his coming implied consciously and unconsciously that man by himself could not master his destiny or reach his goal. Instead, a divine agent would either have to bring about or at least complete the messianic, i.e. perfect human society. And historically it is true that, as Israel's historic situation became increasingly hopeless, the concept of the Messiah became increasingly supernatural, for the greater the need the more powerful had to be the person who would triumph over it. "The burden of exile narrowed their horizon.

---

16 Quoted in *Israel-Volk und Land*, p. 31.

17 Glatzer, *Rosenzweig—His Life and Thought*, p. 350f.; cf. Rosenzweig, *Jehudah HaLevy*, p. 239.

They could see no other way of re-demption from their abject position than by supernatural events.[18] Or as Baeck put it impressively: "It was especially true in the centuries of despair: only by seeing before him a mirage was many a man able to procure the strength with which to keep on marching through the desert which life had become for him.[19] Now, in the 19th century, it was be-lieved that such pessimism about the nature of man and the prospects of his-tory had once and for all been refuted.

Certainly, the political development of the times seemed to indicate that the Jewish despair which had so largely formed the concept of the Messiah had become a thing of the past. Everywhere and increasingly Jews were being en-franchised and at least promised, often also given, equal rights with their fel-low-citizens. Physical persecution, except in some God-forsaken corners of Rus-sia, had almost completely ceased. Lib-eral democracy was making headway everywhere in the West; material and technological developments were fast progressing. And even culturally, the mellowing of Christianity as evidenced by the new liberal theology, Unitarian-ism, ethical humanism and similar phe-nomena, persuaded the usually sober I. M. Wise that America would be Jewish within the foreseeable future. Thus Samuel Hirsch declared: "Everywhere the emancipation of mankind is being striven for so that a morally pure and holy life may be possible of being lived by man on this earth.[20] Auerbach agreed with him: "In our days the ideals of justice and the brotherhood of men have

been so strengthened through the laws and institutions of modern states that they can never again be shattered; we are witnessing an ever nearer approach of the establishment of the Kingdom of God on earth through the strivings of mankind."[21] Herzfeld chimed in: "The conference must declare what it means by redemption; yes, it should state that we are now entering upon the period of redemption. Freedom and virtue are spreading, the world is growing bet-ter."[22] And, of course, the famous Pitts-burgh Platform announced: "We recog-nize, in the modern era of universal culture of heart and intellect, the ap-proaching of the realization of Israel's greatest messianic hope for the estab-lishment of the kingdom of truth, jus-tice, and peace among all men."[23] In this respect, Wiener summarizes the spir-it of the time trenchantly and convinc-ingly: "The new generation was dom-inated by an almost too gay optim-ism... Transcendent, eschatological ideas receded in the face of the confi-dence that this world would soon be the scene of divine justice within the moral life of humanity. By the latter was meant above all the completion of equal-ity of civil rights in all countries—which was an understandable pre-occu-pation, though it became embarrassing by being constantly over-emphasized." He recalls that for Moritz Lazarus the outcome of the Dreyfus Affair was positively "a messianic event." Wiener indicts this entire generation of shal-lowly optimistic, self-centered and self-deceiving leaders when he states: "If it is ever true that religious beliefs are the ideological superstructure of the

---

18 Greenstone, *The Messiah Idea in Jewish His-tory*, p. 264f.
19 *The Essence of Judaism*, 4th ed., p. 273f.
20 *ib.*, p. 178.

21 *ib.*
22 *ib.*
23 *ib.*, p. 356.

economic-political conditions of society, then it was certainly true of this class. It interpreted and accommodated religious doctrines in conformity with its enthusiastic attitude toward civil society which it regarded as final, eternal, and divine."[24]

This outlook no longer deserves a reply. The neo-existentialists, Jewish, Christian, and non-religious, have effectively knocked down this straw-man to build up a case for themselves. Rosenzweig, for example, reports the famous incident in which Hermann Cohen is supposed to have pleaded with him that he must expect the Messiah within no more than fifty years.[25] Thus, he wanted to reveal this vapid optimism for the self-deceiving hallucination that it was —and as a symbol his story serves well enough; although we must add that as a truthful report of Cohen's mind it is a thoroughly incredible tale. It belies everything that Cohen stood for in his affirmation of the infinite messianic process, his violent rejection of all forms of eudaemonism, and even his definition of the Messiah itself. Nonetheless, that the contemporary pessimists have completely and justifiably deflated this hallucination cannot be disputed. We have learned for a fact that the 19th century was profoundly wrong in its vast over-estimation of the social abilities of man. If persecution, pogroms and oppression are indeed the rationale for messianism, then our age is, and by rights ought to be, the most messianic age of all in the history of Israel.

If, then, we must discard the third main reason which the liberals of the 19th century proffered for the abolition of the concept of the personal Messiah, literally not one of their arguments has been found to withstand critical examination. Their anti-nationalism has been repudiated by Jewish history; their anti-miraculousness has been refuted by the necessities of their own position, not to speak of the views of others; their optimism has been repudiated by general history. Furthermore, it turns out that at least two of their reasons were not logically constructed in the first place. In short but brutal fact, their case against the personal Messiah crumbles at the first touch.

We could end the argument at this point. Religious tradition must always be regarded as valid until, and unless, invincible reasons are brought forth against it. The reasons militating against the traditional doctrine under consideration have been shown to be anything but invincible, and we may, therefore, with good and calm consciences return to the original position. Ours is not necessarily the task to prove the doctrine positively; to refute its refutation ought suffice. Nevertheless, without venturing to prove its tenability, there are a few hints which may be given toward the construction of the positive case.

The first is a mere technicality. The liberal prayerbooks of the last century have abounded, and still abound, with phrases which must, if they are to be intellectually acceptable, be interpreted very broadly by the Jews who use them. "The Torah of Moses" is as clear-cut an example as any, although there are many others. Do liberal Jews believe that "the" Torah was given to, by, or from Moses? As a matter of fact, the very ritual reading from the Torah has become a metaphoric act for most of them.

---

[24] *Juedische Religion in Zeitalter der Emancipation*, p. 172f.; *Der Messiasgedanke, op. cit.*, p. 153.
[25] Glatzer, *loc. cit.; Jehudah HaLevy, loc. cit.*

A very high percentage, certainly well over half, of everything read from it, if it is to be acceptable at all, must be homiletically decontaminated of its original historical, theological, moral, or social intent. And nonetheless these things are retained—re-interpreted but retained. Yet the phrase "Who brings a redeemer" cannot be so treated; it must be changed!? All that was required to bring the traditional text into conformity with liberal belief was the interchange of a single letter of the Hebrew alphabet, an *Heh* at the end for a *Vav* in the middle of the word. But this had to be done through a surgical operation on the prayerbook, when much more serious problems were solved with exegetical palliatives. We may assuredly draw two conclusions from this observation: 1. There was more to this than meets the eye; more fundamental interests were involved than those that were expressed; 2. A return to the original phrase is justified if only because it will violate no one's conscience; completely free exegesis will still be offered to anyone who wishes to take advantage of it.

In analyzing the views of Hermann Cohen, we pointed out the intimate connection between the belief in the personality of the Messiah and the belief in the personality of God. For him, as for the liberal mentality in general, the entire concept of personality as such was a terrible stumbling-block. As Kierkegaard and existentialism never tire of pointing out, the existence of the individual personality defies all the universal and theoretical laws of science as well as of idealism. They, therefore, try to dissolve it into general propositions. God as an idea, the Messiah as an age—these are entities with which theoretical reason can deal. The persons of God and

of the Messiah, on the other hand, are hard, stubborn, even—as it were—empiric realities that defy classification. But then, so does every individual. And thus, the de-personalization process does not stop with God or the Messiah so far as liberalism was concerned.

A change was likewise introduced into the second benediction of the *Amidah*. "Praised be Thou, O Lord, who bringest to life the dead" seemed to be a liturgical formulation of the doctrine of resurrection, and this doctrine was regarded as outmoded as the reference to the personal Messiah. Do we not know that the body decomposes in the grave? Where would physical resurrection take place in the spiritual world of God? Does not the belief in the eternity of the body imply a vast over-emphasis on the material aspect of life? And so the modernistic arguments ran. Therefore, again the liturgical formulation was changed, and so remains to this day: "Praised be Thou, who hast implanted within us eternal life." In this manner, belief in the immortality of the soul was substituted for the concept of resurrection of the body.

The rejection of the belief in resurrection is closely connected with the rejection of the personal Messiah—not only because they both found expression at the very beginning of the *Amidah*. Ever since Ezekiel pictured the messianic re-birth of Israel in terms of the famous revived bones, one of the traditional marks of the advent of the Messiah in Jewish thought has been the resurrection of the dead.[26] "May the All-merciful make us worthy of the days of the Messiah and of the life of the world-to-

---

[26] Cf. Greenstone, *op. cit.*, pp. 57-60. Elbogen, *Judaica, Cohen Eestschrift*, p. 671 indicates that resurrection precedes the advent of the Messiah.

come."[27] And at the Conference of American Reform rabbis in Philadelphia in 1869, the rejection of the one doctrine was immediately and logically followed up with the rejection of the other.[28] Thus, the depersonalization process has gone one step further: God is not a person but an idea or a force; the Messiah is not a person but an age; and man is not a person but a universal reason confined in an individualizing and debasing body—a state of affairs fortunately remedied in the hereafter!

Herein also lies the most important reason for our time for a return to the to the personalism of the Messiah. Not only have we re-acknowledged the unitary character of the human person: if scientific conclusions have any bearing on this discussion, they tend to assert the indivisibility, even the indistinguishability of "body" and "soul". Martin Buber's philosophy of dialogue is premised on the recognition of persons, human and divine, as the carriers of life. The outlook of the Bible which deals with "the whole man" is re-asserting itself in the form of what is called "personalism." Baeck[29] describes this outlook in these words: "It is particularly true of prophetic thinking that it is far removed from abstract descriptions and instead envisages the figure of a real human being with its views and deeds. The prophets speak less of a future time than of a future person. The ideal of the future becomes for them an ideal personality... The son of David is the future man. As a man of flesh and blood he makes real and vivid what the ideal man ought to be and will be." As Tillich puts it: "Ontology generalizes, while Biblical religion individualizes."[30] And specifically with regard to the Messiah, the "liberal" Wiener puts the case clearly: "It is always the great miracle, the emergence into overpowering visibility of the deeds of God Himself, which characterize the days of the Messiah—the expression of the personal shaping of world-history by the personal God. For this reason so much emphasis is put on the personality of the Messiah... It is precisely in the belief in the Messiah that one can recognize the full vitality of a religiosity for which God is personality and His revelation the tangible guidance by means of miracle. One is inclined to say that at this point piety is most distantly removed from everything abstract, from conceptual ideology—and that it rather becomes faith in the true sense of the word, believing confidence in the revelation of concrete facts."[31] We have learned from religious as well as non-religious existentialism, that all moral reality, as distinguished from nature or mathematics, is the reality of persons. Man, the person, is the *locus* of ethics, not ages, ideas, or forces. The messianic age is a utopia; the Messiah is a concrete, though future, reality.

Let us consider one last objection which will be raised against this view. It will be said again, as it has often been said in the past, that reliance on the messianic fulfillment will lead to moral quietism and passivism. If men expect a divine agent to bring about perfection, they will sit back, relax their own efforts toward the good, and leave to him the work they themselves ought to do. This has, indeed, often happened.

---

[27] Grace after the meal.
[28] Phillipsohn, *op. cit.*, p. 263.
[29] *op. cit.*, pp. 269f.

[30] *Biblical Religion and the Search for Ultimate Reality*, p. 39.
[31] *Der Messiasgedanke, op. cit.*, p. 154f.

Was it not a delegation of Orthodox rabbis of the *Aggudah* type who requested the British mandatory governor not to withdraw his troops since Zionism was human superorogation anyway, and the Messiah was to come in 1999? But the drawing of an improper conclusion does not mean that the doctrine ought be abolished. It ought rather be protected against false interpreters.

"Perish all those who calculate the end,"[32] was the motto of the Talmudic rabbis who opposed the view that the messianic time was fixed mechanically without regard to the human contribution to its hastening. They taught emphatically that the arrival of the Messiah was dependent upon man's actions: if they were good it would be sooner, if evil—later. "God said: everything depends on you. Just as the rose grows with its heart toward heaven, so do you repent before Me and turn your hearts heavenward, and I will thereupon cause your redeemer to appear."[33] There is even the view, which commends itself on ethical grounds, that the Messiah will appear after the messianic state has been established, leaving its attainment to humanity but guaranteeing its maintenance thereafter. Even Mendelsohn seems to have held this view.[34] The 19th century proto-Zionist, R. Hirsch Kalischer stipulated the return to Zion as a pre-requisite, not consequence, of the messianic advent.[35] And even the man who was later to become one of the foremost and most radical leaders of American Reform, Samuel Hirsch, in the days before he went to greater extremes, advanced this same thought. "It is up to us to turn to God, for the Messiah cannot come before we have become completely good... No, it is not the duty of the Messiah but that of the entire household of the vanguard against evil, the entire house of Jacob, to wage this battle on behalf of all the inhabitants of the world, and the root of Jesse cannot shoot forth out of its midst until it has fulfilled this duty and carried out its task."[36]

Therefore, not only is it untrue that the doctrine of the personal Messiah must necessarily lead to quietism. On the contrary, it can help in suppressing the peculiar modern variant of pseudo-messianism. One of the most horrible and disastrous illusions to which modern men have fallen prey is that they have actually accomplished the messianic state. It is on the basis of this self-deception that our contemporary dictatorships have ruthlessly eliminated all dissent, for they maintain that dissent from perfection is, by definition, falsehood. Whereas in the Middle Ages pseudo-messianisms operated around a central, individual pseudo-messianic person, in our time it is characteristic of our collectivist and societally-minded frame of references that pseudo-messianisms take the form of national movements. More than ever, therefore, the absence of the person of the redeemer should constitute a constant warning against such blasphemous exaggerations. This warning is, furthermore, not without its applicability to the present Jewish world-situation. The messianic undercurrent in the history of modern Zionism has in turn led to the far-reaching secularization of "the messianic

32 *Sanh.* 97b.
33 *Midr. Tehillim* 45:3; cf. generally, A. H. Silver, *Messianic Speculation in Israel*, "Opposition to Messianic Speculation," pp. 195-206.
34 Cf. Wiener, *op. cit.*, p. 170.
35 Cf. Greenstone, *op. cit.*, p. 267.

36 *Die Messiaslehre der Juden*, pp. 402, 404.

thought in Israel," as a result of which, as Leon Roth has pointed out, we no longer ask in the words of the Bible: "Who will recount the mighty deeds of God?" but rather in the words of the Israeli song: "Who will recount the mighty deeds of Israel?" What is even much more dangerous is the hazy notion floating through the minds of a not inconsiderable number of super-Zionists that the establishment of the State itself constitutes the messianic fulfillment. Here lies the road to certain disaster!

When Rabbi Kurt Wilhelm, formerly of Jerusalem and now chief-rabbi of Sweden, and this writer dared point out in a series of articles that Jewishly there is a vast difference between *yeshuah*, historical salvaging, and *ge'ulah*, redemption, an Israeli newspaper attacked us vehemently as new *Pretestrabbiner!*[37] If this journalist had only been waiting for the Messiah!

---

[37] *Yedi'ot Chadashot*, 10/3/50.

# Jewish Mysticism in the Modern Age

## NOCHUMM J. SCHEALTIEL

MYSTICS AND THEIR SYMPATHIZERS ARE OFTEN asked what Kabbalah and Ḥassidism have to tell us today. Morever, since Jewish mysticism assumed prominence relatively late (only since mediaeval and early modern times), of what concern, then, is it to the "historical Jew?" Granting the legitimacy of a Jewish mystical tradition, we must also recognize that it has generally been contained, and involvement had been left to a minimum by the Talmudic and later sages, and no less so by the mystics themselves. Why, then, this "flood" of mystic literature and teaching in recent times, the attempts to popularize mystic tradition?

Such questions have been asked or were anticipated ever since the mystics sought to remove the screens that kept their teachings the sole heritage of *yeḥidei segulah*. And once they furthered their aims by publishing introductory tracts and expositions, they usually spent a good number of pages dealing with the answers, which are addressed to the committed Jew. They trace the historical validity of the Kabbalah, its integral place within normative Judaism, the new vistas which it opens that prove of great philosophic as well as Halakhic consequence, and the fact, particularly since the beginning of the sixth millenium ("on the heels of the Messiah"), that these teachings *could* and *should* be made public and popular.[1]

With slight modifications, especially as regards terminology, their answers, though well-seasoned by age, would seem no less relevant to our age. But as I will try to commit to writing just a few of the points of this vast world of thought, I should preface them with some clarifications. These will, I hope, help the not-mystically-inclined to hurdle some oft-held misconceptions that stand in the way of appreciating our mystical tradition. My sole concern here is with *Jewish* mysticism, and in this I include the authoritative Kabbalah and Ḥassidism as one. That some of its ideas may be found elsewhere, in non-Jewish sources, is interesting but irrelevant. Alleged common sources, textual criticism, arguments about who drew from whom, are all fascinating hunting-grounds for

---

1. R. Meir ibn Gabbai, *Avodat Hakodesh;* R. Chayim Vital, Introduction to *Sha'ar Hahakdamot;* R. Joseph Irgass, *Shomer Emunim;* R. Chaim Moshe Luzatto, *Ḥoker Umekubbal.* See also R. Shneur Zalman of Liadi, *Iggeret Hakodesh* (my references are to the English edition by J. I. Schochet, New York, 1968), sect. XXVI and the literature cited there. For an additional, interesting source on the timing to the beginning of the sixth millenium, cf. Maimonides, *Epistle to Yemen.*

---

NOCHUM J. SCHEALTIEL *is the Pen-name of a Rabbi who has been identified with Contemporary Ḥassidism.*

mysticists that offer them unlimited scope for their speculative theories and ingenious hypotheses, but they are of no practical significance whatever. Jewish mystics do not claim the monopoly on all truth. For example, the Zohar interprets the Midrashic comment that Numbers 19:2 "that is without blemish" as a reference to the Greeks—"because they are very close to the way of the (true) Faith, more than any of the others" (and the commentators add that this refers specifically to the pre-Aristotelians) .[2]

·The point is that Jewish mysticism is Kabbalah, a time-and-source-hallowed tradition strictly within the framework of historical, normative Judaism, involving its recognized authoritative teachers in both Talmudic and later times, and placing all of its premises and doctrines within, and subject to, Torah and Halakhah. This fact lends to it, just as to the remainder of the Oral Tradition, authoritative objectivity and legitimacy as an authentic and integral part of Judaism proper. This intimate relationship with, and dependency on, Halakhah, cannot be sufficiently emphasized. A favorite contention of the mystic, as erroneous as it is mischievous, creates an imaginary tension between Halakhah and Kabbalah. There is absolutely no ground for this contention; authentic Jewish mysticism cannot be taken without Halakhah.[3]

This is not to deny that there are a number of instances where Talmud-Halakhah and Zohar-Kabbalah appear to conflict. However, while the Torah is essentially absolute and unalterable (eighth and ninth of Maimonides' thirteen principles of faith) , yet inasmuch as "it is not in heaven" but entrusted into the earthly hands of the Halakhic authorities and teachers within the unbroken chain of tradition, it will manifest itself on a number of levels reflecting earthly categories. This is quite evident within the Halakhic process which recognizes and legitimizes valid disagreements. Thus, from the beginning of the history of *mahloket*, which essentially started with Hillel and Shammai, we note different types of disagreements, related not only to specific principles of interpretation, or to individual penetrating insights, but also to psychological tendencies[4] or the general perspective of the authorities involved[5] and the different traditions received.[6] In each case of disagreement we must, for pragmatic reasons, decide one way or another, and Halakhah lays

---

2. *Zohar* II:237a; *Zohar Ḥadash*, Yitro, 38b; *Shomer Emunim* II:37.
3. A number of attempts have been made, and some quite successful, to show an intimate relationship between Talmud-Halakhah and the Kabbalah, by revealing the basic premises of the one in the other. Of recent works in this field are notable the writings of R. Chaim Eleazar Schapiro of Munkasc, and, *yibadel leḥayim*, of R. Menaḥem M. Schneerson of Lubavitch. A wealth of material is also to be found in the writings of R. Reuben Margolius.
4. *Iggeret Hakodesh*, sec. XIII.
5. See R. Menaḥem M. Schneerson, *Likutei Siḥot* First series (N.Y., 1962), vol. I, p. 146f, and vol. II; S. J. Zevin, *Leor Hahalakhah* (Tel Aviv, 1964), pp. 302–9.
6. *Eduyot*, end of ch. V.

down the rules for its workings and decisions. Even so, it is also agreed that "both opinions are the words of the living God" and are *objectively valid*.[7] Highly relevant in this respect is the unique "Oven of Aknin incident" in which R. Eliezer the Great is overruled by the majority of his colleagues in spite of the indisputable celestial support of his opinion —for the very reason that the Torah "is not in heaven."[8]

The great giants who excelled in both Halakhah and Kabbalah utterly reject any dissension between Talmud and mysticism. Thus, R. Chaim of Voloszin quotes the Gaon of Vilna to the effect that it is absolutely impossible to speak of a conflict between Talmud and Zohar, between the "revealed" and the "mystical" faces of the Torah.[9] Likewise, R. Hillel of Paritsz quotes the Rav of Liadi to the effect that it is inconceivable that the mystics oppose the Talmud or the *posskim* who derive their decisions from the Talmud.[10]

Now I am not so naïve as to expect my readers to come, to see and, immediately, to be conquered, convinced and converted. I am very suspicious of uncritical, quickie-conversions and do not give them much chance of survival. What I do ask, is an open mind, a complete and sincere objectivity—no less, and perhaps more, than one is prepared to give to the study of other branches of knowledge. To be appreciated properly, Jewish mysticism requires a complete reorientation of thought and attitude from what we are attuned to by our Western backgrounds. With Kabbalah and Hassidism one enters, not so much a new, as a *different* world, a different plane of thought that transcends previously held modes and categories. One must cast away all prejudices imposed by rationalism and scientism and, at the very least, allow a measure of admissibility to the possibility of an order of reality that is not our phenomenal one, and to allow the possibility of methods of perception that differ from our usual ones. While this will reduce our phenomenal world to no more than a partial reality, it would surely be highly unscientific to deny these possibilities. I know of no better formulation of this act of preparation than the following statement: When R. Zeyra emigrated to the land of Israel he fasted one hundred fasts to forget the Babylonian Gemarah so that it should not trouble him in the study and acquisition of the Jerusalem Gemarah.[11]

---

7. *Erubin* 13b, and commentaries, in particular *Ritba*, ad loc.; Rashi on *Ketubot* 57a; commentaries on *Abot* V:16, s.v. *kol mahloket*.
8. *Baba Metzia* 59b.
9. See the bibliographical notes and quotations cited in B. Landau, *Hagaon Hahasid MeVilna* (Jerusalem, 1967), pp. 140–1.
10. His reasons parallel those given by R. Judah ben Barzilai, *Perush Sefer Yetzirah*, p. 157, and *Responsa of Haham Tzvi*, no. 36.
11. *Baba Metzia* 85a (see commentaries a.l., and Maharal of Prague, *Netibot Olam, Netib Hatorah*, ch. 13). This statement is doubly apt, as the Talmudic distinctions between the Babylonian and Jerusalem Talmud (cf., e.g., *Sanhedrin* 24a) are acutely descriptive of the two perspectives we are dealing with here.

The so-called modern attitude to the universe is one of rational inquiry. This method, in its contemporary manifestation, seeks in the phenomenal world, which is its only realm of concern, a scientific uniformity to which all empirical facts and factors must conform. As often as not, the search is endless. But this does not deter our searcher, who will not admit defeat or the possibility of exceptions to his ruling scientific theory. The non-uniform is simply a token of present ignorance. Thus, "scientism" and "objective rationalism" slide into an uncritical dogmatism second to none and a new "religion" is born; a religion of ever-new and changing revelations with an endless chain of high-priests reflecting the moods, conditions and revelations of their times. All this may still be legitimate, and indeed, despite its glaring shortcomings, is often responsible for tremendous technological advances.

However, in attempting to establish this type of unity and uniformity, the modern rationalist creates, in effect, an increasingly disturbing pluralism and an alienating division. By converting the universe into a mammoth machine he simultaneously breaks it up into innumerable, non-related particulars, for his self-contained physiomonistic pantheism can concern itself only with species and universals. Related particulars, personality, individualism, are sacrifices offered for the sustenance of the *deus* in *machina*. The human individual diminishes in proportion to the growth of nature and the universe in the scientific, experimental grasp or consciousness. Human individual life is hedged in by a precarious day-to-day, here-and-now, existence.

Again, this situation may be just too bad; nothing can stand in the way of progress and the chips must fall wherever they do. But here there enters a new factor: a natural, categorical and transcendental sense of morality, deeply embedded in the soul and mind of man, which (often emboldened by a host of empirical facts) revolts against a materialism that is so callous that it leaves us with only barren factualism. The resulting tension between the haunting Lorelei of modern rational inquiry and the groping attempts at human self-assertion lies at the root of many, if not all, of our present-day neuroses and vexations, and "he that increases knowledge increases pain."

The apparent alternatives are resignation or rejection: resignation to the admittedly frustrating paradox, and making the best of it, or the elimination of either the modern method or the recognition of human individuality. Obviously, these alternatives are not satisfactory. And at this point mysticism offers something quite valuable and viable for modern man: its own *Weltanschauung*. No doubt this fact accounts for the recent popularity of mysticism, though, from our point of view at least, this offer of a viable alternative happens to be an incidental fringe-benefit. For mysticism is able to reconcile universality and particularity, uniformity and individuality, macrocosm and microcosm. It is able to adopt scientific method *and* results, to deal with species and universals, even while retaining and giving meaning to that most unique of all particulars, the individual human being.

*Yiḥud* and *pirud,* unity and division, are, perhaps, the two principal concepts in Jewish mysticism around which everything revolves. *Yiḥud* is at the core of everything. All being, the whole of the creation, is as one body, the numerous members of which, therefore, are fully interrelated and interdependent. But, just as in the physical body, the organs and members are bound up one in the other yet each retains its own unique character and quality. Problems for the whole, or for the part, arise where this dual meaningfulness is ignored, where the particular shirks his universality, his membership in, and responsibility to, the others, the whole. and is preoccupied with himself. He commits an act of *pirud,* of division, mutilating the universe, "cutting down the shoots." This *pirud,* this self-assertion and ego-centricity, in the mystic's view, is *the* cardinal sin, the very root of all sins. Such particularized self-assertion is tantamount to idolatry, pluralism, an infringement upon the unity and one-ness of the all-pervading absolute. One who maintains that stance establishes himself as a *yesh,* a substantial reality, a being outside of, and next to, whatever other being there is.[12] The consequences of this tragic division are not limited to that individual. The severance of a part from the whole implies not only the rejection of the whole by the part, but, also, the loss of the part to the whole. The whole body is rendered incomplete, deficient, incapacitated, with regards to the unique qualities and functions of that member. Hence, the concept of *bittul hayesh,* the duty to efface, to annihilate, the ego qua ego,[13] and the imperative dissolution in the whole, the concept of *d'vekut,* to strive for the *unio mystica.*[14]

It may appear paradoxical, but this emphasis on the universal also emphasizes the particular. For, just as everything that is created (thus, everything that is part of the universal) , is created for a distinct purpose with a distinct task in relation to the whole, so it is, in a concrete sense,

12. Cf. the Talmudic sentiments expressed in *Shabbat* 105b and *Sotah* 4b and 5a. Hence the mystics' great aversion to pride and its offshoots, like anger or melancholy (see *Iggeret Hakodesh,* sect. XI, and note 17 ad loc.; sect. XXV; and cf. *Tanya,* ch. 22 and 27).

13. That man is not a self-contained and self-possessed entity is mirrored in an interesting Halakhic ruling. In a famous passage in his edition of the *Shulḥan Arukh,* R. Shneur Zalman of Liadi writes: "It is prohibited to smite a person even if he gives permission to smite him, for *a human being has no authority over his own body at all,* neither to smite it nor to shame it nor to afflict it in any manner of affliction even by withholding some food or drink" (unless for a legal, truly beneficial purpose); *Ḥoshen Mishpat, Hilḥot Nizkei Guf Vanefesh,* par. 4.

14. Here enters also the crucial concept of *teshuvah:* as sin is an act of *pirud* (*ḥet* denoting defect, as in I-Kings I:21) so *teshuvah* is an act of *yiḥud,* reunification, at-one-ment (*teshuvah* denoting return, restoration, restitution, as explained throughout the mystical writings dealing with this subject).

indispensable. The toe-nails, no less than the heart and the brain, have their individual purpose, each one necessary to, and complementing, the other for the complete and perfect functioning of the body. The affectations of toes become affectations of the brain. The ill-health and pain of the one affect the well-being and functioning of the other. To be sure, we distinguish quite clearly between them. We speak of higher and lower, vital and non-vital, more and less important organs. We set up a qualitative, as well as a quantitative, scale of levels and values. Still, they are all intertwined, interdependent, with every particular adding its own contribution for which it was created. And this contribution alone is its function, its raison d'être. Achieving it means to contribute to the well-being, the *yihud*, of the whole; neglecting it leads to *pirud*, a division and defect in the whole.[15] The significance of individuality is poignantly expressed in the words of R. Zusya of Anipoli when he said of his day of judgment that he did not fear the Heavenly Judge's question as to why he had not attained the levels of the partriarchs, why he was not an Abraham, Isaac or Jacob; after all, who was he to compare to them? But, said R. Zusya, "I do fear the question, 'why were you not Zusya of Anipoli?' "

This leads us to another crucial concept, that of the cosmic significance of man's actions. This can be understood, not only in terms of the body-analogy, but, more so, by certain empirical phenomena. Radio and television have shown that even the most innocuous activities of man leave an impression on the whole atmosphere. The voice of a man muttering to himself, and the motions of his playful jumping about on the moon are, by means of instruments, visible and audible hundreds of thousands of miles away. Sound-waves, light-rays, are realities, as are atoms and various forces of energy and radiation. Psychiatry and psycho-analysis show how apparently innocuous mental perceptions create specific consequences. The mystic translates these facts from the phenomenal to the nouminal, from physics to metaphysics. Every activity of man, every word, deed, and even intention, affects the whole cosmic order.[16] *Mizvot*, good deeds, proper intentions and acts, contribute to the *yihud*; sins, evil deeds, improper actions, cause disorder, *pirud*. And in that sense, man, every individual, shapes, as it were, his own destiny and that of the world; he becomes, as it were, a partner in *ma'aseh bereishit*.[17]

---

15. This is essentially the concept of *areyvut*, the intermingling within, and responsibility for, each other, with all its far-reaching implications.

16. See *Zohar* III:31b and 105a, and numerous parallel passages. Compare also the significant Midrashic concept, much elaborated in mysticism, of "adding strength to the heavenly power" and its reverse, in *Eykha Rabbati* I:33; *Pessikta de R. Kahana*, ed. Buber, sect. XXVI (p. 166) and the parallel passages cited in the notes.

17. R. Chayim Vital, *Shaarey Kedushah*, III:2. Cf. *Bereishit Rabba* III:9; *Shabbat* 10a, and *ibid.* 119b; also *ibid.* 114a, and the Rabbinic comments on the last word of Genesis II:3.

Thus, mysticism bridges the gap between universalism and individuality, between the universe as a whole and man as a unique individual. The oftheard accusation that this tends to erode the reality of life, and, in particular, of normative Judaism with its alleged pluralism involving commands and prohibitions, *issur* and *hetter, kasher* and *passul, tammeh* and *tahor,* is at best to be blamed on an ignorance of the principles of mysticism. In fact, it would seem to me that nowhere do these Halakhic categories emerge as clearly delineated as in mysticism, and it is also here that the mystics, and in particular Ḥassidim, make an inestimable contribution of significant practical consequence to our mundane involvements.

Existents are divided into three principal categories. There is the realm of *kedushah,* of holiness, in which belong all the activities enjoined by the Torah (*miẓvot*) and all that is directly related to these (the absolute "good"). Diametrically opposed to it is the "other side" (*sitra aḥara*), the realm of impurity and evil, which comprises all those activities that are prohibited and all that is directly related to them (the actual "evil"). The bulk of existents, which are not, per se, subject to a command (that they *must* be used) or a prohibition (that they *may not* be used), are somewhere in between those two categories, in a realm of *kelipat nogah.*[18]

How we are to relate to *kedushah* and to *sitra aḥara* is self-evident: *kum ve'aseh,* active participation, with regards to the former, and *sheiv ve'al ta'aseh,* conscious passivity, with regards to the latter. When we relate to them thus, in their divinely intended context, they both serve their purpose and achieve their ends; *kedushah* is strengthened and the *sitra aḥara* is subdued, in the world as a whole and in the individual in particular. The real test relates to the vast realm of *kelipat nogah,* which is a "neutral," a profane realm; profane in the sense of not-yet-hallowed, not-yet-defiled. It is potentially holy, or potentially impure. Whether it will ascend to the one or descend to the other depends on how it is used by man. The same piece of skin may become sacred parchment for a Torah-scroll, or a viciously evil cat-o'-nine-tails; the same coin may serve to save someone in need, or may be used for a bribe and corruption. Thus it is also with the myriads of daily activities like eating, drinking, sleeping, walking, talking and all the (permissible) objects related thereto.

The ascetic individual, generally speaking, opts out. Here, immediately, a qualification must be made, for many of our greatest mystics were ascetics, and far be it from us to say that their way of life was an escape. We must distinguish between the two types of asceticism, one of which is not only a legitimate, but noble, albeit unique way for *yeḥidei segulah,*

---

18. See more on these categories and their implications in the Introduction to *Iggeret Hakodesh,* pp. 72 ff.

or is imposed by certain, distinct circumstances, as for example, *teshuvah.* It is the other type which is more a form of escapism. The advocate of it evades reality, he avoids involvement and adheres to the minimum essentials for bare survival. He rejects the world of *nogah,* scared off by seeing only its negative side, the evil-in-potency. The true mystic casts his eye upwards; he sees the not-yet-hallowed, the Divine sparks hidden in the as-yet-not-consecrated. He does not withdraw, but contemplates the Divine creation, the effects of the Divine workings, the particulars of the Divine universe in himself and in the world around him. He chooses, nay, he feels compelled to adopt the more difficult, and admittedly often tortuous, road of involvement. He feels compelled to expose and actualize, to bring out into the open the latent "for My honour I have created it, formed it, and made it," for, again, he sees that without it the universal body is deficient; every particular is essential for the perfection of the whole in its Divinely intended context. The sublimation and transformation of *nogah* is an act of redemption, not only for the *nogah,* but also for the transformer, the agent, and, ipso facto, for the universe as a whole. It is a step towards, and a contribution to, the ultimate total redemption realized in the ultimate, absolute *yiḥud,* the final goal towards which everything strives, when "in that day the Eternal will be One and His Name will be One."

Of this involvement with *nogah* there is a typical teaching of the Baal Shem Tov in his comment on Exodus 23:5: "When you see a "*ḥamor*"—(*matter*) (relating *ḥamor* to *ḥomer*), i.e. the matter of corporeality, you will see that it is "your enemy," as it interferes with the aspirations of your soul, or spirit, "lying under its burden" the burden of its task to become refined and sublimated by means of the *Torah* and *miẓvot* with respect to which the body is indolent. But lest you think that "you shall abstain from helping it" carry out its task, and you will undertake self-mortifications to break the body and crush matter, know that this is not the way of Torah; rather, "you shall surely help along, with it," to refine and sublimate the body, and not to crush it.[19]

A poignant anecdote is told of the Mezeritch Maggid who, one

19. As was said, this is the more difficult, and at times risky, approach in the way of which one must take heed not to lose his spiritual equilibrium and beware of becoming bound up with the evil (cf. *Aboth* I:7). Even while mysticism emphasizes the positive, the "do good" rather than the psychologically dangerous preoccupation with "turn away from evil," the love of, and attachment to, God rather than just fear of God, it stresses no less that the one cannot go exclusively without the other: fear of God, the "beginning of wisdom," is a prerequisite step, a necessary condition and preparation to the love of God; avoidance of evil is a basis to involvement in good deeds. It is just that, once these foundations are established, that the emphasis (the principal, though not the exclusive concern) is shifted to the positive. When bound to the heavens one can safely reach down into the earth. But "one should not be so foolish as to attempt the sublimation of the evil while evil is still rooted in his own heart; for how can he raise it as long as he is himself bound below" (see *Tanya,* ch. 28).

Friday, after retiring to his room for a rest, sent his attendant to stop his disciple, R. Aaron of Karlin, from reciting *Shir haShirim*, for R. Aaron's recital stormed and aroused all the worlds, thus preventing the Maggid from sleeping. The point of this story is not the greatness of R. Aaron and the sublimity of his form of worship, but that the sleep of the Maggid is still more important, a still higher form of worship. And this leads us to the last point I wish to make.

Halakhah, ritual, is at least as essential to the mystic as it is to the non-mystic. Where the mystic differs, first and foremost, is in his *consciousness* of its importance, his *awareness* of its dynamic significance. He is so conscious of the concepts of universality and individuality, of *yiḥud* and *pirud,* that his religious acts are not merely meaningful, but they are living realities; his whole life, every one of his actions and motions, becomes a religious act. R. Leib Sarah's, a disciple of the Maggid, was wont to say that man's purpose is to become a personification of Torah, and he related that he came to his master, not to hear Torah from him, but to see how he laces and unlaces his shoes! Such a meaningfulness of being and living, harboring the impulse of inevitable redemption, is mysticism's contribution that is often imitated but never equalled by others. Implicitly, it is the all-inclusive, all-pervading exhortation of "you shall be holy" (in a positive, active sense, rather than in a passive separation) that sanctifies the totality of life and world, that precludes perfunctory observance, let alone being a reprobate, even while remaining within the four ells of the Halakhah.

There is a well-known expression referring to a certain person as a "donkey laden with books."[20] The implication is that he is loaded with learning and knowledge, perhaps phenomenally erudite; however, just as the donkey is not related to its load, the donkey and the books remain two fully separate entities. So it is with that scholar. He is non-affected by his learning; he stores numerous data for strictly technical use and purposes. He is not aware, he is not conscious, he ignores the principle that the sole purpose of all wisdom is that it lead to *teshuvah,* to *ma'asim tovim (Berachot* 17a), to *yiḥud.* The mystics wittily extend the above expression by reading the Hebrew word for donkey as an acrostic for *ḥaham mufla verav rabbanan*: a wondrous scholar and supreme master, an authority on the undoubtedly important Talmudic nuances and an expert in the pilpulistic method, but ignorant of the deeper meaning, of the soul, of Torah.[21]

This sterile type of life and "scholarship" is quite symptomatic of our present age and its method of rational inquiry, of logical positivism with

---

20. *Zohar Ḥadash,* Tikunim, 101c; *Ḥovot Halevovot,* Avodat Elokim, ch. 4. An obvious parallel appears in the Talmud, *Megillah* 28b ("a basket full of books;" see *Rashi* ad loc.).
21. *Zohar* III:275b; *Tikunei Zohar,* Addenda, X:147b.

its atomizing games of linguistic analysis. Jewish mysticism forcefully counters it and bears a very relevant message for modern man by means of which he is able to extricate himself from contemporary mind- and soul-polluting forces that threaten to stifle him, and to find himself. Paraphrasing Psalms 42:8, mysticism is the *zinor*, the conduit, the voice which causes "deep to call unto deep," the profound depth of man's soul calling unto the profound depth of the universal soul to find and absorb itself therein.

# B. Torah

# The Elusive Revelation

## JACOB M. CHINITZ

ABOUT THE ONLY CENTER THAT CAN BE ACCU-
rately located is that of the circle, but since there are no perfect circles
in nature centers are never really located. Physicists reach the atom,
only to find it swarming with neutrons, positrons, electrons. Biologists
reach the cell, even its nucleus, only to find more ultimate centers within the center. In religion, often the finger of the theologian is laid upon
Revelation, as he proclaims: here is the hub of the wheel of faith. Maimonides, in his *Epistle to Yemen,* writes: "Keep well in mind the Revelation at Sinai, and impress it upon the minds of our children, for the
event is the pivot of our religion."[1] In his Thirteen Articles, the eighth
is devoted to Revelation: "I believe with perfect faith that the entire
Torah which is found in our hands at present is the one given to
Moses." Of course, it is supported by Article Seven which posits the
uniqueness of Moses: ". . . that the prophecy of Moses our master was
true and that he was the greatest of the prophets."[2] The unique and
central Revelation is given through the instrumentality of the unique
and central prophet. And yet, neither the festival which celebrates Revelation, *Shavuot,* nor Moses, the agent of Revelation, achieves any centrality in Judaism.

Shavuot is the shortest of the three Pilgrim Festivals, as compared
to the festivals of freedom and the harvest; in one Talmudic version it
is called *Atzeret,* which would make it a mere appendage to *Pesach.* Its
title of *Z'man Matan Toratenu,* "the time of the giving of our Torah,"
is not mentioned in the Torah. While in the case of the other festivals
the agricultural theme is prior to the historical associations, in the case
of *Shavuot* the association with the Revelation is not even mentioned
by Philo or Josephus.[3] It is almost as if the celebration of the Revelation were an afterthought. Curiously, too, *Shavuot* commemorates not
the figure of Moses, the master of Revelation, but that of David, whose
*yahrzeit* the Tradition assigns to *Shavuot.* Certainly, it can be said there
is no cult of Moses. It is *Torat Moshe;*[4] but it is the God of Abraham
and of the people of Israel. Moses is the Man of God;[5] but it is not the

1. *A Treasury of Judaism,* Philip Birnbaum, Hebrew Publishing Co., N.Y. 1957, p. 339.
2. *Siddur.*
3. *Jewish Encyclopedia,* 1905, article on "Pentecost."
4. *Midrash Rabbath, Ruth,* ch. 30.
5. *Deuteronomy* 33:1. An attribution of centrality to Moses would be implied in
*Exodus* 19:9: ". . . and they will also believe in you forever."

JACOB M. CHINITZ *is rabbi of Beth Ami synagogue in Philadelphia. His essays
have appeared in several national Jewish publications.*

God of Moses. Tribute is paid to Moses as the greatest prophet, and, therefore, the proper medium for the greatest Revelation. But he is primarily titled *Moshe Rabbenu,* Moses the Teacher, not the Prophet. Moreover, according to Yehudah Halevi, if not for Israel there would be no Torah. He did not believe the Torah was binding because of Creation, but "because He led us out of Egypt and remained attached to us."[6]

Religion seems not to be able to get along without Revelation, and is also not completely happy with it. It has been said, "Revelation explains all mysteries except her own."[7] The concept is caught in various fields of tension, and we would like to point out four of these fields. First, there is a tension between the insistence that God can and has revealed Himself, and an equally strong insistence that He cannot be known. Second, there is a need for the stress upon one specific, historic, and definitive Revelation on the one hand; and on the other hand we find both anticipatory and postscript Revelations. Third, there is the heroic attempt to harmonize Revelation with Reason, while the very need for Revelation is put in terms of the irrational information it conveys. Fourth, in the very breath that Revelation pleads for faith on its behalf it invokes skepticism towards all "false" revelations.

## I

THE VERY CRUX OF THE FIRST PARADOX in Revelation is presented in the Bible this way: "The Lord spoke to you out of the midst of the fire. Ye heard the voice of words, but ye saw no form; only ye heard a voice."[8] Even in the case of Moses, whose communion with God is "face to face" and who looks through "the clear lens," the ultimate vision is denied. "Show me Thy Glory . . . for no man shall see Me and live."[9] In the very act of Revelation there is a concealment. Even as the Israelites prepare to receive the Revelation, they are roped off from the mountain and warned not to come too close.[10] The Midrash emphasizes the point that God never descends below, and Moses never ascends above.[11] Thus, even Revelation is suspended between transcendence and immanence. The Bible pleads eloquently not only for the desirability of the knowl-

6. See *Great Jewish Books,* ed. Caplan and Ribalow, Horizon Press, N.Y. 1952, p. 156 (Selections from *Kuzari*): "He did not say 'I am the Creator of the world and your Creator.' . . . But 'I am the God whom you worship, Who hath led you out of the land of Egypt'." It is because of these particular historical considerations that it is possible for Torah to apply only to Israel, even though God is the God of all men.
7. William Cowper, *The Task,* 1785; quoted in *Dictionary of Quotations,* H. L. Mencken, Knopf, N.Y. 1942.
8. *Deuteronomy* 4:12.
9. *Exodus* 33:18 ff.
10. *Exodus* 19:12.
11. *Sukkah* 5a.

edge of God by man but also for the possibility of such knowledge: "I will put my law in their inward parts and will write it upon their hearts. And I will be their God and they shall be My people. They shall no more teach one his neighbor and his brother, 'Know the Lord,' for they shall all know Me from the least of them to the greatest."[12] But with equal strength does it plead the ignorance of man and the unrevealed God: "Where wast thou when I laid the foundations of the earth? Declare if thou hast intelligence. Who determined its measures? —if you possess knowledge. Whereupon were its foundations fastened? Oh, who laid its cornerstone?"[13] Presumably, this ignorance exists even after Revelation.

THE LOGIC OF THEOLOGY WORKS IN TWO DIRECTIONS. In one direction we go from the fact of Revelation to the fact of the existence of God, the Author of Revelation. Also, the text of the Revelations tells us about God. In the other direction, we go from the existence of God to the assumption that He would not leave man without the benefit of His Revelation. Dr. J. H. Hertz, in his commentary on the Pentateuch, writes: "Judaism stands or falls with its belief in the historic actuality of the Revelation at Sinai. . . . The moment we assert the existence of a Supreme Mind as the Fountain and Soul of all the infinite forms of matter and life, revelation, or communication between God and man, becomes a logical and ethical necessity."[14] But as important as it is for man to have God revealed, God remains hidden nevertheless. "For My ways are not your ways."[15]

One way out of the dilemma is to say that Revelation is partial: "Thou shalt see My back, but My face may not be seen."[16] The question is, what part is revealed and what part not? The usual approach is to distinguish between different degrees of knowledge. Thus, according to one Midrash, Moses is afforded "forty-nine degrees of wisdom."[17] At the Red Sea, the merest handmaiden sees more than the prophet Ezekiel, so that all Israel can proclaim, "This is my God."[18] A more

---

12. *Jeremiah* 31:33, 34. See also *Isaiah* 40:21: "Do you not know? Have you not heard? It has been told from the beginning to you. You have been given to understand the foundations of the earth."
13. *Job* 38:4, 5, 6. See also *Isaiah* 40:12: "Who measured the waters in the hollow of his hand, and meted out heaven with the span, and comprehended the dust of the earth in a measure, and weighed the mountains in scales, and the hills in a balance?"
14. *Pentateuch and Haftorahs*, Soncino, London 1961, p. 402.
15. *Isaiah* 55:8.
16. *Exodus* 33:23. It is interesting that God speaks to Moses, and in one place even the people are taken into this process, "face to face." See *Deut.* 5:4.
17. *Rosh Hashanah* 21b: "Fifty gates of wisdom were created in the world and all but one were given to Moses, as it is written, 'And thou hast made him but little less than the angels.'"
18. *Exodus* 15:2, see *Mechilta*.

fruitful approach is the distinction hinted at by Scripture when it considers the Revelation as being verbal rather than visual. Sight is more related to knowledge than hearing. In the legalities of testimony, for instance, the "eyewitness" can testify, but not the witness who must rely on "hearsay" evidence.[19] Hearing is also related, especially in Hebrew, to obedience. "Hear, O Israel" means, "obey, Israel."[20] And this is precisely the great response of Israel to the Revelation of Sinai: "We shall do and we shall hear-obey."[21] For it is not knowledge that is revealed at Sinai, or in prophecy in general, but the will of God. "Ten words"[22] are revealed, which are really "ten commandments." Revelation in essence is moral, not cognitive. Response to Revelation is an act of the will, as the Revelation is that of a will.

THIS DISTINCTION BETWEEN THE EYE AND THE EAR, between seeing and hearing, can be elaborated upon with the reference to many areas of Jewish myth. The Jewish emphasis is upon the word. The world is created with words.[23] Creation itself is a moral response: "Let there be light—and there was light."[24] In prophecy there are various gradations of seers, dreamers, visionaries, but the highest type of prophet is the *Navi*—a word related to speaking, not to seeing. God gives Himself Names, but no pictorial representations.[25] Where such representations do occur, they have to be interpreted as special creations, intended to provide a setting for the words to follow; but the visions do not contain the communication. They could not, because the communication of prophecy and Revelation is always one of an imperative nature, and imperatives cannot be communicated in visions, only in words. (From this stems the Jewish prejudice against the visual arts.) The essence of Jewish Revelation and Jewish religious experience is verbal, not visual. "The voice is the voice of Jacob."[26]

We find Maimonides going to great pains to avoid the assumption

---

19. Even the interpreter cannot substitute for the witness. Certainly, one witness cannot report the testimony of another witness. Only in the case of the report of the death of a husband were these types of evidence, including even the *Bat Kol*, admitted. See *Yebamoth* 87b, 122a; *Makkot* 5a.
20. See *Deut.* 4:1: *shema el hachukim*, "listen to the laws."
21. *Exodus* 24:7. It is sometimes not noticed that this verse refers only incidentally to the Covenant, while at the giving of the Decalogue the people respond: *Na'ase*—"we will do." In *Deut.* the phrase is in reverse: *Nishma ve-na'ase*—"we will do and we will hear."
22. *Exodus* 34:28.
23. *Aboth*, ch. 1, *mishna*, 5.
24. *Genesis* 1:3.
25. *Exodus* 6:3, *Deut.* 4:12.
26. *Genesis* 27:22.

of the visual aspects even of the writing involved in the Two Tablets. In the *Guide* we find the following:[27]

> "And the writing was the writing of God."[28] The relation in which the writing stood to God has already been defined in the words, "written with the finger of God,"[29] and the meaning of this phrase is the same as that of "the work of Thy fingers,"[30] this being said of the heavens; of the latter it has been stated distinctly that they were made by a word, "By the word of the Lord were the heavens made."[31] Hence you learn that in the Bible the creation of a thing is figuratively expressed by terms denoting word and speech. The phrase "written by the finger of God" is therefore identical with "written by the word of God."

So that even in the realm of the Written Law, the word is emphasized above the visual writing. It is from the same concept that the stress upon the Oral Law comes, and the prohibition against its writing —the fear of the visual and the preference for the verbal.

There is one scene, within the complex of the Sinaitic Revelation, where the text of Scripture is quite explicit about a visual experience: "They saw God and they ate and drank."[32] The vision includes the "whiteness of sapphire and the purity of heaven."[33] But here too the symbolism of Midrash removes the vision from the area of the cognitive and puts it into the area of the aesthetic. From this text the Rabbis draw the conclusion: "This world is not like the next world. In the next world there is no eating and no drinking and no reproduction, no business and no jealousy, no hatred and no competition. Only the righteous sit with their crowns upon their heads and enjoy the sight of the Presence, as it is written, 'They saw God and ate and drank.' "[34]

Some scholars see a contrast between the noisy Revelation at Sinai and the quiet Revelation given in the same place many years later to Elijah.[35] The contrast need not be put in terms of publicity and privacy, external and internal perception. This contrast is already made at the first Revelation between the public nature of its first installment, in the presence of all Israel,[36] and the private nature of its second installment when only Moses[37] comes to the mountain to prepare the second set of Tablets. Perhaps the significance of the contrast between the two Revelations, several centuries apart, lies as well in the distinction between the visual and verbal. For the final form of the Revelation to Elijah is "the still small voice."[38] In universal literature and psychol-

---

27. *Guide to the Perplexed*, Friedlander, Hebrew Publishing Co., N.Y., Part I, p. 247.
28. *Exodus* 32:16.
29. *Ibid.* 31:18.
30. *Psalms* 8:4.
31. *Ibid.* 33:6.
32. *Exodus* 24:11.
33. *Ibid.* 10.
34. *Berachot* 17a.
35. See *I Kings*, 19.
36. *Exodus* 19:17.
37. *Ibid.* 34:3.
38. *I Kings* 19:12.

ogy, this small voice has been interpreted not in terms of knowledge but in terms of conscience. Which is to say, Revelation is moral and not intellectual.

BUBER'S COMMENT UPON THE TWO REVELATIONS reflects the reaction of the modern mind to the problem. He writes:

> It is precisely when we make the most earnest efforts to establish a reality, a reality consisting of actual facts, that we are possessed by the feeling that the words of the covenant, the Ten Words, could surely not have entered the world thus, in such optical and acoustical pomp and circumstance. . . . We the late-born, oppressed as we are by the merciless problems of Truth, feel in our own minds a singular belated echoing of the protest which found its expression in the story of the Revelation to Elijah at Sinai. The voice comes not out of the storm, not out of the fury and the fire, but in "a small whisper."[39]

While in Rome there was an altar to the Unknown God, Judaism worshipped the Unseen God. His voice emanates from the top of the Ark, the repository of the Tablets, the symbol of the authority for the Law, His revealed Will; but He cannot be seen, even in the Holy of Holies. When Pompey in 63 C.E. stormed Jerusalem, he forced his way into the Holy of Holies, much to the horror of the Jews, in order to see for himself what was the inmost secret of this unusual religion. And there he found—nothing but an empty room. The general from the image-ridden West was truly amazed.[40]

Perhaps we find here a key to the question of why the theme of Revelation is associated more with the liturgy of *Rosh Hashanah* than with the liturgy even of *Shavuot*. In the *Musaph* of the Day of Judgment, we find three themes, the third of which is *Shofarot*, highlighting the Revelation at Sinai as well as the Revelation of Judgment in the end of days. Since the essence of Revelation is moral, it is intimately connected with judgment, both the Day of Judgment and the instrument which represents the call to judgment, the *Shofar*, which is also an instrument of sound, not of sight.

This distinction between will and knowledge would also help to explain why the Revelation to Israel is consumated in a Covenant with Israel. For assent to knowledge no pact is necessary, only intellectual agreement or conviction. But the acceptance of obligations requires agreement with guarantees, a Covenant with pledges on both sides. It is, therefore, that the willingness to receive the Revelation is itself construed as a moral act on the part of Israel, not as an act of understanding. The "generation of the desert," therefore, need not be intellectually superior to other generations in order to stand at Sinai. It is

---

39. *Moses*, Martin Buber, Oxford, 1947, pp. 110–111.
40. *The Old Testament*, William A. Irwin, H. Schuman, N.Y. 1952, p. 43.

also possible for them, by the same token, to violate the agreement, as soon as it is consummated, through a moral lapse (as in the incident of the golden calf). Part of this very moral lapse is the willingness to exchange the world for the vision. They preferred the visible god to whom they owed no obligations to the God Who prefaces His command-ments by an appeal to the gratitude owed Him for taking His people out of the bondage of Egypt. In the words of Abravanel, "the purpose of this encounter was not to inform Israel of certain philosophic con-cepts which are not available to speculation, for these concepts do not bring man to happiness. . . . In these Ten Words He rooted them in the knowledge of His Providence, His Mercy, and His love of good deeds."[41]

## II

THE TRADITION BETRAYS ANOTHER AMBIVALENCE when it comments upon Revelation. On the one hand, it has many terms for Revelation, other than that of Sinai. As a matter of fact, there is no direct term for Rev-elation as it took place at Sinai other than *Matan Torah,* the giving of the Torah. Whenever terms are used for the phenomenon of Reve-lation, such as *Nevuah* (prophecy), *Ruach Hakodesh* (the holy spirit), *Bat-kol* (the heavenly voice), *Urim Vetumim* (the priestly oracles)—they refer to pre-Sinaitic or post-Sinaitic occasions of Divine Communication. Revelation is obviously not restricted to Sinai.

Also, the Midrash seems to make a great effort to make Revelation inclusive. Various commentaries include not only the unborn souls, the future legislation and elucidation of the Sages, the entire legal process of Torah, but even aspects of nature are embraced into the communion of Revelation. "Birds did not fly"[42] during the Revelation at Sinai. It is explained that the Torah was handed down in the desert, in the public domain so to speak, so that no nation can say it was deprived of its benefits.[43]

Within Israel, the effort is made not to confine Revelation to the immediate generation that witnessed it. Revelation not only has a last-ing effect, but it is also prepared for. "From the very first there must have been a predisposition in the nature of the Jewish people to re ceive the Message of Sinai. The Rabbis point out that all the precepts of the Decalogue had been practiced by the Patriarchs and had become the family tradition of their children."[44] Not only in the preparation for Revelation, but at the moment of receiving it, all Israel is involved.

41. Quoted on p. 481, *Hebrew Union College Annual,* Vol. 26, Cincinnati 1955.
42. *Shir Hashirim Rabbah* 29:9; quoted by Ginzberg, *Legends of the Jews,* Vol. 3, p. 97.
43. *Ibid.*
44. Ginzberg, *ibid.,* p. 82; Hertz, *ibid.,* p. 403.

"The supreme revelation in the life of the Lawgiver . . . that of the Covenant at Mount Sinai, he shared with the whole of Israel. To all of them was then vouchsafed the psychic experience of a direct communion with God."[45] So that both in time and in space, Revelation is not exclusive. And its echoes roll down into the future. Prophecy continues, even though the great Revelation is perfect in its completion. And it continues not only for the Biblical period, but, potentially, it is always available. For Maimonides, for instance, it is exile that keeps prophecy from Israel:

> Prevalence of sadness and dullness was undoubtedly the direct cause of the interruption of prophecy during the exile; for can there be any greater misfortune for man than this: to be a slave bought for money in the service of ignorant and voluptuous masters and powerless against them as they unite in themselves the absence of true knowledge and the force of animal desires?[46]

AND YET WITH THE SWEEP OF REVELATION in its various forms, cutting across the boundaries of historical eras, there is a tremendous accent on the uniqueness of what happened at Sinai. For if Revelation is universal, then it is nothing. Then every human mind, every flower, every burst of lightning, become instruments of Revelation, and there is no distinct doctrine. And so distinctions are made between the fore-Revelations and the post-Revelations, on the one hand, and the central Revelation, on the other hand.

"Abraham did not tell the people that God had sent him to them with the command concerning things which should or should not be done. Even when it was commanded that he, his sons, and his servants should be circumcised, he fulfilled that commandment, but he did not address his fellowmen prophetically on this subject. Abraham induced his fellowmen to do what is right, telling them only his own will."[47] The demarcation is thus not only between knowledge and will, but also between private legislation and public legislation. Other forms of Revelation and prophecy are available for private guidance, or for momentary legislation for the nation, but there is only one permanent and public legislation, that of Sinai.

Maimonides continues on the special mission of Moses: " . . . this distinction alone qualified him for the office of proclaiming the Law, a mission without parallel in the history from Adam to Moses, or among the prophets who came after him; it is a principle in our faith that there never will be revealed another Law." And again: "The object of all this is to say to the Israelites, 'This great sight witnessed by you,

---

45. *Ibid.*
46. *Guide,* Part II, p. 178. In the Messianic period prophecy will return.
47. *Ibid.* p. 186. Maimonides also differentiates between the public and the private Revelation.

the revelation on Mount Sinai, will not continue forever, nor will it ever be repeated.' "[48]

The issue between the doctrine of the "unique" Revelation as opposed to that of "progressive" Revelation is not that of the possibility of further communion between God and man. The most dogmatic position admits of such communion, but not for the purpose of altering the original Covenant. The issue becomes one of legality and legislation rather than one of information and knowledge. When Robert Gordis writes: "Sinai marked the commencement, not the conclusion, of Revelation,"[49] Maimonides would agree insofar as Revelation continues. But then this kind of Revelation did not commence at Sinai but with Adam. Legal Revelation, he would insist, did cease with Sinai.

We recall asking a teacher of Jewish ethics whether the particular gradations of legal authority, and the strata of sacred literature in which they are contained, were foreseen by the original Revelation, or whether the system of Torah, Prophets and Writings, followed by Mishna, Gemara, Codes could have developed differently in a different Jewish history. Was the progression of Prophet, *Tanna, Amora, Gaon, Rishon* and *Acharon* ordained, or was this particular structure of legal authority an accident of history? We forget his reply.

## III

THE THIRD AREA OF TENSION IN REVELATION is that between Reason and Revelation.

Already in the Pentateuch itself we find two different attitudes. There is an oft-repeated appeal to the reasonableness of the commandments. "For who is such a great nation that is possessed of such righteous laws and statutes as those of this Torah?"[50] On the other hand there is a stress upon the unquestioned nature of the commandments, at least some of them. *Zot chukat ha-Torah*—"this is the law."[51] It is this aspect of the law, perhaps, which needs the support of miraculous evidence for its acceptance.

One extreme view would be to claim that only Revelation discloses truth. God is prior to the universe, and He sets the standards for reality through the process of creation. Truth, as the verbal reflection or description of reality, therefore, emanates from God and enters the mind of man through the process of Revelation. The independent use of man's mind in the reasoning process is faulty because it is influenced

---

48. *Ibid.* p. 185.
49. *Judaism for the Modern Age*, Robert Gordis, N.Y. 1955, p. 158. Dr. Gordis notices the Talmudic phrase is *Torah min ha-shamayim*, not *Torah mi-Sinai*.
50. *Deut.* 4:8.
51. *Numbers* 19:1.

by the senses; and therefore reason yields only the mirage of truth but not truth itself. On this view, the only possibility of concord between Reason and Revelation exists where Reason conforms to the dictates of Revelation.

In this connection, the remarks of Benjamin Kidd and G. H. Lewes, as referred to by Ducasse in his *Philosophical Scrutiny of Religion,* are of some interest:

> No form of belief is capable of functioning as a religion in the evolution of society which does not provide an ultra-rational sanction for social conduct in the individual. From this it logically follows that a rational religion is a scientific impossibility, representing from the nature of the case an inherent contradiction in terms. There is an inherent antagonism between religion and philosophy, the aim of the latter having always been to establish a rational sanction for conduct. G. H. Lewes contends that the various attempts which have been made to establish a religious philosophy are innately impossible because the doctrines of religion have always been held to have been revealed, and therefore beyond and inaccessible to reason. Metaphysical problems, the attempted solution of which by reason constitutes philosophy, are solved by faith, and yet the name of philosophy is retained. But the very groundwork of religion is faith. There cannot, consequently, be a religious philosophy: it is a contradiction in terms.[52]

The other extreme view is to say the opposite: only Reason discloses truth. Revelation is a mirage, either because it never occurs, or because even if it does occur the content of the Revelation cannot be understood without the use of Reason. The only possibility of concord on this view is to make Revelation conform to the demands of Reason. This view would reverse the remark of the Caliph Omar on the fall of Alexandria in 641: "Burn the libraries, for all their value is in the Koran."[53] Reason can turn this around and say: "Dispense with your Revelations, for even if they have any truth in them, they are the truths of Reason."

It is safe to say that even where one of these extreme views is held, it is only with regard to the question of ultimate authority, not with regard to the use of Reason and Revelation. That is to say, where you have an already existing conflict in opinion and belief, either Reason or Revelation will be appealed to as the arbiter of the conflict. But in the discovery of truth, and the formulation of opinion, Reason will at least consider the testimony of Revelation, and Revelation will have to use Reason to explain and understand itself. As a matter of record, neither one of the expreme positions is really held in pure form.

ON THE PART OF REVELATION, THERE IS A TENDENCY to admit Reason as itself one of the agencies of Revelation. After all, God can reveal

---

52. Chapter 1.
53. *Dictionary of Quotations, ibid.* p. 685.

Himself, or His will, or His truth, by the means of a voice on Sinai, in the dream of a prophet, in the working of a miracle—why not through the workings of the human mind? In fact, in Jewish tradition, Maimonides makes it a prerequisite for Revelation that the reason of man be properly developed and prepared for Revelation. Thus he finds it impossible to admit that the Revelation at Sinai was received by all Israel directly, because they were not intellectually prepared to receive it. He maintains that Moses alone heard the voice and transmitted the message verbatim to the people. Maimonides' comment on this point is interesting:

> It was only Moses who heard the words, and he reported them to the people. . . . There is, however, an opinion of our Sages expressed in the Midrashim, and found also in the Talmud, to this effect: The Israelites heard the first and the second commandments from God, that is to say, they learned the truth of the principles contained in these two commandments in the same manner as Moses, and not through Moses. For these two principles, the existence of God and His Unity, can be arrived at by means of reasoning, and whatever can be established by proof is known by the prophet in the same way as by any other person; he has no advantage in this respect. These two principles were not known through prophecy alone. But the rest of the commandments are of an ethical and authoritative character, and do not contain truths thus perceived by the intellect.[54]

We draw three conclusions from this extract: 1) that Revelation is available only through the agency of a developed Reason; 2) that Revelation is unnecessary for the area of truth which is accessible to Reason; 3) that Revelation deals only with values and not with cognition.

The third of these was stated explicitly by Moses Mendelssohn in the 18th century: "I believe that Judaism knows nothing of a revealed religion. Supernatural legislation has been taken for supernatural revelation. The eternal verities comprise the natural religion of all humanity and may be discovered by the rational process. In Judaism faith is not commanded, but conduct is."[55] Thus Mendelssohn remained true to the deism of his day by assigning belief and practice to separate compartments of the mind. This may not be entirely satisfactory, but it reflects on the roles of reason and Revelation. G. E. Moore and others in modern philosophy have also dissociated the area of ethics and values from the area of cognition.[56] An ethics based on intuition is thus close to an ethics based on Revelation, at least in this respect.

The above represents one type of effort on the part of religion to make a place for Reason alongside of Revelation in the life of man. But this does not solve the problem. For unless you empty the notion of

---

54. *Guide,* Part II, p. 167.
55. *Jewish Encyclopedia,* article on "Revelation."
56. *Principia Ethica,* George Edward Moore, 1903: "Good is good and that is the end of the matter."

Revelation of any content of authority, or unless you redefine it into an indefinite vagueness consistent with any position, there will be a conflict between Revelation and Reason. This conflict is at its greatest when Reason is confronted with the claim of a specific Revelation at a particular place and a particular time to a particular person or persons. Thus the historical religions face the challenge of direct examination bearing upon their very specific claim of Revelation. The demands of archaeology, anthropology, and the critical study of sacred texts will have to be satisfied by those who claim a literal Revelation in space and time.[57] The conflict is at its mildest when religion falls back upon such notions as continuous Revelation; when it equates Revelation with insight and intuition; when it puts the poet and the scientist on a par with the prophet. But it is difficult to see how the element of authority can still remain in such revelation. Reason would seem to have the field to itself, almost on its own conditions.

LET US EXAMINE A CONTEMPORARY THEOLOGIAN on the subject. A. J. Heschel, in *God in Search of Man,* writes:

> The surest way of misunderstanding Revelation is to take it literally, to imagine that God spoke to the prophet on a long-distance telephone. Yet most of us succumb to such fancy, forgetting that the cardinal sin in thinking about ultimate issues is literal-mindedness. . . . It is not historical curiosity that excites our interest in the problem of Revelation. As an event of the past which subsequently affected the course of civilization, Revelation would not engage the modern mind any more than the Battle of Marathon or the Congress of Vienna. . . . We attempt to debate the question whether to believe that there is a voice in the world that pleads with us in the name of God. . . . No one who has sensed the terrifying seriousness of human history or the earnestness of individual existence can afford to ignore that problem. He must decide, he must choose between yes and no.[58]

Heschel tells us what Revelation is not; he does not tell us what it is. He thinks the possibility of Revelation today is more important than the Revelation of yesterday. But where is the Revelation of today found? To decide that there is a "voice" is very different from hearing it. To decide that there is a need for the "voice" is far from determining its existence or its message. We cannot go, logically (and even psychologically it may not be safe), from the need for Revelation to the fact of Revelation, any more than we can proceed from the need for God to the fact of God.

Heschel is willing to make peace with Reason, at the cost of downgrading the reliability of Reason:

---

57. See Introduction to Solomon Schechter's *Studies in Judaism*, where Bazilai is quoted: "Nature and simple meaning are our misfortune."
58. *God in Search of Man*, A. J. Heschel, N.Y. 1955, p. 168.

> We have discovered that reason may be perverse, that science is no
> security. . . . The prophetic claim that the eternal God addressed Him-
> self to a mortal mind is not inimical to reason. The very structure of
> matter is made possible by the way in which the endless crystallizes in
> the smallest. If the stream of energy that is stored up in the sun and
> the soil can be channeled into a blade of grass, why should it be *a priori*
> excluded that the spirit of God reached into the minds of men?[59]

Heschel's language and imagery are very appealing. One has to grant
that it is not *a priori* excluded that the spirit of God reached into the
minds of men. Perhaps nothing is *a priori* excluded. If *a priori* is a
term within the realm of logic, and if logic deals with the relations among
propositions, no proposition is ever excluded if it is first. But some
things are excluded, or at least have been excluded up to now, from
experience. Those who claim such experience can only tell others about
it, but they cannot duplicate the experience for their listeners. The
listeners must have answers to these questions: How do you recognize
Revelation? Which Revelation do you accept? At what point does Reason step in and take over in religious deliberations? If the choice is based
on an arbitrary commitment—then it is not the Revelation but the commitment that is the basis of a theological position.

Heschel pleads not so much for Revelation but for the desertion
of Reason's certainty:

> The idea of Revelation remains an absurdity as long as we are un-
> able to comprehend the impact with which the realness of God is pur-
> suing man, every man. However, collecting the memories of the sparks
> of illumination we have perceived, the installments of insight that have
> been bestowed upon us throughout the years, we will find it impossible
> to remain certain of the impossibility of Revelation.[60]

It is a great distance from finding it impossible to remain certain of
the impossibility of Revelation to being certain that Revelation took
place.

A LESS EMOTIONAL POSITION IS TAKEN BY MORDECAI KAPLAN. With reference to the holidays, he asks:

> Can *Shavuot,* the festival of Revelation, thrill the modern Jew as it
> did his forebears, now that the tradition with which its celebration has
> become associated is no longer viewed by him as a historic event? . . .
> The meaning which *Shavuot* will acquire, if it is to retain anything of
> its traditional character, can be none other than the one we arrive at
> by the process of revaluation. This involves emphasizing whatever im-
> plications the concept of Torah as divinely revealed may prove to have
> validity and relevance for our day.[61]

59. *Ibid.*
60. *Ibid.*
61. *Meaning of God in Modern Jewish Religion,* M. M. Kaplan, Reconstructionist
Press, N.Y. 1953, chapter on *Shavuot.*

What is the relevance for our own day? Kaplan gives up not only the naive long-distance telephone idea, but the idea of any event in time. This is how he puts it in his *Meaning of God in Modern Jewish Religion:*

> The human mind is so constituted that it has to find the fulcrum for the leverage of the moral laws not within but outside human life itself: that is, today the moral law must be regarded not as some prudential arrangement or social convention but as inherent in the very nature of reality. . . . The unique element in the Jewish religion consisted in the conscious recognition that the chief function of the belief in God was to affirm and fortify the moral law . . . that the moral law is the principal manifestation of God in the world. The identification of God as the author of righteousness was thus translated into the identification of God as the author of the Torah. We should therefore recognize in the doctrine of *Torah Min Hashamayim,* of the Torah as divinely revealed, the original prophetic discovery of the moral law as the principal self-revelation of God.[62]

Kaplan's naturalistic pragmatism is only slightly more satisfactory than Heschel's existentialist pragmatism. In the case of both the plea is not that Revelation occurred, but that we need it. In Heschel's view we need the voice of God. In Kaplan's view we need the backing of reality for the moral law. Also we must note that, whereas in the tradition the Revelation is the authority for the moral law, in Kaplan's view the moral law is the authority for the Revelation—except that he claims this was the subconscious reasoning of the tradition itself. Of course, on this view there cannot be any conflict at all between Reason and Revelation.

Another more traditional method of making Revelation conform to Reason is to make of Reason the arbiter of what is to be taken as literal, and what as metaphorical, in the Revelation. Maimonides, therefore, while he acknowledges that "a boundary is undoubtedly set to the human mind which it cannot pass. . . . The whole object of the prophets and the Sages was to declare that a limit is set to human reason where it must halt,"[63] at the same time leaves himself free to use reason by giving it the following role:

> Employ your reason, and you will be able to discern what is said allegorically, figuratively, or hyperbolically, and what is meant literally, exactly according to the original meaning of the words. You will then understand all prophecies, learn and retain rational principles of faith pleasing in the eyes of God Who is most pleased with truth, and most displeased with falsehood. Your mind and heart will not be so perplexed as to believe or accept as law what is untrue or improbable, whilst the Law is perfectly true when properly understood.[64]

---

62. *Ibid.*
63. *Guide,* Part I, ch. 31.
64. *Ibid.*

On the basis of this approach, Ahad Ha-Am sees Maimonides not as a reconciler of Reason and Revelation but as one who subordinated Revelation to Reason:

> Necessity compels him [Maimonides] to subordinate religion absolutely to the demands of philosophy; in other words, to explain the words of the Torah throughout in conformity with the truth of philosophy, and to make the Torah fulfill in all its parts the function which philosophy imposes upon it. . . . Just as the laws of nature are eternal and universally valid, though their usefulness is only general, and in some individual cases they cause injury as well, so also the divine guidance contained in the Torah must be absolute and general, and does not suffer change and modification according to the different conditions of persons and times. . . . If everything in the universe is the result of fixed laws, nature does not change, and there is nothing supernatural. There is therefore no room for revelation which upsets the order of nature.[65]

The position for Maimonides would be untenable, except that for him, as well as for all proponents of reason in religion, there is an ultimate escape from universal necessity. For behind reason there is will: "But if the world is the result of a creative act, and nature is consequently nothing but a Revelation of the divine will . . . then a second supernatural Revelation of the divine will is no longer impossible. . . . If we ask: why has God inspired a certain person and not another? why has He revealed his Torah to one particular nation, and at one particular time? we answer . . . He willed it so."[66]

## IV

AN IMMEDIATE CONSEQUENCE OF A CLAIM OF REVELATION is a disclaimer of other so-called Revelations. Once the unique role of Moses as Lawgiver is established, the establishment immediately issues a list of instructions as to how to ferret out the false prophet.[67] The historical religions have had to appeal, therefore, both to the credulity of man and also to his skepticism. Believe this! Disbelieve that! For this set of dogmas exercise all your reserves of faith—force yourself when necessary! For the other summon up all your critical faculties—demand proof! "I believe with perfect faith that the entire Torah which is found in our hands at present is the one given to Moses—I believe with perfect faith that this Torah will not be changed, and that there will be no other Torah given by the Creator." The eighth and ninth of Maimonides' Thirteen Articles are thus a set; without the second the first is useless.

To retain the commitment to the "true" Revelation there is an entire arsenal of weapons available to use against the "false" revelations.

---

65. *Philosophia Judaica,* Ahad Ha-Am, East and West Library, Oxford 1946, p. 153 and ch. "The Supremacy of Reason."
66. *Ibid.*
67. *Deut.* 18.

There is the appeal to loyalty, akin to the loyalty inherent in the monogamous marriage relationship. Thus we have such imagery of the prophets as the faithless wife and the straying lover. "And I will visit upon her the days of the Baalim wherein she offered unto them, and decked herself with her earrings and her jewels, and went after her lovers, and forgot Me, saith the Lord."[68] Another weapon is skepticism and denial. It is as if the religious mind must open once to receive the true Revelation, and then close with a stubborn disbelief of all false revelations and prophets. This skepticism, traditional in Jewish theology and Jewish history, is exemplified in the Talmudic dictum: "He who denies idolatry is as if he affirms the entire Torah." This denial can reach the borders of ridicule and humor, as when Elijah taunts the false prophets of Ahab: "Pray ye louder, for he is a god; perhaps he talketh or walketh or taketh a journey; or perhaps he sleepeth and must be awaked."[69] The underground humor aimed at the founder of one of its daughter religions illustrates one of the tactics of denial in Judaism. Other religions have aimed similar darts of skepticism against each other.

IN SELF-DEFENSE THE STRATEGY GOES EVEN FURTHER. Temptations offered by other revelations and other prophecies, even when they appear plausible, even when they are supported by miracles, are considered tests of loyalty and faith. "Thou shalt not hearken unto the words of that prophet, or unto that dreamer of dreams; for the Lord your God putteth you to proof, to know whether ye do love the Lord your God with all your heart and with all your soul."[70] The Biblical test is a simple one: does the new revelation call for the recognition of a new god, or even for the introduction of a permanent change, addition or subtraction, in the Revelation of Sinai? If so, it is false.

In Maimonides we have more subtle considerations. Momentarily standing outside of the gates of the tradition and using the criterion of common reason, he poses the question of the character of the Revealer:

> You may have a test by which you may distinguish between the guidance of human legislation, of the divine law, and of teachings stolen from prophets. . . . You will find laws which tend to improve the state of the faith of man, to create first correct notions of God, and of angels, and to lead then the people by instruction and education to an accurate knowledge of the universe; this education comes from God; these laws are divine. Is the person who proclaimed these laws the same perfect man that received them by prophetic inspiration, or a plagiarist who has stolen these ideas from a true prophet? We must examine the merits of the person. The best test is the rejection, abstention and contempt of

---

68. *Hosea* 2:15.
69. *I Kings* 18:27.
70. *Deut., ibid.*

bodily pleasures; for this is the first condition of men, and *a fortiori* of prophets; especially sense of touch which, according to Aristotle, is a disgrace to us.[71]

Caught between necessity and impossibility, uniqueness and continuity, reason and mystery, faith and skepticism, the doctrine of Revelation is seen as neither the beginning, nor the central, step in the religious process. Like almost all of theology, it is an after-thought and a construct based on other factors and other approaches than those under discussion. The choice between the traditional position and the critical version, the choice between the pleading attitude of Heschel and the cool formulation of Kaplan, will be made, not on the grounds of logic alone, but according to the temperament of the chooser. In fact, he will probably never consciously do the choosing. He will either be in the mystic, intuitional, supernatural stream of human thought, or he will be in the rational, empirical, naturalist tradition.

"Revelation explains all mysteries, except the mystery of revelation."[72] For the believer this is no impediment. To the believing Jew, the verse in which it is said the Lord spoke to Moses "face to face,"[73] strikes a responsive chord. Even for the non-believer for whom this has become a lost chord, the response is still there. Ahad Ha-Am, for instance, the agnostic, ignores the Moses of historical fact and accepts the Moses created by the imagination of his people.[74] One suspects that this was the attitude of the masters of Jewish tradition. They were men of reason and only reluctantly, in the words of a 15th-century commentator, did they "surrender some of reason's rights to the divine revelation."[75]

Even among the pious there were some quite subtle notions on this subject. Thus the Ba'al Shem Tov is supposed to have said: "He conceals Himself in His manifestations, and reveals Himself in His concealments."[76] Drawn out a bit, this would imply that the line between official Revelation and non-revelations is a thin one indeed. Even in Talmudic times the literal doctrine is stretched by metaphor. One sage says: "Each word uttered by God split itself into the seventy languages of the world"[77]—and we have here intimations of universal Revelation. Or, as Shneur Zalman, the master of intellectual Hasidism, put it: "All that man sees—sky, earth, and its fullness—are God's outer garments, manifesting an inner spirit, the divine vital élan which permeates

71. *Guide*, Part II, p. 76.
72. See note 7.
73. *Deut.* 34:10.
74. *Selected Essays*, Philadelphia 1912, essay on "Moses."
75. *Arama, Akedat Yitzhak*, ch. 25; quoted in Baron, *Treasury of Jewish Quotations*.
76. Baron, *ibid.*
77. See note 42.

them."[78] Bergson would have accepted this; Einstein, too, though he would not have put it quite that way. Perhaps Reason and Revelation meet somewhere in the realm of the reasonable.

We can grant this: Revelations can be real experiences and often are remembered by a people. They are impressions of moments of ecstasy —exaggerated but real nevertheless. The one unique Revelation which establishes authority is a product of systematic theology.

BECAUSE OF THE FOUR FIELDS OF TENSION in which the doctrine of Revelation finds itself, we must come to the conclusion that it is never the starting point in theology. The delineated doctrine of Revelation—i.e., the exact documents in which it is contained, how much God has revealed, the extent of its authority in time and in the area of human experience, what interpretative techniques have the stamp of legitimacy conferred upon them—is always a theological construct. An undelineated doctrine of Revelation can be a starting point.

The following naive syllogism has an irresistible attraction for the religious mind: 1) It would be cruel of God not to let man know Him; 2) God is not cruel; 3) *ergo*, God has revealed Himself.[79] Is the Bible this Revelation, as the Tradition claims? Is the Bible the vessel of this Revelation, as neo-Traditionalism claims? To answer "yes" to either of these questions, more sophisticated syllogisms are necessary.

An example of the more advanced web of logic in which the concept of Revelation becomes pinned down, but also somewhat hollow, is found in the opening words of Rabbi Aaron Halevi's introduction to his *Sefer Hachinuch*. There the syllogism is more pointed, more demanding, and yet, also less convincing: 1) All the world accepts the testimony of witnesses; 2) we have the testimony of 600,000 witnesses to the Revelation of Sinai; 3) *ergo*, we should accept the Revelation at Sinai.[80]

As with quicksilver, the more you try to pinpoint Revelation the more elusive it becomes.

---

78. Baron, *ibid.*
79. See note 14.
80. "Truth for the human species is that which has been agreed upon by the majority of men. There has been universal agreement to believe the testimony of men . . . to accept the testimony of grandfathers concerning the events of their day. God gave the Torah to Israel, in the presence of 600,000 adult males, beside women and children, so that all this host might be authentic witnesses to the fact of Revelation."

# REVELATION AND LAW

*Reflections on Martin Buber's Views on Halakah*

ARTHUR A. COHEN

## I

THE "relational event" in which man confronts the reality of God is indeed the center of any genuine religious experience. There can be no doubt that Martin Buber has discerned a fundamental structure which contemporary Jewish thought must reperceive and emphasize. The existential fact, by its very nature, however, indicates an order of truth not so easily grasped by intuition. The meaning of the "relational event" presses us into the assessment of the substance of revelation. It is therefore of critical moment to ascertain whether the meeting with God is structurally identical with revelation, in which case the revelation at Sinai is rendered indistinguishable from the experience of the *baal teshubah;* or whether the "relational event" is posterior in time, structure, and truth to revelation, in which case its value, however real, is rendered tenuous without the complementary acknowledgment that Sinai is enduringly normative.[1]

The struggle of Jewish theology is to establish the bases and purposes of Halakah as the way of God. It is impossible

to consider with seriousness any religious answer which does not meet the reality of the law. If the "relational event" of God and man is one that exists beyond the pale of a revealed teaching, its pertinence to Jewish religion is rendered questionable.

Unfortunately, Buber has not afforded us a *locus classicus* from which to derive his conception of revelation. His reflections on revelation are scattered throughout numberless essays. At the risk of failing to perceive some critical nuance, I shall attempt to summarize his treatment of the problem.

Revelation, Buber contends, may be understood in three possible ways. (1) To conceive of revelation as but the aesthetic consciousness, rapt in the mythopoeic fancies of past ages, surrenders God's speech in history to the relativizing passions of the modern age.[2] It is on such grounds that Buber rejects it. (2) To receive revelation as a supernatural event "severs the intelligible sequence of happenings we term natural by interposing something unintelligible."[3] Buber regards the consequence of such supernaturalism to be an inevitable dualism, which thrusts God out of the totality of life into an abstracted domain of religion.[4] (3) Revelation, rightly conceived, is to be recognized as the response of man to the given of his experience. The event, even the

---

[1]Martin Buber, "The Man of Today and the Jewish Bible", *Israel and the World*, pp. 93ff.

ARTHUR A. COHEN, a student on a fellowship at the Jewish Theological Seminary, is completing his Ph.D. dissertation, "Metaphysics and Method in the Novel", for the University of Chicago.

[2]Buber, *op. cit.*, p. 97.
[3]Buber, *ibid.*
[4]Buber, *ibid.*

natural event, is experienced as revelation when it is capable of transforming the receiver. Revelation is accounted the gift of God when, through its hearing, the entrance of man into life is radically altered.[5] The Bible is to be understood, therefore, as the relational meeting of Israel and God, as the community of Israel addressing its eternal Thou. The task of Israel is seen as that of reconsecrating itself to the Thou, of constantly recalling itself from the abominations of the object-world into the service of its Thou.[6]

The heart of revelation, according to Buber, is located in the dialogue of Presence and apprehension. It is not possible to speak of an unalterable center, a fixed middle point, in the movement from creation to redemption. "The revelation at Sinai is not this mid-point itself, but the perceiving of it, and such perception is possible at any time."[7] It is thus impossible to authorize revelation. Revelation cannot be frozen into the life of tradition. It can be seen only as the repetitive consciousness of its believers, each drawing out of himself the capacity to see it anew, to hear it more deeply, to fix its command to him with clearer direction.[8]

Buber's conception of revelation certainly has its profound appeal, for it succeeds, where the arid literalism of much Jewish thought fails, in bringing

---

[5]Buber, *op. cit.*, pp. 98f. "He who takes what is given him, and does not experience it as a gift, is not really receiving; and so the gift turns into theft. But when we do experience the giving, we find out that revelation exists. And we set foot on the path which will reveal our life and the life of the world as a sign of communication."

[6]Buber, *op. cit.*, p. 89; "What Are We to Do About the Ten Commandments?", *op. cit.*, pp. 85–88.

[7]Buber, "The Man of Today and the Jewish Bible", *op. cit.*, p. 94.

[8]See Buber, *Two Types of Faith*, pp. 62–65, where his conception of heart and intention in relation to Torah is explained.

Israel before the Bible itself. Yet this conception seems to me to raise many questions and difficulties, and it is to these that I would like to turn.

## II

It is significant that Buber does not adequately explain the apparent fact that God, according to the Bible, is capable of treating the community of Israel as a manipulable object. The perfect Thou, to whom the I of each creature ultimately turns, is capable of chastising with seeming heartlessness, of brutalizing His people with tyrannical leaders and corrupt seers, of sending His people into endless captivity. Where, then, is the Thou of meeting and responsiveness manifest? I am not here dealing with the problem of evil, for a more pressing question is involved. God is Thou, not because Israel has met Him as Thou, not because Israel has, at a past moment of its history, addressed God with wholeness of intent, but rather because God has revealed Himself. Revelation is deeply autonomous. It is neither the labor nor the fruit of the divine-human relation. The issue of relation comes after and without necessary connection to the reality of revelation. The revelation cannot, as revelation, be diagrammed in relational terms. Being autonomous, having purposes that elude the apprehension of His creatures, God can work the seemingly monstrous. Moreover, if the experience of relation within time is used as the reference by which time is seen before eternity, there is great risk indeed of destroying the eternity of the divine Thou.

It would be foolish to deny that man speaks out of his situation to God and that God responds in terms adequate to the situation. God indicates to the patriarchs the specific task which they are bound to fulfill. He does not offer thereby a statement of historical purpose. The commands to the patriarchs are distinguished by a repetitive emphasis upon activities within and conditioned by space — movement, travel, the purchase of land, the building of sanctuaries. The single line of generalized statement is the assertion, frequently reaffirmed, that the patriarchs shall inaugurate a great people whose service will be to the eternal God. It is only with Sinai, however, that the history of persons and the purposes of God are commingled. It is through revelation, in which content can only at our peril be separated from form, that God manifests Himself at Sinai.

The patriarchs were met by God. It is somewhat difficult to believe that every meeting was desired. God can compel the attention of man, forcing him to hear with the outer ear. God not only hears the pleading voice and answers. He can speak; He can disclose, He can reveal, He can make himself heard. He does not, however, coerce acknowledgment and belief. The reality of revelation is here too prior to the relation of meeting. Revelation is the call to meeting, but it is not identical with the meeting itself, as Buber insists.

The notion of revelation which Buber unfolds[9] indicates the legitimacy of this criticism. The identification of revelation with meeting permits Buber to state that the essence of revelation is that "a man does not pass, from the moment of the supreme meeting, the same being as he entered it."[10] But surely it is not inconceivable that revelation may bring about no such transformation. Revelation is surely in some sense independent of the structure of apprehension. When the content of revelation is appropriated as *mine*, God is truly met.[11] If we deny the primary significance of content in revelation, it would be possible to affirm that whatever God did at Sinai is irrelevant to the fact that it was God who did it. What God in fact said, each "And He spoke", is surely of equally profound value as the single statement "And God descended." The form of revelation, the Presence of God, may actually be of less pressing importance than the assessment and appropriation of His objective disclosures.

"Man receives, and he receives not a specific 'content' but a Presence, a Presence as power."[12] Buber continues this formulation with an indication of the threefold reality which the Presence of God confirms. The reality of relation, "the inexpressible confirmation of meaning,"[13] and finally the assurance that this meaning is one to be released into *this* life, are, Buber believes, contained within the meeting with God. It is noteworthy, however, that with the exception of the meeting itself, each of the other two aspects is possible only on the assumption that there is something verifiable in faith or experience about the content of God's revelation. Presence as Power will yield neither meaning nor "worldliness", unless *what* God says is acknowledged as a primary reality. To derive meaning and relevance from the content-bare Presence of God is difficult, if not impossible. It remains a fact that the biblical description of God's incursion into time commences with words of specific content (Ex. 19:3–6). As meeting is contingent upon revelation, so meaning is dependent upon content.

The content of revelation indicates the manifest reality of Presence. It is God speaking commandments of history for history out of the fulness of eternity that constitutes the wealth of revelation.

The role of meeting is to be found in

---

[9]Buber, *I and Thou*, pp. 109–112.
[10]Buber, *op. cit.*, p. 109.
[11]Cf. Franz Rosenzweig, *Briefe*, Letters, 398, 413, 435.
[12]Buber, *op. cit.*, p. 110.
[13]Buber, *ibid.*

its personalizing function. Each man appropriates the content for himself. But even though no man may receive the word of God for himself, the House of Israel has received the covenant. The act of meeting is the act whereby each man accepts for himself the word of God; notwithstanding, the word has already been received. The person, as person, can reject the word or meet it; yet for all time, as son of Israel, he must know that the law has been accepted for him.

Revelation is the act of God whereby He has disclosed the way and destiny of Israel. Meeting is the act whereby that destiny, that way, and its divine source are drawn into the inner life. The former is possible and valid for God without the latter, though its fulfilment cannot come until the latter is consummated. Both must ultimately join for salvation to be realized. Revelation is preeminently the disclosure of divine intention. As such, it is rich with content. The task of man is to take it from God, with indescribable delicacy of hand, so as to avoid shattering its divinity.

### III

Once the possibility is denied that revelation discloses content, once the reality of revelation is restricted to its formal, numinous dimension, the Halakah is inescapably voided. Buber is not averse to writing that "just as the meaning itself does not permit itself to be transmitted and made into knowledge generally current and admissible, so confirmation of it cannot be transmitted as a valid Ought; it is not prescribed, it is not specified on any tablet, to be raised above all men's heads."[14] His reasoning is thoroughly consistent. If revelation is addressed to the receptivity of the "single one," its meaning is beyond historical transmission, its confirmation eludes the prescription of

commandments. The generalizing function of revelation is thus neutralized. The sealing of the covenant carried by revelation is rendered inconceivable. Buber's argument rests here as previously upon the identification of revelation with meeting. If revelation is but the meeting of God and the person, clearly no commandment requiring universal obedience can possibly be forthcoming. The individual carries to God his inadequacies and doubts, his perplexities and longings. He receives in return the assurance of divine concern, sympathy, and understanding. The Presence is indeed confirmed in the heart of the seeker, but the seeker is not impelled thereby to normative conduct. The tradition of commandments in the Halakah can therefore be interpreted only as the illicit deduction of imperatives from the deeply private encounter of the "relational event." The uniqueness of meeting, the varying structure of dialogue, the differences that separate seeking persons one from another, render any generalizing statement of conduct spurious, and perhaps, to use a harsher word, idolatrous. Halakah is thus the misconceived projection of attitudes characteristic of false relation,[15] a rupture of the meeting between God and Israel.

The commandments are not, however, rational imperatives; nor do they offer themselves in the disguise of the "valid Ought." They are, to the extent that we acknowledge the ineluctable spirit of divine truth and will in the halakic portions of the Bible, full expressions of God. The commandment becomes an external "Ought" only when its inner freedom has been sapped by the life of habit.[16]

---

[15]This real, however false, relation is designated by Buber as I-It; see Buber, *op. cit.*, pp. 12–14, 35–39.

[16]Buber, "The Education of Character," *Between Man and Man*, p. 113.

---

[14]Buber, *op. cit.*, p. 111.

To disobey the commandments is not to betray the moral law. It is to desert God, to rebel against His authority. It is sin, but not therefore moral wrong. The moral law has been, in the history of the West, variously constructed on natural or rational grounds. It is a very different matter, however, when God proclaims the commandments, projects them without any suggestion of reasonable ground or social function, without allusion to any *raison d'être*. In such case, the holiness of God alone validates the law. The commandment is not a rational "Ought", because a man may conceivably reject the claim of the commandments, whereas no man conscious of his reasonableness can repudiate the fruits of his own reason. To reject the commandments is to reject the will of the eternal One, who notwithstanding our "likeness" to Him, is yet other than we. To reject the imperatives of reason is to reject what is wholly ours. Law can be conceived as the "Ought" only when, as with Buber, the relation of law and revelation has been severed. The law then becomes the product of obscurantist religiosity which the modern spirit can with justice renounce. It reflects an essential betrayal of man's meeting with God; it cannot be the consequence of man's struggle to appropriate the explicit content of revelation.

It is of course true that the Bible is the record of dialogue, but we are not given thereby the principles wherewith to disentangle the revealed word from the received interpretation. The miracle of revelation is the entrance of God into time; the truth of revelation is the word of God sealed into the language of time. The quest for the true law — that is, the quest for the true authority and divine will — is begun aright when one seeks to extricate revelation from the documents of encounter. This is not to deny the relation of the I and Thou, for such rela-

tion is of ultimate pertinence to the individual, being his dialogue of appropriation; nor is it to denigrate the Bible. The Bible is all from God; yet His word is channelled through the mouths of men. The word is one which, in virtue of generalizing beyond the individual, is a statement of eternal purpose; the meeting is disclosure of personality, both God's and man's. Revelation is God's effective commandment to history.

## IV

The historical dimension through which revelation is properly seen uncovers a further problem of perhaps greater seriousness in Buber's thought — the problem of time. Buber has written that the relation of an I to its Thou is achieved in the present. This present is not, however, a point, a simple moment. It is the "real, filled present"[17] which exists only insofar as actual presentness, meeting, and relation exist. "The present arises only in virtue of the fact that the Thou becomes present."[18] Every moment wherein the Thou is spoken becomes a *kairos*, a center-point, for the I, since relation to man and relation to God are contained within it. In contrast to the present of the Thou, the world of It, of things, is of the past. This is to be understood, however, in perspective. Obviously, an act of cognition, an experience, a feeling, a using — all in the world of It — occurs to a subject in some present moment. It is not past in fact, but in meaning. A world experienced as a mere multiplicity lacks a filled present, for the intrinsic richness, foreboding, and consummation realized in the I-Thou is lacking. Man accumulates the world of It; he stores it, labels it, and dispatches it into the darker realms of the remembered past.

Buber notes that the tragedy of ex-

[17]Buber, *I and Thou*, p. 12.
[18]Buber, *ibid*.

istence lies in the fact that the meeting of I and Thou is fated to pass. The Thou will become an object again. The most poignant love, the most dedicated piety, suffers loss. What, then, is the relation between man's dealing with the It and his meeting with the Thou? Is there total discontinuity between the experience of objects and the meeting of subjects? Clearly, the Thou will be different for the having of a past. Every Thou is both particular and general. The Thou is not an abstract essence; it is full concreteness. The Thou is the individuated "image of God". This is otherwise suggested when Buber interprets the much disputed phrase in Exodus: *Ehyeh asher ehyeh*. This phrase is understood by many to mean, "I am that I am," in the sense that YHVH describes Himself as the Being One or even the Everlasting One. Buber criticizes such an exegesis saying: "...that would be an abstraction of a kind which does not usually come about in periods of increasing religious vitality; while in addition, the verb in the biblical language does not carry this particular shade of pure existence. It means: happening, coming into being, being there, being present, being thus and thus; but not being in an abstract sense."[19] The past, the intermediate faltering from the present fulness of the Thou, must contribute value to man's speaking again. The woman loved and lost, but loved again, is something new for having been lost. This is not adequately accounted for in Buber's analysis. There is the tendency to make the fulfilled present static.

The consequences of this difficulty for Buber's conception of law and revelation are far-reaching. In the effort to draw the Thou of God into the heart of life, Buber exhibits a strange contrariness.

Where once the world and time were for God contemplated in love, drawn into eternity, fixed before His gaze, judged before His immutable throne, they have now become the point of fixity before which God moves. Where once time was real before the mark of eternity, eternity has become an accessible dominion before the "filled present" of time. Time has been sealed into the inner life of meeting. It may be suggested by contrast to this view that God is not in time, nor time in God, but eternity is time drawn into the equanimity of God.[20]

The immense struggle to release inwardness into the world, the effort of Hasidism to redeem evil, is misconceived when the role of revelation and law in Jewish tradition is misconceived. Inwardness without the law of God, sanctification without the benediction, is the forsaking of eternity for the vulnerable fortress of time. The crisis of Halakah is met in the tension of time and eternity, of history and messianic redemption. Since all man knows of God is what God has spoken and what man believes, it is only too easy to draw God out of eternity into time, to make of God the Thou before the struggling I, to abolish the objective word in the attempt to appropriate it as one's own. Whatever the magnificence of Buber's conception of I-Thou, the whole reality of relation between God and man can be seen as meeting and encounter only if it has been forgotten that God is, whatever our formulations, mysterious, inaccessible, unpredictable. God can be counted on, but not accounted for. To annihilate the law, the single instrument by which time and eternity, the profane and the holy, the ordinary and the unique, are locked together is either to

---

[19]Buber, *Moses*, pp. 51f; *The Prophetic Faith*, pp. 28–29; "Faith of Israel", *Israel and the World*, pp. 22–23.

[20]*Des Angelus Silesius*, ed. Wilhelm Bölsche, p. 177: "Im Grund ist alles Eins. Man red't von Zeit und Ort, von Nun und Ewigkeit. Was ist denn Zeit und Ort und Nun und Ewigkeit?"

lead man into the mystic way of self-evaporation or to render God submissive to the demands of life-relations. Time is not static before God. It is not only from the present of our relations that we learn. To make the I-Thou into the antithesis of the object-world, into its suspension, denies to the I the opportunity of making of its past a Thou, of redeeming it of evil by having learned from it its mistakes.

The Halakah is the way by which Israel's path through creation is signalled. It is the means of ultimate reference, through which the spirit is turned to its source and guided into its task. It does not permit us to overlook the fact that the separation of the holy and profane, the pure and the impure, the good and the evil, is essentially arbitrary. The rest, that which falls out on the other side of all distinctions, is the area of risk that no man is free wholly to exploit or wholly to ignore.[21] The Hasidim knew of the other side, the side of risk, the side neither touched by the arbitrariness of commandment and prohibition nor consumed by victorious evil. This is the side into which the commandments lead us, the commandments being neither the instrument whereby we flee from evil nor the amulet by which we are guarded from its poison. It is the area in which we are compelled to seek sanctification. The error is to imagine that without law the struggle can be waged. Without the seal of revelation, without the means whereby inner demand and living deed are compelled, each Jew would be cast into the desert of human groping unprovided with the power to withstand its blandishments of despair.

---

[21]*Hasidism*, pp. 44–46.

# REVELATION AND LIBERAL JEWISH FAITH

## JOSEPH H. GUMBINER

### I

Writing almost a decade ago in *Commentary,* Emil Fackenheim set forth the logical problems and described the genetic-evolutionary theory of religious history which had issued in the fact that "in modern Jewish theology, the concept of revelation lies dead and buried." He went on to note the possibility that the burial might have been premature, that it might have proved, "not the demise of the interred, but an indecent haste on the part of the undertakers."

The consequences of such speedy interment, even the possibility that indecent haste was involved in arranging the obsequies for so cardinal a root of Judaism, have not been grasped as yet by most leaders and spokesmen for non-orthodox Jewish religious movements. Here everything moves along as before on the smooth surface of people-centered Jewishness. Efforts are concentrated on fund raising, public relations

Revelation, the author contends, remains the Archimedes point of Jewish theology, and indeed, of authentic Jewish existence. And yet, in non-Orthodox circles, it continues to be by-passed in a non-committal attitude, or waved off with side-stepping, irrelevant references to God in nature and history. Following Buber and Rosenzweig, the writer sets forth a "liberal" interpretation of revelation that seeks to restore the centrality of the doctrine to its classical pre-eminence.

and the drive of each segment of the American Jewish religious community to elaborate on the techniques whereby its institutions may claim the laurel of representing a truly successful mass movement in the current American scene. Jewish secular culture, so far as that actually exists, and the State of Israel derive tangible benefits as an indirect result of such activity. The cause of quickening vital religious faith among the many young people now affiliated with synagogues, however, is poorly served. Policy makers for front organizations do not ask serious religious questions. They do not hear such questions even when they are addressed to them. As a result it is quite natural that they do not spend their time seeking for possible answers to questions which, for them, in their area of concern, do not exist as part of the problematics of human existence.

Beneath the polished surface of things as they are, the questions persist, questions about the ultimate meaning of a man's life, the motivation for maintaining a separate Jewish religious existence in the absence of a divine commandment, the relevance for life in the postmodern era of a liberal Judaism which denies the revelation of the living God. One place where such questions are asked is the college campus. To be sure, most students are entirely preoccupied with breaking into the American success story, while others have retreated to passivity as a way out of a dehumanizing society. There still remain, however a goodly number of seekers, of young people with questions. One such was a deeply disturbed, highly intelligent young man who put his questions to a prominent Jewish religious leader following the latter's keynote address at a week-end convocation of students. The crowd had departed when I came upon the two of them locked in mortal spiritual combat, at the front of the empty auditorium.

"My father told me to be a Jew," the boy spoke in a loud, frightened voice. " 'Yes, father,' I replied then. 'I love you. I'll do what you say.' Now, my father is dead. I ask you, rabbi, why should I remain a Jew?"

The distinguished guest answered in terms of group loyalty and the aesthetic value of Jewish customs and ceremonies. The young man countered by saying that what he wanted to know was why he should be loyal to the Jewish group, why, and in what sense. He ventured the opinion that other people also had customs and ceremonies of aesthetic appeal, that the French language was as beautiful as Hebrew, the Virginia reel as good a dance as the hora, and perhaps, for that matter, just as Jewish. That is how the discussion went: the boy pleading for his spiritual life as a Jew, the rabbi telling him over and over again in varied ways that it was really fun to sing Israeli folk songs. The two remained as far apart as Jews who have ultimate questions to ask remain separated from and untouched by the official answers of contemporary Jewish spokesmen.

Traditionally, theistic religions in general and Judaism in particular have placed the revelation of God at the center of their theological concern. The most basic texts of biblical and rabbinic tradition bear out this claim with respect to Jewish religion. The climax of all that went before in the Bible is the revelation of God at Sinai. In the Talmud and throughout Midrashic literature, as in the writings of philosophers, theologians and poets, the central problem has always been how to understand the statement that "the Lord came down upon Mount Sinai," along with the subsequent and equally puzzling series of revelatory events involved in Hebrew prophecy. We need recall merely that in the Mishnah it is stated that one who denies the divine revelation of Torah has no share in the world to come; that Saadia tried to deal with the question in rationalist terms by his simile of money, in which the proper amount may be arrived at either by calculation or by weighing the residue, thus making of revelation a kind of short cut whereby men receive a law of life without having to wait for the laborious processes of reason to arrive at the same conclusions; that Maimonides made of the revelation of Torah a fundamental principle of Jewish faith; that even Joseph Albo, critic of Maimonides, held that there were three roots of Judaism so basic that they could never be changed, and that one of these was revelation.

In the history of religions, revelation has been thought of traditionally as an authoritatively communicated body of truth. Some part of this truth, it was held might have been possible of attainment by man's own efforts, or at least could have been verified in that way, but essentially it was looked upon as the product of a specific revelation. Beginning with Immanuel Kant many philosophers and theologians abandoned the task of dealing with the meaning of revelation. They could no longer believe literally in the verbal or conceptual communication of truth to men by God. They knew of no other way of construing the significance of revelatory events.

It appears that many rabbis and scholars within liberal Judaism are still beset by the same kind of problems, problems stemming from the identification of revelation with the communication of a definite body of knowledge and code of conduct. Their reasoning has been something like this: Revelation is equated with the supernatural communication of the contents of the Torah. We have studied the Torah historically, comparatively and critically. It is impossible for us to accept the liberal truth of the Torah, its plenary inspiration, its alleged nature as being all of one time or one piece in origin, its character as the very words of God. Therefore, the term "revelation" no longer signifies a fruitful concept.

## II

In order to deal with the question of revelation certain distinctions must be made and consequent problems must be considered. First, we must distinguish clearly between discovery and revelation. When we work hard over a period of time on the solution of a problem and the answer is finally achieved, we are prone to think and speak as if the answer had come to us as revelation.

But a conclusion which results from the application of reason to the fruits of our experience is something which we have discovered. It has not been revealed to us in any precise sense. In the act of discovery, the initiative is man's. What he discovers stands in the relation of object to his cognitive thought. It has

no will, no means of revealing itself. It is just there, part of what is given in the data of the aesthetic continuum of nature, or the theoretic continuum of mind, where concepts derive their meaning from formal relationships with other concepts. In either case, what man learns here is the result of discovery not of revelation.

What is true of discovery is also true of invention, but in the latter case it is much more clearly discernible. When a person working in the field of applied science successfully arrives at a new formula, process, or product, it may seem at the conclusion of his work that the correct method was revealed. Upon reflection, however, it becomes apparent that the invention is the result of the worker's reason applied to the material at hand, including the researches of basic scientists which preceded the application of his inventive talent. In sum, the second law of thermo-dynamics was discovered, not revealed. The incandescent light bulb was invented, not revealed.

The problem of isolating the character of revelation becomes more difficult when we turn to the relationship between inspiration and revelation. Inspiration is a very general category of mind. We may be inspired by the beauty or orderliness of nature, by the quality of human love, by the intellectual joy of thought, by the possibility of service to our fellow men. The possibilities of inspiration are endless. In this sense the Torah and the later books of the Bible are certainly inspired works, as are those of Plato and Goethe, of Shakespeare and Flaubert. Inspiration is a mood in which we respond to the potentialities of our existence on a high plane. If we cannot go beyond inspiration with respect to the categories of religious existence, then we should rest well content at that point. The result would be a kind of universal religion founded upon the sacred scriptures of mankind as a whole, perhaps enriched by the effort to merge the individual person with the cosmic soul through mystical prayer and practice. But one of the most marked characteristics of revelation is its quality of singularity, of concreteness.

Although revelation and inspiration cannot be construed as identical, there is a close relationship between them. Inspiration is the illumination of the mind which serves as a necessary counterpart of revelation, as the receptive mood in revelatory situations. It is through inspiration that man knows who speaks in the still, small voice; it is the state of mind in which man recognizes that he is entering the holy dimension of life. The initiative comes from beyond the community or the person addressed, but the revelatory act cannot be completed unless it is received by a human mind or minds enabled by inspiration to understand that revelation is taking place.

Whatever else it may be, revelation is an event which makes known something which was not known before. If that which becomes known in this way is knowledge in the usual sense, then we must ask whether the knowledge gained through revelation is such that it could have been attained by the unaided use of human reason applied to the data of experience. If so, then revelation is a superfluous concept, and the demands of honesty as well as of elegance require that we apply Occam's razor to it without delay.

However, if whatever is conveyed in revelation is such that it could not have been known by the unaided use of human reason applied to the data of experience, then we must ask by means of

what aspect of the mind of man the result of revelation could possibly have been received and understood. The problem of revelation as usually stated thus poses the seemingly inexorable dilemma of superfluity versus incomprehensibility. Contemporary man will hardly be satisfied with Saadia's attempt at reconciliation.

Again, we are confronted by the paradoxical problem of the eternity of God over against the finitude of human life and history. Revelation implies that there is an incursion of the eternal into time, that God breaks through into the human realm at the time of revelatory events. But if God moves into time, is not His nature as eternal destroyed? And if man, be it Moses or any other man, moves out of temporality into eternity, does it not follow that his human character is destroyed? The Christian solution by means of the incarnation results in destroying the true nature of both God and man, and issues in a kind of christolatry, a serious dilution of monotheistic faith. In Judaism, God remains God and man remains man. The problem inheres in understanding the manner of their meeting.

Leaving aside a specific revelatory event, we may ask whether we do not find the revelation of God in nature and through history as a whole. If we look upon the natural universe with no preconception of faith, there seems to be no reason to find it revelatory of any principle or person beyond itself. Such study will discover certain patterns of uniform behavior which men call "laws of nature." It may also indicate that the natural universe is understandable by men because it evinces mathematical forms which are in consonance with certain canons of human thought. Looked at through the eye of the artist, it may impress the mind with its beauty, order-liness, richness and diversity. But neither the detached observer nor the artist is at any time required to move on to the point of finding a divine creator, law-giver, or master artisan beyond what he observes or studies.

If, with the deists, we posit the exist-ence of God as the creative force neces-sary to place the universe in existence or in motion, we are not much closer to the revelation of God than we were in the role of objective observers with no preconception whatever. It is true that in a very general sense we may speak of the world as the revelation of God. But in that case the application of the term "revelation" is so general that it applies to anything. We may assume that God is manifested in the law of gravity, or in process, or in polarity, or in any other aspect of nature which we describe and believe to be constitutive of the natural universe. It is surely true that: "The heavens declare the glory of God, and the firmament showeth His handiwork." However, the *kavod,* the glory of God referred to, is related to *kaveyd,* weight. When we look at the heavens and the wonders of the firma-ment we feel the weight, the pressure, the glory of God upon His universe and all its creatures. But we sense the divine presence through the natural world only because we look at it through the eyes of faith. Without any faithful precon-ception at all, it is difficult to see how we should find traces of the handiwork of God in the natural world. Even if we posit the prior existence of a Creator who, having created, then left the uni-verse, including mankind, to its own devices, we are no closer to a confronta-tion with the living God.

Our reflections on history will bring us to similar conclusions. If human his-tory is looked upon merely as the chron-icle of events in the lives of very clever, but rather weak and relatively short-lived individuals making up a species known as *homo sapiens,* then history is stripped bare of essential meaning. What matters in history is not so much what happened, or against which nat-ural forces human skill has had to con-tend, but the meaning and significance attached to the eventful struggle. With-out any reference to a principle of in-terpretation and judgment outside of history, the tragic meaning of the par-tially fulfilled, partially frustrated hu-man drama is lost. The chronicle of events tends to appear as a rather repeti-tive cycle, moving towards no goal, sig-nifying nothing much.

Even if we accept the creative first principle of the deists and add thereto the idea that in the end God will some-how redeem the world, we are not much closer to a meeting with God through history. Creation and redemption are the theological first and last terms of the universe, but history is what hap-pens in between. We are living in his-tory, and if the mighty acts of God are not understood and interpreted as rev-elatory events in history, then history it-self, looked at with objective detach-ment, will not provide answers to our ultimate questions.

Such are the limitations of natural religion. Through the uses of reason as applied to the natural universe we may arrive at a cosmological approach to deity which yields an unmoved mover, on first cause. There is no cognitively directed step from this to the conviction that "the heavens declare the glory of God." This is another way of saying with Kierkegaard that Hegel transcended the limits of his own method when he intro-duced motion and progress through logical concepts. Through the uses of reason as applied to history we may arrive at a teleological approach to deity which yields a final cause or highest purpose. But again there is no cognitively directed step from this to an understanding of the acts of God in history. By a supreme effort of human reason turned in upon itself we may finally reach the ontological conclusion that a perfect being of whom we have formed such an admirably drawn concept should not suffer the deprivation of non-existence. Such intellectual legerdemain will not help us find answers to the ultimate questions about our life. We cannot turn in prayer to a God, or perhaps we should say more precisely, to a God-concept, which is merely a high abstraction in our minds. Men ask for bread to sustain life. Without the God of revelation, naturalist thinkers, with all the good will and ingenuity at their command, can feed them only symbols and metaphors.

### III

The problems raised concerning revelation remain insoluble as long as revelatory acts are construed in the traditional terms of the authoritative communication of information from a divine source. The modernist approach through nature, history and the use of cognitive thought fails to bring us to a confrontation with the living God of Judaism. New light illumines the problem when we set aside both former viewpoints and consider revelation as the self-disclosure of God. The self-disclosure of God as referred to here does not mean the disclosure of the essential nature of God, which remains forever hidden from men. It has reference to the concrete acts of God in the history

of peoples and the lives of individual persons.

It is clear that such an approach to revelation is based on certain prior assumptions, even as the traditional and the modernist viewpoints arise out of prior assumptions. The nature of revelation inheres in the fact that it is not merely a psychological process, but that in revelation the mind of man is acted upon by a power outside that mind. In order to accept the reality and understand the consequences of such revelation, we must be prepared to make the unproved but not irrational assumption that real men inhabit a real world under the sovereignty of a real God. Such language may have a metaphorical aspect or a poetic tone, but it is not meant here as metaphor or poetry. The subjects under discussion are men with persistent personalities, living in a world that exists in their minds, over against a God who created them and it.

It is the great merit of Franz Rosenzweig that he began his "new thinking" with these basic principles:

Reality too has its past and its future, an everlasting past and an eternal future. To have cognition of God, the world, and man, is to know what they do or what is done to them in these tenses of reality, and to know what they do to one another or what is done to them by one another. And here we presuppose that these three have separate existence, for if they were not separate, they could not act upon one another.

Rosenzweig sums up the position whereby we may take revelation seriously without assuming the fundamentalist belief to the effect that the contents of revelation are literally written down in a book or books. "All that God ever reveals in revelation is—revelation. Or, to express it differently, he reveals nothing but himself to man."

H. Richard Niebuhr makes the same point within a liberal Christian content:

> Revelation means God, God who discloses Himself to us through our history as our knower, our author, our judge and our only savior.

If revelation means the self-disclosure of God, then it should issue in knowledge of God. The Bible speaks of *da'at elohim,* the knowledge of God; yet it is expressly stated that man cannot know the essential nature of God. Such knowledge as men have of the divine comes about through observing the acts of God in communal and personal life in history. This was also the conclusion of Maimonides, for whom the attributes of God were not thought of as descriptive of His being, but of His acts. The knowledge of God which comes to man in revelation is knowledge in the sense of acquaintance, not of cognitive understanding or capacity to manipulate. It is the knowledge of *connaître,* not of *savoir.* Such knowledge is acquired as a result of the completed act of revelation, which requires man's response in faith to the self-disclosure of God. An inspiration is the state of mind which serves as counterpart of revelation, so faith is the active response, the human correlate of God's initiative in the revelatory act. Faith is an aspect of the practical reason, of the reason of the heart rather than the theoretical reason of the head. It does not follow from this that reason as customarily understood has no role to play in religious understanding. It has a very important function to fulfill, but the initial acquaintance, or knowledge of God which is the result of revelation, is received through the faithful response of practical reason.

We have observed that what is revealed is not a body of information, but God, himself. In consonance with this Martin Buber writes:

> My own belief in revelation . . . does not mean that I believe that finished statements about God were handed down from heaven to earth. Rather it means that the human substance is melted by the divine fire which visits it, and there now breaks forth from it a word, a statement, which is human in its meaning and form, human conception and human speech, and yet witnesses to Him who stimulated it and to His will.

Since objects do not reveal themselves, although they may be discovered, it follows that revelation always takes place from subject to subject, from person to person. If God reveals Himself, then God is the subject of revelation, and the God of revelation is a personal God. In order to affirm his faith in a personal God, one who lives in our culture must be prepared to brush aside the theological straw man fabricated by naturalist thinkers from an idea of personality reduced to an absurd and childish concept.

When one human person sets out to reveal himself to another he has only a limited number of ways of doing so. Indeed, his capacity for self-revelation is so limited that he frequently fails to make himself understood even to those closest to him. More often than not, whatever degree of self-revelation is achieved comes about through unconsciously revealing words, gestures and deeds. Since God is infinite person, the means of His self-disclosure are limitless. That is why, after a revelatory occasion has once been received in faith, man finds other events taking on a revelatory character to a degree. The man of faith finds the word of God in Scripture, traces of His glory in nature, His mighty acts in history, intimations of Him in the postulates of thought and the promptings of conscience. Above all, God reveals Himself in action which results in the radical transformation of life. Through revelation Jacob becomes Israel, a slave people is oriented towards becoming a kingdom of priests and a holy nation, your life and mine are infused with new meaning as we gather courage to pronounce the "Thou" of the benediction in an unredeemed world.

Since revelation requires, for its completion the faithful receptivity of some person or community, it is imperative to deal with the problem of the human side of the occasion, the problem of mediation, understanding, interpretation and transmission.

## IV

What Orthodox Jews call the contents of revelation may be conceived by the liberal Jew (who is critical of the attempt to view Judaism in terms of humanism alone and who seeks to take the revelation of God seriously) as the record of Israel's response to the self-disclosure of God in the Sinai event. In studying this record we should expect to find evidences of the original, motivating divine revelation as well as marks of the process of human mediation. This is precisely what we do find when we read the record without orthodox or modernist preconceptions.

Our problem, then, is not to find out what are the contents of revelation. We know what the contents consist in: the self-disclosure of God. Our problem is one of finding criteria whereby, as we read the record of Jewish response to the Sinai event, we may be enabled to decide which elements more clearly re-

flect the revelation of God in its pristine character, and which are more clearly the result of human attachments to existing ideas and institutions. The question of criteria is of the most crucial character. Without such instrumentalities we shall either be forced back upon the orthodox position to the effect that there are none available, that the Torah is all of one piece, that, for example, it is equally incumbent upon us to follo the injunction, "thou shalt love thy neighbor as thyself," and to avoid the transgression of wearing, "a garment two kinds of stuff mingled together"; or we shall be moved on to the modernist position which holds that such criteria are not needed because there was really no revelation in the first place. But positing such a choice is to pose a false alternative. There is a path beyond archaic literalism, on the one hand, and the generalized humanitarianism of latter-day humanists, tinted, in our case, with the coloration of people-centered Jewishness.

What does a critical but reverent study of Torah disclose at the heart of the teaching of Judaism? The following is one formulation, for which no claim is made respecting either perfection or comprehensiveness:

1) The one God demands obedience to moral law.
2) Man is free to respond to this demand, positively or negatively.
3) Israel is a people chosen to bear witness to this demand and to this freedom.
4) In the fulfillment of this task a double responsibility is required of Jews through their covenant relationship with God: to teach and give living exemplification to the imperatives of moral law; to fulfill additional commandments not of direct ethical import, commandments which help them sustain

their separate religious existence as they seek to sanctify the things and activities of daily life.

Proceeding from this kind of starting point it should be possible for liberal Jews to develop criteria to help evaluate the implications of the revelation of God as recorded in the Bible, throughout the rabbinic tradition, through the creations of the medieval period, in modern attempts at reformulation, and in the experiences of their own lives. Among the possible criteria to utilize in such a task are congruity with the main stream of the tradition; reason, not autonomous reason, but reason conceived of as the endowment of God in man; experience, the funded experience of the Jewish people, and the personal experience of individual lives; historic confirmation; consistency with ideas of truth, beauty, goodness and holiness derived from sources outside the Torah tradition of Judaism; and subjective appropriation—"to know what is knowable" and "to do what is doable," for *you* and for *me*.

With respect to the problem of the progressive character of revelation, the liberal interpreter of Judaism is placed in a dilemma similar to that which he confronts concerning the very possibility of revelation in the first place. He cannot accept the orthodox position to the effect that revelation occurred at only one time in the specific locale of the Sinai wilderness, or that prophecy ceased at the time of the activity of Malachi. Neither can he agree with modernist interpretations of the recent past to the effect that revelation is everywhere at hand, that our understanding of God's will becomes progressively more clear, that we are destined soon to enter the messianic era.

Still, we may say that the revelatory event upon which Judaism and the Jewish people are founded is progressive in two ways. The more we realize that our very existence as a people of faith, our history and our present tasks, can be integrated and understood only as the result of God's self-disclosure, the more convinced we become of the primary import of the Sinai event. This means that present history and life serve progressively to validate the original event of revelation.

We may also say that revelation in Judaism is progressive in the sense that through application to new life situations the meaning of God's revelation may be more clearly understood by men of faith in terms of contemporary events. A kind of dialectic is thus set up whereby new events strengthen our conviction about the self-disclosure of God; while the application of the revelatory event to new situations helps us to understand the implications of revelation for the changing conditions of life. Thus the God of revelation continues to reveal Himself. Within Judaism the progressive revelation of God is always related to the initial covenant made by Israel at the mount of revelation, thus providing the possibility of sharpened conviction and heightened understanding. That is perhaps the meaning of the Hasidic saying to the effect that, "God reveals the Torah every day."

Like the relationship of the basic assumption regarding the uniformity of nature, or the intelligibility of the universe through the manifestation of mathematical forms, to science, so is the relationship of revelation to Judaism. It is the point of departure, the necessary first principle of theism. It is the *cogito ergo sum* of religion. It is so in the sense of being the ultimate principle which enables us to understand what follows in history and in our personal lives.

However, the principle under consideration here is not one of cognitive thought, as it was in the Cartesian formula, but one of faith in the Hebraic sense of *Emunah*, signifying both the active state of fidelity and the receptive condition of trusting. Of especial interest is Martin Buber's translation of Isaiah 7:9 as, "If you do not trust, you will not remain entrusted." The state of remaining entrusted implies an original placing of trust. This original placing of trust by God is the revelatory event of divine self-disclosure. It is the first principle of Jewish faith. Although it occurred in the past, it is always of contemporary concern. To remain entrusted requires that we continue to trust. This is our basic axiom.

Although we cannot go back of this principle to approach it critically by means of other religious categories (since it is the principle which contains within itself the means of critically examining what follows), this does not mean that we are dealing with something esoteric, mystical (in a precise sense), or utterly private in character. Related to Jewish history by internal relationships, taking our stance within the religious community of Israel, we should seek to discuss the basic principle of revelation in reasonable terms. Surely, all religious Jews, including liberal or Reform Jews, who affirm the existence and unity of God at every visit to the synagogue, whenever they pray in private, and who propose to make such affirmation at the moment of approaching death, should be able to think and speak about so fundamental an element of Jewish faith as the self-disclosure of God through Israel. Surely, we should all realize that this original placing of trust in Israel requires for its fulfillment that men of faith daily renew their trust, as Isaiah reminded Ahaz.

The road back to Orthodoxy can never be traversed by many contemporary Jews. Naturalist and humanist approaches will not suffice to sustain vital religious life. Men seek to understand the meaning of their existence in a time of confusion and upheaval. The great opportunity of Reform Judaism inheres in this very situation. By using the tools of liberal interpretation, contemporary Judaism can help restore faith in the living God whose revelation is the rock upon which Judaism and the Jewish people are founded.

# TOWARD A THEOLOGY OF ETHICS

## JACK J. COHEN

### I

This paper aims to explore the theological implications of a simple ethical command, "Thou shalt not murder". The exploration arrives at three conclusions. The first is that the prohibition of murder cannot be logically derived from an analysis and an understanding of the meaning of "Thou." The second point is that the meaning of "Thou" can be derived from the meaning of "Shalt not murder." And finally, we shall seek to demonstrate that "God" cannot be understood until the meaning of both "Thou" and "shalt not murder" is grasped.

By way of preliminary, it ought to be made clear that the traditional concept of *"beyn adam lamaqom"*, (between man and God), is not strictly speaking

*Traditionally, ethics has been viewed as finding its ultimate warrant in the nature of God. This classic conception has been challenged by those who have sought to establish ethics independent of any reference to the nature of either reality or the Divine Being. Here, Rabbi Jack J. Cohen, leader of the Society for the Advancement of Judaism, seeks to make explicit some theological implications revealed by an analysis of the Sixth Commandment. This paper was originally delivered as a lecture for the B'nai B'rith Institute.*

an ethical category. It covers mainly violations of ritual obligations and only tangentially, as in the case of vows affecting our fellowmen which are made to oneself, but not carried out, does it embrace ethical considerations. Ethics, in Jewish tradition, occupies that realm of human experience subject to human reason. Variously termed,[1] ethical laws have been consistently held to be discoverable by man. Revelation of ethical laws was deemed necessary only to speed up the process of discovery, to prevent error by unintelligent men, or to enhance the reward for their observance. Yet we should misinterpret the tradition if we were to assume that it contemplates naturalistic ethics. In all revealed traditions, reason plays an inferior role to faith, and faith always resides in an established tradition. Reason receives the approval of the rabbis whenever it substantiates revealed doctrine, moral or ritual; when reason contradicts that doctrine, or when it is powerless to find supporting grounds for the tradition, it is dismissed as a human and therefore fallible instrument.

The argument of this paper is that ethics is a rational enterprise which, far from being revealed by God to man, re-

---

1 *"Chovot halevavot"*, (duties of the heart), *"mitzvot sichliyot"*, (rational commandments), *"dat tivit"*, (natural religion) are among the designations of ethical laws to be found in medieval Jewish philosophy.

veals God, or at least provides some insight into the nature of reality which man calls God. This is the sense in which ethical values and laws or conventions bespeak a relationship between man and God. It is a dangerous relationship, because while man must rely on God for the ethical meaning of life, he can never be certain that he has correctly understood the demands upon his conscience. Are they divine, or are they demonic? Let us now see what the man-God polarity can mean in relation to ethics?

## II

When one asks oneself who is the "Thou" in the Sixth Commandment, one is either struck by the profundity of the question or its silliness. Thou, you, I—these terms all apply to an irreducible phenomenon, the conscious being who understands when addressed. Is it not ridiculous to inquire for any other meaning to the term? In truth, if one is interested simply in consciousness as such, there are only the physiological fact of the organization of the human body and the psychological reality of consciousness. Epistemologists may worry about the status of the objects of consciousness, but for the ordinary affairs of life, it is enough that there are men and women who can think and express themselves.

In ethical concern, however, the question of "Thou" is far from simple. The fact that there is a thinking being in no way suggests how that being ought to behave. As he can think evil thoughts, so can he perform evil deeds.

Suppose "Thou" is not simply consciousness but a spiritual substance, called a soul. It has been said that the soul has an independent existence—at least after death. During life it functions through a body, but it is sacred and destined for immortality, provided, of course, that it has earned its reward. Those who define "Thou" in this way conclude that murder is precluded by the nature of the Thou. The argument is weak, for the prohibition of murder depends on the truth of the definition of the Thou as sacred and immortal. The soul's immortality, however, is highly hypothetical, depending on a reality beyond human ken. Are we to assume that if the "Thou" proves to be mortal, murder is permitted? Are we further to assume that there is a difference between being sacred and being immune from murder? Is not the latter an aspect of what we mean by being sacred? Thus, the command turns out to be an ethical tautology, with the object of our inquiry, the relationship between Thou and shalt not murder, self-evident. We know, however, from human experience that the prohibition of murder is not self evident at all. Nor was it self-evident to those who conceived this commandment. They sought to counteract a conception of Thou in which murder was apparently possible and perhaps a normal and legitimate quality of human behavior. It would seem to follow that the Thou in whose very conception murder is forbidden must not be self-evident. Therefore, before we can derive the prohibition from Thou, we need a more satisfactory method than mere assertion to arrive at a definition of Thou which, in turn, would legitimize the deduction banning murder.

It has been said that Thou is the spirit of God in man, the divine spark, which calls man to life. Murder, therefore, would be a violation of the divine in man. But God is the destroyer of life as well as its creator and sustainer. He destroys human life by tornadoes, floods and disease. God made man mortal. Why should man live by standards less arbitrary? Far from helping us, the claim that every man has a touch of divinity within him confuses us. For if we can explain away the seemingly unjust consequences of natural evil, why should we not be able to justify the murder of enemies of society, oppressors and power mad men? Yet we are appalled at the mere thought that we have the right to weigh the worth of a human life in our own hands, however unworthy that life may be. So we establish courts and systems of justice to safeguard to the nth degree even those who have destroyed the lives of others and who might continue to do so if given the chance again.

There is, in the traditional approach to ethics, in the system of deduction from God to man, an inherent paradox. Man who is capable of murdering must restrain himself from using his power. Meanwhile, the God who can create life causes death; and yet He commands man to preserve life. Evidently, in the divine scheme, life is natural, and death requires explanation. But how can man be required to preserve life when his own end, decreed by the God of all living things, is death. From God, we can deduce only a paradoxical concept of man, one that is not at all to be identified with the prohibition against murder.

We conclude, then, that Thou is the object of ethical search, rather than the fulcrum upon which an understanding of ethics rests. Is is not our knowledge of man which determines our ethics but as we shall see, our ethical presupposi-

tions which determine our concept of man. This does not mean that a concept of man, once achieved, has no bearing on our ethical attitudes; but it implies that to reach that concept we must first have established our ethical standards.

## III

It has often been pointed out that the Sixth Commandment prohibits murder, not killing. Jewish religion has not, by and large, preached pacifism, Individual self-defense and, *"milchemet mitzvah"* (a war for securing territory belonging to Eretz Yisrael or for defending it) were considered morally necessary in Biblical and Rabbinic tradition. Yet if Jewish religion has not been pacifistic, it has nevertheless considered killing an evil, even when necessary. Beginning with the humanization of slavery, the prevention of blood revenge and other Biblical legislation designed to reduce the spilling of human blood, continuing with Rabbinic limitations on capital punishment through the banning of capital punishment except in cases of treason in modern Israel, the Jewish people has sought to reduce and ultimately to eliminate all killings.

Both in the prohibition against killing and in that against murder there is implicit a conception of Thou as sacred and inviolable. But that sacredness and inviolability are absolute only in potentiality and not necesarily in actuality. The conception of Thou emerges from the meaning attached to murder. Murder is not at all, as we have seen, a self-evident term. To the religious extremist of India, murder is the killing, consciously or unconsciously of any living thing. Thou, therefore, means anything above the realm of vegetation. To the pacifist of the West, murder is the killing of another man in war or as punishment for a capital crime. The pacifist is generally vague as to whether killing in self-defense is permissible and therefore not included in the category of murder. His vagueness follows necessarily from his conception of murder as identical with killing. His Thou is man *qua* man, and it is therefore impossible for him to conclude from this premise which life, his own or his attacker's, is to be preserved.

In Jewish tradition, Thou is man, but not necessarily any man, not man merely by virtue of the fact that he lives. It is man as a potentiality who is implied in the Jewish conception of murder. For murder is the wanton destruction of a human being who himself respects the life of man *qua man*. Human existence, by its very nature, is a conditional existence. It is conditional, in the first place, in man's very mortality. Man is dependent for his life on a process of existence over which he has no ultimate control. Man's life is conditional also upon his ability to understand the forces conducive to life and those making for death. Both in the physical and moral aspects of life, man is subject to the workings of the cosmos. This is an obvious fact in the physical realm where disease and natural events highlight the limits of human power. It is not so obvious in the moral realm, except insofar as social disturbances and conflicts are sometimes predictable when certain types of behavior are practiced in a group.

The Thou, then, of the Sixth Commandment, is man *in potentia*, man as ideal, man as the embodiment of life. It is mortal man who does not resent death and can therefore concentrate on life. It is man whose potential, however, cannot be understood until the fact of murder is grasped, until its implications for man's future are fully appreciated.

In brief, "shalt not murder" leads logically to the traditional religious view of man as sacred. But where does the prohibition itself have its genesis? In the process of life. Call it thought, faith, revelation, intuition, valuation—the answer is still that man is ever a potentiality realizing himself in the process of his existence. There is a circularity here. The Thou is understood as new insights into life are gained. But it is the Thou, in its consciousness, which gains those insights. How can we break through the circle? Only by a conception of transcendence that we have become accustomed to term "God".

## IV

The Ten Commandments are introduced by the presentation to man of the Great Thou, I am the Lord thy God. It is fashionable today in certain theological circles to speak of religion as a cosmic dialogue between man and God. I and Thou are the two poles of reality. Just as in intercourse between men there can be no communication unless there is a clear recognition both of the distance between the I and the Thou and the lines of commonality that draw them together, so man would be lost in chaotic loneliness were he unable to experience a dialogic relationship with the Absolute reality.

Psychologically, it is easy to understand the many ways in which this need for avoiding cosmic loneliness or solipsism expresses itself. Man seems to crave company. He is a social animal. Hence he depicts an ultimate reality which he calls Thou or Mind or Cosmic Consciousness, and to which he can relate in a fashion analogous to his relationship with fellow men. Man speaks to God in words of prayer, and God answers in acts of revelation.

When not pressed too hard, this conception of the cosmos expresses poetically the truth of human psychology, that man cannot stand the pain of loneliness and meaningless existence. As a description of cosmic reality, however, it is a misleading and intellectually dangerous view. For it is an example of the human propensity for making the wish the father to the thought. A wish can never establish the truth or the reality of a thought. A conception of God as Thou, as speaking to man, may give one psychologically a feeling of I-Thou, but existentially, there is only the I and its thoughts. The thoughts may have reference to the outside world, but human as a whole. To believe that one has communicated with the Ground of Being, or with Cosmic Mind, or with God is to mistake Truth for possible truth. Certainty is no guarantee of truth; it only seduces man into arrogance, if he believes in the finality of his own power of apprehension, or into idolatry, if he takes as an expression of final Truth, the object of his apprehension.

Thus, whatever man thinks of God as a result of his need for feeling he lives in a cosmos and not in a chaos is mediated through his own consciousness and has a status no higher than any other well-considered idea. Like other ideas it is an interpretive construction placed upon his experience of the world around him. I believe it is a necessary idea, necessary, that is, in its having to

be formulated. Man cannot live without interpreting his experience. But it is man who does the interpreting, and the results of his thinking must necessarily be relative to his limited experience. The Thou he calls God can thus be a greater or a lesser approximation of ultimate reality but never identical with it.

These considerations must be borne in mind as we try to extrapolate the meaning of God from our moral experience. To put the matter succinctly, we have to turn the tradition upside down. We are told that, "as He is so merciful so should you be merciful." But how is man to know God's mercy, except as he himself interprets it? How is man to attribute mercy to a God who has often seemed to disclose His wrath, unless man refuses to accept these manifestations at face value and instead imposes his own human evaluations on an otherwise intolerable situation? It is man who conceives God in His own image. "As you are merciful, so must He be merciful."

God has to be merciful because man's life is meaningless without this divine quality.

We are now in a position to inquire as to the bearing of the conception of man and moral values on the meaning and existence of God. To say that the murder of a human being is morally wrong is meaningless unless the quality of sacredness belongs to man by his nature. But that identity of man and sacredness cannot be deduced from what man is as an outgrowth of natural process. It can have logical standing only under a transcendent category of divinity in which the relationship between man and his sanctity is a necessary factor. All this may sound like a repetition of traditional supernaturalism in which it is declared that ethical values are absolute because God decreed them. The argument advanced here, however, differs in several respects from that of supernaturalism. In the first place, ethical values are conceived as products of human imagination, having the same logical status as other ideas. An idea, as modern pragmatism claims, is a plan of action whose validity is determined by its workability—not in the vulgar sense of agreeing with the wishes of the thinker but in casting the light of reason and reasonableness on a previously problematic situation. Values are ideas which suggest an organization of human behavior to fit human needs under specific social conditions. These values are conceived by men with the same process of thought that characterizes the solution of problems involving nature.

Secondly, I am suggesting that transcendence and not supernaturalism is all that is necessary to establish a logical connection between the concept of man and the prohibition of murder. It is only when the idea of man and the idea of life's sanctity are integrated in the transcendent conception of the necessity of man's striving for a society of love and fellowship that the specific imperative against murder has a logical context. I am suggesting further that the capacity to project his behavior against moral backgrounds far wider than his own experience draws for him is a native quality of man's nature. Man requires no supernatural deity to act as a legislator of his values or as a judge of his behavior in order to cultivate for himself a system of ethics which is both logical and compelling. Every ethical valuation is itself an act of self-transcendence, whereby man judges his own conduct in a perspective more inclusive than his own self-interest.

But thirdly, all these wider perspectives are man made inferences, guesses, projections, programs. They have no necessary status independent of the human mind. They are, therefore, instrumental to human ends. All that man can do is to hope that his aims in life accord with a transcendent realm that he counts upon to give meaning to his spiritual strivings.

God thus comes to mean in ethical terms the Value of all values, the guarantee that man is not chasing the wind. But He is known only by inference. His existence is a necessary assumption in order to make sense of man's proneness to evaluate life, but man's conceptions of what that existence implies are also natural inferences from limited experience. They fall short, and always will, of exhausting that ultimate reality.

When, therefore, we conceive of man as a Thou, a being whose existence must be dedicated to life, we are not describing an actuality but a potentiality and a hope. That potentiality, in turn, rests for its consummation, not on the hope, but on the existence of a force in the universe that enables man's potentiality to be realized. Belief in that force, in God if you will, is essential to man's morale; but a knowledge of it must forever elude man's grasp. But given God, then human striving in all areas of life makes sense, for then we live in a cosmic order; given God, however, it is the striving alone, the process of searching for the good in which man can place his full faith. For the existence of God, a reality far more encompassing than man can apprehend, makes man's efforts to turn his finite insights into cosmic truths a joke or an idolatry.

The moral venture of man requires, therefore, a liberal sprinkling of skepticism, doubt and agnosticism. The great religious personalities and the sacred scriptures of human history all exhibit these qualities which are noticeably absent from so many pages of intricate and clever theological disputation. But the skepticism has not been directed at the validity of those ethical values which mankind has developed over the centuries and which have become well-nigh universal. No civilized society today, for example, disputes the immorality of murder, although there is still a degree of disagreement as to its difference from mere killing. There is a remarkable consensus among peoples throughout the world as to what is right and wrong. Rather has skepticism always been aroused by the question of the ultimate resolution of man's moral search. Man yearns for peace because he needs it and recognizes it as a divine quality. But what guarantee can he find that his wanting peace can bring it about? Apparently none, except the intensity of his yearning. Yet the skepticism passes, and the doubter returns to his faith with increased vigor until the next crisis, when the cycle of spiritual uncertainty begins again.

We maintain, then, that the ethical business of man is to pursue the search for Thou by refining the values by which he conducts his life. Values can be refined only by permitting the full light of experience to be refracted through the prism of human intelligence. Intelligence, which includes the faculties of imagination and reason, is the only instrument available to man for the understanding of reality. The moment when human imagination suggested the moral wrong in murder a whole new insight into the nature of man became possible, an insight that revealed, too, a dimension in the universe as a whole which had hitherto been unknown.

It is only fair to point out the danger in the approach to ethics I have been describing. I have been saying, in essence, that man is the measure. But we must understand in what sense this is true. As far as we know, man is the only conscious power in the universe. If God has a mind, it is so utterly different from that of man as to be inconceivable. Even if God has a mind, however, it is man alone who ascribes that quality to Him. It is man alone who advances values as good or bad. He alone aspires to know what is divine and what is demonic. In this sense, he is the measure. But man cannot determine the truth of his values. Occasionally, what he calls good is proved to be evil and *vice versa*. The ultimate meaning and value of earthly existents and existence lie in the realm of transcendence far beyond the power of any generation of man ever to exhaust. Man is, therefore, the measure only of what is in his power to measure; namely, his experience.

Insofar as man can tell, therefore, having found the immorality of murder, he has found a divine value. He has discovered in himself and his fellowmen a portion of the meaning of their existence, the preservation and the enhancement of life within the limits of their mortality. And in order to sustain this belief, in order also to give it more than a subjective status, he declares that this understanding is descriptive of the larger reality of God on which all human life must depend in order to make its venture worthwhile. In this faith lies the hope of mankind and also the pitfall.

The psychological necessity of positing a God belief and a God concept too frequently results in the deification of man and his beliefs and orders.

It is at this point that we Jews have a distinct contribution to make to the evolution of ethical thought. Individual philosophizing is valuable and necessary for ethical advance, but the history of a people as old and as widespread as our own can be a corrective to too facile ethical judgments. We should have learned from our history that the long view of things is as necessary to human affairs as the immediate advantage to be gained by moves which patently violate our best ethical insights. It may be difficult for men to put their own lives into the service of values from which they themselves derive little benefit, but having caught a glimpse of what those values mean, life itself is worthless without them. It may be, however, that mankind needs both types of men—those who hold onto life even at the expense of values they hold dear and those who become martyrs to a cause. Jewish history seems to be the resultant of the interaction of both types. It would be comforting to think that martyrdom rewards mankind without fail, that human values operate in society with an absolute cause and effect mechanism. But even this modicum of concession to the quest for ethical certainty is denied to man. The workings of Divine Providence are mysterious indeed, and only the man who can find inspiration in the act of ethical striving will be able to catch a glimpse of redemption. In that spiritual adventure has our people found God.

# PRAYER, HUMILITY AND COMPASSION

## SAMUEL H. DRESNER

WHERE DOES God dwell? This was the question with which the Rabbi of Kotzk surprised a number of learned men who happened to be visiting him. They laughed at him: "What a thing to ask? Is it not written "The whole world is full of His glory?" Then he answered his own question: "God dwells wherever man lets Him in".

God's glory does indeed fill the world, and the Rabbi of Kotzk did not mean to deny it. But just as the radiance of the sun, reaching everywhere, can be closed off by the palm of a fragile hand before the face, so can the glory of God be shut out by the fragile will of mortal man. God constantly pursues man, seeking him in all places, at all times, yearning to enter his life. And yet, in the weakness of folly, man flees Him "down the nights and down the days, down the arches of the years; down the labyrinthine ways"[1] of his own mind. God wants to enter our lives, but time and again we shut Him out, closing the door to the divine.

Through the ages, God has pursued after man, sometimes drawing close, but more often than not forbidden to enter

---

[1] Francis Thompson, *The Hound of Heaven.*

RABBI SAMUEL H. DRESNER is a graduate of the Jewish Theological Seminary. He is presently the Director of the Hillel Foundation at the College of the City of New York, Downtown Branch.

by the obstacles man, himself, had set in the way: paganism, materialism, humanism — all have played their historical role. In our own time, we, too, have erected barriers to God. Our infatuation with the amazing achievements of natural science led many to conclude that only that which could be seen, touched or measured existed. And since God could not be placed in a test tube or rendered visible by a microscope, He was thought to be a fantasy, bred as the product of primitive man's imagination. With the recent breakdown of scientific utopianism, however, such misconceptions have diminished. But another barrier to God has been raised, stronger than the first, which is particularly prevalent among intellectuals, who are exposed to the regnant rationalism which still rules at centers of higher learning—the tendency to think of God as a hypothesis or concept. God, they assert, exists in this latter sense; He is no fantasy, but He exists only in a remote sort of way. He is the God of Aristotle, the prime mover, who created the world, gave it a push and then let it spin on, not caring where it went or what happened to its creatures. To the philosopher, God may be necessary as a supposition or even a process and is fit securely into the pigeon-hole of some well-reasoned system, but whatever His role may be, He is surely not a God who wishes to enter the life of man.

"The God of the philosophers is all indifference, too sublime to possess a heart or to cast a glance at our world. His wisdom consists in being consciou. of Himself and oblivious to the world. In contrast, the God of the prophets is all concern, too merciful to remain aloof to his creation. He not only rules the world in the majesty of His might: He is personally concerned and even stirred by the conduct and fate of man. 'His mercy is upon all His work.' "[2]

Pascal sewed into the lining of the coat that he wore until the day of his death, a scrap of paper upon which were written the words: "Not the God of the philosophers, but the God of Abraham, Isaac and Jacob". Not the remote, aloof God of the philosophers, who is but a concept or a process and cares little for the concerns of man, but the God of Abraham, Isaac and Jacob, the God of the Bible, the God who reveals His will, who hears our prayers, who shares our suffering, the God who has mercy for those in need and compassion for those in privation, the God who searches after the righteous people and seeks the righteous man. We stand in need, not of the God of the philosophers but of the God of our fathers who pursues us "down the nights and down the days, down the arches of the years",[3] seeking to enter our hearts and souls and lives.

There are three ways in which God enters the life of man which I shall attempt to discuss: prayer, humility and compassion.

Prayer is one of those things which stands on the heights of the world and at which men mock. How precious, how sweet is prayer and how rarely is it found. Its soft whisper is crushed by the thundering gallop of the herd in search of power and glory. Our lives are so filled with noise, confusion and excitement, that there is little room for prayer. We are always in a hurry, though to be asked our destination might prove startling. Continually taken up with one thing or another, we are almost afraid to be alone with ourselves.

"And, behold, the Lord passed by, and a great and strong wind rent the mountains, and broke in pieces the rocks before the Lord; but the Lord was not in the earthquake; and after the earthquake, a fire; but the Lord was not in the fire; and after the fire, a still, small, voice. And it was so, when Elijah heard it, that he wrapped his face in his mantle and went out and stood in the entrance of the cave."[4]

All of us stand in the cave with Elijah. We spend the many days of our years in that cave. It is our world. Some hear only the wind and the earthquake and the rending of rocks, while others have the discerning wisdom of spirit which was the prophet's. Prayer is a surrendering to the stillness that surrounds us, a withdrawal from the market place and a yielding to the quiet that is everywhere. For there is another world about and within each of us which we neither see nor touch; there is One who speaks to us constantly, but it is in a tone barely audible, a still, small voice, and we must clear away the din of daily living and open our ears to hear it.

Prayer is not a liturgical slot-machine into which we insert words of coin and expect miracles to jump forth at the

---

[2] A. Heschel, *Man Is Not Alone*, p. 244.
[3] Thompson, Op. Cit.

[4] Kings 1, 19: 11-13.

press of a lever. In Greek, to pray means to wish and in German, to beg, but this is not the central meaning of Jewish prayer. Nor is prayer simply a psychological exercise in which one converses with his better self. Man cannot lift himself by his own bootstraps. To say, I am getting better and better every day in every way, may be a clever trick but has nothing to do with prayer. There are so many misconceptions of prayer that we sometimes wonder why men pray at all. Perhaps the best answer was given by William James. "We pray," he said, "because we cannot help praying."

Prayer implies another dimension of reality, beyond the human, to which man attempts to relate himself. In prayer we open ourselves to God; we lower the barriers and let Him come into our lives. In prayer, God enters the life of man. We do not know God in prayer but we make ourselves known to Him. We do not discover Him, but expose ourselves to His constant yearning to be with us. "Thou shalt love the Lord try God with all thy heart, with all thy soul and with all thy might and these words, which I command thee this day shall be *upon* thy heart (al l'vav'khah) ."[5] The verse does not say "*in* thy heart" (bil'vav'khah), said the Rabbi of Kotzk, as one might expect, for the heart of man is shut fast so that the word of God cannot enter and must remain suspended *upon* the heart of man. But there are holy hours, hours of prayer, when man surrenders himself to the stillness of the universe, and then the heart opens and God's words sink down deep into it.

"As a tree torn from the soil, as a river separated from its source, the human soul wanes when detached from

what is greater than itself."[6] Man is part beast and part angel. When he forgets the angel within him, the heavens above him, his spirit grows sick and weak. Man cannot live without something more than man. "Prayer is our attachment to the utmost. Without God in sight we are like scattered rungs of a broken ladder. To pray is to become a ladder on which thoughts mount to God, to join the movement to Him which surges throughout the entire universe."[7]

Prayer teaches us what to cherish. The mind of the man at prayer meets the imperishable ideals of our faith: peace and righteousness, mercy and holiness, justice and humility, love for the Torah, love for God and love for our fellow man. In the midst of wordly living, when our thoughts are scattered and our wills often weak, the classic words of the Hebrew Siddur keep before our eyes what might so easily be forgotten. "That you go not about after your own desires and your own fancies after which you go astray; that you remember and do all my commandments and be holy unto your God."[8] Prayers are signposts along the way, visible even in the fog, pointing the right direction and reminding us what to remember.

In prayer we find strength for life. Temptation and passion, as well as irritation and torment, plague us constantly. Each day has its ordeals and at times we wonder if we shall survive them. Judge Harold Medina, in a recent speech, declared that his custom of daily prayer gave him the strength to carry on in such a remarkable fashion, through

---

5 Deut. 6:6.

6 A. Heschel, *Prayer*, Review of Religion, Jan., 1945, p. 155.
7 Ibid., p. 155.
8 Numbers, 24:40.

the crushing pressures entailed in the trial of the eleven Communists. "I tell you, as I stand here, that my unguided will alone and such self-control as I possess were unequal to the test. If ever a man felt the presence of someone beside him, strengthening his will and giving him aid and comfort, it was I on those days. And so it was later, toward the end of August, when I finally left the courtroom one day and went to lie down, I thought that perhaps I should never go back. But after ten or fifteen minutes, I was refreshed and I did go back: and I gained in strength from that moment to the end."[9]

Perhaps the most difficult act to imitate is true prayer. For in prayer we learn to tell the truth. "The Lord does not see as man sees, for man looks on the outward appearance, but the Lord looks at the heart."[10] We cannot lie when speaking to God. Our pride, our outward charm, our achievements, our cleverness are all stripped from us when, naked in spirit, we stand before the Lord of all creation. Prayer without inwardness is like the body without the soul. "My words fly up, my thoughts remain below."[11] It is not the words alone which are important but, even more, what is behind them, what lies beneath the words. "God desires the heart"[12] is the way the Talmud puts it. It is the inner feeling, the *kavana*, which God wants in our prayer, not the rote recital of memorized phrases.

When we speak of Jewish contributions to civilization, we usually mention Einstein's theory of relativity or Freud's theory of psychoanalysis while prayer is rarely or never alluded to. And yet Western man, whatever his land and whatever his religion, has adopted the Jewish way of prayer. We have taught most of the world how to pray and should not forget it. The Church is but a copy of the Synagogue while its liturgy is largely patterned after ours, and the Psalms, in a thousand different languages, are the golden links in that great chain which binds man to God.

A Gentile scholar, G. Biddle, gives vivid testimony to the glory of our books of prayer. "When we come to view the half-dozen or so great liturgies of the world, purely as religious documents and to weigh their value as devotional classics, the incomparable superiority of the Jewish convincingly appears ... Certainly the Jew has cause to thank God and his fathers before him for the noblest liturgy the annals of faith can show."

These are words of Jewish prayer:

A prayer before going on a journey.

"May it be thy will, O Lord my God, to conduct me in peace, to uphold me in peace and to deliver me from every enemy and ambush by the way. Send a blessing upon the works of my hands and let me obtain grace, loving kindness and mercy in thine eyes and in the eyes of all who behold me. Blessed art thou, O Lord, who hearkenest unto prayer."

A private prayer of Rabbi Hiyya bar Abba.

"Let our hearts be united in the fear of thy name; bring us near to what thou lovest; keep us far from what thou hatest."

A prayer of Rabbi Tanhum.

"May it be thy will, O Lord our God and God of our fathers, that thou break, and cause to cease, the yoke of the evil

---

[9] *Current Religious Thought*, May, 1952.
[10] Sam. 1;16:7.
[11] Hamlet.
[12] *Sanhedrin*, 106b.

*yetzer* in our hearts, for thou hast created us to do thy will, and we are bound to do thy will: thou desirest it, and we desire it, and what prevents us? The dough in the leaven (i.e. the evil *yetzer*). It is revealed and known before thee that we have not within us the strength to resist it: therefore may it be thy will to cause it to cease from us, and to crush it; and then we will do thy will with a perfect heart."

Rabbi Pedat's prayer.

"May it be thy will, O Lord my God and God of my fathers, that no hatred against any man come into our hearts, and no hatred against us come into the hearts of any man, and may none be jealous of us, and may we not be jealous of any; and may thy Law be our labour all the days of our lives, and may our words be as supplications before thee."

And yet, despite all the poems we write and all the songs we sing, prayer is no cure-all. It takes us from the noise of the world into the stillness of the soul, not that we may escape the world in some mountain retreat or island monastery, but to return us into the world to do our task there. Moses had to experience the shepherd's solitude in the land of Midian, where God found him at the burning bush, before he could know how to lead his people out of Egypt. So it is with all of us. Prayer removes us from the market-place of life only to heal us, to wash us clean, to purify us, to strengthen us, and then to send us back to the crossroads of creation so that we may live out the dreams of prayer. "It is like a beam thrown from a flashlight before us into the darkness. It is in this light that we, who grope, stumble and climb, discover where we stand, what surrounds us and the course we should choose. Prayer makes visible the right, and reveals the hampering and the false. In its radiance we behold the worth of our efforts, the range of our hopes, and the meaning of our deeds."[13]

If *prayer* is the way God enters our life, in terms of man's relation to heaven, then *humility* is the way He enters our life in terms of man's relation to himself.

The discovery of the "self" is modern psychology's claim to fame. The great popularity of this "science", in all its aspects, stems primarily from the realization that many of man's problems are not due to external causes, such as earthquakes, or soil erosion, or forest fires, terrible as they may be, but to internal causes of which man himself is the source. Not only how to live with the Asiatics or how to live with the gadgets of science, but perhaps even more important, how to live with one's self, with that obstinate, elusive, ever-present fellow we call the ego.

It is said of Disraeli that he was a self-made man who worshipped his creator. Power not only lends to corruption, as Lord Actor put it, but it, likewise, leads to pride—the pride of the general over his soldiers, the employer over his employees, the teacher over his students, the father over his children. If we examine the records of the divorce cases which are swamping our courts, we find that while some of them are clearly unavoidable, many are simply the result of two egos which could not learn to live together. Likewise, if we try to understand the conflicts which arise, from time to time, between political leaders, economists or even physicists, there is always, to be sure, some valid ground for disagree-

---

13 A. Heschel, Op. Cit., p. 157.

302

ment whether it be a question of isola-
tionism, Marxism or nuclear physics.
But is it only that? Is there not also
embedded somewhere in the complex
fabric of human conflict, no matter what
the level of that conflict be or how
objective the issue seems at first glance,
the pride of the one man struggling
with the pride of the other? We cannot escape from the human situation.
How to live with ourselves is the problem.

The coat of pride, furthermore, has
many colors. There is overweening conceit, pretentious opinion, garish glitter,
punctilious mummery, pernicious jealousy. There is even—most dangerous of
all—the pious gray of false humility.
"The Devil did grin, for his darling sin
Is pride that apes humility".[14]

The problem of pride is an ancient
as well as a central problem in Judaism. Nothing is condemned so repeatedly and so emphatically as the sin of
pride. "The proud man's sin is as if
he had committed every kind of un-
chastity. It is as if he had denied God.
Pride is equivalent to idolatry. The
proud man deserves to be cut down as
one cuts down a symbol of idolatry.
Over such a one the *Shekhinah* laments
and God declares, "He and I cannot
dwell in the world together".[15] Concerning the verse in Scripture: "I stood between the Lord and you". Rabbi Mi-
khal of Zlotchov said "the I, the ego,
stands between God and ourselves." It is
our own self which blocks God out of
our life, our own "I" which forms an
impenetrable wall, a crust of ego which
gradually winds itself around us, envel-
oping us, blinding us to all but our

own interests, our own desires and closing off the stream of light which God
sheds for our sake.

Nor can this wall be broken down so
easily or so completely. Before the Baal
Shem died, his disciples asked how they
should know who was to be their leader in his stead. He told them to go and
ask how pride could be cured. Whoever would tell them a permanent way,
they would know was not the man. The
struggle with pride is a constant struggle, one which we carry on every day
of our life and from which no man,
rich or poor, learned or ignorant, master
or slave, is every completely free. "Vanity is so anchored in the heart of man",
said Pascal, "that a soldier's servant, a
cook, a porter, brags and wishes to have
his admirers. Even philosophers wish
for them. Those who write against it
want to have the glory of having written well; and those who read it desire
the glory of having read it. I, who wrote
this, have perhaps this desire, and, perhaps . . . those who will read it."[16]

There is only one way of dealing with
the ego and that is through the realization that *man is not alone* in the world,
that there is a "holy dimension"[17] of
all reality which pervades the universe
and transcends it; that man is not his
own master, but the servant of the Lord.
To realize that there is a God in the
world is a shattering experience in the
life of man, exploding his ego in the
tremendous apprehension of the divine,
filling him with shame and the discovery
of his littleness. The prophet Isaiah
discloses how God entered his life when
he was in the Temple in Jerusalem. "In
the year King Uzziah died, I saw the
Lord sitting upon a throne high and

---

14 Coleridge, *The Devil's Thoughts.*
15 *Sotah,* 4b-5a.

16 Pascal, *Pensées,* p. 56.
17 A. Heschel, *Man Is not Alone,* p. 237.

lifted up and his train filled the temple. Above him stood the angels... And one called to the other and said:
'Holy, holy, holy is the Lord of hosts; The whole earth is full of His glory...' Then said I:
Woe is me; for I am undone; Because I am a man of unclean lips And I dwell in the midst of a people of unclean lips;
For mine eyes have seen the King"[18]

When God enters the life of man, he becomes aware of a higher authority, of interests beyond his own, of ideals that surpass his own self. A sense of awe and reverence settles upon such a man and then his *ani* turns to *ayin,* his pride becomes humility. His self is attached to a higher Self. Neither praise nor scorn have effect now. The ego is no longer the center of his life, but God becomes the center, and he understands that life is not for the sake of acquiring possessions for himself, nor for the sake of seeking power over others, but that life is for the sake of God, that we are not autonomous rulers of our own kingdoms, but servants of the Lord, children of the most High, created by him with a spirit and placed upon earth that we might serve Him through our deeds of love. How do we know if a man fulfills the verse "I shall set the Lord before me at all times",[19] asked a Jewish scholar? If he displays humility.[20] In other words, humility is the mark by which the man who dwells in God's presence can be recognized. Humility, then, is the highest virtue of religion.

"Ever let a man be humble in Torah and good works, humble with his par-

ents, teacher and wife, with his children, with his household, with his kinsfolk near and far, even with the heathen in the street, so that he becomes beloved on high and desired on earth."[20a]

In true greatness there is true humility and in true humility there is true greatness. When God enters, the ego becomes nothing, but that nothing, that emptiness, is, in a sense, everything.

It is not enough, however, to read about humility. To understand humility and to don the softness of its garment, one must have walked at the side of a humble man—if only for a moment. To have had a humble teacher, a humble parent, a humble servant is a blessing we often fail to appreciate until years have passed and the depth of experience which breeds wisdom opens our heavy eyes to the treasure we once possessed. For the humble man, no matter what else he may be, is a precious creature, the true nobility of humankind. In his presence we feel a purity of purpose, a sincerity of speech and a clearness of action which invites confidence and trust. Here is one with whom the *Shekhinah* is not ashamed to dwell.

And is this not what we look for in seeking friendship, one who wants our companionship, not for the sake of ulterior motives which corrode the link of unity, but for what we are in ourselves? Clearly, what we seek in others and, therefore, in ourselves as well, is humility. It is not easily found in this confused and harassed world of ours, but it is, nonetheless, worth the seeking. For humility is not a kind of weakness, as some are prone to believe, whereby one is stepped on and pushed around. It is not the lack of something, but the presence of something; not weakness

---

18 Isaiah, 6:1-5.
19 Psalms 16:8.
20 Jacob Emden, *Perush al Aboth* 4:4.

20a *Tanna de be Eliyahu,* p. 78.

but a strength in that which is higher than the self.

When Alexander the Great had returned from his many victories over the nations, he called all of his army together, according to legend, and declared in a mighty voice, "now that we have conquered all the earth, let us prepare to do battle with yet a greater foe —ourselves". Each of us possesses an ego and each of us is engaged in a constant battle, not only an outer battle with the world, but an inner battle as well. It is by throwing open the weighty doors of the spirit and letting God enter our lives in the wonder of humility that we learn how to fight that battle and how to live with ourselves.

If *prayer* is the way God enters our life, in terms of man's relation to heaven, and *humility* is the way God enters our life, in terms of man's relation to himself, then *compassion* is the way he enters our life, in terms of man's relation to his fellow man.

Just as prayer and humility are rare in our time, so is there little compassion in our world today. And no wonder, since this is what one of the most influential thinker of modern times has to say about it: "Pity is opposed to the tonic passions which enhance the energy of the feeling of life; its action is depression. A man loses power when he pities. On the whole, pity thwarts the law of development which is the law of selection. It preserves that which is ripe for death. It fights in favor of the disinherited and the condemned of life; thanks to a multitude of abortions of all kinds which it maintains in life, it lends life, itself, a sombre and questionable aspect. Nothing is more unhealthy, in the midst of an unhealthy modernity, than . . . pity".[21] Earlier in the same work, Nietzsche sheds tears of grief over the beautiful "blond beasts" (his phrase) of Germany, whom religion had caged in and perverted by the subversive doctrine of compassion.

Nietzsche has had his way. Compassion was removed from that blond teutonic beast and the world has been able to view it in all its ghastly beauty. The rise of Nazism was, in no small part, due to taking this philosopher and others like him[22] seriously. We have seen revealed in all its naked fury the wickedness which lies chained in the dark depths of every human breast.

Compassion shuns our world. There has been so much cruelty, so much suffering that the senses have become dulled, so much spilled blood that the sight no longer frightens us, so many rotted bodies that the stench no longer sickens us. The festering hand of moral leprosy has touched us as well.

To see this most clearly we need not turn to weighty philosophical volumes, or momentous questions of national interest, but to the little things of life, our own individual lives. Do we resist the temptation to insult? Do we forgive a wrong? Do we treat rich and poor alike? These questions are partial answers. Compassion is not only for great issues, but for small ones as well, and in both respects the world and we have grown callous, dangerously so.

God enters the life of man in compassion. When man receives the bounty of God's love, he cannot use it simply

---

21 Nietzsche, *The Twilight of the Gods*, p. 45, translated by A. Ludov.

22 George Bernard Shaw stated that, "Compassion is the fellow-feeling of the unsound." *Maxims for Revolutionists*.

to fill the pool of his own soul, nor is it sufficient to express it in prayer, for hidden in God's love of man is God's love for all men. And so it is that the man who feels God's love for him, feels also God's love for other men and he too participates in that love. It is this love of man for his fellow man, which is God's love for all men, that we call compassion.

Compassion means, first of all, the *recognition* of the others' existence, the realization that there are other people, who have the same desires, dreams and pains as we. But compassion is much more than mere recognition of our neighbor, it is an attitude to him, a *going out of ourselves toward him,* to meet him, to embrace him, to love him, "Am I my brother's keeper", was Cain's question and the implicit answer is, "yes, you are". One of the first lessons in the Bible, then, is that every man is our brother and we are his keeper. All men are somehow bound together in an eternal bond of life and death. "Thou shalt love thy neighbor as thyself" is the classic statement of the Bible. But what does it mean to love our neighbor? Rabbi Moshe Leib of Sasov tells us from an experience in his life. "How to love men is something I learned from a peasant. He was sitting in an inn along with other peasants, drinking. For a long time he was silent as all the rest, but when he was moved by the wine, he asked one of the men seated beside him: 'Tell me do you love me or don't you love me?' The other replied: 'I love you very much.' But the first peasant replied: 'You say that you love me, but do you know what I need. If you really loved me, you would know.' The other had not a word to say to this, and the peasant who had put the question fell silent again. *To know the needs of men*

*and to bear the burden of their sorrow* —that is the true love of man."

This, then, is the true meaning of compassion: to know the needs of men and to bear the burden of their sorrow, and this is the true way in which we love our neighbor, by knowing his need, by feeling his pain, by sharing his anguish, by bearing the burden of his sorrow, by pouring forth from our heart the love which God sends us. Only from such understanding and sympathy, from such compassion, can real help come.

A Jewish saint was dissatisfied with himself because he had not yet overcome the "weakness" of loving his own children more than others. A man came to the Baal Shem, complaining about his renegade son. Love him more, was the Baal Shem's advice.

We cannot all live on the spiritual heights of the Baal Shem or the Rabbi of Sasov, but compassion can become an attitude when God enters our lives. The Talmud characterizes Jews as *Rachmanin b'nai Rachmanim,* compassionate one's and the children of compassionate ones. We are taught that the great name of the Lord signifies compassion. It is not an exaggeration to say that one of the few remaining distinctively Jewish traits, despite our rapid assimilation, is compassion. To some extent, we still feel it, it has become embedded too deeply in the lives of our people to be lost in a few generations. Jews do respond to charitable needs with an extraordinary measure of generosity. Some say that Jews are a soft-hearted people. If it be true, then it is one of the rarest of possessions in a century outstanding in its lack of compassion.

The prayer of God Himself, the Talmud says, is a prayer for compassion: "May it be My will that My compassion may overcome Mine anger and that it may prevail over My Justice, and that I may deal with My children according to the attribute of compassion..."[23].

Prayer, humility and compassion, these, then, are three ways in which God enters the life of man. In terms of man's relation to heaven, He enters our lives in prayer; in terms of man's relation to himself, in humility; in terms of man's relation to his fellow man, in compassion. But these are not three lonely paths, each leading to a dead end. They are connected one to the other, for at the root of them all is God's love for man, and this can be expressed in the following way:

When God enters our lives, we are overwhelmed by the stream of his love, and our self-love, which is pride, gives way, making room for love for God, which is prayer. But our love for God, caused by the steady flow of God's love for us that we return,[24] cannot be con-

tained in the silver chalice of prayer, and so pours over into love for our fellow man, which is compassion.

The drama of our life intertwined with the life of God, receiving His love, sharing it and bestowing it upon others, is surely the most profound action of human existence, but for that love to enter us at all, we must first raise the many heavy barriers to our heart that we have so carefully erected over the years, opening the doors of the spirit we have locked in the way of His entrance. He loves us and yearns to be with us, but must stand outside the windows of our lives ever peering at shades which are tightly drawn—until *we* act. That is why it is best to end this essay with what we began:

The Rabbi of Kotzk surprised his learned friends with the question: Where does God dwell?, and had to answer his own query.

"God dwells," he replied, "wherever man lets Him in".

---

[23] *Berakhot,* 7a.

[24] That God's love for man precedes man's love for God is clearly indicated in the *Daily Prayer Book,* Singer, pp. 47-8.

# C. Israel

# UNIVERSAL AND PARTICULAR IN JUDAISM

SAMUEL S. COHON

TWO FACTS impress us as we reflect upon the world's religions: their essential likeness and their striking diversity. The likeness stems from the kinship of the human mind and from the similarity of men's basic needs. Religion is born of the soul's response, in reverent awe and humility, to the mysterious source of its being. All religions reach out after the divine and strain to discover the way of deliverance from the evils that threaten the individual and society and to endow life with significance and with worth. The diversity of religion represents variations of the common response to the holy.

What some brand as "the scandal of plurality" in religion is neither accidental nor incidental, but a necessary phase of individuality which inheres in the entire realm of human experience. Entering deeply into man's inner being, religion is by no means a purely personal matter. The individual exists not in isolation; he is inextricably bound up with society. This fact conditions his cultural as well as his physical being. His religious life too is inseparable from the community which maintains its distinctiveness and stamps it with a character of its own.

SAMUEL S. COHON is professor of Jewish theology at Hebrew Union College in Cincinnati. He edited the theology section of the Universal Jewish Encyclopedia, and is the author of *What We Jews Believe*, *Judaism: A Way of Life*, and other studies in Judaism.

## I

Both as personal and as social experience, religion reflects the character of the community which fosters it. Its development involves deviation from the original form, diversity. Like language, so religion expresses itself in the course of its growth in varied dialects and jargons. The factors that make for its differentiation must be sought in the mode of life of the people, in their physical environment, their political order and economic conditions as well as in the various psychic qualities which control their thinking and dreaming, and in the genius of their gifted leaders.

Religions are as particular as societies and civilizations are particular. Each religion is in fact the distillation of the particular civilization's attitude toward life and destiny. Even the rites, symbols, and ideas which religions have in common assume different significance among them. The beliefs in God, revelation, retribution, sin, atonement, soul, immortality, etc., are flavored by the emotions and cravings of the different religious bodies and are variously combined and interpreted.

Religion never appears in its pure essence or in its generic state, but in concrete, individualized forms, whether in the tribal and national cults of primitive society and antiquity or in the advanced faiths of Hinduism, Buddhism, Judaism, Christianity, and Islam. Their adjectival differentia are no less important for the understanding of religions than their common substantive. The universal comes to life and to power in the particular. Not religion in general, but the specific religions, have stirred the hearts of men.

The universal and the particular are organically interrelated. On all levels of its development, religion evolves a body of rites, ceremonies, and symbols related to the sacred. These practices are shaped by the processes of group life and by its adaptation to the geographic conditions, to its very flora and fauna. The climate, the fertility of the soil, and tribal or national vicissitudes affect the people's mores and religion. Practices of desert peoples naturally differ from those of fertile regions. Northern peoples react to the sense of the holy even as to the sense of beauty in ways that are foreign to men in the tropics.

The ceremonies and the symbols thus arising are not mere hollow forms. They are precious vessels preserving the feelings, the memories, and the ripe experience of the group and serve to unite their past with their present. Removed from ordinary use, reserved for special occasions and places, and entrusted to the guardianship of sacred persons, they acquire significance and value in the spiritual economy of the group.

The cult further contains the seed of moral and creedal development. It generally combines group mores with its ritual procedure and nurtures the standards of personal and group behavior which form the moral code of the community. Primitive religions produce simple legends and myths to express their notions of the totems and spirits that claim their reverence. In advanced religions, reflective thought concerns itself with the nature of the sacred and evolves philosophies and theologies which assign

meaning and purpose to the world and to human life. Reaching out beyond common experience to the invisible and the transcendent, the sacred turns into a life with God. Through the application of reason, it is formulated into beliefs and doctrines, which evoke the highest loyalties of the adherents of the particular religion, and help to unite them into a community.

These elements of cult, code of conduct, and creed belong together. Cut down one and the others are impaired. Once formed into a pattern, they become the abiding heritage of the community and continue long after the community has changed its original abode or its modes of economic and political life.

The civilization, culture and traditions of a people may be radically modified by gifted individuals. The role of leadership is decisive in every religion. In its primitive forms, medicine men, soothsayers and diviners exercise authority. In higher religions, organized priesthoods establish control, and often take over the political and cultural affairs as well. The great religions are dominated by prophetic personalities. Sages appear by their side to enrich faith with wisdom and holiness with righteousness and with compassion. Saints emerge to bear witness to the supreme values of the spirit. While these men of genius build upon the experience of their particular peoples, they enrich their traditions and raise them to universal heights.

A number of personalities so impressed themselves upon their faiths and so modified them with their original insights as to have created new religions. Through their own zeal or through the zeal of their devotees, their teachings were transfered to distant lands, and, in some instances, were forced upon nations with whose life-roots they had little or no connection. By virtue of the basic kinship of the human spirit, the new faiths found lodgement in the lives of the converted nations. Not alone the universal elements of creed and ethics but also the particularities of ritual and even the communal organization were transplanted through moral suasion or conquest. Such is the story of the missionary campaigns of Buddhism, Christianity, and Islam. In some places, the missionary faith was so thoroughly adjusted to the national spirit as to have shed some of its distinctive characteristics. Even where the conversion has been complete, the original faiths of the people have not been completely eradicated. Beneath the surface of the new religious forms and professions flow the deep currents of the old national habits and customs. Much of Norse and Roman paganism course beneath western Christianity. Periodically, the old heathenism bursts through the Christian consciousness to reassert its power over the souls of its people. The history of the church represents a continuous split into secular churches, which made peace with the deep-rooted mores and customs of the nations, and into ascetic monasticism, which fled from the world it set out to save. The one gave all to the Caesars; the other claimed all for God. Not being the natural fruitage of the experience of the nations, Christianity often remained a mere ornamentation, which easily disintegrated in times of stress. In their frenzy, the Nazis readily cast off the restraints of Christian belief and morality and took the German nation back to the abysmal depths of teutonic paganism and to the cult of the bloody heroes of the Valhalla. Consequently, instead of realizing the original inspiration of its founders of becoming the universal religion of humanity, Christianity itself has branched out into almost as many divisions as there are nations in Christendom, each of them encrusted in a hard shell of particularities of its own.

The complaint is often heard that religious diversity promotes divisiveness. Instead of achieving world unity, it keeps men apart in competing and conflicting bodies. To overcome this "scandal of plurality", some have persistently proposed the establishment of a universal faith to replace the existing religions. We must note that every missionary religion has set out to achieve this end, and has only added to the confusion it set out to remove. Even when free from zealotry and aggressiveness and inspired by the purest motives, the hope of the religious unification of all humanity fails to reckon with the actualities of life. Diversity rather than sameness characterizes human culture. It is as reasonable to expect all historical religions to merge into or to be replaced by one synthetic faith as it is for all national tongues to be reduced to one language. The history of the Volapuks and the Esperantos merely records artificial creations added to the existing dialects of men. So with religion. No *ersatz* can replace the historical faiths in evoking the devotion and the sacrifices of men. The cure for the "scandal of plurality" is not the impossible dream of converting all religions to one of them, but the process of education, of cultivating the spirit of understanding among religious leaders, of widening their sympathies for each other's faiths, and of perceiving and appreciating value wherever it may be found.

## II

The interconnection between the universal and the particular sheds light upon the nature and structure of Judaism. It is most literally immersed in the corporate life of Jewry and derives its name and individuality from its vital union therewith. Judaism represents the universal religious consciousness expressed in the particular historical experience of the Jewish people. Like the soul within the body, Judaism has animated and given direction to the Jewish people through the ages. It has shaped the Jewish social structure, and has colored its entire texture of culture, language, thought, tradition, art, and folkways.

Unlike Christianity, Judaism is fostered and preserved not by a church (or churches), held together by ecclesiastical and creedal bonds, but by the people that gave it birth and whose destiny is bound up with it. As the Jewish community, or *Keneset Yisrael,* differs from church communities, whether Catholic or Protestant, so Judaism differs from these faiths. Even the elements of ceremony and belief which the Church took over from Judaism have acquired distinctive meanings in consequence of the varying experiences of the respective bodies. The distinctions are clearer in some instances than in others, but they are present everywhere and can be ignored only at the cost of flattening out both religions and even of impairing their vitality and effectiveness.

Judaism traditionally traces its origin to supernatural revelation, i.e., to the disclosure of the divine purpose to the patriarchs, to Moses and to the prophets. The revelations concern themselves not with abstract principles but with the concrete needs and the well-being of the people. The prophetic personalities that lend glory to Judaism were called to their tasks by the crises that confronted Israel and Judah. In their highest flights, they did not lose touch with the hard realities of national life. They were children of their time and of their country. Hence the imprint of their genius upon their contemporaries and upon posterity. The student of Judaism can trace the rise and growth of its law and ritual, its ethical precepts and theological concepts, wheth-

er of biblical or of later times, to the changing economic, political, and social conditions of the people as well as to the insights of its leaders.

The fact that Judaism is the creation of the collective spirit of the Jewish people rather than of a single personality accounts for much that is distinctive in its forms of worship and in its attitude toward life. For example, its feasts and fasts commemorate not the birth or death of any founder but historic events in the life of Israel. The ancient pilgrim festivals — products of Canaanitic agricultural economy, in the first place — were invested with historical memories: Passover of the Exodus, Pentecost of the Sinaitic covenant and Tabernacles of the divine care during Israel's desert wandering. The minor festivals of Hanukkah and Purim, whatever their distant origins, celebrate the deliverance of the Jews from the threat of extermination. The fasts similarly commemorate black letter days in Jewish history. Even so spiritual a day as the Sabbath has been associated with the Exodus. Likewise, the great days of Rosh Hashana and Yom Kippur have been filled with devout striving for Jewish moral and spiritual well-being. Furthermore, they were not left as mere folk festivals, but were charged with deep religious significance. They have voiced the eternal ideals of human freedom, of divine law, of God's providence, sovereignty, and compassion, of man's chastening sense of sin and contrition, and of humanitarianism and joy in religion. The rituals of the holy days dwell on these themes and apply them to every phase of personal and social experience.

The ethics of Judaism, too, bears the stamp of the Jewish people. This fact becomes evident when we compare Christian with Jewish ethics. While the sanctification of life in all of its relations forms their common ideal, they differ in their emphasis and in mode of expression. In Christianity, the center of gravity is the individual. Without overlooking society, it has — as Mazzini noted — "for its end the salvation of the individual; for its means, the belief in a mediator between God and the individual; for its condition, grace". Godlikeness is manifested through Jesus, who is the pattern of divinity and the inspiration and cause of spiritual life for Christian believers. *Imitatio Christi* represents the highest ideal of Christian ethics. Judaism admits of no mediator between God and man, and consequently regards *Imitatio Dei* as its supreme ideal. Without ignoring the individual, its ethics is social. Its chief aim is the wellbeing of society, and its hope rests in the perfectibility of the human race. Its Messiah is not a personal redeemer from sin and from death, but a Davidic prince who establishes a righteous social order on earth. Its condition is not grace alone, but grace combined with righteousness. In its vision, the divine attribute of mercy is inseparable from the attribute of justice. Singly, they fall short of man's highest interests. Unitedly, they call forth moral order out of the chaos resulting from self-centeredness and from passion. Justice is tempered with love and is saved thereby from hardness; love is invigorated by justice and is consequently saved from dissolving into vapid sentimentality.

The social character of Jewish ethics is exemplified in the Pentateuchal legislation regarding the Sabbath, the sabbatical and jubilee years, and land tenure, and in its charity laws. It is reflected in the prophetic ideal of justice as the foundation of the state and the condition of peace between warring nations and between clashing classes within the nation. The social emphasis accounts likewise for Judaism's preoccupation with morality rather than with eschatology. Its

primary goal is not salvation of souls from damnation in the hereafter but the hallowing of the lives of men in the here and now. When the belief in the other world took hold of the Jewish mind, it was conceived as a moral balance for men's behavior while on earth.

While flowing within a channel of its own, the religious stream of Judaism was kept pure from the taint of narrow and self-seeking nationalism. Its response to the holy, its attitude toward life and duty, its ideas of God, of the individual and of the nation are of the very essense of universal religion. Historical circumstances prevented Judaism from carrying out its initial impulse of spreading its message in all lands and among all races of men. Rival religions, backed by the power of political states, drove Judaism from the field of missionary endeavor. But they have not obscured the universality of Judaism's message. The Torah did not remain the exclusive heritage of the congregation of Jacob. According to the rabbis, it was given in the wilderness, in a no-man's land, and proclaimed in all the seventy tongues of men so that no one nation might claim proprietary rights in it. At Sinai, another midrash states, the souls of all the future proselytes along with those of the coming generations of Jews were present. The light of the Torah was intended for all men. The prophets, too, while addressing themselves to their own people and dealing with local and particular conditions, transcended the bounds of their nation, and made an irresistible appeal to all who hunger and thirst for the word of the living God.

Out of Zion thus went forth the law both in its universal forms of ideas and ethical standards and in its particular expression as modes of worship and even as conceptions of the religious community. The phophet's word, "My house shall be called a house of prayer for all peoples", was actualized in a surprising manner. The church set itself up as the "new Israel". Its organization, its worship and its teaching were in great part derived from the synagogue. Literally from the ends of the earth, men have turned to the word of God which came from Jerusalem for salvation. Western civilization has had Judaism as one of its parents. The thought and conduct of a large part of humanity have been shaped by the Hebrew Bible and by its standards of right. Its very literalism still sets the pattern of faith and duty for vast numbers of men of many races and tongues. Directly, through the labors of the Jewish people and the Bible, and indirectly, through the church and the mosque, Judaism has leavened a great part of civilization and has affected its moral standards, laws, thought, rituals, creed, art, and literature.

### III

The organic relationship between the universal and the particular has been maintained throughout the history of Judaism. There were times when they almost fell apart and appeared in opposition to one another. Like two rival souls, they seemed to struggle against each other for the exclusive possession of the Jewish body. When storms raged, the nationalistic-particularistic elements asserted themselves, and the entire aim and purpose of Judaism was confined to the struggle for Jewish self-preservation. When the skies brightened and the winds died down, the universalistic element came to the fore with the emphasis on the world mission of Judaism. In reality, as we have pointed out, the two do not contradict but supplement each other. They constitute the centripetal and centrifugal forces that help keep Judaism effective. Its particularism saves it from sinking into characterless theism or from becoming a mere variant of natural

religion. Its universalism preserves it from the no less serious danger of becoming self-sufficient, separatistic and narrow.

The contemporary task of Judaism is to safeguard both the unity and the harmonious balance of the two elements. The liberal temper among Jews as among other people tends to underestimate and to disregard the particular and to stress the universal to the point of reducing religion to psychological states of feeling and to humanistic ideals. With some liberals universalism may serve as a cloak for the destruction of the specific character of Judaism. As in Paulinian thought so in certain contemporary conceptions of Judaism, what is left of the Torah is a series of negations. The concrete embodiment of its spirit in definite observances and forms congenial to the Jewish people and their way of life are discarded as obsolete and worthless. Like disembodied souls, the universal ideas are expected to float on the ether. The very concept of community as applied to the Jews has been challenged by representatives of this trend.

Jewish liberals defeat the universalistic ideals they profess by limiting themselves to vague sentiments and broad principles without translating them into modes of living. Ideas of the holy like those of the good, the true, and the beautiful are deprived of power when denied expression in community life and when not supplied with educationally potent media of ritual observance on the personal, domestic, and congregational levels. The monition of the ancient sages against separating oneself from the community has not lost its pointedness for our day. He who does not share the life and tasks of the congregation impairs the effectiveness of its spiritual values, no matter how interested he may be in them intellectually. Platonic religion like platonic love is a poor substitute for the real thing.

Particularism, in turn, runs the danger of self-insulation, of becoming parochial and bigoted. Sectarianism replaces the idea of *Kelal Yisrael*. Cutting itself off from the high tide of the spirit, it refuses to recognize truth and value outside of its own cabined view. Every manifestation of Jewish belief and practice that is not in accord with its particular tradition or *minhag* is ipso facto spurious and a perversion of true Judaism. This type of zealotry strangely appears among certain liberals as well as among some conservatives. The boundary assumes sanctity for them as an end in itself, and differences rank above agreements. External distinctions rather than inner worth form their test of value.

The chief hazard of particularism consists in the shift of interest from religion to the community. In this country, for example, we have thrown ourselves with might and main in the effort to integrate ourselves into American life and have attained marked success. How to preserve our favorable position and how to remove the irritants of anti-Jewish prejudice and discrimination, which crop up here and there, have claimed the solicitude of our local and national leaders and defence organizations. However, while protecting the Jewish body, we run the danger of losing the Jewish spirit and of shedding our religious ideals. Vast numbers of Jews, both in the large cities and in rural communities, are detached from religious life. A large percentage of our children receive no religious training whatever. The various bodies devoted to the propagation of Judaism and of Jewish knowledge have barely scratched the surface. For all the magnificent synagogues and social centers, to which we point with pride, a great part of American Jewry remains untouched by the spirit of Judaism. Even for many affiliated Jews, religion has become a mere side interest. This situation demands the most earnest attention of our lay and rabbinical leadership. From a people of bearers of a religious covenant we are being transformed into a mere aggregate of Jews by the accident of birth. We can have no illusions as to the fate that awaits such an amorphous body in democratic America, where the melting pot operates with sure thoroughness. Without our spiritual heritage, we are lost.

The shift from the religious to the national presents the State of Israel with special problems. The chain of events that has led to her establishment as a political state has imposed upon her the inescapable obligation of devoting her best energies in defence against the various threats to her existence amid the hostile forces of the Near East. Fighting for her place in the sun and concentrating upon her economic, military, and diplomatic problems, Israel must be specially on her guard against losing her historic character as a religious people. History abounds in instances in which the attributes of secular nationalism have crowded out the religious spirit or relegated it to the background. We remember how readily religious elements were absorbed into the national ethos in Nazi Germany and how certain church bodies subordinated themselves to the will of National Socialism. Religious symbols, festivals, and rituals were diverted from their original purpose and turned into instruments of national pride and aggressive militarism.

Jewish nationalism, we trust, will never sink to such depths of depravity. Nevertheless, there is the danger of its coming to dominate the religious conscience of the people or of even setting itself up as a substitute for religion. In fact, the state of religion in Israel is itself quite confused. Instead of serving as a steady light for the entire country, religion in Israel seems to have set itself up along political lines, serving as a party platform and thereby inviting the opposition of the other parties. It is bent on winning elections, holding parliamentary seats, and forming part of coalition governments with the view to securing power and prestige. The ghost of ancient Sadduceeism seems to be stalking in the guise of present-day political clericalism.

The cry persists for the separation of "church and state" in Israel. If by such separation is meant the removal of ecclesiastical control from the government and its agencies, both religion and the state stand to benefit. An unfettered state with full guarantees of freedom of thought and conscience can be of greatest service to religion. However, if — as there is ground for fearing — the removal of all influence of Judaism upon the conduct of the state is intended, separation would mean spiritual disaster. In healthy democracies, religion works like a leaven in the life of the public, affecting the thinking and the action of the people, exercising the right to criticize the government, the political parties, the labor unions, and the policies of the nation. In Israel, too, religion's prophetic task cannot be confined to singing hallelujahs about whatever the governing bodies design and execute. Religion must ever probe all domestic and foreign policies in the light of its highest visions and standards, to approve when there is ground for approval and to condemn when occasion demands.

True to its own character, Judaism sums up the profoundest truths of universal religion about life's deepest problems and stamps with its own genius the conceptions of God, the soul, faith, and duty. It is an ever-growing body of spiritual values, centering around the Fatherhood of God and the brotherhood of man, and held together as a historical entity by its organic connection with the Jewish people. As an unbroken chain of tradition, Judaism links all the generations of Israel. As the goal of the future, it must ever keep alive its original insights. As a Torah, it must continue to chart the way for the individual and for society. As prophecy, it must preserve the passion for righteousness and strive for the establishment of the kingdom of God. As wisdom, it must discover the way of overcoming evil and teach men how to invest their lives with meaning and with purpose.

# A CONTEMPORARY ATTEMPT AT THE PERENNIAL QUESTIONS

## Z. M. SCHACHTER

Philosophy and theology have been in the business of answering mankind's basic questions for thousands of years. The questions have not varied. They are basic ones. Only the degree of emphasis given to a particular question has changed. But the answers to these questions have differed due to changes in societies as well as in the psychology of individuals who constitute them. Thus each generation has given its own answers to the basic questions, for each generation creates its own vocabulary created in its own imagery.

We Jews have an unbroken history of answering the basic questions in terms of Torah and Mitzvoth set in a framework of Divine values and a general willingness to respond to the cosmic challenge. The willingness expresses itself in actualizing the response in terms of behavior, structured as Divine Commandments, into which the naming of historic and personal experience is read.

The "perennial questions" of Jewish theology —God, Torah and Israel—have in our days been interpreted in conceptual contexts that may be denominated as theistic, naturalistic and existential. Here, employing a dialogic framework but going beyond it to include the categories of *It* and *He*, the author essays a fresh solution of the problems, perennial and contemporary, implicit in the Jewish triad. The use of certain Kabbalistic concepts in the scheme of thought here advanced bespeaks a new and unconventional use of Kabbalistic and Hasidic teaching.

The challenge of the *great questions* is the problem of the so-called great "scandal": If there is a God Who is infinite in power, how can He be Personal? And if He is Personal and loves, how can He permit disease and pain and evil? And if He permits disease and pain and evil, how can we believe that He loves? If He is Omnipotent, why does He not help when we pray to Him? And if He loves and yet does not help, can we still believe that He is Omnipotent? The problem *as stated* does not admit a solution. This is not to say that there have not been many attempts at solving the problem as stated. There have been attempts, for instance, to provide answers in terms of free-will and determination. Some of these answers have made God more Absolute than Loving, others have made Him more Loving than Absolute. To retain both seemed impossible. The only feasible thing was to compromise the—for the individual—less important loading of the word God, for the sake of the one that was more important. The fullness contained in the word God consequently was emptied; thus compromised God began to suffer from an anemic "mereness."

Possibly a different way of looking at the problem might yield a more satisfactory answer, one which would not empty the human God-idea of His di-

319

vine fullness, of multi-dimensionality. We need a God Who is Personal, yet Infinite, Who is loving, yet unmoved by human demands, some One Who can fit the description of "Thou Who changest not"; while yet enabling us to petition "abide with me"; some One Who is Creator, Father, Friend, yet is Eternal, Omnipotent, the Prime Mover, Who while being All-Inclusive is still Infinitely Unique. We have these needs because on the one hand we *feel* that only a Personal God would care, love and help. On the other hand we *reason* that the Infinite, all-remote Power is the only God concept we can permit ourselves, for only that would make sense and not reduce God to a fetish. And intuition tells us that *feeling* and *reason* are not mutually exclusive. We need both the person and the impersonal aspects of the Divine to deal with the problems of our human complexity. God, to be sure, is One and Simple. However, our ideas of God are caught in words, and words being dimensions of thought, create complexities.

Let us start out with the premise of the Infinite God in an Infinite number of co-ordinate dimensions and let us explore first three of these infinite dimensions: the dimension of *It*, the dimension of the *He,* and the dimension of the *Thou.* By calling them "co-ordinate dimensions" we indicate that we are dealing with conceptual tools, whose descriptive utility help us to systematize our thinking.

We define the *It* dimension of God as the concept of the Supreme Being—the philosopher's God—all Powerful and all fulfilled, in perfection. This God of consummate Equilibrium, not needing, not seeking nor wanting anything, is identical with the traditional *Eyn Soff* (the Endless) of the Kabbalah. In the *Eyn Soff* there is no distinction between Creator and creature, since in *It* neither of these terms apply. There is no differentiation between "space" and "time," since the Infinite fills and *is* all. The *Eyn Soff* existed before time began, before space was "made," and is now the very same, the *Eyn Soff*.

The simplicity of the One rules supreme; He is the God Who was and Who will be, without change and without a peer. This is the God of the mystic and the atheist, because while the theist insists that the God in Whom he does not believe could only be an *It*-God, the mystic is intoxicated with the Absoluteness the *It* concept of God implies. While reason dictates that God must be as remote as all this, yet we must face creation, nature and thinghood. We must explore another dimension: the *He* of God.

The *He* of God stands for the concepts of the Creator of Nature and the universe, the Prime Mover, the Planner and Originator of space and time. To the *He* of God we can give a name. The Biblical name is *Elohim*. *Elohim* is a plural form and provides room for the plurality of existence and for a God Who emanates creation and Who is Omnipotent. In these roles of the absolute God is not to be influenced and cannot be reached by our prayers. There is no way of making Him change the laws of His creation. As a result, *He* is blamed for permitting suffering. But *He* is the God Who causes evolution and being without Himself becoming involved. *He* exists without being and relating. *He* is in nature's terms a permissive God Who does not care. Moral and ethical criteria do not apply to Him. *He* creates man only to forsake him, as it were. *He* is the scientists' God. *He* is the expert Designer Whose Mind is discernible in His works. But in our human predicaments, we have no concern for the purposes of His plans. *He* overwhelms us. We stand in awe before His unbendingness, and cannot do anything but submit to Him. We conclude that *He* has some purpose, but this purpose cannot be discerned by us. And, just as we cannot reach Him, we cannot elicit a response from Him. Consequently, other than realizing His plan and design, an intellectual need (or luxury?), we as human beings have no need of Him. The God Who can help and Who relates to us, cannot be found in the *He* dimension. We must look for Him on a different level—the level of *Thou*.

God as *Thou* is Father and Helper. He needs us as much as we need Him. He is the moral God Who cares enough to reveal Himself and to relate to man. *Thou* is the One Who redeems even if it impinges on the majesty of His Omnipotence. He restricts His Power because He-as-*Thou* so loves us that He joins us in our limitations. Jewish tradition identifies the *Thou* with the *Sh'chinnah*, the Divine Presence which we are capable of encountering. *Thou* is the God Whom our mothers addressed as "*Gottenyu*," of Whom the Bible states that "in all their oppression was He oppressed." (Isaiah 63:9) All our striving, our life and our love, relates us to *Thou*. Since *Thou* relates to us, *Thou* demands a *Thou*-like life, morally and ethically, and sets conditions for His dwelling with us. *Thou* is the loving Father Who bears the prayers, of His children and helps them. *Thou* is the Benign King Who directs the lives of His subjects. *Thou* is the Teacher. *Thou* is He Who remains forever our Father. And *Thou* is person, if by person we mean personality possessed of will, drive, intelligence, feeling, joy and empathy.

God is this and more. In our limited way we have merely touched three conceptual aspects of God. But this is not enough, we must attempt to understand how *It* can be *He* and *Thou*—and so much more, simultaneously. An analogy is presented by the dimension of length, width and depth of corporeal things. Length, width, and depth do not preclude other dimensions in terms of weight, time, electrical capacity, heat and nuclear radiation. We must remember, however, that we have never seen any of these dimensions in isolation. We have met them only joined inseparably together. A prayerful approach now yields the attitude in which it is possible to think of the *It*, *He*, and *Thou* as One.

The motive of the personal *Thou* and the infinite potential of the transcendental *It* explains why *He* creates the actual universe. In the *He*-created universe, the *It* cannot be met save as *Thou*. The *Thou* and the *He* derive their Divine transcendental value from their identity with the *It*.

We can now begin to see that the scandal was our own doing. Because we flattened (at least) three dimensions into a one-dimensional line, we created "scandalous" contradictions. Perpendicular concepts relate in a "plastic" manner. Their angular coherence constitutes no inner contradiction. Besides resolving the "scandal" this approach helps us in other ways also. An absolutist's concept of God leaves little room for man to act. His questions are often answered in terms of "My thoughts are not your thoughts." (Isaiah 55:8). A purely immanentist relativism leaves us without the "Highest," without God. For the traditional *HVYH*, the *Thou*, one claims on the one hand utter transcendence—"I *HVYH* have not changed"(Mal.

3:6)—while at the very same time, this statement is addressed to man.

*Thou* is the Infinite-Minus-One, never quite finite. *Thou* makes room for man in the cosmic scheme of things. *Thou* challenges man to add his own one to the Infinite-Minus-One. *Thou* thus is the self-limitation of the *It-He,* in Whom we see ourselves as true partners, sharing with God the anticipation of a blessed state of things, His efforts to bring about this state, and His *Naches* over the conversion of evil. The root of *real* evil (not merely the evil which results from an absence of good) inheres in His self-limitation to become a *Thou.* *It* is not opposed by a non-It, *He* is not opposed by a non-He; *It* and *He* are infinitely Infinite. But *Thou* is *Thou* only when faced by the "I" (of man). When man does not face *Thou,* he faces "Non-Thou," another side of reality, the *Sittra Achra.* "Non-Thou" is a vast energy system in its own right. While boldly real (on the *Thou* continuum) it has no transcendental reality of its own. Its main function is to energize the man who chooses not to face the *Thou.* It is dynamic because when enough men yield to its charms, (and these are great because they allow man to live in a self-centered conceit in which he is not answerable to a *Thou*) it grows to catastrophal proportions. Man is thus the cosmic valve which can choose to divert *He*-energies to the "other side," and *He*-energies are amoral to begin with. Or, if man chooses to yield his will to the *Thou,* the slow redemptive process of *T'shuvah* begins. Not only is man redeemed in his "turning" to face the *Thou* but also God is extricated from the energy system of Non-Thou. The "other side" is weakened to the extent that it finally needs the proviso of the "scapegoat" and the after-meal finger-bowl water to stay in business.

We are not in isolation when we work with other "ones" of the Infinite-Minus-One equation. *"Love thy neighbor"* who *"like Thyself"* is capable of redeeming Me. *"I am HVYH"* and stand in need of being redeemed by man. In this sense the Torah is not only not Man's theology, but it is the Thou-ing guide in God's anthropology. It shows how man, facing a chunk of reality, can call forth from it the *Thou* in the four ells of Halakhah, which our sages termed God's Sanctuary in an upset world. In the face of such Divine need, Israel has no choice but to say "We shall do and obey." (Exodus 19:8) Were it not for the Messianic hope that "On that day He will be One and His Name One" (Zachariah 14:9) one would tend to despair. The hope that the "Non-Thou" will ultimately be annihilated, the growing joy which the little victories gained by Mitzvoth against the "Non-Thou" afford, are, to one sensitive to the *Thou's* plight, reward enough. The echo resounds every day: "Turn children" and "Woe to creation for despising Torah!" He who gives ear, hears it and responds.

If our method of reappraising the perennial questions has shown some usefulness, we may apply it to the problems which are specific to Jews, the problems of Torah and revelation. Again we examine the three co-ordinates, while realizing that they do not exhaust the possible dimensions. We then posit the dimension of *Torah where it is altogether Divine.* On that level, God by Himself and for Himself studies the Torah. There, it is God's Will and Wisdom relating to Himself as thought. The process of Divine Intellection and Volition is for us this first dimension of Torah, *It*-Torah.

Then we posit the level of *Thou*-Torah where the *dialogue between God and* man takes place. This dialogue occurs even right now, in the most immediate fashion, without the mediation of the written word, or despite the revelation of the written word. Our self-referring concern with *this* problem makes it Torah. This is so if a prayerful readiness for consecrated action is the ground for our study and concern. At the very moment when this is being written, and when this is being read, some of this dialogue-process occurs; therefore this can truly be called Torah.

The *revelation event, He*-Torah, constitutes our third coordinate. A series of acts once took place and established certain norms and data. At that time, and in succeeding times, we related to these data in a definite fashion. Yesterday's dialogue Torah, as a written document, is today's *He*-Torah! A fact is a numinous entity. It possesses its own "so-be-ingness" regardless of the definition we give it today and of who gives it definition and meaning. But this fact, like other facts, brings with itself certain phenomena. From its internal frame of reference, the Torah-documents before us today claim to be a literal revelation of God in terms of ritual, moral and ethical demands upon man, within a framework of historic events, in which the Exodus factor is the hub. Our liturgy constantly reminds us to give meaning to observances in terms of the Exodus factor: *"Zecher Li'ytziath Mitzrayim."* The corollary of *He*-Torah is the factor of Mitzvoth which establish the renewal of the God-human event in a total God and total man fashion.

In the aspect of Mitzvoth the Torah seeks to unite man and to relate him to the Will of God. This is not a self-seeking factor of conscience, but a unitive process. It takes place simultaneously in the many dimensions of man and the many dimensions of God. It unites and frees the *It-He-Thou* to respond as a Whole to man. The revelation event which in this field becomes defined, stands immutably in the past. Yet, since it is man whom God addresses in the Torah, He must speak man's language. (The rabbis said that He did: *"Dib'ra Torah bil'shon b'nai adam."*)

God reduces Himself by speaking man's langauge. This language, *Lashon Hakodesh*, no matter how perfect and Divine, communicates to us. It is bound by the law of semantics. This law simply states that different words mean different things to different people at different times. It is for this reason that *He*-Torah alone is not enough. Halakhic principle recognizes this and consequently gives rules for interpretation, plus the dicta of *"Halakhah l'Moshe missinai"* to man in order that he may engage in *"Torah she b'al Peh,"* dialogue-Torah.

*Dialogue-Torah* by itself can lead one into the error of subjectivism. Event-and-fact-**Torah** can lead one into the tomb of the dead letter. Neither dialogue-Torah nor event-Torah would be of value if it were not for the level on which God for Himself and by Himself studies it. Each one of these Torah levels represents another dimension of the very same thing. The level of *He*-Torah on which *"Eyn hamikro yotze mip'shuto"* (no Bible verse altogether loses its patent meaning) is intersected by the *dialogue*-Torah, which permits the gaining and testing of meaning to gain semantic clarity and the growth of reinterpretation in terms of *Chiddush*-dynamics. *Chiddush* is the gaining of new insights and new approaches and the deriving of new meaning from a given sentence or Halakhah. *Chiddush* is constantly at work in *dialogue*-Torah. *Chiddush*, a necessity in the Halakhic field, rejects *Shinnua* (change of the text and the intention). The dialogue approach demands the prayerful humility of man, the pupil before God his Teacher. In this dialogue-paradox of unassuming humility, the presumptious arrogance that man can determine what God wants him to do, is present. The student tacitly affirms that his Divine Teacher right now concerns Himself with Halakhah.

There are at least four recognized levels of dialogue passing between men and God: (a) the evident—the *P'shatt;* (b) the inferred—the *Remez;* (c) the implied-associated—the *D'rash;* and (d) the most individual secret—*Sod.* The *P'shatt* relates to action, the *Remez* to yet undefined actions, the *D'rash* to meaning for the group and the individual, and the *Sod* to the meaning most highly individual in man's intercourse with God. The *P'shatt*-decreed action becomes legislation (*Gesetz*) in *Remez.* *D'rash* turns it into commandment (*Gebot*). In *Sod,* it has been transformed in mystery (*Geheimnies*). So high can one reach in Torah, that one almost is able to attain to this level of Torah where God studies Torah Himself. A person so united with God, so identified with Him, so yearning to know what Torah means to God Himself, would merit to share a reflection of the dimension of *Sod.*

The Torah which God studies for Himself is not given to everyone. Those who have been graced with *Sod*-insights realize that these insights grow out of the dialogue situation. Highly subjective and individual, they are meaningful only to one's own self. Such Torah must never be made to bind others. But each individual is quite free to merge with it for all that it is worth to himself in terms of deeper living. *"Drosh v'Kabbel s'char* (Expound and receive your reward)."

It seems clear that man's part in the Torah is quite great. Moses' part in the written Torah is immense. Chassidism has it that Moses got God to commit Himself to a certain set of actions in which He would allow Himself to be swerved. The field of Mitzvah-actions is described in the Talmud as the four ells of Halakha: God's sanctuary with each individual Jew. In this private domain, man frees and unites God.

In this *Gestalt* of God-Torah-Jew the question of whether God revealed Himself to other nations is meaningless. This field of God-Torah-Jew does not appear anywhere else. But no man can prevent God from holding dialogue with anyone else. God is yet free to relate and establish covenants with whomever He wants. "I will favor whom I will favor and I will pity whom I will pity." (Exodus 33:19).

All three levels, *It-, He-* and *Thou*-Torah, of which we have spoken, are the levels of *Torath HVYH.* We also gain insights from nature and its laws. *Thou*-Torah or *HVYH*-Torah relates only to the God-Torah-Jew field. The insights of nature belong to *Elokim*-Torah and transcend the insights of *HVYH*-Torah. *Elokim*-Torah does not permit dialogue, only observation and experiment. In the Sinai experience, *He*-Torah does not enter. God did not state: "I am the God Who created heavens and earth," but rather "I am the Lord your God Who redeemed you out of Egypt."

Do *Thou-(HVYH)*-Torah and *He-(Elohim)*-Torah ever conflict or contradict one another? Yes, as subject and object they contradict one another. But object may also be subject. Reality is One, and as *Thou*-Torah and *He*-Torah are dimensions of that Reality, they cannot contradict one another but are merely perpendicular to one another. Both *Thou*-Torah and *He*-Torah meet ("as if") with the *It*-Torah on the level on which God studies the Torah. Thus, we now see where the three levels which we posited in Torah also coincide. We might allow ourselves to step back, look at all this at once, and feel the complex pluralities melt and merge into a monistic whole. This almost visual experience can serve as a springboard for a leap of faith.

Continuing our method in the realm of Israel, we may posit an *It*-Jew, a *He*-Jew and a *Thou*-Jew.

Each time we face the question "What is a Jew?" we find that racial, national, and religious definitions are offered. Mutually exclusive, these definitions give all kinds of Jews a hold on their Jewishness. Somehow, we find solace in statistics dealing with finger-prints, in which those of the Litvack, the Yemenite and the Cochin Jew have a closer relationship than those of non-Jews. Figures on IQ's and alcoholism, cancer of the penis and womb, etc., all give us, if not absolute proof, then at least a crutch for our favorite prejudice that a Jew is somehow different. Despite our affirmations that we are just like everybody else, we take a hidden pleasure in being "only more so."

Hitler's campaign was directed against the *It*-Jew: one who has a whole row of maternal Jewish ancestors, is still a Jew in our books. The *He*-Jew is the one who acts for his people, he is a part of his people. He is deeply concerned with the survival of a Jewish people and culture. The individual matters less than the whole in this dimension. All means are considered good if they are conducive to survival. The *He*-Jew lives not in the supernatural realm. He is at home with the *He*-God. His is a religion without supernaturalism. His Torah is a historic event and valuable if it will make for a vague survivalist salvation. The *He*-Jew feels entitled to modify *He*-Torah so that it may yield the greatest pragmatical survival results.

The *Thou*-Jew is the one who unites God, who in studying Torah evolves a continuous dialogue of revelation. The *Thou*-Jew unites the *It*-Jew and the *He*-Jew with God and with Torah. This he does not by *being* a Jew but by *jewing* (read this as a verb).

Other languages relish nouns and adjectives. Biblical Hebrew relishes the verb. It is not the best language for abstraction. Qualities and entities are not its forte. If God, Torah, or Jew are seen as such (that is as entities and qualities) it may help one to construe them in universes of discourse that are useful, but not for *jewing*. The sacred Name *HVYH* denotes the constant action of giving-being. Torah denotes the action of teaching. *Ivri*—Jew—denotes the action of transcending. The *Thou*-Jew unites God, Torah and Israel into a dynamic whole by *jewing*. And a Jew *jews* when he *"davens," "learns,"* and does Mitzvoth.

# JEWISH EXISTENCE AND SURVIVAL:

# A THEOLOGICAL VIEW

WILL HERBERG

## I

I T IS the purpose of this paper to present some comments on the problem of Jewish existence and survival from a theological point of view. This is obviously not the only standpoint from which the problem may be discussed; there are as many standpoints as there are levels of existence and categories of explanation. But to the believing Jew the theological standpoint must in some sense be primary and normative, for it is the standpoint from which all problems are seen in their ultimate bearing. If theology is to mean anything at all, if it is to be more than idle speculation or scholastic word-play, it must be recognized as relevant to all concerns of life and as providing a frame of reference more comprehensive than that provided by any less ultimate standpoint and yet including them all within its scope. Less than any other, it seems to me, can the problem of Jewish existence be understood apart from the perspectives of theology; any attempt to deal with it in exclusively or even mainly non-theological terms must necessarily result in danger-

ous distortion and falsification. The findings of psychology, sociology, and history are obviously important, here as elsewhere, but they can have no real meaning in this context unless they are integrated into the conception of the nature and destiny of Israel with which theology provides us.

## II

No one seriously concerned with the problem of Jewish existence will challenge the conclusion of the distinguished sociologist, Carl Mayer, to the effect that "the Jewish people represent a sociologically unique phenomenon and defy all attempts at general definition" ("Religious and Political Aspects of Anti-Judaism", *Jews in a Gentile World*, ed. Graebner and Britt, p. 312). Being a Jew does not in itself mean belonging to a particular race, or to a particular nation, or to a particular culture, or even to a particular religious denomination. Many and diverse "racial" strains are to be found among Jews; Jews have the most varied national origins, allegiances, and cultures; and even those Jews who renounce the Jewish religion or religion in general somehow remain Jews. Yet though we must recognize that Jewishness is neither a racial nor a national nor a cultural nor a religious fact, we cannot deny that somehow each of these factors is in some

WILL HERBERG is author of *Judaism and Modern Man: An Interpretation of Jewish Religion*, recently published by Farrar Straus and Young and the Jewish Publication Society.

way relevant to it. But what Jewish existence is does not emerge from any of them singly, nor from any combination of them nor even from all of them together. The "secret" of Jewish existence is obviously something that transcends these or any other categories that the social scientist is able to devise. "The phenomenon [of Jewish existence] does not fit any of the usual patterns — idealistic or positivistic — by which we try to read the pages of history" (Mayer, *op. cit.*, p. 316).

Calling the Jews a "people" does not help very much. For if "people" is used in the familiar sense of ethnic and cultural community (as in "German people", "Irish people", "American people"), it obviously does not apply to the Jews, and if it is used in a different and unique sense, it does not tell us anything about the nature of Jewish existence. The term "people" may, of course, be employed, but it has to be defined in some fundamental way or else it will possess no meaning and merely serve to confuse and obscure the real problem.

Nor does it make much sense to speak of the "plural sources" of Jewishness. Granted that one or another aspect of Jewish existence may be most prominent in Jewish life in a particular time or situation, the question still remains as to what unites all the varied forms of existence under the one category of "Jewishness" and permits us to speak of phenomena that apparently have nothing in common as if they were all manifestations of a single reality. If Jewish existence is really and irreducibly plural, then it is not one, and the term "Jewish existence" or "Jewishness" is meaningless. If, on the other hand, the term has meaning, it must point to a reality that transcends and underlies all "plural" manifestations.

This reality cannot be indicated or defined in purely naturalistic, purely empirical terms. "The existence of Israel is something unique, unclassifiable. This name...marks the community as one that cannot be grasped in the categories of sociology or ethnology" (Martin Buber, in *Theologische Blätter*, Sept. 1933). Every attempt to give meaning to the concept of Jewishness in naturalistic terms must necessarily end in failure and lead to the conclusion that the concept is empty of intrinsic content and really refers to a "nothing" generated out of a persistent historical delusion shared by Jew and non-Jew. This, in essence, is Sartre's view and it has been held, in more or less sophisticated forms, by a considerable number of people in the past century. On a naturalistic and positivistic basis, there is no other conclusion to reach. The obvious implication is total assimilation.

Jewish existence seems to me to acquire meaning only in terms of the categories of biblical and rabbinic theology. In the normative biblical-rabbinic view, Israel is not a "natural" nation; it is, indeed, not a nation at all like the nations of the world. It is a *supernatural* community, called into being by God to serve his eternal purposes in history. It is a community created by God's special act of covenant, first with Abraham whom he "called" out of the heathen world and then, supremely, with Israel collectively at Sinae. Jewish tradition emphasizes the unimportant and heterogeneous character of the People Israel apart from God's gracious act of election which gives it the significance it has in the scheme of world destiny. The covenant of election is what brought Israel into existence and keeps it in being, today just as truly as at Sinai; apart from the covenant, Israel is as nothing and Jewish existence a mere delusion. The covenant is at the very heart of the Jewish self-understanding of its own reality.

We miss the entire meaning of the covenant if we think of it as something that depends for its power and reality upon the voluntary adherence of the individual Jew. The covenant, in biblical-rabbinic faith, is not a private act of agreement and affiliation; it is not a contract that becomes valid only when the individual Jew signs it. Indeed, the individual Jew would not be a Jew in any intelligible sense were he not *already* under the covenant, whether he knows it or not, whether he likes it or not. The covenant is an objective supernatural fact; it is God's act of creating and maintaining Israel for his purposes in history.

The vocation for which Israel was created through the covenant is made clear in the biblical and rabbinic writings. Israel is to be unto God a "kingdom of priests and a holy nation". It is to stand witness, in word and deed, to the living God against the idolatries of the world. It is to be a "light to the nations", the dedicated Servant of the Lord appointed to serve mankind. That this vocation involves suffering and martyrdom all history testifies; how could it be otherwise? But it is this vocation and this vocation alone that gives meaning to *Jewish* existence whether individual or collective. "He [God] chose Israel" — so Dr. Louis Finkelstein summarizes the Jewish teaching on the subject — "to be his suffering servant, to bear persecution with patience, and by precept and example to bring his word to all the peoples of the world" (*The Beliefs and Practices of Judaism*, p. 25). This remains the vocation of Israel just as much, though in a somewhat different way, after the emergence of Christianity as divine instrument for bringing the God of Israel to the gentiles as it was before. It will continue to be the God-appointed vocation of Israel until the "last day".

Israel as covenant-folk is a community running through history but also transcending it. Professor Baron describes the prophetic conception of Israel as "the idea of a Jewish people beyond state and territory, a divine instrument in man's overcoming of 'nature' through a supernatural process in the course of 'history'" (*A Social and Religious History of the Jews*, vol. i, pp. 83–4). It is this duality of Jewish existence in time and in eternity that is responsible both for the tension of "abnormality" of Jewish life and for its spiritual creativity. To try to overcome it — to try to "normalize" Jewish existence in any fundamental sense — means to try to make the People Israel "like unto the nations" and thus to rob it of its very reason for existence. However much confusion such efforts may produce, they cannot succeed, for they run counter to the divine purpose in the creation and election of Israel.

Israel lives in both time and eternity. The People Israel, supernatural and superhistorical though it is, because it lives *in* history must always find concrete embodiment in some particular historical form. Or rather it would be more accurate to say, various sections of the covenant-folk find particular historical embodiments, depending on time, place, and circumstance — sometimes as a nation, as once and now again in Palestine; sometimes as a national minority, as in eastern Europe for many centuries; sometimes as a self-contained cultural group, as formerly in the United States; sometimes as a religious "denomination", though paradoxically including non-religious Jews as well, as in this country today. But whatever may be the particular forms of Jewish existence — and I have mentioned only some — they are all merely relative, transient, and localized; underlying and yet transcending them is Israel as covenant-people. Were it not for the identity of Israel as covenant-people there would be no basis of existence for these particular communities and no bond of unity among them.

In this light, we can understand the nature of Judaism. *Judaism is the Jew's authentic covenant-existence.* Every Jew is under the covenant, whether by birth or adoption; and once under the covenant, his covenant-existence is an objective fact independent of his will. His position is analogous to that of a son, whose sonship confers a status upon him independent of his will or consent. The son is indeed confronted with a crucial decision: to be a good son or a bad son, to live up to or to repudiate the responsibilities of sonship — but no matter what he does or desires to do, he cannot make himself not a son of his father. So too the Jew. He is confronted with a crucial, life-determining choice; to acknowledge and try to live up to or to repudiate the responsibilities of his Jewish covenant-existence — but no matter what he does, he cannot remove himself from under the covenant and its obligations. The fateful decision confronting every Jew is therefore not: Shall I or shall I not come under the covenant?, but: Shall I affirm my covenant responsibility and live an *authentic* life or shall I deny it and as a consequence live an *inauthentic* one? Judaism is living out the affirmative decision, and from this decision flows everything that is characteristic of Jewish religion, including the halakic concept and the so-called "ritual observances".

The consequences of this decision, both for the individual and the collectivity, are vast and far-reaching. Covenant-existence for the Jew is not a mere figure of speech; it is an objective though supernatural fact. It enters into the structure of the Jew's very being and every attempt to deny it or to repudiate its responsibilities must lead to deep inner division which may manifest itself disastrously in various psychological, social and cultural forms. Ezekiel's thunderous words against the faithless community of his time apply with equal force to the Jewish individual and Jewish community of all times: "And that which comes into your minds shall not be at all, in that you say: We will be as the nations, the races of the lands, to serve wood and stone. As I live, says the Lord God, with a mighty hand, with an outstretched arm and an outpoured fury, will I be king over you" (20:32–33). Against those who repudiate it in word or deed, the divine election under the covenant turns into the wrath of God. All the more, therefore, does wholehearted affirmation of the covenant — to the degree that it is made operative in life — bring with it the divine blessing of authentic existence.

Israel's relation to Palestine — to Zion — is implicit in its nature as covenant-folk. As covenant-folk, Israel has no native land. The individual Jew, of course, has his nation and his land, whether it be France, America, or the new State of Israel; but Israel as covenant-folk is bound to no land, not even to the Holy Land. As Ignaz Maybaum so well points out *(Synagogue and Society,* pp. 159–60), when in the Wilderness the Israelites were told to place the Ark, the visible symbol of the divine presence and covenant, in a tabernacle, they were forbidden to remove the staves that were used to carry it: "The staves shall be in the rings of the Ark; they shall not be taken out" (Ex. 25.15). Even after Canaan had been conquered, and a great empire established under David and Solomon, even after a magnificent Temple had been erected in which the Ark was to be "permanently" lodged, the staves were still not to be removed (I Kings 8.8). Israel was indeed in possession of the Land, but it was not *fixed* to it: it stood ever ready to take up the Ark and begin its wanderings anew. Under judgment of the Lord of history and in loyalty to Him, it could make no concessions to the gods of space.

Yet Zion *is* the Land of Israel — not its native, but its promised land. The destiny of Israel *begins* and *ends* with Zion: it is the land to which, in the beginning, God called Abraham and to which he led the children of Israel from out of Egypt; it is also the land to which, in the promise of the final fulfilment of the Messianic Age, the People Israel will be restored. But *between* the beginning and the end, there is the "great parenthesis" when Jewish existence and Jewish destiny are irremediably dual, centering around *both* Zion *and* the Galut. These two aspects are related as two poles or foci, standing in dialectic tension with each other, each functioning as a norm and balance for the other. Each has its own characteristic strength and weakness, its own peculiar needs and resources. In a sense, the two complement each other, but the tension between them can never be eliminated; it is this tension that points to the full depth of Jewish existence in history.

The duality of existence is naturally reflected in a differentiation of the vocation of Israel in the Land and in the Galut. The Dispersion came not only as a judgment upon Israel but also as a new way and a new field of service to God: "The Holy One scattered Israel over the earth that many might be gained for his service" (B. Pesahim 87b). In the Land, the Jews are called upon to establish their national life so that the "true community" enjoined by the divine law may be built (Buber). For this purpose, political independence, or at least a high degree of autonomy, is obviously required. In the Diaspora, the primary emphasis of the vocation of Israel is upon gaining — directly or indirectly, by word and

by witness of life — the "nations" for the service of God. Under both aspects, the vocation of Israel places heavy responsibility upon the individual Jew and the Jewish community alike.

The "return" of Israel to Zion is in Jewish tradition conceived as a messianic task, part of the work of the Messianic Age. "The idea of the kingdom [of God]", Schechter tells us, "is so often closely connected with the redemption of Israel from exile, the advent of the Messiah, and the restoration of the Temple as to be inseparable from it" *(Some Aspects of Rabbinic Theology,* p. 98). The establishment of the State of Israel in Palestine is a great historic event of the utmost consequence to the Jews of the whole world, but to interpret it, as so many have done, as the beginning of the final "ingathering of the exiles" and the definitive dissolution of the Galut seems to me little better than a new version of false messianism, bound to lead to serious confusion wherever Jews are found and to a dangerous complication of relations between the State of Israel and Galut Jewry. It is equivalent, at bottom, to saying that there is no longer any room for responsible Jewish life in the Galut except for the purpose of rendering auxiliary service to the State of Israel. Such a view, it seems to me, cannot possibly be admitted by anyone really concerned with Jewish vocation and destiny as revealed in faith. The vocation of Israel and the Jew's covenant-existence transcend, though they are involved in, all the relativities of history and come to fulfilment only with the fulfilment of history at the "last day".

### III

Preoccupation with "survival" — that is, with group survival — appears to be well-nigh universal among those sections of American Jewry who think of themselves as Jews. Survival seems to be the binding idea — one might almost call it the binding "faith"—that unites all varieties of so-called "positive" Jews, secular or religious, Orthodox, Conservative, and Reform. It is the one platform upon which all seem to be agreed. In its name, institutions are built, programs launched, and multiple activities undertaken. Even religion is, among religious and non-religious alike, commended in its name. It appears to be the one unquestioned value and concern in American Jewish life today.

And yet, it seems to me, much of this preoccupation with survival, if not the very idea itself, reflects the advanced stage of secularization of Jewish life in this country. American Jews have the urge to exist as a group, but by and large having lost all sense of the covenant, they do not know what they are to exist for or why. Survival is therefore converted into an ultimate and self-justifying value and everything else made subject to it. But this absolutization of survival must obviously be rejected from the standpoint both of social reality and Jewish tradition. From the standpoint of social reality, it is clear that all cultural development is the outcome of the dissolution and fusion of nations and cultures and that no *natural* community can without absurdity make pretensions to eternal self-perpetuation. From the standpoint of authentic Jewish faith, the survival of the Jewish community is merely instrumental to the vocation of Israel. Dr. Finkelstein puts this normative Jewish viewpoint very clearly when he states: "The Jewish people must be maintained in order that their tradition may live; it is not the tradition that must live in order that the Jewish people should be maintained" *(Tradition in the Making,* p. 20). In other words, group survival is not a self-evident and self-justifying

value; if it is to have any claim upon us, it must be validated in terms of some higher consideration, and that higher consideration can in the end only be expressed in terms of the divine covenant and the vocation of Israel. Holding to group survival as if it were itself the ultimate consideration is merely corporate self-absolutization, a form of idolatry no more tolerable than any other.

On another ground too, the anxious preoccupation with survival seems to me to run counter to the tradition of Jewish faith. In Jewish faith, Israel is eternal; whatever may happen in history, Israel as covenant-people cannot be destroyed: the "remnant" will always remain to bear witness to God and to continue the vocation of Israel. "Israel will never cease to be" (B. Men. 53b); "Empires come and go but Israel will live on forever" (Tos. Derek Eretz, Perek Shalom). This conviction that "the election...for a definite destiny serves as the guarantee for the imperishability of Israel" (Meyer Waxman, *A Handbook of Judaism,* p. 149) shines forth from the heartrending lamentations and prayers growing out of the many catastrophes of Jewish history until recent times. The very conception of survival in the modern sense — not the survival of individual Jews, of course, or of this or that Jewish community, but of the Jewish people as such — seems to have been largely alien to traditional Jewish thinking. Jews may wander from one place to another and many may fall by the wayside; particular communities may arise, flourish and decline — but Israel as such goes on forever; it is eternal. To the degree that we modern Jews have lost this conviction, to that degree have we begun to be obsessed with the problem of survival.

I do not mean that in the assurance of God's providence we are to remain idle, watching God's purposes being effected without our participation. God's purposes in history are generally effected through the work of men, and we are all of us called to responsible service. But we must never lose our sense of proportion; we must never forget that there *is* a divine plan and purpose which it is for us to serve. In all our "survivalistic" activities, however necessary and valuable they may be, we must never permit ourselves to slip into the delusion that we are the ultimate power in history and that the fate of Israel really depends upon our wisdom and planning. The arrogant self-sufficiency of modern man has wrought enough havoc in the world in recent centuries to warn us against introducing the same delusion into Jewish life. Here as elsewhere, the consequence of this attitude is bound to be unrestrained self-assertion on the one hand and bitter disillusionment on the other — both equally destructive. Let us try rather to apprehend in faith the divine purpose and to take up our task in the realization of the responsibility placed upon us but in the conviction, too, that God is the Lord of history and will in the end, despite our confusions, perversities, and failures, bring his purposes to fulfilment. In this conviction, we can proceed all the more effectively to carry out our responsibilities as Jews and as men.

What then is our great responsibility as Jews? It seems to me that our great and basic concern should be not so much to devise strategies for survival, but each and every one of us to live an authentic covenant-existence. Our effort should primarily be to bring ourselves and our fellow-Jews to a vital understanding, each in his own experience, of the meaning of life under the covenant. All our efforts should be bent on awakening this sense of vocation and on implementing it in terms of individual life and social re-

sponsibility. It is not a question of instilling an intellectual "belief in the existence of God" — the very phrase is offensive, as if God, the Supreme Reality, needed an intellectual argument to establish his being. Nor is it a question of recommending "faith" for its utility in promoting psychological wellbeing ("happiness", "morale", "security") and group survival. These things, insofar as they are worthy, may come as by-products of opening our life to God; they cannot be made the goals to which our relationship to God is to be subordinated as means to end. The end, the supreme end, is the establishment of right relations with God in love and obedience — and this, for the Jew, can only mean authentic covenant-existence. If that is achieved, and to the degree that it is achieved, everything else will follow. Strategies of community organization and functioning, even strategies of survival, have their place if they are conceived in such terms. Particular programs of religious education, cultural enrichment, the recruitment and training of youth, relations with Israel, all become significant if they are undertaken as the implementation of authentic covenant-existence. But it is existence-in-faith under the covenant that is primary and decisive; it is itself the supreme value in Jewish life and without it nothing means or can amount to anything.

From my own experience, limited though rather varied, with Jewish young men and women on the campus, I think I can say that a straightforward proclamation of what Scripture and rabbinic tradition tell us to be the ultimate truth of existence has a much better chance of arousing their spirit and enlisting their fervor and enthusiasm than any half-hearted apologetic attempt to accommodate the affirmations of faith to the momentary trends of secular thought. The shallow half-truths of the naturalism and positivism that once constituted "modern thought" are being rapidly discredited; a new thirst for the "existential", for a philosophy of life that takes into account the full dimensions of human existence, is everywhere being felt. If secularism — believing and behaving as though man were sufficient unto himself — is the mark of the "modern" mind, then we can say that there is already beginning to emerge a mind that is *post-modern*. It is to this mind, free from the smug self-sufficiency of secularist humanism, keenly aware of the limitations and ambiguities of naturalistic science, and therefore at last open to the power of the word of God, that we must appeal. These "post-modern" young men and women are not concerned so much with busy programs and bustling activities, although they are ready to assume responsibility if it can be made to mean something to them. What they are really searching for is some glimpse of the meaning of life in its ultimate terms and some way of living on a level of really significant existence. They are only disgusted and alienated by the ostentatious parading of idealistic platitudes and the stale commonplaces of yesterday's humanist philosophy that are so often served up to them as the last word of Jewish religion. They, and many like them in other sections of American Jewry, need and are increasingly ready to receive the authentic message of the biblical-rabbinic faith. No substitute will do.

In any case, I do not think it is possible for any one who understands and affirms this faith to question that our primary and, in a sense, our all-inclusive responsibility at this moment is to recall ourselves and our fellow-Jews to the life-in-faith under the covenant for which we are meant. It is not so much the externals of community organization that we need — although that too has its place — as the restoration of a "community of believers" — and believers are those who *live* in faith.

## IV

From what I have said, I think it will be seen that I do not believe it to be possible to maintain an enduring Jewish community on a secular basis. Cases of such secular community existence from recent European history provide no evidence to the contrary, for whatever may have been their overt character, these communities were in fact living on the resources of solidarity bequeathed to them by earlier generations, and these resources were undeniably religious. Their own viability was quite limited, and even nationalism, the pressure of antisemitism and the national-minority system of eastern Europe would not have been able to keep them going much beyond the period of effectiveness of the religious resources they were fortunate enough to inherit. However that may be, it seems certain that in this country, with conditions so vastly different from those of eastern Europe, if the Jewish group is to survive at all, it can do so only as a religious community. Saadia's dictum, "Our people is a people only by virtue of its Torah", seems to me to be eminently and emphatically true of our present situation in America.

But again I want to get back to the fundamental fact. There *is* such a thing as being too anxious about life and thereby losing it. Less anxiety about survival and the techniques of survival and more about bringing ourselves into obedience to God under the covenant might, paradoxically enough, turn out to be the attitude most favorable to group survival. For there is one and only one way of survival as Jews: *authentic, responsible covenant-existence.*

# ISRAEL AND GOD:
## REFLECTIONS ON THEIR ENCOUNTER

THAT GOD AND MAN communicate with each other is basic in Judaism. The dialogue is not limited to Jews. The Bible itself reveals that Balaam, a non-Jew, was endowed with the gift of prophecy. Nor did Judaism assume that God communicates no law to Gentiles. Even before a solitary Hebrew lived God had commanded Noah and his descendants, as He subsequently commanded Abimelech, Laban and others. Moreover, the encounter between God and Israel is a continuous one, and its form and content are subsumed in the concept of Torah, the totality of the Written and Oral traditions. Jews experience the Divine principally through His word, and God still communicates in every newly discovered insight of both the Halacha and the Aggadah. God also communicates by His participation in Jewish history and, as an integral part of that history, in the judicial process of Israel's duly appointed doctors of the law. Yet, remember one must that the ongoing dialogue between God and Israel involves *both* God and man.

Emanuel Rackman, who serves as rabbi of Congregation Shaaray Tefila in Far Rockaway, N. Y., and also teaches political science at Yeshiva University, was recently appointed Assistant to the President of Yeshiva University. He was last represented in these pages with his essay "Truth and Wisdom: An Orthodox Approach," in the Spring 1961 issue.

Despite their differences, some of the most articulate Jewish theologians of our day concur in this conclusion. Heschel, Fackenheim, Petuchowski, Soloveichik, and a host of their disciples in the Orthodox, Reform and Conservative camps, accept the challenge of this encounter. Their controversialists, on the other hand, also to be found in all camps, are Orthodox rabbis who denigrate the role of man in the unfolding of Torah, and Reconstructionists—Conservative and Reform—who denigrate the role of God. The former shun virtually any Halachic development, except perhaps to provide more stringent safeguards about the law. The latter see no reason for Jews to be deterred from doing anything that furthers their humanistic aspirations. Most Jews, alas, are on the side of the controversialists. They prefer rabbis who play it safe with God, or rabbis who assure them that God is harmless. Only a minority regard Torah as an encounter between God and Israel, in which there is a continuous dialogue between finite man and his Infinite Creator. Yet only this minority can help to prevent Judaism from becoming either the faith of a small group, withdrawn from the intellectual currents of our time, or the folk-pattern of a larger group whose Jewishness will only be a function of their social and psychological situation rather than a commitment to God, Whom they can address as "Thou."

The minority cannot transmit its conviction by argument. In the final analysis faith is never induced by reason. However, the minority must—like the prophets of old—speak what they hold to be the truth. They may never be at the helm of Jewish states, communities, or even future Sanhedrins, but they do offer much to those who look to Judaism for something more than merely the culture of a people or the inflexible imperative of a code.

## I

As MAN is God's partner in continuous creation, so the Jew is God's partner in the process called Torah. In that process the Jew is more than God's obedient servant. He participates in the discovery of God's Word for every situation and, therefore, his own needs must enter into the dialogue. It thus appears, for example, that in those areas of life in which the greatest change is likely —man's economic and social life—pure logic and authorities were never, and are not now, the only factors in Halachic exegesis. By way of contrast, an analysis of the Talmudic folios dealing with the duties of the priests in connection with animal offerings reveals almost exclusive reliance upon Biblical texts, Oral traditions, and extensive deductive reasoning with respect to the texts and traditions. Logic is the life of this branch of Jewish law. One of the greatest Talmudic experts of our day is wont to say that he loves to study this branch of Jewish law not only because he believes in the immanence of the Messianic era and the restoration of the Temple and its rituals, as a result of

which Jews wil again have need of this learning, but also because this branch of the law is so "Seicheldik"—so charged with pure reason. In another branch of the law, that dealing with festivals, one discovers more preoccupation with the lives and needs of Jews. In family law and civil law the demands of life are as important as the logical implications of the texts.

This is as it must be. If in the Halachic process there is a Divine encounter, then, as in prayer, the process cannot be oblivious of life. What is more, as in prayer the same texts are discovered to be meaningful throughout the millenia and amid the diversity of human situations in every age, so the same legal texts address themselves to many new legal problems and permit extensive discovery. The Talmud, and several medieval philosophers, visualize the revealed will of God as the blacksmith's anvil which causes a multitude of sparks to fly. In the case of the blacksmith the sparks do not endure. The sparks of God's Word do endure, and in time kindle a fire as the encounter between God and Israel continues. The Jew constantly discovers these sparks which at one time may even have appeared to be ambiguous, contradictory, and multi-directional. Study them night and day, and they speak to one of everything, for every situation, past, present and future.

In the case of the lex talionis we have ambiguity in the Bible. Does an "eye for an eye" require exact retribution as in the case of "a life for a life" when applied to a homicide? Or does it require monetary compensation as in the case of "a life for a life" when used in *Leviticus* in connection with the killing of another's animal? In connection with the phylacteries we have contradiction between the Biblical text and the Oral tradition. The word *Yad* in the Bible means "hand," not "arm." Yet *tefilin* are placed on the arm. Are the ambiguities and contradictions errors, or are they means of involving Jews in the flowering of the law so that they cannot find security in certainty but must always traverse God's path with awe and trembling and ascertain His Will?

THE SOURCE MATERIALS necessitate the intellectual and emotional participation of the Jew for their exposition, classification, and application. One great medieval scholar points to the fact that even a problem resolved in one generation may be reconsidered and resolved differently in another generation. Maimonides differed. Maimonides held that once a majority of the Sanhedrin had arrived at a conclusion as to what the law was, no succeeding Sanhedrin could overrule it unless its personnel was greater in quantity and quality; otherwise, a succeeding Sanhedrin which agreed with the minority in the earlier tribunal could subsequently, by majority vote, make the earlier minority view the authentic one. Somehow, the very fact that the earlier Sanhedrin was closer to the earliest encounter of God with Israel makes it *prima facie* the superior authority.

Rabbi Abraham ben David yielded to no such presumption. In the ongoing encounter, the later tribunal may adopt what was theretofore only a minority view. The later tribunal may even be inferior to its predecessor in quality but that does not gainsay that the view of the minority in the earlier tribunal may have been the truth which only became apparent to a succeeding generation. Maimonides, the rationalist for whom a dialogue with God was less thinkable than for the sage of Posquières, made man's continuous participation in the Divine encounter less productive of Halachic change than did his controversialist. Maimonides made of both God and His word ultimates far beyond the grasp of ordinary men. Rabbi Abraham ben David placed both within our reach.

Perhaps this, too, is the essence of the difference between the two men in theology. Maimonides allegorically interpreted all references in the Bible to the corporeality of God and regarded as pagan any conception of God which was anthropomorphic. Rabbi Abraham ben David seems to say to him: "Don't pontificate." One should not pronounce absolutes even in theology. Binding the generations to one view and anathemizing dissenters is a dangerous course.

Because the view of yesterday's minority may become the view of tomorrow's majority, the Talmud devotes almost as much space to minority as to majority views, as students of Talmud well know. Students of Talmud are frequently exasperated by the seeming futility of trying to fathom positions which did not prevail. Yet in an ongoing encounter between God and Israel, and the progressive Revelation which the encounter entails, minority views are important. Who can understand this better than students of American constitutional law wherein the erstwhile dissents of Holmes, Brandeis, Stone, Black, and Douglas finally become the law of the land!

Thus one should not only master the views of dissenters but encourage them. In one's practice of the Law one should not be a sect unto oneself. This was the heresy of the Karaites and the basic reason for their virtual oblivion. However,

Jews as individuals are expected to engage in the encounter and contend with God and the tradition. It is thus that the study of Torah can rank with prayer as a means of confronting God. It is thus also that a theocentric law is always found viable. Humility in the encounter there must be, but not blind obedience exclusively.

The Halacha supports this position. The *Zaken Mamreh*, the dissenter who defies the Sanhedrin, is punishable only for *acts* in defiance of a superior authority which, by majority vote, arrives at a rule of law. However, he is not punished for persisting in his view that the Sanhedrin erred nor for arguing his position publicly.

If Orthodox rabbis continue to denigrate the role of man in Halachic creativity then they shall bear the guilt for failing to reach many of our contemporaries who want to "return" but resent an uncompromising authoritarianism. They must be helped to see that man plays a role in the development of Halacha.

However, God does also.

## II

WITH REGARD to God's role in the encounter there is even more controversy than with regard to man's. Many theologians, even among those who are committed to the belief in a historic Revelation at Sinai, maintain that it happened once and will never happen again. Those who deny an original Revelation are certainly reluctant to believe in the progressive unfolding of that which never existed. But many Orthodox Jews regard the Law as having been given once, and what Jews have done with it thereafter—within the limits and according to the exegesis originally prescribed—is their doing, and their authority is set forth in *Deuteronomy*, where Jews are ordered to hearken to all that their future judges would teach.

The view that God no longer shares in Torah is supported by texts which deny the validity of supernatural voices (*Bat-Kol*) and of omens in the resolution of Halachic questions. It is also supported by Judaism's resistance to Christian and Muslim revelations. Maimonides made of the finality of Torah a cardinal dogma of the faith. However, texts as well as experience support the view that, while there shall never be another Torah, sages relied on Divine help and even apocalyptic prophecy to discover God's will in countless Halachic situations. Indeed, it could not be otherwise, for then no religious experience whatever would be involved in the resolution of new Halachic problems. Certainly the saintliness of the scholar would be inconsequential, since what he opines must stand the test of reason alone. Yet, in Halachic development it was the scholar who was also saintly whose views prevailed over those more learned but less devout. Piety was at least as much the hallmark of authority as genius, and unless religious experience is involved in Halachic exegesis this requisite makes no sense.

Heschel has fully documented the thesis that prophecy played an important role in Halachic decisions during the Middle Ages. Certainly it was through the immediacy of their experience of God that Hasidic teachers suspended many binding rules of the law. Moreover, even the most avid of Jewish rationalists know only by mystical illumination when a particular discourse in Talmud is the truth and when it is only intellectual acrobatics.

Yet, the greater threat to the Halacha comes not from those who regard God's role as ended but from those who regard the Law as without a transcendent source. They may not adversely affect the status of the Jewish people or the Jewish State in our days as does the American Council of Judaism. However, theologically speaking, their heresy is of the same calibre. One group denies the role of people in the encounter; the other denies the role of God. That is why Reconstructionists can so readily extend the invitation to secularists to join hands in a common humanistic endeavor for Jews.

But those for whom God is the ultimate source of all law and law-making —and the cause of all mutations in our ethical and religious insights—the ongoing encounter between Him and man is the cornerstone of all their commitment.

Nelson Glueck claims that archaeology sustains his faith in a transcendent Being. Excavating in the area traversed by Abraham four millenia ago, he discovers a remarkable homogeneity in cultural patterns everywhere. The emergence of a new faith in the midst of all this sameness is a mutation that could either be accidental or the result of a Divine encounter. He chooses the latter alternative as the basis for his religious commitment.

Henri Bergson derives it rather from the prophets. He cannot concur in the view that justice is exclusively the product of social need. He poses the famous question:

> What should we do if we heard that for the common good, for the very existence of mankind, there was somewhere

a man, condemned to suffer eternal torment? Well, we should perhaps agree to it on the understanding that some magic philter is going to make us forget it, that we shall never hear anything more about it, but if we are bound to know it, to think of it, to realize that this man's hideous torture was the price of our existence, that it was even the fundamental condition of existence in general, no. A thousand times no! Better to accept that nothing should exist at all! Better let our planet be blown to pieces.

"Now what has happened?" asks Bergson. How does a sense of justice which may have emerged originally from social need suddenly soar above it, categorical and transcendent, so that in its name we defy the social need? "Let us recall the tone and accents of the Prophets of Israel. It is their voice we hear when a great injustice has been done and condoned. From the depths of the centuries they raise their protest. They imparted to justice the violently imperative character which it has kept, which it has since stamped on a substance grown infinitely more extensive. Could it have been brought about by mere philosophy? There is nothing more instructive than to see how the philosophers have skirted round it, touched it, and yet missed it."

FOR ORTHODOX JEWS it is in the Pentateuch, even more than in the Prophets, that not only the record of Israel's encounter is to be found but also the warrant for the authenticity of its transcendent source. The twenty-fifth chapter of *Leviticus*, which in modern times inspired a Henry George, is an eloquent illustration.

A people—every one of whom expected to share in the distribution of the land after its conquest—is unequivocally told that the land will not be theirs. It will always belong to God (verse 23). And because it is God's it will not be exploited every seventh year. Nothing will be gained by this other than a demonstration as to who is truly the owner. Yet, if law is to be defined as the expression of universal self-interest, how can one explain this law which denies the self-interest of everyone in the legal order! Furthermore, if law is to be defined as an expression of the self-interest of the dominant economic group, how can one explain that verse in the same chapter which lets the masters of slaves know that God alone is a Master! It was He Who took His people out of bondage in Egypt to serve Him (verse 55). Any servitude to humans is, therefore, always subject to His will and limited by it.

Nor is law the will of the king, the human sovereign, to aggrandize his authority. For it is obedience to God's law, not obedience to the king, that will insure the peace and permit one to live securely on the land (verse 18). The king has his duties and his rights, but domestic tranquility is God's gift, not his. What human sovereign would ever promulgate such a preamble to his constitution! Nor is law for the greatest good of the greatest number. The minority of non-Jews is also not to be put at a disadvantage. Their proprietary rights shall be safeguarded (verse 48). And even human nature is not the source of the law. To the contrary, one of the law's principal functions is to alter human nature. The bully in man is to be shrunk (verse 46).

How other than from a transcendent will could such a code emerge! The sages of the Talmud so thought. In a very incisive comment they made their point. They observed that in the open-ing verse of Chapter 25 of *Leviticus* reference is made to the fact that the laws therein contained were given on Mount Sinai. According to the tradition the entire law of Moses was given at Sinai. Why, then, the special mention of the mountain in introducing this particular chapter? The answer is obvious. Only from Sinai—only from God—could such a chapter come. Who could believe otherwise! Therefore, let all know that as this chapter can only emanate from Him, so all the Law is from Him.

Moses did not transmit the Law as if from God to strengthen his authority and the authority of his successors. That kings in the ancient world were wont to do this gives one no right to assume that Moses must have followed suit. It is the uniqueness of his presentation that bears the certification of its origin in God. For it was only His authority that was being established. Most of the Law was irrelevant to Moses' times. Most of it was to be obeyed only after his death —when Jews would have conquered the Promised Land. And Moses could not have tried to insure the security of his successors. He had none. His own authority he diffused among priests, judges, elders, and kings. Nor would any of them ever have ultimate authority. Authority would forever reside in the One, transcendent and omnipotent.

Buber noted one interesting exception in the phraseology of most of the commandments that were given for fulfillment in the land of Canaan. Most of them would be binding after entry into the land. Two would be binding only after entry, conquest, and division among the tribes of Israel. These two laws pertained to the coronation of a king and the annual ceremony of bringing *Bikurim*—the first fruits—to the shrine in the city where the king would reign. That the performance of these two commandments was to await the conquest of the land and its division among the conquerors was God's way of preventing feudalism with its system of land tenure as derived from the sovereign. Jews were not to have a king before they acquired their land. Then they would know that from God they received it and not from a human majesty. Moreover, if after the coronation of a king the king might be inclined to forget this, he was to be annually reminded of his error, when all Jews would appear in the very city in which he held his court with their first fruits which they presented to the priests with a declaration of gratitude *to God* from Whom they received the gift of the land. And if feudalism might emerge later, as the king and others accumulated land unto themselves, the Law has its antidote in the form of a redistribution of the land every fifty years. Alienation of the land in perpetuity was well-nigh impossible. It takes more credulity to believe that Moses by himself was the visionary social engineer of his day than to believe that he had an encounter with God and transmitted God's will!

### III

**B**UT GOD AND ABRAHAM also had an encounter. For an understanding of Israel's role among the nations this encounter is even more important than the one at Sinai. And what emerged from Abraham's encounter was equally exceptional and warrants belief in a transcendent source. Kierkegaard made the story of the sacrifice of Isaac the cornerstone of his theology. However, as Milton Steinberg conclusively demonstrated,

Judaism does not subscribe to any suspension of the ethical. In Judaism God and the good are as related as a circle to roundness. But that Abraham was commanded to withdraw from his world to become a blessing to all the world is a mandate too revolutionary not to be regarded as a mutation of major importance in universal history. He was ordered to leave his country, the city of his birth, even his forbears, so that in his aloneness he might ultimately bring benefit to all the families of the earth— an altruistic goal five times articulated in *Genesis* to the patriarchs. And Abraham's withdrawal and other-directedness became the hallmark of Israel's existential situation.

Even the rationale for God's choice of Israel differs radically, as Theodore Reik pointed out, from similar conceptions among other tribes and peoples. The Hebrews were not "chosen" because of their quality. Indeed, the Bible indicates that their number least merited God's recognition. Moses was frequently even more insulting. But it was Abraham who merited being chosen, and to his seed fell the lot of fulfilling the promise that through him all humanity would be blessed. This was God's will for Israel and all humanity. And a dialogue which altered the life and career of Abraham became an "I-Thou" relationship for the benefit of third parties.

This component of Judaism is the object of Toynbee's unrelenting criticism. He cannot fathom Israel's separateness, which to him is only a vestigial ethnicism. But the ambivalence involved in a withdrawal for the purpose of ultimate service to those from whom one withdraws is the essence of Abraham's encounter with God and its continuance with his seed. A later confluence of Hebraic and Hellenic ideas in Stoicism yielded the same ambivalence. The Stoic, too—as inspired by Zeno, Epictetus and Aurelius—would have man withdraw unto himself in virtual obliviousness of external facts and circumstances at the same time that he makes empathy and philanthropy for others the basis of his activity as a man. Perhaps the ambivalence involves what are contradictories by logic, but the logic of life and experience transcend the limitations of pure reason. In Stoicism, individualism and universalism are the antitheses; in Judaism they are particular peoplehood and universalism.

FAILURE to fathom the unique significance of Abraham's, and then Israel's, encounter with God has also led to an exaggeration of the significance of the Hellenic tradition for the values of humanism and the denigration of the Hebraic tradition. John Bowle, for example, in his *Western Political Thought,* regards as "typically Jewish" Paul's "blinding vision of God's omnipotence, of the abject condition of man, the overwhelming sense of sin, the passion for 'salvation.'" Daniel Bell, writing in *Commentary,* also subscribes to the idea that Jewish Orthodoxy induced such resignation on the Jew's part to his fate that he did not resist Hitler's decrees.

If any tradition made man the captive of the gods it was Hellenism and not Hebraism. Indeed, the optimism of an Aristotle—or to a lesser degree of a Plato—with regard to man's capacity to mold life and institutions to his will was the exception rather than the rule. Hebraism, on the other hand, because of Abraham's encounter with God, catapulted man to such an exalted position that in dialogue with his Creator he

could insure the peace and plenty of the earth. Righteousness, which is man's *raison d'être* and wholly within his reach, even binds God to fulfill His covenanted obligations. God is the obligee of man!

Furthermore, it was because all men are created in His image that the equality of man is a Hebraic doctrine, while in Hellenism the emphasis is on man's inequality. And since justice was to Abraham God's most pronounced attribute, preoccupation with justice was the hallmark of Judaism throughout the millenia. Notions of equity and equality were, therefore, more Hebraic than Hellenic, and again via Stoicism Hebraic ideas humanized Roman law for the greater happiness of man in the Western world. Subsequently, through Christianity, Biblical Judaism gave to the world the very weapon by which the tyranny of the state—including Rome—could be mitigated and human freedom expanded. This weapon was the faith that there was a right that transcended imperial power—a right derived from God. The individual in opposition to the state, in the name of God, was a conflict unthinkable to an Athenian; but it was the very heart of prophecy in the Bible. This is one of many ways in which it was Hebraism rather than Hellenism that advanced the cause of humanism. And it was Abraham who first held even God to be bound to do the right! The Sovereign of all the earth was also bound by a higher law—albeit His own.

V

WHAT the West will now do in its controversy with the East may well lead to the end of human life and civilization as we know it. However, if the West should capitulate—to prevent the holocaust—then there can be no hope for freedom at any time in the next millenium unless more people individually, because of their personal encounter with God, are prepared to resist the spread of tyranny. Perhaps prudence will dictate that collectively free nations withdraw, suffer shame, and forfeit influence. The responsibility will then fall to solitary humans, in martyrdom, to keep alive the hope that some day the right will prevail.

D.  God, Israel and The Holocaust

# Death of a God

## ELIEZER BERKOVITS

1

"RADICAL THEOLOGY," AT THE CORE OF WHICH
stands the confession that God is dead, is not all of one piece. One may
discern different trends and motives within this latest development of
religious thought, which its spokesmen insist upon calling a theology.
We shall limit ourselves to a discussion of four points which seem to be
the ever-recurring theme in all forms of this type of theology. They concern man's new self-understanding, his new understanding of the universe, his contemporary experience of the presence of God, and, finally,
his awareness of the relationship between God and man as it derives
from modern man's God experience.

As to man, it is maintained, often not without a sense of pride, that
he has come of age, he has reached maturity, and he accepts responsibility for himself and the world. He is, therefore, no longer in need of
God. As to the universe, man's interpretation of its nature and functioning is now purely scientific. Scientifically, the world is self-explanatory.
In our days, so it is affirmed, the universe has become self-sufficient. It
requires no transcendental reference for its meaning. Objective knowledge has banished God from the cosmos. There is no longer any need
for the idea of a Creator, nor is it possible for modern man to have any
experience of the presence of God. Since all knowledge is to be derived
from experience, the realm of the transcendental itself, that of the Beyond, has collapsed. All Absolutes have disintegrated. Man can know
nothing of an Absolute Being. The very fact that God as the Wholly
Other is wholly different from everything human places Him outside
every possible human knowledge. The only Absolute which is still recognized is absolute immanentism, the idea that the world is complete
within itself and has its meaning within its own confines. Needless to
say, on the basis of such a premise, there is no possibility for any form
of God-man relationship. God has departed this earth. We know nothing of His presence. If anything, we experience His absence. It matters
little whether He exists or not. In short, God is dead in our time and in
our existence. With some "radical theologians" this development is the
source of a new optimism. Now we may trust the world; we trust man,
who has come of age. Others speak of the awesome autonomy that man
is assuming now and see in it a tragic form of human existence.

It would seem to us that in the light of philosophical and theologi-

ELIEZER BERKOVITS is *Chairman of the Philosophy Department of The
Hebrew Theological College, Skokie, Illinois.*

345

cal scholarship all of this is a rather meager fare. Neither the problems nor the conclusions drawn from them are in any way new. What is original is the formulation of a not very original atheism as a theology. We have great sympathy with Paul van Buren's secular meaning of the Gospel, yet what he has done is to apply the methodology of logical positivism and language analysis to the New Testament. Now, though logical positivism and language analysis have their value, they also have their limitations. It is rather naive to assume that the metaphysical problem of transcendence has now been philosophically resolved completely in favor of immanence. That the realm of transcendence has finally collapsed is treated by radical theologians as an axiom which requires no further elucidation, and the idea appears in their writings more like a proclamation than as a philosophical standpoint. But the matter cannot be decided by proclamation. To maintain that the scientific interpretation of the universe renders the idea of a Creator unnecessary shows no sign of either philosophical or theological sophistication. It may be so, or it may not be so, but one should not affirm it axiomatically, without entering into a significant discussion of the philosophical or theological issues involved in such an assertion. Finally, that the absence of God, the lack of personal experience of His presence means the death of God, be it the death of faith in God or—as some would have it—God's death in a very real sense as an event happening in time, is a most superficial way of meeting the problem of the *deus absconditus* of metaphysics or of the *el mistater*, the hiding God of the prophets of Israel.

We believe that the "radical theology" is neither a theology nor a philosophy. In its essence, it is an attitude, and its thought-content is a rationalization of that attitude. This comes to clear expression in a statement by Mircea Eliade, who deeply influenced Thomas J. J. Altizer, who, in turn, is probably the most significant spokesman of "radical theology." Eliade has the following to say on the subject:

> God has died as the result of an existential choice made by modern man. Modern man has chosen the realm of the profane; he assumed autonomy; he manages by himself; he has made himself a profane being.[1]

This rationalization of the existential choice into a "theology" is not terribly interesting, but the reason for the choice certainly is. It is of the utmost importance for Jews to understand what is happening in the God-is-dead camp of post-Christian theologians and why it is happenings. They call themselves Christian, even Christian atheists, because the God they talk about and whose death concerns them is the God of Christianity. They are rightly to be known as post-Christian. They all have in common the theme of the collapse of Christendom, of Christian teaching and civilization.

---

1. Thomas J. Altizer, *Mircea Eliade and the Dialectic of the Sacred* (Philadelphia: The Westminster Press, 1963), p. 27.

2

What surprises a Jew most is, I believe, the realization that for the radical theologian modern man is God's competitor. God and man face each other as enemies. It is either God or man. The radical theologian does not content himself with saying that because of the scientific interpretation of the universe there is no need for a Creator. He adds that since man has no more need of God, he, himself, becomes the Creator.[2] It is not only that man has come of age and accepts responsibility, but man may accept responsibility for his life and for the world only now that God is dead.[3] Especially at this point the radical theologian leans heavily on Nietzsche and Camus. This relationship of a competition to the death between God and man is again succinctly delineated in the words of Eliade when he says: "Man cannot be free until he kills the last God."[4] "Radical theology" implies—as its positive aspect—"the turning from the cloister to the world."[5] But, strangely enough, only now that God has died in man's "existence," can man leave the cloister and turn to the world; only now, because he has lost his God, can he live in the secular city in freedom and responsibility. We mentioned earlier that some of the radical theologians speak of a new optimism of trusting man and the world. It is, however, noteworthy that for them this optimism is a direct result of God's death. Thus, Hamilton, for instance, maintains: "I am persuaded that the death of God made this new optimism possible."[6]

This competitive relationship between God and man is utterly foreign to the Jewish mentality. That the scientific interpretation of the universe requires no God hypothesis may be right or wrong; it has been held by numerous Jews. However, the idea that the throne vacated by God really belongs to Man, the Creator, is clearly not a logical thought, but one aspect of modern man's "existential choice" of a profane existence. It is a choice which, I dare say, is existentially alien even for an atheistic Jew. The casual nexus between God's death and human responsibility is equally foreign to the Jew. Within Judaism, from the very beginning, it was God who called man to responsibility and entrusted the earth into his responsible safe-keeping. Far from being able to "turn from the cloister to the world" as a result of God's death, it was God who never let the Jew turn to the cloister, but sent him into the world "to work it and to preserve it." We may understand that it is possible for a man to be optimistic about life and the world even

2. Thomas J. Altizer, *Radical Theology and the Death of God* (New York: Bobbs-Merrill Co., 1966), p. 99.
3. Harvey Cox, *The Secular City* (New York: The Macmillan Co., 1967), pp. 71–72.
4. Altizer, *Mircea Eliade*, p. 26.
5. William Hamilton, *Radical Theology and the Death of God* (New York: Bobbs-Merrill Co., 1966), p. 36.
6: Ibid., p. 165; see also Altizer, *Radical Theology*, p. 182 and *Mircea Eliade*, p. 18.

without faith in God, but what kind of distortion of the mind would require the death of God as the foundation of optimism? In Judaism, God is the only cause of optimism. For a Jew, the strangest aspect of "radical theology" is that, according to it, man, in his very being, feels crushed by God. In keeping with the Nietzschean exclamation, "If there were gods, how could I bear not to be a god?" "radical theology" has man killing God in order to be able to choose himself in freedom and responsibility. What is the reason for this strange competitive relationship between God and man?

We believe that this "theology" could have arisen only in the midst of Christendom as an understandable reaction, long overdue, to some aspects of fundamental Christian teaching and dogma. Harvey Cox makes a penetrating comment on the philosophy of Camus who recognized the essential contradiction between the traditional Christian doctrine of God and the full freedom and responsibility of man. And he adds: "A God who emasculates man's creativity and hamstrings his responsibility for his fellow man must be dethroned."[7] According to Cox, such emasculation of man in Christianity is due to the absorption of Platonic and Aristotelian ideas about the idea of the Good as well as about God, which represented a fateful departure from the teachings of the Hebrew Bible. We believe that Cox does not go far enough in his analysis. The reason for man's emasculation by Christianity is much more fundamental; it goes to the very heart of Christianity, and it is the direct outcome of the dogma of Original Sin. As the result of the Fall, human nature became corrupted. Because of it, man can never save himself; he can do nothing good and worthwhile in this world; he cannot act with responsibility; he is completely subjugated by his fallen condition. He can be saved only by the miracle of divine intervention. This miracle occurred in the Incarnation, and because of it, and through his faith, man is re-born a new and pure being. But what happens if the act of redemption does not take place in fact; if, as a matter of historic experience, man is not renewed and the new Adam does not appear? Be the reason for it what it may, once the miracle of man's rebirth does not materialize, man remains degraded, robbed of his dignity as a human being. G. Vahanian is right in stating that "Christianity has often degraded, enslaved man, deprecated his creative imagination, the intrinsic worth of his finitude."[8]

However, in the teaching of the Fall, not only has man became degraded, but the whole of creation as well. Nature itself became corrupt, the entire universe fell into disarray; this world lost its value and meaning. Whereas man was to be redeemed, the earth was to be replaced by

---

7. Hamilton, *Op. cit.*, p. 72.
8. Gabriel Vahanian, *The Death of God* (New York: George Braziller, 1961), p. 8; see also pp. 175, 181-3.

the Kingdom of God which was not of this world. Christianity is an other-worldly religion. It has no use for this world and no respect for it. But what happens when the promised Kingdom does not come? The original Christian position called for "the end of time" and "the end of the world." But ever since then, time has been going on, the world, this world, has not come to an end, and man is left with an earth degraded, fallen, and corrupt. Seen against the background of the Christian teaching about the world, one may well understand, for example, Altizer's insistence that the Christian concept of the Kingdom of God and the dignity of the cosmos, as conceived by modern science, are antithetical concepts. The affirmation of the one implies the necessary denial of the other.[9]

Vahanian sees correctly that a sound instinct led the founders of Christianity to look for a speedy dissolution of the present world order,[10] as was required by the intrinsic logic of the Christian idea of redemption and the dogma of the incarnation. What we see today in "radical theology" is a rebellion among Christians against a concept of God and redemption that, indeed, treats man as a worthless creature, incapable of responsibility on his own, as well as a radical rejection of the notion of a world that is so fallen and so corrupt that its only hope is to be replaced by an other-worldly Kingdom of God.

### 3

Christianity is unable to cope with man, who has come of age, by deciding to accept responsibility for managing his own life and building "technopolis," the secular city. This problem has been inherent in Christianity from its inception. The "secular city" is *olam hazeh*, this world. The problem arises from what is known as "the delayed parousia." Jesus came and went, but, to use a Talmudic phrase, *olam k'minhago noheg*, the world continued according to its established rules as before and the promise of an other-worldly redemption remained unfulfilled. Yet, according to the teaching, "the Kingdom" was at hand. It was to be revealed by the second coming of the savior, which, according to the expectations of faith, was to be immediate. He never came again. What was to be done with this fallen, rejected, corrupt world, with the secular city of an unredeemed humanity? Troeltsch has aptly commented on the Christian embarrassment, stating that because of the delayed parousia Christianity had to adjust itself to some compromise between the demands of a utopian other worldly Kingdom and the actual conditions of human existence.[11] This process of compromising between unfulfilled promise and reality has been continuous and

---

9. Altizer, *Radical Theology*, pp. 103, 109.
10. Ibid., p. 46.
11. Quoted by Vahanian, *Op. cit.*, p. 46.

it is possible to interpret the various phases in the development of Christian theology in its terms. In essence, at the very heart of Christianity there is a split between civilization and faith, between culture and redemption, between the city of man and the city of God. All Christian culture and civilization are the result of a compromise, a partial surrender of the original sacred to the inescapably secular. This process of secularization, the death of God, started with the delayed parousia.

Implied in the basic Christian position, in the Christian concept of redemption and the Kingdom of God, is a denial of history. Within Christianity there is no room for it. Mircea Eliade puts it this way:

"... it must not be lost sight of that Christianity entered into History in order to abolish it: the greatest hope of the Christian is the second coming of Christ, which is to put an end to all History."[12]

Another author, quoted by Bultman, formulates the idea in the following manner:

"To the Christian the advent of Christ was not an event in that temporal process which we mean by history today. It was an event in the history of salvation, in the realm of eternity, an eschatological moment in which rather this profane history of the world came to an end. And in an analogous way, history comes to an end in the religious experience of any Christian who is in Christ."[13]

That is nobly said. However, history has not come to an end and the overwhelming majority of Christians kept on living in history. They lived in society, got married, raised children, paid income tax, went to war, built cities, governed themselves and ruled the world. They were very much part and parcel of this world of time and quite removed from the realm of eternity. What was to be done? According to the compromise, salvation applies only to the individual soul, the inner man; the world, history, remains unredeemed. Bultman, for instance, distinguishes between universal history, to which Christianity cannot grant *de iure* recognition, and "personal history," consisting of the religious experiences of the inner man. As the Christian Kingdom and the cosmos are antithetical concepts, so, also, are the Christian teachings about redemption and history. Kierkegaard may define faith as absurd because it is, and must be, outside history. From the Christian point of view, all history is Fall and all culture Fall into history. Modern man is choosing the realm of the secular because he lives in history and accepts it. Following in the footsteps of his master, Eliade, Altizer reveals one of the roots of his "radical theology" by saying: "We must have the courage to recognize that it is the Christian God who has enslaved man

12. Altizer, *Mircea Eliade*, p. 65.
13. Paul M. Van Buren, *The Secular Meaning of the Gospel* (New York: The Macmillan Co., 1963), p. 111; cf. also Rudolf Bultmann, "History of Salvation and History" in *Existence and Faith* (New York: Meridian Press, 1960).

to the alienation of being and the guilt of history."[14] But the City is in history. If history is guilt and alienation, then the city of man is rooted in profanity. In order to shatter this concept of history so that he may be able to accept responsibility for his City, modern man has to desire the death of that God who does not let him be.

It is only now that we may analyze what may be called the basic issue involved in our discussion. Altizer refers to Dilthey and Troeltsch, according to whom historicism is a product of the decomposition of Christianity, to which he adds that historical consciousness is a product of modern man's choice of the profane.[15] Altizer may be confusing the cause with the effect; all-important for an understanding of "radical theology" is the equation between the historical and the profane. What is the meaning of the sacred and the profane that will yield such an equation? As has been shown in the researches of Eliade on the subject, in archaic religions, as well as in Hinduism, the profane and the sacred are dialectically related to each other. The definition of the profane contains the negation of the sacred, just as included in the definition of the sacred is the exclusion of the profane. An either-or relationship prevails between them: one lives either in the realm of the altogether sacred or in that of the altogether profane. The sacred is the primordial Totality, it is the Real. Fall is separation from, as Redemption is return to the original whole, submerging in the Real, the Sacred. There is no possibility here for a gradualness of transformation. One submerges oneself completely and becomes miraculously reborn, as if in a flash. What happens happens Now, and Now is Eternity. In the salvation religions, the transformation in a Now is the result of the mystical ritual.

Altizer is anxious to distinguish between the backward-directed return of archaic religions and the forward-reference of Christian redemption. Be that as it may, the dialectical relationship between the profane and the sacred is also found within Christianity. The act of creation brought into being a perfect world, the primordial wholeness, the Sacred. Because of the dialectical nature of the sacred, the Fall is, of necessity, a fall into complete profanity. The transformation of redemption is transfiguration; it is the miraculous death of the Old Adam and the birth of the New in a Now. Redemption is not a process but an "event," the transposition from the realm of the profane into that of the sacred outside of time. In this context there is no possibility of gradualness of transformation, no room for the acknowledgment of history, since history itself is the Fall. One must die to history and be reborn in the timeless miracle of Salvation. Outside the miracle of salvation, outside of the Kingdom of the sacred, there can be only profanity. Existence in his-

---

14. Altizer, *Radical Theology*, p. 110.
15. Altizer, *Mircea Eliade*, p. 33.

tory is, of necessity, existence without God, existence against God. This world, the city of man, is, therefore, not only secular, but profane. History equals profaneness.

Indeed, the Christian position confronts man with the choice: either the Kingdom of God or History; either divine redemption or human freedom and responsibility; either the city of God or the city of Man. All along this line modern man has rejected the Christian position. He has embraced history, assumed freedom and responsibility, and seeks the fulfillment of his life in the secular city. In terms of Christian teaching, he has chosen a profane existence. "Radical theology," seeking a way out of the dilemma, has dethroned the God that presented man with the either-or choice between the "cloister" and the world.

4

Let us now attempt to define the Jewish position as it relates to the issues under discussion. The major difference between the Jewish and the Christian position with reference to our subject lies in the differing concepts of the Sacred. Within Judaism, the sacred and the profane are not dialectically related. One might say that, within Judaism, the sacred, as far as it may be a human concern at all,[16] is found, not in the realm of Being, but in that of Becoming. The sacred *is* not, but has to be brought into being as the result of someone's action or behavior. The seventh day *is* not holy, but *becomes* holy when God sanctifies it. Israel is *made* holy by God and *becomes* holy by sanctifying itself. "Thou shalt be unto Me a kingdom of priests and a holy nation" is not a divine promise of other-worldly transfiguration and redemption, but a challenge to Israel, a task, a responsibility. Man is called upon to sanctify himself; to sanctify this earthly Adam in this world. *K'dusha*, holiness, is sanctification, and sanctification is a process in time, not a miracle outside of time.

Creation, within Judaism, is, from the very beginning, the cosmos, as it is given to man to experience it and to understand it. In it there has never been a cosmic disaster of the nature of a Fall into corruption and profaneness. Furthermore, the cosmos of Biblical creation is not the "primordial Totality" of being, which, as the Real, is identical with the sacred. Since the sacred is the result of sanctification, the Real, in the primordial sense, is neither sacred nor profane, but amenable to both sanctification and profanation. From its very inception the cosmos is secular. However, in Judaism, the secular is not the profane, but the not-yet profane or the not-yet sanctified Real.

The idea may be found expressed in numerous variations in the

---

16. We add this qualification in order to avoid the need for a discussion of the idea of the holy as a divine attribute.

Talmud and the Midrash, so we shall let one example stand for many. At the conclusion of the story of the creation the Bible tells us that God saw everything that he had made and behold it was *"tov m'od,"* very good. Rabbi Samuel, the son of Naḥman, comments: "tov," good, that is the *yeẓer tov,* the good inclination in man; "tov m'od," very good, that is the *yeẓer ra,* the evil urge in him. How is this to be understood? How can one call man's inborn inclination for evil "very good"? And the explanation is offered: This means to teach you that were it not for "the evil inclination," man would not bother to build a house for himself; he would neither marry nor beget children; nor would he attend to the affairs of human existence.[17] In other words, the "evil urge" in man is the basic life drive within him. It is neither sacred nor profane. It is the reality of man's vitality, it is the original givenness of man's existence. It is the secular raw material out of which all human culture and civilization is to be shaped in the sight of God. It is there for man to use for building houses, begetting children, building the city of man. But as one uses it, one is also called upon to sanctify it. At the conclusion of the creation, God looked around and saw his "secular" creation and believed it was "very good." That is all that man ought to know about it. The primordial real is the secular and the secular is very good because it, alone, is capable of being sanctified. In the primordial Sacred there is no room for man. There, all is whole, all is All. There, if man wants to be, he must fall. Yet once he has fallen, he is doomed. He cannot help himself. He can be saved only from "without." Not so in the not-yet holy secular creation of Judaism. From the very beginning man has been placed into this world, not in order to die to it, so that he might be saved by the miracle of divine intervention for a Kingdom which is not of this world, but he has been placed on earth that he may sanctify the secular, *l'taken olam b'malkhut shaddai,* and establish the city of man as the Kingdom of God. It is not either God or Man. Man, according to his own strength, continues the work of creation and becomes, urged on by God's call, a humble associate of the Creator.

One may see the difference between the Christian and the Jewish approach reflected in a midrashic passage, where, in typical midrashic style, the subject is couched in the form of a dialogue between God and Israel:

> Israel said to the Holy One, blessed be He: Thou knowest the hard power of the evil inclination! To which God replied: Remove ye it slowly, gradually in this world; and I shall remove it from you completely in the world to come. As it is written: Cast up, cast up the highway, gather out the stones. And it also said: Cast ye up, cast ye up, clear the way, take up the stumbling block out of the way of My people. . . .[18]

One may well say that the opening of the dialogue is the attempt to es-

17. *Bereshit Rabba,* 9, 9.
18. *Bamidbar Rabba,* 15, 12.

tablish, as valid, a position which, indeed, is identical with the Christian stand. The suggestion is made that the evil in man is too strong for him, and the man is helpless against it. He is a profane creature, and only God can save him. This is as far as Christianity got in the evaluation of the human condition. But this stance is rejected by Judaism. A complete transformation of man may not be possible without divine salvation, but that can wait until "the world to come." In the meantime, there is a task for man in this world: the burdensome struggle of man with himself, the process of slow, gradual self-transformation.

Expressing it in philosophical terms, one ought to say that in Christianity the sacred and the profane are ontological categories, categories of Being; in Judaism they are axiological principles, standards of value. Between ontological categories there is no possibility of gradual transformation. The profane must die in the transfiguration of the mystery of redemption, and the sacred must perish completely in the Fall. The profane is always altogether profane and the sacred is forever altogether sacred. But as axiological principles, the sacred or the profane are processes of becoming. The profane is never completely lost, for the secular, which has been profaned, is always capable of sanctification; while, on the other hand, the sacred is never perfect, for what has been sanctified may also be defiled. Redemption, itself, is a continuous process and is never final in this world. Sanctification proceeds by degrees; it is inseparable from the time process. This is implied in the words: "Remove ye it slowly, gradually." It is the stuff out of which history is made, and it is the essence of the Jewish concept of history. The sacred is life's sanctification on earth. History is man's responsibility; it is one of the dimensions of sanctification. Here, within the God-given task of sanctification, is the source of man's freedom as well as of his responsibility. The God who calls man to responsibility is the guarantor of his freedom to act responsibly. As man accepts responsibility, he enters upon his God-given heritage of freedom. Or, as the rabbis read it: "Freedom —on the Tablets."[19] Granting him freedom and calling him to responsibility, God has expressed confidence in His creature, man. This remains for the Jew the foundation of his optimism, notwithstanding man's disappointing performance in history.

The concept of the Law in Judaism is closely linked to this aspect of our subject. If the profane and the sacred are ontological categories, dialectically related to each other, then, of course, there is no possibility for history. One is either damned or saved. That is why the "Kingdom" has to abolish history. It is also quite logical to say that the "Kingdom" also abolishes the Law. In the "Kingdom," in a state of salvation realized in eternity, there is no need for the Law. This, also, is authentic Jewish teaching. At "the end of the days" the Law is fulfilled. Only man

19. *Pirkei Avot*, 6, 2.

354

who lives in time needs the Law; the redeemed soul, existing in an other-worldly kingdom outside of history is in no need of it. However, once the parousia was delayed, once the compromise between the utopian other-worldly kingdom and the actual conditions of man's this-worldly existence became necessary, once redemption had to be relegated to the inner personal history of the Christian, leaving universal history untouched, the anti-nomian attitude of Christianity lost its logic and validity. While in a Kingdom, which brings all history to an end, there is no need for the Law, outside such a Kingdom, in the world of time in which man continues to live, man cannot manage without law. Abolishing the Law of God there was, itself, an act of profanation of human existence in time and history.

We have to point here to a rather naive aspect of "radical theology." In Christianity, faith in Jesus replaces the Law. As indicated, this has its own logic, on the premise that the Kingdom is at hand and this world is to come to an end. This premise is rejected, however, by the radical theologian. On the contrary, the world, this world is just about to come into its own. What, then, of Jesus? If God is dead, Jesus can no longer be looked upon as the Supreme Lord who descended from the Heavens.[20] All the Absolutes and all transcendence have collapsed. Therefore, he was a man, but one with a unique significance. On that significance, "radical theology" speaks rather vaguely and unconvincingly. Jesus is said to have liberated man from his old being and made him free for the future, or else it is maintained that Jesus made man free for his fellow-man; or again, that he liberated man from the Law. It is not quite clear how, if God is dead, he could have accomplished any of these functions, though he might be considered a noble human being whose example may well deserve imitation. One of the authors calls him "'the standpoint alongside the neighbor."[21] For Altizer, again, in keeping with his predilection for mystical opacity, Jesus represents "the Total Divine Humanity,"[22] whatever that may mean. What we have here is rather old-fashioned humanism that would consider it a pity to let go of the historic figure of Jesus because of its humanitarian significance. These interpretations tend to confirm Feuerbach's thesis that God is a projection of man's ideal inspirations. God is the Ideal Man. Having lost God, the radical theologians hold on to the Divine Ideal Man. Except that, in history, ideals and noble intentions alone may not be a sufficient basis for optimism. Is freedom from the Law and from God, by itself, enough guarantee that man will, indeed, take his place alongside his neighbor? Has man, indeed, come of age in our days, in which the air is still contaminated by the moral stench of the crematoria of

20. Altizer, *Mircea Eliade*, p. 18; *Radical Theology*, p. 128.
21. Hamilton, *Op. cit.*, p. 18.
22. Altizer, *Radical Theology*, p. 187.

Auschwitz and Treblinka? The Kingdom is to be built here on this earth. The Ideal Man is still only an ideal. Before he becomes reality, freedom will have to find its place in the context of the Law. Freedom and Law are the two foci of human existence in time and history.

Christianity maintains that it has its roots in Judaism. But it has departed from Judaism in essentials. In the past, it could not do enough to denigrate the womb from which, according to its own confession, it sprang. What we witness today in radical theology is a theological retreat all down the line along which Christianity departed from Judaism in order that, under Greco-Pagan influence, it might become an otherworldly salvationist mystical religion. As a Jew, one notes with interest a trend in this new departure which, in the search for a way out of the predicament, is, in fact, a return to some of the teachings of the Hebrew Bible. The radical theologians have been greatly influenced by Bonhoeffer, who, of course, was not one of them. But, already in the writings of Bonhoeffer, there is a strong tendency to return to the Hebrew Bible, especially in his preference for the prophetic concept of salvation in history over that of the New Testament's salvation of the soul in a condition of eternity.[23] Cox and Vahanian, both clearly influenced by Bonhoeffer, are the other writers in whom the turning to the Hebrew Bible in search of solutions is strongest.[24] Whereas in the past, Christian theologians were wont to interpret the Hebrew Bible in the light of the teachings of the New Testament, we discern now a significant tendency of re-interpreting the New Testament in the light of the Hebrew Bible. The old method of the Christian reading of the Hebrew Bible under the impact of the Gospels created the Old Testament of Christianity. One cannot help wondering what may be the eventual outcome of the new trend of reading the New Testament with the help of the Hebrew Bible.

23. Dietrich Bonhoeffer, *Letters and Papers from Prison* (New York: Macmillan Paperbacks, 1967), pp. 168, 205.
24. Cf. Cox' open chapter, "The Biblical Sources of Secularization" in *The Secular City*; also pp. 19, 72–73; Vahanian, *Op. cit.*, pp. 61, 67–68.

# The Question and the
# Answers After Auschwitz

## SEYMOUR CAIN

"During the war I had no belief, and I had always disliked the ways of the Orthodox. I saw that God was not impressed by death. Hell was his indifference. But inability to explain is no ground for disbelief. Not as long as the sense of God persists. I could wish that it did not persist. The contradictions are so painful. No concern for justice? Nothing of pity? Is God only the gossip of the living? . . ." (Mr. Sammler, in *Mr. Sammler's Planet*, by Saul Bellow).

From the moment when a national disaster appears inevitable and especially after it has become a reality, it can, like every great torment, become a productive force from the religious point of view; it begins to suggest new questions and to stress old ones. Dogmatized conceptions are pondered afresh in the light of the events, and the faith relationship that has to stand the test of an utterly changed situation is renewed in a modified form. But the new acting force is nothing less than the force of extreme despair, a despair so elemental that it can have but one of two results: the sapping of the last will of life, or the renewal of the soul. (Martin Buber, *The Prophetic Faith*)

AUSCHWITZ, OR "THE HOLOCAUST," LOOMS AS the stumbling block of contemporary Jewish theology. Whatever may be the case with Christian theologians, for whom it seems to play no significant generative or transformative role,* the Jewish religious thinker is forced to confront fullface that horror, the uttermost of evil in Jewish history. The response has not only been a timid or benumbed silence, as some complaints and accusations would lead us to believe (and sometimes silences are deeply meditative and constructive); in fact, there have been sermons, addresses, papers, and, for some years now, a small body of books on this theme. Naturally, the response has not been univocal; it has varied with the particular thinker and his mode of envisioning Judaism, God, history, and the human situation. Hence, I propose here to look at the work of three quite different thinkers, each of whom has his own individual (and typical) interpretation of the Auschwitz event.

---

* No doubt, many Christian theologians, especially those of the Auschwitz generation, have been deeply affected in their hearts and minds, and in their ecumenical interfaith intentions and activities, by the event. I am simply saying that it is not dwelt on (usually not even mentioned) in their considered, explicit theological works, even when they deal with such themes as God's action in history or the historicity of God. I will be happy to be proved mistaken in this impression.

---

SEYMOUR CAIN *is Senior editor, Religion, of the Encyclopaedia Britannica.*

## I.

Let us turn first to the question and answer as put by Ignaz Maybaum in his work, *The Face of God after Auschwitz,* a collection of sermons and essays that appeared in 1965. (The author states that he had been discussing the theme since 1933.) Maybaum, a refugee from Hitler's Germany who found a haven in England, speaks eloquently, in magnificent English, out of the German Reform tradition, to the question "What happened?" or, in its more acute Jobian form, "Where is God?" and, implicitly, to the more radical question, "Is God?" (in the light of what has happened).

Maybaum's basic concept in elucidating the question of "the face of God after Auschwitz" is *churban,* defined as "a catastrophe which makes an end to an old era and creates a new era" (p. 32). *Churban* is epochal and awful, "a day of awe, of awe beyond human understanding," of *nora.* Previous examples of *churban* are the falls of the First and Second Temples; Auschwitz, then, is the third *churban* in Jewish history (and the Temple was the body of the Jewish people). For this usage of the term Maybaum claims no originality; his own special contribution, as he sees it, lies in his viewing the deeper and fuller meaning of *churban* as "progress achieved through sacrifice," specifically through the sufferings of the Jews, through the destruction wrought on them by the Gentiles. A *churban* is a turning point into a new (and better) age, an apocalyptic catastrophe, a messianic event; not merely a *gezerah,* a "severe decree" that is wrenching and painful but not epochal, such as the 15th-century expulsion of the Jews from Spain or the 18th-century Ukrainian massacres. A *gezerah* need not happen (penitence, prayer, and charity may avert it), whereas a *churban* (a world-historical event) is the unavoidable work of God; "it thrusts the history of mankind into a new chapter" (p. 61), as in the creation of the Diaspora after the fall of the First Temple and the establishment of the Synagogue after the fall of the Second.

Progress, that modern notion, is here linked with the traditional Judaic concepts of sin and atonement and of culminating messianic advent and divine judgment. Progress here means the advancement from old (and bad) forms and ways to new (and good) ones; and it comes through atonement by sinners or by those who suffer vicariously for them. In the first and second *churbans,* according to tradition, the Jews suffered for their own sins; in the third *churban,* the so-called Holocaust, according to Maybaum, the Jews died for the sins of mankind, as Suffering Servant, High Priest, and Sacrificial Lamb, all in one. The sins in question, he avers, were the stubbornly retained remnants of feudalism, social and political conservatism and reaction, and medieval religious patterns (and also apparently, and somewhat contradictorily, the godless nihilism and idolatry of technical progress of modern man). The epochal goal achieved has been the End of the Middle Ages (for both Jews and Christians) and advancement into the "the new age . . . of democracy and Western civilization" (p. 63). Maybaum sees this as nothing less than an Exodus into a new realm, the future of mankind, where the "justice, kindness, freedom, and peace" (p. 200) planned by God may finally be achieved.

Maybaum is not unaware of the embarrassing, possibly offensive, and seemingly incredible connotations of his interpretation of Auschwitz as *churban*. He notes frankly the strikingly Christian pattern of his schema (Auschwitz is the analogue of Golgotha); indeed, paradoxically, that is one of his main points. It is the *akedah*, in which Isaac was *not* sacrificed, that is the Jewish model of progress, the happy and fulfilled life, *without sacrifice*, as against the heroic tragedy and sacrificial suffering of the Cross. (Let us leave aside whether this is a true, full picture of Judaism and Christianity, respectively.) But in world-history, ruled by the Gentiles, it is necessarily *churban*, not *akedah*, that prevails, for they seem to need the blood of sacrificed scapegoats to become cleansed and truly Christian—that's the way the Goyim are! Maybaum also does not flinch from the abhorrent logical consequence of his interpretation—that Hitler must be recognized as the instrument of God. "Hitler, My Servant," he ventures, on the analogy of "Nebuchadnezzar, My Servant" (Jer. 27:6), indicating the divinely instrumental role of that monstrously evil man (like Satan, a servant and messenger of God) in the purification and punishment of a sinful world. And Maybaum continues to praise and adore God—whom he pictures (p. 61) at Auschwitz in the role of surgeon performing a necessary operation, cutting out a part, for the renewal of the body of mankind—as still the loving kind Redeemer of old. He cites Isaiah (54:7, 8): "For a small moment have I forsaken thee/But with great compassion will I gather thee/In a little wrath I hid my face from thee for a moment/But with everlasting kindness will I have compassion on thee/Saith the Lord, thy Redeemer;" and on the analogy of the destruction of the 6th-century B.C.E. catastrophes designates those of 1933–1945 as but " 'a small moment,' 'a little wrath,' " (p. 65) measured against the eternal love which God showers on His people. Yet he is conscious and expressive of the awfulness, as well as the glory, of these presumed works of God. "How *nora*, how awful are the acts of God who is 'merciful and gracious, long suffering, and abundant in goodness and truth,' but also beyond our comprehension" (p. 199). He appeals to the model of Job who submits to, though still protesting against, and who extols, though still not comprehending, God and his acts (as against Ivan Karamazov, who revolts against God and rejects His universe). It is no great thing, says Maybaum, to praise God in a happy and prosperous time; it takes deep religious understanding to do so out of the depths of the abyss, in the terrible days of wrath, out of the most intense suffering and horror. This is the response which he, as a rabbi in the sermonic role, calls on his congregants, the Jewish people, and mankind to give to the Auschwitz event.

Despite his, no doubt, sincere insistence that he cannot understand this essentially incomprehensible event, his whole work is an attempt to discover, as he says, "both a logical and religious response" (p. 21). He does so through a synthesis of Biblical, classical Reform, and German philosophical concepts and themes: the Jews suffer to bring in the Rule of God over the world and its peoples; their God-appointed mission is to serve the course of historical progress and the bringing of mankind into a new era; out of the evil done unto them and out of their sufferings surely will come goodness and joy for them and for all mankind. Auschwitz must be seen not only as sacrifice but as salvation, not merely as an analogue of Calvary but rather as an event on the pattern of Exodus, in which we survivors—"the Remnant"—were saved from "Pharaonic persecution" and "medieval tyranny" through the miraculous intervention of God: "*Adonai yarad.* God came down. . . . Ours is the authority of the eyewitness. We were there" (p. 88). Only a part, even if a traumatically large part, of the Jewish people, Maybaum emphasizes, were exterminated; the planned genocide did *not* take place; as before in the history of the Jews, the aims of those who would wipe them out were frustrated. *Am yisrael chai!* The people Israel lives! This calls not only for perpetual lamentations for the Six Million who were sacrificed, but for hallelujahs for the Nine Million (and their children and children's children) who were saved.

But Jewish survival is not merely a biological or ethnocentric good; the Remnant saved has been selected by God as a "perennial witness" to his presence in the world and in the historical process, as the Servant to whom God's purpose and will for man and the world has been specially revealed, and as the herald who will lead in bringing in the new eschatological, progressive age that opens before us. "Our Holy Land is mankind's future. Mankind's future and nothing else is our goal" (p. 68). This eschatological advent is asserted not only as aspiration, but as actual fact in the experienced here-and-now. Of the sacrificial victims of Auschwitz he says flatly: "Their death purged Western civilization so that it can again become a place where man can live, do justly, love mercy, and walk humbly with God" (p. 84). To this assertion of realized eschatology one may respond as Jews have done in response to the Christian assertion of a world saved through Christ's atoning sacrifice and continuing presence. To our ordinary senses and judgment the world looks essentially the same: nation lifts up sword against nation, men struggle with one another, kill and torture and loot and subjugate one another, act like mad, vicious beasts and devouring monsters. My Lai recalls certain awful scenes in the history of the third *churban;* this and other incidents in the Indochina war inform us that one need not be a German or a Nazi to be engaged individually or corporatively in such actions. Obviously, such deeds may (and do) occur repetitively *after Auschwitz*, and apparently refute the thesis that that event has purified mankind.

Maybaum, too, recognizes this to some extent and, despite his frequent paeans to the new day, he is careful, at times, to speak of it only as a possibility which may or may not occur. Auschwitz—and Hiroshima —may or may not have redeemed us from the evil. "After Auschwitz a new era begins which will lead away from everything which led to Auschwitz or will continue in the vein of Auschwitz. . . . After Auschwitz and Hiroshima we must face a hitherto unknown element of human existence. We have looked into an abyss which we know now to be very close to us" (p. 38). Maybaum looks to the Biblical view of man as God's image and the world as God's creation as the source of that greater charity and responsibility which is the sole hope for saving mankind from a nuclear holocaust or genocidal barbarism. The note of inevitability that marks his reading of the third *churban*—the historical era which produced Hitler did so "with the necessity in which evil creates evil" (p. 82)—is a bit muted when looking forward to the future and the golden age of justice and peace which has been bought by the tortures and deaths of the Six Million. Yet, although the words are often the words of long-view, world-historical, German philosophy—with advance marked by the annihilation of the centers of Eastern European (read "medieval") Jewish culture and religion, and with the bulk of Jewry now "in the Western camp" and, hence, with the forces of progress—the voice is often the voice of the oldtime, prophetic hope and messianic reform. Auschwitz and Hiroshima are pointed to as absolutely unique events that have transformed human imagination, and the future into which they lead is described as "something new . . . the door to the new heaven and new earth" (p. 200). Nevertheless, Maybaum's response is couched in the old terms; he repeats the concepts of the Prophets read according to the Reform dispensation; he accepts the old image of God and His actions in the world and, especially, toward Israel. Though the situation out of which the question arises is frankly recognized as a mad inferno placing the old beliefs and assurances in jeopardy, the answer still sounds out as unproblematic and unperplexed, with the old assurance, joy, and hope. This demonstrates that whatever some dogmatic commentators may say, the old words, images, and concepts may still figure in a present-day response to Auschwitz. Whether such a response is satisfactory and convincing, however, is another matter.

## II.

Richard Rubenstein, the young American radical theologian, stands diametrically opposed to Maybaum, and speaks also with remarkable lit-

361

erary power and deftness. Auschwitz, for Rubenstein, is the utter and decisive refutation of the traditional Judaic affirmation of a providential God acting in history, watching especially over the Jewish people whom He has selected out from among the peoples of the earth to serve His will for the world. In his challenging manifesto, *After Auschwitz* (1966), he replied indirectly to Maybaum when he responded to the noted, heroic anti-Nazi German clergyman Heinrich Gruber, who also continued to interpret Auschwitz and the catastrophe that befell the Jews there in the traditional way, often citing the same Biblical verses and analogies as did Maybaum. To Rubenstein's question, in an interview in 1961, "Was it God's will that Hitler destroyed the Jews?" the old man replied with the verse from Psalms, "For Thy sake are we slaughtered every day" (44:23) and went on to the Biblical analogue of Hitler with Nebuchadnezzar as one of the "rods of God's anger" with which He had punished His chosen people. Not being a Reform Jew but an Evangelical Protestant, Gruber did not point toward some eschatological-progressive Mission as justification of the hard ways of God, but contented himself merely with the statement that, "For some reason it was part of God's plan that the Jews died. . . . He is the Lord, He is the Master, all is in His keeping and ordering" (pp. 53, 54).

Rubenstein revolted against this application of what he calls "the normative Judaeo-Christian theology of history" to the murder factories, and completely rejected that theology as obsolete and unbelievable by any reasonably intelligent person with some experience of our times. This interview (capped by a journey to Auschwitz in the early 60s) proved to be "a theological point of no return" (p. 46) for Rubenstein; he could not, and would not, any longer affirm a God who was the omnipotent Lord over history and who would use an Adolf Hitler as His instrument to kill six million of His chosen people; nor could he "believe in Israel as the chosen people of God *after Auschwitz*" (ibid.).

The world, he asserts, is a tragic and meaningless place, where men have no basis for hope in divine aid, or in any ultimate solution of the ills that beset them; the only Messiah is death, and each of us must come to an acceptance of the tragic vision of our evanescence, loneliness, vulnerability, and ultimate destruction in a universe which is unconcerned with us, our prayers, and our hopes. He stands with Albert Camus, particularly the Camus of *The Plague,* in passionately revolting against the view that sees human suffering as a payment for sin and guilt exacted by a transcendent Father-God who stands in judgment against us. Instead, Rubenstein asserts human solidarity and a variety of alternative theological views.

In the first place, he insists, the Auschwitz experience has resulted not only in a rejection or demythologization of the traditional Judaic theology of history, but also in the positive affirmation of the value of human life in and for itself, without any need for sanction by "super-ordinate values," "special theological relationships," or "metahistorical meanings." Joy and fulfillment are to be sought, as pain and suffering are to be endured, in this temporary life here and now, not in some mystical future or *eschaton*. On the one hand, this connotes a reliance on human will and power, instead of on the traditional omnipotent Lord of history; this is the way that Rubenstein reads the return to Zion, which, for him, is, with Auschwitz, one of the "two moments of *kairos*," of decisive transformation, in our time. But it also involves a return to the God (or gods) of nature, to the affirmation of the basic processes and rhythms of nature, and to an emphasis on man's involvement with them and submission to their inevitable powers and cycles. This, too, is part of Rubenstein's reading of the return to Zion: it means not only a return to the Land but also to the old gods of the Land, to the Canaanite paganism of our early ancestors (or at least of a good many of them). We have renewed contact, he insists, "with those powers of life and death which engendered men's feelings about Baal, Astarte, and Anath. These powers have again become decisive in our religious life" (p. 70). Apparently this is intended more as prophetic insight into the future than as observation of the present, and to apply especially (or only) to Israel. It does not mean, literally, a return to the actual worship of Baal and Astarte, he cautions, but simply "that earth's fruitfulness, its vicissitudes, and its engendering power will once again become the central spiritual realities of Jewish life, at least in Israel" (p. 136). The "dionysian" quality of Israeli folk music is for him an example of this return to the archaic religion. Thus, against Maybaum and his exaltation of progress and modernity, the forward march of humanity, Rubenstein champions the return to the archaic past, to primitive modes of religious experience and expression.

He dwells on the destructive aspect of divinity in this archaic view. "Earth is a Mother, but . . . a cannibal Mother. Sooner or later it consumes what it gives birth to" (p. 125). The return of the blood of a slaughtered animal to earth in ancient sacrifice and in still continuing *kashrut* is an indication of traditional Judaism's recognition of this. So is the ceremony of the redemption of the firstborn son. So is Auschwitz, in the context of this discussion of the transmoral, destructive aspect of divine holiness. It fits into the archaic religious consciousness and observance of the universal natural cycle of death and rebirth. The mass death of European Jewry was followed by a rebirth of the Jewish people in the land of Israel.

Moreover, God is not only the "true substance" in contrast with our nothingness, He is also, in Rubenstein's version, the ultimate Nothing or No-thing-ness of the Lurianic Kabbalah, the primordial Godhead out of which the world and the resultant "God" created by this subtraction

363

arose. To this original divine nothingness, man and the world are ultimately to return. God as primal ground remains the reality against which
all finite human concerns and aspirations are measured. Yet there is no
hope of salvation for the human order; man's ultimate destiny is to be
nothinged as his individual personal self (and implicitly also as a species along with the whole finite world) and to be returned to the divine
nothingness.

With this doctrine of God—and of the world and history—goes a doctrine of man, especially of the Jewish people and its relation to other
peoples. The main cause of Jewish disaster, particularly during the
Christian era, according to Rubenstein, has been its claim to be especially holy and chosen, the Priest-People among the nations. With the
assumed sacrality has gone the accompanying vulnerability to become
the sacrificial offering of the wider human community in times of crisis;
inevitably the servant becomes the scapegoat, the priest the sacrifice.
Philo-semitic as well as anti-semitic stereotypes of the Jew (*e.g.*, as especially good and holy) cater to the dark atavistic needs of a mankind that
suffers from its sense of sin and guilt, and in times of great social stress
this may lead to what are, in effect, acts of ritual murder, with the Jews
as the victims. This, he claims, is what happened in Nazi Germany: "The
death camps were one huge act of ritual murder in which the perpetra-
tors were convinced that only through the elimination of the Jews could
Germany's safety be vouchsafed" (*After Auschwitz*, 74). But the main
result of Rubenstein's considerations is to opt for a more modest, ordinary, human, all-too-human role for the Jews, because their previous
claims to special election are unfounded, illusory, and, more urgently,
because they are inherently and ultimately suicidal.

Hence, he ends with a kind of Reconstructionist view of the Jews
as a people like other peoples, with a peculiar ethnic history, culture,
folkways, and religion; but he also concludes with a deepened awareness
of the evil imbedded in men's hearts and of the ultimate nothingess of
human achievements. Though separated from other men by our differing tradition and commitment, we are one with them in our common
guilt and sin (if that term may still be used in this context) and in our
standing forth for a moment against our common inevitable end and
annihilation in death. Religious observances and participation are even
more necessary now, in the time of the Death of the providential, redeeming God of Biblical faith—than ever before; they give the order,
discipline, and restraint without which most men would become anarchic
beasts; and they give the appearance of meaning and value to an essentially meaningless existence. Rubenstein's call is for a Jewish paganism,
centered on the enjoyment of earthly, sensual pleasures, reined in by
reasonable restraints, and guided by sober realism in the difficult task of
human existence in an impassive and uncaring cosmos. For such "real-

364

ism" he claims a traditional basis (*e.g.*, in the allegedly this-worldly and life-centered orientation of the Rabbis).

One is naturally inclined to marvel at and admire the varieties of erudition and the gifts of expression of this talented young man, but if ones moves on to meditate, his protests seem far more cogent than do his proposals. Just how does his theme of God the Destroyer solve the human and religious problem of Auschwitz and how does it link up with the other themes in his variegated presentation? Are the six million victims of the Nazi holocaust simply to be considered part of the rhythmic alternations of birth-death-rebirth in the natural order, and are Hitler and the Nazis simply to be regarded as the apotheosized natural process, which has replaced the providential-redeeming God of history? There is something fundamentally askew here, stemming, I hazard, from the subsuming of the historical under the natural order and its explanatory concepts (and perhaps a basic misreading of Mircea Eliade); moreover, even if the explanation is granted, it is just as irrational and absurd— and indeed even more so—to accept the degrading death of millions of Jews as immanently designed to keep the economy of nature in a state of balance as to accept it as divinely willed to glorify God and serve His purposes. Also, there is a considerable discrepancy between the emphasis on the inevitable, cyclic character of creation and destruction and the alternative emphasis on a psychoanalytically enlightened stratagem to restrain our destructive impulses, and on the traditional, liturgical religious forms to channel and rein in potentially catastrophic human passions. At this point, one is inclined to sympathize once again with Elie Wiesel's resentment of the various highfaluting intellectual attempts of the theologians to make Auschwitz intelligible. How much does talk of Earth as the cannibal Mother and God as the ground of being, or analysis of the presumed anal and fecal obsessions of the Nazis have to do with the reality of Auschwitz and the agonizing traumatic question which it raises for us? However, Rubenstein stands out in one important respect from practically all of the other Jewish commentators on Auschwitz, in his emphasis on the involvement of the Jews in the common passions, instincts, or potentialities of the human race. Auschwitz indicates the ultimate evil in all of us, that we are all, historically or potentially, murderers.

## III.

Emil Fackenheim, the distinguished German refugee and now Canadian philosopher and theologian, has explicitly denied Rubenstein's contention that Auschwitz destroyed the grounds for belief in the traditional historical God of Judaism and made any theology espousing that belief intellectually indefensible. He has done so in a series of publications between 1968 and 1970, culminating in his little book *God's Presence in History*. He is in basic agreement with Rubenstein that

Auschwitz has placed the traditional faith in a historically present and particularly redemptive God in grave jeopardy. He, too, emphasizes Jewish ethnicity and survival as central aims and values in the post-Auschwitz era, with its necessities of staying alive, enduring, and remaining united as a distinctive identifiable people. He cites with approval the statement by the Israeli journalist Amos Kenan: "After the death camps we are left with only one supreme value; existence" (*God's Presence*, 87), and extols the sacredness of Jewish life above that of Jewish death. *"Am yisrael chai*—the people Israel lives," he proclaims, in the context of the establishment and existence of the State of Israel and the events of May-June, 1967.

But here the resemblance ends. To Fackenheim, such an attitude is not merely a healthy, life-affirming human response to the situation, but is, above all, a reply to the command of a God who still remains present in history and in a special relation to His elected people. Jewish existence, survival, unity, and positive action in everyday, this-worldly life are commanded by God, the God of the ancient covenant, now speaking out of the furnaces and through the sufferings and ashes of the victims of Auschwitz. Auschwitz, for Fackenheim, is a revelation-event bearing Torah to mid- and late-20th century Jews.

The faithfulness required by Auschwitz is, however, not merely passive obedience to a divine command; it is an active fidelity, a loyalty to the dead, a refusal to blot them out as if they had never been, and to make Adolf Hitler ultimately the victor. The Jew is contradictorily commanded to remember the apparently God-denying event and, yet, to remain true to the God-affirmation of the past.

This "command from Auschwitz" resolves this dilemma to some extent. But admittedly, in Fackenheim's own presentation, it is a fragmentary, opaque, and contradictory commandment, and the response is, accordingly, mixed. Obviously, the God of Auschwitz cannot be presented as a saving and loving God; indeed, he calls forth protest and defiance from faithful Jews, and Fackenheim approves of those voices of protest as the new form of the age-old Jewish contention with God, as the voices of "Jewish authenticity." Continuing Jewish existence and endurance involve as much a stubborn defiance of God as of man. But where, then, is the redeeming God, the especially saving God of Israel, divine redemption in history, as at the Red Sea in the 13th century B.C.E.?

Historical redemption in our time, says this former staunchly anti-Zionist, anti-nationalist German Jew, is to be found in the reestablishment of the State of Israel and has been especially disclosed in the victory of the Israelis in the Six Day War of 1967. While not an "answer" (in the sense of an explanation), the State of Israel is, for him, a "response" to Auschwitz, the reply of new life and construction to death and destruction. And the Six Day War, the event that he calls "Jerusalem

1967," is almost declared a theophany, a moment of divine revelation and redemption, "when at Jerusalem the threat of total annihilation gave way to sudden salvation," and there was present the "radical astonishment" which marks events experienced as miracle (*Quest for Past and Future*, 25f.).

That Israel is a secular state, that Zionism has represented a reversal of Diaspora Jewry's religious stance toward the world, that Israel's achievements loom rather as the work of human power, skill, and virtue—none of these considerations disturb Fackenheim in his view that divine Providence has been involved here. He has visited Israel and been impressed by *"the religious quality of the 'secularist' Israeli Jew"* (*Christian Century*, May 6, 1970, 567). What this consists of he does not specify, but in context it must have to do with the endurance, the carrying-on of the Jewish people, with the commitment to survival which s testified to, explicitly or implicitly, by every Jew anywhere in the world who has decided to remain a Jew after Auschwitz. The State of Israel is a testimony to the ecumenical unity of "religious" and "secular" Jews, which Fackenheim sees as commanded by the Voice coming out of Auschwitz. Thus, survival is not for him, as for Rubenstein, a merely human and biological fact that carries its own validation, without need for a "superordinate" index and value. Fackenheim reads it as carrying divine sanction and valuation. Survival of the Jews is also not merely of ethnocentric significance, but has a universal meaning, for, as at Auschwith the Jew stood for all mankind, so "Jerusalem" stands for the survival of all peoples and against genocide universally. "Israel is collectively what every survivor is individually: a No to the demons of Auschwitz, a Yes to Jewish survival and security—and thus a testimony to life against death *on behalf of all mankind"* (*Christian Century*, July 29, 1970, 923).

So, here again, we have an eloquent, moving interpretation of the meaning and consequences of Auschwitz, and yet again the author's protests seem more convincing than his proposals. The Jews did not die in the Holocaust for their own sins, or vicariously for the sins of others, he says, nor did they die for their own faith and commitment; they died because they were singled out and identifiable as Jews, and this occurred because their forebears decided to remain Jews and raise their children as Jews—they died because of the commitment and the virtues (or the rashness) of their great-grandparents. Therefore, the decision of the present-day Jew to remain a Jew and raise his children as Jews is, humanly speaking, an absurdity, the willful courting or risking of self-destruction. It must, therefore, be a response, consciously or not, to a divine command, to "the commanding voice of Auschwitz." Fackenheim presents us, indeed, with an extraordinary dialectic: *because* the Nazis tried, almost successfully, to exterminate the Jews and Judaism, *therefore* we must and shall affirm and preserve them—the people and the faith or tradition. His deep,

367

central emphasis is on piety toward the dead, the resolve that their deaths and sufferings shall not have been in vain, that Auschwitz should be the horrible but unavoidable starting point of rebirth and regeneration, of a whole new era and condition for the Jews and Judaism. There is also in his vision an extraordinary magnification and glorification of human will and power, even if it be in carrying out the divine command—to the verge, indeed, of magic or theurgy—in the face of divine powerlessness. "We shall persist without hope and recreate hope—and, as it were, divine Power—by our persistence" (*God's Presence*, 88).

It should be noted that Fackenheim refuses to say that Auschwitz is explained or redeemed by the new unity of the Jewish people and the establishment and preservation of the State of Israel. He does not read it with German world-historical detachment as the cruel and evil event that brings forth value and progress. But if Auschwitz is not for him, in some sense, a Good Friday of ignominious suffering and death before an Easter and resurrection of the Jewish folk, how, then, does he see the event? What becomes of the God of absolute monotheism who is the maker of light and darkness and the creator of peace and evil? Is Auschwitz, then, to be interpreted as a divine trial, a test of Jewish faith and endurance? Or is Auschwitz outside of the divine realm and plan?

Despite his insistence on the preservation of the belief in the God who is present in history and in the historical world as His domain, which, he explicitly emphasizes, must include Auschwitz, at the same time Fackenheim assigns Auschwitz to the unquestioned sway of "the demons," "the devil," or "Satan." Jewish faith involves not merely a protest against God, but a defiance of "the forces of hell itself" (*God's Presence*, 92). When this demonic, unstoppable power is contrasted with the powerlessness of God in these events, we are apparently very close to a two-power, two-reality doctrine, reminiscent not only of classical Gnosticism, but also of the two-God expressions of the Auschwitz survivor and voice Elie Wiesel, to whom, incidentally, *God's Presence in History* is dedicated. The bad God of Auschwitz in this version is the God present in history; the just, good God is banished to the heavens, beyond the sphere of care and concern, of address and response. Indeed, the secular Jew, for one, says Fackenheim, "knows that the devil, if not God, is alive" (p. 82).

It would seem, then, that Fackenheim, reflecting on these terrible events—what Maybaum calls the *churban*—honestly, and in the basic terms of the religious tradition to which he is committed, sounds a refrain which goes counter to his main theme. He wishes, and urges us, to hold fast to the traditional, covenant God who is present in, and Lord of, history; but, impressed to the core of his mind and being by the Auschwitz event, he harps on a dark, demonic force that is the Prince of this world. Although this is no new thing in the history of Judaism and Christianity, and certainly to be taken seriously as an understandable response to the way of the historical world, it does not, any more than Rubenstein's response, save the loving and redeeming God of Israel, much as the author so intensely struggles to do. It leaves questionable both the goodness and the power of God, or at the least, raises anew the question of the nature of God and the place of radical evil in the divine reality.

## V.

Whatever one may think of these three writers, they deserve honor for their spiritual honesty and courage in confronting this epochal traumatic theme. One is reluctant to speak of "this essentially incomprehensible event," because of the ever-present legacy of pain involved, the sense of common guilt and responsibility, the inhibition against theologizing about—making intellectual capital of—the *churban;* but, above all, because of the gigantic religious questions that are raised and that call exigently for equivalent answers, not only intellectually, but also personally, existentially. They push one to the verge of belief and unbelief; they call for an illuminated awareness of what one really believes or disbelieves.

It must be granted immediately, however, that this is not the way Auschwitz appears to all those committed or linked to the Judaic tradition. Not only is belief in the traditional God of Judaism possible (and actual) after Auschwitz, but the *churban* may not raise the ultimate questions noted here. Conversations I have had with ordinary Jewish congregants, including some European survivors, show this; they ascribe evil acts to the wickedness of men and do not hold them against God or consider them a refutation of His existence or His goodness (no more, by the way, than the deeply pious American Negro slaves blamed God for their sufferings and oppression). Possibly this is because ordinary Jews are unreflecting and ignorant or inadequately informed of the traditional doctrines of divine power, providence, and grace, or the covenant-relation. But there are also learned rabbis and theologians who see Auschwitz as just another and more terrible instance of the disasters and trials through which Israel has walked throughout history, and Death-of-God talk as impetuous, irreflective rhetoric. The historical acuteness and the fairness of this judgment may well be questioned, but Mr. Sammler's point in our epigraph above still stands: "inability to explain is no ground for disbelief . . . as long as the sense of God persists." With this, however, goes, as he notes, an anguished awareness of the painful contradictions, the apparent divine indifference to mass death, injustice, and suffering, and the possible reduction of God to mere human "gossip." Hence, as Martin Buber says in our other epigraph, "a national disaster" and the "extreme despair" resulting from it may constitute "an utterly changed situation" that requires a rethinking of the traditional concepts and, thus, not a rejection but a renewal of the "faith relationship," though "in a modified form"—perhaps drastically so.

This raises the question of what is expected in historical events that will justify belief in God as sole Power, Presence, Helper, etc. Is it empirical, worldly success, prosperity, fruitfulness, the physical overcoming of evils and dangers, military victories over our enemies, and the like? There are certainly layers in the Biblical tradition where this is what God and the Covenant mean, but, just as certainly there are different and deeper meanings elsewhere in the Bible and in the post-Biblical tradition. Long before the disasters attending the fall of the Second Temple, the Jews, or at least their spiritual leaders, were aware that the innocent and righteous suffer, are oppressed and even exterminated by the more powerful, that worldly success and triumph may go to evil men or to sheer might alone—for the time being that is the time of men's lives.

Is Jewish faith and religion—"Judaism"—guaranteed to give us release from suffering in a tangible, material sense, to rescue us literally in sorely pressed spots, like the Biblical heroes of old (to be held up on the wings of angels, to be lifted out whole from the furnaces, to have the waters part before us and engulf our pursuers)? How then, would Judaism have survived its numerous failures, defeats, catastrophes, and massacres? Or does Jewish faith rather inculcate a certain response to suffering (and the evil and contradiction out of which it arises), bestow on it a certain meaning and valuation that help us to cope with it creatively, to live with it and in it, and even ultimately, we hope, to overcome or redeem it?

There also arises the question as to whether Jewish faith is contingent only upon what happens to the Jews. Some post-Auschwitz spokesmen resent this question, on the grounds of the absolute uniqueness of the Auschwitz event, and because it is the special covenant with the Jewish people that is at stake here. Elie Wiesel puts it flatly that the divine promise to protect the existence of the Jewish people was broken at Auschwitz, hence the theological terror and confusion (JUDAISM, Summer 1967, 281). Maybaum, alone, contends that God did, indeed, save (the bulk of) His people, but this at the cost of making God both slayer and savior, both the wielder and the foiler of His Nazi instrument. Rubenstein has insisted on the voiding (really the nonexistence or unbelievability) of the covenant as the crucial point, dismissing the general theistic problem of God and evil as irrelevant to his thesis (*Christian Century*, May 21, 1969, 716–718). But one wonders: would faith in the God of the Covenant be justified or undisturbed if only non-Jewish peoples—say, "Aryan" German Communities and Jehovah's Witnesses and ethnic Poles, Russians, and lesser breeds without the Law—had been among the masses of those turned to ashes and smoke, and the Jews had been miraculously saved? Would God then elicit our unreserved praise and adoration, and would we then sing joyous hallelujahs? Or would not the same crucial doubts have arisen about God's presence and action in history, even if only one small folk (say, the Gypsies) had been systematically and completely exterminated? Joined with Hiroshima, such an event would have raised the possibility of the extermination of the human race and put in question the general and not inconsequential covenant with mankind. Despite the protestations of Fackenheim and others, I am convinced that there is a definite link between war and genocide, and a basic similarity between Auschwitz and certain events and policies in Vietnam. As for the alleged criterion of "rational" purpose, one people's or generation's rationality is another's madness in these matters. The whole idea of the special covenant has to be reexamined in the light of the existence of other special peoples and faiths (which are apparently taken seriously, on a worldwide scale, only by Rubenstein among the authors surveyed) and also of other claimed special covenants, *e.g.*, the contention of Black Theology for a special status for black people (especially black Americans) as God's suffering servant, witness, and messenger to mankind.

In the end, everyone of us is faced with Ivan Karamazov's question, in the context, not of one hypothetical tortured innocent child, but of the hundreds of thousands and tens of millions of children and adults who have been burned, fragmented, exploded, and machine-gunned in ditches for no culpable reason. The radical, nihilistic questions are the only right ones—the ones that demand an answer—for our time. They salutarily counteract the shameful collaboration with, and virtual apologia for historical evil that so often goes with traditional thought and scholarship, with a so-called wider view and a self-alleged realism, practicality, and rationality. But we are not, therefore, bound ineluctably to accept the radical nihilistic answer, to reject the world and say "No" to God's creation, as Ivan did.

Somehow, someday, all that has happened to us and from us will have to be affirmed as connected with the ultimate source of existence and value, to be asserted as grace, to be accepted as stemming from grace. This seems a shocking, incomprehensible, impossible feat at the present moment. Yet there are hopeful signs, meager and frail though they be. The world goes on (perhaps it should not have after Auschwitz, as Arthur Hertzberg has observed, but nevertheless it does), and Jews carry on and mankind carries on. And, though often it seems otherwise, everything in the relations between men and peoples is not done on the model of Auschwitz and Hiroshima. At My Lai, not all who were ordered to participate in the massacre did so; some refused and one or two tried to stop it, even in the allegedly explicatory and exculpating situation of

371

battle and comrade-casualties. In the Introduction to his *Secular Chris-tianity*, that excellent Protestant theologian and translator of Buber, Ronald Gregor Smith, notes that his image of modern man stems from "the Germany of the pre-war years, and then of the Third Reich and the brutality and terror of the Nazi regime" (p. 15). But, strikingly, he does not summon up the expected figures of the Nazi leaders, as one would expect; instead, he singles out such heroic resistants to the Nazis as Paul Schneider, Karl Barth, Pastor Niemoeller, Dietrich Bonhoeffer, and Helmut James von Moltke, men who said "No" to the Nazis, and three of whom lost their lives in so doing. This strange notion, that such may be the representative modern men, gives me pause and serves to complement, though not to refute, my sweeping statement above that we are all murderers, historically or potentially. Some of us also try to stop or protest the murders, and in so doing put our existence at stake. There are also heroes and saints in our time, albeit unpretentious and devoid of vainglory. The frightening and troubling question of the face of man after Auschwitz seems to require a complex and polychromatic answer.

Emil Fackenheim is certainly right that we are commanded to hope; hope, of course, being understood not as self-deceptive, sentimental opti-mism, but as an ontological virtue and function, rooted in personal, human, and universal being, and ultimately in the bond with, or aspira-tion toward, the transcendent that may become present. This means to say "Yes" to reality, no matter what. This—or its opposite—is the basic act out of which all else flows. The rest is commentary.

# God and the Holocaust

### CHARLES W. STECKEL

THE INQUIRY INTO THE HOLOCAUST AND GOD'S silent role in it originated in Palestine immediately after 1945, long before Elie Wiesel's passionate *din Torah* with God and his piercing accusation of the entire world, or the radical theology of Richard L. Rubenstein and his psychoanalytical interpretation of God in Auschwitz. It began before the soothing theodicy of Emil L. Fackenheim and the learned explanataions of Samuel E. Karff about the Aggadah and the problem of evil and suffering. Theologians, writers from all walks of life, and rabbis representing all branches of Judaism have addressed themselves to this greatest of all evils. These men are trying to come to grips with the imminent meaning and far-reaching religious implications of our recent tragedy. When World War II ended and the results of cannibalism became known, historians and theologians began to interpret its meaning, and this process of grappling with the catastrophe still continues. It is fair to characterize the Holocaust theology as having alarmed our dormant conscience and having raised pertinent questions without bringing us closer to an acceptable answer. Victor E. Frankl quotes Lessing who once said, "There are things which must cause you to lose your reason or you have none to lose."[1]

Why then are we Jews trying to reason, analyze, rationalize something as ugly, perverted and evil as the Holocaust? We must, for two reasons: Firstly, a Jewish people and a Judaism which survived at the price of ignoring Auschwitz would not deserve to survive.[2] Secondly, because if we Jews do not keep on reminding the world, humankind will soon forget completely and deny that anything ever happened. We are duty-bound to search relentlessly and painstakingly, and it is an encouraging sign that mankind has not forgotten. Neither Jews nor Christians can afford to ignore Auschwitz. Civilized people must grapple with the problem continuously and meticulously.

## THEODICIES

### Thesis—Antithesis—Synthesis

If we are to continue with theodicy as a religious philosophy of traditional monotheism, then the following three alternatives are open to us. The first is Fundamentalism, whose exponents believe that man

---

1. *Man's Search for Meaning* (Boston: Beacon Press, 1963), p. 18.
2. E. L. Fackenheim, "Jewish Faith and the Holocaust," reprint by Atid, p. 2.

---

CHARLES W. STECKEL *is Rabbi of Temple Beth Torah, Pasadena, California.*

cannot always grasp the mysteries surrounding him. In this respect there is no disagreement among traditionalists of all faiths. In the past, Jeremiah's outcry (12:1) was heard in the land: "Why is the way of the wicked prosperous?" and our forefathers were perplexed as they realized and observed the existence of the problem.

Today, it is fashionable to discuss how meaningless is the Fundamentalist point of view. It is, indeed, unacceptable to the "educated and mature" mind, but the fact remains that some well-educated, mature and pious men still adhere to it. Their piety and faith are stronger than reason. The traditionalist simply declares that God's ways are inscrutable and there is no point in trying to find the reasons behind them. Though His ways may appear unjust to our faulty perception, they are not really so. The Fundamentalists claim that man is good, but suffers from an insufficiency of both knowledge of what God expects of him and of genuine reverence and "fear of the Lord." Elie Wiesel quotes a Ḥasidic saint, who said, "For the faithful there are no questions; for the non-believer there are no answers."[3] Does this mean that the "sophisticated" believer, who believes and questions, has no place in the congregation of the faithful?

Mordecai M. Kaplan writes, "Not a single one of the numerous theodicies, or attempts of thinkers to reconcile the goodness of God with the existence of evil, has ever proved convincing."[4] The modern, educated mind will not accept the Holocaust as the result of our sins, or as an unexplainable mystery. Kaplan notes that it is not surprising that none of the great minds, from Samson Raphael Hirsch to Leo Baeck and Martin Buber, came up with a satisfactory solution of the problem of evil.[5] Neither can an adult mind accept Hermann Cohen's explanation that "misery and pain are needed in order to awaken the conscience of men and thereby to advance the cause of ethical progress." "Evil is the necessary background of good; it is the chair for the good," and "evil appears evil to our limited understanding." Cohen also has the answer as to why the poor suffer. "The suffering of the poor is a kind of sacrifice for the sins of all mankind . . . as the price of progress. It is the saints that suffer. God loves the miserable."[6] In other words, the nicest children of God are to pay the price for all of us.

The second alternative, presented by Richard L. Rubenstein and his radical theology, claims that in the face of the German atrocities only two answers are possible in regard to the Holocaust. Either we accept the "traditional answer" that Hitler was used as an instrument of bringing divine visitation upon the Jewish people—or we must assume that "God

---

3. *Jewish Existence in an Open Society* (Los Angeles: The Ward Ritchie Press), p. 41.
4. *Judaism as a Civilization* (New York: Reconstructionist Press, 1957), pp. 115, 329, and *Questions Jews Ask* (New York: Reconstructionist Press, 1956), p. 116.
5. *Questions Jews Ask*, p. 118.
6. Jacob B. Agus, *Modern Philosophies of Judaism* (New York: Behrman's Jewish Book House, 1941), pp. 108–111.

is dead." His pessimism concerning our civilization is based on psychology and the inability of man to discipline himself. Freud's pessimistic predicament about human potentialities dominates Rubinstein's philosophy when he writes, "The fantasy of a world without restraints, the world in which God is dead, can be imagined at many levels."[7]

I confess my regret that a promising, almost brilliant, mind, has not found a different language to convey his message. I might eventually understand that Rubenstein, by joining the ranks of contemporary Protestant radical theologians, has sentenced God to die,[8] but I cannot understand why he continues to disturb Him. To describe "God after-the-death-of-God" as "Holy Nothingness," or the "omnipotent Nothingness is Lord of creation," tells the reader nothing at all, certainly about Nothingness.[9]

As we study the books of Jewish theologians of previous generations dealing with the eternal quest, men who were critics, dissenters and innovators, from Maimonides to Kaplan, we hear soft and God-inspired voices: *divrei Elohim hayym*, words of a living God. Except for the Karaites, who were involved in theological as well as personal polemics with the Rabbanites, Jewish theologians always were soft spoken whenever they disagreed with their predecessors or their contemporaries. Whether Cox is right that "the rise of urban civilization and the collapse of traditional religion are the main hallmarks of our time" remains to be seen. Only the future will tell to what extent any contemporary theologian or thinker was right or wrong, but one thing is sure. Rubenstein the theologian, radical, original and often brilliant, has decided to travel the road to a "very private subjectivity." He has made some friends and gained some followers, but he has also galvanized the great majority of American rabbis to a condemnation of his Auschwitz and post-Auschwitz rhetoric. Surely, there must be better ways in which a rabbi can express his dissent from his own teachers as well as from those of the past.

The third alternative in pursuing the idea of resolving the dilemma of evil and suffering generally, and the Holocaust particularly, is rationalism. Robert Gordis, in his early writings, introduced the Biblical concept of theodicy with special emphasis on Job and Deutero-Isaiah[10] and reiterated and expanded this idea in both "The Book of God and Man— A Study of Job" and in the new edition of "A Faith for Moderns." The justification of God in a world of undeserved suffering is based on a socio-theological analysis of the Biblical text, and Gordis introduces into

---

7. *After Auschwitz*, p. 36.
8. *Ibid.*, p. 243.
9. In Neusner's review of Rubenstein's book, *Morality and Eros. Midstream*, October 1970, p. 73.
10. *Judaism for the Modern Age* (New York: Farrar, Straus and Cudahy, 1955), and, particularly, the essay on the Book of Job in *Great Moral Dilemmas* (New York: Harper and Brothers, 1956), pp. 155–178.

his theodicy two doctrines which, when combined, represent a "realistic and more compassionate" answer.

The first, often expressed in the Holy Scriptures, is the idea of the mutual, moral interdependence of men. Men are organically related to one another. Therefore, when some men sin, other men suffer. Mankind is like the human organism. Each individual organ can, and will, influence the well-being or the aching of the whole body. The Germans[11] committed monstrous crimes and the Jews became the victims. Not God, but the Germans, brought suffering and inflicted it upon Jews and others.

The second doctrine of "vicarious suffering" is found in the writings of the Prophets, particularly in Deutero-Isaiah. "When one loves another human being, one is bound to suffer with and for the loved one."[12] Humankind is likened to a family, and a crime committed by one of the members will cause anguish and pain to all the other members, no matter how innocent they are.

Let us assume that we follow Gordis approvingly to this point and accept his rationale. Our difficulty remains how to explain it to the educated but Jewishly uncommitted Jew. Why were we Jews chosen to suffer for Europeans, most of whom had failed to stand up and to be counted? The annihilation of over one million innocent Jewish children can hardly be explained by vicarious suffering alone and will not satisfy the critic; neither will it help to explain why innocent Biafran children had to die because Africans failed to act rationally. Although we perpetuate tradition, we must realize that we are not living in an age of the Prophets who spoke to their generation in a prophetic language but were, nonetheless, often discouraged, for their contemporaries simply did not understand them. Only if we find our own semantics and the ability to speak of, and about, the Holocaust in our own language will we find some satisfaction and, eventually, an answer to this very agonizing question.

## THE IRRELEVANCE OF THEODICY

The problem of theodicy is as old as Judaism itself, or as religion, for that matter. Joseph Klausner defined the theodicy of the Holocaust as the "question of all questions"[13] and admitted that Jewish thinkers of all ages found answers but not "the answer" to the question of why the righteous suffer and evil exists.

As we enter the second quarter of a century of research—theological, philosophical and historical—into the problems of the Holocaust, the ques-

---

11. Leon Poliakov, in *Harvest of Hate* (Syracuse, N.Y.: Syracuse University Press, 1954), p. 8 and p. 156, writes: ". . . genocide, because it affects the deepest levels of man's spirit cannot be carried out without the concurrence of all the people."
12. Robert Gordis, *Jewish Existence In An Open Society* (Los Angeles: The Ward Ritchie Press, 1970), p. 14.
13. "The Question of all Questions and Answers," *Mibayit* (Tel Aviv: Agudat Hasofrim Haivrim B'eretz Yisrael, 1946), pp. 7–30.

tion is being raised whether our tragedy should be considered as a theological or a socio-political problem.[14] It would be quite reasonable to expect that man today should behave differently from his less educated and less sophisticated ancestors of thousands or even of hundreds of years ago. But reality tells us that man only sometimes behaves better than did his forefathers, and often does not. Man has failed to make of man a better human being. It looks as if God left this educational opportunity to humans, and they have failed to take advantage of the opportunities which are theirs. In the words of Erich Fromm, "Man's life is determined by the inescapable alternative between regression and progression, between return to animal existence and arrival of human existence. Any attempt to return is painful, it inevitably leads to suffering."[15]

Louis M. Shifier, a Gentile who was an inmate of a concentration camp, wrote in the *Davar,* in 1961 "that one can write about War, even if one has not participated in it, but it is impossible to write about concentration camps unless one has lived in one."[16]

Two men survived in concentration camps. One, Wiesel, speaks of "a mystical dimension" when he writes, "We still do not know what took place there, let alone why certain events took place there the way they did."[17] The other, Frankl, being a psychoanalyst, uses the "existential dimension" in discussing the psychology of the concentration camp. He writes, "While the outsider was too far removed from the strange world of the concentration camp and could scarcely empathize, the person who was in the midst of it had grown hardened to its laws and had no distance. It can therefore be said that we have no adequate description of just what took place since we have to allow for a considerable degree of distortion in the mentality of the viewer."[18]

In a letter addressed to Robert Gordis in May, 1968, I wrote, in part:

> The purpose of my letter is twofold. Firstly, permit me to call your attention to the fact that the question of "God is dead" was raised by American rabbis and not by survivors of the Holocaust. It is, therefore, misleading when you state that "one can not only understand but empathize with those who, having gone through the hell-fires of Nazism, continue to feel the iron of persecution in their own being and are therefore unable to accept any rational approach to this darkest of all riddles." This sentence creates the impression that the "God is dead" theology came from the ranks of the survivors while, indeed, the rabbis who introduced it into American Judaism lived thousands of miles away from the scene of the crime. They, then, and not the survivors, are responsible for this discussion of theodicy in Judaism. This is a fact which ought to be stressed clearly.

---

14. Trude Weiss-Rosmarin, in *The Jewish Spectator,* October, 1970, p. 31.
15. *The Sane Society* (Greenwich, Conn.: Fawcet Publications, Inc., 1965), pp. 31–3.
16. K. Shabbetai, *As Sheep to the Slaughter* (New York and Tel Aviv: World Association of the Bergen Belsen Survivors Assoc., 1963), p. 46.
17. *Jewish Existence in an Open Society,* p. 41.
18. *The Doctor and the Soul* (New York: Bantam Books, 1969), p. 75.

I lived in Budapest from February, 1942 until June, 1948, and spoke to a goodly number of rabbis (not only from Hungary, but from central and eastern Europe, as well), who had returned from concentration camps and I don't remember any of them making God responsible and declaring Him dead because of the inhumanity of the Germans and others. It is true that these survivors asked questions and revolted, too, but they rebelled against society, rather than against God. Their rebellion was against the socio-political system which tolerated "man's inhumanity to man." Some of them became leftists and preachers of a new socio-political order, but they did not challenge or deny the existence of God.

I confess that I find the following individuals, who survived the Holocaust, to be more profound as spokesmen of Auschwitz than are the writers of radical theology:

*Rabbi Yekutiel Yehudah Halberstam* of Klausenburg lost his wife and eleven children at Auschwitz. When asked whether he still believed that the Jews were the Chosen People he answered, "that precisely then, after all that had happened to him and the Jewish people, had he been confirmed in his belief in the chosenness of his people, because it was not the Jews who had committed the acts of horror, but the gentiles. . ."[19]

Victor E. Frankl writes:

One cannot claim that these men (i.e. concentration campers) had undergone a regression; on the contrary they experienced a moral progression— moral, and religious. For there broke out in many a prisoner in confinement, and because of confinement, what I have designated as a subconscious or a repressed relationship to God. Let no one judge this religiosity disparagingly, or dispose of it as "foxhole religion . . ." In any event, many prisoners came forth from prison with the feeling of having learned to fear nothing except God.[20]

It seems that our generation will be divided between those who experienced, through the Holocaust, the "hiding of God," and those who feel that the "hidden God" was absent in Auschwitz and elsewhere because He was dead. We might do well to be reminded of the parable of the Ḥasidic saint, Rabbi Barukh, who tried to explain the game to his grandson who was playing hide-and-seek with another boy, that "God, too, says: 'I hide, but there is no one to look for me.'" Or, to put it in other words, "The problem of religion is precisely the problem of one's supreme loyalty or devotion."[22]

*Eva Picková*, a twelve year old girl in the camp at Terezin, wrote a poem entitled "Fear," whose last stanza reads:

---

19. K. Shabbetai, *op. cit.*, p. 36.
20. *Psychotherapy and Existentialism* (New York: Simon and Schuster, 1968), pp. 99–100.
21. Abraham J. Heschel, *Man Is Not Alone* (Philadelphia: Jewish Publication Society, 1951), p. 154.
22. Will Herberg, *Judaism and Modern Man* (New York: The Macmillan Co., 1951), p. 371.

No, no, my God, we want to live
Not watch our numbers melt away.
We want to have a better world,
We want to work—we must not die.[23]

The inscription on the walls of a cellar in Cologne, where Jews were hiding from Nazis, touches the hearts of many, while contemporary radical Jewish theologians appeal only to a few. How inadequate is the statement and the comparison that "Judaism and Christianity are in process of becoming neo-archaic, pagan religions in fact if not in name" as compared with the inscription: "I believe in the sun even when it is not shining. I believe in love even when feeling it not. I believe in God even when He is silent."[24]

*Mordecai Bar-On,* head of the education program of the Israeli Armed Forces once wrote, "I belong to the generation which was born without faith. When I read the literature about the Shoah my reaction is, 'I shall not die, but live.' I say to myself, what can I do in response to this horrible act? My answer is to strengthen my faith in, and my attachment to, Judaism."[25]

---

23. Gerald Green, *The Artists of Terezin* (New York: Hawthorne Books, Inc., 1969), p. 172.
24. Glatstein, Knox and Margoshes, eds., *Anthology of Holocaust Literature* (Philadelphia: Jewish Publication Society, 1969), p. 340.
25. *Petaḥim,* Elul 5727.

## THE CONTRIBUTORS

ALEXANDER ALTMANN is Professor of Jewish philosophy at Brandeis University. Among his recent works are: *Studies in Religious Philosophy and Mysticism; Moses Mendelssohn's Early Metaphysical Writings Analyzed and Interpreted*, and a two-volume biography of Mendelssohn.

ELIEZER BERKOVITS has been Chairman of the Department of Jewish Philosophy, Hebrew Theological College, Skokie, Illinois, since 1958. He is a theologian, educator, author, lecturer. Among his publications are: *Judaism: Fossil or Ferment; God, Man and History; A Jewish Critique of the Philosophy of Martin Buber; Prayer; Man and God, Studies in Biblical Theology; T'nai Binsuin u'Bget*.

SEYMOUR CAIN has been a workingman, a soldier and a freelance writer. He did his graduate work in religion and philosophy at the U. of Chicago and is currently Senior Editor, Religion, for the Encyclopaedia Britannica. He is the author of *Gabriel Marcel* and several introductory guides to basic reading in religion, philosophy, ethics and literature.

JACOB CHINITZ was ordained by Yeshiva University and studied semitics at Dropsie. He edited the sermons of Rabbi Morris Adler, served on the faculty of the American College in Jerusalem, and as the moderator for 175 programs of "Ask the Rabbi" on Philadelphia TV. He is spiritual leader of Beth Ami in that city.

ARTHUR A. COHEN is the author of, among other books, *Martin Buber, The Natural and the Supernatural Jew, The Myth of the Judeo-Christian Tradition*, and editor of *Arguments and Doctrines*.

JACK J. COHEN is Director of the B'nai B'rith Hillel Foundations in Israel. He was formerly Rabbi of the Society for the Advancement of Judaism in New York and taught the philosophy of religion and education at The Jewish Theological Seminary (1955-1961). He is the author of *The Case for Religious Naturalism* and *Jewish Education in Democratic Society*.

SAMUEL S. COHON was, from 1923 until his death, professor of theology at Hebrew Union College. He was also editor, Department of Theology, of the Universal Jewish Encyclopaedia, and the author of *Judaism—A Way of Life, Judaism and War*, and *What We Jews Believe*.

SAMUEL H. DRESNER received his Rabbinical and D.H.L. degrees from the Jewish Theological Seminary. He is currently Rabbi of North Suburban Synagogue Beth El in Highland Park, Illinois. A former editor of *Conservative Judaism*, he is the author of *Prayer, Humility and Compassion, The Jew in American Life*, and *The Sabbath*.

EMIL L. FACKENHEIM is Professor of Philosophy at the U. of Toronto. He is the author of: *Paths to Jewish Belief, Metaphysics and Historicity, The Religious Dimension in Hegel's Thought, Quest for Past and Future: Essays in Jewish Theology*, and *God's Presence in History*.

MARVIN FOX is Professor of Philosophy at The Ohio State University. He was also Visiting Professor at the Hebrew University and at Bar-Ilan University. He has published more than one hundred monographs, articles and reviews on general and Jewish philosophy and on Jewish theology.

MAURICE S. FRIEDMAN is Professor of Religion at Temple University, Philadelphia. He is the author of *Martin Buber: The Life of Dialogue; Problematic Rebel: Melville, Dostoievsky, Kafka, Camus; To Deny Our Nothingness: Contemporary Images of Man; Touchstones of Reality: An Opening Way;* and *The Worlds of Existentialism*.

ROBERT GORDIS is currently Professor of Bible at the Jewish Theological Seminary, and Professor of Religion at Temple University in Philadelphia. He has written more than a dozen books on Bible and religion, as well as scores of articles. He is now rabbi-emeritus of Temple Beth-El of Rockaway Park, and editor of JUDAISM.

JOSEPH H. GUMBINER was ordained at Hebrew Union College and holds graduate degrees from the College-Institute and the U. of Arizona. He is now completing a book on contemporary Jewish life, to be titled *Judaism for Here and Now*.

JACOB LEV HALEVI, a graduate of Hebrew Union College, Cincinnati, served as U.S. Army Chaplain in World War II, and then pursued post-graduate studies at the U. of Southern California, where he first came to embrace Kierkegaard as a favorite author. His doctoral dissertation was *A Critique of Martin Buber's Interpretation of Kierkegaard*.

MONFORD HARRIS is Professor of Religious Studies at Trinity College, Toronto, Canada. Along with his interest in Jewish theology, he is interested in the history of ideas, and has published articles on medieval Jewish dream interpretation and sexuality.

WILL HERBERG is Graduate Professor of Philosophy and Culture at Drew University. He is well known for his work in two fields—social philosophy and theology. Among his writings are: *Judaism and Modern Man: An Interpretation of Jewish Religion*, and *Protestant-Catholic-Jew: An Essay in American Religious Sociology*.

ABRAHAM JOSHUA HESCHEL is the Ralph Simon Professor of Jewish Ethics and Mysticism at The Jewish Theological Seminary of America. Actively concerned with contemporary problems, he has become an authoritative voice on the moral issues facing our nation.

AVRAHAM HOLTZ is a graduate of The Jewish Theological Seminary of America where he is currently Associate Professor of Modern Hebrew Literature. He compiled and edited *The Holy City: Jews on Jerusalem* and has written a book on I. D. Berkowitz.

SIMON KAPLAN, Professor Emeritus of St. John's College, Annapolis, Md., is the author of "Das Problem der Geschichte" in H. Cohen's *System der Philosophie* and the translator of Hermann Cohen's *Religion of Reason out of the Sources of Judaism.*

SAMUEL E. KARFF is Lecturer in Jewish Thought and American Culture at the U. of Chicago, and Rabbi of Chicago Sinai Congregation. He is the editor of the forthcoming Centennial Volume of Hebrew Union College—Institute of Religion, as well as the author of essays and articles in Jewish and professional journals.

JOSEPH KLAUSNER has written voluminously on Jewish history, literature and philology. He is best known for his work in the period of the Second Temple and on the relationship between Judaism and Christianity.

ZVI ERICH KURZWEIL was Inspector of Education for the Central Council of Jewish Education in Great Britain until he emigrated to Israel, where he is now Professor of Education at the Technion-Israel Institute of Technology. He has written extensively on education in English and Hebrew.

JAKOB J. PETUCHOWSKI is Professor of Rabbinics and Theology at HUC-JIR in Cincinnati, and served as visiting Professor of Jewish Philosophy at Tel-Aviv University in 1971. He is the author of several books and numerous articles, and a member of JUDAISM's editorial board.

EMANUEL RACKMAN, Rabbi of the Fifth Avenue Synagogue in N. Y., and formerly Provost and Professor of Judaic Studies at Yeshiva University, is presently Professor of Judaic Studies and Consultant to the Chancellor on Judaic Studies at City University of New York. He is the author of *Israel's Emerging Constitution,* and *One Man's Judaism.*

NOAH H. ROSENBLOOM was ordained by Yeshiva University and received his Ph.D. from New York University. Formerly a member of Hunter College faculty, he presently serves as Professor at Stern College, Yeshiva University. His most recent book is *Luzzatto's Ethico-Psychological Interpretation of Judaism.*

RICHARD L. RUBENSTEIN is currently Professor of Religion at Florida State University. He received his M.H.L. and Rabbinic ordination from J.T.S., his Ph.D. from Harvard. The article reprinted here is a chapter from a book, *The Religious Imagination,* which also has been translated into French. He is the author of *After Auschwitz, Morality and Eros,* and *Paul, My Brother.*

ZALMAN M. SCHACHTER heads the Department of Judaic and Near Eastern Studies at the U. of Manitoba in Winnipeg. He is Musmakh Rabbi of the Lubavitcher Yeshivah, and has degrees from Boston University and H.U.C. He also served as Director of B'nai B'rith Hillel Foundation at the U. of Manitoba.

NOCHUMM J. SCHEALTIEL is a pseudonym for a rabbi identified with contemporary Hasidism who also teaches philosophy at a Canadian college. He is the author of a number of books, monographs and articles dealing with Jewish theology, philosophy and mysticism.

STEVEN S. SCHWARZSCHILD is Professor of Judaic Studies and Philosophy at Washington University, St. Louis. He was editor of JUDAISM, 1961-1969, and is the author of, among others, *Franz Rosenzwieg—Guide of Reversioners.*

DAVID S. SHAPIRO is the author of *Midrash David,* and *Torath Moshe Veha-Neviim.* He is on the editorial committee of *Tradition,* contributing editor of JUDAISM, and associate editor *Hadarom.* He was associate professor at Hebrew Theological College, Chicago, in Bible and Jewish Thought, and lecturer in History of Jewish Civilization, University of Wisconsin, Milwaukee.

SOLOMON SIMON was a prolific writer in, and about, Yiddish. He was one of the founders of the Yiddish secular school system in this country, and was a leader of the Sholom Aleichem Folk Institute from 1940-1955.

CHARLES W. STECKEL, ordained Jewish Theological Seminary, Breslau, Ph.D. University of Breslau. Wrote: *The Influence of the Bible on Polish Literature, Historiography of the Post-Exilic Prophets, Chaim Weizmann on His Way to a Jewish State.* Serves: Temple, Gardena, City of Hope, Duarte, California.

MORRIS STOCKHAMMER became Doctor of Political Science in 1927 in Vienna, and subsequently emigrated to the United States. He has published six German and four English books, and his biography appears in *Contemporary Authors* and in *The Directory of British and American Writers.*

PAUL J. TILLICH emigrated from Germany after the rise of the Nazis and became distinguished as one of the most outstanding American Protestant theologians. His primary concern was with the attempt to incorporate scientific methods and a critical viewpoint into religion.

ISADORE TWERSKY is Littauer Professor of Hebrew Literature and Philosophy at Harvard University, and was formerly Chairman of the Department of Near Eastern Languages and Literatures. He is the author of books and articles on rabbinic literature and intellectual history.

RUTH B. WAXMAN taught English and Comparative Literature at Roosevelt College in Chicago, and at Adelphi University and C. W. Post College in New York, before becoming Managing Editor of JUDAISM.

# SOURCES OF ARTICLES

387